All the Promises
are Yes in Christ Jesus

BY LORI PAGEL

All the Promises Are Yes In Christ Jesus

Lori Pagel copyright © 2016. All rights reserved
2nd edition

This book includes a compilation of Scripture, quotes, and other public domain materials. As such, only materials exclusive to the author may not be reproduced without written permission from the author.

Except where otherwise indicated, all Scripture quotations are taken from the KJV.

All Hebrew and Greek words are taken from www.biblehub.com

All Scripture quoted in part using various versions are noted in the introduction.

All Scripture quoted in completion marked "NIV" are taken from the Holy Bible, New International Version. Copyright © 1973, 1984 by International Bible Society, used by permission of Zondervan Bible Publishers.

Cover Design: by Lori Pagel & Kim McDougal

Printed in the United States – all rights reserved

Dedication

I thank God for all the answers to prayers, and for all the precious promises in His Word.

I would like to dedicate this book to my husband for putting up with all the inconvenience this book has caused in our lives, for being patient with me, and for all his support.

I'm thankful also for my mother who has walked this journey with me and is always there for me and all my family members, whom I love so much!

My prayer is that God would touch lives with this book and that it would be a blessing!

Introduction

This book includes all the promises along with the condition of that promise, blessings, what God did for people, miracles, some commentary, prayers, using the promises, personal answers to prayers using the promises, and the names of the New Jerusalem and of God because every name of God contains a promise.

I have never been so blessed as when I was putting this book together. To read and type all these positive Scriptures of God's promises to us for hours on end was so faith-building. This is a book that you should read over and over to increase your faith. I like to read a little bit every day because I love to have these positive Scriptures running through my thoughts and increasing my faith every day.
"So then Faith comes by hearing, and hearing by the Word of God". Rom. 10:17

I encourage you to get a good yellow highlighter to mark the verses that apply to your situations so that you can find them easily and read them over and over, or get a notebook to write down the Scriptures that mean the most to you with your notes.

I also suggest that you get a journal and write your prayers and requests along with the promises that go with that request. Read, pray, and speak them every day, then write down the date when you receive the answer to your prayer. Your faith will build when you read the promises every day and when you see how God has answered your prayers. By looking back and seeing how God has answered your many requests, it will help you not to forget the great things that God has done for you. I wish that I had kept a journal all my life of answered prayer.

We read these precious promises so that we can know what God has given us. These are the promises of the Covenant, Is. 59:19-21. When we enter into Covenant with God, we inherit the promises through Jesus.
"Whereby are given to us great and exceeding great and precious promises..." II Pet. 1:4
"God is not a man that He should lie... hath He said, and shall He not do it? Or hath He spoken, and shall He not make it good?" Num. 23:19
"... since He (God) has blessed, I cannot change it." Num. 23:20

"He considers no disaster for Jacob; He sees no trouble for Israel. The Lord their God is with them, and there is rejoicing... among them." Num. 23:21
It is the Holy Spirit who helps us know what God has given to us!
"... now we have received... the Spirit which is of God; that we might know the things that are freely given to us of God." I Cor. 2:10-14

I heard David Jeremiah say in a sermon once, *"God never gives a promise He does not keep... God does not view time as we do. God views time in the eternal present. Which means when God says it, it's already as if it has happened. God keeps His promises when we go through periods of uncertainty..."*
Sermon titled, *"The Town Christmas Forgot"* by David Jeremiah.

What does the word *"promise"* mean?
The Merriam-Webster Dictionary
"A statement telling someone that you will definitely do something or that something will definitely happen in the future:
1. *an indication of future success or improvement*
2. *a reason to expect that something will happen in the future*
3. *a: a declaration that one will do or refrain from doing something specified*

   b: a legally binding declaration that gives the person to whom it is made a right to expect or to claim the performance or forbearance of a specified act reason to expect something... ground for expectation..."

Faith is expecting and hoping for something that you cannot see.
"Now faith is the substance of things hoped for, the evidence of things not seen." Heb. 11:1
"Now faith is confidence in what we hope for and assurance about what we do not see." Heb 11:1 NIV
"Now faith is the assurance of things hoped for, the conviction ("certainty" BSB) of things not seen." Heb. 11:1 ESV

What the Bible says about the Word
- hear the Word - Jms. 1:22;Rom. 10:17
- Study the Word - Acts 17:11;II Tim. 2:15
- Read the Word – Rev. 1:3
- Believe the Word – Rom. 4:20;10:17
- Obey the Word – Lk. 11:28;Jms. 1:22

- Do the Word Mt. 7:24,21,26;Jn.14:15;Acts 5:9;Jms.122,25;13:17
- Cherish the Word – Job 23:12
- Share the Word – II Tim. 4:2
- Store the Word in my memory (memorize) so I won't sin – Ps. 119:11
- Receive the Word – Prov.2:1-5;Acts 17:11;Jms.1:21
- Rightly handle the Word – II Tim. 2:15
- "I have put my hope in Your Word." Ps. 110:14 NIV

The Word is profitable for:
    Teaching
    Reproof
    Correction
    Doctrine
    Training in righteousness

So that you may be:
    Competent and equipped for every good work – II Tim. 3:14-17

The Word:
    is a cure for deception – II Thess. 2:10-12;Jms. 1:22

Scriptures about the Word and the promises in the Word
"... there hath not failed one Word of all His good promises, which He promised..." I Kings 8:56
"Know now that there shall fall unto the earth nothing of the Word of the Lord..." II Kings 10:10
"Thou... hast promised this goodness unto Thy servant ..." II Chron. 17:26,27
"Thy Word is settled in heaven." Ps. 119:89
"Your Word, O Lord, is eternal." Ps. 119:89 NIV
"The Lord is faithful to all His promises." Ps. 145:13 NIV
"Not one of these (promises) *shall fail."* Is. 34:16
"I will hasten My Word to perform it." Jer. 1:12
"I am watching to see that My Word is fulfilled." Jer. 1:12 NIV
"He will keep His Word." I Thess. 5:24 PB

Jesus has given us these promises so that we can partake of the divine nature.
"Whereby are given unto us exceeding great and precious promises: that by these (promises) *ye might be partakers of the Divine nature..."* II Pet. 1:4

"For by these He has granted to us His precious and magnificent promises..." II Pet. 1:4 NASB

We need to memorize these promises so that when the hard times come, we can stand on them and say them over and over to build our faith.
We can be sure that *"God is faithful..."* (I Cor. 1:9) and that God is *"... ever true to His promise..."* (I Cor. 1:9 AMP).
"Faithful is He that calleth you, who also will do it." I Thess. 5:24
"I stir up your pure minds by way of remembrance: that ye may be mindful of the words which were spoken before..." II Pet. 3:1,2
"So shall My Word be that goeth forth out of my mouth; it shall not return unto Me void, but it shall accomplish that which I please, and it shall prosper in the thing whereto I sent it." Is. 55:11
"He staggered not at the promise of God through unbelief; but was strong in faith, giving glory to God..." Rom. 4:20
"Now, O Lord God, let Thy promise... be established..." II Chron. 1:9
"There failed not ought of any good thing which the Lord had spoken unto the house of Israel; all came to pass." Josh. 21:45
"... let Thy Word... be verified..." I Kings 8:26

Jesus is the same now as He was back then, and we can claim the miracles, promises, and blessings in Jesus' name.
Heb. 13:8 *"Jesus Christ the same yesterday, and today, and forever."*
He can do the same things for us that He did for those in the Bible.

Jesus fulfilled all the conditions by keeping God's laws perfectly, so the promises are ours in Christ Jesus. We inherit all the promises through Him, but the conditions are something we strive for, just like we strive to do His will all of our life. When we apply the conditions, it increases our faith, and sometimes we can see why God is not answering our prayers. We are all sons and daughters of God through faith in Jesus. And if we are sons, then we are heirs, but He put the conditions there for a reason.
"For all the promises of God in Him (Jesus) *are yea, and in Him Amen, unto the glory of God..."* I Cor. 1:19,20
"For no matter how many promises God has made, they are 'Yes' in Christ. And so through Him the 'Amen' is spoken by us to the glory of God." I Cor. 1:19,20 NIV
That should build your faith right there!
"Now to Abraham and his Seed were the promises made... which is Christ." Gal. 3:16
"... if you belong to Christ... you are heirs to all the promises." Gal. 3:26-28

"And if ye be Christ's, then are ye Abraham's seed, and heirs according to the promise." Gal. 3:29

"Now therefore ye are no more strangers and foreigners, but fellow citizens with the saints, and of the household of God…" Eph. 2:19

"… God, willing more abundantly to shew unto the heirs of promise the immutability of His counsel, confirmed it by an oath…" Heb. 6:17

"For the promise is unto you, and to your children, and to all that are afar off, even as many as the Lord our God shall call." Acts 2:39

"And, behold, this day I am going the way of all the earth and ye know in all your hearts and in all your souls, that not one thing hath failed of all the good things which the Lord your God spake concerning you; all are come to pass unto you, and not one thing hath failed thereof. Therefore it shall come to pass, that as all good things are come upon you, which the Lord your God promised you…" Josh. 23:14,15

If you disobey and serve other gods, then the bad things He promised will also come to pass.

"… so shall the Lord bring upon you all evil things, until He have destroyed you from off this good land which the Lord your God hath given you. When ye have transgressed the Covenant of the Lord your God, which He commanded you, and have gone and served other gods, and bowed yourselves to them; then shall the anger of the Lord be kindled against you, and ye shall perish quickly." Josh. 23:15,16

"For thus saith the Lord; like as I have brought all this great evil upon this people, so will I bring upon them all the good that I have promised them." Jer. 32:42

"Blessed be the Lord, that hath given rest unto His people Israel, according to all that He promised: there hath not failed one Word of all His good promise, which He promised by the hand of Moses His servant." I Kings 8:56

"Through faith subdued kingdoms, worked righteousness, obtained promises, stopped the mouth of lions, quenched the violence of fire, escaped the edge of the sword, out of weakness were made strong." Heb. 11:34

"And we declare unto you glad tidings, how that the promise which was made unto the fathers, God hath fulfilled the same unto us their children…" Acts 13:32,33

"And now I stand and am Judged for the hope of the promise made of God unto our fathers: unto which promise our twelve tribes, instantly serving God day and night, hope to come." Acts 26:6,7

What God promised He is able to perform.
"And being fully persuaded that, what He had promised, He was able also to perform." Rom. 4:21
"Who hast kept with Thy servant David my father that Thou promisedst him: Thou spakest also with Thy mouth, and hast fulfilled it with Thine hand, as it is this day." I Kings 8:23,24
"... who carries out the words of His servants and fulfills the predictions of His messengers..." Is. 44:26 NIV
"Behold, the days come, saith the Lord, that I will perform that good thing which I have promised ..." Jer. 33:14
We must have faith; the Word will not work if it is not mixed with faith.
"And He said, I will hide My face from them, I will see what their end shall be: for they are a very forward generation, children in whom is no faith." Deut. 32:20
"Yea, they despised the pleasant land, they believed not His Word: but murmured in their tents, and hearkened not unto the voice of the Lord." Ps. 106:24
"Then believed they His words; they sang His praise." Ps. 106:12
"... thy faith has made thee whole." Mk. 10:56
"Let us therefore fear, lest, a promise being left us of entering into His rest... but the Word preached did not profit them, not being mixed with faith in them that heard it." Heb. 4:1,2

Sometimes we must wait to see the promises fulfilled.
"... after he had patiently endured, he obtained the promise." Heb. 6:15

Our prayer is *"...Lord... (please) keep (or do) what You promised..."* I King 8:25 HCSB

Jesus paid the price with His blood for me to receive these promises.
  I can claim it!
  I can believe it!
  I can receive it!
  I thank God for it!

Questions we need to ask ourselves.
Do I trust God's will for me?

Do I have sin in my life that needs to be confessed & let go?
Do I want to consume it on my own selfishness and lusts?

Prayer:
Lord, I know these promises are mine in Christ Jesus, and I have done your will to the best of my ability (which is accepted in Jesus); with the help of the Holy Spirit. So please fulfill your Word to me today. Let it be according to Your Word and will; I stand on Your Word. Thank you. In Jesus' name, Amen!

How do I get my prayers answered?
This is the question we all ask and would like to know the answer. Jesus asked, *"What do you want Me to do for you?"* Matt. 20:32.
Jesus' prayers were heard because He feared God and submitted to His will.
"During the days of Jesus' life on earth, He offered up prayers and petitions with fervent cries and tears... He was heard because of His reverent submission ("because that He feared" KJV)." Heb. 5:7 NIV
1. Through the power of the sevenfold Holy Spirit
   "... from the sevenfold Spirit before His throne..." Rev. 1:4 NLT

Know that the Word is powerful.
"Whereby are given unto us exceeding great and precious promises..." II Pet. 1:4
"For I am not ashamed of the Gospel of Christ: for it is the power of God unto Salvation to everyone that believeth..." Rom. 1:16

The Word keeps me from sinning.
"Thy Word have I had in mine heart, that I might not sin against Thee." Ps. 119:11

I ate the Word. I Study and seek to understand God's Word through the power of the Holy Spirit.
"Thy Words were found, and I did eat them; and Thy Word was unto Me the joy and rejoicing of mine heart…." Jer. 15:16

The Word was written for our learning.
"For whatsoever things were written aforetime were written for our learning, that we through patience and comfort of the Scriptures might have hope." Rom. 15:4

"Through faith subdued kingdoms, worked righteousness, obtained promises, stopped the mouth of lions, quenched the violence of fire, escaped the edge of the sword, out of weakness were made strong." Heb. 11:34

We know that *"With God nothing is impossible"*. Lk. 1:37
"There failed not ought of any good thing which the Lord had spoken unto the house of Israel; all came to pass." Josh. 21:45
"... then will I perform My Word with thee, which I spake..." I Kings 6:12
"Know now that there shall fall unto the earth nothing of the Word of the Lord, which the Lord spake..." II Kings 10:10
"... I have said I would do it, and I will." Is. 46:11 NLT
"And being fully persuaded that, what He had promised, He was able also to perform..." Rom. 4:21
"... I have purposed it, I will also do it." Is. 46:11
"... what I have said, that will I bring about; what I have planned, that will I do" Is. 46:11 NIV
"So shall My Word be that goeth forth out of My mouth: it shall not return unto Me void, but it shall accomplish that which I please, and it shall prosper in the thing whereto I sent it." Is. 55:11
"For I am the Lord: I will speak, and the Word that I shall speak shall come to pass; it shall be no more prolonged: for in your days, O rebellious house, will I say the Word, and will perform it, saith the Lord God... there shall none of My Words be prolonged anymore, but the Word which I have spoken shall be done, saith the Lord God." Ez. 12:25,28 (Matt.11:22-24;17:20-22;21:22;Mk.9: 23,24;Lk.8:50;11:9-13;17:5,6,19)

1. **Ask**
   This is obvious, but the first thing we have to do is ask! The Bible says, You don't have because you don't ask, Jms. 4:39. (Matt.6:6-13;7:7,11;Jms.4:23;I Jn.3:22)
   Jesus said, What do you want me to do for you? Mk. 10:51

2. **Pray to the Father which is in heaven (Jer. 29:11,12)**
   Jesus prayed to the Father in heaven in the Lord's Prayer, *"Our Father which art in heaven"* Matt. 6:9 (Jn.14:13,14;15:16)

3. **Pray in the name of Jesus, the Messiah; our Creator, Redeemer**
   There is no other way to the Father in heaven but through the name of Jesus!
   Jesus said, *"... no man comes to the Father except through Me..."* Jn. 14:6 ESV

Jesus said, Ask anything **in My name**, Jn. 14:13;16:23
We must believe that Jesus is God come in the flesh and receive Him as our Lord, Master, and Saviour because it is in His name that we pray!

4. **Ask according to His will**
   Matt. 6:9-13;I Jn. 5:14
   The next thing we must do is ask according to God's will. This is the one we are always afraid to say because for some reason we think that God is harsh and unbending and doesn't want to give us any-thing. But we should never be afraid of God's will. We can know that He wants the best for us. The safest place to be is in God's will. He sees the whole picture and knows what is best for us in the long run.
   We pray in the Lord's Prayer:
   "Thy wil be done on earth as it is in heaven" Matt. 6:10

   a. The Bible says that it is God's will that we prosper and be in health!
   "Beloved, I wish above all things that thou mayest prosper and be in health, even as thy soul prospereth." III Jn. 1:2
   "... the Lord... which hath pleasure in the prosperity of His servant." Ps. 35:27 (the key here is to be His servant).
   "For I know the plans I have for you, declares the Lord, plans to pros-per you and not to harm you, plans to give you hope and a future." Jer. 29: 11 NIV

   b. It is God's will that we be saved and our family.
   "... who wants all people to be saved..." I Tim. 2:4
   "... not willing that any should perish..." II Pet. 3:9

   c. It is His will to give us His Holy Spirit.
   "If ye then, being evil, know how to give good gifts unto your child-ren, how much more shall your Father which is in heaven give good things ("the Holy Spirit" Lk. 11:13) to them that ask Him?" Matt. 7:11;Lk. 11:13

   d. God wants your joy to be full (Joy is not necessarily pleasure).
   "... that your joy be full." I Jn. 1:4

   The Bible says that we can know we have the answer if it's according to His will, I Jn. 5:14.

"And this is the confidence that we have in Him, that, if we ask any-thing according to His will, He heareth us: and if we know that He hear us, whatsoever we ask, we know that we have the petitions that we desired of Him." I Jn. 5:14,15

5. **Believe - If God said it, He will do it!**

   You need faith to receive the promises, and if you want faith you must hear (or read) the Word of God. How do you know how to pray without knowing the Word, and how do you know what God has promised if you don't know the Word?

   "Faith comes by hearing and hearing by the Word of God." Rom. 10:17

   God will fulfill His promises and we can know that God hears us. Their requests were not mixed with faith, Heb. 4:1,2.

   "... followers of them who through faith and patience inherit the promises." Heb. 6:12

   The one who *"... does not doubt but believes that what they say will happen, it will be done for them..."* Mk. 11:23

   "Who through faith... obtained the promises." Heb. 11:35

   "Let us hold fast the profession of our faith without wavering; (for He is faithful that promised)..." Heb. 10:23

   The one who doubts will not receive, *"that person shouldn't expect to receive anything from the Lord."* Jms. 1:6,7 NIV.

   Jesus said to doubting Thomas, *"... be not faithless but believing... because thou hast seen Me, thou hast believed: blessed are they that have not seen, and yet have believed."* Jn. 20:27,29

   Sometimes we need to say, like the man who wanted Jesus to deliver his son, *"Lord, I believe, help my unbelief."* Mk. 9:24

   "And being not weak in faith, he considered not his own body now dead, when he was about an hundred year old, neither yet the deadness of Sara's womb: he staggered not at the promise of God through unbelief; but was strong in faith, giving glory to God; and being fully persuaded that, **what He had promised, He was able also to perform.** *And therefore it was imputed to him for righteousness."* Rom. 4:19-22

   "Faithful is He that calleth you, who also will do it." I Thess. 5:24
   "The One who calls you is faithful and He will do it." I Thess. 5:24 NIV

"... and *He also will bring it to pass.*" I Thess 5:24 NASB
"*Those He promised to help would be perfectly sure.*" Heb. 6:17-19 LB
"*Whereby are given unto us exceeding great and precious promises: that by these ye might be partakers of the Divine nature, having escaped the corruption that is in the world through lust.*" II Pet. 1:4
"*For I am not ashamed of the Gospel of Christ: for it is the power of God unto Salvation to everyone that believeth...*" Rom. 1:16

6. **Speak the promises out loud!**
   Prov. 10:11 "*The mouth of a righteous man is a well of life...*"
   Deut. 30:14 "*But the Word is very nigh unto thee, in thy mouth...*"
   "*... pay attention to the words... for it is pleasing if you keep them within you and if they are constantly on your lips.*" Prov. 22:17-19 HCSB
   "*A good man out of the good treasure of his heart bringeth forth that which is good... for of the abundance of the heart his mouth speaketh.*" Lk. 6:45
   "*And since we have the same Spirit of faith in keeping with what is written, I believed, therefore I spoke, we also believe, and therefore speak.*" II Cor. 4:13 HCSB
   "*So shall My Word be that goeth forth out of My mouth: it shall not return void, but it shall accomplish that which I please.*" Is. 55:11
   Believe it and speak it, Rom. 10:10
     I am healed by the grace of God!
     I have eternal life by the grace of God!
     My God will supply all my needs in Jesus' name!
     I can do all things through Christ, etc.
     Say, I believe; Amen!
   Proclaim liberty, Is. 61:1;Lk.17:5,6Mk.11:22-24

"*Faith means:*
- *a conviction of the truthfulness of God*
- *constancy in such profession – (this definition of faith means a consistent act of openly declaring or publicly proclaiming a belief)*
- *have confidence*
- *obey*

What does it mean to add faith to God's promises? According to the definition, when you really put your faith in the promises of God, you'll speak what you believe.

Real faith is made complete by obedience. When you add real faith to God's word, you'll meet the conditions of His promises. If you truly believe His promise, you'll be obedient to His Word... II Cor. 4:13 also reveals what it means to add real faith to God's promises: It is written: 'I believed; therefore I have spoken.' With that same Spirit of faith we also believe and therefore speak. (NIV)"
God's Great & Precious Promises p. 23

7. **We inherit the promises in Jesus**
   "And if ye be Christ's, then are ye Abraham's seed, and heirs according to the promise." Gal. 3:29
   "Let us hold fast the profession of our hope without wavering; (for He is faithful that promised)..." Heb. 10:23
   "Cast not away therefore your confidence, which hath great recom-pence of reward. For ye have need of patience, that, after ye have done the will of God, ye might receive the promise." Heb.10:35-37
   We can trust Him; His ways are higher than our ways, Is. 55:8,9. Abraham waited patiently and received what was promised, Heb. 6:13-18.
   Paul in the Bible said, "Blessed be the God and Father of our Lord Jesus Christ, who has blessed us in Christ with every Spiritual blessing in the heavenly places..." Eph. 1:3

8. **We can pray using God's promises.**
   Throughout this book I have included prayers using the promises. We can say, Lord, You said in Your Word (_____quote vs._____), now please let Your Word be fulfilled to me in Jesus, name, Amen.

9. **Say "Amen" to God's promises.**
   "For all the promises of God in Him are yea, and in Him Amen, unto the glory of God by us." II Cor. 1:20.
   "... so through Him the 'Amen' is spoken by us..." II Cor. 1:20 NIV
   "For all of God's promises have been fulfilled in Christ with a resounding 'Yes'! and through Christ, our 'Amen' (which means 'Yes') ascend to God for His glory." II Cor 1:20 NLT

Mary said, let it *"... be unto me according to Thy Word."* Lk. 1:38

10. Get knowledge of the promises through the Word
"My people are destroyed for lack of knowledge..." Hosea 4:6
"... through knowledge shall the just be delivered." Prov. 11:9

11. Don't be afraid!
"Don't be afraid, for I am with you." Is. 41:10 NLT

12. Abide in God and let His Word abide in you
We abide through baptism, communion, obedience, and love, Jn. 6:56;15:7,10;I Jn. 2:6,17;3:6.

13. Do what is right and what pleases God
The Bible says that He hears the prayers of the righteous, Prov. 15:29.
"And whatsoever we ask, we receive of Him, because we keep His Commandments, and do those things that are pleasing in His sight." I Jn. 3:22
"No good thing will He withhold from them that walk uprightly." Ps. 84:11
"The eyes of the Lord watch over those who do right, and His ears are open to their prayers..." I Pet. 3:12

Sin separates us from God
What do we do if we have sin in our life? We all sin and come short of God's glory, Rom. 3:23.

1. First, we repent of our sins and confess them, Is.30:15;Jer. 31:19;Matt.3:8;4:17;21:32;Lk.5:31,32;17:3;24:47;Acts 3:18,19; 5:31;11:18;20:21;Rom.2:4,5;II Cor.7:9,10;Rev.2:5;3:3.

2. Second, we ask for forgiveness and cleansing through the blood of Jesus. Who *"... washed us from our sins in His own blood."* Rev. 1:5 NKJV
"... you were slain and have Redeemed us to God by Your blood..." Rev. 5:9 NKJV
"... they have washed their robes and made them white in the blood of the Lamb." Rev. 7:14 NKJV
(more verses - Rom.3:25;Eph.1:7;Heb.9:14;13:12)

3. Third, we must get rid of sin. Jesus said to the man that was healed at the pool of Bethesda, Now go and sin no more lest a worse thing happen to you, Jn. 5:14. He also told the woman caught in adultery, *"Go and sin no more"*, Jn. 8:11.
If a sin has us in its grip, then we must strive to overcome through the power of the Holy Spirt until we get the victory. Keep confessing it and asking for forgiveness and cleansing by the blood until God gives you the victory; in this way you keep your sins under the blood. Put all your sins on the altar. That means you are willing for God to take them. If you like your sin ask God to make you willing to give it up.

14. Be considerate of your wife

The Bible even says that being inconsiderate of your wife could hinder God from hearing and answering your prayers.
"Husbands... be considerate as you live with your wives, and treat them with respect... so that nothing will hinder your prayers." I Pet. 3:7
"... the Lord turns His face against those who do evil." I Pet. 3:12

15. Fast and pray

Sometimes when we need God to intervene, and we can't get a breakthrough in prayer; that is when we must fast. Fasting is the strongest weapon we have to defeat the enemy; it is also the hardest thing to do.
Start out small, maybe cut one meal and work up to a larger fast. Don't fast so often and so long that it causes health problems., Joel 1:14, 2:12;Matt.17:20-22;Mk.9:29.
A true fast is without any food but there are other tyes of fasts that you can do. You could do only fruit, or fruit and vegetables. A Daniel fast is only plant food, Dan. 1:12. Sometimes you can give up something like T.V. or video games or the computer for a time. When fasting, you should spend time in prayer. One time I fasted and prayed for ten days for my husband to be healed and God did heal him. (Some people may not be able to do any type of fast because of health issues. Always consult your doctor to see if you are physically capable of fasting.

16. Always pray with thanksgiving!

The Bible tells us to mix our prayers with giving thanks.

"Don't worry about anything; instead, pray about everything. Tell God what you need, and thank Him for all He has done." Phil. 4:6 NLT

"... make your requests with thanksgiving." Phil. 4:6

We thank Him ahead of time for what He will do, and we thank Him after we receive the answer to our prayer. Don't be like the nine lepers who did not go back to give thanks, but be like the one leper who did go back and give thanks, Lk. 17:11-19.
(More Scriptures Jn.11:42;Eph.5:20;Phil.4:6;I Thess.5:18)

17. Don't be double-minded

"... ask in faith, nothing wavering. For he that wavereth is like a wave of the sea driven with the wind and tossed. For let not that man think that he shall receive anything of the Lord. A double-minded man is unstable in all his ways." I Jn. 1:8-10

18. Sometimes God says to wait and sometimes He says No!

This is the answer we don't like to hear but if we trust God, we can trust that God knows what is best.

"Wait on the Lord: be of good courage, and He shall strengthen thine heart: wait, I say, on the Lord." Ps. 27:14

"My soul, wait thou only upon God; for my expectation is from Him." Ps. 62:5

"... through faith and patience inherit the promises." Heb. 6:12

"... after he had patiently endured, he obtained the promise." Heb. 6:15

If we keep asking for something when God has said no, then some-times He gives us what we desire even when it's not the best thing for us, and we will usually suffer the consequences! God gave them the meat they asked for in the wilderness because they lusted after it, but then many of them died.

"... they tempted God in their heart by asking meat for their lust... for He gave them their own desire..." Ps. 78:18,29

We also see that with Balaam. God gave him his request because he persisted in asking for what he already knew God had said no! (Num. 22:12.13,20). We know that Balaam wanted the money so badly that he convinced them to entice the Israelites to be unfaith-ful to God, Num. 31:16. Eventually he died in battle, (Josh. 13:22) I think that he died without God because it says in Rev. 2:14, *"... there are some among you who hold to the teaching of Balaam, who taught Balak to entice the Israelites to sin..."*

He gave them up to their own desires, Rom. 1:24
"So I let them follow their own stubborn desires, living according to their own ideas." Ps. 81:12

19. Don't pray to consume it on your lust and pleasures
The Bible tells us that *"When you ask, you do not receive, because you ask with wrong motives, that you may spend what you get on your pleasures."* Jms. 4:3

20. Be humble
God keeps His distance from the proud, Ps. 138:6 NLT
The Lord lifts up the humble, Ps. 147:6 NKJV.

21. Forgive and make things right with others
Reconcile with others before you come before God, Matt. 5:23
If you forgive others, God will forgive you, Matt. 6:14

22. Give your tithes and offerings to God
God promises to open the windows of heaven and bless you and rebuke the devourer if you pay your tithes and offerings to Him. Tithe is 10% and an offering is your choice of how much to give.
"Bring ye all the tithes into the storehouse, that there may be meat in Mine house, and prove Me nowherewith, saith the Lord of hosts, if I will not open you the windows of heaven, and pour you out a blessing that there shall not be room enough to receive it. And I will rebuke the devourer for your sakes, and he shall not destroy the fruits of your ground; neither shall your vine cast her fruit before the time in the field, saith the Lord of hosts." Mal. 3:10,11
God tells us to store our money in heaven.
"Lay not up for yourselves teasures upon earth, where moth and rust doth corrupt, and where thieves break through and steal..." Matt. 6:19

You might think this is a lot to think about when you pray. You might think, I just want to come to God and pray and get answers. Well, I say go ahead and pray and expect an answer, but if you're not getting an answer to your prayers, then go through the checklist and see what could be hindering your prayers.
Are you asking God's will?
Do you have assurance that it's God's will?

Is there sin in your life separating you from God?
Is God asking you to wait?
Are you really asking in faith and not being double-minded?
Are you coming to the Father in heaven through Jesus Christ, Creator, Redeemer?

Satan doesn't want us to know what is ours in Jesus
Satan wants to steal, kill, and destroy, but God wants to give you abundant life, Jn. 10:10.
Sometimes we must bind the strongman (with the blood of Jesus) so that we can plunder his house, Matt. 12:29;Mk. 3:27.
Prayer: Father in heaven, please bind the strongman by the blood of Jesus so that he can no longer steal from me in the name of Jesus, my Creator, Redeemer. Thank You, Amen!
Jesus gave us the keys of binding and loosing in Matt. 16:19
"I will give unto thee the keys of the kingdom of heaven: and whatsoever thou shalt bind on earth shal be bound in heaven: and whatsoever thou shalt loose on earth shall be loosed in heaven."
Sometimes God has given us things, and it is the Devil who steals it away. We can ask God to rebuke the Devourer for us!
I had a dream years ago that Jesus was standing in front of me and handing me an amazing gift and the Devil used someone I knew to steal it away from me, saying, You can't have that! Sometimes we think that God isn't giving us the things we need when it is really the Devil who is stealing it away from us.

Verses on the promises:
"For He remembered His Holy promise given to His servant Abraham." Ps. 105:42 NIV
"Then believed they His words…" Ps. 106:12
"Then they believed His promises…" Ps. 106:12 NIV
"Then at last His people believed Him…" Ps. 106: 12 LB
"I rejoice at Thy Word, as one that findeth great spoil." Ps. 119:162
"I rejoice in Your promise like one who finds great ("treasure" NLT)." Ps. 119:162 NIV

God magnified His Word above His name
"I will worship toward Thy Holy Temple (in the O.T.), *and praise Thy name for Thy loving kindness and for Thy truth for* **Thou hast magnified Thy Word above all Thy name**." Ps. 138:2 AMP

In the N.T. we look to the New Jerusalem in heaven, Gal. 4:25
"... yea, I have spoken it, I will also bring it to pass; I have purposed it, I will also do it." Is. 46:11
"... what I have said, that will I bring about; what I have planned, that will I do." Is. 46:11 NIV
"... I have said I would do it and I will." Is. 46:11 LB
"Is the law then against the promises of God? God forbid... that the promise by faith of Jesus Christ might be given to them that believe." Gal. 3:21,22

God is reliable
"Let us hold fast the profession of our hope without wavering; (for He is faithful that promised)..." Heb. 10:23
"... let us go right into the presence of God, with true hearts fully trusting Him." Heb. 10:23 NLT
God bound Himself with an oath and promise, Heb. 6:17,18.
This proves God is committed to fulfilling His Word.

The Promises were given to Abraham and his Seed (Jesus). We inherit those promises when we come through Jesus (Gal. 3:14).
"He Redeemed us in order that the blessing given to Abraham might come to the Gentiles through Christ Jesus... by faith... we receive the promise ..." Gal. 4:14

God will fulfill His Word
("Thou art the God that doest wonders" Ps. 77:13-20)
Num. 23:19 "God is not a man, that He should lie; neither the son of man, that He should repent: hath He said, and **shall He not do it**? Or hath He spoken, and **shall He not make it good**?"
I Jn. 5:14,15 "And this is the confidence that we have in Him, that, if we ask anything according to His will, He heareth us: and if we know that He hear us, whatsoever we ask, **we know that we have the petitions that we desired of Him**."

His promises will not fail!
I Kings 8:56 "There hath not failed one Word of all His good promise(s)..."
Jer. 32:42 "... so I will bring upon them all the good that I have promised them."

God's words will never pass away!

Matt. 24:35 "*Heaven and earth shall pass away, but **My words shall not pass away***."
II Chron. 1:9 "*Now, O Lord God, **let Thy promise... be established**...*"

We are glad for the things God has given us!
Deut. 26:11 "*And thou shalt rejoice in every good thing which the Lord thy **God hath given unto thee**, and unto thine house ...*"
God wants to give us the desires of our heart!
Ps. 21:2 "*Thou hast given him his heart's desire, and hast not withholden the request of his lips...*"
Ps. 37:4,5 "*Delight thyself also in the Lord; and He shall give thee the desires of thine heart... He shall bring it to pass.*"
We can hold on to the promises with confidence because God doesn't lie.
"*That by two immutable things, in which it was impossible for God to lie, we might have a strong consolation, who have fled for refuge to lay hold upon the hope set before us...*" Heb. 6:18

We need the Holy Spirit!
I Cor. 2:12 "*Now we have received... the Spirit which is of God; that we might know the things that are freely given to us of God.*"

We need to always pray Lord, "*Thy will be done!*" Matt. 6:9-13

The ABC's of prayer
    A. Ask
        "*Ask and it shall be given to you...*" Matt. 7:7; Jms. 4:3
    B. Believe
        "*If you believe, you will receive whatever you ask for in prayer.*" Matt. 21:22
    C. Claim
        Claim means, "*An assertion of the truth of something*". If you claim your inheritance, you are declaring your right to that inheritance because you were named as the inheritor by the death of someone.
    D. Decree or Declare
        "*Thou shalt also decree a thing, and it shall be established unto thee.*" Job 22:28
        "*What you decide on will be done!*" Job 22:28 NIV
    E. Examine
        "*Examine yourself to see if you're in the faith...*" II Cor. 13:5

F. Faith
"*Therefore the promise comes by faith...*" Rom. 4:16
G. Give glory and thanks to God!
"*Let them give glory to God...*" Is.42:12;Phil.4:6
H. Humble
"*... humble yourself under the mighty hand of God...*" I Pet. 5:6
I. Inquire
"*... inquire of God...*" Judges 8:5
J. Jesus – ask in the name of Jesus our Creator, Redeemer!
"*He that spared not His own Son, but delivered Him up for us all, how shall He not with Him also freely give us all things?*" Rom. 8: 22;Ps.14: 14
K. Kneel
"*... let us kneel before the Lord...*" Ps. 95:6
L. Learn
"*... learn of Me* (and My promises)..." Matt. 11:29
M. Memorize
Memorize the promises so that you can stand on them, Ps. 119:11!
N. New
"*... His compassions* (#7356 "*mercies, compassion*") *fail not. They are new every morning...*" Lam. 3:22,23
O. Obey
"*... we will receive from Him whatever we ask because we obey Him and do the things that please Him.*" I Jn. 3:22 NLT
P. Pray
"*... be ye therefore sober, and watch unto prayer.*" I Pet. 4:7
Q. Quench not
"*Quench not the* (Holy) *Spirit.*" I Thess. 5:19
R. Rejoice
"*Rejoice in the Lord always.*" Phil. 4:4
S. Study
"*Study to show thyself approved unto God...*" II Tim. 2:15
T. Test
"*... test Me now... saith the Lord...*" Mal. 3:10
U. Understand
"*... I will pray with the understanding...*" I Cor. 14:15
V. Voice
"*... lift your voice like a trumpet...*" Is. 58:1
W. Word
"*Faith comes by hearing, and hearing by the Word...*" Rom. 10:17

X. Exalt God's name
    "Glorify the Lord... let us exalt His name together." Ps. 34:3 NIV
Y. Yes
    "For no matter how many promises God has made, they are 'Yes' in Christ (Jesus).*"* II Cor. 1:20
Z. A to Z
    "I am the Alpha and Omega... first and last" Rev.1:8;22:13

Books of the Bible Abbreviations

Old Testament
Genesis - Gen.
Exodus - Ex.
Leviticus - Lev.
Numbers - Num.
Deuteronomy - Deut.
Joshua - Josh.
Judges - Judges
Ruth - Ruth
I & II Samuel - Sam.
I & II Kings - Kings
I & II Chronicles - Chron.
Ezra - Ezra
Nehemiah - Neh.
Esther - Esther
Job - Job
Psalms - Ps.
Proverbs Prov.
Ecclesiastes - Eccl.
Song of Solomon - Song of Songs
Isaiah - Is.
Jeremiah - Jer.
Lamentations - Lam.
Ezekiel - Ez.
Daniel - Dan.
Hosea - Hosea
Joel - Joel
Amos - Amos
Obadiah - Ob.
Jonah - Jonah
Micah - Mic.
Nahum - Nah.
Habakkuk - Hab.
Zephaniah - Zeph.
Haggai - Hag.
Zechariah - Zech.
Malachi - Mal.

New Testament
Matthew - Matt.
Mark - Mk.
Luke - Lk.
John - Jn.
Acts - Acts
Romans - Rom.
I & II Corinthians - Cor.
Galatians - Gal.
Ephesians - Eph.
Philippians - Phil.
Colossians - Col.
I & II Thessalonians - Thess.
I & II Timothy - Tim.
Titus - Titus
Philemon - Phil.
Hebrews - Heb.
James - Jms.
I & II Peter - Pet.
I, II, & III John - Jn.
Jude
Revelation - Rev.

Bible Versions
(Used in this book)
ABPE = Aramaic Bible in Plain English
AMPC = Amplified Bible Classic Edition
BSB = Berean Study Bible
CEB = Common English Bible
ESV = English Standard Version
GWT = God's Word Translation
HCSB = Holman Christian Standard Bible
JPS Tanakh 1917
KJV = King James Version
LB = Living Bible
LBT = Living Bible Translation
NHEB = New Heart English Bible
NIV = New International Version
NIV fn = New International Version footnote
NIV Reader's Version
NLT = New Living Translation
PB = Peshitta Bible (Peshitta means, "*simple, common, straight*" - sometimes called the "*Syriac Vulgate*" - "*The general, but not universal, consensus is that the Old Testament of the Peshitta was translated into Syriac from the Hebrew, probably in the 2nd century AD, and that the New Testament of the Peshitta was translated from the Greek.*")
RSV = Revised Standard Version
UKJV = Updated King James Version
YLT = Young's Literal Translation
WEB = Word English Bible

Old Testament

The Promises in Chronological Order

Genesis

God blessed the waters and sky
"And God said, Let the waters bring forth abundantly the moving creature that
hath life, and fowl that may fly above the earth in the open firmament of heaven... and God blessed them, saying, Be fruitful, and multiply, and fill the waters in the seas, and let fowl multiply in the earth." Gen. 1:20,22

God gave man dominion over the earth
"... let them have dominion over the fish of the sea, and over the fowl of the air, and over the cattle, and over all the earth, and over every creeping thing that creepeth upon the earth." Gen. 1:26

God blessed mankind to replenish the earth
"And God blessed them, and God said unto them... be fruitful, and multiply, and replenish the earth, and subdue it: and have dominion over the fish of the sea, and over the fowl of the air, and over every living thing that moveth upon the earth." Gen. 1:28

Blessed
"And on the seventh day God ended His work which He had made; and He rested on the seventh day from all His work which He had made. And God blessed the seventh day, and Sanctified it: because that in it He had rested from all His work which God created and made." Gen. 2:2,3

Adam finds a mate
"And the Lord God said, It is not good that the man should be alone; I will make him a help meet for him... and He (God) brought her to the man... and they shall be one flesh" Gen. 2:18,22,24
You can use this verse in your prayer when looking for a mate. Remember that it was God who gave Adam a mate and brought her to him. He can do the same for you or your loved one. You can pray something like this:
Prayer: Father in heaven, You knew that it wasn't good to be alone so I ask that You bring me a helpmate just like You did for Adam. I pray that it would be the right person for me, the one that You have made just for me. Thank You in Jesus' name, Amen!

The 1st promise of a Savior

The Promise:

" *thy seed and her seed; it shall bruise ("crush" NIV) thy head, and thou shalt bruise His heel."* Gen. 3:15

Right at the beginning of the Bible God promises us that Satan will someday be destroyed. And now because of Jesus, God will "...*crush Satan under your feet*" Rom. 16:20

The woman is the church and God puts hatred in the woman for the serpent. Jesus is the Seed that was bruised by dying on the cross and ultimately He will crush the head of the serpent, Satan, by destroying him, Mk.1:24;Lk.4:33. The demons asked Jesus, "... *are You come to destroy us?*" *"In verse 24, the English word 'destroy' is a translation of the Greek word 'appolumi', which means 'to destroy fully', 'complete destruction', 'to perish', or 'to die'. This same word is used many times to describe the utter destruction of individuals and places* (Matt.10:28;12:14;21:41;Lk.17:29). *All of these examples of the word 'apollumi' are used to convey utter or complete destruction. Both the Hebrew and the Greek words for destroy mean 'the destruction and cessation of existence'.*

'Forasmuch then as the children are partakers of flesh and blood, He also Himself likewise took part of the same; that through death He might destroy him that had the power of death, that is, the devil' Heb.2:14 KJV (II Thess.2:8).

"In verse 14, the English word 'destroy' is a translation of the Greek word 'katargeo', which comes from the root 'argeo', which means 'to render entirely useless.' It can also mean 'to abolish', 'to cease', 'to vanish away', or 'to utterly destroy'. Christ will utterly destroy Satan.

About Satan it says, *"Your heart was lifted up because of your beauty, you have corrupted your wisdom by reason of your brightness: I will cast you to the ground, I will lay you before kings, that they may behold you. You have defiled your sanctuaries by the multitude of your iniquities, by the iniquity of your traffic; therefore will I bring forth a fire from the midst of you, it shall devour you, and I will bring you to ashes upon the earth in the sight of all them that behold you. All they that know you among the people shall be astonished at you: you shall be a terror, and **never shall you be anymore**, (Ez.28: 17-19 KJV)."* By B.L Cocherell; File a9pws 7/07

Because of what Jesus did on the cross we have authority to "... *tread on serpents and scorpions, and over all the power of the enemy: and nothing shall by any means hurt you."* Lk. 10:19

"Thou shalt tread upon the lion and adder: the young lion and the dragon shalt thou trample under feet." Ps. 91:13

"And the God of peace shall bruise Satan under your feet shortly ..." Rom. 16:20

"... put their feet upon the necks of them... for thus shall the Lord do to all your enemies against whom ye fight." Josh. 10:25

God promised Cain, Do what's right and God will accept you.

The Condition:
"If thou doest well..." Gen. 4:7

> **The Promise:**
> *"... shalt thou not be accepted?"* Gen. 4:7

"... and if thou doest not well, sin lieth at the door." Gen. 4:7

It's the same for us today – if we don't do what is right, sin is right there to trip us up and cause us, or those we love, to have pain and suffering.

Blessed

"Male and female created He them; and blessed them, and called their name Adam, in the day when they were created." Gen. 5:2

After the flood, Noah offered sacrifices and God accepted his sacrifices and promised that He would not curse the ground again.

"And the Lord smelled a sweet savour; and the Lord said in His heart..." Gen. 8:21

> **The Promise:**
> *"... I will not again curse the ground anymore for man's sake... neither will I again smite anymore everything living, as I have done. While the earth remaineth, seedtime and harvest, and cold and heat, and summer and winter, and day and night shall not cease."* Gen. 8:21,22

Blessed

"God blessed Noah and his sons, and said unto them, 'Be fruitful, and multiply, and replenish the earth. And the fear of you and the dread of you shall be upon every beast of the earth, and upon every fowl of the air, upon all that moveth upon the earth, and upon all the fishes of the sea; into your hand are they delivered. Every moving thing that liveth shall be meat for you; even as the green herb have I given you all things..."' Gen. 9:1-4

Covenant with Noah

"And I will establish My Covenant with you; neither shall all flesh be cut off

anymore by the waters of a flood; neither shall there anymore be a flood to destroy the earth. And God said, This is the token of the Covenant which I make between Me and you and every living creature that is with you, for perpetual generations..." Gen. 9:11,12

The rainbow is a promise that God will never flood the entire earth again. *"I do set My bow in the cloud..."* Gen. 9:13

> **The Promise:**
> *"... and it shall be for a token of a Covenant between Me and the earth. And it shall come to pass, when I bring a cloud over the earth, that the bow shall be seen in the cloud: and I will remember My Covenant, which is between Me and you and every living creature of all flesh and the waters shall no more become a flood to destroy all flesh. And the bow shall be in the cloud; and I will look upon it, that I may remember the everlasting Covenant between God and every living creature of all flesh that is upon the earth. And God said unto Noah, This is the token of the Covenant, which I have established between Me and all flesh that is upon the earth."* Gen. 9:13-17

Blessed
"And He said, Blessed be the Lord God of Shem; and Canaan shall be his servant. God shall enlarge Japheth, and he shall dwell in the tents of Shem; and Canaan shall be his servant." Gen. 9:26,27

Covenant with Abraham (see note after Gen. 17:13 & 24:35)
> **The Promise:**
> *"And I will make of thee a great nation, and I will bless thee, and make thy name great; and thou shalt be a blessing: and I will bless them that bless thee, and curse him that curseth thee: and in thee shall all families of the earth be blessed."* Gen. 12:2,3

God's promise to give Abraham and his descendants the land
"And the Lord appeared unto Abram, and said..." Gen. 12:7

> **The Promise:**
> *"... unto thy seed will I give this land..."* Gen. 12:7

Blessed
"And Abram was very rich in cattle, in silver, and in gold." Gen. 13:2

And now we are adopted children of Abraham and we inherit the promises given to him through Jesus.
"The promises were spoken to Abraham and his seed..." Gal. 3:16
We *"... through faith and patience inherit the promises."* Heb. 6:12
(We are adopted by Abraham if we believe and receive Jesus, Rom. 9:8;Gal.3:1 -3,7,29)

God's promise to Abraham
"Arise, walk through the land in the length of it and in the breadth of it; for I will give it unto thee." Gen. 13:15-17

Blessed
"And he... said... blessed be Abram of the Most High God, possessor of heaven and earth: and blessed be the Most High God, which hath delivered thine enemies into thy hand..." Gen. 14:19,20

God's promise to Abraham
"After these things the Word of the Lord came unto Abram in a vision, saying, Fear not, Abram..." Gen. 15:1

> **The Promise:**
> *"... I am thy shield, and thy exceeding great reward."* Gen. 15:1

More promises to Abraham
"And He (God) brought him (Abraham) forth abroad, and said, Look now toward heaven, and tell the stars, if thou be able to number them: and He (God) said unto him (Abraham)..." Gen. 15:5

> **The Promise:**
> *"... so shall thy seed be."* Gen. 15:5

Abraham believed.
"And he believed in the Lord; and He counted it to him for righteousness. And He said unto him, I am the Lord that brought thee out of Ur of the Chaldees, to give thee this land to inherit it... and he said, Lord God, whereby shall I know that I shall inherit it..." Gen. 15:6-14

> **The Promise:**
> *"... and afterward shall they come out with great substance. And thou shalt go to thy fathers in peace; thou shalt be buried in a good old age. But in the fourth generation they shall come hither again..."* Gen. 15:14-16

"... for the iniquity of the Amorites is not yet full... in the same day the Lord made a Covenant with Abram, saying..." Gen. 15:16-18

> **The Promise:**
> "Unto thy seed have I given this land, from the river of Egypt unto the great river, the river Euphrates..." Gen. 15:18

Promise to Sarah
"And the angel of the Lord said unto her (Sarah)..." Gen. 16:10

> **The Promise:**
> "... I will multiply thy seed exceedingly, that it shall not be numbered for multitude." Gen. 16:10

"... because the Lord heard your affliction." Gen. 16:11
God sees
"... You are the God who sees..." Gen. 16:13

The Covenant
"And when Abram was ninety years old and nine, the Lord appeared to Abram, and said unto him, I am the Almighty God..." Gen 17:1

The Condition:
"... walk before Me, and be thou perfect ("upright or sincere." KJV fn)" Gen. 17:1

> **The Promise:**
> "And I will make My Covenant between Me and thee, and will multiply thee exceedingly." Gen. 17:2

"And Abram fell on his face: and God talked with him, saying, As for Me, behold..." Gen. 17:3

> **The Promise:**
> "My Covenant is with thee, and thou shalt be a father of many nations." Gen. 17:4

"Neither shall thy name anymore be called Abram, but thy name shall be Abraham..." Gen. 17:5

> **The Promise:**
> "... for a father of many nations have I made thee. And I will make thee exceeding fruitful... kings shall come out of thee... I will establish My Covenant between Me and thee and thy seed after thee... to be a God unto thee, and to thy seed... I will be their God." Gen. 17:6-8

"And God said unto Abraham, Thou shalt keep My Covenant therefore, thou, and thy seed after thee in their generations. This is My Covenant, which ye shall keep, between Me and you and thy seed after thee ..." Gen. 17:9,10

The Condition:
"Every man child among you shall be circumcised... he that is born in thy house, and he that is bought with thy money, must needs be circumcised ..." Gen. 17:10

> **The Promise:**
> "... and My Covenant shall be in your flesh for an everlasting Covenant." Gen. 17:13

In the Old Covenant, you had to be circumcised to enter into the Covenant with God, but in the New Covenant you must be circumcised in the heart; through a change of heart, with the help of the Holy Spirit, and through baptism (You must be born of water and Spirit - Jn. 3:5).

God's promise to Sarah
"... but Sarah shall her name be." Gen. 17:15

> **The Promise:**
> "And I will bless her, and give thee a son also of her: yea, I will bless her, and she shall be a mother of nations; kings of people shall be of her." Gen. 17:16

God's promise to Abraham concerning Ishmael

> **The Promise:**
> "... and I will make him a great nation." Gen. 17:20

God's promise concerning Isaac
"... which Sarah shall bear unto thee at this set time in the next year." Gen. 17:21

> **The Promise:**
> "But My Covenant will I establish with Isaac..." Gen. 17:21

God promises Sarah a son
"And he said, I will certainly return unto thee according to the time of life; and, lo..." Gen. 18:10

> **The Promise:**
> "... Sarah thy wife shall have a son." Gen. 18:10

The Promise:
"*Is anything too hard for the Lord? At the time appointed I will return unto thee, according to the time of life, and Sarah shall have a son.*" Gen. 18:14

Nations blessed through Abraham
"*And the Lord said, Shall I hide from Abraham that thing which I do; seeing that Abraham shall surely become a great and mighty nation, and all the nations of the earth shall be blessed in him? For I know him, that he will command his children and his household after him, and they shall keep the way of the Lord, to do justice and Judgment; that the Lord may bring upon Abraham that which he hath spoken of* (promised) *him.*" Gen. 18:17-19

God chose Abraham because He knew Abraham would teach his children to obey God.
God promised Abraham, "*I will not destroy it* (Sodom) *for the sake of ten.*" Gen. 18:32
Lot wanted to go to a small city for a while and God let him but eventually he had to leave that one also.

"*... I have favored you concerning this thing also...*" Gen. 19:21
God said to Lot, "*All right... I will grant your request...*" Gen. 19:21 NLT

After a time of deliberation, God saved Lot for Abraham's sake
"*... God remembered Abraham* (and saved) *Lot out of the midst of the overthrow, when He overthrew the cities in the which Lot dwelt.*" Gen. 19:29
Prayer:
Father in heaven, if You saved Lot because of Abraham, then please save my family because I love You and serve You. In Jesus' name, Amen!

God kept king Abimelech from sinning against Sarah
"*And God said unto him in a dream, Yea, I know that thou didst this in the integrity of thy heart; for I also withheld thee from sinning against Me: therefore suffered I thee not to touch her.*" Gen. 20:6
Prayer:
Father in heaven, if you kept Abimelech from sinning, then please keep me and my family from sinning against You also. In Jesus' name, Amen!

"*... Abraham prayed to God, and God healed...* (them) *so that they bore children.*" Gen. 20:17 ESV

God does what He promises
"... *the Lord was gracious to Sarah as He had said, and the Lord did for Sarah what He had promised.*" Gen. 21:1,2 NIV

Hagar was about to die for lack of water
To Hagar "... *God opened her eyes and she saw a well of water...*" Gen. 21:19 NKJV
She called God, The-God-who-sees, Gen. 16:13 (see names of God, p. 694)

King Abimelech said to Abraham

The Promise:
"*God is with thee in all that thou doest...*" Gen. 21:22

"*And Abraham said, My son (Isaac)...*" Gen. 22:8

God provides
"*And Abraham called the name of that place Jehovah-Jireh: as it is said to this day...*" Gen. 22:14

The Promise:
"*... God will provide Himself a lamb...*" Gen. 22:8

The Promise:
"*... in the Mount of the Lord it shall be seen ("provided" NIV)*" Gen. 22:14

"*And Abraham called the name of the place, The-Lord-Will-Provide; as it is said to this day, In the Mount of the Lord it shall be provided.*" Gen. 22:14 NKJV
Jesus was the true Lamb of God that was provided as a sacrifice for our sins. Jehovah-Jireh means the Lord provides!

God's blessing to Abraham
"*That in blessing I will bless thee, and in multiplying I will multiply thy seed as the stars of the heaven, and as the sand which is upon the sea shore; and thy seed shall possess the gate of his enemies; and in thy seed shall all the nations of the earth be blessed*" Gen. 22:17,18

The Condition:
"*... because thou hast obeyed My voice.*" Gen. 22:18
We are the seed of Abraham through adoption and the promises. The prom-ise of possessing the gates of our enemies is for us also!
"*If you belong to Christ, then you are Abraham's seed.*" Gal. 3:29 NIV

"... *you are heirs and God's promise to Abraham belongs to you.*" Gal. 3:29 NLT

Blessed
"... *the Lord blessed Abraham in all things.*" Gen. 24:1 NKJV
"*The Lord God of heaven, which took me from my father's house, and from the land of my kindred, and which spake unto me, and that sware unto me, saying...*" Gen. 24:7

> **The Promise:**
> "... *unto thy seed will I give this land...*" Gen. 24:7

"*And he* (Laban) *said,* (to Jacob) *Come in, O blessed of the Lord.*" Gen. 24:31 NKJV

God helps him find a wife for Isaac
"... *He shall send His angel before thee, and thou shalt take a wife unto my son from thence.*" Gen. 24:7

Blessed
Laban said to Eliezer (Abraham's servant) "... *Come in, O blessed of the Lord...*" Gen. 24:31 NKJV

"... *the Lord hath blessed my master greatly; and he is become great.. Sarah my master's wife bare a son to my master when she was old: and unto him hath he given all that he hath.*" Gen. 24:35,36

"*And he said unto me...*" Gen. 24:40

> **The Promise:**
> "... *the Lord, before whom I walk, will send His angel with thee, and prosper thy way...*" Gen. 24:40

Abraham to Eliezer
"... *and thou shalt take a wife for my son of my kindred, and of my father's house...*" Gen. 24:40

Eliezer said, "... *the Lord has prospered my way.*" Gen. 24:56 NKJV

The Blessing
"... *be thou the mother of thousands of millions, and let thy seed possess the gate of those which hate them.*" Gen. 24:60

Prayer:
Father in heaven, if You sent Your angel to help Eliezer find Abraham's son a wife, then please send Your angel to help my child/children find a Godly spouse. And let me and my child/ children possess the gates of those who hate us. Thank You in Jesus' name, Amen!

Blessed
"... *God blessed his son Isaac...*" Gen. 25:11 NKJV

Rebeckah conceived
"... *and the Lord granted his* (Jacob's) *plea, and Rebekah his wife conceived.*" Gen. 25:21 NKJV

Promise to Abraham
> **The Promise:**
> "... *I will be with thee, and will bless thee; for unto thee, and unto thy seed... I will make thy seed to multiply as the stars of heaven, and will give unto thy seed all these countries; and in thy seed shall all the nations of the earth be blessed...*" Gen. 26:3,4

The Condition:
"*Because that Abraham obeyed My voice, and kept My charge, My Command-ments, My Statutes, and My laws.*" Gen. 26:5
The reason God chose Abraham was because he was obedient and because he would teach his children to be obedient (Gen. 18:17-19;22:18).

Blessed
"*Then Isaac sowed in that land, and received in the same year an hundredfold: and the Lord blessed him. And the man waxed great, and went forward, and grew until he became very great: for he had possession of flocks, and possession of herds, and great store of servants: and the Philistines envied him.*" Gen. 26:12-14

God gives Rebekah children
"*And Isaac intreated the Lord for his wife, because she was barren: and the Lord was intreated of him, and Rebekah his wife conceived... and the Lord said unto her, Two nations are in thy womb, and two manner of people shall be separated from thy bowel; and the one people shall be stronger than the other people; and the elder shall serve the younger.*" Gen. 26:21,23
Here is a prayer you can pray if you want God to give you children.

Prayer:
Father in heaven, You listened to Isaac's prayer and gave him children. Please give me children as You did for him, if it's Your will. Thank You in Jesus' name, Amen!

"And the Lord appeared unto him the same night, and said, I am the God of Abraham thy father" Gen. 26:24

> **The Promise:**
> *"... fear not, for I am with thee... will bless thee, and multiply thy seed for My servant Abraham's sake."* Gen. 26: 24

"... we have certainly seen that the Lord is with you." Gen. 26:28 NKJV

Blessed
"... blessed of the Lord." Gen. 26:29 NKJV

Isaac said to Jacob, *"And make me savoury meat, such as I love, and bring it to me, that I may eat; that my soul may bless thee before I die."* Gen. 27:4
Blessed
God has blessed the fields of the earth
The fields *"which the Lord hath blessed..."* Gen. 27:27
The Bible says that He sends rain on the good and the bad, Matt. 5:45.
Isaac's blessing to Jacob
"Therefore God give thee of the dew of heaven, and the fatness of the earth, and plenty of corn and wine: let people serve thee, and nations bow down to thee: be lord over thy brethren, and let thy mother's sons bow down to thee: cursed be everyone that curseth thee, and blessed be he that blesseth thee." Gen. 27:28,29

Blessed
"... I have blessed him – and indeed he shall be blessed." Gen. 27:33 NKJV

Blessed
"Then Isaac called Jacob and blessed him..." Gen. 28:1

The Blessing of Abraham
"And God Almighty bless thee, and make thee fruitful, and multiply thee, that thou mayest be a multitude of people; and give thee the blessing of Abraham, to thee, and to thy seed with thee; that thou mayest inherit the land wherein thou art a stranger, which God gave unto Abraham." Gen. 28:3,4

We inherit the blessings of Abraham through Christ Jesus.
"May He give you and your descendants the blessing given to Abraham, so that you may take possession of the land where you now reside as a foreigner, the land God gave to Abraham." Gen. 28:4 NIV
"That the blessing of Abraham might come on the Gentiles through Jesus Christ; that we might receive the promise of the Spirit through faith." Gal. 3:14

Jacob's Ladder
"And behold, the Lord stood above it ("at the top of the stairway" NLT), and said, I am the Lord God of Abraham thy father, and the God of Isaac..." Gen. 28:13

The Promise:
"... the land... to thee will I give it, and to thy seed; and thy seed shall be as the dust of the earth, and thou shalt spread abroad to the West and to the East, and to the North, and to the South: and in thee and in thy seed shall all the families of the earth be blessed. And behold I am with thee, and will keep thee in all places whither thou goest and will bring thee again into this land; for I will not leave thee, until I have done that which I have spoken to thee of." Gen. 28:13-15

God is the One who opens and closes the womb
"And when the Lord saw that Leah was hated, He opened her womb: but Rachel was barren. And Leah conceived, and bare a son... she said Surely the Lord hath looked upon my affliction; now therefore my husband will love me. And she conceived again, and bare a son; and said, Because the Lord hath heard that I was hated, He hath therefore given me this son also..." Gen. 29:31-33

God listens
"And God listened to Leah, and she conceived..." Gen. 30:17 NKJV
"And God remembered Rachel, and God hearkened to her, and opened her womb. And she conceived, and bare a son; and said, God hath taken away my reproach..." Gen. 30:22,23
We see here that it is God who opens and closes the womb.

Laban blessed because of Jacob
"And Laban said unto him (Jacob)... the Lord hath blessed me for thy sake..." Gen. 30:27

Blessed
And Jacob said to Laban, "... and it is now increased unto a multitude; and the Lord hath blessed thee since my coming..." Gen. 30:30

Blessed
"And the man (Jacob) increased exceedingly, and had much cattle, and maidservants, and menservants, and camels, and (donkeys)." Gen. 30:43
"So the man became exceedingly prosperous..." Gen. 30:43 NASB

"... I will be with you." Gen. 31:3 NKJV

God sees our affliction
"Except the God of my father, the God of Abraham, and the fear of Isaac, had been with me, surely thou hadst sent me away now empty. God hath seen mine affliction and the labour of my hands, and rebuked thee (last)... night." Gen. 31:42

Jacob reminds God of His promises
"And Thou saidist, Return unto thy country, and to thy kindred, and I will deal well with thee ..." Gen. 32:12

> **The Promise:**
> "... I will surely do thee good, and make thy seed as the sand of the sea, which cannot be numbered..." Gen. 32: 9, 12

Bless me!
"... I will not let Thee go, except Thou bless me." Gen.32:26

Blessed
"... and He blessed him there." Gen. 32:29

Jacob to Esau
"Take, I pray thee, my blessing that is brought to thee; because God hath dealt graciously with me, and because I have enough." Gen. 33:11

God answered
"... God, who answered me in the day of my distress, and was with me in the way which I went." Gen. 35:3

God protects
"And they journeyed: and the terror of God was upon the cities that were

round about them, and they did not pursue after the sons of Jacob." Gen. 35:5

God put fear on the nations around Jacob so he would not be hurt by them.
Prayer:
Father in heaven, please put fear in anyone who would hurt me. Thank You in Jesus' name, Amen!

God repeats the promise of Abraham to Jacob
"And God said unto him, Thy name is Jacob; thy name shall not be called anymore Jacob, but Israel shall be thy name: and He called his name Israel. And God said unto him, I am God Almighty: be fruitful and multiply; a nation and a company of nations shall be of thee, and kings shall come out of thy loins; and the land which I gave Abraham and Isaac, to thee I will give it, and thy seed after thee will I give the land." Gen. 35:10,11

Jacob blessed

> **The Promise:**
> *"... be fruitful and multiply; a nation and a company of nations shall be of thee, and kings shall come out of thy loins; and the land which I gave Abraham and Isaac, to thee I will give it, and to thy seed after thee will I give the land."* Gen. 35:11,12

Prayer:
Father in heaven, please give me the blessings of Abraham, Isaac, and Jacob. Thank You in Jesus' name, Amen!

God's blessing on Joseph
"And the Lord was with Joseph, and he was a prosperous man... the Lord was with Joseph, and shewed him mercy, and gave him favour in the sight of the keeper of the prison. And the keeper of the prison committed to Joseph's hand all the prisoners that were in the prison; and whatsoever they did there, he was the doer of it. The keeper of the prison looked not to any thing that was under his hand; because the Lord was with him, and that which he did, the Lord made it to prosper. And Joseph found grace in His sight... the Lord blessed the Egyptian's house for Joseph's sake; and the blessing of the Lord was upon all that he had in the house, and in the field. And he left all that he had in Joseph's hand... Joseph was a goodly person, and well favoured." Gen. 39:2-6
Prayer: Father in heaven, please give me Your favor in Jesus' name, Amen!

God gave Joseph mercy and favor
"But the Lord was with Joseph, and shewed him mercy, and gave him favour in the sight of the keeper of the prison. And the keeper of the prison committed to Joseph's hand all the prisoners that were in the prison; and whatsoever they did there, he was the doer of it. The keeper of the prison looked not to anything that was under his hand; because the Lord was with him, and that which he did, the Lord made it to prosper." Gen. 39:21-23

God gives the interpretation of dreams
"... do not interpretations belong to God?" Gen. 40:8

Joseph gives all the glory to God who gives us the answers
"... it is not in me: God shall give Pharaoh an answer of peace." Gen. 41:16

Joseph was full of the Holy Spirit
Pharaoh says, *"... can we find such a one as this is, a man in whom the Spirit of God is?"* Gen. 41:38

Pharaoh tells Joseph to tell his family
"... I will provide for you, lest you and your household, and all that you have, come to poverty..." Gen. 45:11 NKJV

The fat of the land
"... and I will give you the good of the land of Egypt, and ye shall eat the fat of the land... for the good of all the land of Egypt is yours." Gen. 45:18,20

God tells Jacob that He is with him
"And he said, I am God, the God of thy father: fear not to go down into Egypt; for I will there make of thee a great nation: I will go down with thee into Egypt; and I will also surely bring thee up again: and Joseph shall put his hand upon thine eyes." Gen. 46:3,4

Jacob blesses Ephraim and Manasseh
And Jacob asked Joseph, *"Who are these? And Joseph said unto his father, They are my sons, whom God hath given me in this place. And he said, Bring them, I pray thee, unto me, and I will bless them."* Gen. 47:8,9

Blessed
"And Jacob blessed Pharaoh..." Gen. 47:10

Blessed by God
"... God Almighty appeared unto me at Luz in the land of Canaan, and

blessed me, and said unto me..." Gen. 48:3,4

The Promise:
"... Behold, I will make thee fruitful, and multiply thee, and I will make of thee a multitude of people; and will give this land to thy seed after thee for an everlasting possession." Gen. 48:4

Joseph's two sons.
"And now thy two sons, Ephraim and Manasseh, which were born unto thee in the land of Egypt before I came unto thee into Egypt, are mine; as Reuben and Simeon, they shall be mine." Gen. 48:5

Blessed
"... I will bless them." Gen. 48:9

Joseph brings Ephraim and Manasseh to Jacob to be blessed.
"And he brought them near unto him; and he kissed them, and embraced them. And Israel said unto Joseph, I had not thought to see thy face: and lo, God hath shewed me also thy seed... and he blessed Joseph, and said, God, before whom my father's Abraham and Isaac did walk, the God which fed me all my life long unto this day, the Angel which Redeemed me from all evil, bless the lads; and let my name be named on them, and the name of my fathers, Abraham and Isaac; and let them grow into a multitude in the midst of the earth. And when Joseph saw that his father laid his right hand upon the head of Ephraim, it displeased him: and he held up his father's hand, to remove it from Ephraim's head unto Manasseh's head. And Joseph said unto his father, not so, my father: for he is the firstborn; put thy right hand upon his head. And his father refused, and said, I know it, my son, I know it: he also shall become a people and he also shall be great: but truly his younger brother shall be greater than he, and his seed shall become a multitude of nations. And he blessed them that day, saying, In thee shall Israel bless, saying, God make thee as Ephraim and as Manasseh: and he set Ephraim before Manasseh. And Israel said unto Joseph, Behold, I die: but God shall be with you, and bring you again unto the land of your fathers. Moreover I have given to thee one portion above thy brethren..." Gen. 48:10-22

Promise of Messiah
"Judah, thou art he whom thy brethren shall praise... thy father's children shall bow down before thee. The scepter shall not depart from Judah, nor a lawgiver from between his feet until Shiloh come; and unto Him shall the gathering of the people be." Gen. 49:8,10

Bless thee with blessings
"Even by the God of thy father, who shall help thee; and by the Almighty, who shall bless thee with blessings of heaven above, blessings of the deep that lieth under... blessings of thy father have prevailed above the blessings of my progenitors unto the utmost bound of the everlasting hills ..." Gen. 49:25,26

Blessed
"All these are the twelve tribes of Israel: and this is it that their father spake unto them, and blessed them; every one according to his blessing he blessed them." Gen. 49:28
See Jacob's blessing over his 12 sons in Topical section.

God turns bad things into good!
"... ye thought evil against me; but God meant it unto good, to bring to pass, as it is this day, to save much people alive. Now therefore fear ye not: I will nourish you, and your little ones. And he comforted them, and spake kindly unto them." Gen. 50:20,21

Joseph reminds his brothers of God's promises
"And Joseph said unto his brethren, I die ..." Gen. 50:24

> **The Promise:**
> *"... and God will surely visit you, and bring you out of this land unto the land which He sware to Abraham, to Isaac, and to Jacob... God will surely visit you..."* Gen. 50:24,25

"... and ye shall carry up my bones from hence." Gen. 50:24,25

Exodus

God provides for those who fear Him
"God dealt well with the midwives... because the midwives feared God, that He provided households for them." Ex. 1:20,21 NKJV

God remembered His Covenant
"... and their cry came up unto God by reason of the bondage. And God heard their groaning, and God remembered His Covenant with Abraham, with Isaac, and with Jacob. And God looked upon the children of Israel, and God had respect unto them." Ex. 2:23-25

A land flowing with milk and honey
"And the Lord said, I have surely seen the affliction of My people which are in Egypt, and have heard their cry by reason of their taskmasters; for I know their sorrows; and I am come down to deliver them out of the hand of the Egyptians, and to bring them up out of that land unto a good land and a large, unto a land flowing with milk and honey… bring forth My people the children of Israel out of Egypt." Ex. 3:7-10
Here is a prayer you could pray using this verse.
Prayer:
Father in heaven, look down from heaven and see my afflictions and sorrows. Deliver me from those stronger than me as You did for them and bring me to the true land of promise, the New Earth. In Jesus' name, Amen!

God's promise to Moses
> **The Promise:**
> I will be with you and "… *ye shall serve God upon this Mountain* (Mt. Horeb/Mt. Sinai)" Ex. 3:12

"And God said unto Moses I Am that I Am: and He said, Thus shalt thou say unto the children of Israel, I Am hath sent me unto you. And God said moreover unto Moses, Thus shalt thou say unto the children of Israel, the Lord God of your fathers, the God of Abraham, the God of Isaac, and the God of Jacob, hath sent me unto you: this is My name forever, and this is My memorial unto all generations. Go, and gather the elders of Israel together, and say unto them, the Lord God of your fathers, the God of Abraham, of Isaac, and of Jacob, appeared unto me, saying, I have surely visited you, and seen that which is done to you in Egypt: and I have said, I will bring you up out of the affliction of Egypt unto the land (I promised you)… *unto a land flowing with milk and honey"* Ex. 3:14-17
The name of God, "*I Am*" is actually a promise: a promise He makes that I Am:
- your healing
- your life
- your power
- your riches
- your strength
- your sufficiency
- everything that you need!

Jesus identified Himself as the "*I Am*" in Jn. 8:58 when He said, "*Before Abraham was, I Am*". The Jews understood what He said and tried to stone Him for blasphemy. Now if you're not God and you say you're God, then that is blasphemy, but Jesus was God, so it was not blasphemy for Him to declare Himself to be who He really is. In fact, it would have been a lie if He had said He wasn't God because He really is. He said, Believe that I Am who I say I Am because of the miracles.

"... though you believe not Me, believe the works... that the Father is in Me, and I in Him." Jn. 10:38

"... the Father who dwelleth in Me, He doeth the works... believe Me for the very work's sake." Jn. 14:10

Remember that one of Jesus' names is Immanuel meaning, "God with us". Thomas said to Jesus, My Lord and my God in Jn. 20:28.

God gives favor

"And I will give this people favour in the sight of the Egyptians: and it shall come to pass, that, when ye go, ye shall not go empty: but every woman shall borrow of her neighbor, and of her that sojourneth in her house, jewels of silver, and jewels of gold, and raiment: and ye shall put them upon your sons, and upon your daughters; and ye shall spoil the Egyptians." Ex. 3:21,22

Prayer:
Father in heaven, give me favor as You did for them. Thank You in Jesus' name, Amen!

The Israelites had been slaves and worked with very little pay and now God was giving them recommence.

God will teach us what to say

"... who hath made man's mouth? Or who maketh the dumb, or deaf, or the seeing, or the blind? Have not I the Lord? Now therefore go..." Ex. 4:11,12

The Promise:
"... and I will be with thy mouth, and teach thee what thou shalt say... and... what ye shall do." Ex. 4:11,12,15

Prayer:
Father in heaven, please be with my mouth and teach me what to say and do as You were with Moses. Help me to say a kind word to those who need it – help me to speak life when needed – Keep my tongue from hurting others or speaking foolishly. Thank You in Jesus' name, Amen!

Jethro blesses Moses
"... go in peace." Ex. 4:18

God's promises to Moses

The Promise:
"Then the Lord said unto Moses, Now shalt thou see what I will do to Pharaoh: for with a strong hand shall he let them go, and with a strong hand shall he drive them out of his land..." Ex. 6:1

"And I appeared unto Abraham, unto Isaac, and unto Jacob, by the name of God Almighty, but by My name, Jehovah, was I not known to them." Ex. 6:3

Covenant
"And I have also established My Covenant with them, to give them the land of Canaan, the land of their pilgrimage, wherein they were strangers." Ex. 6:4

God's promise to the children of Israel
"I have also heard the groaning of the children of Israel, whom the Egyptians keep in bondage; and I have remembered My Covenant. Wherefore say unto the children of Israel, I am the Lord, and..." Ex. 6:5,6

The Promise:
"... I will bring you out from under the burdens of the Egyptians... I will rid you out of their bondage... I will Redeem you with a stretched out arm, and with great Judgments... I will take you to Me for a people, and I will be to you a God... ye shall know that I am the Lord your God, which bringeth you out from under the burdens of the Egyptians. And I will bring you in unto the land... for an heritage..." Ex. 6:6-8

"... I Am the Lord." Ex. 6:8

Prayer:
Father in heaven, please bring me out from my burdens and take me out of all bondage. Redeem me with Your outstretched arm; be my God and let me be Yours. Bring me at last to the land of promise – the New Earth. Thank You in Jesus' name, Amen!

"And the Lord said unto Moses... I will... multiply My signs and My wonders in the land of Egypt... and bring forth Mine armies... and the Egyptians shall know that I am the Lord, when I stretch forth Mine hand upon Egypt..." Ex. 7:1-5

"So the Lord did according to the word of Moses." Ex. 8:13 NKJV

The Promise:
"And I (God) will put a division between My people and thy people..." Ex. 8:23

"And the Lord did according to the word of Moses..." Ex. 8:31

"But the Lord will make a distinction between the livestock of Israel and the livestock of Egypt, so that nothing of all that belongs to the people of Israel shall die." Ex. 9:4 ESV

God said to Moses
"And in very deed for this cause have I raised thee up, for to shew in thee My power; and that My name may be declared throughout all the earth." Ex. 9:16
God did not let hail come down on the Israelites and He can keep us from evil also, Ex. 9:26.

The Earth is the Lord's
"... that thou mayest know how that the earth is the Lord's ... and Moses... spread abroad his hands unto the Lord: and the thunders and hail ceased, and the rain was not poured upon the earth." Ex. 9:29,33

"Then the Lord said to Moses, Go to Pharaoh, for I have hardened his heart and the hearts of his officials so that I may do these miraculous signs of Mine among them, and so that you may tell your son and grandson how severely I dealt with the Egyptians and performed miraculous signs among them, and you will know that I am Yahweh." Ex. 10:1,2

When all of Egypt had darkness from the plagues of Moses *"... all the children of Israel had light in their dwellings."* Ex. 10:23

God's promise to Moses
"And the Lord said unto Moses, Yet will I bring one plague more upon Pharaoh, and upon Egypt; afterwards..." Ex. 11:1

> **The Promise:**
> *"... he will let you go hence..."* Ex. 11:1

"... when he shall let you go, he shall surely thrust you out hence altogether. Speak now in the ears of the people, and let every man borrow of his neighbor,
and every woman of her neighbor, jewels of silver, and jewels of gold." Ex. 11:1,2

> **The Promise:**
> *"And the Lord gave the people favour in the sight of the Egyptians."* Ex. 11:3

God made Moses great
"Moreover the man Moses was very great in the land of Egypt, in the sight of Pharaoh's servants, and in the sight of the people..." Ex. 11:3

God's promises to the Israelites
> **The promise:**
> *"... but against any of the children of Israel shall not a dog move his tongue, against man or beast..."* Ex. 11:7

"... that ye may know how that the Lord doth put a difference between the Egyptians and Israel." Ex. 11:7
"Then shall ye return, and discern between the righteous and the wicked, between him that serveth God and him that serveth him not." Mal. 3:18
"He that is unjust, let im be unjust still: and he which is filthy, let him be filthy still: and he that is righteous let him be righteous stll: and he that is Holy, let him be Holy still." Rev. 22:11

Wonders multiplied
"... that My wonders may be multiplied in the land of Egypt. And Moses and Aaron did all these wonders before Pharaoh. And the blood shall be to you for a token upon the houses where ye are..." Ex. 11:9,10

> **The Promise:**
> *"... and when I see the blood, I will pass over you, and the plague shall not be upon you to destroy you..."* Ex. 12:13

"... when I smite the land of Egypt." Ex. 12:13
"... no plague shall be upon you." Ex. 12:13 AMP

> **The Promise:**
> *"... the Lord will pass over the door, and will not suffer the Destroyer to come in unto your houses to smite you."* Ex. 12:23

God now sees the blood of Jesus on us and rebukes the Destroyer or Devourer for our sakes; Satan is the Destroyer! I have this promise hanging over my front door.
Prayer:
Father in heaven, please stand guard over my doors and windows and don't let the Destroyer come in. Thank You! In the name of Jesus, Amen!

"And it shall come to pass... according as He hath promised... that ye shall say, It is the sacrifice of the Lord's Passover, who passed over the houses of

the children of Israel in Egypt, when he smote the Egyptians, and delivered our houses. And the people bowed the head and worshipped." Ex. 12:25-27

> **The Promise:**
> "And the Lord gave the people favour in the sight of the Egyptians so that they lent unto them such things as they required. And they spoiled the Egyptians." Ex. 12:36

God did what He promised
"It is a night to be much observed unto the Lord for bringing them out from the land of Egypt..." Ex. 12:42
"... the Lord did bring the children of Israel out of the land of Egypt by their armies." Ex. 12:51

> **The Promise:**
> "... for by strength of hand the Lord brought you out from this place... (to) a land flowing with milk and honey..." Ex. 13:3,5

"... for with a strong hand hath the Lord brought thee out of Egypt... By strength of hand the Lord brought us out from Egypt, from the house of bondage..." Ex. 13:9,14,16

"And Moses took the bones of Joseph with him: for he had straitly sworn the children of Israel, saying..." Ex. 13:19

> **The Promise:**
> "... God will surely visit you; and ye shall carry up my bones away hence with you." Ex. 13:19

Cloud by day and pillar of fire by night
"And the Lord went before them by day in a pillar of a cloud, to lead them the way; and by night in a pillar of fire, to give them light; to go by day and night: He took not away the pillar of the cloud by day, nor the pillar of fire by night, from before the people." Ex. 13:21,22

Salvation of God
"... fear ye not, stand still, and see the Salvation of the Lord, which He will shew to you today..." Ex. 14:13
"... and ye shall hold your peace... go forward..." Ex. 14:13-15

> **The Promise:**
> "The Lord shall fight for you..." Ex. 14:14

Miracle
"... the Lord caused the sea to go back by a strong East wind all that night,

and made the sea dry land, and the waters were divided. And the children of Israel went into the midst of the sea upon the dry ground..." Ex. 14:21,22

God fights for you
And the Lord "... took off their chariot wheels... for the Lord fighteth for them against the Egyptians... the Lord overthrew the Egyptians in the midst of the sea... there remained not so much as one of them." Ex. 14:25,27,28
It says, "... not so much as one of them remained..." Ex. 14:28 NKJV – which includes Pharaoh. That meant that Egypt had no leader or men of army age; therefore it was left unprotected!

They saw and believed!
"And Israel saw that great work which the Lord did upon the Egyptians: and the people feared the Lord, and believed the Lord, and His servant Moses." Ex. 14:31

Moses' Song (A song of God's triumph – they also sing this in Rev. 15:3)
"The Lord is my strength and song, and He is become my Salvation: He is my God, and I will prepare Him an habitation... I will exalt Him. The Lord is a man of war... Thy right hand, O Lord, is become glorious in power: Thy right hand, O Lord, hath dashed in pieces the enemy. And in the greatness of Thine excellency Thou hast overthrown them that rose up against Thee: Thou sentest forth Thy wrath, which consumed them as stubble... the floods stood upright as an heap, and the depths were congealed in the heart of the sea. The enemy said, I will pursue, I will overtake, I will divide the spoil; my lust shall be satisfied upon them; I will draw My sword, my hand shall destroy them. Thou didst blow with Thy wind, the sea covered them: they sank as lead in the mighty waters. Who is like unto Thee, O Lord, among the gods? Who is like Thee, glorious in Holiness, fearful in praises, doing wonders? Thou stretchedst out Thy right hand, the earth swallowed them. Thou in Thy mercy hast led forth the people which Thou hast Redeemed: Thou hast guided them in Thy strength unto Thy Holy habitation. The people shall hear, and be afraid... (they) shall melt away. Fear and dread shall fall upon them; by the greatness of Thine arm they shall be as still as a stone... the Lord shall reign forever and ever... sing ye to the Lord, for He hath triumphed gloriously; the horse and his rider hath He thrown into the sea." Ex. 15:2-21

The waters of Marah
"And he cried unto the Lord; and the Lord shewed him a tree, which when he had cast into the waters, the waters were made sweet..." Ex. 15:25
The tree was a symbol of the cross.

The Condition:
"... *if thou wilt diligently hearken to the voice of the Lord thy God, and wilt do that which is right in His sight, and wilt give ear to His Commandments, and keep all His Statutes...*" Ex. 15:26

> **The Promise:**
> "... *I will put none of these diseases upon thee, which I have brought upon the Egyptians: for I am the Lord that healeth thee.*" Ex. 15:26

The miracle of Manna
"*Then said the Lord unto Moses, Behold, I will rain bread from heaven for you...*" Ex. 16:4

The Condition:
"... *that I might prove them whether they will walk in My law, or no.*" Ex. 16:4

> **The Promise:**
> "... *it* (the manna) *shall be twice as much* (on Friday) *as they gather daily...* " Ex. 16:5

Miracle
"... *then ye shall see the glory of the Lord for He hears* (you)... *the Lord shall give you in the evening flesh to eat, and in the morning bread to the full; for that the Lord heareth* (you)... *at even ye shall eat flesh, and in the morning ye shall be filled with bread; and ye shall know that I am the Lord your God. And it came to pass, that at even the quails came up...*" Ex. 16:7-9,12,13

Miracle
"*And when the dew that lay was gone up, behold, upon the face of the wilderness there lay a small round thing, as small as the hoar frost on the ground* (Manna)". Ex. 16:14
Jesus is the true bread that came down from heaven, Jn. 6:58.

"... *he that gathered much had nothing over, and he that gathered little had no lack...*" Ex. 16:18

God is a banner over me
"*And Moses built an altar, and called the name of it Jehovah-Nissi.*" (*"That is, The Lord my banner"* KJV fn)" Ex. 17:15
Jethro blesses God for all He had done!
Moses' son, Eliezer means "... *for the God of my father... was mine help, and delivered me from the sword...*" Ex. 18:4

Blessed
"And Moses told his father-in-law all that the Lord had done... for Isarel's sake... and how the Lord delivered them. And Jethro rejoiced for all the good-ness which the Lord had done to Israel, whom he had delivered... and Jethro said, Blessed be the Lord, who hath delivered you out of the hand of the Egypt-ians, and out of the hand of Pharaoh... now I know that the Lord is greater than all gods: for in the thing wherein they dealt proudly He was above them." Ex. 18:8-11

> **The Promise:**
> "... God will be with you..." Ex. 18:19 NKJV

Jethro tells Moses to appoint 70 men
"If you do this, God will direct you, you will be able to endure, and all this people also will go to their place in peace." Ex. 18:23 ESV

"... I bare you on eagles' wings, and brought you unto Myself. Now there-fore..." Ex. 19:4
The Condition:
"... if ye will obey My voice indeed, and keep My Covenant..." Ex. 19:5

> **The Promise:**
> "... then ye shall be a peculiar treasure unto Me above all people: for all the earth is Mine: and ye shall be unto me a Kingdom of priests, and an Holy nation." Ex. 19:5,6

Now we are all priests if we are in Christ Jesus (I Pet.2:9;Rev. 5:10).

Believe
"And the Lord said unto Moses, Lo, I come unto thee in a thick cloud, that the people may hear when I speak with thee, and believe thee forever." Ex. 19:9

Blessed:
"... the Lord blessed the seventh day and hallowed It (made it Holy)..." Ex. 20:11

The Condition:
"Honour thy father and thy mother..." Ex. 20:12

> **The Promise:**
> "... that thy days may be long upon the land which the Lord thy God giveth thee." Ex. 20:12

The first Commandment with promise, Eph. 6:2.
"*And Moses said unto the people, Fear not: for God is come to prove you, and that His fear may be before your faces, that ye sin not... and the Lord said unto Moses, Thus thou shalt say unto the children of Israel, ye have seen that I have talked with you from heaven.*" Ex. 20:20,22
The fear of the Lord is the beginning of wisdom, Prov. 9:10. And when we fear God, we don't want to sin against Him.
The Condition:
"*... ye shall not make with Me gods of silver, neither shall ye make unto you gods of gold...*" Ex. 20:23,24

> **The Promise:**
> "*... in all places where I record My name I will come unto thee, and I will bless thee...*" Ex. 20:24

The Condition:
"*If thou lend money to any of My people that is poor by thee, thou shalt not be to him as an usurer, neither shalt thou lay upon him usury...*" Ex. 22:25

> **The Promise:**
> "*... and it shall come to pass, when he crieth unto Me, that I will hear; for I am gracious.*" Ex. 22:27

> **The Promise:**
> "*Behold, I send an Angel before thee, to keep thee in the way, and to bring thee into the place which I have prepared.*" Ex. 23:20

The Condition:
"*Beware of him, and obey his voice, provoke him not; for he will not pardon your transgressions: for My name is in him...*" Ex. 23:21

The Condition:
"*But if thou shalt indeed obey his voice, and do all that I speak...*" Ex. 23:22

> **The Promise:**
> "*... then I will be an enemy unto thine enemies, and an adversary unto thine adversaries. For Mine Angel shall go before thee, and bring thee in... and I will cut them off.*" Ex. 23:22,23

The Condition:
"*Thou shalt not bow down to their gods, nor serve them, nor do after their works: but thou shalt utterly overthrow them, and quite break down their images. And ye shall serve the Lord your God...*" Ex. 23:24,25

Blessed
> **The Promise:**
> *"... and He shall bless thy bread, and thy water; and I will take sickness away from the midst of thee. There shall nothing cast their young, nor be barren, in thy land: the number of thy days I will fulfil. I will send My fear before thee, and will destroy all the people to whom thou shalt come, and I will make all thine enemies turn their backs unto thee. And I will send hornets before thee, which shall drive out the Hivite, the Canaanite, and the Hittite, from before thee. I will not drive them out from before thee in one year; lest the land become desolate, and the beast of the field multiply against thee. By little and little I will drive them out from before thee until thou be increased, and inherit the land. And I will set thy bound from the Red Sea even unto the sea of the Philistines, and from the desert unto the river: for I will deliver the inhabitants of the land into your hand; and thou shalt drive them out before thee."* Ex. 23:25-32

The Condition:
"Thou shalt make no covenant with them nor with their gods. They shall not dwell in thy land, lest they make thee sin against Me: for if thou serve their gods, it will surely be a snare unto thee." Ex. 23:32,33

Moses reminds God of His promise to Israel
"And let them make Me a Sanctuary; that I may dwell among them" Ex. 25:8

God promised to meet with them
"And there I will meet with thee, and I will commune with thee from above the mercy seat from between the two Cherubims which are upon the Ark of the Testimony, of all things which I will give thee in Commandment unto the children of Israel." Ex. 25:22

"And I have filled him with the Spirit of God, in wisdom, and in understanding, and in knowledge, and in all manner of workmanship ..." Ex. 31:3

> **The Promise:**
> *"... I will multiply your seed as the stars of heaven, and all this land that I have spoken of will I give unto your seed, and they shall inherit it forever."* Ex. 32:13

Blessed
"Consecrate yourselves... that He may bestow on you a blessing this day." Ex. 32:29 NKJV

God speaks to Moses
"And the Lord spake unto Moses face to face, as a man speaketh unto his friend... I know thee by name, and thou hast also found grace in My sight." Ex. 33:12

"And He said..." Ex. 33:14

> **The Promise:**
> *"... My presence shall go with thee, and I will give thee rest."* Ex. 33:14

Grace
"... I will do this thing also that thou hast spoken: for thou hast found grace in My sight, and I know thee by name." Ex. 33:17

"And (God) said, I will make all My goodness pass before thee (Moses), and I will proclaim the name of the Lord before thee..." Ex. 33:19

> **The Promise:**
> *"... and will be gracious to whom I will be gracious, and will shew mercy on whom I will shew mercy."* Ex. 33:19

"And the Lord passed by before him, and proclaimed, The Lord, The Lord God, merciful and gracious, longsuffering, and abundant in goodness and truth. Keeping mercy for thousands, forgiving iniquity and transgression and sin, and that will by no means clear the guilty; visiting the iniquity of the fathers upon the children, and upon the children's children, unto the third and to the fourth generation." Ex. 34:6,7

"And he said, Behold, I make a Covenant: before all thy people I will do marvels, such as have not been done in all the earth, nor in any nation: and all the people among which thou art shall see the work of the Lord: for it is a terrible ("awesome" ESV) thing that I will do with thee." Ex. 34:10

> **The Promise:**
> *"... My presence shall go with thee, and I will give thee rest."* Ex. 34:14

God's promise to those working on the Tabernacle
"And He hath filled him with the Spirit of God, in wisdom, in understanding, and in knowledge, and in all manner of workmanship... them hath He filled

with wisdom of heart, to work all manner of work, of the engraver, and of the cunning workman, and of the embroiderer... even of them that do any work, and of those that devise cunning work." Ex. 35:31,35

"... every wise hearted man, in whom the Lord put wisdom and understanding to know how to work all manner of work for the service of the Sanctuary, according to all that the Lord had commanded... and every wise hearted man, in whose heart the Lord had put wisdom, even every one whose heart stirred him up to come unto the work to do it..." Ex. 36:1,2

Prayer:
Father in heaven, if You could put wisdom and understanding in Bezaleel and Aholiab, then please fill me with Your wisdom and understanding also. For You said in Jms. 1:5 that whoever asked for wisdom, You would give it freely to them. Thank you in Jesus' name, Amen!

Sanctified
"... I am the Lord who Sanctifies you." Lev. 22:32 NKJV

The Condition:
"Wherefore ye shall do My Statutes, and keep My Judgments, and do them..." Lev. 25:18

The Promise:
"... and ye shall dwell in the land in safety. And the land shall yield her fruit, and ye shall eat your fill, and dwell therein in safety... then I will command My blessing upon you in the sixth year, and it shall bring forth fruit for three years." Lev. 25:18,19,21

The Prayer:
Father in heaven, if you could keep the Israelites safe in their land and let their gardens and vineyards flourish, then please do the same for me. Help me to obey You in everything. Thank you in Jesus' name, Amen!

The Jubilee
"... and in the (year of) Jubilee it shall be released, and he shall return to his possession." Lev. 25:28
The ultimate Jubilee is when Jesus comes and gives us back everything that was taken from us.

The Condition:
"If ye walk in My Statutes, and keep My Commandments, and do them ..." Lev. 26:3

> **The Promise:**
> "... then I will give you rain in due season, and the land shall yield her increase, and the trees of the field shall yield their fruit. And your threshing shall reach unto the vintage, and the vintage shall reach unto the sowing time: and ye shall eat your bread to the full, and dwell in your land safely. And I will give peace in the land, and ye shall lie down, and none shall make you afraid: and I will rid evil beasts out of the land, neither shall the sword go through your land... and five of you shall chase an hundred, and an hundred of you shall put ten thousand to flight: and your enemies shall fall before you... for I will have respect unto you, and make you fruitful, and multiply you, and establish My Covenant with you. And ye shall eat old store, and bring forth the old because of the new. And I will set My Tabernacle among you: and My soul shall not abhor you. And I will walk among you, and will be your God, and ye shall be My people. I am the Lord your God... and I have broken the bands of your yoke, and made you go upright." Lev. 26:4-13

The Prayer:
Father in heaven, please let these promises be fulfilled in my life because of Jesus' righteous life and because He kept all the conditions required. Help me to be obedient and walk as He walked through the power of the Holy Spirit. Please keep me safe and let my land produce abundantly, as You promised in Your Word; let me have peace and deliver me from my enemies. Keep me safe from wild animals and make me and my family fruitful as You promised. Be my God and break every bondage in my life. If you did it for them, I know you can do it for me. Thank you for hearing and answering my prayer. In Jesus' name, Amen!

Promise to the Israelites
The Condition:
"If they shall confess their iniquity, and the iniquity of their fathers, with their trespass which they trespassed against Me, and that also they have walked contrary unto Me... if then their uncircumcised hearts be humbled, and they then accept of the punishment of their iniquity..." Lev. 26:40,41

> **The Promise:**
> "... then will I remember My Covenant with Jacob, and also My Covenant with Isaac, and also My Covenant with Abraham will I re - -

... member; and I will remember the land... yet for all that, when they be in the land of their enemies, I will not cast them away, neither will I abhor them, to destroy them utterly, and to break My Covenant with them: for I am the Lord their God. But I will for their sakes remember the Covenant of their ancestors, whom I brought forth out of the land of Egypt in the sight of the heathen, that I might be their God: I am the Lord" Lev. 26:42,44,45

God promises in I Jn. 1:9 that if we confess our sins to Him, He will forgive us and cleanse us by the blood of Jesus. Even in the Old Testament God wanted their hearts to be circumcised and to obey from the heart.

Numbers

This book is called Numbers because there are a lot of numbers in it and therare two census taken; one at the beginning and one at the end.

Bless
"This is the way you shall bless (them)..." Num. 6:23 NKJV
"... ye shall bless the children of Israel, saying unto them ... the Lord bless thee, and keep thee: the Lord make His face shine upon thee, and be gracious unto thee: the Lord lift up His countenance upon thee, and give thee peace. And they shall put My name upon the children of Israel; and I will bless them." Num. 6:24-27
This is a good promise to put on the wall of your home.
Prayer
Father in heaven, please bless me and my family and be gracious to us. Give us Your peace and put Your name on us, I pray. Thank you in Jesus' name, Amen!

The Condition:
"The sons of Aaron, the priests, shall blow with the trumpets ..." Num. 10:8

> **The Promise:**
> *"... and ye shall be remembered before the Lord your God, and ye shall be saved from your enemies... "* Num. 10:9,10

Promise to the Israelites
"And Moses said unto Hobab (Jethro, Moses' father-in-law)... we are journeying unto the place of which the Lord said ..." Num. 10:29

The Promise:
"... I will give it you... we will do thee good; for the Lord hath spoken good concerning Israel." Num. 10:29

Moses said to Jethro, *"If you come with us, we will share with you whatever good things the Lord gives us."* Num. 10:32 NIV

God's promise to Moses
"... I will come down and talk with thee there: and I will take of the Spirit which is upon thee, and will put it upon them..." Num. 11:17
"... ask, and it shall be given you... for everyone that asketh receiveth... how much more shall your heavenly Father give the Holy Spirit to them that ask Him?" Lk. 11:9-13
Prayer:
Father in heaven, please baptize me with Your Holy Spirit. Thank You in Jesus' name, Amen!

God's Word will come to pass
"And the Lord said unto Moses, Is the Lord's hand waxed short? Thou shalt see now whether My Word shall come to pass unto thee or not." Num. 11:23

"... would God that all the Lord's people were prophets, and that the Lord would put His Spirit upon them!" Num. 11:29
Moses desired that all God's people would receive the Holy Spirit, and in the New Testament we all can receive the Holy Spirit through Jesus.

God promised Moses that He would speak with him mouth to mouth, Num.12:8.

A promise to give the land to Israel
"And the Lord spake unto Moses, saying, send thou men, that they may search the land of Canaan, which I give unto the children of Israel: of every tribe of their fathers shall ye send a man, everyone a ruler among them." Num. 13:1,2

A land flowing with milk and honey
"And they returned from searching of the land after forty days... and brought back word unto them, and unto all the congregation, and shewed them the fruit of the land. And they told him, and said, We came unto the land whither thou sentest us, and surely it floweth with milk and honey; and this is the fruit of it." Num.13:25-27

Prayer:
Father in Heaven, let my life flow with all the blessings that You have for me. Thank You in Jesus' name, Amen!

Caleb speaks faith
"*And Caleb stilled the people before Moses, and said, Let us go up at once, and possess it; for we are well able to overcome it.*" Num. 13:30
The promise for today is that we can overcome through the power of the Holy Spirit and we can come into God's Kingdom.

A good land - Caleb confessed that God would help them
"*And Caleb... spake unto all the company of the children of Israel, saying, The land, which we passed through to search it, is an exceeding good land.*" Num. 14:7,8

The Condition:
"*If the Lord delight in us...*" Num. 14:8

> **The Promise:**
> "*... then He will bring us into this land, and give it us; a land which floweth with milk and honey.*" Num. 14:8

The Condition:
"*Only rebel not ye against the Lord, neither fear ye the people of the land; for they are bread for us...*" Num. 14:9

> **The Promise:**
> "*... their defence is departed from them, and the Lord is with us: fear them not...*" Num. 14:9

How long until you believe?
"*And the glory of the Lord appeared in the Tabernacle of the congregation before all the children of Israel. And the Lord said unto Moses, How long will this people provoke Me? and how long will it be ere they believe Me, for all the signs which I have shewed among them?*" Num. 14:10,11
Jesus said, Believe Me because of the miracles I do in My own name, Jn. 10:38;14:11,12.
We can also ask ourselves the question, when will we believe God?

By God's mighty power
"*... for by Your might You brought these people up from among them...*" Num. 14:13 NKJV

On the New Earth
The Promise:
"But as truly as I live, all the earth shall be filled with the glory of the Lord." Num. 14:21

Promise to Caleb
"But My servant Caleb..." Num. 14:24

The Condition:
"... because he had another Spirit with him, and hath followed Me fully..." Num. 14:24

The Promise:
"... him will I bring into the land where into he went; and his seed shall possess it." Num. 14:24

"But your little ones, which ye said should be a prey, them will I bring in, and they shall know the land which ye have despised." Num. 14:31

Promise to Israelites
"... the place which the Lord hath promised..." Num. 14:40
"... land... I am giving to you." Num. 15:2 NKJV

Your inheritance
"... I am thy part and thine inheritance among the children of Israel." Num. 18:20

The Rock gives water
"And the Lord spake unto Moses... speak ye unto the Rock before their eyes; and it shall give forth his water, and thou shalt bring forth to them water out of the Rock: so thou shalt give the congregation and their beasts drink." Num. 20:8
And that Rock was Jesus, I Cor. 10:4.

God listened
"... the Lord listened to the voice of Israel." Num. 21:3 NKJV

Look and live
"... make thee a fiery serpent, and set it upon a pole: and it shall come to pass, that every one that is bitten, when he looketh upon it..." Num. 21:8

The Promise:
"... shall live." Num. 21:8

This represents Jesus on the cross taking our sins but later they had to destroy it because they made an idol out of it by worshipping it instead of God, II Kings 18:4.

God heard
"And the Lord hearkened to the voice of Israel, and delivered (them)." Num. 21:34

Blessed
"... he whom thou blesses is blessed..." Num. 22:6

Blessed
"... thou shalt not curse the people: for they are blessed." Num. 22:12

Blessed
"And God said unto Balaam, Thou shalt not go with them; thou shalt not curse the people: for they are blessed." Num. 22:12
What is blessed by God cannot be cursed.

The death of the righteous
"Let me die the death of the righteous, and let my last end be like his." Num. 23:10
The promise is that the righteous don't have to fear death.

Blessed
"... You have blessed them bountifully." Num. 23:11 NKJV

Blessed
"God is not a man, that He should lie; neither the son of man, that He should repent: hath He said, and shall He not do it? Or hath He spoken, and shall He not make it good? Behold, I have received commandment to bless: and He hath blessed; and I cannot reverse it..." Num. 23:19,20

The Condition:
"He hath not beheld iniquity in Jacob, neither hath He seen perverseness in Israel..." Num. 23:21

> **The Promise:**
> "... the Lord his God is with him, and the shout of a king is among them. Surely there is no enchantment against Jacob, neither is there any divination against Israel: according to this time it shall be said of Jacob and of Israel, What hath God wrought!" Num. 23:23

As long as God's people were doing His will, He was able to protect them but when they brought rebellious sin into the camp, they stepped outside of His protection and got into trouble until they repented, and stopped sinning, confessed and were washed clean by the blood (of animals in the Old Testament which represented Jesus' blood in the New Testament).

Prayer:
Father in heaven, I pray that you would help me to get rid of any perverseness or sin in my life through the power of the Holy Spirit and the cleansing power of the blood of Jesus, so that I can walk in Your blessings. Thank You in Jesus' name, Amen!

Blessed
"... it pleased the Lord to bless Israel." Num. 24:1 NKJV

Blessed
"He hath said, which heard the Words of God, which saw the vision of the Almighty, falling into a trance, but having his eyes open: How goodly are thy tents, O Jacob, and thy Tabernacles, O Israel! As the valleys are they spread forth, as gardens by the river's side, as the trees of lign aloes which the Lord hath planted, and as Cedar trees beside the waters. He shall pour the water out of His buckets, and His seed be in many waters, and his King (Jesus) *shall be higher than Agag and his kingdom shall be exalted. God brought him forth out of Egypt; He hath as it were the strength of an* (Heb. "ox")*... he couched, he lay down as a lion, ad as a great lion: who shall stir him up? Blessed is he that blesseth thee, and cursed is he that curseth thee... blessed them these three times."* Num. 24:4-10

"lign aloes" tree - *"... a perfume derived from some Oriental tree (Num. 24:6), probably the agallochum or aloe-wood* (tree)*..."* Easton's Bible Dict.
Those who bless us are blessed and those who curse us are cursed.

Promise of a Messiah

The Promise:
"... there shall come a Star out of Jacob, and a Sceptre shall rise out of Israel... Israel does valiantly... out of Jacob shall come He (Jesus) *that shall have dominion..."* Num. 24:17-19

"... firm is your dwelling place and your nest is set in the rock." Num. 24:21 NKJV

Covenant of peace
"Behold, I give unto Him My Covenant of peace..." Num. 25:12

The promise is that if you sin, you will be found out
"... be sure your sin will find you out." Num. 32:23

Deuteronomy

"... ye are this day as the stars of heaven for multitude." Deut. 1:10
The promise given to Abraham was not fulfilled during his lifetime but was partially fulfilled years later, and it will ultimately be fulfilled on the New Earth.

Blessed
"... the Lord God of your fathers make you a thousand times so many more as ye are, and bless you, as He hath promised you..." Deut. 1:11

Promise to Abraham and the children of Israel
"Behold, the Lord thy God hath set the land before thee: go up and possess it, as the Lord God of thy fathers hath said unto thee; fear not, neither be dis-couraged." Deut. 1:21
"It is a good land which the Lord our God doth give us." Deut. 1:25
Prayer:
Father in heaven, please help me to possess everything that You promised to me in Your Word. Thank You in Jesus' name, Amen!

God goes before us
"Then I said unto you, Dread not, neither be afraid of them. The Lord your God which goeth before you..." Deut. 1:29

> **The Promise:**
> *"He shall fight for you, according to all that He did for you in Egypt before your eyes; and in the wilderness..."* Deut. 1:30

Prayer:
Father in heaven; please fight for me as You did for the Israelites when they were in Egypt and in the wilderness. Thank You in Jesus' name, Amen!

Believe
"... where thou hast seen how that the Lord thy God bare thee, as a man doth bear his son, in all the way that ye went, until ye came into this place. Yet in this thing ye did not believe the Lord your God. Who went in the way before you, to search you out a place to pitch your tents in, in fire by night,

to shew you by what way ye should go, and in a cloud by day." Deut. 1:31-33

We must be careful to believe everything that God promises!

Prayer:
Father in heaven, carry me in Your arms wherever I go until I am finally with You in heaven. Please help us to believe. Thank You in Jesus' name, Amen!

> **The Promise:**
> *"... they will be afraid of you..."* Deut. 2:4 NKJV

Blessed
"The Lord thy God hath blessed thee, in all the works of thy hand: He knoweth thy walking through this great wilderness: these forty years the Lord thy God hath been with thee; thou hast lacked nothing." Deut. 2:7

Prayer:
Father in heaven, please help me to lack nothing according to Your Word in Jesus' name, Amen!

> **The Promise:**
> *"This day will I begin to put the dread of thee and the fear of thee upon the nations that are under the whole heaven, who shall hear report of thee, and shall tremble, and be in anguish because of thee."* Deut. 2:25

Prayer:
Father in heaven, please put the fear of God in anyone who would come against me or my family. Thank You in Jesus' name, Amen!

Speaking of the descendants of Esau
"... the Lord thy God hardened his spirit, and made his heart obstinate, that he might deliver him into thy hand, as appeareth this day... our God delivered him before us; and... there was not one city too strong for us: the Lord our God delivered all unto us..." Deut. 2:30,36

"And the Lord said unto me, Fear him not..." Deut. 3:2

> **The Promise:**
> *for I will deliver him, and all his people, and his land, into thy hand..."* Deut. 3:2

God used this promise one night in a very special way to save a friend of ours. See section at end of book, Personal answers to prayer.

Prayer:
Thank You Father in heaven for Your great and precious promises that we can call upon to help us in our time of need. In Jesus' name, Amen!

> **The Promise:**
> *"Ye shall not fear them: for the Lord your God He shall fight for you."* Deut. 3:22

"... what God is there in heaven or in earth, that can do according to Thy works, and according to Thy might?" Deut. 3:24

Prayer:
Father in heaven, You are so mighty and powerful, please fight all my battles for me. Thank You in Jesus' name, Amen!

The Condition:
"... hearken, O Israel, unto the Statutes and unto the Judgments, which I teach you, for to do them..." Deut. 4:1

> **The Promise:**
> *"... that ye may live, and go in and possess the land which the Lord God of your fathers giveth you."* Deut. 4:1

Hold fast to God
"... you who held fast to the Lord your God are alive today, every one of you." Deut. 4:4 NKJV

"Carefully follow them (the Ten Commandments) *for this will show your wis-dom and understanding in the eyes of the peoples. When they hear about all these Statutes, they will say, This great nation is indeed a wise and under-standing people."* Deut. 4:6 HCSB

"But if from thence thou shalt seek the Lord thy God..." Deut. 4:29

> **The Promise:**
> *"... thou shalt find Him..."* Deut. 4:29

Seek and you will find
The Condition:
"... if thou seek Him with all thy heart and with all thy soul. When thou art in tribulation, and all these things are come upon thee, even in the latter days, if thou turn to the Lord thy God, and shalt be obedient unto His voice; (For the Lord thy God is a merciful God)..." Deut. 4:29-31

> **The Promise:**
> *"... He will not forsake thee, neither destroy thee, nor forget the Covenant of thy fathers which He sware unto them."* Deut. 4:31

No god like our God
"... has any god ever attempted to go and take a nation for Himself from the midst of another nation, by trials, by signs, by wonders, and by war, by a mighty hand and an outstretched arm, and by great deeds of terror... which the Lord your God did for you in Egypt... " Deut. 4:34 ESV

He is the only God!
"... that thou mightest know that the Lord He is God; there is none else beside Him." Deut. 4:35
"To drive out nations from before thee greater and mightier than thou art, to bring thee in, to give thee their land for an inheritance, as it is this day." Deut. 4:38

The Condition:
"Thou shalt keep therefore His Statutes, and His Commandments, which I command thee this day..." Deut. 4:40

> **The Promise:**
> *"... that it may go well with thee, and with thy children after thee, and that thou mayest prolong thy days upon the earth, which the Lord thy God giveth thee, forever."* Deut. 4:40

The Condition:
"Honour thy father and thy mother, as the Lord thy God hath commanded thee..." Deut. 5:16

> **The Promise:**
> *"... that thy days may be prolonged, and that it may go well with thee..."* Deut. 5:16

The Condition:
"O that there were such an heart in them, that they would fear Me, and keep all My Commandments always..." Deut. 5:29

> **The Promise:**
> *"... that it might be well with them, and with their children forever!"* Deut. 5:29

"... this is the whole duty of man." Eccl 12:13
"When all has been heard, the conclusion of the matter is: fear God and keep His Commandments, because this is for all humanity." Eccl. 12:13 HXAB

The Condition:
"Ye shall walk in all the ways which the Lord your God hath commanded you..." Deut. 5:33

> **The Promise:**
> *"... that it might be well with them, and with their children forever!"* Deut. 5:33

How many times do we suffer because we disobey God? We would save our-selves a lot of trouble just by our obedience to God. Just think if Adam and Eve had obeyed God, sin would have never entered the world!

The Condition:
"Now these are the Commandments, the Statutes, and the Judgments, which the Lord your God commanded to teach you, that ye might do them in the land whither ye go to possess it: that thou mightist fear the Lord thy God, to keep all His Statutes and His Commandments, which I command thee, thou, and thy son, and thy son's son, all the days of thy life..." Deut. 6:1,2

> **The Promise:**
> *"... and that thy days may be prolonged."* Deut. 6:2

The Condition:
"Hear, O Israel: the Lord our God is **One Lord***: and thou shalt love the Lord thy God with all thine heart, and with all thy soul, and with all thy might. And these words, which I command thee this day, shall be in thine heart: and thou shalt teach them diligently unto thy children, and shalt talk of them when thou sittest in thine house, and when thou walkest by the way, and when thou liest down, and when thou risest up..."* Deut. 6:4-9

Jesus quoted this verse *"the Lord our God is* **One Lord***"* (Deut. 6:4) in Mk. 12:29.

In Hebrew *"one"* can mean, *"united"*

A man and his wife become *"... one flesh"* Gen. 2:24

The two shall be one.

A nation can be considered *"... one people"* Gen. 11:6

The word Elohim is actualy plural for God.

> **The Promise:**
> *"... when the Lord thy God shall have brought thee into the land which He sware unto thy fathers, to Abraham, to Isaac, and to Jacob, to give thee great and goodly cities, which thou buildedst not, and houses full of all good things, which thou filledst not, and wells digged, which thou diggedst not, and houses full of all good things,*

which thou filledst not, and wells digged, which thou diggedst not, vineyards, and olive trees, which thou plantedst not; when thou shalt have eaten and be full..." Deut. 6:10,11

The Condition:
"... then beware lest thou forget the Lord... thou shalt fear the Lord thy God, and serve Him, and shalt swear by His name." Deut. 6:12,13

Miracles
"And the Lord shewed signs and wonders, great and sore, upon Egypt, upon Pharaoh, and upon all his household, before our eyes: and he brought us out from thence, that He might bring us in, to give us the land which He sware unto our fathers. " Deut. 6:22,23
God's Commands are for our good
And the Lord commanded us to do all these Statutes, to fear the Lord our God, for our good always, that He might preserve us alive, as it is at this day." Deut. 6:24

God has chosen you and He is faithful
"For thou art an Holy people unto the Lord thy God: the Lord thy God hath chosen thee to be a special people unto Himself, above all people that are upon the face of the earth... (God set His love on you even though you were the fewest) because the Lord loved you and because He would keep the oath which He had sworn unto your fathers, hath the Lord brought you out with a mighty hand, and Redeemed you out of the house of bondmen, from the hand of Pharaoh... He is... the faithful God..." Deut. 7:6-9

The Condition:
"... know therefore that the Lord your God is God; He is the faithful God, keep-ing His Covenant of love to a thousand generations of those who love Him and keep His ("Commandments" KJV)..." Deut. 7:9 NIV

You will not be afraid
"Thou shalt therefore keep the Commandments, and the Statutes and the Judgments, which I command thee this day, to do them..." Deut. 7:11

The Promise:
"... that the Lord thy God shall keep unto thee the Covenant and the mercy which He sware unto thy fathers: and He will love thee, and, bless thee, and multiply thee: He will also bless the fruit of thy womb and the fruit of thy land, thy corn, and thy wine, and thine oil, the increase of thy kine, and the flocks of thy sheep, in the land which He

sware unto thy fathers to give thee. Thou shalt be blessed above all people: there shall not be male or female barren among you, or among your cattle. And the Lord will take away from thee all sickness, and will put none of the evil diseases... upon thee... thou shalt not be afraid for the Lord thy God is among you a mighty God and terrible... no man shall be able to stand before thee..." Deut. 7:11-26

"... no one will be able to stand up against you." Deut. 7:24 NIV
"... nobody will be able to resist you." Deut. 7:24 NET
"... nobody will be able to stop you." Deut. 7:24 God' Word Translation

Prayer:
Father in heaven, thank You for your love to us. Help me to remember all the wonderful things You did in the Bible and Your promises. I pray that You will bless me and my family and everything that we have. Please help us to obey You in everything and take away all our sicknesses and diseases as You prom-ised in Your Word. Thank You that all the promises are mine in Christ Jesus. Help me to walk as Jesus walked and to try and please You in all that I do. In Jesus' name, Amen!

God's promise to Israel
The Condition:
"All the Commandments which I command thee this day shall ye observe to do..." Deut 8:1

The Promise:
"... that ye may live, and multiply, and go in and possess the land which the Lord sware unto your fathers." Deut. 8:1

Prayer:
Father in heaven, I know that my righteousness is in Jesus who kept every one of Your Commandments. Help me to be like Jesus and walk as He walked. Help me to please You in everything I do because You have done so much for me. Help me to walk worthy of You in everything. I know that I can only do this with Your help. Please accept my efforts and forgive me where I fall short. Let me go in and possess everything that You have given to me. Thank You in Jesus' name, Amen!
"That you might walk worthy of the Lord unto all pleasing being fruitful in every good work, and increasing in the knowledge of God..." Col. 1:10
"... walk worthy of the vocation wherewith you are called." Eph.4:1

God tests you to see what's in your heart
"And thou shalt remember all the way which the Lord thy God led thee these forty years in the wilderness, to humble thee, and to prove thee, to know what was in thine heart, whether thou wouldest keep His Commandments, or no. And He humbled thee, and suffered thee to hunger, and fed thee with manna, which thou knewest not, neither did thy fathers know; that He might make thee know that man doth not live by bread only..." Deut. 8:3

The Promise:
"... but by every Word that proceedeth out of the mouth of the Lord doth man live. Thy raiment waxed not old upon thee, neither did thy foot swell, these forty years." Deut. 8:3,4

The Condition:
"Thou shalt also consider in thine heart, that, as a man chasteneth his son, so the Lord thy God chasteneth thee. Therefore thou shalt keep the Commandments of the Lord thy God, to walk in His ways, and to fear Him." Deut. 8:5,6

Jesus quoted Deut. 8:3 when tempted by the Devil in the wilderness and we can speak these promises when we are tempted also.

"For whom the Lord loveth He chaseneth, and scourges every son whom He receiveth." Heb. 12:6

The promised land – Canaan for Israel & ultimately the New Earth!

The Promise:
"For the Lord thy God bring thee into a good land, a land of brooks of water, of fountains and depths that spring out of valleys and hills; a land of wheat, and barley, and vines, and fig trees, and pomegranates; a land of oil olive, and honey; a land wherein thou shalt eat bread without scarceness, thou shalt not lack anything in it; a land whose stones are iron, and out of whose hills thou mayest dig brass." Deut. 8:7-9

Bless God who gives us good things
The Condition:
"When thou hast eaten and art full, then thou shalt bless the Lord thy God for the good land which He hath given thee. Beware that thou forget not the Lord thy God, in not keeping His Commandments, and His Judgments, and His Statutes, which I command thee this day: lest when thou hast eaten..." Deut. 8:10-12

The Promise:
"... and art full, and hast built goodly houses, and dwelt therein: and when thy herds and thy flocks multiply, and thy silver and thy gold is multiplied, and all that thou hast is multiplied..." Deut. 8:12,13

"... God... who brought water for you out of the flinty rock; who fed you in the wilderness with Manna." Deut. 8:15,16 NKJV

The Condition:
"... then thine heart be lifted up, and thou forget the Lord thy God... who led thee... who fed thee in the wilderness with manna, which thy fathers knew not, that He might humble thee, and that He might prove thee, to do thee good at thy latter end; and thou say in thine heart My power and the might of mine hand hath gotten me this wealth..." Deut. 8:18

The Promise:
"But thou shalt remember the Lord thy God: for it is He that giveth thee power to get wealth, that He may establish His Covenant which He sware unto thy fathers, as it is this day." Deut. 8:18

Prayer:
Father in heaven, when I can find no food or water, help me to remember that You fed the Israelites and gave them food and water. Please feed us and give us clean water when we need it also. Thank You in Jesus' name, Amen!

Promise to Israel
"Understand therefore this day, that the Lord thy God is He which goeth over before thee; as a consuming fire..." Deut. 9:3

The Condition:
*"... what doth the Lord thy God require of thee, but to fear the Lord thy God, to walk in all His ways, and to love Him, and to serve the Lord thy God **with all thy heart** and with all thy soul. To keep the Commandments of the Lord, and His Statutes, which I command thee this day for thy good? Behold, the heaven and the heaven of heavens is the Lord's thy God, the earth also, with all that therein is."* Deut. 10:12-14
The earth belongs to God who created it!

The Promise:
"Only the Lord had a delight in thy fathers to love them, and He chose their seed after them, even you above all people, as it is this day." Deut. 10:15

God chose me
"Ye have not chosen Me, but I have chosen you......" Jn. 15:16
Prayer:
I thank You, Father in heaven, that You chose me. Help me to always do the things that please You from my heart and through the power of Your Holy Spirit. In Jesus' name, Amen!

The Condition:
"Circumcise... your heart, and be no more stiffnecked ("stop your stubbornness" LB). For the Lord your God is God of gods, and Lord of lords (Rev. 19: 16), a great God, a mighty, and a terrible, which regardeth not person, nor taketh reward..." Deut. 10:16,17
Circumcising your heart is not new to the New Covenant. God wanted them to do that in the Old Covenant as well! He wanted them to obey the Commandments from the heart by the Spirit and not by the letter (See these verses II Chron.31:21;34:31;Ps.37:31; Jer.9:36) See *"Heart"* in Topical section.
"... You... have turned their hearts back to You again. Then the fire of the Lord fell ..." I Kings 18:37,38 NKJV

> **The Promise:**
> *"He doth execute the Judgment of the fatherless and widow, and loveth the stranger, in giving him food and raiment..."* Deut. 10:18

The Condition:
"Thou shalt fear the Lord thy God; Him shalt thou serve, and to Him shalt thou cleave, and swear by His name. He is thy praise, and He is thy God, that hath done for thee these great and terrible things, which thine eyes have seen." Deut.10: 20,21

The Condition:
"... if ye shall hearken diligently unto My Commandments which I command you this day, to love the Lord your God, and to serve Him with all your heart and with all your soul." Deut. 11:13
There it is again, we see that God wants us to serve Him from the heart!

> **The Promise:**
> *"That I will give you the rain of your land in his due season, the first rain and the latter rain, that thou mayest gather in thy corn... and thine oil. And I will send grass in thy fields for thy cattle, that thou mayest eat and be full... that your days may be multiplied, and the days of your children, in the land which the Lord sware unto your fathers to give them, as the days of heaven upon the earth."* Deut. 11:14.15.21

God's promise to the Israelites
"*Every place whereon the soles of your feet shall tread shall be yours; from the wilderness and Lebanon, from the river, the river Euphrates, even unto the uttermost sea shall your coast be... no man* (shall) *be able to stand before you: for the Lord your God shall lay the fear of you and the dread of you upon all the land that ye shall tread upon, as He hath said unto you...*" Deut. 11:24-26

A Blessing
"*... behold, I set before you this day a blessing and a curse...*" Deut. 11:26

The Condition:
"*... a blessing, if ye obey the Commandments of the Lord your God which I command you this day: and a curse, if ye will not obey the Commandments of the Lord your God, but turn aside out of the way which I command you this day, to go after other gods, which ye have not known.*" Deut. 11:27,26

A promise for Israel
"*For ye shall pass over Jordan to go in to possess the land which the Lord your God giveth you, and ye shall possess it, and dwell therein.*" Deut. 11:31

The Condition:
"*And ye shall observe to do all the Statutes and Judgments which I set before you this day.*" Deut. 11:32

God will give them rest from their enemies
"*But when ye go over Jordan, and dwell in the land which the Lord your God giveth you to inherit, and when He giveth you rest from all your enemies round about, so that ye dwell in safety...*" Deut. 12:10
"*When a man's ways please the Lord, He maketh even his enemies to be at peace with him.*" Prov. 16:7
Prayer:
Father in heaven, let me dwell in safety and give me rest from my enemies as You promised. Thank You in Jesus' name, Amen!

Blessing
"*Notwithstanding thou mayest... eat... according to the blessing of the Lord thy God...*" Deut. 12:15
The Condition:
"*Observe and hear all these words which I command thee...*" Deut. 12:28

The Promise:
"... that it may go well with thee, and with thy children after thee forever..." Deut. 12:28

The Condition:
"... when thou doest that which is good and right in the sight of the Lord thy God." Deut. 12:28

Blessed
"... the Lord shall greatly bless thee in the land for an inheritance ... for the Lord thy God blesseth thee, as He promised thee ..." Deut. 15:4,6
God will bless your works

The Promise:
"... the Lord thy God shall bless thee in all thy works, and in all that thou puttest thine hand unto ... and ... in all that thou doest." Deut. 15:10,18

Prayer:
Father in heaven, bless me in everything I do. Thank You in the name of Jesus, Amen!

The Blessing
"... every man shall give as he is able, according to the blessing of the Lord thy God which He hath given thee." Deut. 16:17

Promise of a Messiah
"Thou shalt be perfect with the Lord thy God ... the Lord thy God will raise up unto thee a Prophet (Jesus) *from the midst of thee, of Thy brethren, like unto me; unto Him ye shall hearken..."* Deut. 18:13,15

A promise to send the Messiah

The Promise:
"I will raise them up a Prophet (Jesus) *from among their brethren, like unto thee, and will put My words in His mouth; and He shall speak unto them all that I shall command Him."* Deut. 18:18

Jesus said, I speak what My Father tells Me, Jn. 5:19;8:28;12:49;14:31. They called Jesus *"The Prophet"* in Matt. 14:5;21:11;Jn.6:14 (See Names of God p. 694).
"... land, which the Lord thy God giveth thee to inherit ..." Deut. 19:3

The Promise:
"For the Lord your God is He that goeth with you, to fight for you against your enemies, to save you." Deut. 20:4

The Promise:
"... the Lord thy God hath delivered them into thine hands..." Deut. 21:10

Prayer:
Father in heaven, please fight against those who fight against me and deliver me from all evil and save me in Your kingdom. Thank You in Jesus' name, Amen!

"... and when we cried unto the Lord God of our fathers, the Lord heard our voice, and looked on our affliction, and our labour, and our oppression: and the Lord brought us forth out of Egypt with a mighty hand, and with an outstretched arm, and with great terribleness, and with signs, and with wonders: and He hath brought us into this place, and hath given us this land, even a land that floweth with milk and honey..." Deut. 26:7-11

Prayer:
Father hear our voice when we pray to You and see our troubles. Bring us out of our trials and tribulations with a mighty hand. Please give us good things and let us rejoice in what You give. Bring us at last to heaven and finally to the New Earth. Thank You Father for all the good things You do and for everything You give to us. Let our life flow with milk and honey. In Jesus' name, Amen!

The Condition:
"... to keep His... Commandments... and to hearken unto His voice.." Deut. 26:18

The Promise:
"And to make thee high above all nations which He hath made, in praise, and in name, and in honour; and that thou mayest be an Holy people unto the Lord thy God, as He hath spoken." Deut. 26:19

The Condition:
"And it shall come to pass, if thou shalt hearken diligently unto the voice of the Lord thy God, to observe and to do all His Commandments which I command thee this day..." Deut. 28:1

The Promise:
"... that the Lord thy God will set thee on high above all nations of the earth: and all these blessings shall come on thee, and overtake thee..." Deut. 28:1,2

The Condition:
"…. if thou shalt hearken unto the voice of the Lord thy God…" Deut. 28:2

The Promise:
"… blessed shalt thou be in the city, and blessed shalt thou be in the field. Blessed shall be the fruit of thy body, and the fruit of thy ground, and the fruit of thy cattle, the increase of thy kine (herds), *and the flocks of thy sheep. Blessed shall be thy basket and thy store* ("kneading bowl" HCSB). *Blessed shalt thou be when thou comest in, and blessed shalt thou be when thou goest out. The Lord shall cause thine enemies that rise up against thee to be smitten before thy face: they shall come out against thee one way, and flee before thy face: they shall come out against thee one way, and flee before thee seven ways. The Lord shall command the blessing upon thee In thy storehouses, and in all that thou settest thine hand unto; and He shall bless thee in the land which the Lord thy God giveth thee. The Lord shall establish thee an Holy people unto Himself, as He hath sworn unto thee…"* Deut. 28:3-9

Prayer:
Father in heaven, please let all Your blessings come to me according to Your Word in Christ Jesus. Thank You, Amen!

The Condition:
"… if thou shalt keep the Commandments of the Lord thy God, and walk in His ways." Deut. 28:9

The Promise:
"… all people of the earth shall see that thou art called by the name of the Lord; and they shall be afraid of thee… the Lord shall make thee plenteous in goods, in the fruit of thy body… thy cattle… the Lord shall open unto thee His good treasure, the heaven to give the rain unto thy land in His season, and to bless all the work of thine hand: and thou shalt lend unto many nations, and thou shalt not borrow. And the Lord shalt make thee the head, and not the tail; and thou shalt be above only, and thou shalt not be beneath…" Deut. 28:10-13

The Condition:
"… if that thou hearken unto the Commandments of the Lord thy God, which I command thee this day, to observe and to do them: and thou shalt not go aside from any of the words which I command thee this day, to the right hand, or to the left, to go after other gods to serve them." Deut. 28:13,14

Deuteronomy 28 tells us the blessings for obedience and the curses for disobedience. Jesus fulfilled all the requirements for obedience so that we could be saved and blessed us even though we are not perfect and even though we have sinned. He took the curse for us by becoming a curse on the cross but we must remember that we are still striving to please God to the best of our ability every day with the help of the Holy Spirit; to please Him because we love Him, not to be saved. The more we fall in love with Jesus, the more we want to do only those things that please Him and He will reward us someday. When we fulfil the conditions wih God's help, it will increase our faith.

"... it pleased the Lord to make you prosper and increase in number..." Deut. 28:63

The Condition:
"Keep therefore the Words of this Covenant, and do them..." Deut. 29:9

> **The Promise:**
> "... that ye may prosper in all that ye do." Deut. 29:9

Prayer:
Father in heaven, I know that Jesus fulfilled all righteousness for me and that I inherit these beautiful promises through Jesus. Help me to obey You in all things because I love You. Bless me and prosper me in all that I do in Jesus' name, Amen!

The Condition:
"That thou shouldest enter into Covenant with the Lord thy God, and into His oath, which the Lord thy God maketh with thee this day..." Deut. 29:12

> **The Promise:**
> "... that He may establish thee today for a people unto Himself, and that He may be unto thee a God." Deut. 29:13

Secret things revealed
"The secret things belong unto the Lord our God: but those things which are revealed belong unto us and to our children forever, that we may do all the Words of this law." Deut. 29:29

Blessings
"And it shall come to pass, when all these things are come upon thee, the blessing and the curse, which I have set before thee, and thou shalt call them to mind among all the nations, whither the Lord thy God hath driven thee." Deut. 30:1,2

The Condition:
"And shalt return unto the Lord thy God, and shalt obey His voice according to all that I command thee this day, thou and thy children, with all thine heart, and with all thy soul…" Deut. 30:2

> **The Promise:**
> *"… the Lord… will turn thy captivity, and have compassion upon thee, and will return and gather thee from all the nations… if any of thine* (children) *be driven out into the outmost parts of heaven, from thence will the Lord thy God gather thee, and from thence will He fetch thee: And the Lord thy God will bring thee into the land which thy fathers possessed, and thou shalt possess it; and He will do thee good, and multiply thee above thy fathers. And the Lord thy God will circumcise thine heart, and the heart of thy seed, to love the Lord thy God with all thine heart, and with all thy soul, that thou mayest live."* Deut. 30:3-6

Again we see that God wants us to obey from the heart! Ask God to circumcise your heart and the hearts of your children.

Prayer:
Father in heaven, please circumcise our hearts and the hearts of our family members so that we will serve You wholeheartedly. In Jesus' name, Amen!

> **The Promise:**
> *"And the Lord thy God will make thee plenteous in every work of thine hand, in the fruit of thy body, and in the fruit of thy cattle, and in the fruit of thy land, for good: for the Lord will again rejoice over thee for good, as He rejoiced over thy fathers…"* Deut. 30:8,9

The Condition:
"… if thou shalt hearken unto the voice of the Lord thy God, to keep His Com-mandments and His Statutes which are written in this book of the law, and if thou turn unto the Lord thy God with all thine heart, and with all thy soul." Deut. 30:8-10

> **The Promise:**
> *"… I have set before thee… life and good…"* Deut. 30:15

The Condition:
"… and death and evil; in that I command thee this day to love the Lord thy God, to walk in His ways, and to keep His Commandments and His Statutes and His Judgments…" Deut. 30:15-16

The Promise:
"... that thou mayest live and multiply: and the Lord thy God shall bless thee in the land whither thou goest to possess it..." Deut. 30:16

The Condition:
"... I have set before you life and death, blessing and cursing: therefore choose life..." Deut. 30:19

The Promise:
"... that both thou and thy seed may live..." Deut. 30:19

The Condition:
*"... that thou mayest **love** the Lord thy God, and that thou mayest **obey** His voice, and that thou mayest cleave unto Him ..."* Deut. 30:20
We see that "Love" and "obey" always go hand in hand.

"Be strong and of a good courage, fear not, nor be afraid of them ..." Deut. 31:6

The Promise:
"... for the Lord thy God, He it is that doth go with thee; He will not fail thee, nor forsake thee. And the Lord He it is that doth go before thee; He will be with thee, He will not fail thee, neither forsake thee: fear not, neither be dismayed." Deut. 31:6-8

The Promise:
"... for He is thy life, and the length of thy days: that thou mayest dwell in the land which the Lord sware... to give them." Deut. 31:20

When we choose Jesus, we choose life. The opposite is death; the choice is ours. God hasn't changed! He says, *"I change not"* Mal. 3:6. He also says, I am *"the same yesterday, today, and tomorrow"* Heb. 13:8.

The Promise:
"Be strong and of a good courage... I will be with thee." Deut. 31:23

When God says to *"be strong and have courage"* the power is in the words to be strong and have courage! God's Word is powerful and active, sharper than any two-edged sword, Heb. 4:12,13.

Apple of God's eye
"For the Lord's portion is His people; Jacob is the lot of His inheritance. He found him in a desert land, and in the waste howling wilderness; He led him about, He instructed him, He kept him as the apple of His eye. As an eagle

stirreth up her nest, fluttereth over her young, spreadeth abroad her wings, taketh them, beareth them on her wings: so the Lord alone did lead him, and there was no strange god with him..." Deut. 32:9-12

> **The Promise:**
> *"He made him ride on the high places of the earth, that he might eat the increase of the fields; and He made him to suck honey out of the rock, and oil out of the flinty rock; butter of kine* (herds)*, and milk of sheep, with fat of lambs, and rams of the breed of Bashan, and goats, with the fat of kidneys of wheat; and thou didst drink the pure...* (juice) *of the grape."* Deut. 32:13,14

*"... for they are a very forward generation, children in whom is **no faith**."* Deut. 32:20

Prayer:
Father in heaven, help me to be a child of faith who believes Your Word and promises! Thank You, in Jesus' name, Amen!

Set your heart on the Word
"And he said unto them, Set your hearts unto all the Words which I testify among you this day, which ye shall command your children to observe to do, all the Words of this law. For it is not a vain thing for you..." Deut. 32:46,47

> **The Promise:**
> *"... because it is your life: and through this thing ye shall prolong your days in the land, whither ye go over Jordan to possess it."* Deut. 32:47

Blessed (See Topical section for complete blessings to 12 tribes p. 451)
"And this is the blessing, wherewith Moses the man of God blessed the children of Israel before his death." Deut. 33:1

Of Benjamin he said, *"... the beloved of the Lord shall dwell in safety by Him; and the Lord shall cover him all the day long, and he shall dwell between His shoulders."* Deut. 33:12

Prayer:
Father in heaven, carry me like a little child riding on his daddy's shoulders like it says here to *"dwell between His shoulders"*. Thank You in Jesus' name, Amen!

Blessed
"Blessed of the Lord be His land, for the precious things of heaven, for the dew... and for the precious fruits brought forth by the sun, and for the

precious things put forth by the moon, and for the chief things of the ancient mountains, and for the precious things of the lasting hills, and for the precious things of the earth and fullness thereof, and for the good will of Him that dwelt in the (burning) *bush: let the blessing come upon the head of Joseph, and upon the top of the head of him that was separated from his brethren."* Deut. 33:13-16

Blessing to Zebulun
"They will summon peoples to the mountain and there... feast on the abund-ance of the seas, on the treasures hidden in the sand." Deut. 33: 19,20

Blessing to Asher
"... satisfied with favour, and full with the blessing of the Lord: possess thou the West and the South. Let Asher be blessed with children; let him be acceptable to his brethren, and let him dip his foot in oil. Thy shoes shall be iron and brass; and as thy days, so shall thy strength be." Deut. 33:23-25

The Promise:
"There is none like unto the God of Jeshurun, who rideth upon the heaven in thy help, and in His excellency on the sky. The eternal God is thy refuge, and underneath are the everlasting arms: and He shall thrust out the enemy from before thee; and shall say, Destroy them. Israel then shall dwell in safety alone: the fountain of Jacob shall be upon a land of corn and wine; also His heavens shall drop down dew. Happy art thou, O Israel: who is like unto thee, O people saved by the Lord, the shield of thy help, and who is the sword of thy excellency! And thine enemies shall be found liars unto thee; and thou shalt tread upon their high places." Deut. 33:26-29

Joshua

Promise to Joshua
"Every place that the sole of your foot shall tread upon, that have I given unto you, as I said unto Moses. From the wilderness and this Lebanon even unto the great river, the river Euphrates, all the land of the Hittites, and unto the great sea toward the going down of the sun, shall be your coast. There shall not any man be able to stand before thee all the days of thy life: as I was with Moses, so I will be with thee: I will not fail thee, nor forsake thee.

Be strong and of a good courage; for unto this people shalt thou divide for an inheritance the land..." Josh. 1:3-6

The Condition:
"Only be thou strong and very courageous, that thou mayest observe to do according to all the law. This book of the law shall not depart out of thy mouth; but thou shalt meditate therein day and night, that thou mayest observe to do according to all that is written therein." Josh. 1:7,8

> **The Promise:**
> *"... for then thou shalt make thy way prosperous, and then thou shalt have good success..."* Josh. 1:8

"Have not I commanded thee? Be strong and of a good courage; be not afraid, neither be thou dismayed..." Josh. 1:8,9

> **The Promise:**
> *"... for the Lord thy God is with thee whithersoever thou goest."* Josh. 1:8,9

> **The Promise:**
> *"... the Lord your God hath given you rest, and hath given you this land."* Josh. 1:13

Be strong
"... be strong and of good courage." Josh. 1:18

Blessing to Rahab
"And she said unto the men, I know that the Lord hath given you the land, and that your terror is fallen upon us, and that all the inhabitants of the land faint because of you. For we have heard how the Lord dried up the water... and as soon as we had heard these things, our hearts did melt, neither did there remain anymore courage in any man, because of you: for the Lord your God, He is God in heaven above, and in earth beneath. Now therefore, I pray you, swear unto me by the Lord, since I have shewed you kindness, that ye will also shew kindness unto my father's house, and give me a true token: and that ye will save alive my father, and my mother, and my brethren, and my sisters, and all that they have, and deliver our lives from death... and it shall be, when the Lord hath given us the land, that we will deal kindly and truly with thee." Josh. 2:9,11-14

The Condition:
Rahab must put a scarlet cord in the window, Josh 2:18

"*According unto your words, so be it...*" Josh. 2:21
This is what Mary said also in Lk. 1:38. This is a good response we can have for the promises in the Bible.

Promise to Israel during time of Joshua.
"*... truly the Lord hath delivered into our hands all the land; for even all the inhabitants of the country do faint because of us.*" Josh. 2:24
"*Sanctify ("consecrate" NIV; "purify" NLT) yourselves: for tomorrow the Lord will do wonders ("amazing things" NIV; "marvelous things" ISV) among you.*" Josh. 3:5

God's promise to Joshua
"*And the Lord said unto Joshua, This day will I begin to magnify thee in the sight of all Israel, that they may know that, as I was with Moses, so I will be with thee... ye shall know that the living God is among you...*" Josh. 3:7,10
Prayer:
Father in heaven, let others see that the living God is with me. In Jesus' name, Amen!

Miracle
"*And it shall come to pass, as soon as the soles of the feet of the priests that bear the Ark of the Lord, the Lord of all the earth, shall rest in the waters of Jordan, that the waters of Jordan shall be cut off from the waters that come down from above; and they shall stand upon an heap... and the people passed over...*" Josh. 3:13,16
God is Lord of all the earth because He created it and it is His; it belongs to Him.

"*On that day the Lord magnified Joshua in the sight of all Israel; and they feared ("stood in awe" NIV) him, as they feared Moses, all the days of his life... that all the people of the earth might know the hand of the Lord, that it is mighty: that ye might fear the Lord your God forever.*" Josh. 4:14,24
In Acts they prayed, Stretch forth Thy mighty hand of power, Acts 4:30! See Deut. 26;Ps.136:12;Jer.32:21 also.
God gave them "*... a land flowing with milk and honey.*" Josh. 5:6
"*And the Lord said unto Joshua, This day have I rolled away the reproach of Egypt from off you...*" Josh. 5:9
"*... He will remove His people's disgrace ("reproach" ESV) from all the earth...*" Is. 25:8 NIV

"And the Lord said unto Joshua, See, I have given into thine hand Jericho, and the king thereof, and the mighty men of valour." Josh. 6:2

The promise to give Jericho to Israel
The Condition:
"Shout..." Josh. 6:16

> **The promise:**
> *"... for the Lord hath given you the city."* Josh. 6:16

Prayer:
Father in heaven, I claim this city for You. I plead the blood of Jesus over this city and ask You to fight the evil working in this city. Please send the armies of heaven to push back the darkness and send Your Holy Spirit to help those in this city to come to a knowledge of truth and be saved. Let the light dispel the darkness. Thank You in Jesus' name; Amen!
Promise to Rahab
"... Rahab... shall live, she and all that are with her..." Josh. 6:17
Prayer:
Father in heaven, give me all that are with me, my family and friends as you did for Rahab. Thank You in Jesus' name, amen!

"... the Lord turned away from the fierceness of His anger..." Josh. 7:26
Prayer: Father in heaven, I thank You that we are saved from God's wrath through faith in Jesus.
"... being now Justifid by His blood, we shall be saved from wrath through Him (Jesus). Rom. 5:9

Promise to Israel
"... I have given into thy hand the king of Ai, and his people and his city, and his land... for the Lord your God will deliver it into your hand." Josh. 8:1,7
God told Joshua to point his spear toward the city of Ai
"... for I will give it unto your hand..." Josh. 8:18 NKJV
"... so they had no power to flee this way or that.." Josh. 8:20 NKJV

Joshua blessed the people
"... as Moses the servant of the Lord had commanded before, that they should bless the people of Israel. And afterward he read all the words of the law, the blessings and cursings..." Josh. 8:33

"And the Lord said unto Joshua..." Josh. 10:8

The Promise:
"... fear them not; for I have delivered them into thine hand; there shall not a man of them stand before thee." Josh. 10:8

Miracle
And He made the *"... sun, stand ... still upon Gibeon; and* (the) *Moon, in the valley of Ajalon... and there was no day like that before it or after it, that the Lord hearkened unto the voice of a man: for the Lord fought for Israel."* Josh. 10:11-14

Prayer:
Father in heaven, please fight for me as You did for Israel of old. Is anything too hard for You? Thank You in Jesus' name, Amen! (Gen.18:14;Jer.32:27;Lk.18:27)

"... for the Lord your God has delivered them into your hand." Josh. 10:19

The Promise:
"And Joshua said unto them, Fear not, nor be dismayed, be strong and of good courage: for thus shall the Lord do to all your enemies against whom ye fight." Josh. 10:25

"... the Lord God of Israel fought for Israel." Josh. 10:42

The Promise:
"And Moses sware on that day, saying, Surely the land whereon thy feet have trodden shall be thine inheritance, and thy children's forever..." Josh. 14:9

The Condition:
"... because thou hast wholly followed the Lord my God." Josh. 14:9

Promise to Caleb
"... if so be the Lord will be with me, then I shall be able to drive them out, as the Lord said. And Joshua blessed him... Hebron therefore became the inheritance of Caleb... and the land had rest from war." Josh. 14:12-15

The Lord blessed Joseph's children
"And the children of Joseph spake unto Joshua, saying, Why hast thou given me but one lot and one portion to inherit, seeing I am a great people forasmuch as the Lord hath blessed me hitherto?" Josh. 17:14
Sometimes we need to go in and possess what God has already given to us.

"And Joshua said unto the children of Israel, How long are ye slack to go to possess the land, which the Lord God of your fathers hath given you?" Josh. 18:3
"How long will you wait before you begin to take possession of the land?" Josh. 18:3 NIV

Prayer:
Father in heaven, I take back everything that God has already given to me and that Satan has stolen from me, through the power of Jesus' name and by His blood, Amen!

"And the Lord gave unto Israel all the land which He sware to give unto their fathers; and they possessed it, and dwelt therein." Josh. 21:43

> **The Promise:**
> *"(God) gave them rest round about, according to all that He sware unto their fathers: and there stood not a man of all their enemies before them; the Lord delivered all their enemies into their hand. There failed not ought of any good thing which the Lord had spoken... all came to pass."* Josh. 21:44,45

God's promises never fail!
God gives them rest

The Condition:
"Ye... have kept the charge of the Commandment of the Lord your God." Josh. 22:3

> **The Promise:**
> *"And now the Lord your God hath given rest, unto your brethren, as He promised them..."* Josh. 22:4

The Condition:
*"But take diligent heed to do the Commandment and the law, which Moses the servant of the Lord charged you, to **love** the Lord your God, and to walk in all His ways, and to **keep** ("obey" NLT) His Commandments, and to cleave unto Him, and to serve Him with all your heart and with all your soul."* Josh. 22:5
Again we see that "love" and "obey" go hand in hand.

Blessed
"So Joshua blessed them... saying, Return with much riches unto your tents... much cattle... silver... gold... brass... (and) very much raiment: divide the spoil of your enemies with your brethren." Josh. 22:6-8

First we bind the strong man with the blood of Jesus and then we spoil him (Matt.12:29;Mk.3: 27).

It is God who fights for you as promised
"And ye have seen all that the Lord your God hath done unto all these nations because of you; for the Lord your God is He that hath fought for you... and the Lord your God, He shall expel them from before you, and drive them from out of your sight; and ye shall possess their land, as the Lord your God hath promised unto you. Be ye therefore very courageous..." Josh. 23:3,5,6

The Condition:
"... to keep and to do all that is written in the book of the law of Moses, that ye turn not aside... to the right hand or to the left; that ye come not among these nations..." Josh. 23:6,7

"For the Lord hath driven out from before you great nations and strong..." Josh. 23:9

> **The Promise:**
> *"... but as for you, no man hath been able to stand before you unto this day. One man of you shall chase a thousand: for the Lord your God, He it is that fighteth for you, as He hath promised you."* Josh. 23:10

One man shall chase a thousand Deut.32:30;Lev.26:8.

God's promises never fail!

> **The Promise:**
> *"... not one thing hath failed of all the good things which the Lord your God spake concerning you; all are come to pass unto you, and not one thing hath failed thereof. Therefore it shall come to pass, that as all good things are come upon you, which the Lord your God promised you..."* Josh. 23: 14,15

"So Joshua let the people depart, every man unto his inheritance." Josh. 24:7,8

Blessed
"... I would not hearken unto Balaam; therefore he blessed you still: so I delivered you out of his hand." Josh. 24:10

Promise to Israel
"... I delivered them (the surrounding nations) *into your hand. And I sent the hornet before you, which drave them out from before you... and I have given you a land for which ye did not labour, and cities which ye built not, and ye dwell in them; of the vineyards and oliveyards which ye planted not do ye eat.*" Josh. 24:11-13

"*For the Lord our God, He it is that brought us up and our fathers out of the land of Egypt, from the house of bondage, and which did those great signs in our sight, and preserved us in all the way wherein we went and among all the people through whom we passed: and the Lord* (drove) *out from before us all the people...*" Josh. 24:17,18

Judges

"*... and the Lord delivered...* (them) *into their hand...*" Judges 1:4

"*... as I have done, so God hath requited* ("*repaid*" NKJV) *me...*" Judges 1:7
We get back what we do - whether good or bad!

Prayer for blessing
"*... give me a blessing...*" Judges 1:15
"*And the Lord was with Judah...*" Judges 1:19
"*And ... the Lord was with the Judge, and delivered them out of the hand of their enemies all the days of the Judge...*" Judges 2:18

Blessed
"*Blessed above women shall Jael the wife of Heber the Kenite be, blessed shall she be above women in the tent.*" Judges 5:24

"*... let all Thine enemies perish... let them that love Him be as the sun when he goeth forth in his might. And the land had rest forty years.*" Judges 5:31

"*And Israel was greatly impoverished because of the Midianites; and the children of Israel cried unto the Lord. And it came to pass, when the children of Israel cried unto the Lord...* (He) *sent a prophet... which said unto them, Thus saith the Lord God of Israel, I brought you up from Egypt, and brought you forth out of the house of bondage; and I delivered you out of the hand of the Egyptians, and out of the hand of all that oppressed you, and* (drove) them out from before you, and gave you their land; and I said unto you, I am the Lord your God; fear not the gods of the Amorites, in whose land ye dwell..." Judges 6:6-10

The Condition:
"... but you have not obeyed My voice." Judges 6:10

"And the angel of the Lord appeared unto him, and said unto him..." Judges 6:12

> **The Promise:**
> "...the Lord is with thee..." Judges 6:12

"... thou mighty man of valour." Judges 6:12

"And the Lord said unto him..." Judges 6:16

> **The Promise:**
> "... surely I will be with thee and thou shalt smite the Midianites as one man." Judges 6:16

When Gideon saw the angel of the Lord
"And he said, unto Him, If now I have found grace in Thy sight, then shew me a sign that Thou talkest with me." Judges 6:17

"And the Lord said unto him, Peace be unto thee; fear not..." Judges 6:23

The promise to Gideon
"... thou shalt not die." Judges 6:23

God delivered them
"And the Lord said unto the children of Israel, Did not I deliver you from the Egyptians... and (they) did oppress you; and ye cried to Me, and..." Judges 10:11,12

> **The Promise:**
> "... I delivered you out of their hand." Judges 10:12

The Condition:
"Yet ye have forsaken Me, and served other gods: wherefore I will deliver you no more. Go and cry unto the gods which ye have chosen; let them deliver you in the time of your tribulation. And the children of Israel said unto the Lord, We have sinned: do Thou unto us whatsoever seemeth good unto Thee; (but) deliver us only, we pray Thee, this day. And they put away the strange gods from among them, and served the Lord..." Judges 10:13-16

God felt bad for them
"... and His soul was grieved for the misery of Israel." Judges 10:16

"... now let Your Words come to pass..." Judges 13:12
This should be our prayer!
"Let it be according to Your Word." Lk. 1:38

Miracle
"... the Spirit of the Lord came mightily upon him (Samson), and the cords that were upon his arms became as flax that was burnt with fire, and his bands loosed from off his hands." Judges 15:14

Miracle
"But God clave an hollow place that was in the jaw, and there came water thereout; and when he had drunk, his spirit came again, and he revived: wherefore he called the name thereof En-hak-kor-e (Heb. #5875 "spring of the one calling, or fountain")..." Judges 15:19.
Samson prayed for water and God provided water for him. If we ever need water, we can remember that if God gave Samson water from a jawbone then He can provide water for us also.

A full reward
"The Lord recompense thy work, and a full reward be given thee of the Lord God of Israel, under whose wings thou art come to trust." Ruth 2:12
See also Ruth 3:9;Ps.63:7;91:4;Ez.16:8

God blessed Ruth with a son
"... the Lord gave her conception, and she bare a son." Ruth 4:13

The women blessed Ruth
"And the women said unto Naomi, Blessed be the Lord, which hath not left thee this day without a kinsman, that his name may be famous in Israel. And he shall be unto thee a restorer of thy life, and a nourisher of thine old age ..."
Ruth 4:14,15
Jesus is our Kinsman Redeemer – He has legally taken back the land which we lost through Adam. He has become our Bridegroom and we are His Bride. Thank You Jesus!!!

1st Samuel

Eli speaks a blessing to Hannah
Eli, *"Then Eli answered and said, Go in peace: and the God of Israel grant thee thy petition that thou hast asked of Him."* I Sam. 1:17
Hannah, *"For this child I prayed; and the Lord hath given me my petition which I asked of Him."* I Sam. 1:27
Hannah prayed for a child and God gave her what she asked for.
Prayer:
Father in heaven, please give me the answers to my prayers like You did for Hannah. Thank You in Jesus' name, Amen!

It is God who makes you rich.
"The Lord maketh poor, and maketh rich: He bringeth low, and lifteth up. He raiseth up the poor out of the dust, and lifteth up the beggar from the dunghill, to set them among princes, and to make them inherit the throne of glory… He will keep the feet of His saints… the adversaries of the Lord shall be broken to pieces; out of heaven shall He thunder upon them… and He shall give strength unto His king, and exalt the horn of His anointed." I Sam. 2:7-10

Eli blessed Elkannah and Hannah
"And Eli blessed Elkanah and his wife, and said, The Lord give thee seed of this woman… and the Lord visited Hannah, so that she conceived, and bare three sons and two daughters (besides Samuel)." I Sam. 2:20,21

God speaks to Eli
"… them that honour Me I will honour…" I Sam. 2:30
Return to God with all your heart
The Condition:
"If you do return unto the Lord with all your hearts, then put away the strange gods… from among you, and prepare your hearts unto the Lord, and serve Him only…" I Sam. 7:3

> **The Promise:**
> *"… He will deliver you out of the hand of the Philistines."* I Sam. 7:3

Prayer:
Father in heaven, deliver us from anything that would pull us away from You

and help us to serve You with all our hearts! Thank You in Jesus' name, Amen!

Ebenezer – the Lord heped us
"Then Samuel took a stone and set it between Mizpah and Shen, and named it Ebenezer, saying, Thus far the Lord has helped us." I Sam. 7:12 NASB
All through Samuel's lifetime, God's hand was against their enemies, I Sam. 7:13

Samuel speaks a blessing over Saul
   The Promise:
   "And the Spirit of the Lord will come upon thee and thou shalt prophesy with them, and shalt be turned into another man..." I Sam. 10:6

Prayer:
Father in heaven, I pray for _____, that You would send Your Holy Spirit and turn him/her into another person to serve You with all their hearts! In Jesus' name, Amen!

"... and let it be, when these signs are come unto thee, that thou do as occasion serve thee..." I Sam. 10:7

   The Promise:
   "... for God is with thee... God gave him another heart... and the Spirit of God came upon him, and he prophesied among them." I Sam. 10:7,9,10

Prayer:
Father in heaven, please give me and my loved ones another heart to serve You. Thank You, in Jesus' name, Amen!

It is God who saves us out of our trials and tribulations
"And ye have this day rejected your God, who Himself saved you out of all your adversities and your tribulations..." I Sam. 10:19

The Holy Spirit
"And the Spirit of God came upon Saul when he heard those tidings... and the fear of the Lord fell on the people, and they came out with one consent." I Sam. 11:6,7

God sent his prophets
"... and delivered you out of the hand of your enemies on every side, and ye dwelled safe." I Sam. 12:11

God's promise to Israel when Saul was crowned king
"For the Lord will not forsake His people for His great name's sake: because it hath pleased the Lord to make you His people... consider how great things He hath done for you." I Sam. 12:22,24
And now we too are the people of God, if we believe in Jesus, Gal. 3:26;I Pet. 2:4-10.

The Condition:
"But if ye shall still do wickedly, ye shall be consumed, both ye and your king." I Sam. 12:25

Jonathan to his armor bearer
"Come, and let us go over unto the garrison of these uncircumcised: it may be that the Lord will work for us: for there is no restraint to the Lord to save by many or by few." I Sam. 14:6

Prayer:
Father in heaven, please use me to save many or few according to Your will. Thank You in the name of Jesus, Amen!

God delivered them
"... for the Lord hath delivered them into the hand of Israel... there was trembling in the host, in the field, and among all the people... and the earth quaked: so it was a very great trembling." I Sam. 14:12,15

"... and the Spirit of the Lord came upon David from that day forward... the Lord was with him..." I Sam. 16:13,18
God chose David because of the integrity of his heart.
"He also chose David His servant... according to the integrity of his heart..." Ps. 78:70,72 NKJV

"David said moreover, The Lord that delivered me out of the paw of the lion, and out of the paw of the bear, He will deliver me out of the hand of this Philistine. And Saul said unto David, Go, and the Lord be with thee." I Sam. 17:37

"... I come to thee in the name of the Lord of hosts, the God of the armies of Israel, whom thou hast defied." I Sam. 17:45

The battle is the Lord's
"This day will the Lord deliver thee (Goliath) *into mine* (David's) *hand; and I*

will smite thee; that all the earth may know that there is a God in Israel. And all this assembly shall know that the Lord saveth not with sword and spear: for the battle is the Lord's, and He will give you into our hands." I Sam. 17:46,47

God was with David
"And David behaved himself wisely in all his ways; and the Lord was with him. Wherefore when Saul saw that he behaved himself very wisely, he was afraid of him. But all Israel and Judah loved David..." I Sam. 18:14,15

God delivered him
"... Saul sought him (David) every day, but God delivered him not into his hand." I Sam. 23:14

Blessing from David to Naboth
"And thus you shall say to him who lives in prosperity: peace be to you, peace to your house, and peace to all that you have." I Sam. 25:6 NKJV
God put king Saul into a deep sleep
"So David took the spear and the cruse of water from Saul's bolster; and they ... (got) away, and no man saw it, nor knew it, neither awaked: for they were all asleep; because a deep sleep from the Lord was fallen upon them." I Sam. 26:12

"... but David encouraged himself in the Lord his God." I Sam. 29:6
Prayer:
Father in heaven, help me to be encouraged in You, Amen!

God's promise to David.
"And David inquired at the Lord, saying, Shall I pursue after this troop? Shall I overtake them?

> **The Promise:**
> "And He answered him pursue; for thou shalt surely overtake them, and without fail recover all." I Sam. 30:8

If God could help David recover everything he lost, then He can help us also.

2nd Samuel

Blessed
"... you are blessed of the Lord, for you have shown this kindness... and now may the Lord show kindness and truth to you... let your hands be strengthened, and be valiant..." II Sam. 2:5-7 NKJV

About David
"... the Lord God of Hosts was with him." II Sam. 4:10 NKJV

David gives God the credit
"... the Lord hath broken forth upon mine enemies before me, as the breach of waters... for then shall the Lord go out before thee, to smite the host of the Philistines." II Sam. 5:20,24

Blessed
"... and the Lord blessed Obed-edom, and all his household. And it was told king David, saying, The Lord hath blessed the house of Obed-edom, and all that pertaineth unto him, because of the Ark of God. So David went and brought up the Ark of God from the house of Obed-edom into the city of David with gladness." II Sam. 6:12

God chose you
"... the Lord, which chose me..." II Sam. 6:21

God's blessing and promise to David
"And I was with thee whithersoever thou wentest, and have cut off all thine enemies out of thy sight, and have made thee a great name, like unto the name of the great men that are in the earth. Moreover I will appoint a place for My people Israel, and will plant them, that they may dwell in a place of their own, and move no more; neither shall the children of wickedness afflict them anymore, as beforetime... and caused thee to rest from all thine enemies. Also the Lord telleth thee that He will make thee an house. And when thy days be fulfilled, and thou shalt sleep with thy fathers, I will set up thy seed after thee, which shall proceed out of thy bowels, and I will establish his kingdom. He shall build an house for My name, and I will stablish the throne of his kingdom forever. I will be his father, and he shall be My son. If he commit iniquity... My mercy shall not depart away from him... and thine house and thy kingdom shall be established forever before thee: thy throne shall be established forever..." II Sam. 7:9-16

Jesus will sit on the throne of David on the New Earth.

David's response to God's blessing
"... Thou hast promised this goodness unto Thy servant: therefore now let it please Thee to bless the house of Thy servant, that it may continue forever before Thee: for Thou, O Lord God, hast spoken it: and with Thy blessing let the house of Thy servant be blessed forever." II Sam. 7:28,29

God was with David.
"... the Lord preserved David whithersoever he went." II Sam. 8:6,14
"... the Lord gave David victory..." II Sam. 8:6,14 NIV

God does good!!!
"Be of good courage... the Lord do that which seemeth Him good." II Sam. 10:12
"... the Lord will do what is good in His sight." II Sam. 10:12 NIV

God speaks to David after his sin with Bathsheba
"... if that had been too little, I would moreover have given unto thee such and such things." II Sam. 12:8
"If all this had been too little, I would have even given you more." II Sam. 12:8 NIV
"If it had not been enough, I would have given you... more" II Sam. 12:8 LB

The Condition:
"... wherefore hast thou despised the Commandment of the Lord, to do evil in His sight?" II Sam. 12:8

David fled from Jerusalem when Absalom tried to take over
"... if I shall find favour in the eyes of the Lord, He will bring me again, and shew me both it, and His habitation..." II Sam. 15:25

"It may be that the Lord will look on mine affliction, and that the Lord will requite me good for his cursing this day." II Sam. 16:12
Prayer:
Father in heaven, please give me good for the bad things that have happened to me. In Jesus' name, Amen!

The Song of praise from David

The Promise:
"And David spake unto the Lord the words of this song in the day that the Lord had delivered him out of the hand of all his enemies ... and he said, The Lord is my Rock, and my fortress, and my deliverer; the God of my Rock; in Him will I trust: He is my shield, and the horn of my Salvation, my high tower, and my refuge, my Saviour; Thou savest me from violence. I will call on the Lord, who is worthy to be praised: and so shall I be saved from mine enemies, when the waves of death compassed me, the floods of ungodly men made me afraid; the sorrows of hell compassed me about; the snares of death prevented me; in my distress I called upon the Lord, and cried to my God: and He did hear my voice out of His Temple, and my cry did enter His ears." II Sam. 22: 1-7

The Lord fought for them
"The Lord ordered from heaven, and the Most High uttered His voice. He sent out His arrows and scattered them; lightning bolts, and He vanquished them." II Sam. 22:14,15 NKJV

"He sent from above, He took me; He drew me out of many waters; He delivered me from my strong enemy, and from them that hated me: for they were too strong for me. They prevented me in the day of my calamity: but the Lord was my stay. He brought me forth also into a large ("spacious" HCSB) place: He delivered me..." II Sam. 22:17-20

The Condition:
"... because He delighted in me." II Sam. 22:20

The Promise:
"... the Lord rewarded me..." II Sam. 22:21

The Condition:
"... according to my righteousness; according to the cleanness of my hands..." II Sam. 22:21

The Promise:
"... hath he recompensed me..." II Sam. 22:21

The Promise:
"Therefore the Lord hath recompensed me according to my righteousness..." II Sam. 22:25

The Promise:
"And David spake unto the Lord the words of this song in the day that the Lord had delivered him out of the hand of all his enemies... and he said, The Lord is my Rock, and my fortress, and my deliverer; the God of my Rock; in Him will I trust: He is my shield, and the horn of my Salvation, my high tower, and my refuge, my Saviour; Thou savest me from violence. I will call on the Lord, who is worthy to be praised: and so shall I be saved from mine enemies, when the waves of death compassed me, the floods of ungodly men made me afraid; the sorrows of hell compassed me about; the snares of death prevented me; in my distress I called upon the Lord, and cried to my God: and He did hear my voice out of His Temple, and my cry did enter His ears." II Sam. 22: 1-7

The Condition:
"... according to my cleanness in His eye sight. With the merciful..." II Sam. 22:25,26

> **The Promise:**
> "... Thou wilt shew Thyself merciful..." II Sam. 22:26

The Condition:
"... and with the upright ("blameless" NKJV) man..." II Sam. 22:26

> **The Promise:**
> "... Thou wilt shew Thyself upright ("blameless" NKJV)..." II Sam. 22:26

The Condition:
"... with the pure..." II Sam. 22:27

> **The Promise:**
> "... Thou wilt shew Thyself pure..." II Sam. 22:27

"... and with the forward ("devious" NKJV) Thou wilt shew Thyself unsavoury ("shrewd" NKJV)..." II Sam. 22:27

> **The Promise:**
> "... and the afflicted ("humble" NKJV) people Thou wilt save... the Lord will lighten my darkness. For **by Thee I have run through a troop: by my God have I leaped over a wall**. As for God, His way is perfect; the Word of the Lord is tried: He is a buckler to all them that trust in Him. For who is God, save the Lord? And who is a Rock, save our God? God is my strength and power: and He maketh my way perfect. He maketh my feet like hinds' feet: and setteth me

*upon my high places. He teacheth my hands to war; so that a **bow of steel is broken by mine arms**. Thou hast also given me the shield of Thy Salvation: and Thy gentleness hath made me great. Thou hast enlarged my steps under me; so that my feet did not slip. I have pursued mine enemies, and destroyed them... that they could not arise: yea, **they are fallen under my feet**. For Thou hast girded me with strength to battle: them that rose up against me hast Thou subdued under me. Thou hast also given me... mine enemies ... them that hate me..."* II Sam. 22:28-41

What a beautiful promise! With God I can *"run through a troop"* and *"leap over a wall"*; I can *"break a steel bow with my arms"*! This is saying that with God all things are possible and I can do great things with His help.
Thank You Jesus!!!
The Bible says that we have authority to trample snakes and scorpions in Jesus, Lk. 10:19.

God delivers me
"Thou also hast delivered me from the strivings of my people, Thou hast kept me to be head of the heathen: a people which I knew not shall serve me. Strangers shall submit themselves unto me: as soon as they hear, they shall be obedient unto me... the Lord liveth; and blessed be my Rock; and exalted be the God of the Rock of my Salvation. It is God that avengeth me, and that bringeth down the people under me, and that bringeth me forth from mine enemies: thou also hast lifted me up on high above them that rose up against me: Thou hast delivered me from the violent man. Therefore I will give thanks unto Thee, O Lord, among the heathen, and I will sing praises unto Thy name. He is the tower of Salvation for his king: and sheweth mercy to His anointed, unto David, and to his seed forevermore." II Sam. 22:44-51

"The Spirit of the Lord spake by me, and His Word was in my tongue." II Sam. 23:2
I speak the Word of God, the promises, out loud.

God's Covenant lasts forever
"... yet He (God) hath made with me an everlasting Covenant, ordered in all things, and sure: for this is all my Salvation, and all my desire..." II Sam. 23:5
"Is not my house right with God? Has He not made with me an everlasting Covenant, arranged and secured in every part? Will He not bring to fruition my Salvation and grant me my every desire?" II Sam. 23:5 NIV

The Bible says that we can ask anything in Jesus' name and the Father will give it to us so that our joy may be full, Jn. 16:24.

"... the Lord wrought a great victory that day; and the people returned after Him only to spoil." II Sam. 23:10
Plague stopped
"And David built there an altar unto the Lord... so the Lord was entreated for the land, and the plague was stayed ("withdrawn" NKJV) from Israel." II Sam. 24:25

1st Kings

Promise to David and his descendants

The Promise:
"... that thou mayest prosper in all that thou doest, and whithersoever thou turnest thyself: that the Lord may continue His Word which He spake concerning me, saying..." I Kings 2:3,4

The Condition:
"... if thy children take heed to their way, to walk before Me in truth with all their heart and with all their soul..." I Kings 2:4

The Promise:
"... there shall not fail thee... a man on the throne of Israel." I Kings 2:4

Again we see God wants us to serve Him with all our heart and soul.
God said to king Solomon
"In Gibeon the Lord appeared to Solomon in a dream by night: and God said, ask what I shall give thee." I Kings 3:5

Solomon asked for a wise and understanding heart
"Give therefore Thy servant an understanding heart to Judge Thy people, that I may discern between good and bad: for who is able to Judge this Thy so great a people? And the speech pleased the Lord, that Solomon had asked this thing." I Kings 3:9,10

God gives wisdom and understanding to Solomon
"Behold, I have done according to Thy words: lo, I have given thee a wise and an understanding heart; so that there was none like thee before thee, neither after thee shall any arise like unto thee. And I have also given the e

that which thou has not asked, both riches, and honour: so that there shall not be any among the kings like unto thee all thy days." I Kings 3:12,13

The Condition:
"And if thou wilt walk in My ways, to keep My Statutes and My Commandments, as thy father David did walk..." I Kings 3:14

> **The Promise:**
> *"... then I will lengthen thy days."* I Kings 3:14

Solomon failed in the end to keep the conditions of the promise; he married many women who worshipped idols, and he ended up worshipping their gods along with the One true God but God wants us to worship only Him; that is why He is a Jealous God.

"... for they saw that the wisdom of God was in him (Solomon), *to do Judgment."* I Kings 3:28

"And God gave Solomon wisdom and understanding exceeding much, and largeness of heart, even as the sand that is on the seashore. And Solomon's wisdom excelled the wisdom of all the children of the East country, and all the wisdom of Egypt. For he was wiser than all men... his fame was in all nations round about. And he spake three thousand proverbs: and his songs were a thousand and five." I Kings 4:29-32

> **The Promise:**
> *"... until the Lord put them under the soles of his feet. But now the Lord my God hath given me rest on every side, so that there is neither adversary nor evil occurrent* ("disaster" NIV)." I Kings 5:3,4

God fulfills His promise to Solomon
"And the Lord gave Solomon wisdom, as He promised him..." I Kings 5:12
Prayer:
Father in heaven, please let Your promises come true for me and give me wisdom as You did for Solomon. Thank You! In Jesus' name, Amen!

God allows Solomon to build the Temple of God
"Concerning this house which thou art in building..." I Kings 6:12
The Condition:
"... if thou wilt walk in My Statutes, and execute My Judgments, and keep all My Commandments to walk in them..." I Kings 6:12

> **The Promise:**
> *"... I* (will) *perform My Word with thee... I will dwell among the children of Israel, and will not forsake My people.."* I Kings 6:12,13

The Condition:
"And he (Solomon) *said, Lord God of Israel, there is no God like Thee, in heaven above, or on earth beneath..."* I Kings 8:23

Let Your Word come true!
"... (You) who keepest Covenant and mercy with Thy servants that walk before Thee with all their heart... who hast kept with Thy servant David my father that Thou promisedst him: Thou spakest also with Thy mouth, and hast fulfilled it with Thine hand... therefore now, Lord God of Israel, keep with Thy servant David my father that Thou promisedst him, saying, There shall not fail thee a man in My sight to sit on the throne of Israel; so that thy children take heed to their way, that they walk before Me as thou hast walked before Me. And now, O God of Israel, let Thy Word, I pray thee be verified ("come true" NIV), which Thou spakest unto Thy servant David my father." I Kings 8:23-26
God gave Solomon what He promised to David.

Not one of God's promises will fail
"Blessed be the Lord, that hath given rest unto His people Israel, according to all that He promised: there hath not failed one Word of all His good promises, which He promised by the hand of Moses His servant." I Kings 8:56

2nd Kings

Elisha asks Elijah for a double portion of the Holy Spirit
"So he (Elijah) *said, You* (Elisha) *have asked a hard thing. Nevertheless, if you see me when I'm taken from you, it shall be so for you..."* II Kings 2:10 NKJV

Elisha receives a double portion of the Holy Spirit from Elijah
"And he (Elisha) *took the mantle of Elijah that fell from him, and smote the waters, and said, Where is the Lord God of Elijah? and when he also had smitten the waters, they parted hither and thither: and Elisha went over. And when the sons of the prophets which were to view at Jericho saw him, they said, The Spirit of Elijah doth rest on Elisha..."* II Kings 2:14,15

Miracle
"And he (Elisha) *said, Bring me a new cruse, and put salt therein. And they brought it to him. And he went forth unto the spring of the waters, and cast*

the salt in there, and said, Thus saith the Lord, I have healed these waters; there shall not be from thence anymore death or barren land. So the waters were healed unto this day, according to the saying of Elisha which he spake." II Kings 2:20-22

Miracle
"Go and wash in Jordan seven times, and thy flesh shall come again to thee, and thou shalt be clean... his flesh came again like unto the flesh of a little child, and he was clean. And he (Namaan) returned to the man of God, he and all his company, and came, and stood before him: and he said, Behold, now I know that there is no God in all the earth, but in Israel..." II Kings 5:10,14,15
Elijah promised Namaan that if he washed in the Jordan River seven times, he would be healed, and he was.

The Promise:
"... fear not: for they that be with us are more than they that be with them." II Kings 6:16

The Assyrians were coming against Israel. Elisha asked God to "smite this people (the Syrians) ..with blindness. And He (God) smote them with blindness according to the Word of Elisha." Elisha led the Syrians to Samaria, then Elisha prayed, "... Lord, open the eyes of these men that they may see." II Kings 6:20
God opened their eyes
"... and the Lord opened their eyes, and they saw..." II Kings 6:20

"For the Lord had made the host of the Syrians to hear a noise of chariots, and a noise of horses, even the noise of a great host..." II Kings 7:6
They heard the horses of angels and when Jesus comes the second time, the armies of angels are also following on horses, Rev. 19:14.

Restore everything
"... restore all that was hers, and all the fruits of the field since the day that she left the land, even until now." II Kings 8:6
On the new earth, God will restore everything that was taken from us.

The Word will not fail
"Know now that there shall fall unto the earth nothing of the Word of the Lord... for the Lord hath done that which He spake by His servant.." II Kings 10:10
God will do what He says! His Word never fails!

"... and the Lord gave Israel a saviour..." II Kings 13:5
"... a deliverer so that they escaped..." II Kings 13:5 NKJV
God has given us a Savior, Jesus Christ.

"And the Lord was gracious unto them, and had compassion on them, and had respect unto them, because of His Covenant with Abraham, Isaac, and Jacob..." II Kings 13:23

The Condition:
"But the Lord your God ye shall fear..." II Kings 17:39

>**The Promise:**
>*"... and He shall deliver you out of the hand of all your enemies."* II Kings 17:39

He prospered
"And the Lord was with him: and he prospered whithersoever he went forth..." II Kings 18:7
"... the Lord was with him; he prospered wherever he went..." II Kings 18:7 NKJV

>**The Promise:**
>*"... the Lord will surely deliver us...* II Kings 18:30 NKJV

Isaiah told Hezekiah God's promise to him
"... thus saith the Lord, be not afraid of the words which thou hast heard, with which the servants of the king of Assyria have blasphemed me." II Kings 19:6

>**The Promise:**
>*"Behold, I will send a blast upon him, and he shall hear a rumour, and shall return to his own land; and I will cause him to fall by the sword in his own land."* II Kings 19:7

"... the Lord will surely deliver us..." II Kings 19:28 NKJV
Miracle
"Then he (Hezekiah) turned his face to the wall, and prayed unto the Lord, saying, I beseech Thee, O Lord, remember now how I have walked before thee in truth and with a perfect heart, and have done that which is good in Thy sight. And Hezekiah wept sore. And it came to pass, (before) Isaiah was gone out into the middle court, that the Word of the Lord came to him, saying, Turn again, and tell Hezekiah the captain of My people, Thus saith the Lord, the God of David thy father..." II Kings 20:2-5

The Promise:
"... I have heard thy prayer, I have seen thy tears... I will heal thee: on the third day thou shalt go up unto the house of the Lord. And I will add unto thy days fifteen years; and I will deliver thee and this city out of the hand of the king of Assyria; and I will defend this city for Mine own sake, and for My servant David's sake." II Kings 20:5,6

Prayer:
Father in heaven, please hear my prayers, see my tears, and heal me when I need healing like You did for king Hezekiah in Jesus' name, Amen!

Miracle
"And Isaiah said, Take a lump of figs. And they took and laid it on the boil, and he recovered. And Hezekiah said unto Isaiah, What shall be the sign that the Lord will heal me, and that I shall go up into the house of the Lord the third day? And Isaiah said, This sign shalt thou have of the Lord, that the Lord will do the thing that He hath spoken: shall the shadow go forward ten degrees, or go back ten degrees? And Hezekiah answered, It is a light thing for the shadow to go down ten degrees: nay, but let the shadow return backward ten degrees. And Isaiah the prophet cried unto the Lord; and He brought the shadow ten degrees backward, by which it had gone down in the dial of Ahaz." II Kings 20:7-11

God's promise to Hezekiah because he repented
"... and thine eyes shall not see all the evil which I will bring upon this place ..."
II Kings 22:20

I Chronicles

The prayer of Jabez
"... O that Thou wouldest bless me indeed, and enlarge my coast, and that Thine hand might be with me, and that Thou wouldest keep me from evil, that it may not grieve me. And God granted him that which he requested."
I Chron. 4:10

Prayer:
Father in heaven, bless me and let Your hand be with me. Keep me from evil as the Lord's Prayer says, "*deliver us from evil*". Please grant my request as You did for Jabez. Thank You in Jesus' name, Amen!

God answered
"... for they cried to God in the battle, and He was intreated of them; because they put their trust in Him... for there fell down many slain, because the war was of God..." I Chron. 5:20,22
"... He answered them..." I Chron. 5:20 NASB
"... He granted their urgent prayer..." I Chron. 5:20 ESV
"... He granted their request..." I Chron. 5:20 HCSB
According to the promises in God's Word
"So David waxed greater and greater: for the Lord of hosts was with him... according to the Word of the Lord concerning Israel." I Chron. 11:9,10
Prayer:
Father in heaven, please be with me as You were with David according to Your Word in my life. Thank You, in Jesus' name, Amen!

Blessed
"... and the Lord blessed the house of Obed-edom, and all that he had." I Chron. 13:14
"God blessed him because the Ark of the Covenant was with him... and his entire household." II Sam. 6:11 NIV
Prayer:
Father in heaven, please put Your law in my heart (Jer. 31:37) and bless me and my house as You did for Obed-edom. Thank You in Jesus' name, Amen!

"... then David said, God hath broken in upon mine enemies by mine hand like the breaking forth of waters: therefore they called the name of that place Baal-pera-zim... and the Lord brought the fear of him upon all nations." I Chron. 14:11,17

The Condition:
"Be ye mindful always of His Covenant; the Word which He commanded to a thousand generations: even of the Covenant which he made with Abraham, and of his oath unto Isaac; and hath confirmed the same to Jacob..." I Chron. 15:17

Blessed
"... he blessed the people in the name of the Lord." I Chron. 16:2 NKJV

> **The Promise:**
> *"Unto thee will I give the land of Canaan, the lot of your inheritance ... He suffered no man to do them wrong: yea, He reproved kings for their sakes, saying, Touch not mine anointed, and do my prophets no harm."* I Chron. 16:18-22

Prayer:
Father in heaven, suffer no man to do me wrong, as it says in Your Word. Thank You in Jesus' name, Amen.

"Fear before Him, all the earth..." I Chron. 16:30

The Promise:
"... the world also shall be stable, that it be not moved." I Chron. 16:30

The Promise:
"And I have been with thee whithersoever thou hast walked, and have cut off all thine enemies from before thee, and have made thee a name like the name of the great men that are in the earth... they shall dwell in their place, and shall be moved no more; neither shall the children of wickedness waste them anymore, as at the beginning... moreover I will subdue all thine enemies. The Lord will build thee an house... I will raise up thy seed after thee, which shall be of thy sons; and I will establish his kingdom... He shall build me an house, and I will stablish his throne forever. I will be his father, and he shall be My son: and I will not take My mercy away from him, as I took it from him that was before thee: but I will settle him in Mine house and in My kingdom forever: and his throne shall be established forevermore." I Chron. 17:8-14

The God of Israel
"For Thy people Israel didst Thou make Thine own people forever; and Thou, Lord, becamest their God. Therefore now, Lord, let the thing that Thou hast spoken concerning Thy servant and concerning his house be established forever, and do as Thou hast said." I Chron. 17:22,23

Prayer:
Father in heaven, let the thing You have said in Your Word be estabished for me. Thank You in Jesus' name, Amen!

When God blesses, it is blessed forever
"And now, Lord, Thou art God, and hast promised this goodness unto Thy servant: now therefore let it please Thee to bless the house of Thy servant, that it may be before Thee forever: for Thou blessedst, O Lord, and it shall be blessed forever." I Chron. 17:26,27

"So the Lord preserved David whithersoever he went..." I Chron. 18:6,13

"Be of good courage, and let us be strong for our people and for the cities of our God. And may the Lord do what is good in His sight." I Chron. 19:13

God's mercy is great!
"... the Lord... for very great are His mercies..." I Chron. 21:13

Promise to Solomon
"... I will give him rest from all his enemies round about: for his name shall be Solomon, and I will give peace and quietness unto Israel in his days. He shall build an house for My name; and he shall be My son, and I will be his father; and I will establish the throne of his kingdom over Israel forever. Now my son, the Lord be with thee; and prosper thou, and build the house of the Lord thy God as He hath said of thee. Only the Lord give thee wisdom and under-standing, and give thee charge concerning Israel..." I Chron. 22:9-11
"The Lord be with you so that you may prosper" I Chron. 22:11 PB

Prayer:
Father in heaven, please give me wisdom and understanding like You did for king Solomon. Thank You in Jesus' name, Amen!

The Condition:
"... keep the law of the Lord thy God." I Chron. 12:13

> **The Promise:**
> *"... then shalt thou prosper..."* I Chron. 22:13

The Condition:
"... if thou takest heed to fulfil the Statutes and Judgments which the Lord charged Moses with concerning Israel; be strong, and of good courage; dread not, nor be dismayed." I Chron. 22:13
"Then shall you prosper if you take heed to observe these Commandments... then you will be strong..." I Chron. 22:13 PB

"... arise therefore, and be doing, and the Lord be with thee." I Chron. 22:16
"The Lord will help you..." I Chron. 22:16 PB

Set your heart on seeking God
"Is not the Lord your God with you? and hath He not given you rest on every side? For He hath given the inhabitants of the land into mine hand; and the land is subdued before the Lord, and before His people. Now set your heart and your soul to seek the Lord your God..." I Chron. 22:18,19
"He will help you and relieve you on every side." I Chron. 22:18PB

Blessed
"... for God blessed him." I Chron. 26:5

Prayer:
Father in heaven, please bless me as it says in Your Word. Thank You! In Jesus' name, Amen!

God chose Solomon
"And He said unto me, Solomon thy son, he shall build My house and My courts; for I have chosen him to be My son, and I will be his Father. Moreover I will establish his kingdom forever..." I Chron. 28:6-8

The Condition:
"... if he be constant to do My Commandments and My Judgments, as at this day..." I Chron. 28:7,8

> **The Promise:**
> *"... that ye may possess this good land, and leave it for an inheritance for your children after you forever."* I Chron. 28:8

"... Solomon My son, know thou the God of thy father, and serve Him with a perfect heart and with a willing mind: for the Lord searcheth all hearts, and understandeth all the imaginations of the thoughts..." I Chron. 28:9

The Condition:
"... if thou seek Him..." I Chron. 28:9

> **The Promise:**
> *"... He will be found of thee..."* I Chron. 28:9

"Both riches and honour come of Thee (God), and Thou reignest over all; and in Thine hand is power and might; and in Thine hand it is to make great, and to give strength unto all... for all things come of Thee, and of Thine own have we given Thee." I Chron. 29:12,13
"Then Solomon... prospered..." I Chron. 29:13 NKJV
All good things come from God. Even Satan cannot do one thing unless God gives him permission; we see that with Job. The Bible tells us that even a sparrow cannot die without God's permission in Matt. 10:29,30.

Promise to Solomon and his son
"All this, said David, the Lord made me understand in writing by His hand upon me, even all the works of this pattern. And David said to Solomon his son, Be strong and of good courage, and do it: fear not, nor be dismayed: for the Lord God, even my God, will be with thee: He will not fail thee, nor forsake thee, until thou hast finished all the work for the service of the house of the Lord." I Chron. 29:19,20

God blessed king Solomon
"And the Lord magnified Solomon exceedingly in the sight of all Israel, and bestowed upon him such royal majesty as had not been on any king before him in Israel." I Chron. 29:25-28

 2nd Chronicles

"And Solomon the son of David was strengthened in his kingdom, and the Lord his God was with him, and magnified him exceedingly." II Chron. 1:1

God speaks
"... God appear unto Solomon, and said unto him, Ask what I shall give thee. And Solomon said unto God, Thou hast shewed great mercy unto David my father, and hast made me to reign in his stead. Now, O Lord God, let Thy promise unto David my father be established... give me now wis-dom and knowledge, that I may go out and come in before this people: for who can Judge this Thy people, that is so great?" II Chron. 1:7-10

Prayer:
Father in heaven, please let Your promises be established for me as well and give me knowledge, wisdom, and understanding in Jesus' name, Amen!

Solomon asks for wisdom
"And God said to Solomon, Because this was in thine heart, and thou hast not asked riches, wealth, or honour, nor the life of thine enemies, neither yet hast asked long life; but hast asked wisdom and knowledge for thyself, that thou mayest Judge My people over whom I have made thee king: Wisdom and knowledge is granted unto thee; and I will give thee riches, and wealth, and honour, such as none of the kings have had that have been before thee, neither shall there any after thee have the like." II Chron. 1:11,12

"The Lord therefore hath performed His Word that He hath spoken: for I am risen up in the room of David my father, and am set on the throne of Israel, as the Lord promised..." II Chron. 6:10
"So the Lord fulfilled His Word... as (He) promised..." II Chron. 6:10 NKJV
God keeps His Word/promises!

"Thou which hast kept with Thy servant David my father that which Thou hast promised him; and spakest with Thy mouth, and hast fulfilled it with Thine hand..." II Chron. 6:15

"You have kept what You promised. Therefore, Lord God of Israel, now keep what You promised to Your servant..." II Chron. 6:15,16 NKJV

God is good!
"... for He (God) is good; for His mercy endureth forever." II Chron. 7:3
"And the Lord appeared to Solomon by night, and said unto him, I have heard thy prayer, and have chosen this place to Myself for an house of sacrifice." II Chron. 7:12

The Condition:
"If My people, which are called by My name, shall humble themselves, and pray and seek My face, and turn from their wicked ways..." II Chron. 7:14

> **The Promise:**
> "... then will I hear from heaven, and will forgive their sin, and will heal their land." II Chron. 7:14

We come to God in humility. We must never come to God in pride demanding
that He do anything!
"God resists ("opposes" NIV) the proud but gives grace to the humble." Jms. 4:6
The publican cried out to God, Have mercy on me a sinner and God justified him, Lk. 8:13,14.
"Now Mine eyes shall be open, and Mine ears attent unto the prayer that is made in this place... then will I stablish the throne of thy kingdom, according as I have Covenanted with David thy father, saying, There shall not fail thee a man to be ruler in Israel." II Chron. 7:15

The Condition:
"And when the Lord saw that they humbled themselves, the Word of the Lord came to (them) saying, They have humbled themselves..." II Chron. 12:7

> **The Promise:**
> "... therefore I will not destroy them, but I will grant them some deliverance; and My wrath shall not be poured out upon Jerusalem..." II Chron. 12:7

"... God delivered them in their hand... and the children of Judah prevailed, because they relied upon the Lord God of their fathers." II Chron. 13:16,18
"... because the Lord had given him rest." II Chron. 14:6
Jehoshaphat said, I don't know what to do but my eyes are on You, II Chron. 20:12.

The Condition:
"... *because we have sought the Lord our God...*" II Chron. 14:7

> **The Promise:**
> "*...and He hath given us rest on every side. So they built and prospered.*" II Chron. 14:7

"... *and they carried away very much spoil.*" II Chron. 14:13 NKJV

God was with them
"... *for the fear of the Lord came upon them: and they spoiled all the cities; for there was exceeding much spoil in them. They smote also the tents of the cattle, and carried away sheep and camels in abundance, and returned to Jerusalem.*" II Chron. 14:14,15

When they turned to God, He was found by them
"*The Lord is with you, while ye be with Him; and if ye seek Him, He will be found of you... now for a long season Israel hath been without the true God* ("not served their God in truth" PB) *and without a teaching priest, and without law... in their trouble did turn unto the Lord God of Israel, and sought Him...*" II Chron. 15:2-4

> **The Promise:**
> "... *He was found of them.*" II Chron. 15:2-4

Rewarded
"*Be strong therefore, and let not your hands be weak...*" II Chron. 15:7

> **The Promise:**
> "... *for your work shall be rewarded.*" II Chron. 15:7

Sometimes God rewards us now and sometimes we have to wait and be rewarded in heaven.

"*And he gathered all Judah and Benjamin and the strangers with them, out of Ephraim and Manasseh, and out of Simeon: for they fell to him out of Israel in abundance, when they saw that the Lord his God was with him.*" II Chron. 15:9

"... *large numbers had come over to him from Israel...*" II Chron. 15:15 NKJV
"... *the Lord gave them rest all around.*" II Chron. 15:15 NKJV

The Condition:
"... *because thou didst rely on the Lord...*" II Chron. 16:8

The Promise:
"He delivered them into thine hand. For the eyes of the Lord run to and fro throughout the whole earth, to shew Himself strong in the behalf of them..." II Chron. 16:8,9

The Condition:
"... whose heart is perfect ("fully committed" NIV) toward Him." II Chron. 16:9

"And the fear of the Lord fell upon all the kingdoms of the land that were round about Judah, so that they made no war against Jehoshaphat... and Jehosha-phat waxed great exceedingly..." II Chron. 17:3-5,10,12

God has all the power and might
"... O Lord God of our fathers, art not Thou God in heaven? And rulest not Thou over all the kingdoms of the heathen? and in Thine hand is there not power and might, so that none is able to withstand Thee?" II Chron. 20:6-9

God will fight your battles
"Then upon Jahaziel... came the Spirit of the Lord in the midst of the congregation... thus saith the Lord unto you, Be not afraid nor dismayed by reason of this great multitude..." II Chron. 20:14,15

> **The Promise:**
> *"... for the battle is not yours, but God's. Ye shall not need to fight in this battle..."* II Chron. 20:15,17

The Condition:
"... set yourselves, stand ye still, and see the Salvation of the Lord with you, O Judah and Jerusalem: fear not, nor be dismayed; tomorrow go out against them..." II Chron. 20:17

> **The Promise:**
> *"... O Judah and Jerusalem: fear not nor be dismayed; tomorrow go out against them: for the Lord will be with you."* II Chron. 20:17

The Condition:
"... believe in the Lord your God..." II Chron. 20:20

> **The Promise:**
> *"... so shall ye be established: believe... so shall ye prosper...'* II Chron. 20:20

"... His mercy endureth forever. And when they began to sing and to praise, the Lord set ambushments against (them)... they were ("defeated" NIV)." II Chron. 20:21,22

Prayer

Father in heaven, please fight all my battles for me as You did for them. Let me see Your Salvation in Jesus' name, Amen!

Valley of Blessing and praise

"... they found among them in abundance both riches... and precious jewels... more than they could carry away; and they were three days in gathering of the spoil, it was so much... for they blessed the Lord; therefore the name of the same place was called, The Valley of Berachah ("Valley of Blessing" LB), unto this day. Then they returned, every man of Judah and Jerusalem, and Jehosha-phat in the forefront of them, to go again to Jerusalem with joy; for the Lord had made them to rejoice over their enemies." II Chron. 20:25-27
"Baracah means praise" NIV fn; could also be called "Valley of praise".

Prayer: Father in heaven, bring me to the Valley of Blessing and praise in my life. Thank You in Jesus' name, Amen!

God gave them quiet and rest from their enemies

"the fear of God was on all the kingdoms... when they had heard that the Lord fought against the enemies of Israel... the realm of Jehoshaphat was quiet: for his God gave him rest round about." II Chron. 20: 29,30

King Amaziah, from Judah, had hired troops from Israel to help him fight, but God didn't want him to use these troops because He, God, wasn't with Israel at that time.

"But there came a man of God to him, saying, O king, let not the army of Israel go with thee; for the Lord is not with Israel... but if thou wilt go, do it, be strong for the battle: God shall make thee fall before the enemy ("Even if you go and fight courageously in battle, God will overthrow you before the enemy"): for God hath power to help, and to cast down. And Amaziah said to the man of God, But what shall we do for the hundred talents which I have given ("paid" NIV) to the army of Israel? And the man of God answered ..." II Chron. 25:7-9

The Promise:

"... the Lord is able to give thee much more than this." II Chron. 25:9

God has the power to help you or defeat you. So it's better to be on God's side than against Him.

"And he (king Uzziah) did that which was right in the sight of the Lord, according to all that his father Amaziah did. And he sought God in the days of Zechariah, who had understanding in the visions of God..." II Chron. 26:5
The Condition:
"... and as long as he sought the Lord..." II Chron. 26:5

> **The Promise:**
> *"... God made him to prosper."* II Chron. 26:5

"God helped him..." II Chron. 26:7 NKJV
"So Jotham became mighty..." II Chron. 27:6

The Condition:
"... because he prepared his ways ("walked steadfastly" NIV) before the Lord his God." II Chron. 27:6

God is merciful and gracious
"Now be ye not stiffnecked, as your fathers were, but..." II Chron. 30:8

The Condition:
"... yield yourselves unto the Lord, and enter into His Sanctuary, which He hath Sanctified forever: and serve the Lord your God that the fierceness of His wrath may turn away from you..." II Chron. 30:8,9

> **The Promise:**
> *"... for if ye turn again unto the Lord, your brethren and your children shall find compassion before them that lead them captive, so that they shall come again into this land: for the Lord your God is gracious and merciful, and will not turn away His face from you..."* II Chron. 30: 9

The Condition:
"... if ye return unto Him." II Chron. 30: 9
Prayer:
Father in heaven, please let my child/children find compassion from You. Be gracious and merciful to me and my family. Please don't ever turn Your face away from us, and help us not to turn away from You. Thank You in Jesus' name, Amen!

One heart
"Also in Judah the hand of God was to give them one heart to do the Commandment of the king and the prince, by the Word of the Lord." II Chron. 30:12

Prayer:
Father in heaven, please give us one heart to obey You! Thank You in Jesus' name, Amen!

Healed
"And the Lord hearkened to Hezekiah, and healed the people." II Chron. 30:20

Blessed
"Then the priests the Levites arose and blessed the people: and their voice was heard, and their prayer came up to His Holy dwelling place, even unto heaven." II Chron. 30:27

Prayer:
Father in heaven, please let my prayers come up before You and hear my prayers. Thank You in Jesus' name, Amen!

Blessed
"... since the people began to bring the offerings into the house of the Lord, we have had enough to eat, and have left plenty: for the Lord hath blessed His people; and that which is left is this great store." II Chron. 31:10

The Condition:
"And in every work that he began in the service of the house of God, and in the law, and in the Commandments, to seek his God, he did it with **all his heart**..." II Chron. 31:21

> **The Promise:**
> "... and prospered." II Chron. 31:21

God still wants us to serve Him with all our hearts, Jer. 29:13; 31:33.

God fights our battles
"Be strong and courageous, be not afraid nor dismayed for the king of Assyria, nor for all the multitude that is with him..." II Chron. 32:7

> **The Promise:**
> "... for there be more with us than with him..." II Chron. 32:7

"... with him is an arm of flesh..." II Chron. 32:8

> **The Promise:**
> "... but with us is the Lord our God to help us, and to fight our battles." II Chron. 32:8

Are we relying on flesh or on God?
"... and the people rested themselves ("were encouraged" PB) upon the words of Hezekiah king of Judah." II Chron. 32:8

God sent an angel
"And the Lord sent an angel, which cut off all the mighty men of valour, and the leaders and captains in the camp of the king of Assyria..." II Chron. 32:21

> **The Promise:**
> "... the Lord saved Hezekiah... and guided them on every side." II Chron. 32:21,22

"And many brought gifts unto the Lord to Jerusalem, and presents to Hezekiah king of Judah: so that he was magnified in the sight of all nations from thenceforth. In those days Hezekiah was sick to the death, and prayed unto the Lord; and He spake unto him ("answered him" NIV), and He gave him a ("miraculous" NIV) sign." II Chron. 32:23,24

Blessed
"And Hezekiah had exceeding much riches and honour: and he made himself treasuries for silver, and for gold, and for precious stones, and for spices, and for shields, and for all manner of pleasant jewels. Storehouses for the increase of corn, and wine, and oil; and stalls for all manner of beasts ("cattle" NIV), and cotes ("pens" NIV) for flocks. Moreover he provided him cities, and possessions of flocks and herds in abundance; for God had given him substance very much... and Hezekiah prospered in all his works... God left him, to try him, that he might know all that was in his heart." II Chron. 32:27-31
God tested and tried him; sometimes God allows us to be tested to see what is in our hearts like Hezekiah and Job.

Promise to Hezekiah
"... I have even heard thee also, saith the Lord. Behold, I will gather thee to thy fathers, and thou shalt be gathered to thy grave in peace..." II Chron. 34:27,28

> **The promise:**
> "... neither shall thine eyes see all the evil that I will bring upon this place..." II Chron. 34:28

This was the beginning of the seventy-year Babylonian captivity for Judah.

"And the Lord God of their fathers sent ("word" NIV) to them by His messengers, rising up betimes ("again and again" NIV), and sending; because He had compassion ("pity" NIV) on His people, and on His dwelling place..." II Chron. 36:15

"But the eye of their God was upon ("watching over" NIV) the elders..." Ezra 5:5

"... they prospered through the prophesying of Haggai the prophet and Zechariah..." Ezra 6:14

"... for the Lord had made them joyful, and turned the heart of the king of Assyria unto them, to strengthen their hands in the work ..." Ezra 6:22
God is able to turn the hearts of people to help us when we need help also. Thank You Jesus!

The hand of the Lord
"... the king granted him all his request, according to the hand of the Lord his God upon him." Ezra 7:6
"... according to the good hand of his God upon him." Ezra 7:9
"... and I was strengthened as the hand of the Lord my God was upon me..." Ezra 7:28

The Promise:
"... the hand of our God is upon all them for good..." Ezra 8:22

The Condition:
"... that seek Him ..." Ezra 8:22

"... the **hand of our God** was upon us, and He delivered us from the **hand of the enemy**..." Ezra 8:31
The "hand of God" versus "the hand of the enemy"; which hand do you want to be under?

God won't forsake us
"... our God hath not forsaken us in our bondage, but hath extended mercy unto us..." Ezra 9:9

Nehemiah

God keeps His promises

    The Promise:
    "... *God, that keepeth Covenant and mercy for them...*" Neh. 1:5

The Condition:
"... *that love Him and observe ("obey" NLT) His Commandments...*" Neh. 1:5
Love and obey, they always go hand in hand.

Prosper Thy servant
"*Now these are Thy servants and Thy people, whom Thou hast Redeemed by Thy great power, and by Thy strong hand... and prosper, I pray thee, Thy se-vant this day, and grant him mercy...*" Neh. 1:10,11

God's hand upon me
"... *according to the good hand of my God upon me.*" Neh. 2:8
"*Then I told them of the hand of my God which was good upon me...*" Neh. 2:18

"... *the God of heaven...*" Neh. 2:20

    The Promise:
    "*He will prosper us...*" Neh. 2:20

"*Be not ye afraid of them: remember the Lord, which is great and terrible, and fight for your brethren...*" Neh. 4:14,15

    The Promise:
    "... *God has brought their counsel to nought...*" Neh. 4:15

    The Promise:
    "... *our God shall fight for us.*" Neh. 4:20

Prayer:
Father in heaven, when people come against me and/or my family then please bring their counsel to nothing and fight for us. Thank You in Jesus' name, Amen!

"... *this work was wrought of our God.*" Neh. 6:16

    The Promise:
    "... *for the joy of the Lord is your strength.*" Neh. 8:10

"Yet Thou in Thy manifold mercies forsookest them not in the wilderness ..." Neh. 9:19

The Promise:
"Thou gavest also Thy good Spirit to instruct them and withheldest not Thy manna from their mouth, and gavest them water for their thirst. Yea, forty years didst Thou sustain them in the wilderness, so that they lacked nothing; their clothes waxed not old, and their feet swelled not" Neh. 9:20,21

"... and gavest them into their hands... they took strong cities, and a fat land, and possessed houses full of all goods... they did eat, and were filled, and became fat, and delighted themselves in Thy great goodness." Neh. 9:24,25

"... in the time of their trouble, when they cried unto Thee..." Neh. 9:27

The Promise:
"... Thou heardest them from heaven; and according to Thy manifold mercies Thou gavest them saviours, who saved them out of the hand of their enemies." Neh. 9:27

The Condition:
"... yet when they returned, and cried unto Thee..." Neh. 9:28

The Promise:
"Thou heardest them from heaven; and many times didst Thou deliver them according to Thy mercies..." Neh. 9:28

When they returned to God, He heard their prayers!
Prayer:
Father in heaven, if You heard and helped them, then please hear from heaven the prayers that I pray to You. Please deliver me from all my troubles. In Jesus' name, Amen!

Curse turned into a blessing
"... bring them again unto Thy law: yet they dealt proudly and hearkened not unto Thy Commandments... nevertheless for Thy great mercies' sake (You helped them)*... let not all the trouble seem little before Thee, that hath come upon us... for Thou hast done right..."* Neh. 9:29-32
"... do not let all this hardship seem trifling in Your eyes..." NIV
"... seem insignificant..." NLT;NASB
"... do not view lightly all the hardsihps that have afflicted us ..." HCSB
"... do not regard as inconsequential all the hardship that has befallen us..." Net Bible

"... do not consider all the hardships that we have been going through as unimportant ..." God's Word

Prayer:
Father in heaven, please don't let my troubles seem little to You. Thank You! In Jesus' name, Amen!

God turns curses into blesses

   The Promise:
   "... *howbeit* our *God turned the curse into a blessing*." Neh. 13:2

Prayer:
Father in heaven, please turn every curse into a blessing over me and my fam-ily. Thank You in Jesus' name, Amen!

Because Mordecai loved and obeyed God "... (He)*waxed greater and greater.*" Esther 9:4
"As the days wherein the Jews rested from their enemies, and the month which was turned unto them from sorrow to joy, and from mourning into a good day" Esther 9:22
I pray that God will turn all our sorrows into joy and our mourning into a good day! Thank You, Jesus!
"... his wicked device, which he devised against the Jews, should return upon his own head..." Esther 9:25
We must be careful that if we curse someone, that curse could come back on our own head. In the New Testament we are told not to curse but to bless those who curse us, Matt. 5:44.

Satan accused God of protecting and blessing Job, which was true.
"Hast not Thou made an hedge about him, and about his house, and about all that he hath on every side? Thou has blessed the work of his hands, and his substance is increased in the land." Job 1:10
Prayer:
Father in heaven, please put a hedge around me and my family like You did

for Job in the beginning and end of his life that the evil one cannot touch us and bless the work of our hands and our substance. Thank You in Jesus' name, Amen!

Commit it to God
"I would seek unto God, and unto God would I commit my cause: which doeth great things and unsearchable; marvelous things without number: who giveth rain upon the earth, and sendeth waters upon the fields: to set up on high those that be low; that those which mourn may be exalted to safety. He dis-appointeth the vices of the crafty, so that their hands cannot perform their enterprise." Job 5:8-12

"He thwarts the plans of the crafty, so that their hands achieve no success." Job 5:12 NIV

"He frustrates the plans of crafty men. They are caught in their own traps." Job 5:12 LB

Prayer:
Father in heaven, please thwart any evil plans that have been made over me and my family. Thank You in Jesus' name, Amen!

"But He saveth the poor from the sword, from their mouth, and from the hand of the mighty. So the poor hath hope..." Job 5:15

Seven troubles shall not touch you
*"For He maketh sore, and bindeth up: He woundeth, and His hands make whole. He shall deliver thee in six troubles: yea, in **seven** there shall no evil touch thee.*
1. *In famine He shall Redeem thee from **death**:*
2. *and in **war** from the power of the sword.*
   Thou shalt be hid from the scourge of the tongue ("slander" NLT): neither shalt thou be afraid of destruction when it cometh. At destruction...
3. ***famine** thou shalt laugh:*
4. *neither shalt thou be afraid of the **beasts** ("wild animals" NIV) of the earth. For thou shalt be in league with the stones of the field: and the beasts of the field shall be at peace with thee.*
5. *And thou shalt know that Thy Tabernacle shall be in peace ("your **home is safe**" NLT). And thou shalt visit thy habitation, and shalt not sin ("find nothing missing" NIV).*
6. *Thou shalt know also that thy **seed shall be great**, and thine offspring as the grass of the earth ("you'll have many children" ISV).*

7. *Thou shalt come to thy grave in a **full** ("ripe old" NLT) **age**, like as a shock of corn cometh in his season."*

... we have searched it, so it is; hear it, and know thou it for thy good." Job 5:18-27
"Behold, this we have searched out; it is true. Hear it, and know for yourself." Job 5:27 NKJV
Prayer:
"Oh that I might have my request: and that God would grant me the thing that I long for!" Job 6:8

Though you start out small, God will increase you
The Condition:
"If thou wert pure and upright..." Job 8:6

>   **The Promise:**
>   "... surely now He would awake for thee, and make the habitation of thy righteousness prosperous. Though thy beginning was small, yet thy latter end should greatly increase." Job 8:6,7

"... till He fill thy mouth with laughing, and thy lips with rejoicing." Job 8:21
Prayer:
Father in heaven, please fill me with laughing and rejoicing. In Jesus' name, Amen!

>   **The Promise:**
>   "... they that hate thee shall be clothed with shame; and the dwelling place of the wicked shall come to nought." Job 8:22

You cannot harden yourself against God and prosper
"He (God) is wise in heart, and mighty in strength: who hath hardened himself against Him, and hath prospered? Which removeth the mountains..." Job 9: 4,5
You can't prosper if you harden yourself against God! If you have faith you can move mountains, Matt. 17:20!
"You will surely forget your trouble... as waters gone by." Job 11:16 NIV
"You shall call and I will answer you..." Job 14:15 NKJV

God grants life and favor
"Thou hast granted me life and favour, and Thy visitation hath preserved my spirit." Job 10:12
"You gave me life and showed me kindness, and in your providence watched over my spirit." Job 10:12 NIV

You will sleep safely
"For then shalt thou lift up thy face without spot ("with innocence" NLT, "without moral defect" NASB); yea, those shalt be stedfast, and shalt not fear... thine age shall be clearer than the noonday ("Your life will be brigher than noonday"). thou shalt shine forth, thou shalt be as the morning ("life will be brighter than noonday and darkness will become like morning" NIV)..." Job 11:15-17

> **The Promise:**
> *"... thou shalt be secure, because there is hope; yea, thou shalt dig ("look" NIV; Heb. #2658 "search for") about thee, and thou shalt take thy rest in safety... thou shalt lie down, and none shall make thee afraid... many shall make suit unto thee ("many will court your favor" NIV)."* Job 11:18-20

Those with clean hands grow stronger
"The righteous also shall hold on his ("their" NIV) way..." Job 17:9
The Condition:
"... and he that hath clean hands..." Job 17:9

> **The Promise:**
> *"... shall be stronger and stronger."* Job 17:9

"For I know that my Redeemer liveth, and that He shall stand at the latter (#314 *"end, last") day upon the earth* (Heb. #6083 *"dust, dry earth, debris of ruined city, ashes, rubbish, rubble): and though after my skin worms destroy this body, yet in my flesh shall I see God* (at the Resurrection)*: whom I shall see for myself, and mine eyes shall behold, and not another; though my reins be consumed within me ("my heart yearns" NIV; "my heart faints")."* Job 19:25-27

The Condition:
"Acquaint now thyself with Him, and be at peace..." Job 22:21

> **The Promise:**
> *"... thereby good shall come unto thee...."* Job 22:21

The Condition:
"If thou return to the Almighty..." Job 22:23
> **The Promise:**
> *"... thou shalt be built up ("restored" NIV)..."* Job 22:23

The Condition:
"... thou shalt put away iniquity far from thy Tabernacles." Job 22:23

The Promise:
"Then shalt thou lay up gold as dust, and the gold of Ophir as the stones of the brooks. Yea, the Almighty shall be thy defence ("gold" NIV) and thou shalt have plenty of silver... thou shalt make thy prayer unto Him, and He shall hear thee... thou shalt also decree a thing, and it shall be established unto thee: and the light shall shine upon thy ways... He shall save the humble person. He shall deliver the island (Heb. # 336 "non-innocent") of the innocent..." Job 22:24-30

The Condition:
"... and it is delivered by the pureness of thine hands." Job 22:30
"Submit to God and be at peace with Him; in this way prosperity will come to you... if you return to the Almighty, you will be restored: if you remove wickedness far from your tent... then the Almighty will be your gold, the choicest silver for you, surely then you will delight in the Almighty ... you will pray and He will hear... what you decide on will be done, and light will shine on your ways. When men are brought low and you say, 'Lift them up!' then He will save the downcast. He will deliver even one who is not innocent. Who will be delivered through the cleanness of your hands." Job 22:21-30 NIV
"But He knoweth the way that I take..." Job. 23:10

The Condition:
"... when He hath tried me..." Job 23:10

The Promise:
"... I shall come forth as gold." Job 23:10

"... I will emerge as gold" HCSB
"... I will come out like ("as" NLT) gold" ISV

God had richly blessed the beginning of Job's life.
"How I long for the months gone by" Job 29:2 NIV
"... when God preserved me ("took care of me" PB "watched over me" NIV). When His candle (Heb. #4216 "lamps") shined upon my head, and when by His light I walked through darkness. As I was in the days of my youth, when the secret of God was upon my tabernacle ("when God's intimate friendship blessed my house" NIV); when the Almighty was yet ("still" NIV) with me, when my children were about me: when I washed my steps with butter ("my path was drenched with cream" NIV), and the rock poured me out rivers of oil; when I went out to the gate through the city, when I prepared my seat in the street ("public square" NIV)! The young men saw me, and hid themselves ("stepped aside" NIV): and the aged arose, and stood up. The

princes ("chief men" NIV) refrained talking, and laid their hand on their mouth. The nobles held their peace, and their tongue cleaved to the roof of their mouth. When the ear heard me, then it blessed me; and when the eye saw me, it gave witness to me ("whoever heard me spoke well of me, and those who saw me commended me" NIV)..." Job 29:2-11
"Thy Word is a lamp to my feet and a light to my path." Ps. 119:105

The Condition:
"... because I delivered the poor that cried, and the fatherless, and him that had none to help him. The blessing of him that was ready to perish came upon me: and I caused the widow's heart to sing for joy." Job 29:12,13

"Then He is gracious unto him, and saith, Deliver him from going down to the pit: I have found a ransom (in Jesus). *His flesh shall be fresher than a child's: he shall return to the days of his youth..." Job 33:24,25*

> **The Promise:** *"He* (God) *will render unto man his righteousness... He will deliver his soul from going into the pit, and his life shall see the light." Job 33:26,27*

God is mighty in strength and wisdom.
"Behold, God is mighty, and despiseth not any: He is mighty in strength and wisdom..." Job 36:5

> **The Promise:**
> *"(He) giveth right to the poor. He withdraweth not His eyes from the righteous... He doth establish them forever, and they are exalted." Job 36:6,7*

The Condition:
"If they obey and serve Him..." Job 36:11

> **The Promise:**
> *"... they shall spend their days in prosperity, and their years in pleasures ("contentment" NIV; Heb. # 5273 "pleasant, delightful, lovely, beautiful")." Job 36:11*

> **The Promise:**
> *"He delivereth the poor in his affliction, and openeth their ears..." Job 36:15*

"But those who suffer He delivers in their suffering; He speaks to them in their affliction. He is wooing you from the jaws of distress to a spacious place free from restriction to the comfort of your table laden with choice food." Job 36:15,16 NIV

"He shall... give peoples for your sake, and the nations for your life." Job 36:20 PB

God can speak to the ocean and keep it from going past its boundaries.

"... who shut up the sea with doors... and said, Hitherto shalt thou come, but no further: and here shall thy proud waves be stayed?" Job 38:8,11

God tested Job but in the end, blessed him greater than before.

Prayer:
Father in heaven, when I live near water, please keep them in their boundaries for me according to Your Word. Thank You in Jesus' name, Amen!

God helped Job whe he prayed for his friends
"The Lord turned the captivity of Job..." Job 42:10
The Condition:
"...when he prayed for his friends..." Job 42:10
The Blessing:
"... also the Lord gave Job twice as much as he had before... the Lord blessed the latter end of Job more than his beginning: for he had fourteen thousand sheep, and six thousand camels, and a thousand yoke of oxen,, and a thousand (female donkeys). *He had also seven sons and three daughters... and in all the land were no women found so fair as the daughters of Job: and their father gave them inheritance among their brethren. After this lived Job an hundred and forty years, and saw his sons, and his sons' sons, even four generations. So Job died, being old and full of days."* Job 42:10,12-17

Psalms

The Blessing
"Blessed is the man that walketh not in the counsel of the ungodly, nor standeth in the way of sinners, nor sitteth in the seat of the scornful." Ps. 1:1

The Condition:
"... his delight is in the law of the Lord... in His law doth he meditate day and night..." Ps. 1:2

> **The Promise:**
> *"... he shall be like a tree planted by the rivers of water, that bringeth forth his fruit in his season; his leaf... shall not wither; and whatsoever he doeth shall prosper..."* Ps. 1:3

"... for the Lord knoweth the way of the righteous..." Ps. 1:6

The Condition:
"Ask of Me..." Ps. 2:8

> **The Promise:**
> *"... and I shall give thee the heathen for thine inheritance, and the uttermost parts of the earth for thy possession."* Ps. 2:8

Trust Him
"... blessed are all they that put their trust in Him." Ps. 2:12

> **The Promise:**
> *"But Thou, O Lord, art a shield for me; my glory, and the lifter up of mine head..."* Ps. 3:3

"I cried unto the Lord with my voice, and..." Ps. 3:4

> **The Promise:**
> *"... He heard me out of His Holy Hill. Selah."* Ps. 3:4

Prayer:
Father in heaven, please hear my prayers from Your Holy Hill as You promised. In Jesus' name, Amen!

Promise for sleep
"I laid me down and slept; I awaked..." Ps. 3:5

> **The Promise:**
> *"... for the Lord sustained me..."* Ps. 3:5

God blesses His people
"I will not be afraid of ten thousands of people, that have set themselves against me round about. Arise, O Lord; save me, O my God: for..." Ps. 3:6,7

> **The Promise:**
> *"... Thou hast smitten all mine enemies upon the cheek* (Heb. #3895 *"Jaw"*) *bone; Thou hast broken the teeth of the ungodly... Thy blessing is upon Thy people. Selah."* Ps. 3:7,8

> **The Promise:**
> *"... You delivered me in my distress.."* Ps. 4:1

> **The Promise:**
> *"But know that the Lord hath set apart him that is godly for Himself: the Lord will hear when I call unto him."* Ps. 4:3

The Promise:
"Thou hast put gladness in my heart, more than in the time that their corn and their wine increased. I will both lay me down in peace, and sleep: for Thou, Lord, only makest me dwell in safety." Ps. 4:8

Prayer:
Father in heaven, please give me peaceful sleep and safety as You promised in Your Word. Thank You in the name of Jesus, Amen!

"But let all those that put their trust in Thee rejoice: let them ever shout for joy..." Ps. 5:11

The Promise:
"... because Thou defendest them... for Thou, Lord, wilt bless the righteous; with favour wilt Thou compass him as with a shield." Ps. 5:11,12

Prayer:
Father in heaven, please defend me and bless me with Your favor; compass me with Your shield. Thank You in Jesus' name, Amen!

Prayer: *"... I am weak; O Lord, heal me..."* Ps. 6:2 NKJV

God will receive my prayer
"... for the Lord hath heard the voice of my weeping. The Lord hath heard my supplication; the Lord will receive my prayer. Let all mine enemies be ashamed and sore vexed: let them return and be ashamed suddenly." Ps. 6:8-10

Prayer
Father in heaven, thank You that You see my tears and that You hear and re-ceive my prayers. In Jesus' name, Amen!

The Promise:
"My defence is of God, which saveth the upright in heart..." Ps. 7:10

The Promise:
"Thou madest him (man) to have dominion over the works of Thy hands; Thou hast put all things under his feet..." Ps. 8:6

"When mine enemies are turned back, they shall fall and perish at Thy presence. For Thou hast maintained my right and my cause... Thou hast re-buked the heathen..." Ps. 9:3-5

"He shall Judge the world in righteousness..." Ps. 9:8 NKJV

The Promise:
"The Lord also will be a refuge for the oppressed, a refuge in times of trouble. And they that know Thy name will put their trust in Thee: for Thou, Lord, hast not forsaken them..." Ps. 9:9,10

The Condition:
"... that seek Thee." Ps. 9:9,10

God won't forget our prayers
"... He forgetteth not the cry of the humble." Ps. 9:12

The poor should trust in God
"... the poor committeth himself unto Thee..." Ps. 10:14,15

The Promise:
"... Thou art the helper of the fatherless. Break Thou the arm of the wicked and the evil man..." Ps. 10:14,15

Prayer:
"Lord, Thou hast heard the desire of the humble: Thou wilt prepare their heart, Thou wilt cause Thine ear to hear... that the man of the earth may no more oppress." Ps. 10:17,18

God's people love what is right
"For the righteous... loveth righteousness..." Ps. 11:7

God watches over the upright

The Promise:
"... His countenance doth behold the upright." Ps. 11:7

Prayer:
Father in heaven, I thank You that You hold me up because my righteousness is in Jesus, Amen!

"For the oppression of the poor, for the sighing of the needy... will I arise...I will set him to safety from him that putteth at him. The Words of the Lord are pure Words: as silver tried in a furnace of earth, purified seven times." Ps. 12:5,6
"The Word is God... the Word was mde flesh (Jesus), and dwelt among us... the only begotten Son..." Jn. 1:1-14

"*I will set in safety the one whom the wicked one has ensnared.*" Ps. 12:5 Jubilee Bible 2000

> **The promise:**
> "*Thou shalt keep them, O Lord, Thou shalt preserve them from this generation forever.*" Ps. 12:7

"*... for God is in the generation of the righteous... the Lord is his refuge... when the Lord bringeth back the captivity of His people, Jacob shall rejoice, and Israel shall be glad.*" Ps. 14:5-7

The Condition:
"*He that walketh uprightly, and worketh righteousness, and speaketh the truth in his heart. He that backbiteth not with his tongue, nor doeth evil to his neighbor, nor taketh up a reproach against his neighbor... (who) honoureth them that fear the Lord. He that sweareth to his own hurt* ("who keeps his oath even when it hurts" NIV), *and changeth not. He that putteth not out his money to usury, nor taketh reward against the innocent...*" Ps. 15:2-5

> **The Promise:**
> "*... he that doeth these things shall never be moved* ("Heb. #4131 "shaken, slip"))." Ps. 15:5

My righteousness is in Jesus
"*... my goodness cometh from Thee.*" Ps. 16:2 PB

The Lord is my inheritance
"*The Lord is the portion of mine inheritance and of my cup: Thou maintainest my lot... I have a goodly heritage. I will bless the Lord, who hath given me counsel...*" Ps. 16:5-7
"*Thou shalt restore my inheritance.*" Ps. 16:5 PB
The Condition:
"*I have set the Lord always before me: because He is at my right hand...*" Ps. 16:8

> **The Promise:**
> "*I shall not be moved.*" Ps. 16:8

"*Therefore my heart is glad, and my glory rejoiceth: my flesh also shall rest in hope. For Thou wilt not leave my soul in hell; neither wilt Thou suffer Thine Holy One to see corruption* (prophecy of Jesus)." Ps. 16:9,10

> **The Promise:**
> *Thou wilt shew me the path of life: in Thy presence is fullness of joy; at Thy right hand there are pleasures forevermore.*" Ps. 16:11

"Thou hast proved mine heart; Thou hast visited me in the night; Thou hast tried me, and shalt find nothing; I am purposed that my mouth shall not transgress. Concerning the works of men...." Ps. 17:3,4

The Promise:
"... by the Word of Thy lips I have kept me from the paths of the Destroyer." Ps. 17:3,4

The Condition:
"I have called upon Thee..." Ps. 17:6

The Promise:
"... for Thou wilt hear me, O God... O Thou that savest by Thy right hand them which put their trust in Thee from those that rise up against them." Ps. 17:6,7

Prayer:
Father in heaven, please *"Keep me as the apple of* (Your) *eye, hide me under the shadow of Thy wings..."* Ps. 17:8 (Deut.33:27;Ruth2:12;Ps.17:8;36:7;57:1;91:1,4;Is.51:16;Lam.4:20;Hosea14:7

The Condition:
"I will love Thee, O Lord, my strength. The Lord is my Rock, and my fortress, and my deliverer; my God, my strength in whom I will trust; my buckler, and the horn of my Salvation, and my high tower. I will call upon the Lord, who is worthy to be praised..." Ps. 18:1-3

The Promise:
"... so shall I be saved from mine enemies." Ps. 18:3

God hears my prayers
"In my distress I called upon the Lord, and cried unto my God: He heard my voice out of His Temple, and my cry came before Him, even into His ears." Ps. 18:6

God delivers me because He delights in me
"... He sent out His arrows, and scattered them..." Ps. 18:14

The Promise:
"He sent from above, He took me, He drew me out of many waters. He delivered me from my strong enemy, and from them which hated me: for they were too strong for me. They prevented ("confronted" ESV) me in the day of my calamity: but the Lord was my stay ("deliverer" PB). He brought me forth also into a large place; He delivered, because He delighted in me. The Lord rewarded me..." Ps. 18:16-20

"They attacked me at a moment when I was in distress but the Lord supported me" NLT

The Lord rewards me according to my works
The Condition:
"... according to my righteousness; according to the cleanness of my hands..." Ps. 18:20

> **The Promise:**
> "... hath He recompensed me." Ps. 18:20

"The Lord rewarded me for doing right and being pure." Ps. 18:20 LB

> **The Promise:**
> "Therefore hath the Lord recompensed me..." Ps. 18:24

The Condition:
"... according to my righteousness, according to the cleanness of my hands in His eyesight. With the merciful..." Ps. 18:24,25

> **The Promise:**
> "... Thou wilt shew Thyself merciful..." Ps. 18:25

The Condition:
"... with an upright man..." Ps. 18:25

> **The Promise:**
> "... Thou wilt shew Thyself upright..." Ps. 18:25

The Condition:
"... with the pure..." Ps. 18:26

> **The Promise:**
> "... Thou wilt shew Thyself pure... for Thou wilt save the afflicted people... Thou wilt light my candle: the Lord my God will enlighten my darkness. For by Thee I have run through a troop; and by my God have I leaped over a wall. As for God, His way is perfect: the Word of the Lord is tried ("pure" PB)..." Ps. 18:26-30

"In Your strength I can crush an army; with my God I can scale a wall." Ps. 18:29 NIV
"... I can charge against an army..." Ps. 18:29 Net Bible
"... attack a line of soldiers... Ps. 18:29 GWT
"... scattered armies..." Ps. 18:29 JB 2000

> **The Promise:**
> "... He is a buckler to all those..." Ps. 18:30

God's gentleness makes me great
The Condition:
"... that trust in Him." Ps. 18:30
"He is a shield to all those who take refuge and put their trust in Him." Ps. 18:30 AMP

> **The Promise:**
> "... God... girdeth me with strength, and maketh my way perfect. He maketh my feet like hinds' feet... setteth me upright.. on high places... a bow of steel is broken by mine arms... Thou... give(th) me the shield of Thy Salvation ("Shield of faith" Eph. 6:15)... Thy right hand hath holden me up... Thy gentleness hath made me great. Thou hast enlarged my steps under me... my feet did not slip ..." Ps. 18: 32-36

"... for Thou hast girded me with strength unto the battle: Thou hast subdued under me those that rose up against me .." Ps. 18:39,40
"You have armed me with strength..." Ps. 18:39 NKJV

"Thou hast delivered me from the strivings of the people; and Thou hast made Me the head of the heathen: a people whom I have not known shall serve Me. As soon as they hear of Me, they shall obey Me: the strangers shall submit themselves unto Me." Ps. 18:43,44

"It is God that avengeth me, and subdueth the people under me. He delivereth me from mine enemies: yea, thou liftest me up above those that rise up against me: thou hast delivered me from the violent man ... great deliverance giveth He to His king; and sheweth mercy to His anointed, to David, and to His Seed (Jesus) forevermore." Ps. 18:47,48

As a Bridegroom
"Which is as a Bridegroom coming out of His chamber, and rejoiceth as a strong man to run a race. His going forth is from the end of heaven, and His circuit unto the ends of it: and there is nothing hid..." Ps. 19:5,6
This verse is talking about the sun but it can be used as an allegory for Jesus at the second coming, who is the ultimate Bridegroom and brighter than the sun.

"The law of the Lord is perfect..." Ps. 19:7

> **The Promise:**
> "... converting the soul..." Ps. 19:7

"... the Testimony of the Lord is sure..." Ps. 19:7

The Promise:
"... making wise the simple." Ps. 19:7

"The Statutes of the Lord are right..." Ps. 19:8

The Promise:
"... rejoicing the heart..." Ps. 19:8

"... the Commandment of the Lord is pure..." Ps. 19:8

The Promise:
"... enlightening the eyes..." Ps. 19:8

"... the fear of the Lord is clean..." Ps. 19:9

The Promise:
"... enduring forever..." Ps. 19:9

"... the Judgments of the Lord are true and righteous altogether. More to be desired are they than gold, yea, than much fine gold: sweeter also than honey and the honeycomb. Moreover by them is Thy servant warned..." Ps. 19:9-11

The Condition:
"... and in keeping of them (the 10 Commandments)..." Ps. 19:11

The Promise:
".... there is great reward." Ps. 19:11

"Who can understand his errors, cleanse Thou me from secret (#5641 "secret, hide conceal, cover") faults. Keep back Thy servant also from presumptuous (#2086 - we know it's a sin but we do it anyway) sins; let them not have dominion over me; then shall I be innocent from ("of" NIV) the great transgression (#6588 "breach of trust, rebellious" a big sin with terrible consequences) Ps. 19:12-14

God also warns that there is no sacrifice for deliberate sins in Heb. 10:26.
It is presumptuous to think that God doesn't care if we sin, that grace gives me a license to sin.
"... shall we continue in sin, that grace may abound? God forbid." Rom. 6:1,2

Prayer:
"The Lord hear thee in the day of trouble; the name of the God of Jacob defend thee; send thee help from the Sanctuary, and strengthen thee out of Zion; remember all thy offerings... grant thee according to thine own heart, and fulfil all thy counsel... the Lord fulfil all thy petitions." Ps. 20:1-4

Yes, Lord, please hear my prayers in the Day of Trouble and send help from Your Sanctuary in heaven. Send strength from heavenly Zion and please fulfill all my petitions. In Jesus' name, Amen!

May God fulfill all your petitions
"Now know I that the Lord saveth His anointed; He will hear him from His Holy
heaven with the saving strength of His right hand." Ps. 20:6
"Now I know that the Lord saves His anointed; He will answer him ..." Ps. 20:6 NKJV

"... we are risen and stand upright." Ps. 20:8
"May the King answer us when we call." Ps. 20:9 NKJV

> **The Promise:**
> "You have given him his heart's desire, and have not withheld the request of his lips." Ps. 21:2

Blessings
"For Thou preventest him with the blessings of goodness: Thou settest a crown of pure gold on his head. He asked life of Thee, and Thou gavest it him, even length of days forever... His glory is great in Thy Salvation: honour and majesty hast Thou laid upon him. For Thou hast made him most blessed forever: Thou hast made him exceeding glad with Thy countenance ..." Ps. 21:3-6
He who "... trusteth in the Lord and through the mercy of the Most High ..." Ps. 21:7

> **The Promise:**
> "... he shall not be moved." Ps. 21:7

God delivered them.
"Our fathers trusted in Thee: they trusted..." Ps. 22:4

> **The Promise:**
> "... and Thou didst deliver them." Ps. 22:4

"... they cried unto Thee..." Ps. 22:5

> **The Promise:**
> "... and were delivered..." Ps. 22:5

"... they trusted in Thee..." Ps. 22:5

> **The Promise:**
> "... and were not confounded." Ps. 22:5

The Promise:
"... he shall not be moved." Ps. 22:7 NKJV

You were my God even in the womb
"But Thou art He that took me out of the womb: Thou didst make me hope when I was... (a nursing baby) I was cast upon Thee from the womb: Thou art my God from my mother's belly." Ps. 22:9,10 (Ps. 71:6)
"For he hath not despised nor abhorred the affliction of the afflicted; neither hath He hid his face from him; but when he cried unto Him He heard." Ps. 22:24

"The meek shall eat and be satisfied: they shall praise the Lord that seek Him: your heart shall live forever. All the ends of the world shall remember and turn unto the Lord: and all the kindreds of the nations ("Gentiles" PB) shall worship before Thee. For the kingdom is the Lord's: and He is the Governor among the nations." Ps. 22:26-28
"... He rules over the nations." Ps. 22:28 Net Bible
See Names of God pg. 693.
Psalms 23 is a very familiar chapter and is full of promises
"The Lord is my Shepherd..." Ps. 23:1

The Promise:
"... I shall not want. He maketh me to lie down in green pastures: He leadeth me beside the still waters. He restoreth my soul: He leadeth me in the paths of righteousness for His name's sake..." Ps. 23:1-3

"... Yea, though I walk through the valley of the shadow of death, I will fear no evil, for..." Ps. 23:4

The Promise:
"... Thou art with me; Thy rod and Thy staff they comfort me. Thou preparedst a table before me in the presence of mine enemies: Thou anointest my head with oil; my cup runneth over. Surely goodness and mercy shall follow me all the days of my life: and I will dwell in the house of the Lord forever." Ps. 23:4-6

True blessings come from God
"He shall receive the blessing from the Lord, and righteousness from the God of his Salvation." Ps. 24:5

"Good and upright is the Lord: therefore..." Ps. 25:8

The Promise:
"... will He teach sinners in the way. The meek will He guide in Judgment: and the meek will He teach His way." Ps. 25:8,9

"All the paths of the Lord are mercy and truth..." Ps. 25:10

The Condition:
"... unto such as keep His Covenant and His Testimonies." Ps. 25:10

The secret of God is with those who fear Him
"What man is he that feareth the Lord? " Ps. 25:12
"He himself shall dwell in prosperity, and his descendants shall inherit the earth." Ps. 25:13 NKJV

>**The Promise:**
>"... him shall He teach in the way that he shall choose. His soul shall dwell at ease; and his seed shall inherit the earth. The secret of the Lord ..." Ps. 25:12-14

The Condition:
"... is with them that fear Him..." Ps. 25:12-14

>**The Promise:**
>"... and He will shew them His Covenant." Ps. 25:14

>>**The Promise:**
>>"The Lord is my light and my Salvation, whom shall I fear? The Lord is the strength of my life; of whom shall I be afraid?" Ps. 27:1

"Though an host should encamp against me..." Ps. 27:3 NASB

>**The Promise:**
>"... my heart shall not fear: though war should rise against me, in this will I be confident." Ps. 27:3

"... I will even trust in that situation." Ps. 27:3 ISV
"... in spite of this I will be confident." NASB
"... even when war is imminent, I remain confident." Net Bible

God will hide me in the time of trouble
"One thing have I desired of the Lord, that will I seek after; that I may dwell in the house of the Lord all the days of my life, to behold the beauty of the Lord, and to inquire in His Temple." Ps. 27:4

>**The Promise:**
>"For **in the time of trouble He shall hide me** in His Pavilion: in the secret of His Tabernacle shall He hide me; He shall set me up upon **a Rock**. And now shall mine head be lifted up above mine enemies round about me: therefore will I offer in His Tabernacle sacrifices of joy; I will sing, yea, I will sing praises unto the Lord." Ps. 27:5,6

Jesus is the Rock - Ps.18:2;Mt.21:42;Rom.9:32, 33.
I will keep you from the hour of trial, Rev. 3:10
(Gr. #5083 Keep "*guard, watch over, keep intact*")

"*When my father and my mother forsake me...*" Ps. 27:10

The Promise:
"*... then the Lord will take me up.*" Ps. 27:10

"*I had fainted, unless I had believed to see ("I am still confident of this: I will see..." NIV) the goodness of the Lord in the land of the living.*" Ps. 27:13
The Condition:
"*Wait on the Lord: be of good courage...*" Ps. 27:14

The Promise:
"*... and He shall strengthen thine heart...*" Ps. 27:14

The Condition:
"*... wait, I say, on the Lord.*" Ps. 27:14

Blessed
"*Blessed be the Lord, because He hath heard the voice of my supplications.*" Ps. 28:6

The Promise:
"*The Lord is my strength and my shield; my heart trusted in Him, and I am helped: therefore my heart greatly rejoiceth; and with my song will I praise Him. The Lord is their strength, and He is the saving strength of His anointed. Save Thy people, and bless Thine inheritance: feed them also, and lift them up forever.*" Ps. 28:7-9

"*Lord, by Your favor You have made my mountain stand strong...*" Ps. 30:7 NKJV

The Promise:
"*The Lord will give strength unto His people; the Lord will bless His people with peace.*" Ps. 29:11

"*I will extol Thee, O Lord; for...*" Ps. 30:1

The Promise:
"*... Thou hast lifted me up, and hast not made my foes to rejoice over me. O Lord my God I cried unto Thee, and Thou hast healed me. O Lord, Thou hast brought up my soul from the grave: Thou hast kept me alive, that I should not go down to the pit.*" Ps. 30:1-3

The Promise:
"... in His favour is life. Weeping may endure for a night, but joy cometh in the morning... in my prosperity I said, I shall never be moved... Thy favour Thou hast made my mountain to stand strong ... Thou hast turned for me my mourning into dancing... and girded me with gladness..." Ps. 30:5-7,11

"Your favor, O Lord, made me as secure as a mountain..." Ps. 30:7 NLT
"You made me stand like a strong mountain." Ps. 30:7 HCSB

The Promise:
"... for Thou hast considered my trouble... and hast not shut me up into the hand of the enemy: Thou hast set my feet in a large room ("a spacious place" NIV)." Ps. 31:7,8

The Condition:
"I trusted in Thee..." Ps. 31:14

Prayer:
"O Lord: I said, Thou art my God. My times are in Thy hand: deliver me from the hand of mine enemies, and from them that persecute me. Make Thy face to shine upon Thy servant: save me for Thy mercies sake. Let me not be ashamed. O Lord..." Ps. 31:14-17

The Promise:
"Oh how great is Thy goodness, which Thou hast laid up..." Ps. 31:19

The Condition:
"... for them that fear Thee; which Thou hast wrought for them that trust in Thee before the sons of men!" Ps. 31:19

The Promise:
"Thou shalt hide them in the secret of Thy presence from the pride of man: Thou shalt keep them secretly in a pavilion from the strife of tongues." Ps. 31:20

Blessed
"Blessed be the Lord: for He hath shewed me His marvelous kindness in a strong city." Ps. 31:21

"O love the Lord, all ye His saints: for the Lord preserveth the faithful, and plentifully rewardeth (punishes) the proud doer. Be of good courage, and..." Ps. 31:23,24

The Promise:
"He shall strengthen your heart..." Ps. 31:24

"... all ye that hope in the Lord." Ps. 31:23,24

Blessed:
"Blessed is he whose transgression is forgiven, whose sin is covered. Blessed is the man unto whom the Lord imputeth not iniquity, and in whose spirit there is no guile." Ps. 32:1,2

The Condition:
"I acknowledged my sin unto Thee, and mine iniquity have I not hid. I said, I will confess my transgressions unto the Lord; and..." Ps. 32:5

> **The Promise:**
> "... Thou forgavest the iniquity of my sin. Selah." Ps. 32:5

This verse is very similar to I Jn. 1:9

> **The Promise:**
> "Thou art my hiding place; Thou shalt preserve me from trouble; Thou shalt compass me about with songs of deliverance... I will instruct thee and teach thee in the way which thou shalt go: I will guide thee..." Ps. 32:7,8

For He spake, and it was done; He commanded, and it stood fast." Ps. 33:9

> **The Promise:**
> "The Lord bringeth the counsel of the heathen to nought: He maketh the devices of the people of none effect." Ps. 33:10

"Blessed is the nation whose God is the Lord." Ps. 33:12 NKJV

> **The Promise:**
> "... the eye of the Lord is upon them..." Ps.33:18

The Condition:
"... that fear Him..." Ps.33: 18

> **The Promise:**
> "To deliver their soul from death, and to keep them alive in famine. Our soul waiteth for the Lord: He is our help and our shield." Ps. 33:19,20

Prayer:
Father in heaven, I claim this verse that You are my help and shield by the blood of Jesus. Thank You in Jesus' name, Amen!

The Condition:
"*I sought the Lord...*" Ps. 34:4

> **The Promise:**
> "*... and He heard me, and delivered me from all my fears... this poor man cried, and the Lord heard him, and saved him out of all his troubles. The angel of the Lord encampeth round about them that fear Him, and delivereth them.*" Ps. 34:4-7

"*They looked to Him and were radiant, and their faces we're not ashamed.*" Ps. 34:5 NKJV

Blessed
"*O taste and see that the Lord is good; blessed is the man that trusteth in Him.*" Ps. 34:8

The Condition:
"*O fear the Lord, ye His saints...*" Ps. 34:9

> **The Promise:**
> *Thou shalt compass me about with songs of deliverance... I will instruct thee and teach thee in the way which thou shalt go: I will guide thee...*" Ps. 32:7,8

"*Come, ye children, hearken unto Me: I will teach you the fear of the Lord. What man is he that desireth life, and loveth many days, that he may see good? Keep thy tongue from evil, and thy lips from speaking guile. Depart from evil, and do good; seek peace, and pursue it...*" Ps. 34:11-14

> **The Promise:**
> "*The eyes of the Lord are upon the righteous, and His ears are open unto their cry.*" Ps. 34:15

"*... the face of the Lord is against them that do evil, to cut off the remembrance of them from the earth.*" Ps. 34:16
"*The righteous cry...*" Ps. 34:17

> **The Promise:**
> "*... and the Lord heareth, and delivereth them out of all their troubles. The Lord is nigh unto them that are of a broken heart; and saveth such as be of a contrite spirit...*" Ps. 34:17,18

"*... many are the afflictions of the righteous...*" Ps. 34:18,19

> **The Promise:**
> "*... but the Lord delivereth him out of them all. He keepeth all his bones: not one of them is broken* (a prophecy of Jesus).*" Ps. 34:19,20

"... those who hate the righteous shall be condemned." Ps. 34:21 NKJV

> **The Promise:**
> "The Lord Redeemeth the soul of His servants: and none of them that trust in Him shall be desolate ("condemned" PB)." Ps. 34:22

"... Lord, who is like unto Thee..." Ps. 35:10

> **The Promise:**
> "... which deliverest the poor from him that is too strong for him ..." Ps. 35:10

It gives God pleasure to prosper me
"... let the Lord be magnified, which hath pleasure in the prosperity of His servant." Ps. 35:27

"Thy mercy, O Lord, is in the heavens; and Thy faithfulness reacheth unto the clouds. Thy righteousness is like the great mountains; Thy Judgments are a great deep... Ps. 36:5,6
Prayer:
"... O Lord, Thou preservest man and beast. How excellent is Thy lovingkindness, O God! Therefore the children of men put their trust under the shadow of Thy wings. They shall be abundantly satisfied with the fatness of Thy house..." Ps. 36:6-8
See note on Ps. 17:8

> **The Promise:**
> "... and thou shalt make them drink of the river of Thy pleasures. For with Thee is the fountain of life: in Thy light shall we see light." Ps. 36:8,9

"... come... whosoever will, let him take the Water of Life freely." Rev.22:17
"O continue Thy lovingkindness unto them that know Thee; and Thy righteousness to the upright in heart. Let not the foot of pride come against me, and let not the hand of the wicked remove me." Ps. 36:10,11

The Condition:
"Trust in the Lord, and do good..." Ps. 37:3

> **The Promise:**
> "... so shalt thou dwell in the land, and verily thou shalt be fed." Ps. 37:3

The Condition:
"Delight thyself also in the Lord..." 37:4

The Promise:
"... and He shall give thee the desires of thine heart." Ps. 37:4

The Condition:
"Commit thy way unto the Lord; trust also in Him ..." Ps. 37:5

The Promise:
"... and He shall bring it to pass. And He shall bring forth thy righteousness as the light, and Thy Judgment as the nonday." Ps. 37:5,6

The Condition:
"Rest in the Lord, and wait patiently for Him: fret not thyself because of Him who prospereth in his way, because of the man who bringeth wicked devices to pass. Cease from anger, and forsake wrath: fret not thyself in any wise to do evil. For evildoers shall be cut off but those that wait upon the Lord ..." Ps. 37:7-9

The Promise:
"... they shall inherit the earth." Ps. 37:9

"... the wicked have drawn out the sword... to cast down the poor and needy, and to slay such as be of upright conversation." Ps. 37:14

The Promise:
"... their sword shall enter into their own heart, and their bows shall be broken... the arms of the wicked shall be broken: but the Lord, upholdeth the righteous... and their inheritance shall be forever. They shall not be ashamed in the evil time: and in the days of famine they shall be satisfied." Ps. 37:15, 17-19

Blessed
"For such as be blessed of Him ..." Ps. 37:22

The Promise:
"... shall inherit the earth... the steps of a good man are ordered by the Lord: and He delighteth in his way. Though he fall, he shall not be utterly cast down: for the Lord upholdeth him with His hand. I have been young, and now am old; yet have I not seen the righteous forsaken, nor his seed begging bread. He is ever merciful, and lendeth; and his seed is blessed." Ps. 37:22-26

God does not forsake His saints

The Promise:
"For the Lord... forsaketh not His saints; they are preserved forever... the righteous shall inherit the land and dwell therein forever. The mouth of the righteous speaketh wisdom ..." Ps. 37:28-30

The Condition:
"... the law of his God is in his heart..." Ps. 37:31

> **The Promise:**
> "... none of his steps shall slide." Ps. 37:31
>
> **The Promise:**
> "The Lord will not leave him in his hand, nor condemn him when he is Judged." Ps. 37:33

The Condition:
"Wait on the Lord, and keep His way..." Ps. 37:34

> **The Promise:**
> "... and He shall exalt thee to inherit the land..." Ps. 37:34

The Condition:
"Mark the perfect man, and behold the upright..." Ps. 37:37

> **The Promise:**
> "... for the end of that man is peace." Ps. 37:37

"But the transgressors shall be destroyed together: the end of the wicked shall be cut off." Ps. 37:38

> **The Promise:**
> "But the Salvation of the righteous is of the Lord: He is their strength in the time of trouble. And the Lord shall help them, and deliver them; he shall deliver them from the wicked, and save them ..." Ps. 37:39,40

The Condition:
"... because they trust in Him." Ps. 37:40

> **The Promise:**
> "... Thou wilt hear, O Lord my God." Ps. 38:15

The Condition:
"I waited patiently for the Lord..." Ps. 40:1

> **The Promise:**
> "... and He inclined unto me, and heard my cry. He brought me up also out of an horrible pit, out of the miry clay, and set my feet upon a Rock (Jesus), and established my goings. And He hath put a new song in my mouth, even praise unto our God..." Ps. 40:1-3

Blessed
"Blessed is that man that maketh the Lord his trust..." Ps. 40:4

Blessed
"Blessed is he..." Ps. 41:1

The Condition:
"... that considereth the poor..." Ps. 41:1
> **The Promise:**
> *"... the Lord will deliver him in time of trouble. The Lord will preserve him, and keep him alive; and he shall be blessed upon the earth: and thou wilt not deliver him unto the will of his enemies. The Lord will strengthen him upon the bed of languishing: thou wilt make all his bed in his sickness."* Ps. 41:1-3

"The Lord sustains them on their sickbed and restores them from their bed of illness." Ps. 41:3 NIV

"... hope thou in God: for I shall yet praise Him for the help of His countenance." Ps. 42:5;43:5
> **The Promise:**
> *"Yet the Lord will command His lovingkindness in the daytime, and in the night His song shall be with me, and my prayer unto the God of my life."* Ps. 42:8

"... praying to God who gives me life." Ps. 42:8 NLT
"... hope thou in God: for I shall yet praise Him, who is the health ("help" NKJV) of my countenance, and my God." Ps. 42:11

> **The Promise:**
> *"But Thou hast saved us from our enemies, and hast put them to shame that hated us."* Ps. 44:7

Promise to Jesus
"... God hath blessed Thee forever. Thou lovest righteousness, and hatest wickedness: therefore God, thy God, hath anointed thee with the oil of gladness above thy fellows." Ps. 45:2,7

> **The Promise:**
> *"God is our refuge and strength, a very present help in trouble. Therefore will not we fear, though the earth be removed, and though the mountains be carried into the midst of the sea; though the waters thereof roar and be troubled, though the mountains shake with the swelling thereof..."* Ps. 46:1-3

A promise of the New Jerusalem
"There is a river, the streams whereof shall make glad the City of God, the Holy Place of the Tabernacles of the Most High. God is in the midst of her; she shall not be moved; God shall help her, and that right early." Ps. 46:4,5
In the New Jerusalem there is no Temple because the Father and Jesus are the Temple, Rev. 21:3.

The Promise:
"The Lord of hosts is with us; the God of Jacob is our refuge. Selah... He maketh wars to cease unto the end of the (New) *earth; He breaketh the bow, and cutteth the spear in sunder; He burneth the chariot in the fire... the Lord of hosts is with us; the God of Jacob is our refuge."* Ps. 46:7,9,11

The Condition:
"Be still and know..." Ps. 46:10

The Promise:
".. that I am God" Ps. 46:10

The Promise:
"He shall subdue the people under us, and the nations under our feet. He shall choose our inheritance for us..." Ps. 47: 3,4

The Promise:
"... for this God is our God forever and ever: He will be our guide even unto death." Ps. 48:14

"... I will fear not in the days of evil..." Ps. 49:5 PB

The Promise:
"But God will Redeem my soul from the power of the grave: for he shall receive me, Selah." Ps. 49:15

"Our God shall come, and not keep silent..." Ps. 50:3 NKJV
When Jesus comes, it will not be quiet. The heavens will disappear with a roar, the elements will be destroyed by fire, and everything will be destroyed. The heavens will be on fire and dissolved, (see I Pet. 3:10).

The Condition:
"And call upon me in the day of trouble..." Ps. 50:15

The Promise:
"... I will deliver thee, and thou shalt glorify Me." Ps. 50:15

"Whoso offereth praise glorifieth Me: and to him that ordereth his conversation aright will I shew the Salvation of God." Ps. 50:23

Prayer:
"Have mercy upon me, O God, according to Thy lovingkindness..." Ps. 51:1

> **The Promise:**
> "Thou shalt make me to know wisdom." Ps. 51:6

The Condition:
"Purge me with hyssop..." Ps. 51:7

> **The Promise:**
> "... and I shall be clean: wash me, and I shall be whiter than snow." Ps. 51:7

"He will repay my enemies for their evil..." Ps. 53:5 NKJV

"... when God brings back the captivity of His people..." Ps. 53:6 NKJV
".. when God restores the fortunes of His people..." Ps. 53:6 ESV

> **The Promise:**
> "Behold, God is mine helper: the Lord is with them that uphold my soul... for He hath delivered me out of all trouble: and mine eye hath seen His desire upon mine enemies." Ps. 54:4,7

The Condition:
"As for me, I will call upon God..." Ps. 55:16

> **The Promise:**
> "... and the Lord shall save me." Ps. 55:16

The Condition:
"Evening, and morning, and at noon, will I pray, and cry aloud..." Ps. 55:17

> **The Promise:**
> "... and He shall hear my voice. He hath delivered my soul in peace from the battle that was against me; for there were many with me. God shall hear..." Ps. 55:17,18

The Condition:
"Cast thy burden upon the Lord..." Ps. 55:22

> **The Promise:**
> "... and He shall sustain thee: He shall never suffer the righteous to be moved." Ps. 55:22

The Condition:
"What time I am afraid, I will trust in Thee. In God I will praise His Word, in God I have put my trust; I will not fear what flesh can do unto me." Ps. 56:3,4

God is for me
The Condition:
"When I cry unto thee..." Ps. 56:9

> **The Promise:**
> *"... then shall mine enemies turn back: this I know; God is for me... in God have I put my trust: I will not be afraid what man can do unto me... thou hast delivered my soul from death: wilt not thou deliver my feet from falling, that I may walk before God in the light of the living?"* Ps. 56:9,11,13

> **The Promise:**
> *"... then the Lord will take me up* (at the Resurrection)." Ps. 57:10

Prayer:
"Be merciful unto me, O God, be merciful unto me: for my soul trusteth in Thee: yea, in the shadow of Thy wings will I make my refuge, until these calamities overpast. I will cry unto God Most High..." Ps. 57:1,2

> **The Promise:**
> *"... that performeth* ("vindicates" NIV, "will fulfill His purpose for me" NLT, "accomplishes" NASB) *all things for me. He shall send from heaven, and save me from the reproach of him that would swallow me up... God shall send forth His mercy and His truth."* Ps. 57:2,3

God rewards the righteous!
"So that a man shall say..." Ps. 58:11
"Surely there is a reward for the righteous; surely He is God..." Ps. 58:11 ESV

> **The Promise:**
> *"... verily there is a reward for the righteous..."* Ps. 58:11

> **The Promise:**
> *"But Thou, O Lord, shalt laugh at them... God is my defence. The God of my mercy shall prevent me: God shall let me see my desire upon mine enemies."* Ps. 59:8-10

Song to God for what He has done
"I will sing of Thy power; yea, I will sing aloud of Thy mercy in the morning: for Thou hast been my defence and refuge in the day of my trouble. Unto

Thee, O my strength, will I sing: for God is my defence, and the God of my mercy." Ps. 59:16,17

"You are my strength, I sing praise to you; you, God, are my fortress, my God on whom I can rely." Ps. 59:17 NIV

"O my Strength, to you I sing praises, for you, O God, are my refuge, the God who shows me unfailing love." Ps. 59:17 NLT

The Promise:
"Thou hast given a banner to them…" Ps. 60:4

The Condition:
"… that fear Thee…" Ps. 60:4

The Promise:
"Through God we shall do valiantly: for He it is that shall tread down our enemies." Ps. 60:12

The Promise:
"For Thou hast been a shelter for me, and a strong tower from the enemy… Thou hast given me the heritage…" Ps. 61:3,5

"… you have heard…" PS. 61:5 NKJV

The Condition:
"… of those that fear Thy name." Ps. 61:5

The Condition:
"Truly my soul waiteth upon God…" Ps. 62:1

The Promise:
"… from Him cometh my Salvation. He only is my Rock and my Salvation; He is my defence; I shall not be greatly moved." Ps. 62:1.2

The Condition:
"My soul, wait thou only upon God; for my expectation is from Him. He only is my Rock and my Salvation: He is my defence…" Ps. 62:5

The Promise:
"… I shall not be moved." Ps. 62:6

"… *you who* (are His servants and by your prayers) *put the Lord in remembrance* (of His promises) Ps. 62:6 AMP

"In God is my Salvation and my glory: the Rock of my strength, and my refuge, is in God." Ps. 62:7

The Promise:
"... God is a refuge for us..." Ps. 62:8

"... power ("strength" HCSB) belongs to God." Ps. 62:11 NASB

The Promise:
"... Thou renderest to every man according to his work." Ps. 62:12

We are saved by grace but those who do wickedly will be punished, and those who do what is right will be rewarded (Ps. 19:11;Prov.11:23).

Blessed
"Because Thy lovingkindness is better than life, my lips shall praise Thee. Thus will I bless Thee while I live: I will lift up my hands in Thy name. My soul shall be satisfied as with marrow and fatness; and my mouth shall praise Thee with joyful lips: when I remember Thee upon my bed, and meditate on Thee in the night watches. Because Thou hast been my help, therefore in the shadow of Thy wings will I rejoice. My soul followeth hard after Thee: Thy right hand upholdeth me." Ps. 63:3-8
"You satisfy me more than the richest feast..." Ps. 63:5 NLT
"I will be fully satisfied as with the richest of foods..." Ps. 6:5 NIV
"... choicest food..." Ps. 63:5 ISV

"... You will provide Atonement..." Ps. 65:3 NKJV

Blessed
"... as for our transgressions, Thou shalt purge them away. Blessed is the man whom Thou choosest... that he may dwell in Thy courts: we shall be satisfied with the goodness of Thy house... by terrible things in righteousness wilt Thou answer us..." Ps. 65:4,5
"You will answer us..." Ps. 65:5 NKJV

Blessed
"Thou visitest the earth, and waterest it: Thou greatly enriches it with the river of God, which is full of water: Thou prepares them corn, when Thou hast so provided for it. Thou waterest the ridges thereof abundantly: Thou settlest the furrows thereof: Thou makest it soft with showers: Thou blessest the springing thereof. Thou crownest the year with Thy goodness; and Thy paths drop fatness. They drop upon the pastures of the wilderness: and the little hills rejoice on every side. The pastures are clothed with flocks; the

valleys also are covered over with corn; they shout for joy, they also sing." Ps. 65:9-13

> **The Promise:**
> "... *through the greatness of Thy power shall Thine enemies submit themselves unto Thee.*" Ps. 66:3

"*All the earth shall worship Thee...*" Ps. 66:4
This promise will be fulfilled on the New Earth.

Bless God
"*O bless our God, ye people... which holdeth our soul in life, and suffereth not our feet to be moved.*" Ps. 66:8,9
Prayer:
Father in heaven, don't let our feet be moved in Jesus' name, Amen!

God brought me to a wealthy place
"*Thou hast caused men to ride over our heads; we went through fire and through water...*" Ps. 66:12

> **The Promise:**
> "... *but Thou broughtest us out into a wealthy place.*" Ps. 66:12

God will not turn my prayers away
The Condition:
"*If I regard iniquity in my heart, the Lord will not hear me...*" Ps. 66:18

> **The Promise:**
> "... *verily God hath heard me; He hath attended to the voice of my prayer. Blessed be God, which hath not turned away my prayer nor His mercy from me.*" Ps. 66:18,19

God will bless us!
"*Then shall the earth yield her increase; and God, even our own God, shall bless us. God shall bless us; and all the ends of the earth shall fear Him.*" Ps. 67:6,7
Prayer:
Father in heaven, I thank You that You hear and answer my prayers and for Your great mercy and blessings. In Jesus' name, Amen!

> **The Promise:**
> "*God setteth the solitary in families: He bringeth out those which are bound with chains...*" Ps. 68:6

"... Thou, O God, didst send a plentiful rain... O God, hast prepared of Thy goodness for the poor." Ps. 68:9,10
"... God, You provided for the poor." Ps. 68:10 NIV
"... God, provided from Your goodness for the poor." Ps. 68:10 NKJV
"Thou hast ascended on high, Thou hast led captivity captive: Thou hast received gifts for men; yea, for the rebellious also, that the Lord God might dwell among them. Blessed be the Lord, who daily loadeth us with benefits, even the God of our Salvation. Selah. He that is our God is the God of Salvation... I will bring My people again from the depths of the sea (at the Resurrection)..." Ps. 68:18-20,22

Blessed be God!
"O God... He that giveth strength and power unto His people. Blessed be God." Ps. 68:35

"The humble shall see this, and be glad: and your heart shall live that seek God." Ps. 69:32

The Promise:
"For the Lord heareth the poor, and despiseth not His prisoners... for God will save Zion, and will build the cities of Judah: that they may dwell there, and have it in possession. The seed also of His servants shall inherit it..." Ps. 69:32

The Condition:
"... and they that love His name..." Ps. 69:36

The Promise:
"... shall dwell therein." Ps. 69:36

"When the humble see it they will be glad; you, who seek God, let your hearts revive." Ps. 69:32 ESV

"... O Lord... Thou hast given commandment..." Ps. 71:1

The Promise:
"... to save me; for Thou art my Rock and my fortress." Ps. 71:1,3

"For Thou art my hope O Lord God: Thou art my trust ("confidence" NIV; "hope" NAS; "security" Jublilee Bible 2000) since my youth..." Ps. 71:5

Praise God
"By Thee have I been holden up from the womb: Thou art He that took me

out of my mother's bowels: my praise shall be continually of Thee... Thou art my strong refuge." Ps. 71:6,7 (Ps. 22:9,10)

You teach us
"O God, Thou hast taught me from my youth..." Ps. 71:17

God does great things
"Thy righteousness also, O God, is very high, who hast done great things: O God, who is like unto Thee!" Ps. 71:19

"Though You have made me see troubles many and bitter..." Ps. 71:20,21 NIV

> **The Promise:**
> "... You will restore my life again... You will increase my honor and comfort me once again." Ps. 71:20,21 NIV

On the New Earth
"You shall... comfort me on every side." Ps. 71:21 NKJV

> **The Promise:**
> "The mountains shall bring peace to the people, and the little hills, by righteousness... He shall save the children of the needy, and shall break in pieces the oppressor... He shall come down like rain upon the mown grass: as showers that water the earth. In His days shall the righteous flourish; and abundance of peace so long as the moon endureth. He shall have dominion also from sea to sea, and from the river unto the ends of the earth." Ps. 72:3-8

"The kings... shall bring presents... (and) shall offer gifts." Ps. 72:10

> **The Promise:**
> "Yea, all kings shall fall down before Him: all nations shall serve Him. For He shall deliver the needy when he crieth; the poor also, and him that hath no helper. He shall spare the poor and needy, and shall save the souls of the needy. He shall Redeem their soul from deceit and violence... and he shall live, and to Him shall be given of the gold of Sheba; prayer also shall be made for him continually; and daily shall He be praised..." Ps. 72:11-15

There will be an abundance of grain in the earth... its fruit shall wave..." Ps. 72:16 NKJV

The Promise:
"His name shall endure forever: His name shall be continued as long as the sun: and men shall be blessed in the God of Israel, who only doeth wondrous things. And blessed be His glorious name forever: and let the whole earth be filled with His glory (on the New Earth); *Amen, and Amen."* Ps. 72:17-20

"Truly God is good to Israel..." Ps. 73:1

Those with a clean heart have a full cup
The Condition:
"... even to such as are of a clean heart." Ps. 73:1

The Promise:
"... waters of a full cup are wrung out to them." Ps. 73:10
"They shall have everything in abundance." Ps. 73:10 PB
"Therefore their people turn to them and drink up waters in abundance." Ps. 73:10 NIV

The Promise:
"Nevertheless I am continually with thee: Thou hast holden me by my right hand. Thou shalt guide me with Thy counsel, and afterward receive me to glory... God is the strength of my heart, and my portion forever." Ps. 73:23,24,26

"Thou hast set all the borders of the earth..." Ps. 74:17

"... the horns of the righteous shall be exalted.' Ps. 75:10
"... I will increase the power of the godly." Ps. 75:10 NLT
"... I will cut off the horns of the wicked." Ps. 75:10 NIV

"Has His promise failed forevermore? (No!)*..."* Ps. 76:8 NKJV

"When God arose to Judgment..." Ps. 76:9

The Promise:
"... to save all the meek of the earth..." Ps. 76:9

"Thou art the God that doest wonders: Thou hast declared Thy strength among the people. Thou hast with Thine arm Redeemed Thy people..." Ps. 77:14,15
"You are the God who performs miracles; You display Your power among the peoples..." Ps. 77:14 NIV
"Thou leddest Thy people like a flock..." Ps. 77:20

Miracles
To Israel during their 40 yrs. in the wilderness
"He divided the sea, and caused them to pass through; and He made the waters to stand as an heap. In the daytime also He led them with a cloud, and all the night with a light of fire. He clave the Rocks in the wilderness, and gave them drink as out of the great depths. He brought streams also out of the Rock, and caused waters to run down like rivers." Ps. 78:13-16

Manna
"Though He had commanded the clouds from above, and opened the doors of heaven, and had rained down manna upon them to eat, and had given them of the corn of heaven (manna). *Man did eat angels' food; He sent them meat to the full... He rained flesh also upon them as dust, and feathered fowls like as the sand of the sea... He gave them their own desire..."* Ps. 78:23-25,27,29

God is compassionate and forgives
"And they remembered that God was their Rock, and the high God their Redeemer... He, being full of compassion, forgave their iniquity, and destroyed them not: yea, many a time turned He His anger away, and did not stir up all His wrath. For He remembered that they were but flesh." Ps. 78:39

Prayer:
Father in heaven, I thank You that You forgive! Please help me to do the things that please You. Thank You In Jesus' name, Amen!
"The Spirit is willing but the flesh is weak", Mat.26:41;Mk.14:38.

God led His people
"But made His own people to go forth like sheep, and guided them in the wilderness like a flock. And He led them on safely... He brought them to the border of His Sanctuary... and divided them an inheritance..." Ps. 78:42-55
"He... allotted them an inheritance..." Ps. 78:55 NKJV

"Then the Lord awaked as One out of sleep... and He smote His enemies in the hinder parts: He put them to a perpetual reproach." Ps. 78:65,66

Prayer:
Oh Lord, awake from Your sleep as You did for them and deliver me from my trials and tribulations! In the name of Jesus, Amen!
Prayer:
"Turn us again, O God of hosts, and cause Thy face to shine..." Ps. 80:7

> **The Promise:**
> "... we shall be saved." Ps. 80:7,10

"... only then will we be saved." Ps. 80:7 NLT
Prayer:
Father in heaven, let Your light shine on me & my loved ones so that we are saved and please turn our hearts to You. Thank You in Jesus' name, Amen!

"I removed his shoulder from the burden: his hands were delivered from the pots ("heavy tasks" NLT). Thou calledst in trouble..." Ps. 81:6,7

> **The Promise:**
> "... I delivered thee; I answered thee in the secret place of thunder... I proved thee at the waters of Meribah..." Ps. 81:6,7

"I am the Lord thy God, which brought thee out of the land of Egypt: open thy mouth wide..." Ps. 81:10

> **The Promise:**
> "... and I will fill it." Ps. 81:10

"Oh that My people had hearkened unto Me, and Israel had walked in My ways!" Ps. 81:13

> **The Promise:**
> "... I should soon have subdued their enemies, and turned My hand against their adversaries." Ps. 81:14

"He would have fed them also with the finest of wheat; and with honey from the Rock I would have satisfied you." Ps. 81:16 NKJV

Blessed
"Blessed are they that dwell in Thy house: they will be still praising Thee. Selah. Blessed is the man whose strength is in Thee; in whose heart are the ways of them..." Ps. 84:4,5

> **The Promise:**
> "... they go from strength to strength..." Ps. 84:7

God will not withhold good from the upright

> **The Promise:**
> "For the Lord God is a sun and shield: the Lord will give grace and glory: no good thing will He withhold from them that walk uprightly." Ps. 84:11

Blessed
"O Lord of hosts, blessed is the man that trusteth in Thee." Ps. 84:12

God forgives
"Thou hast forgiven the iniquity of Thy people, Thou hast covered all their sin. Selah. Thou hast taken away all Thy wrath: Thou hast turned Thyself from the fierceness of Thine anger." Ps. 85:2,3

"I will hear what God the Lord will speak..." Ps. 85:8

> **The Promise:**
> *"... for He will speak peace unto His people, and to His saints... truth shall spring out of the earth; and righteousness shall look down from heaven."* Ps. 85:8,11

God is good and will forgive
"For Thou, Lord, art good, and ready to forgive; and plenteous in mercy unto all them that call upon Thee..." Ps. 86:5

> **The Condition:**
> *"In the day of my trouble I will call upon Thee..."* Ps. 86:7
>
>> **The Promise:**
>> *"Thou wilt answer me."* Ps. 86:7
>
>> **The Promise:**
>> *"All the nations You have made will come and bow down before You, Lord, and will honor Your name. For Thou art great, and doest wondrous things: Thou art God alone..."* Ps. 86:9,10

This will be fulfilled on the New earth.

> **The Promise:**
> *"For great is Thy mercy ("love" NIV) toward me: and Thou hast delivered my soul from the lowest hell."* Ps. 86:13

> **The Promise:**
> *"But Thou, O Lord, art a God full of compassion, and gracious, longsuffering, and plenteous in mercy and truth."* Ps. 86:15

"Shew me a token ("sign" NLT) for good ("of Your favor" NLT); that they which hate me may see it, and be ashamed ("put to shame" NLT): because..." Ps. 86:17

> **The Promise:**
> *"Thou, Lord, hast holpen ("helped" NLT) me, and comforted me."* Ps. 86:17

"I will sing of the mercies of the Lord forever: with my mouth will I make known Thy faithfulness to all generations. For I have said, Mercy shall be built up forever: Thy faithfulness shalt Thou establish in the very heavens. I have made a Covenant with My chosen, I have sworn unto David My servant, thy seed will I establish forever, and build up thy throne to all generations. Selah. And the heavens shall praise Thy wonders, O Lord; Thy faithfulness also in the congregation of the saints." Ps. 89:1-5

God is strong and faithful
"O Lord God of hosts, who is a strong Lord like unto Thee? Or to Thy faithfulness round about Thee? Thou rulest the raging of the sea: when the waves thereof arise, Thou stillest them... as one that is slain; Thou hast scattered Thine enemies with Thy strong arm... Thou hast a mighty arm: strong is Thy hand, and high is Thy right hand... blessed is the people that know the joyful sound: they shall walk, O Lord, in the light of Thy countenance. In Thy name shall they rejoice all the day: and in Thy righteousness shall they be exalted. For Thou art the glory of their strength: and in Thy favour our horn ("power" ISV) shall be exalted. For the Lord is our defence; and the Holy One of Israel is our king...." Ps. 89:8-25

Blessed
"... then Thou spakest in vision to Thy Holy One, and saidist..." Ps. 89:15-19

The Promise:
"... I have laid help upon one that is mighty; I have exalted one chosen out of the people. I have found David My servant; with My Holy oil have I anointed him: with whom My hand shall be established: Mine arm also shall strengthen him. The enemy shall not exact upon him; nor the son of wickedness afflict him. And I will beat down his foes before his face, and plague them that hate him. But My faithfulness and My mercy shall be with him: and in My name shall his horn be exalted. I will set his hand also in the sea, and his right hand in the rivers. He shall cry unto Me, Thou art my father, my God, and the Rock of my Salvation" Ps. 89:19-26

A promise to Jesus
"Also I will make Him (Jesus) My firstborn, higher than the kings of the earth. My mercy will I keep for Him forevermore, and my Covenant shall stand fast with Him. His seed also will I make to endure forever, and His throne as the days of heaven. Ps. 89:27-29

The Condition:
"... If his children forsake My law, and walk not in My Judgments; if they break My Statutes, and keep not My Commandments..." Ps. 89:30-32

The Promise:
"... My lovingkindness will I not utterly take from him, nor suffer My faithfulness to fail. My Covenant will I not break, nor alter the thing that is gone out of My lips. Once have I sworn by My Holiness that I will not lie unto David. His seed shall endure forever, My Holiness that I will not lie unto David. His seed shall endure forever, and his throne as the sun before Me. It shall be established forever as the moon, and as a faithful witness in heaven. Selah." Ps. 89:33-37

Prayer:
"Blessed be the Lord forevermore. Amen, and Amen." Ps. 89:52

The Condition:
"He that dwelleth in the secret place of the Most High..." Ps. 91:1

The Promise:
"shall abide under the shadow of the Almighty. I will say of the Lord He is my refuge and my fortress: my God; in Him will I trust. Surely He shall deliver thee from the snare of the fowler, and from the noisome pestilence. He shall cover thee with His feathers, and under His wings shalt thou trust: His truth shall be thy shield and buckler. Thou shalt not be afraid for the terror by night; nor for the arrow that flieth by day: nor for the pestilence that walketh in darkness; nor for the destruction that wasteth at noonday. A thousand shall fall at thy side, and ten thousand at thy right hand; but it shall not come nigh thee..." Ps. 91:2-8

"... only with thine eyes shalt thou behold and see the reward of the wicked." Ps. 91:8

The Condition:
"Because thou hast made the Lord which is my refuge, even the Most High, thy habitation..." Ps. 91:9

The Promise:
"... there shall no evil befall thee, neither shall any plague come nigh thy dwelling. For He shall give His angels charge over thee, to keep thee in all thy ways." Ps. 91:10,11

The Condition:
"Because He hath set his love upon Me..." Ps. 91:14

> **The Promise:**
> *"... therefore will I deliver him: I will set him on high..."* Ps. 91:14

The Condition:
"... because he hath known My name." Ps. 91:14

> **The Promise:**
> *"He shall call upon Me, and I will answer him: I will be with him in trouble; I will deliver him, and honour him. With long life will I satisfy him, and shew him My Salvation."* Ps. 91:15,16

"For Thou, Lord, hast made me glad through Thy work: I will triumph in the works of Thy hands." Ps. 92:4

> **The Promise:**
> *"The righteous shall flourish like the palm tree: he shall grow like a cedar... those that be planted in the house of the Lord shall flourish in the courts of our God. They shall still bring forth fruit in old age; they shall be fat ("vital" NLT) and flourishing ("green" NLT)..."* Ps. 92:12-14

"... to shew that the Lord is upright: He is my Rock, and there is no unrighteousness in Him." Ps. 92:15

"... the world also is stablished, that it cannot be moved. Thy throne is established..." Ps. 93:1,2

Blessed
"Blessed is the man whom Thou chastenest, O Lord, and teachest him out of Thy law; that Thou mayest give him rest from the days of adversity..." Ps. 94:12,13

> **The Promise:**
> *"... for the Lord will not cast off His people, neither will He forsake His inheritance."* Ps. 94:14

God is my help
"Unless the Lord had been my help, my soul had almost dwelt in silence." Ps. 94:17
Prayer:
"When I said, My foot slippeth; Thy mercy, O Lord, held me up. In the

multitude of my thoughts within me Thy comforts delight my soul." Ps. 94:18,19

"But the Lord is my defence; and my God is the Rock of my refuge. And he shall bring upon them their own iniquity ("He will repay them for their sins..." NIV), and shall cut them off in their own wickedness; yea, the Lord our God shall cut them off." Ps. 94:22,23

"For He is coming..." Ps. 96:13
Light and joy on the righteous

> **The Promise:**
> *"... He preserveth the souls of His saints; He delivereth them out of the hand of the wicked. Light is sown for the righteous, and gladness for the upright in heart."* Ps. 97:10, 11

"... light shines on the godly, and joy on those who do right." Ps. 97:11 NLT

"The Lord hath made known His Salvation: His righteousness hath He openly shewed in the sight of the heathen." Ps. 98:2

"... they called upon the Lord..." Ps. 99:6

> **The Promise:**
> *"... and He answered them."* Ps. 99:6

God is full of mercy and goodness
"For the Lord is good; His mercy is everlasting; and His truth endureth to all generations." Ps. 100:5
The Condition:
"I will behave myself wisely in a perfect way, O when wilt Thou come unto me? I will walk within my house with a perfect heart. I will set no wicked thing before mine eyes: I hate the work of them that turn aside; it shall not cleave to me." Ps. 101:2,3

> **The Promise:**
> *"Mine eyes shall be upon the faithful of the land, that they may dwell with Me..."* Ps. 101:6

The Condition:
"... he that walketh in a perfect way, he shall serve Me." Ps. 101:6

> **The Promise:**
> *"Thou shalt arise, and have mercy upon Zion: for the time to favour her, yea, the set time, is come."* Ps. 102:13

"So the nations shall fear the name of the Lord..." Ps. 102:15 NKJV

God will hear our prayers
"When the Lord shall build up Zion, He shall appear in His glory. He will regard the prayer of the destitute, and not despise their prayer." Ps. 102:16,17

"For He hath looked down from the height of His Sanctuary; from heaven did the Lord behold the earth; To hear the groaning of the prisoner..." Ps. 102:19,20

>**The Promise:**
>"... to loose those that are appointed to death..." Ps. 102:20
>
>**The Promise:**
>"The children of Thy servants shall continue, and their seed shall be established before Thee." Ps. 102:28

"Their descendants will live securely in Your presence." Ps. 102:28 NB
"... be secure in Your presence." Ps. 102:28 GWT

"Bless the Lord... and forget not all His benefits: who forgiveth all thine iniquities; who healeth all thy diseases; who redeemeth thy life from destruction; who crowneth thee with lovingkindness and tender mercies; who satisfieth thy mouth with good things; so that thy youth is renewed like the eagle's." Ps. 103:2-5

God is full of mercy and grace
"The Lord is merciful and gracious, slow to anger, and plenteous in mercy... He hath not dealt with us after our sins; nor rewarded us according to our iniquities. For as the heaven is high above the earth, so great is His mercy toward them that fear Him. As far as the East is from the West, so far hath He removed our transgressions from us... the Lord pitieth them that fear Him." Ps. 103:8-13
"As a father shows compassion to his children." Ps. 103:13 ESV

>**The Promise:**
>"But the mercy of the Lord is from everlasting to everlasting ..." Ps. 103:17

The Condition:
"... upon them that fear Him, and His righteousness unto children's children to such as keep His Covenant, and to those that remember His Commandments to do them." Ps. 103:18

"... *His Kingdom rules over all.*" Ps. 103:29 NKJV
"*(God) who laid the foundations of the earth, that it should not be removed forever.*" Ps. 104:5

The Promise:
"*... the waters... Thou hast set a bound that they may not pass over; that they turn not again to cover the earth. He sendeth the springs into the valleys, which run among the hills.*" Ps. 104:6,9,10

I claimed this verse when we lived on the Red River. It flooded before we moved in and after we moved out, but not while we lived there for 4 years. Thank You, Jesus! (see Answers to prayers)

Prayer:
Father in heaven, You set the boundaries on the waters, and I ask You to keep the waters within their boundaries where I live. Thank You in Jesus' name, Amen!

The Promise:
"*He causeth the grass to grow for the cattle...*" Ps. 104:14

"*O Lord, how manifold are Thy works! In wisdom hast Thou made them all: the earth is full of Thy riches.*" Ps. 104:24

The Promise:
"*He suffered no man to do them wrong: yea, He reproved kings for their sakes; saying, Touch not Mine anointed, and do My prophets no harm.*" Ps. 105:14,15

Prayer:
Father in heaven, I ask that You would suffer no man to do me wrong nor touch me for harm according to Your Word. Thank You in Jesus' name, Amen!

"*... till what He foretold came to pass, till the Word of the Lord proved Him true.*" Ps. 105:19 NIV
"*... He increased his people greatly; and made them stronger than their enemies.*" Ps. 105:24

God remembered His promise
"*He opened the Rock, and the waters gushed out; they ran in the dry places like a river. For He remembered His Holy promise, and Abraham His servant. And he brought forth His people with joy, and His chosen with gladness; and gave them the lands of the heathen: and they inherited the labour of the people...*" Ps. 105:41-44

The Condition:
"... that they might observe His Statutes, and keep His laws..." Ps. 105:45

"Blessed are they that keep Judgment, and he that doeth righteousness at all times... that I may see the good of Thy chosen... that I may glory with Thine inheritance." Ps. 106:3,5

Then they believed!
"Nevertheless He saved them for His name's sake, that He might make His mighty power to be known. He rebuked the Red sea also, and it was dried up: so He led them through the depths, as through the wilderness. And He saved them from the hand of him that hated them, and Redeemed them from the hand of the enemy. And the waters covered their enemies: there was not one of them left. Then believed they His Words..." Ps. 106:8-12

Some did not believe
"They did not believe His promises... and grumbled... and did not obey." Ps. 106:24 NIV

God wants us to believe the promises and obey!
"Nevertheless He regarded their affliction, when He heard their cry: and He remembered for them His Covenant, and repented according to the multitude of His mercies. He made them also to be pitied of all those that carried them captives." Ps. 106:44-46

"Then they cried unto the Lord in their trouble..." Ps. 107:6

> **The Promise:**
> "... and He delivered them out of their distresses. And He led them forth by the right way..." Ps. 107:6,7

We should praise God for all His wonderful works that He does for us! Ps. 107:8

> **The Promise:**
> "For He satisfieth the longing soul, and filleth the hungry soul with goodness." Ps. 107:9

"Then they cried unto the Lord in their trouble, and..." Ps. 107:13
> **The Promise:**
> "... He saved them out of their distresses. He brought them out of darkness and the shadow of death, and brake their bands in sunder." Ps. 107:13,14

The Promise:
"For He hath broken the gates of brass, and cut the bars of iron in sunder." Ps. 107:16

"Then they cry unto the Lord in their trouble…" Ps. 107:19

The Promise:
"… and He saveth them out of their distresses. He sent His Word, and healed them, and delivered them from their destructions." Ps. 107:19,20

Prayer: Father in heaven, please send Your Word to heal and deliver me in Jesus' name, Amen!

"Then they cry unto the Lord in their trouble…" Ps. 107:28

The Promise:
"… and He bringeth them out of their distresses. He maketh the storm a calm, so that the waves thereof are still. Then are they glad because they be quiet; so He bringeth them unto their desired haven." Ps. 107:28-30

The Promise:
"He turneth the wilderness into a standing water, and dry ground into watersprings. And there He maketh the hungry to dwell…" Ps. 107:35,36

Blessed
"He blesseth them also, so that they are multiplied greatly; and suffereth not their cattle to decrease." Ps. 107:38

"Yet setteth He the poor on high from affliction, and maketh him families like a flock." Ps. 107:41

The Promise:
"Through God we shall do valiantly; for He it is that shall tread down our enemies." Ps. 108:13

The Promise:
"For He shall stand at the right hand of the poor, to save him from those that condemn his soul." Ps. 109:31

The Promise:
"He hath made His wonderful works to be remembered: the Lord is gracious and full of compassion. He hath given meat unto them that fear Him: he will ever be mindful of His Covenant. He hath shewed

His people the power of His works that He may give them the heritage of the heathen." Ps. 110: 4-6

Promise to Jesus
"The Lord said unto my Lord, Sit thou at My right hand, until I make Thine enemies Thy footstool." Ps. 111:4-6
"He sent Redemption unto His people: He hath commanded His Covenant forever: Holy and reverend is His name. The fear of the Lord is the beginning of wisdom: a good understanding have all they that do His Commandments..." Ps. 111: 9,10

Blessed
The Condition:
"... blessed is the man that feareth the Lord, that delighteth greatly in His Commandments." Ps. 112:1

The Promise:
"His seed shall be mighty upon earth; the generation of the upright shall be blessed. Wealth and riches shall be in his house: and his righteousness endureth forever. Unto the upright there ariseth light in the darkness: he is gracious, and full of compassion, and righteous." Ps. 112:2-4

"Their children will be mighty..." Ps. 112:2 NIV
"Their children will be successful..." Ps. 112:2 NLT
"His descendants will be powerful in the land..." Ps. 112:2 HCSB
"Even in darkness light dawns for the upright, for those who are gracious and compassionate and righteous." Ps. 112:4 NIV
"Good will come to those who conduct their affairs with justice." Ps. 112:5 NIV

"Surely he shall not be moved forever: the righteous shall be in everlasting remembrance. He shall not be afraid of evil tidings: his heart is fixed, trusting in the Lord. His heart is established, he shall not be afraid, until he see his desire upon his enemies. He hath dispersed, he hath given to the poor; his righteousness endureth forever; his horn shall be exalted with honour..." Ps. 112:6-10

The Promise:
"He raiseth up the poor out of the dust, and lifteth the needy out of the dunghill (and) *set him with princes, even with the princes of His people. He maketh the barren woman to keep house, and to be a joyful mother of children..."* Ps. 113:7-9

The Promise:
"... He is their help and their shield. The Lord hath been mindful of us: He will bless us; He will bless the house of Israel; He will bless the house of Aaron. He will bless them that fear the Lord, both small and great. The Lord shall increase you more and more, you and your children. Ye are blessed of the Lord which made heaven and earth... the earth hath He given to the children of men." Ps. 115:11-17

"I love the Lord, because He hath heard my voice and my supplications. Because He hath inclined His ear unto me, therefore will I call upon Him as long as I live." Ps. 116:1,2
"Who will hear the voice of my prayer?" Ps. 116:1 ABPE

The Promise:
"... yea, our God is merciful. The Lord preserveth the simple..." Ps. 116:5

"I was brought low..." Ps. 116:5

The Promise:
"... and He helped me." Ps. 116:6

"Return unto thy rest, O my soul; for the Lord hath dealt bountifully with thee." Ps. 116:7

The Promise:
"For thou hast delivered my soul from death, mine eyes from tears, and my feet from falling." Ps. 116:8

The Promise:
"... Thou hast loosed my bonds." Ps. 116:16

"I called upon the Lord in distress..." Ps. 118:5

The Promise:
"... the Lord answered me, and set me in a large place. The Lord is on my side; I will not fear: what can man do unto me? The Lord taketh my part with them that help me..." Ps. 118:5-7

"The Lord is on my side as my helper..." Ps. 118:7 ESV
"The Lord is for me..." Ps. 118:7 NASB
"The Lord is my helper..." Ps. 118:7 HCSB
"The Lord takes my part..." Ps. 118:7 KJ 2000 Bible
Prayer:
Father in heaven, when I am in distress, I will call upon You Thank You for being on my side in Jesus' name, Amen!

The Lord helped me
"*All nations compassed me about; but in the name of the Lord will I destroy them. They compassed me about; yea, they compassed me about: but in the name of the Lord I will destroy them. They compassed me about like bees; they are quenched as the fire of thorns: for in the name of the Lord I will destroy them...*" Ps. 118:10-13

> **The Promise:**
> "*... but the Lord helped me. The Lord is my strength and song, and is become my Salvation.*" Ps. 118:13,14

"*I shall not die, but live, and declare the works of the Lord.*" Ps. 118:17

"*The Lord hath chastened me sore: but He hath not given me over unto death.*" Ps. 118:18

> **The Promise:**
> "*... for Thou hast heard me, and art become my Salvation.*" Ps. 118:21

"*O give thanks unto the Lord; for He is good...*" Ps. 118:29

> **The Promise:**
> "*... for His mercy endureth forever.*' Ps. 118:29

Blessed
"*Blessed are the undefiled ('whose walk is blameless' NIV) in the way, who walk in the law of the Lord. Blessed are they that keep His Testimonies, and that seek Him with the whole heart.*" Ps. 119:1,2

The Word of God keeps us from sinning
"*Thy Word have I hid in mine heart, that I might not sin against Thee.*" Ps. 119:11
"*I have thought much about Your words, and stored them in my heart so that they would hold me back from sin.*" Ps. 119:11 LB

Your promises refresh me
"*Remember thy Word unto Thy servant, upon which Thou hast caused me to hope. This is my comfort in my affliction: for Thy Word hath quickened me.*" Ps. 119:49,50
"*Never forget Your promises to me Your servant, for they are my only hope. They give me strength in all my troubles: how they refresh and revive me!*" Ps. 119:49,50 LB
"*... Your promise renews my life.*" Ps. 119:50 NIV

"This is my comfort in my affliction that Thy promise gives me life." Ps. 119:50 RSV

I expect You to help me
"... I expect Your help, for You have promised it. My eyes are straining to see Your promises come true" Ps. 119:81,82 LB
"My eyes fail, looking for Your promise..." Ps. 119:82 NIV

God's Word is eternal.
"Forever, O Lord, Thy Word is settled in heaven." Ps. 119:89
"Your Word, O Lord, is eternal; it stands firm in the heavens." Ps. 119:89 NIV
Continually think about His promises
"Though the wicked hide along the way to kill me, I will quietly keep my mind upon Your promises." Ps. 119:95 LB

"Thou through Thy Commandments hast made me wiser than mine enemies: for they are ever with me." Ps. 119:97

> **The Promise:**
> "Thy Word is a lamp unto my feet, and a light unto my path." Ps. 119:105

"Thy Testimonies have I taken as an heritage forever: for they are the rejoicing of my heart." Ps. 119:111
"Your laws are my joyous treasure forever. I am determined to obey You until I die." Ps. 119:111 LB

> **The Promise:**
> "Thou art my hiding place and my shield..." Ps. 119:114

"I hope in Thy Word... uphold me according unto Thy Word, that I may live..." Ps. 119:114,116

Prayers:
"Sustain me according to Your promise..." Ps. 119:116 NIV
"Lord, You promised to let me live! Never let it be said that God failed me." Ps. 119:116 LB
Lord, "Uphold me according unto Thy Word, that I may live: and let me not be ashamed of my hope." Ps. 119:116 NASB
This prayer tells us that God will not let us be ashamed if we ask Him for help.

Meditate on the promises
"My eyes stay open through the watches of the night, that I may meditate on Your promises." Ps. 119:148 NIV

God is full of mercy
"Great are Thy tender mercies, O Lord…" Ps. 119:156

"I rejoice at Thy Word, as one that findeth great spoil." Ps. 119:162
"I rejoice in Your promise like one who finds great spoil." Ps. 119:162 NIV
"… like one who finds a great treasure." Ps. 119:162 LB
"… vast treasure" HCSB
"I rejoice at Your Word as one who finds great treasure." Ps. 119:162 NKJV

"Great peace have they which love Thy law: and nothing shall offend them." Ps. 119:165

Deliver me
"… deliver me according to Your promise." Ps. 119:170 NIV

"In my distress I cried unto the Lord…" Ps. 120:1

> **The Promise:**
> *"I will lift up mine eyes unto the hills, from whence cometh my help. My help cometh from the Lord, which made heaven and earth. He will not suffer thy foot to be moved: He that keepeth thee will not slumber. Behold, He that keepeth Israel shall neither slumber nor sleep. The Lord is thy keeper: the Lord is thy shade upon thy right hand. The sun shall not smite thee by day, nor the moon by night. The Lord shall preserve thee from all evil: He shall preserve thy soul. The Lord shall preserve thy going out and thy coming in from this time forth, and even forevermore."* Ps. 121:1-8

The Condition:
They *"… that love Thee (Jerusalem)."* Ps. 122:6

> **The Promise:**
> *"… shall prosper…"* Ps. 122:6

"… so our eyes wait upon the Lord our God, until that He have mercy upon us." Ps. 123:2

God is on our side
"If it had not been the Lord who was on our side... when men rose up against us: then they had swallowed us up quick, when their wrath was kindled against us: then the waters had overwhelmed us, the stream had gone over our soul: then the proud waters had gone over our soul. Blessed be the Lord who hath not given us as a prey to their teeth." Ps. 124:1-6

> **The Promise:**
> *"Our soul is escaped as a bird out of the snare of the fowlers: the snare is broken, and we are escaped. Our help is in the name of the Lord, who made heaven and earth."* Ps. 124: 7,8

The Condition:
"They that trust in the Lord..." Ps. 125:1

> **The Promise:**
> *"... shall be as Mount Zion, which cannot be removed, but abideth forever. As the mountains are round about Jerusalem, so the Lord is round about His people from henceforth even forever... peace shall be upon Israel."* Ps. 125:1,2,5

Some of these promises have their ultimate fulfillment on the New Earth when everything is restored.
When God brought Israel back from the Babylonian captivity
"When the Lord turned again the captivity of Zion, we were like them that dream. Then was our mouth filled with laughter, and our tongue with singing: then said they among the heathen, The Lord hath done great things for them... whereof we are glad." Ps. 126:1-3

Prayer:
Father in heaven, please turn away our captivity and fill us with laughter and singing. Do great things for us as it says in Your Word and make us glad. Thank You for all Your blessings in the name of Jesus, Amen!

The Condition:
"They that sow in tears" Ps. 126:5

> **The Promise:**
> *"... shall reap in joy."* Ps. 126:5

The Condition:
"... he that goeth forth and weepeth, bearing precious seed..." Ps. 126:6

> **The Promise:**
> *"... shall doubtless come again with rejoicing bringing his sheaves with him."* Ps. 126:6

Prayer:
Father in heaven, I thank You for seeing the tears I have shed for my family and loved ones. I pray that they will all be there at the harvest of souls. In Jesus' name, Amen!

> **The Promise:**
> "... for so He giveth His beloved sleep. Lo, children are an heritage of the Lord: and the fruit of the womb is His reward." Ps. 127:2,3

Blessed
 "Happy is the man that hath his quiver full of them (children)..." Ps. 127:5

Blessed
"Blessed is everyone..." Ps. 128:1

The Condition:
"... that feareth the Lord; that walketh in His ways...." Ps. 128:1

> **The Promise:**
> "For thou shalt eat the labour of thine hands: happy shalt thou be, and it shall be well with thee. Thy wife shall be as a fruitful vine by the sides of thine house: thy children like olive plants round about

The Condition:
"... that feareth the Lord." Ps. 128:4

Blessing

> **The Promise:**
> "The Lord shall bless thee out of Zion: and thou shalt see the good of Jerusalem all the days of thy life. Yea, thou shalt see thy children's children, and peace upon Israel." Ps. 128:5,6

"Many a time have they afflicted me from my youth; yet they have not prevailed against me... the Lord is righteous: He hath cut asunder the cords of the wicked." Ps. 129:2-4

"Let Israel hope in the Lord: for with the Lord there is mercy, and with Him is plenteous Redemption." Ps. 130:7

> **The Promise:**
> "And He shall Redeem Israel from all his iniquities." Ps. 130:8

The Lord bestows blessings from Mt. Zion

> **The Promise:**
> *"I will abundantly bless her provision: I will satisfy her poor with bread. I will also clothe her priests with Salvation: and her saints shall shout aloud for joy. There will I make the horn (Heb. #7161 "strength") of David to bud... his enemies will I clothe with shame: but upon himself shall his crown flourish."* Ps. 132:15-18

"I will increase the power of David. My anointed will be a light for My people." Ps. 132:17 NLT

"... the Lord commanded the blessing, even life forevermore." Ps. 133:3

"And hath Redeemed us from our enemies: for His mercy endureth forever. Who giveth food to all flesh: for His mercy endureth forever. O give thanks unto the God of heaven..." Ps. 136:24-26

> **The Promise:**
> *"... for His mercy endureth forever."* Ps. 136:26

"In the day when I cried..." Ps. 138:3

> **The Promise:**
> *"... Thou answeredst me, and strengthenedst me with strength in my soul."* Ps. 138:3

> **The Promise:**
> *"... yet hath He respect unto the lowly..."* Ps. 138:6

"Though the Lord be high..." Ps. 138:6

Prayer:
Father in heaven, thank You for Your great mercy toward me. Please strengthen me in my soul. In Jesus' name, Amen!

"... but the proud He knoweth afar off." Ps. 138:6

"Though the Lord is great, He cares for the humble, but He keeps His distance from the proud." Ps. 138:6 NLT

"Though I walk in the midst of trouble..." Ps. 138:7

> **The Promise:**
> *"Thou wilt revive me: Thou shalt stretch forth Thine hand against the wrath of mine enemies, and Thy right hand shall save me. The Lord will perfect that which concerneth me: Thy mercy, O Lord, endureth forever..."* Ps. 138:7,8

> **The Promise:**
> *"... even the night shall be light about me."* Ps. 139:11

"Blessed be the Lord my strength... my goodness, and my fortress; my high tower, and my deliverer; my shield, and He in whom I trust; who subdueth my people under me." Ps. 144:1,2

"He is my loving God and my fortress, my stronghold and my deliverer, my shield, in whom I take refuge, who subdues peoples under me." Ps. 144:2 NIV

God's people happy
"It is He that giveth Salvation unto kings: who delivereth David His servant from the hurtful sword... that our sons may be as plants grown up in their youth; that our daughters may be as cornerstones, polished after the similitude of a palace: that our garners may be full, affording all manner of store: that our sheep may bring forth thousands and ten thousands in our streets: that our oxen may be strong to labour; that there be no breaking in, nor going out; that there be no complaining in our streets. Happy is that people... whose God is the Lord." Ps. 144:10-15

> **The Promise:**
> "The Lord is gracious, and full of compassion; slow to anger, and of great mercy. The Lord is good to all: and His tender mercies are over all His works..." Ps. 145:8,9

"All Thy works shall praise Thee, O Lord; and Thy saints shall bless Thee." Ps. 145:10

God's kingdom will last forever
"Thy kingdom is an everlasting kingdom, and Thy dominion endureth throughout all generations." Ps. 145:13
"... the Lord is faithful to all His promises and loving toward all He has made." Ps. 145:13 NIV

> **The Promise:**
> "The Lord upholdeth all that fall, and raiseth up all those that be bowed down. The eyes of all wait upon Thee ('look to Thee' NIV); and Thou givest them their meat in due season ("You give them their food at the proper time." HCSB; "as they need it" NLT). Thou openest Thine hand, and satisfiest the desire of every living thing... the Lord is nigh unto all them that call upon Him, ("watches over them" NIV)..." Ps. 145: 14-18

The Condition:
"... to all that call upon Him in truth." Ps. 145:18

The Promise:
"He will fulfil the desire of them that fear Him: He also will hear their cry, and will save them. The Lord preserveth ('watches over' NIV) all them that love Him..." Ps. 145: 19,20

Prayer:
Father in heaven, please give me food and water when I need it and fulfill my desires as You promised because I fear You. Hear my prayers and save me ac-cording to Your Word. Thank you in Jesus' name, Amen!

Bless His name
"... all flesh shall bless His Holy name forever and ever." Ps. 145:21 NKJV

The Promise:
"... which giveth food to the hungry... looseth the prisoners... openeth the eyes of the blind... raiseth them that are bowed down... loveth the righteous... (and) relieveth the fatherless and widow..." Ps. 146:7-9

"The Lord lifts up those who are weighed down." Ps. 146:8 NIV

The Promise:
"He healeth the broken in heart, and bindeth up their wounds." Ps. 147:3

"The Lord lifts up the humble." Ps. 147:6 NKJV
God *"Who covereth the heaven with clouds, who prepareth rain for the earth, who maketh grass to grow upon the mountains. He giveth to the beast his food, and to the young ravens which cry."* Ps. 147:8,9
"... the fowls of the air... they sow not, neither do they reap, nor gather... yet your heavenly Father feedeth them..." Matt. 6:26

Prayer:
Thank You Lord for the rain that waters the earth and makes the grass grow which gives food to the animals. You are so great and mighty and wonderful! In the name of Jesus, Amen!

The Promise:
"For He hath strengthened the bars of thy gates; He hath blessed thy children within thee. He maketh peace in thy borders, and filleth thee with the finest of the wheat. He sendeth forth His command-ment upon earth: His Word runneth very swiftly." Ps. 147:13-15

The Promise:
"He casteth forth His ice like morsels: who can stand before His cold? He sendeth out His Word, and melteth them... He sheweth his Word..." Ps. 147:18,19

The Promise:
"For the Lord taketh pleasure in His people: He will beautify the meek with Salvation." Ps. 149:4

Proverbs

The Promise:
"We shall find all precious substance, we shall fill our houses with spoil..." Prov. 1:13

"We will get all sorts of valuable things and fill our houses with plunder." Prov. 1:13 NIV
"Think of the great things we'll get! We'll fill our houses with all the stuff we take." Prov. 1:13 NLT
"We will find all kinds of precious wealth, we will fill our houses with spoil..." Prov. 1:13 NASB
"We will find all kinds of riches" Prov. 1:13 Jubilee Bible
"We will find all His wealth and His stuff and fill our houses with loot." Prov. 1:13 Aramaic Bible in Plain English

The Promise:
"... I (Wisdom) will pour out My Spirit unto you, I will make known My Words unto you." Prov. 1:23

God goes on to say that if we refuse to listen to Him and we insist on doing things our own way, He won't listen or answer our prayers. We will end up eating the fruit of what we do (Prov. 1:23-26).

The Condition:
"But whoso hearkeneth unto Me (Wisdom)..." Prov. 1:33

The Promise:
"... shall dwell safely, and shall be quiet from fear of evil." Prov. 1:33

"... but whoever listens to Me will live in safety and be at ease, without fear of harm." Prov. 1:33 NIV

The Condition:
"My son, if thou wilt receive My words, and hide My Commandments with thee; so that thou incline thine ear unto wisdom, and apply thine heart to understanding; yea, if thou criest after knowledge, and liftest up thy voice for understanding; if thou seekest her as silver, and searchest for her as for hid treasures..." Prov. 2:1-4

> **The Promise:**
> "Then shalt Thou understand the fear of the Lord, and find the knowledge of God." Prov. 2:5

> **The Promise:**
> "For the Lord giveth wisdom: out of His mouth cometh knowledge and understanding. He layeth up sound wisdom for the righteous: He is a buckler to them..." Prov. 2:6,7

The Condition:
"... that walk uprightly." Prov. 2:7

> **The Promise:**
> "He keepeth the paths of Judgment, and preserveth the way of His saints." Prov. 2:8

"To deliver thee from the way of the evil man, from the man that speaketh forward things..." Prov. 2:12

> **The Promise:**
> "For the upright shall dwell in the land, and the perfect shall remain in it." Prov. 2:21

The Condition:
"My son, forget not My law: but let thine heart keep My Commandments..." Prov. 3:1

> **The Promise:**
> "For length of days, and long life, and peace, shall they add to thee." Prov. 3:2

The Condition:
"Let not mercy and truth forsake thee: bind them about thy neck; write them upon the table of thine heart..." Prov. 3:3

> **The Promise:**
> "So shalt thou find favour and good understanding in the sight of God and man." Prov. 3:4

God has always wanted us to obey from the heart, but now we have the Holy Spirit to help us.
Bible verses about the heart!
(Deut.10:16;Ps.37:31;40:8;Prov.7:3;Is.51:7;Jer.9:26; 31:33;32:39;Ez.11:19; 18:31;36:26;Rom.2:14,15;7:22;IICor.3:3;Heb.8:8,10;10: 16)
The Bible says that King Josiah and King Hezekiah kept the Commandments with all their hearts, II Chron. 34:31;31:21.
Prayer:
Father in heaven, please write Your law on my heart so that I will want to do Your will with all my heart; and help me never to forsake Your truth so that I will find favor with God and man. Thank you in Jesus' name, Amen!

The Condition:
"Trust in the Lord with all thine heart; and lean not unto thine own understanding. In all thy ways acknowledge Him..." Prov. 3:5,6

The Promise:
"... and He shall direct thy paths." Prov. 3:6

Prayer:
Father in heaven, please direct my paths according to Your will and help me to always trust that Your ways are better than my ways. In Jesus' name, Amen!

The Condition:
"Be not wise in thine own eyes: fear the Lord, and depart from evil." Prov. 3:7

The Promise:
"It shall be health to thy navel, and marrow to thy bones." Prov. 3:8

Prayer:
Father in heaven, please help me to depart from evil so that I can receive health and healing. Thank You that all the promises are mine in Christ Jesus, Amen!

The Condition:
"Honour the Lord with thy substance, and with the firstfruits of all thine increase..." Prov. 3:9

The Promise:
"... so shall thy barns be filled with plenty, and thy presses shall burst out with new wine." Prov. 3:10

In the New Testament we see that they were not to neglect tithing
*"Woe unto you, Scribes and Pharisees, hypocrites! For ye pay tithe of mint and anise and cummin, and have omitted the weightier matters of the law, Judgment, mercy, and faith: these ought ye to have done, and **not to leave the other undone**."* Matt. 23:23

*"... **you should tithe**, yes, but do not neglect the more important things."* Matt. 23:23 NLT

Prayer:
Father in heaven, please help me to give to You first and fill me with plenty according to Your Word. In Jesus' name, Amen!

"Length of days is in her (Wisdom's) right hand; and in her left hand riches and honour." Prov. 3:16

> **The Promise:**
> *"When thou liest down, thou shalt not be afraid: yea, thou shalt lie down, and thy sleep shall be sweet. Be not afraid of sudden fear, neither of the desolation of the wicked, when it cometh. For the Lord shall be thy confidence, and shall keep thy foot from being taken."* Prov. 3:24-26

Blessed
"... He (God) blesseth the habitation of the just..." Prov. 3:33

The Condition:
"... keep My Commandments..." Prov. 4:4

> **The Promise:**
> *"He giveth grace unto the lowly. The wise shall inherit glory..."* Prov. 3:34-35

> **The Promise:**
> *"... and live."* Prov. 4:4

The Condition:
"Get wisdom, get understanding... forsake her not..." Prov. 4:5,6

The Condition:
"... love her (wisdom)... exalt her..." Prov. 4:6,8

> **The Promise:**
> *"... and she shall preserve thee and she shall keep thee."* Prov. 4:8

> **The Promise:**
> *"... and she shall promote thee: she shall bring thee to honour..."* Prov. 4:8

The Condition:
"... *when thou dost embrace her* (wisdom)." Prov. 4:8

> **The Promise:**
> "... *she* (wisdom) *shall give to thine head an ornament of grace: a crown of glory shall she deliver to thee.*" Prov. 4:9

"*I have taught thee in the way of wisdom, I have led thee in right paths.*" Prov. 4:11

> **The Promise:**
> "*When thou goest, thy steps shall not be straitened* ("hampered" NIV); *and when thou runnest, thou shalt not stumble.*" Prov. 4:11,12

"*But the path of the just is as the shining light, that shineth more and more unto the perfect day.*" Prov. 4:18

The Condition:
"*My son, attend to My words; incline thine ear unto My sayings. Let them not depart from thine eyes; keep them in the midst of thine heart.*" Prov. 4:20,21

> **The Promise:**
> "*For they are life unto those that find them, and health to all their flesh.*" Prov. 4:22

The Condition:
"*My son, keep thy father's commandment, and forsake not the law of thy mother: bind them continually upon thine heart, and tie them about thy neck.*" Prov. 6:20,21

> **The Promise:**
> "*When thou goest, it shall lead thee; when thou sleepest, it shall keep thee; and when thou awakest, it shall talk with thee.*" Prov. 6:22

Follow your father and mother's commands if they are following God and His Commands. We must always obey God over man, if man is telling us to disobey God (Acts 5:29).

The Condition:
"*For the Commandment is a lamp; and the law is light; and reproofs of instruction are the way of life...*" Prov. 6:23

"Receive My instruction, and not silver; and knowledge rather than choice gold. For wisdom is better than rubies; and all the things that may be desired are not to be compared to it." Prov. 8:10,11

Wisdom says, "Counsel is mine, and sound wisdom: I am understanding; I have strength." Prov. 8:14

> **The Promise:**
> "I love them..." Prov. 8:17

The Condition:
"... that love Me; and those that seek Me early..." Prov. 8:17

> **The Promise:**
> "... shall find Me." Prov. 8:17

"Riches and honour are with me (wisdom): yea, durable riches and righteousness." Prov. 8:18
"Unending riches, honor, wealth, and justice are Mine to distribute. My gifts are better than the purest gold, My wages better than sterling silver! I walk in righteousness, in paths of justice." Prov. 8:18-20

Those that love God inherit wealth
The Condition:
"That I may cause those that love Me..." Prov. 8:21

> **The Promise:**
> "... to inherit substance; and I will fill their treasures." Prov. 8:21

"... to inherit wealth, for I fill their treasuries." Prov. 8:21 NLT

"When He assigned to the sea its limit, so that the waters would not transgress His command, when He marked out the foundations of the earth." Prov. 8:29 NKJV

Prayer:
Father in heaven, You have set limits to the sea, so I ask You to keep the sea in its boundaries where I live according to Your Word. Thank You in Jesus' name, Amen!

Blessed:
"Blessed are they..." Prov. 8:32

The Condition:
"... that keep My ways." Prov. 8:32

Find wisdom, find favor
"Blessed is the man who listens to me (wisdom)*..."* Ps. 8:34 NKJV

> **The Promise:**
> *"For whoso findeth me* (wisdom) *findeth life, and shall obtain favour of the Lord."* Prov. 8:35

Forsake foolishness
The Condition:
"Forsake foolishness..." Prov. 9:6 NKJV

> **The Promise:**
> *"... and live..."* Prov. 9:6 NKJV

Fear the Lord
The Condition:
"The fear of the Lord..." Prov. 9:10

> **The Promise:**
> *"... is the beginning of wisdom, and the knowledge of the Holy One is understanding."* Prov. 9:10 NKJV

> **The Promise:**
> *"For by me* (wisdom) *thy days shall be multiplied, and the years of thy life shall be increased."* Prov. 9:11

The Condition:
"Righteousness..."

> **The Promise:**
> *"... delivers from death."* Prov. 10:2 NKJV

> **The Promise:**
> *"The Lord will not suffer the soul of the righteous to famish..."* Prov. 10:3

> **The Promise:**
> *"... the hand of the diligent maketh rich."* Prov. 10:4

Blessed:
"Blessings are upon the head..." Prov. 10:6

The Condition:
"... of the just..." Prov. 10:6

Blessed
"The memory of the righteous is blessed..." Prov. 10:7 NKJV

> **The Promise:**
> "The mouth of a righteous man is a well of life..." Prov. 10:11

"... love covereth all sins." Prov. 10:12
"... for love covers a multitude of sins." I Pet. 4:8 NLT

"The rich man's wealth is his strong city..." Prov. 10:15 NKJV
> **The Promise:**
> "The labour of the righteous tendeth to life... he is in the way of life that keepeth instruction..." Prov. 10:16

"The tongue of the righteous is choice silver." Prov. 10:20 NKJV

> **The Promise:**
> "The blessing of the Lord, it maketh rich, and He addeth no sorrow with it." Prov. 10:22

> **The Promise:**
> "... the desire of the righteous shall be granted... the righteous is an everlasting foundation... the fear of the Lord prolongeth days... the hope of the righteous shall be gladness" Prov. 10:24-28

Prayer:
Father in heaven, thank You that You cover me with the righteousness of Jesus. Please grant to me the desires of my heart and help me to always do the things that please You. In Jesus' name, Amen!

"The way of the Lord is strength to the upright..." Prov. 10:29

> **The Promise:**
> "The righteous shall never be removed..." Prov. 10:30

"... with the lowly is wisdom." Prov. 11:2
The Condition:
"The integrity of the upright..." Prov. 11:3 NKJV

> **The Promise:**
> "... will guide them..." Prov. 11:3 NKJV

The Condition:
"... but righteousness..." Prov. 11:4

> **The Promise:**
> "... delivereth from death..." Prov. 11:4,5

The Condition:
"... the righteousness of the perfect..." Prov. 11:4,5

The Promise:
"… shall direct his way…" Prov. 11:4,5

The Condition:
"The righteousness of the upright…" Prov. 11:6

The Promise:
"… shall deliver them…" Prov. 11:6

The Condition:
"The righteous…" Prov. 11:8

The Promise:
"… is delivered out of trouble…" Prov. 11:8

"An hypocrite with his mouth destroyeth his neighbor…" Prov. 11:9 With our mouth we can speak blessings or curses,; we can do good or harm, Jms. 3:10

The Condition:
"… but through knowledge…" Prov. 11:9

The Promise:
"… shall the just be delivered." Prov. 11:9

Blessing
"By the blessing of the upright the city is exalted…" Prov. 11:11 NKJV
"… but is overthrown by the mouth of the wicked." Prov. 11:11 NKJV

The Condition:
"… in the multitude of counselors…" Prov. 11:14 NKJV

The Promise:
"… there is safety." Prov. 11:14 NKJV

The Condition:
"… he who sows righteousness…" Prov. 11:18 NKJV

The Promise:
"… will have a sure reward." Prov. 11:18 NKJV

The Condition:
"… righteousness…" Prov. 11:19 NKJV

The Promise:
"… leads to life…" Prov. 11:19 NKJV

The Promise:
"... the seed ("*offspring*" PB) *of the righteous shall be delivered.*" Prov. 11:21

Prayer:
Father in heaven, please deliver my child/children from sin, from troubles, and from disasters according to Your Word. Thank You in Jesus' name, Amen!

"There is that scattereth, and yet increaseth; and there is that withholdeth more than is meet, but it tendeth to poverty." Prov. 11:24,25

The Condition:
"The liberal soul..." Prov. 11:25

> **The Promise:**
> *"... shall be made fat..."* Prov. 11:25

The Condition:
"... and he that watereth..." Prov. 11:25

> **The Promise:**
> *"... shall be watered also himself."* Prov. 11:25

"One man gives freely yet gains even more... a generous man ... will prosper; he who refreshes others will himself be refreshed." Prov. 11:25 NIV

Blessing:
"... blessing shall be upon the head of him that selleth it (corn). *He that diligently seeketh good procureth favour..."* Prov. 11:26
"People curse those who hold their grain for higher prices, but they bless the one who sells to them in their time of need." Prov. 11:26 NLT

The Condition:
"If you search for good..." Prov. 11:27

> **The Promise:**
> *"... you will find favor..."* Prov. 11:27

"... but if you search for evil, it will find you!" Prov. 11:27
The Condition:
"... the righteous ("the godly" NLT)..." Prov. 11:28

> **The Promise:**
> *"... shall flourish as a branch."* Prov. 11:28

"... flourish like leaves in spring." Prov. 11:28 NLT

Recompensed

> **The Promise:**
> *"The fruit of the righteous is a tree of life; and he that winneth souls is wise. Behold, the righteous shall be recompensed in the earth..."* Prov. 11:30,31

The Condition:
"... the righteous..." Prov. 12:3

> **The Promise:**
> *"... shall not be moved."* Prov. 12:3

"A virtuous woman is a crown to her husband...." Prov. 12:4
"A wife of noble character..." Prov. 12:4 NIV
"An excellent wife..." Prov. 12:4 NASB
"A worthy wife is her husband's joy and crown..." Prov. 12:4 NLT

The Condition:
"The mouth of the upright..." Prov. 12:6

> **The Promise:**
> *"... will deliver them..."* Prov. 12:6

The Condition:
"... the house of the righteous..." Prov. 12:7

> **The Promise:**
> *"... will stand."* Prov. 12:7

The Condition:
"He that tilleth his land..." Prov. 12:11

> **The Promise:**
> *"... shall be satisfied with bread ("will have abundant food" NIV)..."* Prov. 12:11

> **The Promise:**
> *"... the root of the righteous yieldeth fruit... the just shall come out of trouble."* Prov. 12:12,13

"A man will be satisfied with good by the fruit ("words" NCSB) of his mouth, and the recompense of a man's hands will be rendered him." Prov. 12:14 NKJV

> **The Promise:**
> *"... the tongue of the wise is health."* Prov. 12:18

"There is one whose rash words are like sword thrusts, but the tongue of the wise brings healing." Prov. 12:18 ESV
With your mouth you speak – Rom. 10:10

"The lip of truth shall be established forever..." Prov. 12:19
"Truthful words stand the test of time..." Prov. 12:19 NLT

> **The Promise:**
> *"There shall no evil happen to the just..."* Prov. 12:21

"Anxiety in a man's heart weighs it down, but a good word makes it glad." Prov. 12:25 NASB
"... a kind word cheers him up." Prov. 12:25
Prayer:
Father in heaven, please help us to be kinder, more compassionate, and more sympathetic to others. In Jesus' name, Amen!

"The righteous is more excellent than his neighbor..." Prov. 12:26
The path of life

> **The Promise:**
> *"In the way of righteousness is life; and in the pathway thereof there is no death."* Prov. 12:28

The Condition:
"... the soul of the diligent..." Prov. 13:4

> **The Promise:**
> *"... shall be made fat ("be enriched" PB)."* Prov. 13:4

"Those who work hard will prosper." Prov. 13:4 NLT

> **The Promise:**
> *"Righteousness keepeth him that is upright in the way..."* Prov. 13:6

"The light of the righteous rejoiceth..." Prov. 13:9

The Condition:
"... but he that gathereth by labour..." Prov. 13:11

> **The Promise:**
> *"... shall increase."* Prov. 13:11

"Dishonest money dwindles away, but whoever gathers money little by little makes it grow." Prov. 13:11 NIV

"Hope deferred makes the heart sick, but a longing fulfilled is a tree of life." Prov. 13:12 NIV

Rewarded
The Condition:
"... he that feareth the Commandment..." Prov. 13:13

> **The Promise:**
> "... shall be rewarded." Prov. 13:13

"The law of the wise is a fountain of life, to depart from the snares of death." Prov. 13:14
The Condition:
"Good understanding..."

> **The Promise:**
> "... gains favor." Prov. 13:15

The Condition:
"A faithful ("reliable" NLT) ambassador..." Prov. 13:17 NKJV

> **The Promise:**
> "... brings health." Prov. 13:17 NKJV

The Condition:
"... he that regardeth reproof..." Prov. 13:18

> **The Promise:**
> "... shall be honoured." Prov. 13:18

The Condition:
"... desire accomplished..." Prov. 13:19

> **The Promise:**
> "... is sweet to the soul..." Prov. 13:19

The Condition:
He that walketh with wise men..." Prov. 13:19,20

> **The Promise:**
> "... shall be wise... to the righteous good shall be repayed... the wealth of the sinner is laid up for the just." Prov. 13:20-22

"The righteous eateth to the satisfying of his soul..." Prov. 13:25

"Fools make a mock at sin..." Prov. 14:9
"Fools make fun of guilt..." Prov. 14:9 NLT

> **The Promise:**
> "... but among the righteous there is favour." Prov. 14:9

"The house of the wicked shall be overthrown..." Prov. 14:11

> **The Promise:**
> "... but the tabernacle of the upright shall flourish." Prov. 14:11

The Condition:
"... a good man..." Prov. 14:14 NKJV

> **The Promise:**
> "... will be satisfied from above." Prov. 14:14 NKJV

The Condition:
"... he that hath mercy on the poor..." Prov. 14:21

> **The Promise:**
> "... happy is he... mercy and truth shall be to them that devise good. In all labour there is profit... the crown of the wise is their riches..." Prov. 14:21,24

The Condition:
"In the fear of the Lord..." Prov. 14:26

> **The Promise:**
> "... is strong confidence: and his children shall have a place of refuge. The fear of the Lord is a fountain of life, to depart from the snares of death." Prov. 14:26,27

Prayer:
Father in heaven, help me to fear You and please give my child/children a place of refuge according to Your Word. Thank You in Jesus' name, Amen!

The Condition:
"He that is slow to wrath is of great understanding... (and) a sound heart..." Prov. 14:29,30

> **The Promise:**
> "... is the life of the flesh..." Prov. 14:29,30

"... the righteous hath hope in his death. Wisdom resteth in the heart of him that hath understanding..." Prov. 14:32,33

The Condition:
"A soft answer..." Prov. 15:1

> **The Promise:**
> "... turneth away wrath..." Prov. 15:1

"A wholesome tongue..." Prov. 15:4

> **The Promise:**
> "... is a Tree of Life..." Prov. 15:4

"... in the house of the righteous..." Prov. 15:6

> **The Promise:**
> "... is much treasure..." Prov. 15:6

"Great wealth is in the house of the righteous..." Prov. 15:6 NASB

The Condition:
"A merry heart..." Prov. 15:13

> **The Promise:**
> "... maketh a cheerful countenance..." Prov. 15:13

The Condition:
"... he that is of a merry heart..." Prov. 15:15

> **The Promise:**
> "... hath a continual feast ("tranquility" PB)" Prov. 15:15

The Condition:
"... he that is slow to anger..." Prov. 15:18

> **The Promise:**
> "... appeaseth strife." Prov. 15:18

"A man hath joy by the answer of his mouth... the way of life is above to the wise..." Prov. 15:23,24

"The Lord will destroy the house of the proud..." Prov. 15:25

> **The Promise:**
> "... but He will establish the border of the widow." Prov. 15:25

"The Lord is far from the wicked..." Prov. 15:29

The Condition:
"... he that heareth reproof..." Prov. 15:32

> **The Promise:**
> "... He heareth the prayer of the righteous. The light of the eyes rejoiceth the heart: and a good report maketh the bones fat." Prov. 15:29,30

The Promise:
"... getteth understanding. The fear of the Lord is the instruction of wisdom; and before honour..." Prov. 15:32,33

The Condition:
"... is humility." Prov. 15:32,33

The Promise:
"The preparations of the heart in man, and the answer of the tongue is from the Lord." Prov. 16:1

"The preparations of the heart belong to man but the answer of the tongue is from the Lord." Prov. 16:1 NKJV
We make our own plans, but the Lord is the one directing our paths. We should always say I will do this or that by the grace of God, or Lord willing, to acknowledge that all our plans are in God's hands.

The Condition:
"Commit thy works unto the Lord..." Prov. 16:3
We should commit everything we do and everything that happens to God! A prayer that we could pray:
Father in heaven, I commit (<u>fill in the blank</u>) to You knowing that I can't make things happen but nothing is too big for You. In Jesus' name, Amen

"... iniquity is purged: and by the fear of the Lord men depart from evil." Prov. 16:7

The Promise:
"... and thy thoughts shall be established." Prov. 16:3

The Condition:
"When a man's ways please the Lord..." Prov. 16:7

The Promise:
"He maketh even his enemies to be at peace with him." Prov. 16:7

The Promise:
"... the Lord directeth His steps." Prov. 16:9

The Condition:
"He that handleth a matter wisely shall find good: and whoso trusteth in the Lord..." Prov. 16:20

The Promise:
"... happy is he." Prov. 16:20

"The wise in heart shall be called prudent ("discerning" NIV): and the sweetness of the lips increaseth learning." Prov. 16:21

"The wise are known for their understanding, and instruction is appreciated if it's well presented." Prov. 16:21 NLT

"The heart of the wise teacheth his mouth, and addeth learning to his lips." Prov. 16:23

"A wise man's heart guides his mouth, and his lips promote instruction." Prov. 16:23 NIV

"From a wise mind comes wise speech; the words of the wise are persuasive." Prov. 16:23 NLT

"The heart of the wise instructs his mouth and adds persuasiveness to his lips." Prov. 16:23 NASB

The Condition:
"Pleasant words..." Prov. 16:24

> **The Promise:**
> "... are as an honeycomb, sweet to the soul, and health to the bones." Prov. 16:24
>
> **The Promise:**
> "The... ("silver hair" GWT) is a crown of glory..." Prov. 16:31

The Condition:
"... if it be found in the way of righteousness." Prov. 16:31

"A wise servant... shall have part of the inheritance." Prov. 17:2

"Children's children are the crown of old men..." Prov. 17:6
"A gift is as a precious stone in the eyes of him that hath it: whithersoever it turneth, it prospereth." Prov. 17:8

The Condition:
"A merry heart..." Prov. 17:22

> **The Promise:**
> "... doeth good like a medicine..." Prov. 17:22

"The words of a man's mouth are as deep waters, and the wellspring of wisdom as a flowing brook." Prov. 18:4

The Condition:
"The name of the Lord is a strong tower: the righteous runneth into it..." Prov. 18:10

> **The Promise:**
> "... and is safe." Prov. 18:10

"The spirit of a man will sustain his infirmity... the heart of the prudent getteth knowledge... a man's gift maketh room for him, and bringeth him before great men." Prov. 18:14-16

Prayer:
Father in heaven, please let the gifts and talents you've given to me and my family open doors according to Your will. In Jesus' name, Amen!

"A man's belly shall be satisfied with the fruit of his mouth; and with the increase of his lips shall he be filled. Death and life are in the power of the tongue..." Prov. 18:20,21

"The positive words that a man speaks fill his stomach; he will be satisfied with what his lips produce." Prov. 18:20 ISV

"Out of the same mouth proceedeth blessing and cursing. My brethren, these things ought not so to be." Jms. 3:10.

Some commentaries say that we have to accept the consequences of our words. Words can destroy and words can bring life. We must be very careful what we say.

The Bible says that the one who "... *does not doubt but believes that what they say will happen, it will be done for them*..." Mk. 11:23

"... they *overcame him by the blood of the Lamb, and by the word of their testi-mony*..." Rev. 12:11

"... *whoso findeth a ("good" PB) wife fineth a good thing*..." Prov. 18:22

   The Promise:
   "... *and obtaineth favour of the Lord.*" Prov. 18:22

Condition:
"He that getteth wisdom loveth his own soul: he that keepeth understanding..." Prov. 19:8

   The Promise:
   "... shall find good." Prov. 19:8

"The discretion of a man deferreth his anger; and it is his glory to pass over a
transgression." Prov. 19:11

"House and riches are the inheritance of fathers: and a prudent wife is from the Lord." Prov. 19:14

The Condition:
"He that keepeth the Commandment..." Prov. 19:16

   The Promise:
   "... keepeth his own soul..." Prov. 19:16

"... despising them (the Commandments) *leads to death"* Prov. 19:16 NLT

The Condition:
"... he that hath pity upon the poor lendeth unto the Lord..." Prov. 19:17

> **The Promise:**
> *"... and that which he hath given will He pay him again."* Prov. 19:17

"He who is kind to the poor lends to the Lord, and He will reward him for what he has done." Prov. 19:17 NIV
"Hear counsel, and receive instruction, that thou mayest be wise in thy latter end... the counsel of the Lord, that shall stand." Prov. 19:20,21
"The fear of the Lord tendeth to life ("leads to life" NIV; "gives life" NLT)*: and he that hath it shall abide satisfied; he shall not be visited with evil."* Prov. 19:23
"... so that one may sleep satisfied, untouched by evil" Prov. 19:23 NASB
"... untouched by trouble" Prov. 19:23 NIV
"... and protection from harm." Prov. 19:23 NLT

The Condition:
"The just man walketh in his integrity..." Prov. 20:7

> **The Promise:**
> *"... his children are blessed after him."* Prov. 20:7

The Condition:
"... wait on the Lord..." Prov. 20:22

> **The Promise:**
> *"... and He shall save thee."* Prov. 20:22

"The king's heart is in the hand of the LORD, as the rivers of water: he turneth it whithersoever He will." Prov. 21:1
"Just as water is turned into irrigation ditches, so the Lord directs the king's thoughts. He turns them wherever he wants to." Prov. 21:1 LB
"In the LORD's hand the king's heart is a stream of water that He channels toward all who please Him." Prov. 21:1 NIV
If God has the king's heart in His hand and can turn or direct it any way He wants, then He can turn your loved one's heart to Himself.

Prayer:
Father in heaven, _____'s heart is in Your hands so please turn his/her heart toward You as the rivers of waters. In Jesus' name, Amen!

"The thoughts of the diligent tend only to plenteousness; but of every one that is hasty only to want." Prov. 21:5

"The plans of the diligent lead to profit as surely as haste leads to poverty." Prov. 21:5 NIV

"Good planning and hard work lead to prosperity, but hasty shortcuts lead to poverty." Prov. 21:5 NLT

The Condition:
"He that foloweth after righteousness and mercy..." Prov. 21:21

    The Promise:
    "... findeth life, righteousness, and honour." Prov. 21:21

The Condition:
"Whoso keepeth his mouth and his tongue..." Prov. 21:23

    The Promise:
    "... keepeth his soul from troubles." Prov. 21:23

We need to be careful what we say. Gossip can stir up strife, and we can speak curses over ourselves and others by negative statements. We should practice speaking positive words and blessings over ourselves and others in Jesus' name.
See speak/words, p. 680

God keeps us safe
"... safety is of the Lord." Prov. 21:31

The Condition:
"By humility and the fear of the Lord..." Prov. 22:4

    The Promise:
    "... are riches, and honour, and life." Prov. 22:4

The Condition:
"Train up a child in the way he should go..." Prov. 22:6

    The Promise:
    "... and when he is old, he will not depart from it." Prov. 22:6

The Condition:
"He that hath a bountiful eye..." Prov. 22:9

    The Promise:
    "... shall be blessed..." Prov. 22:9

The Condition:
"... for he giveth of his bread to the poor." Prov. 22:9

"Blessed are those who are generous…" Prov. 22:9 NLT
"The generous will themselves be blessed, for they share their food with the poor." Prov. 22:9 NIV
"Cast out the scorner, and contention shall go out; yea, strife and reproach shall cease." Prov. 22:10
"For the Lord will plead their cause, and spoil the soul of those that spoiled them." Prov. 22:23

The Condition:
"Do you see any truly competent workers?" Prov. 22:29 NLT

> **The Promise:**
> *"They will serve kings rather than ordinary people."* Prov. 22:29 NLT
>
> **The Promise:**
> *"For surely there is an end ("reward" KJV fn)"* Prov. 23:18

"For surely there is a hereafter…" Prov. 23:18 NKJV

"The father of a righteous child has great joy; a man who fathers a wise son rejoices in him." Prov. 23:24

The Condition:
"Through wisdom is a house builded; and by understanding it is established: and by knowledge shall the chambers be filled…" Prov. 24:3

> **The Promise:**
> *"… with all precious and pleasant riches…"* Prov. 24:4

The Condition:
A wise man is strong; yea, a man of knowledge…" Prov. 24:3-5

> **The Promise:**
> *"… increaseth strength."* Prov. 24:5

The Condition:
"… in multitude of counsellers…" Prov. 24:6

> **The Promise:**
> *"… there is safety."* Prov. 24:6

"… and shall not He (God) render to every man according to his works." Prov. 24:12
We are saved by grace alone but the righteous are rewarded for their good works and the wicked are punished for their evil deeds. As we strive to obey and do those things that please God (not to be saved but because we love Him), He will reward us someday in heaven. The Bible says that Paul *"… had respect unto the recompence of the reward."* Heb. 11:26

"... he was looking ahead to his reward." Heb. 11:26 NIV
The Condition:
"... when thou hast found it (wisdom)..." Prov. 24:14

> **The Promise:**
> "... then there shall be a reward, and thy expectation shall not be cut off." Prov. 24:14

"Wisdom is sweet to your soul. If you find it, you will have a bright future, and your hopes will not be cut short." Prov. 24:14 NLT

"... a righteous man may fall seven times..." Prov. 24:16

> **The Promise:**
> "... and rise again..." Prov. 24:16 NKJV

Blessed
"... a good blessing shall come upon them." Prov. 24:25

"A word fitly spoken is like apples of gold in pictures of silver. As an earring of gold, and an ornament of fine gold..." Prov. 25:11,12
"... a gentle tongue breaks a bone." Prov. 25:15 NKJV

The Condition:
"If thine enemy be hungry, give him bread to eat; and if he be thirsty, give him water to drink: for thou shalt heap coals of fire upon his head..." Prov. 25:21,22

> **The Promise:**
> "... and the Lord shall reward thee." Prov. 25:22

"As the bird by wandering, as the swallow by flying..." Prov. 26:2

> **The Promise:**
> "... so the curse causeless shall not come." Prov. 26:2

"... an undeserved curse does not come to rest." Prov. 26:2 NIV
"... an unfair curse will not land on its intended victim." Prov. 26:2 NLT
"... so a curse without cause does not alight." Prov. 26:2 NASB
"... so the curse that is causeless shall be driven away." Prov. 26:2 PB

"And thou shalt have... milk enough for thy food, for the food of thy household..." Prov. 27:27

Prayer:
Father in heaven, I pray that my family and I would always have enough food and water according to Your Word. In Jesus' name, Amen!

"The righteous are bold as a lion." Prov. 28:1

"... but such as keep the law contend with ("resist" NIV) them." Prov. 28:4
"Those who keep the law receive strength." Prov. 28:4 PB
"Whoso keepeth the law..." Prov. 28:7

   The Promise:
   "... is wise..." Prov. 28:7

The Condition:
"... the upright..." Prov. 28:10,11

   The Promise:
   "... shall have good things in possession..." Prov. 28:10,11

"He that covereth his sins shall not prosper: but whoso confesseth and forsaketh them shall have mercy." Prov. 28:13
See I Jn. 1:9

Blessed
"Happy ("blessed" NIV) is the man who is always reverent ("trembles" NIV; "feareth" KJV)..." Prov. 28:14 NKJV

The Condition:
"... he that hateth covetousness..." Prov. 28:16

   The Promise:
   "... shall prolong his days." Prov. 28:16

"Whoso walketh uprightly shall be saved... He that tilleth his land shall have plenty of bread... a faithful man shall abound with blessings..." Prov. 28:18-20

The Condition:
"... he that putteth his trust in the Lord..." Prov. 28:25

   The Promise:
   "... shall be made fat ("will prosper" NIV)." Prov. 28:25

The Condition:
"Discipline your children..." Prov. 29:17

The Promise:
"... and they will give you peace ("peace of mind" HCSB); "comfort" ISV); they will bring you the delights you desire ("bring you happiness" Net Bible)." Prov. 29:17 NIV

The Condition:
"... whoso putteth his trust in the Lord..." Prov. 29:25

The Promise:
They "... shall be safe." Prov. 29:25

The Promise:
"Every Word of God is pure: He is a shield unto them..." Prov. 30:5

The Condition:
"... that put their trust in Him." Prov. 30:5

Blessed
The Condition:
"... a virtuous woman..." Prov. 31:10

The Promise:
"... her children arise up, and call her blessed... many daughters have done virtuously, but thou excellest them all." Prov. 31:28,29

"... a woman that feareth the Lord, she shall be praised. Give her of the fruits of her hands; and let her own works praise her in the gates." Prov. 31:30,31

Ecclesiastes

The Condition:
"For God giveth to a man that is good in His sight..." Eccl. 2:26

The Promise:
"... wisdom, and knowledge, and joy..." Eccl. 2:26

"But to the sinner He giveth travail, to gather and to heap up, that he may give to him that is good before God..." Eccl. 2:26
"To the man who pleases Him, God gives wisdom, knowledge, and happiness but to the sinner He gives the task of gathering and storing up wealth to hand it over to the one who pleases God." Eccl. 2:26 NIV

God is happy with us and loves to reward us when we strive to please Him! Sometimes though we must wait to receive our reward in heaven.

"He has made everything beautiful in its time. Also, He has put eternity in their hearts..." Eccl. 3:11 NKJV

"Behold that which I have seen: it is good and comely for one to eat and to drink, and to enjoy the good of all his labour that he taketh under the sun all the days of his life, which God giveth him: for it is his portion. Every man also to whom God hath given riches and wealth, and hath given him power to eat thereof... this is the gift of God... because God answereth him in the joy of his heart." Eccl. 5:18-20

"Here is what I have seen to be good and fitting: to eat, to drink and enjoy oneself in all one's labor in which he toils under the sun during the few years of his life which God has given him; for this is his reward. Furthermore, as for every man to whom God has given riches and wealth, He has also empowered him to eat from them and to receive his reward and rejoice in his labor; this is the gift of God. For he will not often consider the years of his life, because God keeps him occupied with the gladness of his heart." Eccl. 5:18-20 NASB

"When God gives any man wealth and possessions and enables him to enjoy them to accept his lot and be happy in his work – this is a gift of God. He seldom reflects on the days of his life, because God keeps him occupied with gladness of heart." Eccl. 5:19,20 NIV

The gift of God is to be able to enjoy wealth and possessions and be happy in your labor as long as you are doing God's will and helping others.

The Condition:
"... cast thy bread upon the waters..." Eccl. 11:1
"Give generously..." Eccl. 11:1 NLT

> **The Promise:**
> *"... for thou shalt find it after many days."* Eccl. 11:1

"... for your gifts will return to you later." Eccl. 11:1 NLT
"Give, and it shall be given unto you; good measure pressed down, and shaken together, and running over, shall men give into your bosom. For with the same measure that ye mete withal it shall be measured to you again." Lk. 6:38

Song of Solomon

An allegory of the church and Jesus.

> **The Promise:**
> "He brought me to the banqueting house, and His banner over me was love." Song of Solomon 2:4

Someday we will eat at the Wedding Feast with Jesus in heaven, Matt.8: 11;22: 1-14;25:1-13;Rev.19:7-9.

Isaiah

"Come now, and let us reason together, saith the Lord: though your sins be as scarlet..." Is. 1:18

> **The Promise:**
> "... they shall be as white as snow..." Is. 1:18

> **The Promise:**
> "... they shall be as wool." Is. 1:18

"... though they be red like crimson..." Is. 1:18

The Condition:
"If ye be willing and obedient..." Is. 1:18

> **The promise:**
> "... ye shall eat the good of the land..." Is. 1:18,19

The Condition:
"Say ye to the righteous, that... Is. 3:10

> **The Promise:**
> "... it shall be well with him; for they shall eat the fruit of their doings." Is. 3:10

"And the Lord will create upon every dwelling place of Mount Zion, and upon her assemblies, a cloud and smoke by day, and the shining of a flaming fire by night: for upon all the glory shall be a defence. And there shall be a Tabernacle for a shadow in the daytime from the heat, and for a place of refuge, and for a covert from storm and from rain." Is. 4:5,6

The cloud by day and the fire by night was Jesus who protects us. We know that because Jesus claimed to be the "*I Am*" in Jn. 8:59; and it was the "*I Am*" that was in the cloud and fire.

"... *for... the glory will be a canopy. There will be a shelter to give shade from the heat by day, and refuge and protection from the storm and the rain.*" Is. 4:5,6 NASB

"... *for the glory of the Lord shall be a shelter over all*" Is. 4:5 PB

This promise will ultimately be fulfilled on the New Earth when God will be the Tabernacle and His glory will be a canopy over the New Jerusalem because the Lord is the Temple (Tabernacle) as it says in Rev. 21:3,22.

Promise about the Messiah, Jesus.

"*Ask thee a sign of the Lord thy God. The Lord Himself shall give you a sign; Behold, a virgin shall conceive, and bear a son, and shall call His name Immanuel.*" Is. 7:11,14

Immanuel means "*God with us*" because Jesus was God with us (See Jn. 1).

"... *for God is with us.*" Is. 8:10

We are told in Matt. 1:23 that one of Jesus' names would be Immanuel, which means "*God with us*".

"*Sanctify the Lord of hosts Himself...*" Is. 8:13 PB

> **The Promise:**
> "... *He is your God and He is your helper.*" Is. 8:13 PB

"*Behold, I and the children whom the Lord hath given me...*" Is. 8:18
"*Here am I, and the children* (child) *the Lord has given me.*" Is. 8:18 NIV

Prayer:
Father in heaven, when I get to heaven, please let me be able to say, "*Here I am with my child/children You gave me.*" In Jesus' name, Amen!

Promise of the Messiah, Jesus.

"*The people that walked in darkness have seen a great light: they that dwell in the land of the shadow of death, upon them hath the light shined.*" Is. 9:2

> **The Promise:**
> "*Israel will again be great, and its people will rejoice as people rejoice at harvest time. They will shout with joy like warriors dividing the plunder. For God will break the chains that bind His people and the whip that scourges them, just as He did when He destroyed the army of Midian with Gideon's little band.* **In that day** *battle gear will no longer be issued. Never again will uniforms be bloodstained by war. All such equipment will be burned.*" Is. 9:3-5 NLT

This promise will ultimately be fulfilled on the New Earth, on the *"day of peace"*. That will be the day when *"swords are turned into plowshares... neither shall they learn war anymore"* (Is. 2:4) and there will never again be any kind of war.

"Then at last those left in Israel and Judah will trust the Lord..." Is. 10: 20 NLT

Promise to Israel
"So this is what the Lord, the Lord Almighty, says: My people in Jerusalem, do not be afraid... when they oppress you..." Is. 10:26 NLT
"And it shall come to pass in that day, that his burden shall be taken away from off thy shoulder, and his yoke from off thy neck. And the yoke shall be destroyed because of the anointing." Is. 10:27
"... He will break the yoke of slavery and lift it from their shoulders." Is. 10:27 NLT
"... the yoke will be broken..." Is. 10:27 NASB
The promise was originally given to Judah from Isaiah about the Assyrian and Babylonian captivity but we may need to claim this promise to break the bondage of things in our own lives.

> **The Promise:**
> *"... the haughty shall be humbled."* Is. 10:33

"... the lofty will be brought low." Is. 10:33 ESV
"... the tall ones will be brought low." Is. 10:33 NIV
"O Lord, I will praise Thee: though Thou wast angry with me ..." Is. 12:1

> **The Promise:**
> *"Thine anger is turned away, and Thou comfortedst me. Behold, God is my Salvation; I will trust, and not be afraid: for the Lord Jehovah is my strength and my song; He also is become my Salvation. Therefore with joy shall ye draw water out of the wells of Salvation."* Is. 12:1-3

God does excellent things
"And in that day shall ye say, praise the Lord, call upon His name, declare His doings among the people, make mention that His name is exalted. Sing unto the Lord; for He hath done excellent things..." Is. 12:4,5

"I will make a man more precious than fine gold: even a man than the golden wedge of Ophir." Is. 13:12

"... and they shall rule over their oppressors. And it shall come to pass in the day that the Lord shall give thee rest from thy sorrow, and from thy fear, and from the hard bondage wherein thou wast made to serve, that thou shalt take up this proverb... and say... the Lord hath broken the staff of the wicked, and the scepter of the rulers." Is. 14:2-5

"... then shall His yoke depart from off them, and His burden depart from off their shoulders." Is. 14:25

"The Lord Almighty has sworn this oath: 'It will all happen as I have planned. It will come about according to My purposes. I will break the Assyrians when they are in Israel; I will trample them on My mountains. My people will no longer be their slaves. I have a plan for the whole earth, for My mighty power reaches throughout the world. The Lord Almighty has spoken – who can change His plans? When His hand moves, who can stop Him?' Is. 14:24-27 NLT

No one can change God's plans or stop Him. He is the highest authority!

Prayer:

Father in heaven, I pray that nothing masters me and that I no longer will be a slave to anything. Let Your plans for me be accomplished in Jesus' name, Amen!

> **The Promise:**
> *"... the needy shall lie down in safety..."* Is. 14:30
>
> **The Promise:**
> *"... none shall make them afraid."* Is. 17:2

Blessed

"And the Lord shall smite Egypt: He shall smite and heal it: and they shall return even to the Lord, and He shall be intreated of them, and shall heal them... the Lord of hosts shall bless, saying, Blessed be... My people... the work of My hands... Mine inheritance." Is. 19:22-25

> **The Promise:**
> *"For Thou hast been a strength to the poor, a strength to the needy in his distress, a refuge from the storm, a shadow from the heat, when the blast of the terrible ones is as a storm against the wall."* Is. 25:4
>
> **The Promise:**
> *"... for in the Lord, Jehovah is everlasting strength."* Is. 25:4
>
> **The Promise:**
> *"He will swallow up death forever. The... Lord will wipe away the tears from all faces; He will remove His people's disgrace from all the earth... He will save us..."* Is. 25:8,9 (see Rev. 21:4)

"O death where is thy sting, O grave where is thy victory?" I Cor. 15:55

The Condition:
"Open ye the gates, that the righteous nation which keepeth the truth may enter in..." Is. 26:2

> **The Promise:**
> *"Thou wilt keep him in perfect peace..."* Is. 26:3

The Condition:
"... whose mind is stayed on Thee: because he trusteth in Thee. Trust ye in the Lord forever..." Is. 26:3,4

"My soul yearns for you in the night; in the morning my spirit longs for you. When your Judgments come upon the earth..." Is. 26:9

> **The Promise:**
> *"... the people of the world learn righteousness."* Is. 26:9

Prayer:
"Lord, Thou wilt ordain peace for us: for Thou also hast wrought all our works in us." Is. 26:12
"... all that we have accomplished you have done for us." Is. 26:12 NIV
"O Lord, Thou wilt give us peace..." Is. 26:12 PB
"Come, My people, enter thou into thy chambers, and shut thy doors about thee: hide thyself as it were for a little moment, until the indignation be overpast." Is. 26:20

In that day *"... sing ye unto her a vineyard..."* Is. 27:2

> **The Promise:**
> *"... I the Lord do keep it; I will water it every moment; lest any hurt it, I will keep it night and day."* Is. 27:3

The Condition:
"... let him take hold of My strength, that he may make peace with Me..." Is. 27:5

> **The Promise:**
> *"... and he shall make peace with Me. He shall cause them that come of Jacob to take root: Israel shall blossom and bud, and fill the face of the world with fruit."* Is. 27:5,6

"... and they have filled the face of the earth (with) *increase."* Is. 27:6 YLT

"Therefore thus saith the Lord God, Behold, I lay in Zion for a foundation a Stone, a tried Stone, a precious Corner Stone, a Sure Foundation: he that believeth shall not make haste." Is. 28:16

Jesus is the Cornerstone, Acts 4:1-12; Rom. 9:33; Eph.2:20-22; I Pet. 2:4-8.

"... the one who relies on it will never be stricken with panic." Is. 28:16 NIV
"... the one who maintains his faith will not panic." Is. 28:16 NET Bible
"... whoever believes need never be shaken." Is. 28:16 NLT
"... the one who believes will be unshakable." Is. 28:16 HCSB
"... whoever believes firmly will not act hastily" Is. 28:16 ISV

The Condition:
"... in returning and rest..." Is. 30:15

> **The Promise:**
> *"... shall ye be saved..."* Is. 30:15

The Condition:
"... in quietness and in confidence..." Is. 30:15

> **The Promise:**
> *"... shall be your strength..."* Is. 30:15

"And therefore will the Lord wait, that He may be gracious unto you, and therefore will He be exalted, that He may have mercy upon you: for the Lord is a God of Judgment: blessed are all they that wait for Him. For the people shall dwell in Zion at Jerusalem..." Is. 30:18,19

> **The Promise:**
> *"... thou shalt weep no more: He will be very gracious unto thee at the voice of thy cry; when He shall hear it, He will answer thee."* Is. 30:19
>
> **The Promise:**
> *"And thine ears shall hear a word behind thee, saying, This is the way, walk ye in it, when ye turn to the right hand, and when ye turn to the left."* Is. 30:21
>
> **The Promise:**
> *"Then shall He give the rain of thy seed, that thou shalt sow the ground... and bread of the increase of the earth... it shall be fat and plenteous... shall thy cattle feed in large pastures."* Is. 30:23

"Then He will give you rain for the seed which you will sow in the ground, and bread from the yield of the ground, and it will be rich and plenteous; on that day your livestock will graze in a roomy pasture... on every lofty mountain and on every high hill there will be streams running with water...

the light of the moon will be as the light of the sun, and the light of the sun will be seven times brighter like the light of seven days, on the day the Lord binds up the fracture of His people, and heals the bruise He has inflicted." Is. 30:23-26 NASB

This promise will ultimately be fulfilled on the New Earth.

> **The Promise:**
> "Ye shall have a song, as in the night..." Is. 30:29

This is a promise for Jerusalem

"... the Lord spoken unto me, Like as the lion and the young lion roaring on his prey, when a multitude of shepherds is called forth against him, he will not be afraid of their voice, nor abase himself for the noise of them: so shall the Lord of hosts come down to fight for Mount Zion, and for the hill thereof. As birds flying, so will the Lord of hosts defend Jerusalem; defending also He will deliver it; and passing over He will preserve it." Is. 31:4,5

Prayer:
Father in heaven, please fight my battles for me and defend me and deliver me according to Your Word. Thank You! In Jesus' name, Amen!

A promise about Jesus

"Behold, a King shall reign in righteousness, and princes shall rule in Judgment. And a man shall be as an hiding place from the wind and a covert from the tempest; as rivers of water in a dry place, as the shadow of a great Rock in a weary land." Is. 32:1,2

"Look, a righteous King is coming! And honest princes will rule under him. Each one will be like a shelter from the wind and a refuge from the storm, like streams of water in the desert and the shadow of a great Rock in a parched land." Is. 32:1,2 NLT

This will be fulfilled on the New Earth.

Promise of a New Earth

"Until the Spirit be poured upon us from on high, and the wilderness be a fruitful field, and the fruitful field be counted for a forest. Then Judgment shall dwell in the wilderness, and righteousness remain in the fruitful field. And the work of righteousness shall be peace; and the effect of righteousness quietness and assurance forever..." Is. 32:15-17

> **The Promise:**
> "And My people shall dwell in a peaceable habitation, and in sure dwellings, and in quiet resting places..." Is. 32:18

Blessed
"Blessed are ye that sow beside all waters, that send forth thither the feet of the ox and the (donkey)." Is. 32:20

"And wisdom and knowledge shall be the stability of thy times, and strength of Salvation: the fear of the Lord is His treasure." Is. 33:6

"He will be the sure foundation for your times, a rich store of Salvation and wisdom and knowledge; the fear of the Lord is the key to this treasure." Is. 33:6 NIV

"Now will I rise, saith the Lord; now will I be exalted; now will I lift up Myself." Is. 33:10

"If I be lifted up, I will draw all men to Myself." Jn. 12:32

The Condition:
"He that walketh righteously, and speaketh uprightly; he that despiseth the gain of oppressions, that shaketh his hands from holding of bribes, that stoppeth his ears from hearing of blood, and shutteth his eyes from seeing evil..." Is. 33:15

> **The Promise:**
> *"He shall dwell on high: his place of defence shall be the munitions of rocks: bread shall be given him; his waters shall be sure. Thine eyes shall see the King in His beauty: they shall behold the land that is very far off."* Is. 33:16,17

Jesus is the King that will reign on the New Earth forever and ever.
"For the Lord is our Judge, the Lord is our lawgiver, the Lord is our King..." Is. 33:22

> **The Promise:**
> *"... He will save us."* Is. 33:22

Promise of New Earth
"And the inhabitant shall not say, I am sick: the people that dwell therein shall be forgiven their iniquity." Is. 33:24

"Seek ye out of the Book of the Lord, and read..." Is. 34:16

> **The Promise:**
> *"... no one of these (promises) shall fail, none shall want her mate..."* Is. 34:16

"... not one of these will be missing; none will lack its mate..." Is. 34:16 NASB

Prayer:
Thank You, Lord, that Your promises never fail. I know that if You say it, You will do it (Num. 23:19)! In Jesus' name, Amen!

"... for My mouth it hast commanded, and His Spirit it hath gathered them." Is. 34:16

Promise of the New Earth
"The wilderness and the solitary place shall be glad for them; and the desert shall rejoice, and blossom as the rose. It shall blossom abundantly... rejoice... with joy and singing: the glory of Lebanon shall be given unto it, the excellency of Carmel and Sharon, they shall see the glory of the Lord, and the excellency of our God. Say to them that are of a fearful heart, Be strong, fear not..." Is. 35:1-4

Second Coming and New Earth

The Promise:
"... behold, your God will come with vengeance (at the second Coming), even God with a recompence; He will come and save you. Then the eyes of the blind shall be opened, and the ears of the deaf shall be unstopped. Then shall the lame man leap as an hart and the tongue of the dumb sing: for in the wilderness shall waters break out, and streams in the desert. And the parched ground shall become a pool, and the thirsty land springs of water... and grass with reeds and rushes... a highway shall be there, and a way, and it shall be called The Way of Holiness; the unclean shall not pass over it; but it shall be for those: the wayfaring men, though fools, shall not err therein... the Redeemed shall walk there: and the ransomed of the Lord shall return, and come to Zion with songs and everlasting joy upon their heads: they shall obtain joy and gladness, and sorrow and sighing shall flee away." Is. 35:4-10

"... the Lord will surely deliver us..." Is. 36:15

This was a promise to Hezekiah for Jerusalem
"For I will defend this city to save it for Mine own sake..." Is. 37:35;38:6

Promise to king Hezekiah
"... I have heard thy prayer, I have seen thy tears... I will add unto (your) years. And I will deliver thee and this city... I will defend this city... this shall be a sign unto thee from the Lord, that the Lord will do this thing that He hath spoken..." Is. 38:5-7

Miracle
God told king Hezekiah to ask for a sign and he asked to have the sun go backwards and it did.
"Behold, I will bring again the shadow of the degrees, which is gone down in the sun dial... ten degrees backward. So the sun returned ten degrees, by which degrees it was gone down." Is. 38:8

Hezekiah asked of God
"Heal me and make me live..." Is. 38:15
> **The Promise:**
> *"... so wilt Thou recover me, and make me to live... but Thou hast in love to my soul delivered it from the pit of corruption: for Thou hast cast all my sins behind Thy back."* Is. 38:17

Prayer:
Father in heaven, please heal me, deliver me, and cast all my sins behind Your back. Thank You in Jesus' name, Amen!

Miracle
"For Isaiah had said, Let them take a lump of figs, and lay it for a plaster upon the boil, and he shall recover." Is. 38:21
God answers
Hezekiah had been sick but then was healed, Is. 39:1.

Jerusalem's warfare is over (fulfilled on the New Earth)
"Comfort ye, comfort ye My people, saith your God. Speak ye comfortably to Jerusalem, and cry unto her, that her warfare is accomplished, that her iniquity is pardoned: for she hath received of the Lord's hand double for all her sins. The voice of him that crieth in the wilderness, Prepare ye the way of the Lord, make straight in the desert a highway for our God. Every valley shall be exalted, and every mountain and hill shall be made low: and the crooked shall be made straight, and the rough places plain: and the glory of the Lord shall be revealed..." Is. 40:1-5
> **The Promise:**
> *"Behold, the Lord God will come* (at the 2nd coming of Jesus) *with strong hand, and His arm shall rule for Him: behold, His reward is with Him* (Rev. 22:12), *and His work before Him. He shall feed His flock like a Shepherd: He shall gather the lambs with His arm, and Shepherd: He shall gather the lambs with His arm, and carry them in His bosom, and shall gently lead those that are with young."* Is. 40:10,11

The Promise:
"... but the Word of our God shall stand forever." Is. 40:8

The Promise:
"He giveth power to the faint; and to them that have no might He increaseth strength..." Is. 40:29

"Even the youths shall faint and be weary, and the young men shall utterly fall..." Is. 40:30

The Promise:
"... they that wait upon the Lord shall renew their strength; they shall mount up with wings as eagles; they shall run, and not be weary; and they shall walk, and not faint." Is. 40:31

"... thou art My servant..." Is. 41:9

The Promise:
"... I have chosen thee, and not cast thee away..." Is. 41:9

"... fear thou not... " Is. 41:10

The Promise:
"... for I am with thee..." Is. 41:10

be not dismayed..." Is. 41:10

The Promise:
"... for I am thy God. I will strengthen thee; yea, I will help thee; yea, I will uphold thee with the right hand of My righteousness. Behold, all they that were incensed against thee shall be ashamed and confounded: they shall be as nothing; and they that strive with thee shall perish. Thou shalt seek them, and shalt not find them, even them that contended with thee: they that war against thee shall be as nothing, and as a thing of nought. For I the Lord thy God will hold thy right hand, saying unto thee, Fear not; I will help thee. Fear not, thou worm Jacob, and ye men of Israel; I will help thee, saith the Lord, and thy Redeemer, the Holy One of Israel... and thou shalt rejoice in the Lord, and shalt glory in the Holy One of Israel..." Is. 41:10-14

"When the poor and needy seek water, and there is none, and their tongue faileth for thirst..." Is. 41:17

The Promise:
"... I the Lord will hear them, I the God of Israel will not forsake them. I will open rivers in high places, and fountains in the midst of the valleys: I will make the wilderness a pool of water, and the dry land

springs of water. I will plant in the wilderness the Cedar, the Shittah tree, and the Myrtle, and the Oil tree; I will set in the desert, the Fir tree, and the Pine, and the Box tree together: that they may see, and know, and consider, and understand together, that the hand of the Lord hath done this, and the Holy One of Israel hath created it* (on the New Earth).*" Is. 41: 17-20

Promise of the Messiah (Jesus)
"Behold My servant, whom I uphold; Mine elect, in whom My soul delighteth; I have put My Spirit upon Him: He shall bring forth Judgment to the Gentiles. He shall not cry, nor lift up, nor cause His voice to be heard in the street. A bruised reed shall He not break, and the smoking flax shall He not quench: He shall bring forth Judgment unto truth. He shall not fail nor be discouraged, till He have set Judgment in the earth: and the isles shall wait for His law. Thus saith God the Lord, He that created the heavens, and stretched them out; He that spread forth the earth, and that which cometh out of it; He that giveth breath unto the people upon it, and Spirit to them that walk therein: I the Lord have called Thee in righteousness, and will hold Thine hand, and will keep Thee, and give Thee for a Covenant of the people, for a light of the Gentiles; to open the blind eyes, to bring out the prisoners from the prison, and them that sit in darkness out of the prison house." Is. 42:1-7

The Promise:
"Behold, the former things are come to pass, and new things do I declare: before they spring forth I tell you of them." Is. 42:9

The Promise:
"And I will bring the blind by a way that they knew not; I will lead them in paths that they have not known: I will make darkness light before them, and crooked things straight. These things will I do unto them, and not forsake them." Is. 42:16,18

Prayer:
Father in heaven; please make my paths straight and shine Your light on all my ways as it says in Your Word. Thank You in Jesus' name, Amen!

I called you by name
"... thus saith the Lord that created thee, O Jacob, and He that formed thee, O Israel, Fear not: for I have Redeemed thee, I have called thee by thy name; thou art Mine. When thou passest through the waters, I will be with thee; and through the rivers, they shall not overflow thee: when thou walkest

through the fire, thou shalt not be burned; neither shall the flame kindle upon thee." Is. 43:1,2

I have loved you
"For I am the Lord thy God, the Holy One of Israel, thy Saviour: I gave Egypt for thy ransom, Ethiopia and Seba for thee. Since thou wast precious in My sight, thou hast been honourable, and I have loved thee: therefore will I give men for thee, and people for thy life. Fear not: for I Am with thee: I will bring thy seed from the East, and gather thee from the West; I will say to the North, Give up; and to the South, Keep not back: bring My sons from far, and My daughters from the ends of the earth; even every one that is called by My name: for I have created him for My glory, I have formed him; yea, I have made him, Bring forth the blind people that have eyes, and the deaf that have ears. Let all the nations be gathered together, and let the people be assembled: who among them can declare this, and shew us former things? Let them bring forth their witnesses, that they may be Justified: or let them hear, and say, It is truth. Ye are My witnesses, saith the Lord, and My servant whom I have chosen: that ye may know and believe Me, and understand that I am He: before Me there was no God formed, neither shall there be after Me. I, even I, am the Lord; and beside Me there is no Saviour. I have declared, and have saved, and I have shewed, when there was no strange god among you: therefore ye are My witnesses, saith the Lord, that I am God. Yea, before the day was I am He; and there is none that can deliver out of My hand: I will work, and who shall let it? Thus saith the Lord, your Redeemer, the Holy One of Israel; for your sake I have sent to Babylon, and have brought down all their nobles, and the Chaldeans, whose cry is in the ships. I am the Lord, your Holy One, the Creator of Israel, your King ..." Is. 43:3-15

The Promise:
"... the Lord, which maketh a way in the sea, and a path in the mighty waters; which bringeth forth the chariot and horse... to give drink to My people, My chosen. This people have I formed for Myself; they shall shew forth My praise ..." Is. 43:16-21

Who can make God do anything or who can stop Him from doing anything? No one! No one can say, I let God do anything. God decides what He will do and no one can stop Him. He is above every principality and power (Eph. 1:21-28).

The Promise
"I, even I, am He that blotteth out thy transgressions for Mine own sake, and will not remember thy sins." Is. 43:25

See I Jn. 1:9

God says, *"Put Me in remembrance* (of My promises)*..."* Is. 43:26-28
Prayer:
Father in heaven, You said to remind You of Your promises, so please remem-ber Your promises toward me. Thank You in Jesus' name, Amen!

"... Israel, whom I have chosen." Is. 44:1 NKJV

"Thus saith the Lord that made thee, and formed thee from the womb ..." Is. 44:2

> **The Promise:**
> *"... which will help thee; Fear not, O Jacob, My servant; and thou, Jeshurun* (Israel)*, whom I have chosen. For I will pour water upon him that is thirsty, and floods upon the dry ground, I will pour My Spirit upon your seed and My blessings upon your offspring. And they shall spring up as among the grass, as willows by the water courses."* Is. 44:3,4

Jeshurun is another name for Israel and means, *"upright"*.
Prayer:
Father in heaven, please pour out Your Holy Spirit and Your blessings like water on my child/children. Thank You! In Jesus' name, Amen!
God's promise is that *"... apart from Me there is no God."* Is. 44:6
"Fear ye not, neither be afraid: have not I told thee from that time, and have declared it? Ye are even My witnesses. Is there a God beside Me? yea, there is no God; I know not any." Is. 44:8

"Remember these, O Jacob and Israel; for thou art My servant: I have formed thee; thou art My servant: O Israel" Is. 44:21

> **The Promise:**
> *"... thou shalt not be forgotten of Me. I have blotted out, as a thick cloud, thy transgressions, and, as a cloud, thy sins. Return unto Me; for I have Redeemed thee..."* Is. 44:21,22

God formed you in the womb
"... the Lord hath Redeemed Jacob, and glorified Himself in Israel. Thus saith the Lord, thy Redeemer, and He that formed thee from the womb, I am the Lord that maketh all things; that stretcheth forth the heavens alone: that spreadeth abroad the earth by Myself..." Is. 44:23,24

"Who carries out the words of His servants and fulfills the predictions of His messengers..." Is. 44:26 NIV

"I will go before thee, and make the crooked places straight: I will break in pieces the gates of brass, and cut in sunder the bars of iron: and I will give thee the treasures of darkness, and hidden riches of secret places, that thou mayest know that I, the Lord, which call thee by thy name, am the God of Israel." Is. 45:2,3

"Thus saith the Lord, the Holy One of Israel, and his (Israel's) Maker, Ask Me of things to come concerning My sons, and concerning the work of My hands command ye Me. I have made the earth, and created man upon it: I, even My hands, have stretched out the heavens, and all their host have I commanded. I have raised him up in righteousness, and I will direct all his ways: he shall build My city, and he shall let go My captives, not for price nor reward, saith the Lord of hosts... they shall come over, and they shall fall down unto thee, they shall make supplication unto thee, saying..." Is. 45:11-14

> **The Promise:**
> "Surely God is in thee; and there is none else, there is no (other) God... but Israel shall be saved in the Lord with an everlasting Salvation: ye shall not be ashamed nor confounded..." Is. 45:14-17

"... they shall walk behind you, they shall come over in chains; and they shall bow down to you. They will make supplication to you, saying, Surely God is in you, and there is no other... they shall be ashamed and also disgraced, all of them; they shall go in confusion together, who are makers of idols." Is. 45:14-16 NKJV

"Truly Thou art a shelter..." Is. 45:15 PB

No God besides Me
"Tell ye, and bring them near; yea, let them take counsel together: who hath declared this from ancient time? Who hath told it from that time? Have not I the Lord? And there is no God else beside Me; a just God and a Saviour; there is none beside Me. Look unto Me..." Is. 45:21-22

> **The Promise:**
> "...and be ye saved, all the ends of the earth: for I am God, and there is none else. I have sworn by Myself, the Word is gone out of My mouth in righteousness, and shall not return... that unto Me every knee shall bow every tongue shall swear. Surely, shall one say, in the Lord have I righteousness and strength: even to Him shall men come; and all that are incensed against Him shall be ashamed. In the Lord shall all the seed of Israel be Justified, and shall glory." Is. 45:21-25

Someday those who are angry with God will be ashamed!
"At the name of Jesus every knee shall bow... and that every tongue will confess that Jesus Christ is Lord..." Phil. 2:9,10

"Listen to Me..." Is. 46:3

> **The Promise:**
> *"... you whom I have upheld since you were conceived, and have carried since your birth. And even to your old age I am He; and even to... (grey) hairs will I carry you: I have made, and I will bear; even I will carry, and will deliver you."* Is. 46:3,4

"I will be your God through all your lifetime, yes, even when your hair is white with age. I made you and I will care for you. I will carry you along and be your Savior." Is. 46:4 LB

Prayer:
Thank You, Lord, that You have been there for me and taken care of me all my life, since I was born. I'm thankful that I can trust You to take care of me when I get old as well. In Jesus' name, Amen!

"Remember the former things of old, for I am God, and there is none else; I am God, and there is none like Me, declaring the end from the beginning, and from ancient times the things that are not yet done ("what is still to come." NIV), saying, My counsel shall stand, and I will do all My pleasure..." Is. 46:9-10

> **The Promise:**
> *"... yea, I have spoken it, I will also bring it to pass; I have purposed it, I will also do it."* Is. 46:11

"What I have said, that will I bring about; what I have planned, that will I do. Listen to Me you stubbornhearted ("stouthearted" KJV), that are far from righteousness: I am bringing My righteousness near; it is not far away: and My Salvation shall not be delayed. I will grant Salvation in Zion, My splendor to Israel." Is. 46:11-13 NIV

> **The Promise:**
> *"I have declared the former things from the beginning; and they went forth out of My mouth, and I showed them; I did them suddenly, and they came to pass... I have even from the beginning declared it to thee; before it came to pass I showed it thee..."* Is. 48:5

God will bring to pass the things He has promised and He will do it!

> **The Promise:**
> *"I have made his way prosperous"* Is. 48:15 PB

"... his way will prosper." Is. 48:15 NKJV

"... I am the Lord thy God which teacheth thee to profit, which leadeth thee by the way that thou shouldest go." Is. 48:17
"... I am the Lord God who teaches you not to do wrong ..." Is. 48:17 PB
The Condition:
"O that thou hadst hearkened to My Commandments..." Is. 48:18

> **The Promise:**
> *"... then had thy peace been as a river, and thy righteousness as the waves of the sea: thy seed also had been as the sand, and the offspring of thy bowels like the gravel thereof... the Lord hath Redeemed His servant Jacob."* Is. 48:18-20

"And they thirsted not when He led them through the deserts: He caused the waters to flow out of the Rock for them: He clave the Rock also, and the waters gushed out." Is. 48:21

I said *"... I have labored in vain, I have spent my strength for nothing and futility; yet my vindication is with the Lord, and my reward is with my God ."* Is. 49:4 HCSB
"And now, saith the Lord that formed me from the womb to be His servant, to bring Jacob again to Him, Though Israel be not gathered, yet shall I be glorious in the eyes of the Lord..." Is. 49:5

> **The Promise:**
> *"... and my God shall be my strength."* Is. 49:5

"And He said, It is a light thing that thou shouldest be My servant to raise up the tribes of Jacob, and to restore the preserved of Israel..." Is. 49:6

About Jesus.
"Thus saith the Lord, the Redeemer of Israel, and His Holy One, to Him whom man despiseth, to Him whom the nation abhorreth, to a servant of rulers, kings shall see and arise, princes also shall worship, because of the Lord that is faithful, and the Holy One of Israel..." Is. 49:7

> **The Promise:**
> *"I will also give thee for a light to the Gentiles, that thou mayest be ("bring" NIV) My Salvation unto the end of the earth."* Is. 49:6

> **The Promise:**
> *"... and He shall choose thee. Thus saith the Lord, In an acceptable time have I heard thee, and in a day of Salvation have I helped thee: and I will preserve thee, and give thee for a Covenant of the people*

to establish the earth, to cause to inherit the desolate heritages, that thou mayest say to the prisoners, Go forth; to them that are in darkness, Show yourselves. They shall feed in the ways, and their pastures shall be in all high places. They shall not hunger nor thirst; neither shall the heat nor sun smite them: for He that hath mercy on them shall lead them, even by the springs of water shall He guide them. And I will make all My mountains a way, and My highways shall be be exalted. Behold, these shall come from far: and, lo, these from the North and from the West... sing, O heavens; and be joyful, O earth; and break forth into singing, O mountains: for the Lord hath comforted His people, and will have mercy upon His afflicted." Is. 49:7-13

To the despised and rejected, God has chosen you!
"The Lord, the Redeemer and Holy One of Israel, says to the one who is despised, rejected by mankind, and kept beneath the heel of earthly rulers: 'Kings shall stand at attention when you pass by; princes shall bow low because the Lord has chosen you; He, the faithful Lord, the Holy One of Israel, chooses you.' The Lord says, 'Your request has come at a favorable time. I will keep you from premature harm...'" Is. 49:7-9 LB
"In the time of My favor I will answer you, and in the day of Salvation I will help you; I will keep you..." Is. 49:8 NIV
"Sing, O heavens; and be joyful, O earth; and break forth into singing, O mountains: for the Lord hath comforted His people, and will have mercy upon His afflicted." Is. 49:13

"Can a woman forget her sucking child, that she should not have compassion on the son of her womb? Yea, they may forget..." Is. 49:15

> **The Promise:**
> "... yet will I not forget thee. Behold, I have graven thee upon the palms of My hands; thy walls are continually before me." Is. 49:15,16

Your enemies will be your servants

> **The Promise:**
> "Soon your rebuilders shall come and chase away all those destroying you. Look and see, for the Lord has vowed that all your enemies shall come and be your slaves. They will be as jewels to display, as bridal ornaments." Is. 49:17,18 LB

Promise of Messiah
"And in that day shall the deaf hear the words of the book, and the eyes of the blind shall see out of obscurity, and out of darkness. The meek also shall increase their joy in the Lord, and the poor among men shall rejoice in the Holy One of Israel." Is. 49:18,19

"... all your children will come back to you... they will be like jewels... to display." Is. 49:18 NLT

This will ultimately be fulfilled in heaven.
"The Lord God says, 'See, I will give a signal to the Gentiles and they shall carry your little sons back to you in their arms, and your daughters on their shoulders. Kings and queens shall serve you; they shall care for all your needs. They shall bow to the earth before you, and lick the dust from off your feet; then you shall know I am the Lord. Those who wait for Me shall never be ashamed." Is. 49:22, 23 LB

"... for I will contend with him that contendeth with thee..." Is. 49:25
"... for I will fight those who fight you..." Is. 49:25 LB

> **The Promise:**
> *"... and I will save thy children."* Is. 49:25,26

"... is My hand shortened at all, that it cannot Redeem? Or have I no power to deliver? Behold, at My rebuke I dry up the sea... I clothe the heavens with blackness..." Is. 50:2,3

The promise is that He will Redeem and will deliver, Is. 59:1.

> **The Promise:**
> *"The Lord God hath given me the tongue of the learned, that I should know how to speak a word in season to him that is weary: he wakeneth morning by morning, he wakeneth mine ear to hear as the learned. The Lord God hath opened mine ear, and I was not rebellious, neither turned away back."* Is. 50:3-5

> **The Promise:**
> *"For the Lord God will help me; therefore shall I not be confounded: therefore have I set my face like a flint, and I know that I shall not be ashamed. He is near that Justifieth me; who will contend with me? let us stand together: who is mine adversary? Let him come near to me. Behold, the Lord God will help me; who is he that shall condemn me?"* Is. 50:7-9

"Because the Sovereign Lord helps me, I will not be disgraced." Is. 50:7 NIV
"... who will dare to fight against me now..." Is. 50:8 LV
"... let them trust the Lord, let them rely upon their God." Is. 50:10 LB
Prayer:
Thank You, Lord, that You are near to me and help me in my troubles. I thank You that whoever fights against me has to fight You instead. In Jesus' name, Amen!

Blessed
"... for I called him (Abraham) *alone, and blessed him, and increased him. For the Lord shall comfort Zion: He will comfort all her waste places; and He will make her wilderness like Eden, and her desert like the garden of the Lord; joy and gladness shall be found therein, thanksgiving, and the voice of melody."* Is. 51:2,3

God blessed Abraham and we are blessed through Abraham, Gal. 3:14
"... on My arm they will trust... My Salvation will be forever, and My righteousness will not be abolished." Is. 51:5,6 NKJV

> **The Promise:**
> *"Therefore the Redeemed of the Lord shall return, and come with singing unto Zion; and everlasting joy shall be upon their head: they shall obtain gladness and joy; and sorrow and mourning shall flee away. I called him... and blessed him, and increased him."* Is. 51:11, 12

They came back to Judah after the seventy-year captivity but ultimately we come to the New Earth.
"And I have put My words in your mouth; I have covered you with the shadow of My hand... and say to Zion, you are My people." Is. 51:16

"... Jerusalem loose yourself from the bonds of your neck..." Is. 52:2 NKJV
We are given the keys of bind and loosing in Matt. 16:19;18:18.

> **The Promise:**
> *"... and ye shall be Redeemed without money."* Is. 52:3

We're Redeemed by the blood of Jesus.

"... My people shall know My name..." Is. 52:6 NKJV

"How beautiful upon the mountains are the feet of him that bringeth good tidings, that publisheth peace; that bringeth good tidings of good, that publisheth Salvation; that saith unto Zion, Thy God reigneth!" Is. 52:7
"Break forth into joy, sing together, ye waste places of Jerusalem: for the Lord hath comforted His people, He hath Redeemed Jerusalem. The Lord hath made bare His Holy arm in the eyes of all the nations; and all the ends of the earth shall see the Salvation of our God." Is. 52:9,10
"For ye shall not go out with haste, nor go by flight..." Is. 52:12

The Promise:
"... for the Lord will go before you; and the God of Israel will be your rearward ("rear guard" NIV)." Is. 52:12

"... from behind." Is. 52:12 LB

The Promise:
"So shall He sprinkle many nations (by the blood of Jesus); *the kings shall shut their mouths at Him: for that which had not been told them shall they see; and that which they had not heard shall they consider."* Is. 52:15

Promise about Jesus
"Surely He hath borne our griefs, and carried our sorrows: yet we did esteem Him stricken, smitten of God, and afflicted. But He was wounded for our transgressions, He was bruised for our iniquities: the chastisement of our peace was upon Him; and with His stripes we are healed. All we like sheep have gone astray; we have turned every one to his own way; and the Lord hath laid on Him the iniquity of us all." Is. 53:4-6

Prayer:
Thank You, Lord, that You bear all my sorrows, griefs, and sins. Thank You for taking the lashes that heal me. In Jesus' name, Amen!

"Sing, O barren, thou that didst not bear; break forth into singing, and cry aloud, thou that didst not travail with child..." Is. 54:1

The Promise:
"... for more are the children of the desolate than the children of the married wife, saith the Lord." Is. 54:1

You will not be ashamed
"Enlarge the place of thy tent, and let them stretch forth the curtains of thine habitations: spare not, lengthen thy cords, and strengthen thy stakes; for thou shalt break forth on the right hand and on the left; and thy seed shall inherit the Gentiles, and make the desolate cities to be inhabited. Fear not;

for thou shalt not be ashamed: neither be thou confounded; for thou shalt not be put to shame: for thou shalt forget the shame of thy youth, and shalt not remem-ber the reproach of thy widowhood anymore. For thy Maker is thine husband; the Lord of hosts is His name; and thy Redeemer the Holy One of Israel; the God of the whole earth shall He be called. For thou shalt break forth on the right hand and on the left; and thy seed shall inherit the Gentiles, and make the desolate cities to be inhabited. For the Lord hath called thee as a woman forsaken and grieved in spirit, and a wife of youth, when thou wast refused, saith thy God. For a small moment have I forsaken thee; but with great mercies will I gather thee. In a little wrath I hid My face from thee for a moment; but with everlasting kindness will I have mercy on thee, saith the Lord thy Redeemer." Is. 54:2-8

"For this is as the waters of Noah unto Me: for as I have sworn that the waters of Noah should no more go over the earth..." Is. 54:9

The Promise:
"... I would not be wroth with thee, nor rebuke thee. For the mountains shall depart, and the hills be removed; but My kindness shall not depart from thee, neither shall the Covenant of My peace be removed, saith the Lord that hath mercy on thee. ..." Is. 54:9,10

The Promise:
"... behold, I will lay thy (New Jerusalem) *stones with fair colours, and lay thy foundations with sapphires* (Rev.21:19). *And I will make thy windows of agates, and thy gates of carbuncles, and all thy borders of pleasant stones."* Is. 54: 11,12

Carbuncles are a red gem (can be a garnet).
"... O thou afflicted, tossed with tempest, and not comforted..." Is. 54:11

The Promise:
"And all thy children shall be taught of the Lord; and great shall be the peace of thy children." Is. 54:13

Prayer:
Father in heaven, please teach my child/children and give them peace as You promised in Your Word. Thank You in Jesus' name, Amen!

The Promise:
"In righteousness shalt thou be established: thou shalt be far from oppression; for thou shalt not fear: and from terror; for it shall not come near thee." Is. 54:14

The Promise:
"... whoever attacks you will surrender to you." Is. 54:15 NIV

The Promise:
"No weapon that is formed against thee shall prosper; and every tongue that shall rise against thee in Judgment thou shalt condemn. This is the heritage of the servants of the Lord, and their righteousness is of Me, saith the Lord." Is. 54:17

"Ho, every one that thirsteth, come ye to the waters, and he that hath no money; come ye, buy, and eat; yea, come, buy wine and milk without money and without price. Wherefore do ye spend money for that which is not bread? And your labour for that which satisfieth not? Hearken diligently unto Me, and eat ye that which is good, and let your soul delight itself in fatness. Incline your ear, and come unto Me..." Is. 55:1-3

The Promise:
"... and your soul shall live; and I will make an everlasting Covenant with you, even the sure mercies of David." Is. 55:3

"Behold, I have given him for a witness to the people, a leader and commander to the people. Behold, thou shalt call a nation that thou knowest not, and nations that knew not Thee shall run unto Thee because of the Lord thy God, and for the Holy One of Israel; for He hath glorified thee..." Is. 55:4,5

The Condition:
"... seek ye the Lord while He may be found, call ye upon Him while He is near: let the wicked forsake his way, and the unrighteous man his thoughts: and let him return unto the Lord..." Is. 55:6,7

God's Word will not return void!!!
"For My thoughts are not your thoughts, neither are your ways My ways, saith the Lord. For as the heavens are higher than the earth, so are My ways higher than your ways, and My thoughts than your thoughts. For as the rain cometh down, and the snow from heaven, and returneth not thither, but watereth the earth, and maketh it bring forth and bud, that it may give seed to the sower, and bread to the eater..." Is. 55:8-10

The Promise:
"... so shall My Word be that goeth forth out of my mouth: it shall not return unto Me void, but it shall accomplish that which I please, and it shall prosper in the thing whereto I sent it. For ye shall go out with joy, and be led forth with peace: the mountains and the hills shall break forth before you into singing, and all the trees of the field shall clap their hands. Instead of the thorn shall come up the fir tree, and instead of the brier shall come up the Myrtle tree: and it shall be to the Lord for a name, for an everlasting sign..." Is. 55: 11-13

Prayer:
Father in heaven, please send forth Your Word and let it accomplish Your will in my life and prosper. Thank You in Jesus' name, Amen!

Blessed
"Blessed is the man that doeth this, and the son of man that layeth hold on it; that keepeth the Sabbath from polluting it, and keepeth his hand from doing any evil. Neither let the son of the stranger, that hath joined himself to the Lord, speak, saying, The Lord hath utterly separated me from His people: neither let the eunuch say, Behold, I am a dry tree. For thus saith the Lord unto the eunuchs that keep My Sabbaths, and choose the things that please Me, and take hold of My Covenant; even unto them will I give in Mine house and within my walls a place and a name better than of sons and of daughters: I will give them an everlasting name, that shall not be cut off. Also the sons of the stranger, that join themselves to the Lord, to serve Him, and to love the name of the Lord, to be His servants, every one that keepeth the Sabbath from polluting it, and taketh hold of My Covenant; even them will I bring to My Holy Mountain, and make them joyful in My house of prayer: their burnt offerings and their sacrifices shall be accepted upon Mine altar; for Mine house shall be called an house of prayer for all people. The Lord God, which gathereth the outcasts of Israel saith, Yet will I gather others to Him, beside those that are gathered unto Him." Is. 56:2-8

"He shall enter into peace: they shall rest in their beds, each one walking in his uprightness." Is. 57:2

The Condition:
"... he that putteth his trust in Me..." Is. 57:13

> **The Promise:**
> "... shall possess the land, and shall inherit My Holy Mountain ..." Is. 57:13

"For thus saith the high and lofty One that inhabiteth eternity, whose name is Holy; I dwell in the high and Holy place, with him also that is of a contrite and humble spirit, to revive the spirit of the humble, and to revive the heart of the contrite ones." Is. 57:15

> **The Promise:**
> "I have seen his ways, and will heal him: I will lead him also, and restore comforts unto him and to his mourners. I create the fruit of the lips; Peace, peace to him that is far off, and to him that is near, saith the Lord; and I will heal him." Is. 57:18,19

"I have healed her... I have given comfort to her. I create the (speech) of the lips... I will heal them." Is. 57:18,19 PB

The Promise:
"Then shall thy light break forth as the morning, and thine health shall spring forth speedily: and thy righteousness shall go before thee; the glory of the LORD shall be thy reward. Then shalt thou call, and the LORD shall answer; thou shalt cry, and He shall say, Here I am." Is. 58:8,9

Prayer:
Thank You, Lord, that as soon as I call to You, You answer and say, Here I am!

The Condition:
"If thou take away from the midst of thee the yoke, the putting forth of the finger, and speaking vanity; and if thou draw out thy soul to the hungry, and satisfy the afflicted soul..." Is. 58:9,10

The Promise:
"... then shall thy light rise in obscurity, and thy darkness be as the noon day: and the Lord shall guide thee continually, and satisfy thy soul in drought, and make fat thy bones: and thou shalt be like a watered garden, and like a spring of water, whose waters fail not.. And they that shall be of thee shall build the old waste places: thou shalt raise up the foundations of many generations; and thou shalt be called The repairer of the breach, The restorer of paths to dwell in." Is. 58:10-12

The Condition:
"If thou turn away thy foot from the Sabbath, from doing thy pleasure on My Holy Day; and call the Sabbath a delight, the Holy of the Lord, honourable; and shalt honour Him, not doing thine own ways, nor finding thine own pleasure, nor speaking thine own words." Is. 58:13

The Promise:
"... then shalt thou delight thyself in the Lord; and I will cause thee to ride upon the high places of the earth, and feed thee with the heritage of Jacob thy father: for the mouth of the Lord hath spoken it." Is. 58:14

The Promise:
"Behold, the Lord's hand is not shortened, that it cannot save; neither His ear heavy, that it cannot hear..." Is. 59:1

The Condition:
"... but your iniquities have separated between you and your God, and your sins have hid His face from you, that He will not hear." Is. 59:1,2

Prayer:
Father in heaven, please forgive me of my sins and wash me clean by the blood of Jesus because I don't want anything to keep You from hearing my prayers. Please give me the victory over sin through the power of the Holy Spirit so that I can please You in everything I do. Thank You in Jesus' name, Amen!

"... therefore His (Jesus') own arm brought Salvation for Him; and His own righteousness, it sustained Him!" Is. 59:16 NKJV

"So shall they fear the name of the Lord from the West, and His glory from the rising of the sun. When the enemy shall come in like a flood..." Is. 59:19

The Promise:
"... the Spirit of the Lord shall lift up a standard against him. And the Redeemer shall come to Zion, and unto them that turn from transgression in Jacob, saith the Lord. As for Me, this is My Covenant with them, saith the Lord: My Spirit that is upon thee, and My words which I have put in thy mouth, shall not depart out of thy mouth, nor with them, saith the Lord: My Spirit that is upon thee, and My Words which I have put in thy mouth, shall not depart out of thy mouth, nor out of the mouth of thy seed, nor out of the mouth of thy seed's seed, saith the Lord, from henceforth and forever..." Is. 59:19-21

Prayer:
Father in heaven, when the enemy tries to come in like a flood into my life, I ask that Your Holy Spirit will raise up a standard against him and help me turn away from temptation. Please don't let Your Spirit or Word depart from me or my child/children forever. Thank You in Jesus' name, Amen!

A promise about the New Jerusalem
"Arise, shine; for thy light is come, and the glory of the Lord is risen upon thee. For, behold the darkness shall cover the earth, and gross darkness the people..." Is. 60:1,2

The Promise:
"... but the Lord shall arise upon thee, and His glory shall be seen upon thee. And the Gentiles shall come to thy light, and kings to the brightness of thy rising. Lift up thine eyes round to thee: thy sons shall come from far, and thy daughters shall be nursed at thy side. Then thou shalt see, and flow together, and thine heart shall fear, and be enlarged; because the abundance of the sea shall be converted unto Thee, the forces of the Gentiles shall come unto Thee. The multitude of camels shall cover thee, the dromedaries of Midian and Ephah; all they from Sheba shall come: they shall bring gold and Incense; and they shall shew forth the praises of the Lord. All the flocks of Kedar shall be gathered together unto thee, the rams of Nebaioth shall minister unto thee: they shall come up with acceptance on Mine altar, and I will glorify the house of My glory." Is. 60:2-7

"Who are these that fly as a cloud, and as the doves to their windows? Surely the isles shall wait for me, and the ships of Tarshish first, to bring thy sons from far, their silver and their gold with them, unto the name of the Lord thy God, and to the Holy One of Israel, because He hath glorified thee. And the sons of strangers shall build up thy walls, and their kings shall minister unto thee..." Is. 60:8-10

Speaking of the New Jerusalem

The Promise:
"... in My favour have I had mercy on thee... (Your gates) shall be open continually (Rev. 21:25); they shall not be shut day nor night; that men may bring unto thee the forces of the Gentiles, and that their kings may be brought. For the nation and kingdom that will not serve Thee shall perish; yea, those nations shall be utterly wasted. The glory of Lebanon shall come unto thee, the Fir tree, the Pine tree, and the Box together, to beautify the place of My Sanctuary; and I will make the place of My feet glorious. The sons also of them that afflicted thee shall come bending unto thee; and all they that despised thee shall bow themselves down at the soles of thy feet; and they shall call thee; The City of the Lord, The Zion of the Holy One of Israel." Is. 60:10-14

About the New Jerusalem
The Promise:
"... I will make thee (Jerusalem) *an eternal excellency, a joy of many generations...* ("powerful kings and mighty nations will satisfy your every need, as though you were a child nursing... a queen." vs. 16 NLT) *and thou shalt know that I the Lord am thy Saviour and thy Redeemer, the mighty One of Jacob. For brass I will bring gold, and for iron I will bring silver, and for wood brass, and for stones iron: I will also make thy officers peace, and thine exactors righteousness. Violence shall no more be heard in thy land, wasting nor destruction within thy borders; but thou shalt call thy walls Salvation, and thy gates Praise. The sun shall be no more thy light by day; neither for brightness shall the moon give light unto thee: but the Lord shall be unto thee an everlasting light, and thy God thy glory* (Rev. 21:23). *itself: for the Lord shall be thine everlasting light, and the days of thy mourning shall be ended. Thy people also shall be all righteous: they shall inherit the land forever, the branch of My planting, the work of My hands, that I may be glorified."* Is. 60:15-21

The glory of God will be so great in the New Jerusalem that we won't even see the sun or moon but there will be a sun and moon on the New Earth because it says in Is. 30:26 that the sun will be seven times brighter and the moon will be like the sun.
"All Your righteous people shall inherit the land forever." Is. 60:20 PB
"A little one shall become a thousand and a small one a strong nation." Is. 60:22

Promise about Jesus
"The Spirit of the Lord God is upon Me; because the Lord hath anointed Me to preach good tidings unto the meek... to bind up the brokenhearted, to proclaim liberty to the captives, and the opening of the prison to them that are bound; to proclaim the acceptable year of the Lord, and the day of the vengeance of our God; to comfort all that mourn; to appoint unto them that mourn in Zion, to give unto them beauty for ashes, the oil of joy for mourning, the garment of praise for the spirit of heaviness; that they might be called trees of righteousness, the planting of the Lord, that He might be glorified. And they shall build the old wastes, they shall raise up the former desolations, and they shall repair the waste cities, the desolations of many generations. And strangers shall stand and feed your flocks, and the sons of the alien shall be your plowmen and your vinedressers. But ye shall be named the Priests of the Lord: men shall call you the Ministers of our God:

ye shall eat the riches of the Gentiles, and in their glory shall ye boast yourselves." Is. 61:1-6

A double portion
"For your shame ye shall have double; and for confusion they shall rejoice in their portion: therefore in their land they shall possess the double: everlasting joy shall be unto them. For I the Lord love Judgment, I hate robbery for burnt offering; and I will direct their work in truth, and I will make an everlasting Covenant with them. And their seed shall be known among the Gentiles, and their offspring among the people: all that see them shall acknowledge them, that they are the seed which the Lord hath blessed. I will greatly rejoice in the Lord, my soul shall be joyful in my God; for He hath clothed me with the garments of Salvation, He hath covered me with the robe of righteousness, as a bridegroom decketh himself with ornaments, and as a bride adorneth herself with her jewels. For as the earth bringeth forth her bud, and as the garden causeth the things that are sown in it to spring forth..." Is. 61:7-11
"... you shall have double honor... and they will rejoice in their portion... they shall possess double; everlasting joy shall be theirs." Is. 61:7 NKJV

> **The Promise:**
> "... so the Lord God will cause righteousness and praise to spring forth before all the nations." Is. 61:11

Jerusalem
"For Zion's sake will I not hold My peace, and for Jerusalem's sake I will not rest, until the righteousness thereof go forth as brightness, and the Salvation thereof as a lamp that burneth. And the Gentiles shall see Thy righteousness, and all kings Thy glory: and thou shalt be called by a new name (New Jerusalem), which the mouth of the Lord shall name. Thou shalt also be a crown of glory in the hand of the Lord, and a royal diadem in the hand of thy God. Thou shalt no more be termed Forsaken (Agaubah, the name of the mother of Jehoshaphat); neither shall thy land anymore be termed Desolate ("Shemamah"): but thou shalt be called Hephzibah (means, "My delight is in her"), and thy land Beulah (means, "Married"): for the Lord delighteth in thee, and thy land shall be married. For as a young man marrieth a virgin, so shall thy sons marry thee: and as the bridegroom rejoiceth over the bride, so shall thy God rejoice over thee. I have set watchmen upon thy walls, O Jerusalem, which shall never hold their peace day nor night: ye that make mention of the Lord, keep not silence, and give Him no rest, till He establish, and till He make Jerusalem a praise in the earth. The Lord hath sworn by His right hand, and by the arm of His strength, Surely

I will no more give thy corn to be meat for thine enemies... for the which thou hast labored: but they that have gathered it shall eat it, and praise the Lord; and they that have brought it together shall drink it in the courts of My Holiness. Go through, go through the gates; prepare ye the way of the people; cast up, cast up the highway; gather out the stones; lift up a standard for the people. Behold, the people... behold, the Lord hath proclaimed unto the end of the world, say ye to the daughter of Zion, Behold, thy Salvation cometh; behold, His reward is with Him (Rev.22:12), and His work before Him. And they shall call them, The Holy People, The Redeemed of the Lord: and thou shalt be called, Sought Out, A city not forsaken." Is. 62:1-12

"Never again will you be called 'The Forsaken City' or 'The Desolate Land'. Your new name will be 'The city of God's Delight' and 'The Bride of God', for the Lord delights in you and will claim you as His bride." Is. 62:2 NLT

Hephzibah is only found twice in the Bible; here and in II Kings 21:1. In II Kings she was the wife of king Hezekiah and mother of king Manasseh of Judah; here she is the New Jerusalem.

The church is also the Bride of Christ, Matt.25:1-18;Mk.2:19,20;Jn.3:29;II Cor. 11:2;Eph.5:25-27;Rev.19:7-9;21:2,9-11.

> **The Promise:**
> *"... surely they are My people... so He was their Saviour. In all their affliction He was afflicted, and the angel of His presence saved them: in His love and in His pity He Redeemed them; and He bare them, and carried them all the days of old."* Is. 63:8,9

A promise about Jesus

"Who is this that cometh from Edom, with dyed garments from Bozrah? this that is glorious in His apparel, travelling in the greatness of his strength? I that speak in righteousness, mighty to save." Is. 63:1

This is Jesus, who is the Word, because it says in Rev. 19:13, *"And He was clothed with a vesture dipped in blood: and His name is called The Word of God."* Rev. 19:13

"I will mention the lovingkindnesses of the Lord, and the praises of the Lord, according to all that the Lord hath bestowed on us, and the great goodness toward the house of Israel, which He hath bestowed on them according to His mercies, and according to the multitude of His lovingkindnesses. For He said..." Is. 63:7,8

> **The Promise:**
> *"For since the beginning of the world men have not heard, nor perceived by the ear, neither hath the eye seen, O God, beside Thee... what He hath prepared for him..."* Is. 64:4,5

> **The Promise:**
> "I am sought of them that asked not for Me; I am found of them that sought Me not..." Is. 65:1

"Doubtless thou art our father, though Abraham be ignorant of us, and Israel acknowledge us not..." Is. 63:16

> **The Promise:**
> "For since the beginning of the world men have not heard, nor perceived by the ear, neither hath the eye seen, O God, beside Thee..." Is. 64:4

"... Thou, O Lord, art our Father, our Redeemer; Thy name is from everlasting." Is. 63:16

> **The Promise:**
> "... what He hath prepared for him..." Is. 64:4,5

The Condition:
"... that waiteth for him." Is. 64:4,5
Sometimes we have to wait for God to give us what He has promised.
Prayer:
Father in heaven, help me to wait patiently for all the things You have prepared for me. Thank You in Jesus' name, Amen!

"But now, O Lord, Thou art our Father; we are the clay, and Thou our potter; and we all are the work of Thy hand." Is. 64:8

> **The Promise:**
> "I am sought of them that asked not for Me; I am found of them that sought Me not..." Is. 65:1

"... I said, Behold Me, behold Me, unto a nation that was not called by My name." Is. 65:1
"... Here am I... all day long I have held out My hands to an obstinate people, who walk in ways not good, pursuing their own imaginations – a people who continually provoke Me to My very face..." Is. 65:1-3 NIV

A Blessing
"Thus saith the LORD, As the new wine is found in the cluster, and one saith, Destroy it not; for a blessing is in it: so will I do for my servants' sakes..." Is. 65:8

A promise about Jesus
"And I will bring forth a Seed out of Jacob, and out of Judah an Inheritor of My Mountains: and Mine elect shall inherit it, and My servants shall dwell there." Is. 65:9

Promise of a New Earth:
"That he who blesseth himself in the earth shall bless himself in the God of truth; and he that sweareth in the earth shall swear by the God of truth because the former troubles are forgotten, and because they are hid from mine eyes. For, behold, I create new heavens and a New Earth: and the former shall not be remembered, nor come into mind. But be ye glad and rejoice forever in that which I create: for, behold, I create Jerusalem a rejoicing, and her people a joy. And I will rejoice in Jerusalem, and joy in My people: and the voice of weeping shall be no more heard in her, nor the voice of crying. There shall be no more thence an infant of days, nor an old man... and they shall build houses, and inhabit them; and they shall plant vineyards, and eat the fruit of them. They shall not build, and another inhabit; they shall not plant, and another eat: for as the days of a tree are the days of My people, and Mine elect shall long enjoy the work of their hands. They shall not labour in vain, nor bring forth for trouble; for they are the seed of the blessed of the Lord, and their offspring with them. And it shall come to pass, that before they call, I will answer; and while they are yet speaking, I will hear. The wolf and the lamb shall feed together, and the lion shall eat straw like the bullock: and dust shall be the serpent's meat. They shall not hurt nor destroy in all My Holy Mountain, saith the Lord." Is. 65:16-25

> **The Promise:**
> *"Shall I bring to the birth, and not cause to bring forth? Saith the Lord: shall I cause to bring forth, and shut the womb? Saith thy God."* Is. 66:9
>
> **The Promise:**
> *"... I will extend peace to her like a river, and the glory of the Gentiles like a flowing stream: then shall ye ("nurse" NIV), ye shall be borne upon her sides, and be dandled upon her knees."* Is. 66:12
>
> **The Promise:**
> *As one whom his mother comforteth, so will I comfort you; and ye shall be comforted in Jerusalem. And when ye see this, your heart shall rejoice, and your bones shall flourish like an herb: and the hand of the Lord shall be known toward His servants, and His indignation toward His enemies. For, behold, the Lord will come with fire, and with His chariots like a whirlwind, to render His anger with fury, and His rebuke with flames of fire."* Is. 66:13-15

On the New Earth
"For as the new heavens and the New Earth, which I will make, shall remain before Me, saith the Lord, so shall your seed and your name remain. And It shall come to pass, that from one new moon to another, and from one Sabbath to another, shall all flesh come to worship before Me, saith the Lord." Is. 66:22,23

Jeremiah

Promise to Jeremiah
"But the Lord said unto me, Say not, I am a child: for thou shalt go to all that I shall send thee, and whatsoever I command thee thou shalt speak. Be not afraid of their faces: for I am with thee to deliver thee, saith the Lord. Then the Lord put forth His hand, and touched my mouth. And the Lord said unto me, Behold, I have put My Words in thy mouth. See, I have this day set thee over the nations and over the kingdoms, to root out, and to pull down, and to destroy, and to throw down, to build and to plant." Jer. 1:7-10,

> **The Promise:**
> *"... for I will hasten My Word to perform it."* Jer. 1:12

"... for I am watching to see that My Word is fulfilled." Jer. 1:12 NIV
The promise for us is that God will make sure His words are fulfilled or come true.

> **The Promise:**
> *"For, behold, I have made thee this day a defenced city, and an iron pillar, and brazen walls against the whole land, against the kings of Judah, against the princes thereof, against the priests thereof, and against the people of the land. And they shall fight against thee; but they shall not prevail against thee; for I am with thee, saith the Lord, to deliver thee."* Jer. 1:18,19

"Go and cry in the ears of Jerusalem, saying, Thus saith the Lord... I remember thee, the kindness of thy youth, the love of thine espousals, when thou of thine espousals, when thou sentest after Me in the wilderness, in a land that was not sown." Jer. 2:2
"Go and proclaim in the hearing of Jerusalem, Thus says the Lord, 'I remember the devotion of your youth, your love as a bride, how you followed Me in the wilderness..." Jer. 2:2 ESV

"For of old time I have broken thy yoke, and burst thy bands; and thou saidist, I will not transgress..." Jer. 2:20

New Earth
"At that time (on the New Earth) they shall call Jerusalem the throne of the Lord; and all the nations shall be gathered unto it, to the name of the Lord, to Jerusalem: neither shall they walk anymore after the imagination of their evil heart. In those days the house of Judah shall walk with the house of Israel, and they shall come together out of the land of the North to the land that I have given for an inheritance unto your fathers." Jer. 3:17-19

The Condition:
"Return, ye backsliding children..." Jer. 3:22

> **The Promise:**
> *"... and I will heal your backslidings. Behold, we come unto Thee; for Thou art the Lord our God... truly in the Lord our God is the Salvation of Israel."* Jer. 3:22,23

"And thou shalt swear, The Lord liveth, in truth, in Judgment, and in righteousness..." Jer. 4:2

> **The Promise:**
> *"... and the nations shall bless themselves in Him, and in Him shall they glory."* Jer. 4:2

"O Jerusalem, wash thine heart from wickedness..." Jer. 4:14

> **The Promise:**
> *"... that thou mayest be saved."* Jer. 4:14

"... how long shall thy vain thoughts lodge within thee?" Jer. 4:14
We wash our hearts through repentance, by the Blood of Jesus, and baptism.
"Behold the lamb of God, which taketh away the sin of the world." Jn 1:29

The Condition:
"Thus saith the Lord of hosts, the God of Israel, Amend your ways and your doings, and I will cause you to dwell in this place. Trust ye not in lying words, saying, The Temple of the Lord... are these. For if ye thoroughly amend your ways and your doings; if ye thoroughly execute Judgment between a man and his neighbour; if ye oppress not the stranger, the fatherless, and the widow, and shed not innocent blood in this place, neither walk after other gods to your hurt..." Jer. 7:3-6

The Promise:
"... then will I cause you to dwell in this place, in the land that I gave to your fathers, forever and ever." Jer. 7:7

The Condition:
"But this thing commanded I them, saying, Obey My voice..." Jer. 7:23

The Promise:
"... and I will be your God, and ye shall be My people..." Jer. 7:23

The Condition:
"... and walk ye in all the ways that I have commanded you..." Jer. 7:23

The Promise:
"... that it may be well unto you" Jer. 7:23

"... they hearkened not, nor inclined their ear, but walked in the counsels and... imagination of their evil heart, and went backward, and not forward." Jer. 7:24

"Is there no balm in Gilead; is there no physician there? Why then is not the health of the daughter of My people recovered?" Jer. 8:22
It is implied that there is a balm in Gilead and that there is a physician there!

The Condition:
"Obey My voice, and do them (the Commandments), according to all which I command you..." Jer. 11:4,5

The Promise:
"... so shall ye be My people, and I will be your God: that I may perform the oath which I have sworn unto your fathers, to give them a land flowing with milk and honey..." Jer. 11:4,5

"... then answered I, and said, So be it, O Lord." Jer. 11:5
This is similar to what Mary said to the angel, "... be it unto me according to your Word." Lk. 1:38
We too can pray, "So be it" and "Lord, let it be unto me according to Your Word!".
"And it shall come to pass, after that I have plucked them out..." Jer. 12:15

The Promise:
"... I will return, and have compassion on them, and will bring them again, every man to his heritage, and every man to his land." Jer. 12:15

The Condition:
"And it shall come to pass, if they will diligently learn the ways of My people, to swear by My name, the Lord liveth..." Jer. 12:16

> **The Promise:**
> "... then shall they be built in the midst of My people." Jer. 12:16

The Condition:
"But if they will not obey, I will utterly pluck up and destroy that nation, saith the Lord." Jer. 12:17

"The Lord said, Verily it shall be well with thy remnant; verily I will cause the enemy to entreat thee well in the time of evil and in the time of affliction." Jer. 15:11

"The Lord said: I will certainly set you free and care for you. I will certainly intercede for you in a time of trouble, in your time of distress, with the enemy." Jer. 15:11 HCSB

The Condition:
"Therefore thus saith the Lord, If thou return..." Jer. 15:19

The Condition:
"... and if thou take forth the precious from the vile..." Jer. 15:19

> **The Promise:**
> "...I bring thee again, and thou shalt stand before Me..." Jer. 15:19

> **The Promise:**
> "... thou shalt be as My mouth..." Jer. 15:19

"... let them return unto thee; but return not thou unto them." Jer. 15:19

> **The Promise:**
> "Therefore, behold, I will this once cause them to know, I will cause them to know Mine hand and My might; and they shall know that My name is The Lord." Jer. 16:21

> **The Promise:**
> "And I will make thee unto this people a fenced brazen wall: and they shall fight against thee, but they shall not prevail against thee: for I will deliver thee out of the hand of the wicked, and I will Redeem thee out of the hand of the terrible." Jer. 15:20,21

"Blessed is the man that trustesth in the Lord... whose hope the Lord is." Jer. 17:7

The Promise:
"For he shall be as a tree planted by the waters, and that spreadeth out her roots by the river, and shall not see when heat cometh, but her leaf shall be green; and shall not be careful in the year of drought, neither shall cease from yielding fruit." Jer. 17:8

"I, the Lord, search the heart, I try the reins ("the mind" NIV), even to give every man according to his ways, and according to the fruit of his doings." Jer. 17:10
Our Salvation is free but our reward in heaven is based on what we do now on earth.

"The Lord is the hope of Israel... the fountain of living water." Jer. 17:13 PB
"... the Lord, the fountain of living waters." Is. 17:13 NKJV
Come drink the Water of Life freely, Jn.4:14;7:37,38;Rev.21:6;22:17
"Come all who are thirsty, come to the waters..." Is. 55:1 NIV
"Heal me, O Lord..." Jer. 17:14

The Promise:
"... and I shall be healed..." Jer. 17:14

"... save me..." Jer. 17:14

The Promise:
"... and I shall be saved..." Jer. 17:14

"... for Thou art my praise... Thou art my hope in the day of evil. Let them be confounded that persecute me, but let not me be confounded: let them be dismayed, but let not me be dismayed..." Jer. 17:14,17,18

The Condition:
"If that nation, against whom I have pronounced, turn from their evil..." Jer. 18:8

The Promise:
"... I will repent of the evil that I thought to do unto them." Jer. 18:8

The Promise:
"But the Lord is with Me as a mighty terrible One: therefore My persecutors shall stumble, and they shall not prevail: they shall be greatly ashamed; for they shall not prosper: their everlasting confusion shall never be forgotten." Jer. 20:11

"Sing unto the Lord, praise ye the Lord: for He hath delivered the soul of the poor from the hand of evildoers." Jer. 20:13

The Condition:
"For if ye do this thing indeed..." Jer. 22:4

> **The Promise:**
> "... then shall there enter in by the gates of this house kings sitting upon the throne of David, riding in chariots and on horses, He, and His servants, and His people." Jer. 22:4

> **The Promise:**
> "... did not your father have food and drink?" Jer. 22:15 NIV

"He did what was right and just..." Jer. 22:15 NIV
"He Judged the cause of the poor and needy..." Jer. 22:16

> **The Promise:**
> "... then it was well with him..." Jer. 22:16

"... so all went well with him." Jer. 22:16 NIV
"... was not this to know Me? Saith the Lord." Jer. 22:16
"... they shall fear no more, nor be dismayed, neither shall they be lacking, saith the Lord." Jer. 23:4
"... they will never be afraid again. Not a single one of them will be lost or missing, says the Lord." Jer. 23:4 NLT

A Promise about Jesus
"Behold, the days come, saith the Lord, that I will raise unto David a righteous Branch (Jesus), and a King shall reign and prosper, and shall execute Judgment and justice in the earth. In His days Judah shall be saved, and Israel shall dwell safely: and this is His name whereby He shall be called, The Lord Our Righteousness." Jer. 23:5,6

> **The Promise:**
> "I will keep My eyes on them for their good and will return them to this land. I will build them up and not demolish them; I will plant them and not uproot them. And I will give them an heart to know Me, that I am Yahweh. They will be My people, and I will be their God: for they shall return unto Me with their ("whole" KJV) heart." Jer. 24:6,7 HCSB

Prayer:
Father in heaven, please give me and my family and loved ones a heart to know You; to return to You with all our hearts and be our God we pray in Jesus' name, Amen!

Rewarded according to works
"... and I will recompense them according to their deeds, and according to the works of their own hands." Jer. 25:14

About Israel coming back after the 70 yr. captivity
"... then I will bring them back and restore them ..." Jer. 27:22 ESV

Israelites told to do this in Babylon
"Thus saith the Lord of hosts, the God of Israel, unto all that are carried away captives, whom I have caused to be carried away from Jerusalem unto Babylon; build ye houses, and dwell in them; and plant gardens, and eat the fruit of them; take ye wives, and beget sons and daughters; and take wives for your sons, and give your daughters to husbands, that they may bear sons and daughters; that ye may be increased there, and not diminished. And seek the peace of the city whither I have caused you to be carried away captives, and pray unto the Lord for it: for in the peace thereof shall ye have peace." Jer. 29:4-7
We can pray for our city as well.

A promise concerning the 70 yr. Babylonian captivity
"... you will be in Babylon for seventy years. But then I will come and do for you all the good things I have promised, and I will bring you home again. For I know the plans I have for you... plans for good and not for disaster, to give you a future and a hope. In those days when you pray, I will listen. If you look for Me in earnest, you will find Me when you seek Me. I will be found by you... I will end your captivity and restore your fortunes. I will... bring you home..." Jer. 29:10-14 NLT

Prayer:
Father in heaven, I pray that You would do all the good things You've promised in Your Word and bring us to our heavenly home. Thank You that Your plans for me are good and not bad. Give me a future and a hope as You promised. Please listen to my prayers and let me find You. Please restore everything that the Devil has stolen from me. Thank You in Jesus' name, Amen!

"For I know the thoughts that I think toward you, saith the Lord ..." Jer. 29:11

The Promise:
"... thoughts of peace, and not of evil, to give you an expected end. Then shall ye call upon Me, and ye shall go and pray unto Me, and I will hearken unto you. And ye shall seek Me, and find Me, when ye

shall search for Me with all your heart. And I will be found of you, saith the Lord: and I will turn away your captivity, and I will gather you from all the nations, and from all the places whither I have driven you, saith the Lord; and I will bring you again into the place whence I caused you to be carried away captive." Jer. 29:11-14

Jacob's Trouble
"Alas! for that day is great, so that none is like it: it is even the time of Jacob's trouble..." Jer. 30:7

The Promise:
"... but he shall be saved out of it. For it shall come to pass in that day, saith the Lord of hosts, that I will break his yoke from off thy neck, and will burst thy bonds, and strangers shall no more serve themselves of him: but they shall serve the Lord their God, and David their king, whom I will raise up unto them. Therefore fear thou not, O My servant Jacob, saith the Lord; neither be dismayed, O Israel: for, lo, I will save thee from afar, and thy seed from the land of their captivity; and Jacob shall return, and shall be in rest, and be quiet, and none shall make him afraid. For I am with thee, saith the Lord, to save thee: though I make a full end of all nations whither I have scattered thee, yet I will not make a full end of thee..." Jer. 30:7-11

"For I will restore health unto thee, and I will heal thee of thy wounds..." Jer. 30:17
"I will give you back your health... says the Lord." Jer. 30:17 NLT
Promise to the Israelites after the seventy-year captivity by Babylon
"Thus saith the Lord; Behold, I will bring again the captivity of Jacob's tents, and have mercy on his dwelling places; and the city shall be builded upon her own heap, and the palace shall remain after the manner thereof. And out of them shall proceed thanksgiving and the voice of them that make merry: and I will multiply them, and they shall not be few; I will also glorify them, and they shall not be small. Their children also shall be as aforetime, and their congregation shall be established before Me, and I will punish all that oppress them." Jer. 30:18-20

The Promise:
"And ye shall be My people, and I will be your God." Jer. 30:22

"At the same time, saith the Lord..." Jer. 31:1

The Promise:
"... will I be the God of all the families of Israel, and they shall be My people." Jer. 31:1

Promise to Jeremiah
"Thus saith the Lord, The people which were left of the sword found grace in the wilderness; even Israel, when I went to cause him to rest. The Lord hath appeared of old unto me, saying, Before I formed thee in the belly I knew thee; and before thou camest forth out of the womb I Sanctified thee, and I ordained thee a prophet unto the nations." Jer. 31:2,3

> **The Promise:**
> *"... I have loved thee with an everlasting love: therefore with loving-kindness have I drawn thee... I will build thee, and thou shalt be built, O virgin of Israel: thou shalt again be adorned with thy tabrets, and shalt go forth in the dances of them that make merry. Thou shalt yet plant vines upon the mountains of Samaria: the planters shall plant, and shall eat them as common things. For there shall be a day, that the watchmen upon the Mount Ephraim shall cry, Arise ye, and let us go up to Zion unto the Lord our God."* Jer. 31:3-6

"For thus saith the Lord; Sing with gladness for Jacob, and shout among the chief of the nations: publish ye, praise ye, and say, O Lord, save Thy people, the remnant of Israel." Jer. 31:7

> **The Promise:**
> *"... behold, I will bring them from the North Country, and gather them from the coasts of the earth, and with them the blind and the lame, the woman with child and her that travaileth with child together: a great company shall return thither. They shall come with weeping, and with supplications will I lead them: I will cause them to walk by the rivers of waters in a straight way, wherein they shall not stumble..."* Jer. 31:8,9

"... for I am a father to Israel, and Ephraim is My firstborn." Jer. 31:9

A promise to Israel at the time of the Babylonian Captivity
"Hear the Word of the Lord, O ye nations, and declare it in the isles afar off, and say, He that scattered Israel..." Jer. 31:10

> **The Promise:**
> *"... will gather him, and keep him, as a Shepherd doth his flock. For the Lord hath Redeemed Jacob, and ransomed him from the hand of him that was stronger than he. Therefore, they shall come and sing in the height of Zion, and shall flow together to the goodness of the not sorrow anymore at all. Then shall the virgin rejoice in the dance, both young men... and old together: for I will turn their mourning*

into joy, and will comfort them, and make them rejoice from their sorrow. And I will satiate the soul of the priests with fatness, and My people shall be satisfied with My goodness, saith the Lord... refrain thy voice from weeping, and thine eyes from tears: for thy work shall be rewarded, saith the Lord; and they shall come again from the land of the enemy. And there is hope in thine end, saith the Lord, that thy children shall come again to their own border" Jer. 31:10-17

"I will fill the soul of the priests with abundance, and My people will be satisfied with My goodness..." Jer. 31:14 NASB
Prayer:
Father in heaven, let my child/children come home to the borders of the heavenly Canaan. Satisfy us with Your goodness as You promised. Deliver us from the enemy and help us to do the works You require of us so that we can share in the rewards. Let our souls be as a watered garden. Thank you for these wonderful promises in Jesus' name, Amen!

"I have surely heard..." Jer. 31:18 NKJV

"I will surely have mercy..." Jer. 31:20 NKJV

Blessed
"Thus saith the Lord of hosts, the God of Israel; as yet they shall use this speech in the land of Judah and in the cities thereof, when I shall bring again their captivity; the Lord bless thee, O habitation of justice, and Mountain of Holiness." Jer. 31:23

"... I have satiated the weary soul, and I have replenished every sorrowful soul. Upon this I awaked, and beheld; and my sleep was sweet unto me. Behold, the days come, saith the Lord, that I will sow the house of Israel and the house of Judah with the seed of man, and with the seed of beast. And it shall come to pass, that like as I have watched over them, to pluck up, and to break down, and to throw down, and to destroy, and to afflict..." Jer. 31:25-28

> **The Promise:**
> *"... so will I watch over them, to build, and to plant, saith the Lord."* Jer. 31:28

> **The Promise:**
> *"Behold, the days come, saith the Lord, that I will make a New Covenant with the house of Israel, and with the house of Judah: not*

according to the Covenant that I made with their fathers in the day that I took them by the hand to bring them out of the land of Egypt; which My Covenant they brake, although I was an husband unto them, saith the Lord: but this shall be the Covenant that I will make with the house of Israel; after those days, saith the Lord, I will put My law in their inward parts, and write it in their hearts; and will be their God, and they shall be My people. And they shall teach no more every man his neighbor, and every man his brother, saying, Know the Lord: for they shall all know Me, from the least of them unto the greatest of them, saith the Lord: for I will forgive their iniquity, and I will remember their sin no more." Jer. 31:31-34

"*If those ordinances* (of sun & moon) *depart from before Me, saith the Lord, then the seed of Israel also shall cease from being a nation before Me forever.*" Jer. 31:36

Prayer:
Father in heaven, please forgive us and remember not our sins. Thank You in the name of Jesus, Amen!

"*For thus saith the Lord of hosts, the God of Israel; houses and fields and vineyards shall be possessed again in this land.*" Jer. 32:15 NKJV

   The Promise:
   "*... there is nothing too hard for Thee...*" Jer. 32:17

"*Great in counsel, and mighty in work: for Thine eyes are open upon all the ways of the sons of men...*" Jer. 32:19

Nothing is too hard for God.
"*Behold, I am the Lord, the God of all flesh: is there anything too hard for Me?*" Jer. 32:27
"*... I taught them rising up early and teaching them...*" Jer. 32:33 NKJV

"*And now therefore thus saith the Lord, the God of Israel, concerning this city* (Jerusalem)*...*" Jer. 32:36,37

   The Promise:
   "*Behold, I will gather them out of all countries, whither I have driven them in Mine anger, and in My fury, and in great wrath and I will bring them again unto this place, and I will cause them to dwell safely: and they shall be My people, and I will be their God: and I will give them one heart, and one way, that they may fear Me forever, for the good of them, and of their children after them: and I will*

make an everlasting Covenant with them, that I will not turn away from them, to do them good; but I will put My fear in their hearts, that they shall not depart from Me. Yea, I will rejoice over them to do them good, and I will plant them in this land assuredly with My whole heart and with My whole soul." Jer. 32:37-41

This promise was given to Israel that God would bring them back to Jerusalem after the seventy years they were taken captive in Babylon but we can use these promises and apply them to our own situations today.
Prayer:
Father in heaven, please give us one heart and help us to walk in truth. Thank You that You don't turn us away and You do good to us. Put Your fear in us so that we will never depart from You. In Jesus' name, Amen!

"For thus saith the Lord..." Jer. 32:42

> **The Promise:**
> *"... so will I bring upon them all the good that I have promised them. And fields shall be bought in this land..."* Jer. 32:42,43

"... whereof ye say, It is desolate without man or beast; it is given into the hand of the Chaldeans. Men shall buy fields for money, and subscribe evidences, and seal them, and take witnesses in the land of Benjamin, and in the places about Jerusalem, and in the cities of Judah, and in the cities of the mountains, and in the cities of the valley, and in the cities of the South..." Jer. 32:43,44

"Thus saith the Lord the maker ("of the heavens and earth" NLT)... *call unto Me..."* Jer. 33:2,3

> **The Promise:**
> *"... and I will answer thee, and shew thee great and mighty things, which thou knowest not."* Jer. 33:3

We see here that the God who created everything is the God we are to call upon. He is the only One worthy of our praise because He created us and Redeemed us!

> **The Promise:**
> *"... I will bring it health and cure, and I will cure them, and will reveal unto them the abundance of peace and truth. And I will cause the captivity of Judah and the captivity of Israel to return, and will build them, as at the first. And I will cleanse them from all their iniquity*

whereby they have sinned against Me, and I will pardon all their iniquities, whereby they have sinned, and whereby they have transgressed against Me. And it shall be to Me a name of joy, a praise and an honour before all the nations of the earth, which shall hear all the good that I do unto them: and they shall fear and tremble for all the goodness and for all the prosperity that I procure unto it" Jer. 33:6-9

Prayer:
Father in heaven, please forgive and cleanse me and my loved ones from our sins. Let all those around me see all the good You do for me. Thank You in Jesus' name, Amen!

God is good!
"... praise the Lord of hosts: for the Lord is good; for His mercy endureth for-ever: and of them that shall bring the sacrifice of praise into the house of the Lord." Jer. 33:11

> **The Promise:**
> *"For I will cause to return the captivity of the land as at the first, saith the Lord."* Jer. 33:11

Again this promise was for the Israelites at the time of the Babylonian captivity but this verse promises us that God is good and that His mercy endures forever and because of that we should praise Him.

God fulfills His promises
"Behold, the days come, saith the Lord..." Jer. 33:14

Promise about Jesus and the New Jerusalem

> **The Promise:**
> *"... that I will perform that good thing which I have promised unto the house of Israel and to the house of Judah."* Jer. 33:14

"In those days, and at that time, will I cause the Branch of Righteousness (Jesus) to grow up unto David; and He shall execute Judgment and righteousness in the land. In those days shall Judah be saved, and Jerusalem shall dwell safely: and this is the name wherewith she shall be called, The Lord our righteousness. For thus saith the Lord; David shall never want a man to sit upon the throne of the house of Israel... and the Word of the Lord came unto Jeremiah, saying, Thus saith the Lord; If ye can break My Covenant of the day, and My Covenant of the night, and that there should

not be day and night in their season; then may also My Covenant be broken with David My servant, and the Levites that minister unto Me. Moreover the Word of the Lord came to Jeremiah, saying, Considerest thou not what this people have spoken, saying, The two families which the Lord hath chosen, He hath even cast them off? Thus they have despised My people, that they should be no more a nation before them. Thus saith the Lord; if My Covenant be not with day and night, and if I have not appointed the ordinances of heaven and earth; then will I cast away the seed of Jacob and David My servant, so that I will not take any of his seed to be rulers over the seed of Abraham, Isaac, and Jacob: for I will cause their captivity to return, and have mercy on them." Jer. 33:15-26

"... *that no one should keep them in bondage anymore*..." Jer. 34:10

King Zedekiah wanted to find Jeremiah and Baruch the scribe to harm them "... *but the Lord hid them.*" Jer. 36:26

"*But Jeremiah said, They shall not deliver thee.*" Jer. 38:20
The Condition:
"... *obey, I beseech thee, the voice of the Lord, which I speak unto thee*..." Jer. 38:20

    The Promise:
    "... *so it shall be well unto thee, and thy soul shall live.*" Jer. 38:20

    The Promise:
    "*But I will deliver thee in that day, saith the Lord: and thou shalt not be given into the hand of the men of whom thou art afraid. For I will surely deliver thee, and thou shalt not fall by the sword, but thy life shall be for a prey unto thee...*" Jer. 39:17,18

The Condition:
"... *because thou hast put thy trust in Me, saith the Lord.*" Jer. 39:17,18
"*But I will rescue you on that day, declares the Lord; you will not be given into the hands of those you fear. I will save you; you will not fall by the sword but will escape with your life, because you trust in Me, declares the Lord.*" Jer. 39:17,18 NIV
"... *you shall have your life as a prize of war*..." Jer. 39:17,18 ESV
"... *you will not be handed over to men you fear.*" Jer. 39:17,18 HCSB
Spoken to Jeremiah
"*And now, behold, I loose thee this day from the chains which were upon thine hand... behold, all the land is before thee: whither it seemeth good and*

convenient for thee to go..." Jer. 40:4
Prayer:
Father in heaven, please loose us from every chain and anything that would put us in bondage. Thank You in Jesus' name, Amen!
"... do not be afraid... it will be well with you." Jer. 40:9 NKJV

"... obey... that it may be well with us..." Jer. 42:6 NKJV

"If ye will still abide in this land, then will I build you, and not pull you down, and I will plant you, and not pluck you up: for I repent ("relented" NIV) Me of the evil that I have done unto you... for I am with you to save you, and to deliver you from his hand. And I will shew mercies unto you, that he may have mercy upon you, and cause you to return to your own land." Jer. 42:10,12
A promise to the Israelites that if they would do what God said, they would be O.K. at the time of the Babylonian captivity.
"I will give your life to you as a prize in all places, wherever you go." Jer. 45:5 NKJV

Promise to Israel at time of captivity
"But fear not thou, O My servant Jacob, and be not dismayed, O Israel: for, behold..." Jer. 46:27

> **The Promise:**
> *"... I will save thee from afar off, and thy seed from the land of their captivity; and Jacob shall return, and be in rest and at ease, and none shall make him afraid..."* Jer. 46:27

"Fear thou not, O Jacob My servant, saith the Lord..." Jer. 46:28

> **The Promise:**
> *"... for I am with thee; for I will make a full end of all the nations whither I have driven thee: but I will not make a full end of thee..."* Jer. 46:28

Your sins will be no more
"In those days, and in that time, saith the Lord, the iniquity of Israel shall be sought for, and there shall be none; and the sins of Judah, and they shall not be found..." Jer. 50:20

> **The Promise:**
> *"... for I will pardon them whom I reserve ("leave as a remnant" RSV)."* Jer. 50:20

The Promise:
"Their Redeemer is strong; the Lord of hosts is His name He shall thoroughly plead their cause, that He may give rest to the land..." Jer. 50:34

Prayer:
Father in heaven, please thoroughly plead my cause because You are strong. Thank You in the name of Jesus, Amen!

"For Israel hath not been forsaken, nor Judah of his God, of the Lord of hosts; though their land was filled with sin against the Holy One of Israel." Jer. 51:5

God will repay good and evil
"... for the Lord is a God of recompence ("retribution" NIV), He will surely repay." Jer. 51:56 (See Rom. 12:19)

Lamentations

God's mercy is new every morning
   The Promise:
   "The Lord hath done that which He had devised; He hath fulfilled His Word that He had commanded in days of old..." Lam. 2:17

   The Promise:
   "It is of the Lord's mercies that we are not consumed because His compassions fail not. They are new every morning: great is Thy faithfulness. The Lord is my portion, saith my soul; therefore will I hope in Him. The Lord is good unto them that wait for Him, to the soul that seeketh Him. It is good that a man should both hope and quietly wait for the Salvation of the Lord ..." Lam. 3:22-26

We must wait for the eternal Salvation that God is giving us.
"But if we hope for that we see not, then do we with patience wait for it." Rom. 8:25
"... the kindness of the Lord never ceases and His mercies never fail." Lam. 3:22 PB

Prayer:
Father in heaven, Thank You that each day You are working out my Salvation. Please give me fresh grace and mercy today and every day in Jesus' name, Amen!

"But though He cause grief ("affliction" PB)..." Lam. 3:32

The Promise:
"... yet will He have compassion according to the multitude of His mercies." Lam. 3:32

Prayer:
Father in heaven, please have compassion on me according to Your great mercy. In the name of Jesus, Amen!

"Turn us back to You, O Lord, and we will be restored..." Lam. 5:21

The Promise:
"Behold, I have made thy face strong against their faces, and thy forehead strong against their foreheads. As an adamant harder than flint have I made thy forehead..." Ez. 3:8,9

"... fear them not, neither be dismayed at their looks..." Ez. 3:8,9

"... so the Spirit lifted me up, and took me away... but the hand of the Lord was strong upon me." Ez. 3:14

The Condition:
"... if you warn the wicked... (to) turn from his wickedness." Ez. 3:19 ESV

The Promise:
"... you have delivered your soul." Ez. 3:19 ESV

The Condition:
"... if you warn the righteous person not to sin, and he does not sin..." Ez. 3:21 ESV

The Promise:
"... he shall surely live because he took warning: and you will have delivered your soul..." Ez. 3:22 ESV

"... the hand of the Lord was upon me there." Ez. 3:22 ESV
"Then those of you who escape will remember Me among the nations... they will loathe themselves for the evils which they have committed... they shall know I am the Lord..." Ez. 6:9,10

"... I have been a Sanctuary for them... where they have gone." Ez. 11:16 HCSB

God Himself is our Sanctuary, our place of refuge. The Bible says "*The name of the Lord is a strong tower, the righteous run into it and are safe*." Prov. 18:10

A promise to Israel after the Babylonian captivity
"... *thus saith the Lord God; I will even gather you from the people, and assemble you out of the countries where ye have been scattered, and I will give you the land of Israel.*" Ez. 11:17

> **The Promise:**
> "*And I will give them one heart, and I will put a new Spirit within you; and I will take the stony heart out of their flesh, and will give them an heart of flesh: that they may walk in My Statutes, and keep mine Ordinances, and do them: and they shall be My people, and I will be their God.*" Ez. 11:19,20

God has always wanted us to love and obey Him from the heart. Verses about the heart – (More Scriptures Deut.10:16;Ps.37:31;40:8;119:34;Is.51: 7;Rom.2:14,15;7:22;II Cor.3:3;Heb.10:16;8:8,10;Jer.32:39;Prov.7:3; Ez.11: 19;36: 26;18:31)

Prayer:
Father in heaven, please give me and my family one heart. Take away our stony hearts and make them flesh through the power of Your Holy Spirit. Help us to love and obey You always and to walk in Your ways from the heart. Make us Your people and be our God. Thank You in Jesus' name, Amen!

> **The Promise:**
> "*For I am the Lord: I will speak, and the Word that I shall speak shall come to pass; it shall be no more prolonged... the Word which I have spoken shall be done*" Ez. 12:25,28

> **The Promise:**
> "*... I will deliver My people out of your hand: and ye shall know that I am the Lord.*" Ez. 13:23

"*That the house of Israel may go no more astray from Me, neither be polluted anymore with all their transgressions; but that they may be My people, and I may be their God, saith the Lord God.*" Ez. 14:11

Prayer:
Father in heaven, please help us not to go astray from You anymore. Thank You in Jesus' name, Amen!

God said to Israel

> **The Promise:**
> "I said unto thee... live... I have caused thee to multiply as the bud of the field, and thou hast increased and waxen great, and thou art come to excellent ornaments..." Ez. 16:6,7

"I said to you... live" Ez. 16:6,7
"I made you grow ("*flourish*" ESV) *like a plant of the field.*"
"I made you thrive like plants of the field. You grew up and matured and became very beautiful." Ez. 16:7 HCSB

God to Israel
"... I sware unto thee, and entered into a Covenant with thee, saith the Lord God, and thou becamest Mine. Then washed I thee with water; yea, I thoroughly washed (you)... and I anointed thee with oil... I decked thee also with ornaments, and I put bracelets upon thy hands, and a chain on thy neck... I put a jewel on thy forehead, and earrings in thine ears, and a beautiful crown upon thine head. Thus wast thou decked with gold and silver; and thy raiment was of fine linen, and silk, and broidered work; thou didst eat fine flour, and honey, and oil: and thou wast exceeding beautiful, and thou didst prosper into a kingdom. And thy renown went forth among the heathen for thy beauty: for it was perfect through My comeliness, which I had put upon thee, saith the Lord God." Ez. 16:8-14

"I will remember My Covenant with thee in the days of thy youth, and I will establish unto thee an everlasting Covenant. Then thou shalt remember thy ways, and be ashamed..." Ez. 16:60,61

> **The Promise:**
> "... and I will establish My Covenant with thee; and thou shalt know that I am the Lord..." Ez. 16:62

"Then when I make atonement for you (on the cross of Jesus) *for all you have done, you will remember and be ashamed and never again open your mouth because of your humiliation.*" Ez. 16:63 NIV

"... for I have forgiven you for all that you have done..." Ez. 16:63 PB
We will never boast when we see how sinful we are and how pure Jesus is, how much God has had mercy on us, and how much Jesus suffered because of our sins!

> **The Promise:**
> "... he shall surely live, saith the Lord God." Ez. 18:8

The Condition:
"He that hath not given forth upon usury, neither hath taken any increase, that hath withdrawn his hand from iniquity, hath executed true Judgment between man and man, hath walked in My Statutes, and hath kept My Judgments, to deal truly; he is just..." Ez. 18:8,9

The Condition:
"But if the wicked will turn from all his sins that he hath committed, and keep all My Statutes, and do that which is lawful and right..." Ez. 18:21

> **The Promise:**
> *"... he shall surely live, he shall not die. All his transgressions that he hath committed, they shall not be mentioned unto him: in his righteousness that he hath done he shall live."* Ez. 18:21,22

God wants us to turn away from sin! Sin can ruin your life!

"... when the wicked man turneth away from his wickedness that he hath committed, and doeth that which is lawful and right, he shall save his soul alive. Because he considereth, and turneth away from all his transgressions that he hath committed, he shall surely live, he shall not die." Ez. 18:27,28

Repent and live!
The Condition:
"... repent, and turn yourselves from all your transgressions; so iniquity shall not be your ruin. Cast away from you all your transgressions... make you a new heart, and a new Spirit: for why will ye die, O house of Israel? For I have no pleasure in the death of him that dieth... turn (away from sin)..." Ez. 18:32

> **The Promise:**
> *"... and live..."* Ez. 18:32

We see the same thing in the New Testament.
Jesus said, *"Go and sin no more"* Jn. 8:11
"Repent and be baptized every one of you in the name of Jesus Christ for the remission (removal) of sins and ye shall receive the gift of the Holy Ghost." Acts 2:38
"If we confess our sins, He is faithful and just to forgive us our sins, and to cleanse us from all unrighteousness." I Jn. 1:9
"... sin not..." I Jn. 2:1
We hurt ourselves, others, and God when we sin because sin always hurts someone and will ruin us or the ones we love.

God promised the Israelites
"... a land ... flowing with milk and honey..." Ez. 20:6
The New Earth is ultimately our land of milk and honey!

The Promise:
"... I will bring you into the bond of the Covenant: and I will purge out from among you the rebels, and them that transgress against Me ..." Ez. 20:37,38

"I will put an end to lewdness in the land... then you will know that I am the Sovereign Lord." Ez. 23:48 NIV

"No longer will the people of Israel have malicious neighbors who are painful briers and sharp thorns. Then they will know that I am the Sovereign Lord." Ez. 28:24 NIV

"They will live there in safety and will build houses and plant vineyards; they will live in safety when I inflict punishment on all their neighbors who maligned them. Then they will know that I am the Lord their God." Ez. 28:26 NIV

The Promise:
"I will seek that which was lost, and bring again that which was driven away, and will bind up that which was broken, and will strengthen that which was sick..." Ez. 34:16

On the New Earth
"And I will Sanctify My great name... and the heathen shall know that I am the Lord, saith the Lord God, when I shall be Sanctified in you before their eyes." Ez. 36:23

The Promise:
"... I will set up One Shepherd over them, ad He shall feed them, even M servant David; he shall feed them, and he shall be their Shepherd... and I will make with them a Covenant of peace, and will cause the evil beasts to cease out of the land: and they shall dwell safely in the wilderness, and sleep in the woods. And I will make them and the places round about My hill a blessing... and there shall be showers of blessing. All the trees of the field shall yield her fruit, and the earth shall yield her increase, and they shall be safe in their land, and shall know that I am the Lord, when I have broken the bands of their yoke, and delivered them out of the hand of those that served themselves of them. And they shall no more be a prey to the heathen, neither shall the beast of the land devour them; but they shall dwell safely

and none shall make them afraid. And I will raise up for them a plant of renown and they shall be no more consumed with hunger in the land, neither bear the shame of the heathen anymore. Thus shall they know that I the Lord their God am with them, and that they, even the house of Israel, are My people, saith the Lord God. And ye My flock, the flock of My pasture, are men, and I am your God, saith the Lord God" Ez. 34:23-31

After the seventy year captivity of Israel

The Promise:
"... for I will take you from among the heathen, and gather you out of all countries, and will bring you into your own land. Then will I sprinkle clean water upon you, and ye shall be clean from all your filthiness, and from all your idols, will I cleanse you. A new heart also will I give you, and a new Spirit will I put within you: and I will take away the stony heart out of your flesh, and I will give you an heart of flesh. And I will put My Spirit within you and ye shall keep My Judgments, and do them. And ye shall dwell in the land that I gave to your fathers; and ye shall be My people, and I will be your God. I will also save you from all your uncleannesses: and I will call for the corn, and will increase it, and lay no famine upon you. And I will multiply the fruit of the tree, and the increase of the field, that ye shall receive no more reproach of famine among the heathen. Then shall ye remember your own evil ways, and your doings that were not good, and shall loathe yourselves in your own sight for your iniquities and for your abominations." Ez. 36:24-31

Prayer:
Father in heaven, I ask that You give me a new heart. Please put Your Holy Spirit in me and help me to obey You from the heart. I lift up _____ to You and ask that You give him/her a new heart and take away the stony heart from them. Please put Your sevenfold Holy Spirit in them and cause them to walk in obedience to Your will. Be their God and let them belong to You. Cleanse them from all uncleanliness and bless them with Your true blessings. Let them hate their sins and turn from them and love You with all their heart. Thank You in the name of Jesus, Amen!

The Promise:
"And they shall say, This land that was desolate is become like the Garden of Eden; and the waste and desolate and ruined cities are become fenced, and are inhabited... then the heathen that are left round about you shall know that I the Lord build the ruined places,

and plant that that was desolate I... will increase them with men like a flock... so shall the waste cities be filled with flocks of men: and they shall know that I am the Lord." Ez. 36:35-38

The Promise:
"Moreover I will make a Covenant of peace with them; it shall be an everlasting Covenant with them: and I will place them, and multiply them, and will set My Sanctuary in the midst of them forevermore. My Tabernacle also shall be with them: yea, I will be their God, and they shall be My people. And the heathen shall know that I the Lord do Sanctify Israel, when My Sanctuary shall be in the midst of them forevermore." Ez. 37: 26-28

On the New Earth there is no Temple because the Father and Jesus are the Temple.
"Behold, the Tabernacle of God is with men... and I saw no Temple therein: for the Lord God Almighty and the Lamb are the Temple of it ..." Rev. 21:3,22
We also are the Temple of God, living stones that make up the Temple with Jesus, the Cornerstone, (I. Cor.3:16;6:19;II Cor.6:16;I Pet.2:5).

"... I will make their people as numerous as sheep." Ez. 36:37 NIV
"Neither will I hide My face anymore from them: for I have poured out My Spirit upon the house of Israel, saith the Lord God." Ez. 39:29

Blessing
"... ye shall also give unto the priest the first of your dough, that he may cause the blessing to rest in thine house." Ez. 44:30

Daniel

"Now God had brought Daniel into favour and tender love with the prince of the eunuchs." Dan. 1:9
Prayer:
Father in heaven, please give me favor and tender love with the people around me as you did for Daniel. Thank you in the name of Jesus, Amen!

Ten times better
The Condition:
"Prove thy servants... ten days; and let them give us pulse (Heb. #2235

"something sown", vegetables) *to eat, and water to drink."* Dan. 1:12

The Blessing:
"And at the end of ten days their countenances appeared fairer and fatter in flesh than all the children which did eat the portion of the king's meat... and in all matters of wisdom and understanding, that the king inquired of them, he found them ten times better than all the magicians and astrologers that were in all his realm." Dan. 1:15,20

Daniel blesses God
"... they would desire mercies of the God of heaven concerning this secret (of the king's dream)*; that Daniel and his fellows should not perish with the rest of the wise men of Babylon. Then was the secret revealed unto Daniel in a night vision. Then Daniel blessed the God of heaven... blessed be the name of God forever and ever: for wisdom and might are His: and He changeth the times and the season: He removeth kings, and setteth up kings: He giveth wis-dom unto the wise, and knowledge to them that know understanding: He re-vealeth the deep and secret things: He knoweth what is in the darkness, and the light dwelleth with Him... God of my fathers, who hast given me wisdom and might, and hast made known unto me now what we desired of Thee: for Thou hast now made known unto us the king's matter."*
Dan. 2:18-23

Prayer:
Father in heaven, You revealed secrets to Daniel because he loved and served You. Please give me Your knowledge, wisdom, and understanding and reveal Your deep and secret truths and mysteries according to Your will in Jesus' name, Amen!

The Promise:
"If it be so, our God whom we serve is able to deliver us from the burning fiery furnace, and He will deliver us out of thine hand, O king..." Dan. 3:17,18

"... but if not, be it known unto thee, O king, that we will not serve thy gods, nor worship the golden image which thou hast set up." Dan. 3:17,18
Shadrach, Meshach, and Abednego knew that God could deliver them. They spoke faith but they were determined to serve Him no matter what happened!

Prayer:
Father in heaven, I know that you can deliver me from all my troubles but by the grace of God I will still serve You no matter what happens. In Jesus' name, Amen!

Miracle
God delivers Daniel from the lion's den
"... thy God whom thou serveth continually..." Dan. 6:16

> **The Promise:**
> "... He will deliver thee." Dan. 6:16

"... the king spake... O Daniel, servant of the living God, is thy God whom thou servest continually, able to deliver thee from the lions? Then Daniel said to the king... my God hath sent His angel, and hath shut the lions' mouths, that they have not hurt me: forasmuch as before Him innocency was found in me; and also before thee, O king, have I done no hurt. My God hath sent His angel, and hath shut the lions' mouths, that they have not hurt me: forasmuch as before Him innocency was found in me; and also before thee, O king, have I done no hurt... so Daniel was taken up out of the den, and no manner of hurt was found upon him, because he believed in his God." Dan. 6:20-23

God saved Daniel from the lions because he was innocent of any wrong doing and he believed God. God promises to send angels to help us also.

"For He shall give His angels charge over thee, to keep thee in all thy ways. They shall bear thee up in their hands, lest thou dash thy foot against a stone." Ps. 91:11,12

"The angel of the Lord encampeth round about them that fear Him, and delivereth them." Ps. 34:7

Prayer:
Father in heaven, please send Your angels to watch over me and my family and deliver us from evil as You promised in Your Word. Thank You for hearing and answering in the name of Jesus, Amen!

The king made a decree
"I make a decree that... men tremble and fear before the God of Daniel: for He is the living God, and stedfast ("endures" PB) forever, and His kingdom that which shall not be destroyed, and His dominion shall be even unto the end. He delivereth ("saves" PB) and rescueth, and He worketh signs and wonders in heaven and in earth." Dan. 6:26,27

God is the One who can deliver and rescue us.

> **The Promise:**
> "... who hath delivered Daniel from the power of the lions. So this Daniel prospered..." Dan. 6:27,28

God keeps His Covenant
"... the great and dreadful God." Dan. 9:4

The Promise:
"... keeping the Covenant and mercy to them..." Dan. 9:4

The Condition:
"... that love Him and... keep His Commandments." Dan. 9:4

The Condition:
"To the Lord our God belong mercies and forgivenesses, though we have rebelled against Him; neither have we obeyed the voice of the Lord our God, to walk in His laws, which He set before us by His servants the prophets..." Dan. 9:9,10

The Promise:
"... the Lord our God is righteous in all His works which He doeth." Dan. 9:14

The Condition:
"For we obeyed not His voice and now, O Lord our God, who didst bring Thy people out of the land of Egypt with a mighty hand, and hast made thee a name..." Dan. 9:15 PB

God sent the angel Gabriel to give Daniel skill and understanding

"... the man Gabriel... informed me, and talked with me, and said, O Daniel, I am now come forth to give thee skill and understanding." Dan. 9:21,22

Prayer:
Father in heaven, please give me skill and understanding when I need it like you did for Daniel. Thank You in Jesus' name, Amen!

God gives Daniel strength.

"Then there came again and touched me one like the appearance of a man, and he strengthened me. And said, O man greatly beloved, fear not: peace be unto thee, be strong, yea, be strong. And when he had spoken unto me, I was strengthened, and said, Let my Lord speak; for Thou hast strengthened me." Dan. 10:18,19

"... but the people that do know their God shall be strong, and do exploits. And they that understand among the people shall instruct many..." Dan. 11:32,33

(*"act valiantly"* Net Bible; *"prevail"* JPS Tanqkh 1917)

The Promise:
"And they that be wise shall shine as the brightness of the firmament; and they that turn many to righteousness as the stars forever and ever." Dan. 12:3

Prayer:
Father in heaven, give me wisdom to help others turn from their sins and start doing what is right. In Jesus' name, Amen!
The wise will understand!

> **The Promise:**
> "*Many shall be purified, and made white, and tried... the wise shall understand.*" Dan. 12:10

Hosea

God told Hosea to marry a woman that was promiscuous and unfaithful as an illustration of how God's people were unfaithful to Him by worshipping other gods. God gave Hosea a promise that would help him get his wife back. This is a promise you can claim if you have an unfaithful spouse.

> **The Promise:**
> "*... I will fence her in with thornbushes, I will block her path with a wall to make her lose her way (to her lovers). When she runs after her lovers, she won't be able to catch up with them. She will search for them but not find them... she will think, 'I might as well return to my husband because I was better off with him than I am now.' She doesn't realize that it was I who gave her everything she has... even the gold and silver... were gifts from Me...*" Hosea 2:6-13 NLT

If you have an unfaithful spouse, you could pray this prayer.
Prayer:
Father in heaven, please fence _____ in with thorns and block his/her path with a wall so that if he/she wanders from You he/she will be pricked and return to You. Close up every avenue to sin and win them back to You again. Help my spouse to realize it is better to go back their marriage. Thank You in Jesus' name, Amen!
I will turn the Valley of Trouble into a gateway of hope
"*Therefore, behold, I will allure her, and bring her into the wilderness, and speak comfortably unto her. And I will give her vineyards... she shall sing there, as in the days of her youth, and as in the day when she came up out of the land of Egypt... and it shall be at that day, saith the Lord, that thou shalt call Me Ishi ("That is, My husband" KJV fn)...*" Hosea 2:14-16

> **The Promise:**
> "*... I will win her back once again. I will lead her out... and speak tenderly to her there. I will... transform the Valley of Trouble into a gateway of hope. She will give herself to Me...*" Hosea 2:14,15 NLT

"... and His Bride has made herself ready." Rev. 19:7 NIV
In Revelation, the church is the Bride of Christ.
You could pray this prayer for your spouse
Prayer:
Father in heaven please win my spouse back to You so that they will be won back to me. In Jesus' name, Amen!

On the New Earth, there will be no more war

> **The Promise:**
> *"And in that day will I make a Covenant for them with the beasts of the field, and with the fowls of heaven, and with the creeping things of the ground: and I will break the bow and the sword and the battle out of the earth, and will make them to lie down safely."* Heb. 2:18

The Bible tells us that we are the Bride of Christ
"I am jealous over you with godly jealousy: for I have espoused you to one husband, that I may present you as a chaste virgin to Christ." II Cor. 11:2
"Husbands, love your wives even as Christ also loved the church, and gave Himself for it; that He might Sanctify and cleanse it with the washing of water by the Word. That He might present it to Himself a glorious church, not having spot, or wrinkle, or any such thing; but that it should be Holy and without blemish." Eph. 5:25-27
"... for the marriage of the Lamb is come, and His wife hath made herself ready." Rev. 19:7

God's mercy
"And I will sow her unto me in the earth; and I will have mercy upon her that had not obtained mercy; and I will say to them which were not My people, Thou art My people and they shall say, Thou art my God." Hosea 2:23
"I will plant her for myself in the land; I will show my love to the one I called 'not My loved one.' I will say to those called 'Not My people', 'You are My people'; and they will say, 'You are my God.'" Hosea 2:23 NIV
"Afterward shall the children of Israel return, and seek the Lord their God, and David their king; and shall fear the Lord and His goodness in the latter days." Hosea 3:5
"Afterward the Israelites will return and seek the Lord their God... they will come trembling to the Lord and to His blessing in the last days." Hosea 3:5 NIV
"... they shall know the Lord and His goodness in the latter days." Hosea 3:5 PB

God says, I will *"reward them their doings."* Hosea 4:9
"Come, and let us return unto the Lord: for He hath torn ..." Hosea 6:1
The Promise:
"... and He will heal us..." Hosea 6:1
The Promise:
"... and He will bind us up. After two days will He revive us: in the third day He will raise us up, and we shall live in His sight. Then shall we know, if we follow on to know the Lord: His going forth is prepared as the morning (#7837 "daybreak, dawn, dawning of the day"); and He shall come unto us as the rain, as the latter and former rain unto the earth." Hosea 6:1-3

The early rain came at Pentecost and before Jesus comes again, there will be a Latter Rain which will be greater than the first. See Rain and Latter Rain in Topical: Deut.11:14;Job29:23;Prov.16:15;Is.44:3;45:8;Jer.3:3;5:24;Ez.34:26; Zech. 10:1;Acts2: 17;ITim.4:1;Jms.5:7,8
"Also, O Judah, He hath set an harvest for thee, when I returned the captivity of My people. When I would have healed Israel..." Hosea 6:11;7:1

God called Israel out of Egypt
"When Israel was a child, then I loved him, and called My son out of Egypt. As they called them, so they went from them... I taught Ephraim also to go, taking them by their arms; but they knew not that I healed them." Hosea 11:1-3
Prayer:
Father in heaven, bring us out from the world and take us in Your arms and heal us we pray in Jesus' name, Amen!

"I bent over them and fed them." Hosea 11:4 PB
"I led them with cords of human kindness with ties of love; I lifted the yoke from their neck and bent down to feed them." Hosea 11:4 NIV

God promised to bring Israel back after the 70 yr. captivity in Babylon.
The Promise:
"... I will place them in their houses, saith the Lord." Hosea 11:11

"I will settle them in their homes..." Hosea 11:11 NIV
"I will bring them back to their dwelling places." Hosea 11:11 PB
"... your help is from Me. I will be your King..." Hosea 13:9 NKJV
The Promise:
"I will ransom them from the power of the grave; I will Redeem them from death..." Hosea 13:14

"O death, where is thy sting? O grave, where is thy victory?" I Cor. 15:55

The Condition:
"Pledge loyalty, and turn to the Lord your God; and pray to Him... that He may forgive your iniquity and receive blessings." Hosea 14:2 PB

> **The Promise:**
> *"I will heal their backsliding, I will love them freely: for Mine anger is turned away from him. I will be as the dew unto Israel: he shall grow as the lily... His branches shall spread, and his beauty shall be as the olive tree, and his smell as Lebanon. They that dwell under his shadow shall return; they shall revive as the corn, and grow as the vine ..."* Hosea 14:4-7

"... your fruit is found in Me." Hosea 14:8
"But the fruit of the Spirit is love, joy, peace, longsuffering, gentleness, goodness, faith, meekness, temperance..." Gal. 5:22,23

Joel

Blessing
"Who knows if He will return and repent ("relent" NIV), and leave a blessing behind Him." Joel 2:14

> **The Promise:**
> *"... the Lord will answer and say unto His people... I will send you corn, and wine, and oil, and ye shall be satisfied there with: and I will no more make you a reproach among the heathen: but I will remove far off from you the Northern army, and will drive him into a land barren and desolate... He hath done great things. Fear not, O land; be glad and rejoice: for the Lord will do great things."* Joel 2:19-21

"... for the Lord has done marvelous things. Do not be afraid..." Joel 2:22 KJV

The Latter Rain
"Be glad then, ye children of Zion, and rejoice in the Lord your God..." Joel 2:23

> **The Promise:**
> *"And I will restore ("recompense" – PB) to you the years that the locusts have eaten."* Joel 2:25

The Promise:
"And ye shall eat in plenty, and be satisfied, and praise the name of the Lord your God, that hath dealt wondrously with you: and My people shall never be ashamed. And ye shall know that I am in the midst of Israel, and that I am the Lord your God, and none else: and My people shall never be ashamed. And it shall come to pass afterward that I will pour out My Spirit upon all flesh; and your sons and your daughters shall prophesy, your old men shall dream dreams, your young men shall see visions... also upon the servant and upon the handmaids in those days will I pour out My Spirit. And I will shew wonders in the heavens and in the earth, blood, and fire, and pillars of smoke. The sun shall be turned into darkness, and the moon into blood, before the great and the terrible day of the Lord come. And it shall come to pass, that whosoever shall call on the name of the Lord shall be delivered: for in Mount Zion and in Jerusalem shall be deliverance, as the Lord hath said, and in the remnant whom the Lord shall call." Joel 2:26-32

There was a literal rain that came in the spring of the year to get the seeds started and a literal rain that came in the fall that helped the seeds to come to maturity and ready for the harvest. This was an allegory of the Spiritual early and latter rain that comes on God's people. The early rain at Pentecost helped to start the church and the latter rain will ripen and mature God's people to be ready for the second coming of Jesus.

"For, behold, in those days, and in that time, when I shall bring again the captivity of Judah and Jerusalem, I will also gather all nations, and will bring them down into the valley of Jehoshaphat, and will plead with them there for My people and for My heritage Israel, whom they have scattered among the nations, and parted My land." Joel 3:1,2

"Behold, I will raise them out of the place whither ye have sold them, and will return your recompence upon your own head..." Joel 3:7
The evil that people do to you will come back on their own heads.

"Beat your plowshares into swords, and your pruning hooks into spears: let the weak say, I am strong." Joel 3:10
Prayer:
Father in heaven, I am weak but You are strong; please give me Your strength. Thank you for your dear and precious promises, in Jesus' name, Amen!

Jerusalem will be Holy again when God dwells there on the New Earth
"So shall ye know that I am the Lord your God dwelling in Zion, My Holy Mountain: then shall Jerusalem be Holy, and there shall no strangers pass through her anymore. And it shall come to pass in that day, that the mountains shall drop down new wine, and the hills shall flow with milk, and all the rivers of Judah shall flow with waters, and a fountain shall come forth of the house of the Lord and shall water the valley of Shittim." Joel 3:17,18
"And he shewed me a pure river of Water of Life, proceeding out of the throne of God and of the Lamb." Rev. 22:1

God will cleanse Jerusalem from bloodshed on the New Earth
"But Judah shall dwell forever, and Jerusalem from generation to generation. For I will cleanse their blood that I have not cleansed: for the Lord dwelleth in Zion." Joel 3:20,21

The Promise:
"Surely the Lord will do nothing, but He revealeth His secret unto His servants the prophets." Amos 3:7

The Condition:
"Seek the Lord..." Amos 5:6

The Promise:
"... and you shall live." Amos 5:6

The Condition:
"Seek good, and not evil..." Amos 5:14

The Promise:
"... that ye may live: and so the Lord, the God of hosts, shall be with you, as ye have spoken." Amos 5:14

The Promise:
"... the days come... that the plowman shall overtake the reaper, and the treader of grapes him that soweth seed... the mountains shall drop sweet wine, and all the hills shall melt. And I will bring again the captivity of My people of Israel, and they shall build the waste cities, inhabit them; and they shall plant vineyards... they shall also make gardens, and eat the fruit of them. And I will plant them upon their land, and they shall no more be pulled up out of their land which I have given them, saith the Lord thy God." Amos 9:13-15

Obadiah

"But upon Mount Zion shall be deliverance, and there shall be Holiness; and the house of Jacob shall possess their possessions ("inheritance" NIV)... Mount Zion... shall be the Lord's" Obadiah 1:17,21

Jonah

"... Thou hast brought up my life from corruption, O Lord my God." Jonah:2:6
"... for I knew that Thou art a gracious God, and merciful, slow to anger, and of great kindness, and repentest thee of the evil." Jonah 4:2
Johan was angry at God for being merciful and kind, which says a lot about God. He didn't want the Ninevites to be saved but God is willing to save anyone who will repent and turn from their sins.

Micah

The Promise:
"... do not My Words do good?" Mic. 2:7

The Condition:
"... to him that walketh uprightly?" Mic. 2:7

On the New Earth
"And many nations shall come, and say, Come, and let us go up to the Mountain of the Lord, and to the house of the God of Jacob; and ..." Mic. 4:2

The Promise:
"... He will teach us of His ways, and we will walk in His paths: for the law shall go forth of Zion, and the Word of the Lord from Jerusalem... they shall beat their swords into plowshares, and their spears into pruning hooks: nation shall not lift up a sword against nation, neither shall they learn war anymore. But they shall sit every man under his vine and under his fig tree: and none shall make them afraid..." Micah 4:2-4

"... for the mouth of the Lord of hosts hath spoken it. For all people will walk every one in the name of his God, and we will walk in the name of the Lord our God forever and ever." Mic. 4:4,5

On the New Earth
"In that day, declares the Lord, I will assemble the lame and gather the outcasts, even those whom I have afflicted. I will make the lame a remnant and the outcasts a strong nation, and the Lord will reign over them in Mount Zion from now on and forever." Mic. 4:6,7 NASB

> **The Promise:**
> "And this man (Jesus) *shall be the peace... thus shall He deliver us..."* Mic. 5:5,6

"... when He treadeth within our borders." Mic. 5:6
Jesus treads the winepress of the wrath of God in Rev. 14:19;19:15.

"Rejoice not against me, O mine enemy: when I fall..." Mic. 7:8

> **The Promise:**
> *"I shall arise..."* Mic. 7:8

"... when I sit in darkness..." Mic. 7:8

> **The Promise:**
> *"... the Lord shall be a light unto me."* Mic. 7:8

Nahum

> **The Promise:**
> *"The Lord is good, a stronghold in the day of trouble..."* Nahum 1:7

The Condition:
"... and He knoweth them that trust in Him." Nahum 1:7

"What do ye imagine against the Lord? What do you plot against the Lord?" Nahum 1:9

> **The Promise:**
> *"... He will make an utter end: affliction shall not rise up the second time."* Nahum 1:9

"... He will make a complete end (of sin); *trouble will not rise up a second time."* Nahum 1:9 ESV
The Promise is that sin and suffering will never rise up a second time.

> **The Promise:**
> *"... O Judah ... the wicked shall no more pass through thee; he is utterly cut off."* Nahum 1:15

Someday, on the New Earth, there will be no more evil or wicked people going through Judah and no more sin or trouble.
"*And there shall in no wise enter into it* (the New Jerusalem) *anything that defileth, neither whatsoever worketh abomination, or maketh a lie: but* (on-ly) *they which are written in the Lamb's Book of Life.*" Rev. 21:27

 Habakkuk

"*Behold ye among the heathen... regard, and wonder marvelously...*" Hab. 1:5

The Promise:
"*... for I will work a work in your days which ye will not believe though it be told you.*" Hab. 1:5

"*... for the vision is yet for an appointed time, but at the end it shall speak, and not lie: though it tarry, wait for it...*" Hab. 2:3

The Promise:
"*... because it will surely come, it will not tarry.*" Hab. 2:3

The Promise:
When God reigns "*... the earth shall be filled with the knowledge of the glory of the Lord, as the waters cover the sea.*" Hab. 2:14

"*Thou wentest forth for the Salvation of Thy people, even for Salvation with Thine anointed; Thou woundedst the head out of the house of the wicked... Thou didst strike through with his staves the head of his villages; they came out as a whirlwind to scatter me: their rejoicing was as to devour the poor secretly. Thou didst walk through the sea, with Thine horses, through the heap of great waters.*" Hab. 3:13-15
Revelation talks about Jesus coming on a white horse and an army following Him on white horses.
"*... and behold a white horse; and He that sat upon him was called Faithful and True, and in righteousness He doth... make war... and the armies which were in heaven followed Him upon white horses...*" Rev. 19:11,14

The Promise:
"*The Lord God is my strength, and He will make my feet like hinds' feet, and He will make me to walk upon mine high places.*" Hab. 3:19

Zephaniah

The Condition:
"Seek ye the Lord, all ye meek of the earth, which have wrought His Judgment; seek righteousness, seek meekness..." Zeph. 2:3

> **The Promise:**
> "... it may be ye shall be hid in the day of the Lord's anger." Zeph. 2:3

"... they lie down in the evening: for the Lord their God shall visit them, and turn away their captivity." Zeph. 2:7

"... the residue of My people shall spoil them, and the remnant of My people shall possess them." Zeph. 2:9

When God reigns on the earth "... men shall worship Him, every one from his place, even all the isles of the heathen." Zeph. 2:11
When "... the **earth shall be devoured by fire**..." Zeph. 3:8

> **The Promise:**
> "... **then** will I turn to the people a pure language, that they may all call upon... the Lord, to serve Him with one consent." Zeph. 3:9

"In that day shalt thou not be ashamed for all thy doings, wherein thou hast transgressed against Me: for then I will take away out of the midst of thee them that rejoice in thy pride, and thou shalt no more be haughty because of My Holy Mountain. I will also leave in the midst of thee an afflicted and poor people, and they shall trust in the name of the Lord." Zeph. 3:11,12

> **The Promise:**
> "The remnant of Israel shall not do iniquity, nor speak lies; neither shall a deceitful tongue be found in their mouth: for they shall feed and lie down, and none shall make them afraid." Zeph. 3:13

> **The Promise:**
> "... the Lord, is in the midst of thee: thou shalt not see evil anymore." Zeph. 3:15

> **The Promise:**
> "The Lord thy God in the midst of thee is mighty; He will save, He will rejoice over thee with joy: He will rest in His love, He will joy over thee with singing." Zeph. 3:17

God sings over you when you get saved – Hallelujah!!!

The Promise:
"Behold, at that time I will undo all that afflict thee: and I will save her that halteth ("is lame" NIV), and gather her that was driven out; and I will get them praise and fame in every land where they have been put to shame. At that time will I bring you again, even in the time that I gather you: for I will make you a name and a praise among all people of the earth, when I turn back your captivity before your eyes, saith the Lord." Zeph. 3:19,20

"At that time I will deal with all who oppressed you..." Zeph. 3:19 NIV
"... I will save the weak and helpless ones; I will bring together those who were chased away. I will give glory and renown to My former exiles, who have been mocked and shamed." Zeph. 3:19 NLT

Haggai

"Yet now be strong, O Zerubbabel, saith the Lord..." Hag. 2:4
The Promise:
"... I am with you, saith the Lord." Hag. 1:13

The Promise:
"I am with you, saith the Lord of hosts... My Spirit remaineth among you: fear ye not." Hag. 2:4,5

"The silver is Mine, and the gold is Mine, saith the Lord of hosts..." Hag. 2:8

The Promise:
"... in this place will I give peace, saith the Lord of hosts." Hag. 2:8,9

(See Ps. 24:;50:10)

Blessed
"... from this day will I bless you." Hag. 2:19

The Promise:
"... I... will make thee as a signet; for I have chosen thee, saith the Lord of hosts." Hag. 2:22,23

Zechariah

The Condition:
"... return to Me.."

> **The Promise:**
> "... and I will return to you... says the Lord of hosts." Zech. 1:3 NKJV

"I am returned to Jerusalem with mercies..." Zech. 1:16

> **The Promise:**
> "... thus saith the Lord of hosts; My cities through prosperity shall yet be spread abroad; and the Lord shall yet comfort Zion, and shall yet

> **The Promise:**
> "For I, saith the Lord, will be unto her (New Jerusalem) *a wall of fire round about, and will be the glory in the midst of her*." Zech. 2:4,5

Prayer:
Father in heaven, please be a wall of fire around me and my loved ones. Thank You in Jesus' name, Amen!

"Sing and rejoice, O daughter of Zion: for, lo..." Zech. 2:10

> **The Promise:**
> "... I come, and I will dwell in the midst of thee, saith the Lord. And many nations shall be joined to the Lord in that day, and shall be My people: and I will dwell in the midst of thee, and thou shalt know that the Lord of hosts hath sent me unto thee. And the Lord shall inherit Judah His portion in the Holy land, and shall choose Jerusalem again." Zech. 2:10-12

On the New Earth "... I heard a great voice out of heaven saying... the Tabernacle of God is with men, and He will dwell with them, and they shall be His people, and God Himself shall be with them, and be their God." Rev. 21:3
The Father and Jesus are the only Temple on the New Earth, Rev. 21: 3, 22.

> **The Promise:**
> "... behold, I have caused thine iniquity to pass from thee, and I will clothe thee with change of raiment (the righteousness of Jesus, Rom. 13:14)..." Zech. 3:4

"And I said, Let them set a fair mitre upon his head. So they set a fair mitre upon his head, and clothed him with garments..." Zech. 3:4,5

The robe of Christ's righteousness!

"Thus saith the Lord of hosts..." Zech. 3:7
The Condition:
"... if thou wilt walk in My ways, and if thou wilt keep My charge..." Zech. 3:7

> **The Promise:**
> *"... then thou shalt also Judge My courts, and I will give thee places to walk among these that stand by."* Zech. 3:7

"And I saw thrones, and they sat upon them, and Judgment was given unto them..." Rev. 20:4

A promise about Jesus the Messiah
"... for, behold, I will bring forth My Servant the Branch (Jesus)*."* Zech. 3:8

> **The Promise:**
> *"... not by might, nor by power, but by My Spirit, saith the Lord of hosts. Who art thou, O great mountain? Before Zerubbabel thou shalt become a plain: and he shall bring forth the Headstone* (Jesus) *thereof with shoutings, crying Grace, grace unto it."* Zech. 4:6,7

On the New Earth

> **The Promise:**
> *"... I will remove the iniquity of that land in one day. In that day, saith the Lord of hosts, shall ye call every man his neighbor under the vine and under the fig tree."* Zech. 3:9, 10

Jesus is the Headstone or Cornerstone the builders rejected, Eph. 2:20. We can also say to our troubles; Who are you O great mountain? Before me you will become a plain in Jesus' name.
"In that day (on the New Earth), *saith the Lord of hosts, shall ye call every man his neighbor under the vine and under the fig tree."* Zech. 3:10

"For who has despised the day of small things." Zech. 4:10 NKJV
"Do not despise these small beginnings." Zech. 4:10 NLT

Children playing in the streets
"Thus saith the Lord; I am returned unto Zion, and will dwell in the midst of Jerusalem: and Jerusalem shall be called a City of Truth; and the Mountain of the Lord of host, the Holy Mountain. There shall yet old (Gr. #2205 "elders") *men and old* (Gr. #2205 "elders") *women dwell in the streets of Jerusalem... and the streets of the city shall be full of boys and girls playing*

in the streets thereof... behold, I will save My people. And I will bring them, and they shall dwell in the midst of Jerusalem: and they shall be My people, and I will be their God, in truth and in righteousness." Zech. 8:3,7,8
When does this happen? When God dwells in Jerusalem

>**The Promise:**
>"For the seed shall be prosperous; the vine shall give her fruit, and the ground shall give her increase, and the heavens shall give their dew; and I will cause the remnant of this people to possess all these things... so will I save you, and ye shall be a blessing: fear not, but let your hands be strong." Zech. 8:12,13

"The seed will grow well." Zech. 8:12 NIV
If you have faith as small as a mustard seed, you can say to this mountain – be removed and cast into the sea and it will happen for you, Matt. 17:20;Lk. 17:6.

On the New Earth
"... even He, shall be for our God, and He shall be as a Governor in Judah..." Zech. 9:7

>**The Promise:**
>"... no oppressor shall pass through them anymore..." Zech. 9:8

A promise about Jesus
"... for now have I seen with mine eyes. Rejoice greatly, O daughter of Zion; shout, O daughter of Jerusalem: behold, thy King cometh unto thee: He is just, and having Salvation; lowly, and riding upon (a donkey), and upon a colt the foal of (a donkey)." Zech. 9:8,9
"As for thee also, by the blood of Thy Covenant I have sent forth thy prisoners out of the pit wherein is no water." Zech. 9:11
They entered into the Covenant through the blood of animals in the Old Testament but we enter into the New Covenant through the blood of Jesus.
"... I will render double unto thee..." Zech. 9:12
"... I will restore twice as much to you." Zech. 9:12 NIV

>**The Promise:**
>"The Lord of Hosts ("Almighty" NIV) shall defend ("shield" NIV; "protect" ESV) them..." Zech. 9:15

>**The Promise:**
>"And the Lord their God shall save them, in that day as the flock of His people: for they shall be as the stones of a crown, lifted up as an ensign upon His land. For great is His goodness, and how great is His beauty! Corn shall make the young men cheerful, and new wine the maids." Zech. 9:16,17

"Ask ye of the Lord rain in the time of the latter rain..." Zech. 10:1

The Promise:
"... so the Lord shall make bright clouds, and give them showers of rain, to every one grass in the field." Zech. 10:1

This promise was originally given to Israel after the 70 yr. captivity

The Promise:
"And I will strengthen the house of Judah, and I will save the house of Joseph, and I will bring them again to place them; for I have mercy upon them: and they shall be as though I had not cast them off: for I am the Lord their God, and will hear them. And they of Ephraim shall be like a mighty man, and their heart shall rejoice as through wine: yea, their children shall see it, and be glad; their heart shall rejoice in the Lord. I will hiss (Gr. "whistle") for them, and gather them; for I have Redeemed them: and they shall increase as they have increased. And I will sow them among the people: and they shall remember Me in far countries; and they shall live with their children, and turn again. I will bring in them again also out of the land of Egypt, and gather them out of Assyria; and I will bring them into the land of Gilead and Lebanon; and place shall not be found for them. And he shall pass through the sea with affliction, and shall smite the waves in the sea, and all the deeps of the river shall dry up: and the pride of Assyria shall be brought down, and the scepter of Egypt shall depart away. And I will strengthen them in the Lord; andand they shall walk up and down in His name, saith the Lord." Zech. 10:5-12

"... and they shall look upon Me (Jesus) whom they have pierced..." Zech. 12:10

"When I (Jesus) be lifted up, I will draw all men unto Me." Jn. 12:32

The Promise:
"In that day there shall be a fountain opened to the house of David and to the inhabitants of Jerusalem for sin and for uncleanness. And it shall come to pass in that day, saith the Lord of hosts, that I will cut off the names of the idols out of the land, and they shall no more be remembered: and also I will cause the (false) prophets and the unclean spirit to pass out of the land." Zech. 13:1,2

"And I will bring the third part through the fire, and will refine them as silver is refined, and will try them as gold is tried..." Zech. 13:9

> **The Promise:**
> *"... they shall call on My name, and I will hear them: I will say, It is My people: and they shall say, The Lord is my God."* Zech. 13:9

On the New Earth
"And it shall be in that day, that living waters shall go out from Jerusalem... and the Lord shall be King over all the earth... and men shall dwell in it, and there shall be no more utter destruction; but Jerusalem shall be safely inhab-ited." Zech. 14:1,8

God promises to never change.
"For I am the Lord, I change not..." Mal. 3:6

I will return to you
"Even from the days of your fathers ye are gone away from Mine Ordinances, and have not kept them..." Mal. 3:7

The Condition:
"... return unto Me..." Mal. 3:7

> **The Promise:**
> *"... and I will return unto you, saith the Lord of hosts..."* Mal. 3:7

Tithing
The Condition:
"Bring ye all the tithes into the storehouse, that there may be meat in Mine house, and prove Me now herewith, saith the Lord of hosts..." Mal. 3:10

> **The Promise:**
> *"... I will... open... the windows of heaven, and pour you out a blessing, that there shall not be room enough to receive it. And I will rebuke the Devourer for your sakes, and he shall not destroy the fruits of your ground; neither shall your vine cast her fruit before the time in the field, saith the Lord... all nations shall call you blessed: for ye shall be a delightsome land, saith the Lord...."* Mal.3:10-12

God writes down every word that we speak about Him
"Then they that feared the Lord spake often one to another: and the Lord hearkened, and heard it, and a Book of Remembrance was written before

Him for them that feared the Lord, and that thought upon His name." Mal. 3:16

The Promise:
"... they shall be Mine, saith the Lord... in that day when I make up My jewels; and I will spare them, as a man spareth his own son... Then shall ye return, and discern between the righteous and the wicked, between him that serveth God and him that serveth Him not." Mal. 3: 17,18

On the New Earth
The Condition:
"... unto you that fear My name..." Mal. 4:2

The Promise:
"... shall the Sun of righteousness arise with healing in His wings; and ye shall go forth, and grow up as calves of the stall. And ye shall tread down the wicked; for they shall be ashes under the soles of your feet in the day that I shall do this, saith the Lord of hosts." Mal. 4:2,3

The coming of Elijah

The Promise:
"Behold, I will send you Elijah, the prophet before the coming of the great and dreadful day of the Lord: and he shall turn the heart of the fathers to the children, and the heart of the children to their fathers..." Mal. 4:5,6

New Testament

Matthew

"... and thou shalt call His name Jesus ("Yeshua or Yahshuah – which means Adonai saves" JNT; His name is a promise that He saves.)..." Matt. 1:21

The Promise:
"... for He shall save His people from their sins." Matt. 1:21

"Behold, a virgin shall conceive, and bear a son, and shall call His name Immanuel (meaning, *"God with us"*)." Is. 7:14
This prophecy about Jesus in Is. 7:14 was fulfilled here in Matthew about 700 yrs. later.

"... they shall call His name Emmanuel, which being interpreted is, God with us." Matt. 1:23
Jesus' name is a promise that He will be with us – the name Immanuel means *"God with us"* because He is God!
Jesus asked Peter, *"Who do you say I am?"* And Peter answered and said, *"You are the Christ, the Son of the living God"* Matt. 16:13-20 NIV.
Nicodemus said, *"Rabbi, we know that You have come from God..."* Jn. 3:2 NASB
They wanted to stone Jesus for declaring Himself the *"I Am"* in Jn. 5:58. This verse tells us that Jesus was the God of the Old Testament; the same God that talked to Moses in the burning bush.
They said that Jesus was a blasphemer because He claimed to be God in Matt. 26:65. Now it is true that it is blasphemy to claim to be God if you aren't God; that is the definition of blasphemy. But it isn't blasphemy to claim to be God if You are indeed God. So it wasn't blasphemy for Jesus to claim to be God because He was God and He did the miracles to prove it. In fact, it would have been a lie if Jesus had said He wasn't God because He actually was God. He was the very God of the Old Testament that the people were claiming to worship and serve. He is the only man who is also God!
"Search the Scriptures; for in them ye think ye have eternal life (and you do): *and they are they which testify of Me."* Jn. 5:39
"The Jews answered him, We have a law, and by our law He ought to die, be-cause He made Himself the Son of God." Jn. 19:7
The Bible says, *"And the Word was made flesh* (Jesus), *and dwelt among us... as of the only begotten of the Father...."* Jn. 1:14
It also says, *"In the beginning was the Word and the Word was with God and the Word was God... all things were made by Him".* Jn. 1:1,3
We can put these things together to know that:

Jesus is the Word! Jesus is God! Jesus is the Creator and Jesus was with God in the beginning. Jesus is the God of Israel (on the cross it was written *"King of the Jews"*). Thomas said to Jesus, My Lord and my God, Jn. 20:28. Jesus said that the Father and He were One in Jn. 10:30. God the Father says in Heb. 1:6 NLT, *"Let all the angels of God worship Him (Jesus)"*. The leper worshipped Him in Matt. 8:2, the leader of the Synagogue worshiped Him in Matt. 9:18, the blind man worshipped Him in Jn. 9:38, the Canaanite woman worshipped Him in Matt. 15:25, and the disciples worshipped Him in Matt. 28:9,17 and Lk. 24:52 (and we are to worship only God). Jesus is called the *"Lord of glory"* in Jms. 2:1. He is above angels in Heb. 1:6,13 and above every principality, power, might, dominion, and every name, Eph. 1:21, Phil. 2:9-11.

"And without controversy great is the mystery of godliness: God was manifest in the flesh..." I Tim. 3:16

"... He that cometh after me is mightier than I, whose shoes I am not worthy to bear..." Matt. 3:11

The Promise:
"... He shall baptize you with the Holy Ghost, and with fire: whose fan is in His hand, and He will thoroughly purge His floor, and gather His wheat into the garner..." Matt. 3:11, 12

When Jesus was tempted in the wilderness, He quoted Scriptures to overcome the Devil and we can do the same thing.
"But he answered and said, It is written, Man shall not live by bread alone, but..." Matt. 4:4

The Promise:
"... by every Word that proceedeth out of the mouth of God." Matt. 4:4

The Promise:
"... He shall give His angels charge concerning thee: and in their hands they shall bear thee up, lest at any time thou dash thy foot against a stone." Matt. 4:6

Satan was quoting Ps. 91:11 here but Jesus showed that we are never to be presumptuous with the promises.

"The people which sat in darkness saw a great light; and to them which sat in the region and shadow of death light is sprung up." Matt. 4:16
The Condition:
"And He saith unto them, Follow Me..." Matt. 4:19

The Promise:
"... and I will make you fishers of men." Matt. 4:19

Prayer:
Jesus, help us to follow You so that we too can be fishers of men! Thank You, Amen!

Miracles
"... Jesus... healing all manner of sickness and all manner of disease among the people... and they brought unto Him all sick people that were taken with divers diseases and torments, and those which were possessed with devils, and those which were lunatick, and those that had the palsy; and He healed them." Matt. 4:23,24
Prayer:
Jesus, please heal me and my family when we need it as You did when on earth; according to Your Word. Thank You! Amen!

Blessings
The Condition:
"Blessed are the poor in spirit..." Matt. 5:3

The Promise:
"... for theirs is the kingdom of heaven." Matt. 5:3

The Condition:
"... blessed are they that mourn..." Matt. 5:4

The Promise:
"... for they shall be comforted." Matt. 5:4

The Condition:
"Blessed are the meek..." Matt. 5:5

The Promise:
"... for they shall inherit the earth." Matt. 5:5

The Condition:
"Blessed are they which do hunger and thirst after righteousness..." Matt. 5:6

The Promise:
"... for they shall be filled." Matt. 5:6

The Condition:
"Blessed are the merciful..." Matt. 5:7

> **The Promise:**
> *"... for they shall obtain mercy."* Matt. 5:7

The Condition:
"Blessed are the pure in heart..." Matt. 5:8

> **The Promise:**
> *"... for they shall see God."* Matt. 5:8

The Condition:
"Blessed are the peacemakers..." Matt. 5:9

> **The Promise:**
> *"... for they shall be called the children of God."* Matt. 5:9

The Condition:
"Blessed are they which are persecuted for righteousness' sake..." Matt. 5:10

> **The Promise:**
> *"... for theirs is the kingdom of heaven."* Matt. 5:10

The Condition:
"Blessed are ye, when men shall revile you, and persecute you, and shall say all manner of evil against you falsely, for My sake. Rejoice, and be exceeding glad..." Matt. 5:11,12

> **The Promise:**
> *"... for great is your reward in heaven..."* Matt. 5:12

> **The Promise:**
> *"For truly I say to you, until heaven and earth pass away, not the smallest letter or stroke shall pass from the Law until all is accomplished."* Matt. 5:18

The Condition:
"But I say unto you, Love your enemies, bless them that curse you, do good to them that hate you, and pray for them which despitefully use you, and per-secute you..." Matt. 5:44

> **The Promise:**
> *"... that ye may be the children of your Father which is in heaven..."* Matt. 5:45

*"... for He maketh His sun to rise on the evil and on the good, and sendeth rain on the just and on the unjust. For if ye love them which love you, what reward have ye... and if ye salute your brethren only, what do ye more than

others... be ye therefore perfect even as your Father which is in heaven is perfect." Matt. 5:44-48

Your reward comes in loving those who don't love you back and greeting those who don't greet you back. The God who sees in secret, will reward you openly, Matt. 6:4.

"Take heed that ye do not your alms before men... otherwise ye have no reward of your Father which is in heaven." Matt. 6:1

If we do our good works expecting the praises of men, we will not have a reward in heaven.

The Condition:
"But thou, when thou prayest, enter into thy closet, and when thou hast shut thy door, pray to thy Father which is in secret; and thy Father which seeth in secret..." Matt. 6:6

> **The Promise:**
> "... shall reward thee openly... for your Father knoweth what things ye have need of, before ye ask Him..." Matt. 6:6

The Condition:
"For if ye forgive men their trespasses..." Matt. 6:14

> **The Promise:**
> "... your heavenly Father will also forgive you..." Matt. 6:14

"But thou, when thou fastest, anoint thine head, and wash thy face; that thou appear not unto men to fast, but unto thy Father which is in secret: and thy Father, which seeth in secret..." Matt. 6:17,18

> **The Promise:**
> "... shall reward thee openly." Matt. 6:18

"But lay up for yourselves treasures in heaven, where neither moth nor rust doth corrupt, and where thieves do not break through nor steal..." Matt. 6:20

God promises us treasures in heaven where they are secure and cannot be stolen away from us.

The Condition:
"The light of the body is the eye: if therefore thine eye be single..." Matt. 6:22

> **The Promise:**
> "... thy whole body shall be full of light." Matt. 6:22

"Behold the fowls of the air: for they sow not, neither do they reap, nor gather into barns; yet your heavenly Father feedeth them. Are ye not much better than they? Which of you by taking thought ("worrying" NKJV) can add one cubit unto his stature? And why take ye thought for raiment? Consider the lilies of the field, how they grow; they toil not, neither do they spin: and yet I say unto you, That even Solomon in all his glory was not arrayed like one of these. Wherefore, if God so clothe the grass of the field, which today is, and tomorrow is cast into the oven..." Matt. 6:26-30

> **The Promise:**
> *"... shall He not much more clothe you..."* Matt. 6:30

"... O ye of little faith? Therefore take no thought, saying, What shall we eat? or, What shall we drink? or, Wherewithal shall we be clothed... for your heavenly Father knoweth that ye have need of all these things." Matt 6:30-32

Lk. 12:25 NIV *"Who of you by worrying can add a single hour to your life?"*

The Condition:
"But seek ye first the kingdom of God, and His righteousness..." Matt. 6:33

> **The Promise:**
> *"... all these things shall be added unto you." "* Matt. 6: 33

"Take therefore no thought for the morrow: for the morrow shall take thought for the things of itself. Sufficient unto the day is the evil thereof." Matt. 6:34

The Condition:
"Ask..." Matt. 7:7

> **The Promise:**
> *"... and it shall be given you..."* Matt. 7:7

The Condition:
"... seek..." Matt. 7:7

> **The Promise:**
> *"... and ye shall find..."* Matt. 7:7

The Condition:
"... knock..." Matt. 7:7

> **The Promise:**
> *"... and it shall be opened unto you: for everyone that asketh receiveth; and he that seeketh findeth; and to him that knocketh it shall be opened."* Matt. 7:7,8

"If ye then, being evil, know how to give good gifts unto your children..." Matt. 7:11

The Promise:
"... how much more shall your Father which is in heaven give good things to them..." Matt. 7:11

The Condition:
"... that ask Him?" Matt. 7:11
"... Lord, if Thou wilt, Thou canst make me clean. And Jesus put forth His hand, and touched him, saying..." Matt. 8:2

The Promise:
"... I will; be thou clean..." Matt. 8:3

"... and immediately his leprosy was cleansed." Matt. 8:3

Miracle
"And Jesus saith unto him, I will come and heal him." Matt. 8:7

Miracle
"... speak the Word only, and my servant shall be healed. Go thy way; and as thou hast believed, so be it done unto thee..." Matt. 8:8,13
Because he believed - it was done for him.

Miracle
"And when Jesus was come into Peter's house, He saw his wife's mother... sick of a fever. And He touched her hand, and the fever left her: and she arose, and ministered unto them." Matt. 8:14

Miracles
"When the even was come, they brought unto Him many that were possessed with devils: and He cast out the spirits with His Word, and healed all that were sick! That it might be fulfilled which was spoken by Esaias the prophet, saying, Himself took our infirmities, and bare our sicknesses." Matt. 8:16,17

Miracle
"And His disciples came to Him, and awoke Him, saying, Lord, save us: we perish. And He saith unto them, Why are ye fearful, O ye of little faith? Then He arose, and rebuked the winds and the sea... what manner of man is this, that even the winds and the sea obey Him!" Matt. 8:25-27
Jesus said that they had little faith but He calmed the storm anyway.

Prayer:
Jesus, I thank You that even when we are faithless, You are faithful! (II Tim. 2:13)

Miracle
"... they brought to... (Jesus) *a man sick of the palsy, lying on a bed: and Jesus seeing their faith said unto* (him); *Son, be of good cheer; thy sins be forgiven thee... but that ye may know that the Son of man hath power on earth to forgive sins (... He* [said] *to the sick of the palsy), Arise take up thy bed, and go unto thine house... but when the multitudes saw it, they marveled, and glorified God, which had given such power unto men."* Matt. 9:2,6,18

Miracle
"And, behold, a woman, which was diseased with an issue of blood twelve years came behind Him, and touched the hem of His garment: for she said within herself, If I may but touch His garment, I shall be whole. But Jesus turned Him about, and when He saw her, He said, Daughter, be of good comfort; thy faith hath made thee whole." Matt. 9:21,22
And the woman was made whole from that hour; her faith made her whole.

Miracle
Jesus brings the twelve year old girl back to life, Matt. 9:23-25.
"And the fame hereof went abroad into all that land." Matt. 9:26
I have heard preachers use the woman with the issue of blood to illustrate the Old Covenant with the continual flow of blood from animal sacrifices and this young girl as an illustration of the New Covenant. Though you were dead in trespasses and sin now you're alive in Christ Jesus!
Old woman = Old Covenant
Young girl = New Covenant
Issue of blood = continual flow of animal sacrifices
12 = 12 tribes of Israel

Miracle
"... *two blind men followed...* (Jesus), *crying, Thou Son of David, have mercy on us... Jesus saith unto them, Believe ye that I am able to do this? They said unto Him, Yea, Lord. Then touched He their eyes, saying, According to your faith be it unto you."* Matt. 9:28,29

Mracle
Jesus cast out the evil spirit *"and when the devil was cast out, the dumb*

spake: and the multitudes marveled, saying, It was never so seen in Israel." Matt. 9:33

Miracles
"And Jesus went about all the cities and villages, teaching in their Synagogues, and preaching the Gospel of the kingdom, and healing every sickness and every disease among the people, but when He saw the multitudes, He was moved with compassion on them, because they fainted, and were scattered abroad, as sheep having no shepherd…" Matt. 9:35,36

Jesus gave His disciples power over unclean spirits and to heal
"And when He had called unto Him His twelve disciples, He gave them power (#1849 "power, authority") against unclean spirits, to cast them out, and to heal all manner of sickness and all manner of disease." Matt. 10:1;Lk.10:19
Prayer:
Father in heaven, we are Your disciples. Please give us Your power and authority to heal in the name of Jesus, Amen!

The Great Commission
"And as ye go, preach saying, The kingdom of heaven is at hand. Heal the sick, cleanse the lepers, raise the dead, cast out devils: freely ye have received, freely give." Matt. 10:7,8
Prayer:
Father in heaven, please give freely to us so that we can freely give to others. Thank You in Jesus' name, Amen!

"But when they deliver you up, take no thought how or what ye shall speak…" Matt. 10:19

> **The Promise:**
> *"… for it shall be given you in that same hour what ye shall speak. For it is not ye that speak, but the Spirit of your Father which speaketh in you."* Matt. 10:19,20

"And ye shall be hated of all men for My name's sake…" Matt. 10:22

The Condition:
"… but He that endureth to the end…" Matt. 10:22

> **The Promise:**
> *"… shall be saved."* Matt. 10:22

The Condition:
"Whosoever therefore shall confess Me before men..." Matt 10:32

> **The Promise:**
> *"... him will I confess also before My Father which is in heaven."* Matt. 10:33

The Condition:
"He that receiveth you..." Matt. 10:40

> **The Promise:**
> *"... receiveth Me..."* Matt. 10:40

The Condition:
"... and he that receiveth Me..." Matt. 10:40

> **The Promise:**
> *"... receiveth Him that sent Me* (the Father).*"* Matt. 10: 40

The Condition:
"He that receiveth a prophet in the name of a prophet..." Matt. 10:41

> **The Promise:**
> *"... shall receive a prophet's reward..."* Matt. 10:41

There are different rewards for different things and we will each receive rewards according to what we've done here on earth (see "*rewards*" in Topical section).

"But I keep under my body, and bring it into subjection: lest that by any means, when I have preached to others, I myself should be a castaway." I Cor. 9:27

Prayer:
Father in heaven, please help me to do my best here now so that I will not lose anything that You have for me in heaven. In Jesus' name, Amen!

The Condition:
"And whosoever shall give to drink unto one of these little ones a cup of cold water only in the name of a disciple, verily I say unto you..." Matt. 10:42

> **The Promise:**
> *"... he shall in no wise lose his reward."* Matt. 10:42

Miracles
"The blind receive their sight, and the lame walk, the lepers are cleansed,

and the deaf hear, the dead are raised up, and the poor have the Gospel preached to them." Matt. 11:5

Blessed
"And blessed is he, whosoever shall not be offended in Me." Matt. 11:6

The Condition:
"Come unto Me, all ye that labour and are heavy laden..." Matt. 11:28

    The Promise:
    "... and I will give you rest." Matt. 11:28

The Condition:
"Take My yoke upon you, and learn of Me; for I am meek and lowly in heart..." Matt. 11:29

    The Promise:
    "... and ye shall find rest unto your souls." Matt. 11:29

"For My yoke is easy, and My burden is light." Matt. 11:30
If we cast our burdens and cares on God (Ps.55:22;I Pet.5:7), we can find rest and trust that what He says He will do; we can trust His promises.

Miracle
"Then saith He (Jesus) to the man (with the withered hand). And he stretched it forth; and it was restored whole, like as the other." Matt. 12:13

Miracles of Jesus
"... Jesus... healed them all..." Matt. 12:15
Prayer:
Jesus, You healed so many when You were here on this earth; please heal us now when we need healing like You did then. Thank You, Amen!

Promise to Jesus
"Behold My servant (Jesus), whom I have chosen; My beloved, in whom My soul is well pleased: I will put My Spirit upon Him, and He shall shew Judgment to the Gentiles." Matt. 12:18
Prayer:
Father in heaven, please fulfill Your promises to me because of Your dear and precious Son, Jesus, who pleased You in everything He did. I acknowledge that my righteousness is in Jesus! Thank You in Jesus' name, Amen!

Prophecy about Jesus
"*A bruised reed shall He not break, and smoking flax shall He not quench, till He send forth Judgment unto victory.*" Matt. 12:20
"*And in His name (Jesus) shall the Gentiles trust ("hope" Gr.).* Matt. 12:21
God opened the way for Gentiles to be saved through Jesus.

Miracle
"*Then was brought unto Him (Jesus) one possessed with a devil, blind, and dumb: and He healed him, insomuch that the blind and dumb both spake and saw.*" Matt. 12:22

Bind the strong man
"*... if I cast out devils by the Spirit of God, then the kingdom of God is come upon you... how can one enter into a strong man's house, and spoil his goods except he first bind the strong man?*" Matt. 12:28,29

> **The Promise:**
> "*And then he will spoil his house...*" Matt. 12:29

Jesus said to the woman who had an infirmity for 18 years, "*Woman, thou art loosed from thine infirmity.*" Lk. 13:12
Jesus said, "*... I will give unto thee the keys of the kingdom of heaven: and whatsoever thou shalt bind on earth shall be bound in heaven: and whatsoever thou shalt loose on earth shall be loosed in heaven.*" Matt. 16:19
"*Verily I say unto you, Whatsoever ye shall bind on earth shall be bound in heaven: and whatsoever ye shall loose on earth shall be loosed in heaven.*" Matt. 18:18
It is through the blood of Jesus that we have victory over the Devil.
"*And they overcame him* (the Devil) *by the blood of the Lamb, and by the word of their testimony...*" Rev. 12:11
Prayer:
Jesus, I thank You that You have already bound Satan, the strong man, by Your precious blood and in Your name. Give me the spoils that You have won by Your sacrifice on the cross. Thank You for Your precious blood and Word that gives us the victory!
"*Wherefore I say unto you...*" Matt. 12:31

> **The Promise:**
> "*All manner of sin and blasphemy shall be forgiven unto men...*" Matt. 12:31

Except the "*... blasphemy against the Holy Ghost... and whosoever speaketh a word against the Son of man...*" Matt. 12:31

The Promise:
"... it shall be forgiven him..." Matt. 12:32

"But I say unto you that every idle word that men shall speak, they shall give account thereof in The Day of Judgment." Matt. 12:36

The Promise:
"For by thy words thou shalt be Justified..." Matt. 12:37

"... and by thy words thou shalt be condemned." Matt. 12:37
The Bible says that if we believe and receive Jesus, we have passed from Judgment to Life, Jn. 5:24. So if you are a Christian, you don't need to fear the Judgment but all of our works go through the fire to see what they're made of, I Cor. 3:15. So we see that we still have to give an account to God, Rom. 14:12, II Cor. 5:10. Some will have lots of rewards and some very few, even though they are saved but everyone will be happy just to be saved and be with Jesus.

The Condition:
Jesus said, "For whosoever shall do the will of My Father which is in heaven..." Matt. 12:50

The Promise:
"... the same is My brother, and sister, and mother." Matt. 12:50

The Parable of the four soils

The Promise:
Some seed "... brought forth fruit, some an hundredfold, some sixty-fold, some thirtyfold." Matt. 13:8

Here we see that we get different rewards; some get thirty percent, some sixty percent, and some a hundred percent.

The Promise:
"... it is given unto you to know the mysteries of the kingdom of heaven... for whosoever hath, to him shall be given, and he shall have more abundance..." Matt. 13:11,12

The Condition:
"... be converted," Matt. 13:15

The Promise:
"... and I should heal them." Matt. 13:15

Blessed
"But blessed are your eyes, for they see: and your ears, for they hear." Matt. 13:16

The Condition:
"But he that received seed into the good ground is he that heareth the Word, and understandeth it..." Matt. 13:23

> **The Promise:**
> *"... which also beareth fruit, and bringeth forth, some an hundred-fold, some sixty, some thirty."* Matt. 13:23

"... for great is your reward in heaven." Matt. 5:12
Again we see that we are saved by grace alone but saved to do good works (Eph. 2:10) and we will be rewarded for those works someday in heaven.

Miracles
"And Jesus went forth, and saw a great multitude, and was moved with compassion toward them, and He healed their sick." Matt. 14:14

Miracle
Jesus multiplied the bread and fish, He blessed it *"and they did all eat, and were filled..."* Matt. 14:19,20
Miracle
Jesus walks on water, Matt. 14:25.

Jesus takes our fears away
"... Jesus spake unto them, saying, Be of good cheer; it is I; be not afraid." Matt. 14:27

Peter walks on water
"And He said, Come. And when Peter was come down out of the ship, he walked on the water, to go to Jesus. But when he saw the wind boisterous, he was afraid; and beginning to sink, he cried, saying, Lord save me. And immediately Jesus stretched forth His hand, and caught him, and said unto him, O thou of little faith, wherefore didst thou doubt? And when they were come into the ship, the wind ceased." Matt. 14:29-32
"... then immediately the ship was at land" Jn. 6:21
Do we have little faith?
Prayer:
Father in heaven please strengthen our faith in Jesus' name, Amen!

Miracles
"And when the men of that place had knowledge of Him, they sent out into all that country round about, and brought unto Him all that were diseased; and besought Him that they might only touch the hem of His garment: and as many as touched were made perfectly whole." Matt. 14:35,36

Miracle
"Then Jesus answered and said unto her, O woman, great is thy faith: be it unto thee even as thou wilt. And her daughter was made whole from that very hour." Matt. 15:28

Miracles
"And great multitudes came unto Him, having with them those that were lame, blind, dumb, maimed, and any others, and cast them down at Jesus' feet; and He healed them. Insomuch that the multitude wondered, when they saw the dumb to speak, the maimed to be whole, the lame to walk, and the blind to see: and they glorified the God of Israel. Then Jesus called His disciples unto Him, and said, I have compassion on the multitude, because they continue with Me now three days, and have nothing to eat: and I will not send them away fasting, lest they faint in the way." Matt. 15:30-32
Jesus fed 4,000 men, plus women and children.

Blessed
"And Jesus answered and said unto him, Blessed art thou, Simon Barjona: for flesh and blood hath not revealed it unto thee, but My Father which is in heaven. And I say also unto thee, That thou art Peter (#4074 Gr. *"petrus"* Pebble; *"a piece of the rock"*) *and upon this Rock* (#4073 Gr. *"petra"* means the rock; cliff - the substratum of soil, ledge which is Jesus)..." Matt. 16:17,18

The Promise:
"... I will build My church; and the gates of hell shall not prevail against it. And I will give unto thee (the church) *the keys of the kingdom of heaven: and whatsoever thou shalt bind on earth shall be bound in heaven: and whatsoever thou shalt loose on earth shall be loosed in heaven."* Matt. 16:18,19

Jesus promised that the church would prevail - being built on Himself. *"No other foundation than Christ Jesus"* I Cor. 3:11
"That Rock was Christ" Matt. 21:42; I Cor. 10:4; the Stone the builders rejected Rom. 9:33; a stumbling Stone, Rock of offense I Pet. 2:4,6-8l; Mt.16:16.

God gave the church two keys; we can bind and loose by the blood of Jesus. They overcame by the blood of Jesus and the word of their testimony, Rev. 12:11.

Promise of His Second Coming
"For the Son of man shall come in the glory of His Father with His angels; and then He shall reward every man according to his works." Matt. 16:27
Again we see that we are saved by grace and rewarded for our works. Even though our works are as filthy rags, He still rewards us because He is a good, merciful, and gracious God. Even our rewards are by grace. Even though we are saved by grace, we should strive to please Him because we love Him! Salvation is a free gift of God but the rewards are for our works.

Miracle
"And Jesus rebuked the devil; and he departed out of him; and the child was cured from that very hour." Matt. 17:18
The Condition:
"And Jesus said unto them, If ye have faith as a grain of mustard seed ye shall say unto this mountain, Remove hence to yonder place ..." Matt. 17:20

> **The Promise:**
> *"... and it shall remove; and nothing shall be impossible unto you."* Matt. 17:20

The Condition:
"... howbeit this kind goeth not out but by prayer and fasting." Matt. 17:21
Promise to save the lost
"For the Son of man is come to save that which is lost." Matt. 18:11
"Even so it is not the will of your Father which is in heaven, that one of these little ones should perish." Matt. 18:14

> **The Promise:**
> *"Verily I say unto you, Whatsoever ye shall bind on earth shall be bound in heaven: and whatsoever ye shall loose on earth shall be loosed in heaven. Again I say unto you, That if two of you shall agree on earth as touching anything that they shall ask, it shall be done for them of My Father which is in heaven. For where two or three are gathered together in My name, there am I in the midst of them."* Matt. 18:18-20

The Amplified Bible puts it a little differently.
"Whatever you forbid and declare to be improper and unlawful on earth must be what is already forbidden in heaven, and whatever you permit and

declare proper and lawful on earth must be what is already permitted in heaven." Matt. 18:18 AMP

"And great multitudes followed Him; and He healed them there." Matt. 19:2

"... He which made them at the beginning made them male and female, and said, For this cause shall a man leave father and mother, and shall cleave to his wife..." Matt. 19:4,5

> **The Promise:**
> *"... and they twain shall be one flesh? Wherefore they are no more twain, but one flesh."* Matt. 19:5,6

"What therefore God hath joined together, let not man put asunder." Matt. 19:6
God is the One who joins a man and a woman together as one flesh in marriage (Gen. 2:27,28). The promise is that God will make us one flesh when we do things His way and He will help us fight to save our marriage. See Top-ical section on marriage.

"... if thou wilt enter into (Gr. 3588 *"the"*) [path of] *life..."* Matt. 19:17
The Condition:
"... keep the Commandments." Matt. 19:17

"Jesus said unto him, If thou wilt be perfect (#5046 *"full grown, full age, completeness of Christian character, perfect"*) Matt. 19:21

The Condition:
"... go and sell that thou hast, and give to the poor..." Matt. 19:21

> **The Promise:**
> *"... and thou shalt have treasure in heaven..."* Matt. 19:21

"... and come and follow Me." Matt. 19:21
Jesus wasn't telling the rich young ruler that he would be saved by giving away his wealth because if that was the way to be saved, then most of us would be lost. He was telling him how to get the greater reward in heaven because that was what he really wanted.
He said, *"If you want to enter into* (Gr. *"the"*) (path of) *life, keep the Command-ments."* Matt. 19:17.
The path to life is the Ten Commandments but you would have to keep them perfectly to get to heaven. Since no one has kept them perfectly except Jesus, then no one can be saved by keeping them. In fact, we deserve the

penalty of eternal death for breaking God's law. That is why we need Jesus, who is God, and who kept the Commandments perfectly and never committed even one sin, to save us by His blood because He took our punishment for us by dying on the cross. Because, He, even though innocent, paid the penalty for breaking the Commandments and we can believe in Him and die with Him through baptism and be raised with Him in the newness of life through the Holy Spirit. It is Jesus who saves us but then we strive to obey because we love Him and want to please Him; not to be saved. We are saved by grace and someday He will reward us according to our works. Our works are as filthy rags (Is. 64:6) so even our rewards are by grace.

The rich man was seeking the highest rewards and Jesus told him that by giving away his wealth and following Jesus He could get what he desired. And, who knows, he might have become one of the twelve disciples when it was time to pick a replacement for Judas. Anyway, I don't think that this man was lost but I think he missed out on the greater reward in heaven.

I Cor. 3:15 tells us that all our works go through the fire and that some will have all their works be burned up but they will still be saved.

"If any man's work shall be burned, he shall suffer loss: but he himself shall be saved; yet so as by fire."

"Watch yourselves, so that you should not lose what things we have worked for, but you may receive a full reward." II Jn. 1:8

God can save the rich and the poor
"But Jesus beheld them, and said unto them, With men this is impossible…" Matt. 19:26

The Promise:
"… but with God all things are possible." Matt. 19:26

He was saying here that whether you are rich or poor, it is impossible to be saved without Jesus. Both need to put their trust in God and not in money; and money is no indication of your acceptance with God! Today some still think that if they are rich, then that must mean God is pleased with them and accepts them based on the fact that they have wealth but that is not the standard by which we measure God's acceptance of us. Look at the parable of the rich man and Lazarus; Lazarus was a poor beggar and he was saved. The rich man, well, he was rich, of course, and we see that he didn't make it.

I think that the rich man had a false sence of confidence because of his riches and didn't concern himself with his own Salvation until it was too late. Then he wanted someone to go to his brothers from the dead but it is very clear in this parable that the dead are not allowed to come back and talk to us. If you think that you are talking to your dead loved one then you better consider who you're really talking to because the Bible says the dead cannot come back to talk to us.

The promise Jesus made to the twelve disciples
"... ye also shall sit upon twelve thrones, Judging the twelve tribes of Israel." Matt. 19:28
We see that the twelve disciples also get their names written on the twelve foundations of the New Jerusalem in Rev. 21:14.
And they get to sit at Jesus' table at the wedding Feast, Lk. 22:30. Because they were with Jesus and were there at the beginning of the church and suffered many things, they will have a very special reward in heaven.

The Condition:
"And everyone that hath forsaken houses, or brethren, or sisters, or father, or mother, or wife, or children, or lands, for My name's sake ..." Matt. 19:29

The Promise:
"... shall receive an hundredfold, and shall inherit everlasting life. But many that are first shall be last; and the last shall be first." Matt. 19:29,30

We are rewarded in heaven for giving up anything on earth for Jesus. This doesn't save us; it only puts our treasures in heaven for us where nothing can destroy, or steal it.
"Where your treasure is, there will your heart be also" Matt. 6:21.
Some will have a lot of riches in heaven and some will have very few rewards in heaven according to what they did while on this earth; but you must get to heaven first if you want to receive your rewards. See *"How to be reconciled to God"* on p. 713 for more notes.
"Saying, These last have wrought but one hour, and thou hast made them equal unto us, which have borne the burden and heat of the day." Matt. 20:12
"... to sit on My right hand, and on My left, is not Mine to give, but it shall be given to them for whom it is prepared of My Father." Matt. 20:23

Miracle
"And Jesus stood still, and called them, and said, What will ye that I shall do unto you? They say unto Him, Lord, that our eyes may be opened. So Jesus had compassion on them, and touched their eyes: and immediately their eyes received sight, and they followed Him." Matt. 20:32-34

Miracles
"And the blind and the lame came to Him in the Temple; and He healed them." Matt. 21:14

Miracle
"And when He (Jesus) saw a fig tree in the way, He came to it, and found nothing thereon, but leaves only, and said unto it, Let no fruit grow on thee henceforward forever. And presently the fig tree withered away. And when the disciples saw it, they marveled, saying, How soon is the fig tree withered away! Jesus answered and said unto them, Verily I say unto you..." Matt. 21:19-21

The Condition:
"... if ye have faith, and doubt not..." Matt. 21:21 (Mk.11:23,24)

> **The Promise:**
> *"... ye shall not only do this which is done to the fig tree, but also if ye shall say unto this mountain, Be thou removed, and be thou cast into the sea; it shall be done. And all things, whatsoever ye shall ask in prayer, believing, ye shall receive."* Matt. 21:21,22

The Fig Tree was an illustration of our works. We can bear a little fruit or a lot of fruit in our lives but if we have no fruit, we are in trouble. The dead branches are thrown into the fire, Jn. 15:2.

The Condition:
"... he that shall humble himself..." Matt. 23:12

> **The Promise:**
> *"... shall be exalted."* Matt. 23:12

The Condition:
"But he that shall endure unto the end..." Matt. 24:13

> **The Promise:**
> *"... the same shall be saved. And this Gospel of the kingdom shall be preached in all the world for a witness unto all nations; and then shall the end come."* Matt. 24:13,14

"Immediately after the tribulation of those days..." Matt. 24:29

> **The Promise**
> *"... shall appear the sign of the Son of man in heaven (at the 2nd Coming): and then shall all the tribes of the earth mourn, and they shall see the Son of man coming in the clouds of heaven with power and great glory. And He shall send His angels with a great sound of*

trumpet, and they shall gather together His elect from the four winds, from one end of heaven to the other." Matt. 24: 29-31

The Promise:
"... this generation shall not pass, till all these things be fulfilled. Heaven and earth shall pass away, but My words shall not pass away." Matt. 24:34,35

Parable of the talents
"For the kingdom of heaven is as a man travelling into a far country, who called his own servants, and delivered unto them his goods. And unto one he gave five talents, to another two, and to another one; to every man according to his several ability... then he that had received the five talents went and traded with the same, and made them other five talents. And likewise he that had received two, he also gained other two... his lord said unto him..." Matt. 25:14-21

The Condition:
"... well done, thou good and faithful servant thou hast been faithful over a few things..." Matt. 25:21

The Promise:
"... I will make thee ruler over many things: enter thou into the joy of thy Lord. For unto every one that hath shall be given, and he shall have abundance:" Matt. 25:21,23

"... but from him that hath not shall be taken away even that which he hath." Matt. 25:29

Here we see that God knows our abilities and that we're rewarded for what we did with what God gave us.

"Then shall the King say unto them on His right hand, Come ye blessed of My Father..." Matt. 25:34

The Promise:
"... inherit the kingdom prepared for you from the foundation of the world..." Matt. 25:34

The Condition:
"... for I was ("hungry"), and ye gave Me meat: I was thirsty, and ye gave Me drink: I was a stranger, and ye took Me in: naked, and ye clothed Me: I was sick, and ye visited Me; I was in prison, and ye came unto Me. Then shall the righteous answer Him, saying, Lord, when saw we Thee ("hungry"), and fed

Thee? Or thirsty, and gave Thee drink? When saw we Thee a stranger, and took Thee in? or naked, and clothed Thee? Or when saw we Thee sick, or in prison, and came unto Thee? And the King shall answer and say unto them, Verily I say unto you, Inasmuch as ye have done it unto one of the least of these My brethren, ye have done it unto Me." Matt. 25:35-40*

Communion
The Condition:
"And as they were eating, Jesus took bread, and blessed it, and brake it, and gave it to the disciples, and said Take, eat; this is (a symbol of) *My body. And He took the cup, and gave thanks, and gave it to them, saying, Drink ye all of it; For this is* (a symbol of) *My blood of the New Testament, which is shed for many..."* Matt. 26:26-28

> **The Promise:**
> *"... for the remission* (removal) *of sins."* Matt. 26:28

"remission" Gr. #859 means, *"deliverance, pardon, complete forgiveness, release, free; releasing someone from obligation or debt.*
"... pardon, of sins (... as if they had not been committed... remission of their penalty...)."
Here we see the problem of sin. Sin separates us from God and keeps Him from answering our prayers, Is 59:1,2. First we must understand how heineous sin is and that sin is treason against God and deserves death, Ez. 18:20. Adam and Eve would have died (Gen. 2:17) if it hadn't been for the promise that Jesus would come and crush the serpent's head (Gen. 3:15) and He clothed them with animal skins (Gen. 3:21), which probably came from the lamb's sacrificed to cover them as a promise that He would be the true lamb of God which takes away the sins of the world (otherwise how would Abel have known to sacrifice a lamb).

When we really understand how sin hurts God, ourselves, and others, we will desire to live a sinless life. If we fully understand this, then we can see how amazing it is that God is willing to put all our sins on Jesus and let Him pay the penalty for them and give us a complete pardon and release us from the obligation of our sins. In the Old Testament they had to lay their hands on the head of the sheep (or whatever animal they were sacrificing) and confess or put all their sins on that animal. When we confess our sins, we are also putting all our sins on Jesus and He bears the guilt and shame for them. Somebody has to die for those sins, and He did.

The Bible says that before we come to Jesus we are *"dead in sins"*.
*"But God, who is rich in mercy, for His great love wherewith He loved us, even when we were **dead in sins**, hath quickened us together with Christ, (by*

grace ye are saved); and hath raised us up together, and made us sit together in heavenly places in Christ Jesus: that in the ages to come He might shew the exceeding riches of His grace in His kindness toward us through Christ Jesus. For by grace are ye saved through faith: and that not of yourselves: it is the gift of God.." Eph. 2:4-8

We should never take this for granted or think that God doesn't care if we sin. He didn't die to make us free to sin but free from sin (Jn.8:36;Rom.6:18; 8:1-4;Gal.5:1,13;II Cor. 3:17;I Pet.2:16). He paid a high price to release us from the penalty of our sins and wants us to walk as He walked.

"*See then that ye **walk circumspectly**, not as fools, but as wise, Redeeming the time because the days are evil. Wherefore be ye not unwise, but understanding what the will of the Lord is.*" Eph. 5:15,16

What is sin? Sin is the transgression of the law, I Jn. 3:4. It is the will of God that we don't sin. Paul says that, as Christian's, we should walk worthy of Him and strive to please Him, bearing fruit.

"*That ye might walk worthy of the Lord unto all pleasing, being fruitful in every good work, and increasing in the knowledge of God...*" Col. 1:10

He knows we will sin but we are not given permission to sin. He has provided a way that we can continue to be forgiven and cleansed by His blood, I Jn. 1:9, Rev. 5:9. I heard someone say once that forgiveness is our greatest weapon against Satan.

"*What shall we say then? Shall we continue in sin, that grace may abound? God forbid...*" Rom. 6:1

Paul says, "*O wretched man that I am! Who shall deliver me from the body of this death? I thank God through Jesus Christ our Lord...*" Rom. 7:24,25

So what do we do?
1. We realize that we are sinners (Rom. 3:23)
2. We come to Jesus, receive Him as our Lord and Master (Jn. 3:15)
3. Then we get baptized (Matt.28:19,20;16:16)
4. And take Communion (I Cor. 11:24).
4. Then we strive to please God by not sinning but if we do sin, we repent (Rev. 3:19) and ask for forgiveness (I Jn. 1:9) and continue to strive to do God's will.

It is our "*... goal to be pleasing... to Him.*" II Cor. 5:9 ISV

We continue this process of striving against sin and repenting when we sin until Jesus comes.

Let's be thankful for this amazing grace and strive to please Him by obeying Him and someday He will reward us for overcoming our sins. Grace is free but works are rewarded.

"Whosoever therefore shall break one of these least Commandments, and shall teach me so, he shall be called the least in the kingdom of heaven: but whosoever shall do and teach them, the same shall be called great in the kingdom of heaven." Matt. 5:19

It doesn't say you will be lost but that you will be lesser or greater in God's kingdom.

I find rest in Jesus but I strive to enter that rest, Heb. 4:11.
I can rest in the fact that Salvation is a free gift of God and cannot be earned but I strive to do the things that please God and overcome my sins, which pleses God and He will reward me someday.

  Salvation – free

  Works – rewarded

Each of the Seven Churches are promised a reward for overcoming in Rev. 2:1-3:18.

"... work out your own Salvation with fear and trembling" Phil. 2:12

We are to Judge ourselves (I Cor. 11:31) but we are not to judge others (Matt. 7:13)

 (See the section on How to Be Reconciled to God p. 713)

Jesus promised

"But I say unto you, I will not drink henceforth of this fruit of the vine, until that day when I drink it new with you in My Father's kingdom." Matt. 26:29

If Jesus won't drink wine until He is with me, then I don't want to drink any wine until I am with Him.

The Great Commission

"And Jesus came and spake unto them, saying, All power is given unto Me in heaven and in earth. Go ye therefore, and teach all nations, baptizing them in the name of the Father, and of the Son, and of the Holy Ghost: teaching them to observe ("obey" NIV) all things whatsoever I have commanded you..." Matt. 28:19,20

  The Promise:

  "... and, lo, I am with you always, even unto the end of the world. Amen." Matt. 28:18-20

Mark

John the Baptist, speaking of Jesus, said,

The Promise:
"... He shall baptize you with the Holy Ghost." Mk. 1:8

"And straightway coming up out of the water, He saw the heavens opened, and the Spirit like a dove descending upon Him: and there came a voice from heaven, saying, Thou art My beloved Son, in whom I am well pleased." Mk. 1:10,11

"Repent, and be baptized every one of you in the name of Jesus Christ for the remission of sins, and ye shall receive the gift of the Holy Ghost." Acts 2:38
For this is my blood of the New Tesament which is shed for many for the remission of sins." Matt.26:28

The Condition:
"And Jesus said unto them, Come ye after Me..." Mk 1:17

The Promise:
"... and I will make you to become fishers of men." Mk. 1:17

Jesus delivered a man from an unclean spirit,
"... for with authority commandeth He even the unclean spirits, and they do obey Him." Mk. 1:27
And Jesus gives us authority, Matt.10:1 NIV;Mk.3:15 NIV;Lk.10:19 NIV.

Miracle
"And He (Jesus) came and took her by the hand, and lifted her up; and immediately the fever left her..." Mk. 1:31

Miracle
"And at even, when the sun did set, they brought unto Him (Jesus) all that were diseased, and them that were possessed with devils. And all the city was gathered together at the door. And He healed many that were sick of divers diseases, and cast out many devils; and suffered not the devils to speak, because they knew Him." Mk. 1:32-34

Miracle
"If Thou wilt, Thou canst make me clean. And Jesus, moved with compassion, put forth His hand, and touched him, and saith unto him, I will:

be thou clean. And as soon as He had spoken, immediately the leprosy departed from him, and he was cleansed." Mk. 1:40-42

Miracle
"When Jesus saw their faith, He said unto the sick of the palsy, Son, thy sins be forgiven thee... but that ye may know that the Son of man hath power on earth to forgive sins, (He saith to the sick of the palsy), I say unto thee, Arise, and take up thy bed, and go thy way into thine house. And immediately he arose, took up the bed, and went forth before them all; insomuch that they were all amazed, and glorified God, saying, We never saw it on this fashion." Mk. 2:5,10-12

"... He (Jesus) saith unto the man (with withered hand), Stretch forth thine hand. And he stretched it out: and his hand was restored whole as the other." Mk. 3:5

Miracle
"For He (Jesus) had healed many; insomuch that they pressed upon Him for to touch Him, as many as had plagues. And unclean spirits, when they saw Him, fell down before Him, and cried, saying, Thou art the Son of God." Mk. 3:10,11

Jesus gave His disciples power
"And He (Jesus) ordained twelve, that they should be with Him, and that He might send them forth to preach, and to have power (Gr. #1849 "power, authority") to heal sicknesses, and to cast out devils..." Mk. 3:15

Bind the strong man
"No man can enter into a strong man's house, and spoil his goods, except he will first bind the strong man..." Mk. 3:27

> **The Promise:**
> "... and then he will spoil his house..." Mk. 3:27

Remember that we've been given the keys of the Kingdom to bind and loose in Matt. 16:18,19 (See notes on Matt. 12:29).

Verily I say unto you..." Mk. 3:27,28

> **The Promise:**
> "... all sins shall be forgiven... and blasphemies wheresoever they shall blaspheme..." Mk. 3: 28

The Condition:
"... but he that shall blaspheme against the Holy Ghost hath never forgiveness, but is in danger of eternal damnation..." Mk. 3:29
The sin against the Holy Spirit was when they said Jesus did His miracles by the power of Satan, Mk. 3:22,23. It is true that we should never say that something of God is of the Devil but we also must be careful not to say some-thing is of God when we know for sure that it is not!

Jesus said, "... who is My mother, or My brethren? And He looked round about on them which sat about Him, and said, Behold My mother and My brethren!" Mk. 3:33,34

The Condition:
"For whosoever shall do the will of God..." Mk. 3:35

> **The Promise:**
> "... the same is My brother... sister, and mother." Mk. 3:35

Promise to the twelve disciples
"... unto you it is given to know the mystery of the kingdom of God: but unto them that are without, all these things are done in parables..." Mk. 4:11

"For there is nothing hid, which shall not be manifested; neither was anything kept secret, but that it should come abroad." Mk. 4:22
The Condition:
"... what measure ye mete..." Mk. 4:24

> **The Promise:**
> "... it shall be measured to you: and unto you that hear shall more be given. For he that hath, to him shall be given..." Mk. 4:24,25

Miracle
"And he arose, and rebuked the wind, and said unto the sea, peace, be still. And the wind ceased, and there was a great calm. And He said unto them, Why are ye so fearful? How is it that ye have no faith... and said one to another, What manner of man is this, that even the wind and the sea obey Him?" Mk. 4:39-41

Jesus delivers the demoniac Mk. 5:13-23

Miracle
"... she... touched His garment. For she said, If I may touch but His clothes, I shall be whole. And straightway the fountain of her blood was dried up; and

she felt in her body that she was healed of that plague. And Jesus, immediate-ly knowing in Himself that virtue had gone out of Him, turned Him about in the press, and said, Who touched My clothes... thy faith hath made thee whole; go in peace, and be whole of thy plague." Mk. 5:27-30,34

Miracle
"... be not afraid, only believe... and He took the damsel by the hand, and said unto her, Talitha cumi; which is, being interpreted, Damsel, I say unto thee, arise. And straightway the damsel arose, and walked; for she was of the age of twelve years. And they were... (astonished) with a great astonishment." Mk. 5:36,41,42 (See notes on Matt. 9:23-25)

"And He could there do no mighty work, save that He laid His hands upon a few sick folk, and healed them. And He marveled because of their unbelief. And he went round about the villages, teaching." Mk. 6:5,6
Jesus could not perform many miracles in His home town because of their lack of faith.

Jesus sent His disciples out two by two
"... and gave them power over unclean spirits... and they cast out many devils, and anointed with oil many that were sick, and healed them." Mk. 6:7,13

Miracle
"He answered and said unto them, Give ye them to eat... and they did all eat, and were filled." Mk. 6:37,42

Miracle
"For they all saw Him, and were troubled. And immediately He talked with them, and saith unto them, Be of good cheer: it is I; be not afraid." Mk. 6:50

Miracles
"And whithersoever He entered, into villages, or cities, or country, they laid the sick in the streets, and besought Him that they might touch if it were but the border of His garment: and as many as touched Him were made whole." Mk. 6:56
When we see the miracles that Jesus performed while on earth, we can know that if He did it for them, He can do it for us.

Miracle
"... they bring unto Him one that was deaf, and had an impediment in his speech (they asked) Him to put His hand upon him... He took him aside... and put His fingers into his ears... spit, and touched his tongue... looking up to heaven, He sighed, and saith unto Him Eph-pha-tha... be opened. And straightway His ears were opened, and the string of his tongue was loosed, and he spake plain... and were beyond measure astonished, saying... He maketh both the deaf to hear, and the dumb to speak." Mk. 7:32-37

Miracle
"I have compassion on the multitude, because they have now been with Me three days, and have nothing to eat; and if I send them away fasting to their own house, they will faint by the way: for divers of them came from far... He took the seven loaves, and gave thanks, and brake, and gave to His disciples to set before them; and they did set them before the people. And they had a few small fishes: and he blessed, and commanded to set them also before them. So they did eat, and were filled..." Mk. 8:2-8

Miracle
"... and they bring a blind man unto Him, and besought Him to touch him. And He took the blind man by the hand, and led him out of the town; and when He had spit on his eyes, and put His hands upon him, He asked him if he saw ought. And he looked up, and said, I see men as trees, walking. After that He put His hands again upon his eyes, and made him look up: and He was restored, and saw every man clearly." Mk. 8:22-25

"... whoever shall lose his life for My sake and the Gospel's..." Mk. 8:35

   The Promise:
   "... the same shall save it." Mk. 8:35

Believe
The Condition:
"Jesus said unto him, If thou canst believe..." Mk. 9:23

   The Promise:
   "... all things are possible to him that believeth." Mk. 9:23

The disciples asked Jesus why they couldn't cast out the demons
"And He (Jesus) said unto them..." Mk. 9:29
The Condition:
"... this kind can come forth by nothing, but by prayer and fasting." Mk. 9:29

The Condition:
"For whosoever shall give you a cup of water to drink in My name, because ye belong to Christ, verily I say unto you ..." Mk. 9:41

The Promise:
"... he shall not lose his reward." Mk. 9:41

"... from the beginning of the creation God made them male and female. For this cause shall a man leave his father and mother, and cleave to his wife; and they twain shall be one flesh... they are no more twain, but one flesh. What therefore God hath joined together, let not man put asunder." Mk. 10:6-9

The promise is that God will make us one flesh with our spouse. This is a mystery but it is also a symbol of how we are one with Christ. He is the Bridegroom and the church is the Bride (Jn.3:29; Eph. 5:32).

Blessed
"And He (Jesus) *took them* (the children) *in His arms, put His hands upon them, and blessed them."* Mk. 10:16

Treasures in heaven
"Then Jesus beholding him loved him, and said unto him, One thing thou lackest: go thy way, sell whatsoever thou hast, and give to the poor, and thou shalt have treasure in heaven: and come, take up the cross, and follow Me." Mk. 10:21
Selling what he had was not to earn Salvation but to earn the treasures stored up in heaven.

"And Jesus looked round about, and saith unto His disciples, How hardly shall they that have riches enter into the kingdom of God... how hard is it for them that trust in riches to enter into the kingdom of God... who then can be saved? And Jesus looking upon them saith, With men it is impossible but not with God..." Mk. 10:27

The Promise:
"... for with God all things are possible." Mk. 10:27

If God blesses us with riches then we should make sure we give our tithes and offerings to God first and then to share what we have with those in need, Matt. 6:19,20; then we will be blessed! Sometimes we have to leave our possessions behind to follow Jesus but He reassures us that we will be rewarded in heaven for everything that we have to give up for Him. God says that the Christian who is poor will be exalted in heaven so we should not look down on them (See notes on Matt. 19:21).

"Let the brother of low degree rejoice in that he is exalted: (in heaven) but the rich, in that he is made low..." Jms. 1:9,10

"My brethren, have not the faith of our Lord Jesus Christ, the Lord of glory, with respect of persons. For if there come unto your assembly a man with gold ring, in goodly apparel, and there come in also a poor man in vile raiment. And ye have respect to him that weareth the ("fine") clothing, and say unto him, Sit thou here in a good place; and say to the poor, Stand thou there, or sit here under my footstool: are ye not then partial in yourselves, and are become Judges of evil thoughts? Hearken, my beloved brethren, Hath not God chosen the poor of this world rich in faith, and heirs of the kingdom which He hath promised to them that love Him? But ye have despised the poor..." Jms 2:1-6

The Condition:
"And Jesus answered and said, Verily I say unto you there is no man that hath left houses, or brethren, or sisters, or father, or mother, or wife, or children, or lands, for My sake, and the Gospel's..." Mk. 10:29

> **The Promise:**
> "... but he shall receive an hundredfold now in this time, houses, and brethren, and sisters, and mothers, and children, and lands..." Mk. 10:29,30

The Condition:
"... with persecutions..." Mk. 10:30

> **The Promise:**
> "... and in the world to come eternal life. But many that are first shall be last; and the last first." Mk. 10:30,31

Here God tells us that we will be rewarded for anything we give up for Him. Sometimes we are rewarded now and sometimes we have to wait for our rewards in heaven. Everyone will be glad just to be in heaven but we will be surprised who is greater (Matt. 5:19)! It may not be the way we think it should be because God doesn't Judge the same way that man Judges. God looks on the heart while man looks on the outward appearance, (I Sam. 16:7). The Bible says that those who do their good works for men to see have already received their reward, Matt.6:1, 2;Lk.6:24. Which means they lose their heavenly reward. I Cor. 3:15 says that our works go through the fire and that some will have all their works burned up but they will still be saved.

Miracle
"And Jesus answered and said unto him, What wilt thou that I should do unto thee? The blind man said unto Him, Lord, that I might receive my sight. And Jesus said unto him, Go thy way; thy faith hath made thee whole. And immediately he received his sight, and followed Jesus in the way." Mk. 10:51,52

Miracle
"And seeing a fig tree afar off having leaves, He came, if haply He might find anything thereon: and when He came to it, He found nothing but leaves; for the time of figs was not yet. And Jesus answered and said unto it, No man eat fruit of thee hereafter forever. And His disciples heard it... and in the morning, as they passed by, they saw the fig tree dried up from the roots. And Peter calling to remembrance saith unto Him, Master, behold, the fig tree which Thou cursedst is withered away. And Jesus answering saith unto them, Have faith in God. For verily I say unto you, That whosoever shall say unto this mountain, Be thou removed, and be thou cast into the sea; and shall not doubt in his heart, but shall believe that those things which he saith shall come to pass; he shall have whatsoever he saith. Therefore I say unto you, What things soever ye desire, when ye pray, believe that ye receive them, and ye shall have them." Mk. 11:13, 14,20-24

"For this reason I am telling you, whatever you ask for in prayer, believe (trust, be confident) that it is granted to you, and you will (get it)." Mk. 11:24 AMP

"But the Gospel must first be published among all nations. But when they shall lead you, and deliver you up, take no thought beforehand what ye shall speak, neither do ye premeditate..." Mk. 13:11

The Promise:
"... but whatsoever shall be given you in that hour, that speak ye: for it is not ye that speak, but the Holy Ghost." Mk. 13:11

The Condition:
"And ye shall be hated of all men for My name's sake: but he that shall endure unto the end..." Mk. 13:13

The Promise:
"... the same shall be saved." Mk. 13:13

We should not be surprised that some hate us for being Christians. Jesus said, they hated me first, Matt.10:22;Jn.15:18-25.

The Condition:
"And he said unto them, Go ye into all the world, and preach the Gospel to every creature. He that believeth and is baptized..." Mk. 16:16

The Promise:
"... will be saved... and these signs will accompany those who believe: in My name they will drive out demons; they will speak in new languages..." Mk. 16:17 HCSB

The Promise:
"...they shall take up serpents; and if they drink any deadly thing, it shall not hurt them; they shall lay hands on the sick, and they shall recover... and they went forth, and preached everywhere, the Lord working with them, and confirming the Word with signs following. Amen." Mk. 16:17,18,20

This verse says that these signs are given to anyone who believes... how can we do the works He does? Believe on Jesus, Jn. 6:27-29.

Promise to Zaccharias and Elisabeth
"Fear not, Zacharias: for thy prayer is heard; and thy wife Elisabeth shall bear thee a son, and thou shalt call his name John. And thou shalt have joy and gladness; and shall rejoice at his birth... many of the children of Israel shall he turn to the Lord their God. And he shall go before him in the Spirit and power of Elias, to turn the hearts of the fathers to the children, and the disobedient to the wisdom of the just; to make ready a people prepared for the Lord." Lk. 1:13- 17

Blessed
The angel Gabriel's promise to Mary, the mother of Jesus
"And the angel came in unto her, and said, Hail, thou that art highly favoured, the Lord is with thee: blessed art thou among women... and the angel said unto her, Fear not, Mary: for thou hast found favour with God. And, behold thou shalt conceive in thy womb, and bring forth a son, and shalt call His name Jesus..." Lk. 1:28,30,31

Promise about Jesus
"... He shall be great, and shall be called the Son of the Highest: and the Lord God shall give unto Him the throne of His father David: and He shall reign

over the house of Jacob forever; and of His kingdom there shall be no end... the Holy Ghost shall come upon thee, and the power of the Highest shall overshadow thee: therefore also that Holy Thing which shall be born of thee shall be called the Son of God..." Lk. 1:31-35

The Promise:
"*For with God nothing shall be impossible.*" Lk. 1:37

Mary believes the angel
"*And Mary said, Behold the handmaid of the Lord; be it unto me according to Thy Word...*" Lk. 1:38
Mary had a great response to the angel and when we see a promise we can also say, Let it "*be... unto me according to The Word.*"

Blessed
"*... Elisabeth was filled with the Holy Ghost: and she spake out with a loud voice, and said, Blessed art thou among women, and blessed is the fruit of thy womb (Jesus).*" Lk. 1:41,42

Blessed
"*And blessed is she that believed: for there shall be a performance of those things which were told her from the Lord... and all generations shall call me blessed... His mercy is on them that fear Him from generation to generation. He hath shewed strength with His arm; He hath scattered the proud in the imagination of their hearts. He hath put down the mighty from their seats, and exalted them of low degree. He hath filled the hungry with good things; and the rich He hath sent empty away. He hath...* (helped) *His servant Israel, in remembrance of His mercy...*" Lk. 1:45,50-54

The promise to John the Baptist
"*... and the hand of the Lord was with him.*" Lk. 1:66
Prayer:
Father in heaven, let Your hand be with me like it was with John. Thank you in Jesus' name, Amen!

Blessed
"*Blessed be the Lord God of Israel, for He hath visited and Redeemed His people, and hath raised up an horn of Salvation for us in the house of His people... in the house of His servant David; as he spake by the mouth of His Holy prophets... that we should be saved from our enemies, and from the hand of all that hate us; to perform the mercy promised to our fathers, and to remember His Holy Covenant; the oath which He sware to our father*

Abraham, that He would grant unto us, that we being delivered out of the hand of our enemies might serve Him without fear, in Holiness and righteousness before Him, all the days of our life. And Thou, Child (Jesus), *shalt be called The Prophet of the Highest* (See Names of Jesus p. 694): *for Thou shalt go before the face of the Lord to prepare His ways; to give knowledge of Salvation unto His people by the remission of their sins, through the tender mercy of our God; whereby the Dayspring from on high hath visited us, to give light to them that sit in darkness and in the shadow of death, to guide our feet into the Way of Peace."* Lk. 1:68-79

Prayer:
Father in heaven, You delivered us from our enemies. Give us the mercy that You've promised and remember Your Covenant. Help us to serve You and re-move our sins by the blood of Jesus so that we can overcome and serve You in Holiness and righteousness. Thank You that You came down and visited us and gave us Your tender mercies; help us to be merciful to others. Guide our feet in Your ways so that we can have Your peace. Thank You in Jesus' name, Amen!

"For unto you is born this day in the city of David a Saviour, which is Christ the Lord." Lk. 2:11
Is. 9:6 is fulfilled here – the promise of a Savior

Simeon blesses God
"And, behold, there was a man in Jerusalem, whose name was Simeon; and the same man was just and devout, waiting for the consolation of Israel: and the Holy Ghost was upon him. And it was revealed unto him by the Holy Ghost, that he should not see death, before he had seen the Lord's Christ. And he came by the Spirit into the Temple: and when the parents brought in the child Jesus, to do for Him after the custom of the law, then took he Him up in his arms, and blessed God, and said, Lord, now lettest Thou Thy servant depart in peace, according to Thy Word: for mine eyes have seen Thy Salvation, which Thou hast prepared before the face of all people; a light to lighten the Gentiles,
and the glory of Thy people Israel." Lk. 2:25-32

Blessed
"And Simeon blessed them, and said unto Mary his mother, Behold, this child (Jesus) *is set for the fall and rising again of many in Israel; and for a sign which shall be spoken against..."* Lk. 2:34

"And all flesh shall see the Salvation of God." Lk. 3:6

Miracle
Jesus "*said to the man which had the withered hand, Rise up, and stand forth in the midst. And he arose and stood forth... He said unto the man, Stretch forth thy hand. And he did so: and his hand was restored whole as the other...*" Lk. 3:8

> **Promise**
> "*... He shall baptize you with the Holy Ghost and with fire...*" Lk. 3:16

Prayer:
Lord, baptize me fresh and new each day with Your Holy Spirit in Jesus' name, Amen!
"*.... His compassions fail not. They are new every morning...*" Lam. 3:23

"*For it is written, He shall give His angels charge over thee, to keep thee: and in their hands they shall bear thee up, lest at any time thou dash thy foot against a stone.*" Lk. 4:10,11 (Quoting from Ps. 91:11,12)

> **The Promise:**
> "*The Spirit of the Lord is upon Me, because He hath anointed Me to preach the Gospel to the poor He hath sent Me to heal the broken-hearted, to preach deliverance to the captives, and recovering of sight to the blind, to set at liberty them that are bruised, to preach the acceptable year of the Lord. And He closed the book, and... sat down... and He began to say unto them, This day is this Scripture fulfilled in your ears.*" Lk. 4:18,19,21

Jesus proclaims that the promise about the Messiah is fulfilled through Him.
Prayer:
Father in heaven, please heal our broken hearts and deliver us from any bondage; give sight to those who are blind and heal our bruised hearts according to Your Word in Jesus, Amen!

Miracle
"*And in the Synagogue there was a man, which had a spirit of an unclean devil, and cried out with a loud voice, saying, Let us alone; what have we to do with Thee, Thou Jesus of Nazareth? Art Thou come to destroy us? I know Thee who Thou art; the Holy One of God. And Jesus rebuked him, saying, Hold thy peace, and come out of him. And when the devil had thrown him in the midst, he came out of him, and hurt him not. And they were all amazed, and spake among themselves, saying, What a Word is this! For*

with authority and power He commandeth the unclean spirits, and they come out." Lk. 4:33-36

And Jesus has given us authority, LK. 10:19.

"However, do not rejoice that the spirits submit to you, but rejoice that your names are written in heaven." Lk. 10:20

Miracle
"And He stood over her, and rebuked the fever; and it left her: and immediately she arose and ministered unto them. Now when the sun was setting, all they that had any sick with divers diseases brought them unto Him; and He laid His hands on every one of them, and healed them. And devils also came out of many crying out, and saying, Thou art Christ the Son of God. And He rebuking them suffered them not to speak..." Lk. 4:39-41

Jesus promise to Peter
"And Jesus said unto Simon, Fear not; from henceforth thou shalt catch men." Lk. 5:10
Prayer:
Father in heaven, please help us to bring others to You also and be fishers of men! Thank You in Jesus' name, Amen!

Miracle
"And it came to pass, when He was in a certain city, behold a man full of leprosy: who seeing Jesus fell on his face, and besought Him, saying, Lord if Thou wilt, Thou canst make me clean. And He put forth His hand, and touched him, saying, I will: be thou clean. And immediately the leprosy departed from him." Lk. 5:12,13
Prayer:
Father in heaven, I know that You are willing. Please forgive us of our sins and wash us by the blood of Jesus so that we can be clean. In Jesus' name, Amen!

Miracles
Great multitudes came to hear Jesus and be "... *healed by Him.*" Lk. 5:15

Miracles
"... *and the power of the Lord was present to heal them. And, behold, men brought in a bed a man which was taken with a palsy: and they sought means to bring him in, and to lay him before Him. And when they could not find by what way they might bring him in because of the multitude, they went upon the housetop, and let him down through the tiling with his couch*

into the midst before Jesus. And when He saw their faith, He said unto him, Man, thy sins are forgiven thee… but that ye may know that the Son of man hath power upon earth to forgive sins, (He said unto the sick of the palsy), I say unto thee, Arise, and take up thy couch, and go into thine house. And immediately he rose up before them, and took up that whereon he lay, and departed to his own house, glorifying God. And they were all amazed, and they glorified God, and were filled with fear, saying, We have seen strange things today." Lk. 5:16-20,24-26

Prayer:
Father in heaven, let Your power be present to heal us when we need it. Thank You for hearing and answering in the name of Jesus, Amen!

Jesus calls sinners to repent
The Scribes and Pharisees ask Jesus "*Why do Ye eat and drink with publicans and sinners? And Jesus answering said unto them, They that are whole need not a physician; but they that are sick. I came not to call the righteous, but sinners to repentance.*" Lk. 5:30-32
The truth is that we are all unrighteous and need Christs' righteousness.

Prayer:
Father in heaven, I acknowledge that I am a sinner and need Your righteousness and blood to cover my sins; I also acknowledge my need for The Great Physician. In Jesus' name, Amen!

Miracles
"… *He came down with them, and stood in the plain, and the company of His disciples, and a great multitude of people out of all Judaea and Jerusalem, and from the sea coast of Tyre and Sidon, which came to hear Him, and to be healed of their diseases; and they that were vexed with unclean spirits: and they were healed. And the whole multitude sought to touch Him: for there went virtue out of Him, and healed them all…*" Lk. 6:17-19

Blessed
"*And He* (Jesus) *lifted up His eyes on His disciples, and said, Blessed be ye poor…*" Lk. 6:20

The Promise:
"*… for yours is the kingdom of God.*" Lk. 6:20

"*Blessed are ye that hunger now* (for righteousness, Mt. 5:6)*…*" Lk. 6:21

The Promise:
"*… for ye shall be filled.*" Lk. 6:21

"Blessed are ye that weep now..." Lk. 6:21

The Promise:
"... for ye shall laugh." Lk. 6:21

"... blessed are ye, when men shall hate you, and when they shall separate you from their company, and shall reproach you, and cast out your name as evil, for the Son of man's sake. Rejoice ye in that day, and leap for joy: for..." Lk. 6:22-23

The Promise:
"... your reward is great in heaven..." Lk. 6:23

"... for in the like manner did their fathers unto the prophets." Lk. 6:23
We see here that if you endure the hard times, God will make sure you are rewarded in heaven.

"... as ye would that men should do to you, do ye also to them likewise. For if ye love them which love you, what thank have ye? For sinners also love those that love them. And if ye do good to them which do good to you, what thank have ye? For sinners also do even the same. And if ye lend to them of whom ye hope to receive, what thank have ye? For sinners also lend to sinners, to receive as much again... love ye your enemies... do good, and lend, hoping for nothing again..." Lk. 6:31-35

The Promise:
"... and your reward shall be great, and ye shall be the children of the Highest..." Lk. 6:35

"... for He is kind unto the unthankful and to the evil." Lk. 6:35
The reward is in loving those who don't love you back. God is kind to sinners and the ungrateful. If God can be kind to the evil, then maybe we should also be kind to those who do things we don't approve of.

The Condition:
"Be ye therefore merciful, as your Father also is merciful. Judge not..." Lk. 6:36,37

The Promise:
"... and ye shall not be Judged..." Lk. 6:37

The Condition:
"... condemn not..." Lk. 6:37

The Promise:
"... and ye shall not be condemned..." Lk. 6:37

The Condition:
"... *forgive...*" Lk. 6:37

> **The Promise:**
> "... *and ye shall be forgiven...*" Lk. 6:37

The Condition:
"... *give...*" Lk. 6:38

> **The Promise:**
> "... *and it shall be given unto you; good measure, pressed down, and shaken together, and running over, shall men give into your bosom. For with the same measure that ye mete withal it shall be measured to you again.*" Lk. 6:38

"*A good man out of the good treasure of his heart bringeth forth that which is good... for of the abundance of the heart his mouth speaketh.*" Lk. 6:45

Miracle
"*... the centurion sent friends to Him, saying unto Him, Lord, trouble not Thyself: for I am not worthy that Thou shouldest enter under my roof: wherefore neither thought I myself worthy to come unto Thee: but say in a Word, and my servant shall be healed. For I also am a man set under authority, having under me soldiers, and I say unto one, Go, and he goeth; and to another, Come, and he cometh; and to my servant, Do this, and he doeth it. When Jesus heard these things, He marveled at him, and turned him about, and said unto the people that followed Him, I say unto you, I have not found so great faith, no, not in Israel. And they that were sent, returning to the house, found the servant whole that had been sick.*" Lk. 7:6-10
Prayer:
Father in heaven, please let me have faith like the Centurion. Thank You in Jesus' name, Amen!

Miracle
"*And when the Lord saw her, He had compassion on her, and said unto her, Weep not. And He came and touched the bier; and they that bare him stood still. And He said, Young man, I say unto thee, Arise. And he that was dead sat up, and began to speak. And He delivered him to his mother. And there came a fear on all: and they glorified God, saying, That a great Prophet is risen up among us; and, That God hath visited His people.*" Lk. 7:13-16

Blessed
"*And in that same hour he cured many of their infirmities and plagues, and*

of evil spirits; and unto many that were blind He gave sight. Then Jesus answering said unto them, Go your way, and tell John what things ye have seen and heard; how that the blind see, the lame walk, the lepers are cleansed, the deaf hear, the dead are raised, to the poor the Gospel is preached. And blessed is he, whosoever shall not be offended in Me." Lk. 7:21-23

You will be blessed if you're not offended by Jesus. Jesus promises that if we aren't ashamed of Him, He won't be ashamed of us (Mk.8:38).

"For I say unto you, Among those that are born of women there is not a greater prophet than John the Baptist..." Lk. 7:28

> **The Promise:**
> "... but he that is least in the kingdom of God is greater than he." Lk. 7:28

Jesus speaks about Mary who anointed His feet
"Wherefore I say unto thee, Her sins, which are many, are forgiven; for she loved much: but to whom little is forgiven, the same loveth little. And He said unto her..." Lk. 7:47-50

> **The Promise:**
> "... thy sins are forgiven... and He said to the woman Thy faith hath saved thee..." Lk. 7:50

"... go in peace." Lk. 7:50

Miracle
A woman "... which had been healed of evil spirits and infirmities, Mary called Magdalene, out of whom went seven devils..." Lk. 8:2

> **The Promise:**
> "And He said, Unto you it is given to know the mysteries of the kingdom of God..." Lk. 8:10

"... but to others in parables..." Lk. 8:10
This promise was given to the twelve disciples but if we are a disciple of Jesus Christ, then we too can know the mysteries of the kingdom of God.
Prayer:
Father in heaven, please help me to understand the mysteries of Your kingdom in Jesus' name, Amen!

Jesus, our brother
"And He answered and said unto them..." Lk. 8:21

The Promise:
"... My mother and My brethren are these..." Lk. 8:21

The Condition:
"... which hear the Word of God, and do it." Lk. 8:21

Miracle
"And they came to Him, and awoke Him, saying, Master, Master, we perish. Then He arose, and rebuked the wind and the raging of the water: and they ceased, and there was a calm. And He said unto them, Where is your faith? And they being afraid wondered, saying one to another, What manner of man is this! For He commandeth even the winds and water, and they obey Him." Lk. 8:24,25

Prayer:
Father in heaven, when the sea becomes rough to the point we are in danger, please calm it for us like You did for them. Lord please rebuke the wind and waves when we need it in Jesus' name, Amen!

Miracle
"... there came a man named Jairus, and he was a ruler of the Synagogue: and he fell down at Jesus' feet, and besought Him that He would come into his house: for he had one only daughter, about twelve years of age, and she lay a dying. But as He went the people thronged Him... while He yet spake, there cometh one from the ruler of the Synagogue's house, saying to Him, Thy daughter is dead; trouble not the Master. But when Jesus heard it, He answered him, saying, Fear not: believe only, and she shall be made whole. And when He came into the house, He suffered no man to go in, save Peter... James, and John, and the father and the mother of the maiden. And all wept, and bewailed her: but He said, Weep not; she is not dead, but sleepeth. And they laughed Him to scorn, knowing that she was dead. And He put them all out and took her by the hand, and called, saying, Maid, arise. And her spirit came again, and she arose straightway: and He commanded to give her meat. And her parents were astonished..." Lk. 8:41,42, 49-56

Miracle
"And a woman having an issue of blood twelve years, which had spent all her living upon physicians, neither could be healed of any, came behind Him, and touched the border of His garment: and immediately her issue of blood stanched (stopped). And Jesus said, Who touched Me? When all denied, Peter and they that were with Him said, Master, the multitude throng Thee and press Thee, and sayest Thou, Who touched Me? And Jesus said,

Somebody hath touched Me: for I perceive that virtue is gone out of Me. And when the woman saw that she was not hid, she came trembling, and falling down before Him, she declared unto Him before all the people for what cause she had touched Him, and how she was healed immediately. And He said unto her, Daughter, be of good comfort: thy faith hath made thee whole; go in peace." Lk. 8:43-48

Prayer:
Father in heaven, let me have the faith to be whole like this woman. Thank You in Jesus' name, Amen!

Jesus gives power and authority to His disciples
"Then He called His twelve disciples together, and gave them power and authority over all devils, and to cure diseases. And He sent them to preach the kingdom of God, and to heal the sick... and they departed, and went through the towns, preaching the Gospel, and healing everywhere." Lk. 9:1,2,6

Jesus gave His twelve disciples power and authority but He also promised in Mk. 16:17 that these signs would follow those who believe. He said that *".. these signs shall follow them that believe; in My name ..."* Mk. 16:17.

Miracle
"And the people... followed Him: and He received them, and spake unto them of the kingdom of God, and healed them that had need of healing." Lk. 9:11

The Condition:
"... whosoever will lose his life for My sake ..." Lk. 9:24

> **The Promise:**
> *"... the same shall save it."* Lk. 9:24

Miracle
"And, behold, a man of the company cried out, saying, Master, I beseech Thee, look upon my son: for he is mine only child. And, lo, a spirit taketh him, and he suddenly crieth out... and I besought Thy disciples to cast him out; and they could not. And Jesus answering said, O faithless and perverse generation, how long shall I be with you, and suffer you? Bring thy son hither... and Jesus re-buked the unclean spirit, and healed the child, and delivered him again to his father. And thy were all amazed at the mighty power of God." Lk. 9:38-43

We have power and authority over evil spirits in Jesus' name if we believe in Jesus, Mk. 16:17.

The Condition:
Jesus *"... said unto them, Whosoever shall receive this child in My name receiveth Me: and whosoever shall receive Me receiveth Him that sent Me: for he that is least among you all..."* Lk. 9:48

> **The Promise:**
> *"... the same shall be great."* Lk. 9:48

"For the Son of man is not come to destroy men's lives, but to save them..." Lk. 9:56

Jesus tells His disciples to *"... heal the sick... and say... the kingdom of God is come nigh unto you."* Lk. 10:9

"And the seventy returned again with joy, saying, Lord, even the devils are subject unto us through Thy name. And He said unto them, I beheld Satan as lightning fall from heaven." Lk. 10:17,18

> **The Promise:**
> *"Behold, I give unto you power (Gr. #1849 "authority") to tread on serpents and scorpions, and over all the power of the enemy: and nothing shall by any means hurt you."* Lk. 10:19

We see here that it wasn't just the twelve disciples who had power and authority but seventy of Jesus' followers; we see that Paul also had power to heal in Acts 19:12.

We are not to rejoice that God has given us power over evil spirits but that our names are written in the Book of Life.

"Notwithstanding in this rejoice not, that the spirits are subject unto you; but rather rejoice, because your names are written in heaven." Lk. 10:19,20

The Condition:
"And I say unto you, Ask..." Lk. 11:9

> **The Promise:**
> *"... and it shall be given you..."* Lk. 11:9

The Condition:
"... seek..." Lk. 11:9

> **The Promise:**
> *"... and ye shall find..."* Lk. 11:9

The Condition:
"... knock..." Lk. 11:9

The Promise:
"... and it shall be opened unto you. For everyone that asketh receiveth; and he that seeketh findeth; and to him that knocketh it shall be opened..." Lk. 11:9,10

Holy Spirit given to those who ask
"If ye then, being evil, know how to give good gifts unto your children..." Lk. 11:13

The Promise:
"... how much more shall your heavenly Father give the Holy Spirit to them that ask Him?" Lk. 11:13

Miracle
"But if I with the finger of God cast out devils, no doubt the kingdom of God is come upon you. When a strong man armed keepeth his palace, his goods are in peace: but when a stronger than he shall come upon him, and overcome him, he taketh from him all his armour wherein he trusted, and divideth his spoils." Lk. 11:20-22
Jesus is stronger and took Satan's armor; He divides the spoils with us.

Blessed
"... blessed are they that hear the Word of God, and keep (#5442 *"to observe, as a precept"* Dict. *"precept"* means *"a Commandment or law"*) *it."* Lk. 11:28

"If you are filled with light... then your whole life will be radiant, as though a floodlight were filling you with light." Lk. 11:35,36 NLT

A promise that everything will be revealed in time
"For there is nothing covered, that shall not be revealed; neither hid, that shall not be known. Therefore whatsoever ye have spoken in darkness shall be heard in the light; and that which ye have spoken in the ear in closets shall be proclaimed upon the housetops." Lk. 12:2,3

The Condition:
"Also I say unto you, Whosoever shall confess Me before men..." Lk. 12:8

The Promise:
"... him shall the Son of man also confess before the angels of God... and whosoever shall speak a word against the Son of man, it shall be forgiven him..." Lk. 12:8

"... but he that denieth Me before men shall be denied before the angels of God." Lk. 12:9

"... and when they bring you unto the Synagogues, and unto magistrates, and powers, take ye no thought how or what thing ye shall answer, or what ye shall say..." Lk. 12:10,11

> **The Promise:**
> "... for the Holy Ghost shall teach you in the same hour what ye ought to say." Lk. 12:12

"And He said unto His disciples, Therefore I say unto you, Take no thought for your life, what ye shall eat; neither for the body, what ye shall put on. The life is more than meat, and the body is more than raiment. Consider the ravens: for they neither sow nor reap; which neither have storehouse nor barn; and God feedeth them: how much more are ye better than the fowls? And which of you with taking thought can add to his stature one cubit? If ye then be not able to do that thing which is least, why take ye thought for the rest? Consider the lilies how they grow: they toil not, they spin not; and yet I say unto you, that Solomon in all his glory was not arrayed like one of these. If then God so clothe the grass, which is today in the field, and tomorrow is cast into the oven..." Lk. 12:22-28

> **The Promise:**
> "... how much more will He clothe you, O ye of little faith?" Lk. 12:28

"And seek not ye what ye shall eat, or what ye shall drink, neither be ye of doubtful mind. For all these things do the nations of the world seek after: and your Father knoweth that ye have need of these things. But rather seek ye the kingdom of God..." Lk. 12:29-31

> **The Promise:**
> "... and all these things shall be added unto you. Fear not, little flock; for it is your Father's good pleasure to give you the kingdom." Lk. 12:31

The Condition:
"Sell that ye have, and give alms; provide yourselves bags which wax not old..." Lk. 12:33

> **The Promise:**
> And you will have "... a treasure in the heavens that faileth not, where no thief approacheth, neither moth corrupteth." Lk. 12:33

Alms - from the word *"eleos"* which means *"compassion"*.
"... give to the needy..." Matt. 6:2 NIV
"So that your giving will be in secret" Matt. 6:4 NAS
"Kindness and charity" Acts 9:36

"... *your prayers and alms have ascended...*" Acts 10:4 ESV

"For where your treasure is, there will your heart be also. Let your loins be girded about, and your lights burning; and ye yourselves like unto men that wait for their Lord, when He will return from the wedding; that when He cometh and knoweth, they may open unto Him immediately." Lk. 12:34-36

Blessed
"Blessed are those servants, whom the Lord when He cometh shall find watching: verily I say unto you..." Lk. 12:37

The Promise:
"... that He shall gird Himself, and make them to sit down (#347 Gr. *"to make to recline at table... as at a feast"* like the Wedding Feast) *to meat, and will come forth and serve them. And if He shall come in the second watch, or come in the third watch, and find them so, blessed are those servants."* Lk. 12:37,38

Blessed
"And the Lord said, Who then is that faithful and wise steward, whom his Lord shall make ruler over His household, to give them their portion of meat in the due season? Blessed is that servant, whom his Lord when He cometh shall find so doing. Of a truth I say unto you, that..." Lk. 12:42-44

The Promise:
"... He will make him ruler over all that He hath." Lk. 12:44

Miracle
"And when Jesus saw her, He called her to Him, and said unto her, Woman, thou art loosed from thine infirmity. And He laid His hands on her: and immediately she was made straight, and glorified God." Lk. 13: 12,13

"And ought not this woman, being a daughter of Abraham, whom Satan hath bound, lo, these eighteen years, be loosed from this bond..." Lk. 13:16

Miracles
Jesus said, *"... I cast out devils, and I do cures today and tomorrow, and the third day I shall be perfected."* Lk. 13:32

Blessed
"... ye shall not see Me, until the time come when ye shall say, Blessed is He that cometh in the name of the Lord (at 2nd coming)." Lk. 13:35

Miracle
Jesus healed the man with dropsy, Lk. 14:1-4.

> **The Promise:**
> *"And, behold, there are last which shall be first, and there are first which shall be last."* Lk. 14:30

"For whosoever exalteth himself shall be abased..." Lk. 14:11
The Condition:
"... and he that humbleth himself..." Lk. 14:11

> **The Promise:**
> *"... shall be exalted."* Lk. 14:11

Recompensed at the Resurrection
The Condition:
"But when thou makest a feast, call the poor, the maimed, the lame, the blind..." Lk. 14:14

> **The Promise:**
> *"... and thou shalt be blessed for they cannot recompense thee: for thou shalt be recompensed at the Resurrection of the just."* Lk. 14:14

Parable of the wedding feast
"... He said unto him, Blessed is he that shall eat bread in the Kingdom of God. Then said He unto him, A certain man made a great supper, and bade many: and sent His servant at supper time to say to them that were bidden, Come: for all things are now ready. And they all with one consent began to make excuses... then the master of the house being angry said to His servant, Go out quickly into the streets and lanes of the city, and bring in hither the poor, and the maimed, and the halt, and the blind. And the servant said, Lord, it is done as Thou hast commanded, and yet there is room. And the Lord said unto the servant, Go out into the highways and hedges, and compel them to come in, that My house may be filled." Lk. 14:15-23

The Condition:
"If therefore ye have not been faithful in the unrighteous mammon, who will commit to your trust the true riches?" Lk. 16:11
The promise is that if you are faithful with money in this world He will trust you with the true riches in heaven.

Faith as small as a mustard seed
"And the Apostles said unto the Lord, Increase our faith." Lk. 17:5

The Promise:
"... if ye had faith as a grain of mustard seed, ye might say unto this Sycamine tree, Be thou plucked up by the root, and be thou planted in the sea; and it should obey you." Lk. 17:5,6

Miracle
"And as He entered into a certain village, there met Him ten men that were lepers, which stood afar off: and they lifted up their voices, and said, Jesus, Master, have mercy on us. And when He saw them, He said unto them, Go shew yourselves unto the priests. And it came to pass, that, as they went, they were cleansed. And one of them, when he saw that he was healed, turned back, and with a loud voice glorified God. And fell down on his face at His feet, giving Him thanks: and he was a Samaritan... and He said unto him, Arise, go thy way: thy faith hath made thee whole." Lk. 17:12-19
Only one came back to thank Jesus! We should always be grateful!
Prayer:
Father in heaven, help me to always be thankful and appreciate everything You do for me. In Jesus' name, Amen!

"Behold, the kingdom of God is within you ("or among you" KJV fn)" Lk. 17:21

"Whosoever shall seek to save his life shall lose it..." Lk. 17:33

The Condition:
"... and whosoever shall lose his life..." Lk. 17:33

   The Promise:
   "... shall preserve it." Lk. 17:33

Promise that God will avenge His elect
"And shall not God avenge His own elect, which cry day and night unto Him, though He bear long with them?" Lk. 18:7

The Condition:
"... he that humbleth himself..." Lk. 18:14

   The Promise:
   "... shall be exalted." Lk. 18:14

The Condition:
"But Jesus called them unto Him, and said, Suffer little children to come unto Me, and forbid them not..." Lk. 18:16

   The Promise:
   "... for of such is the kingdom of God..." Lk. 18:16

The Condition:
"... distribute unto the poor, and..." Lk. 18:22

> **The Promise:**
> *"... thou shalt have treasure in heaven..."* Lk. 18:22

"... and come, follow Me (Jesus)." Lk. 18:22
"... the things which are impossible with men are possible with God." Lk. 18:27

"And He said unto them, Verily I say unto you..." Lk. 18:29
The Condition:
"... there is no man that hath left houses, or parents, or brethren, or wife, or children, for the kingdom of God's sake..." Lk. 18:29

> **The Promise:**
> *"... who shall not receive manifold (#4179 – Gr. "many times more")... in this present time, and in the world to come life everlasting."* Lk. 18:29,30

Miracle
"... He (Jesus) asked him, saying, What wilt thou that I shall do unto thee? And he said, Lord, that I may receive my sight. And Jesus said unto him, Receive thy sight: thy faith hath saved thee. And immediately he received his sight, and followed Him, glorifying God: and all the people, when they saw it, gave praise unto God." Lk. 18:40-43

The Promise is that Jesus will seek out the lost to save them
"For the Son of man is come to seek and to save that which was lost." Lk. 19:10
Prayer
Father in heaven, please seek out those who are lost in my family and save them! Thank You in Jesus' name, Amen!

> **The Promise:**
> *"For I will give you a mouth and wisdom, which all your adversaries shall not be able to gainsay nor resist."* Lk. 21:15

Prayer:
Father in heaven, please give me a mouth to speak with wisdom so that no one can resist the truth. In Jesus' name, Amen!
"... ye shall be hated of all men for My name's sake." Lk. 21:17

> **The Promise:**
> *"But there shall not an hair of your head perish. In your patience possess ye your souls."* Lk. 21:18,19

The promise is that Jesus is coming back again!
"*And there shall be signs in the sun, and in the moon, and in the stars; and upon the earth distress of nations, with perplexity; the sea and the waves roaring; men's hearts failing them for fear, and for looking after those things which are coming on the earth for the powers of heaven shall be shaken. And then shall they see the Son of Man coming in a cloud with power and great glory. And when these things begin to come to pass, then look up, and lift up your heads...*" Lk. 21:25-28

The Promise:
"*... for your Redemption draweth nigh.*" Lk. 21:28

God's Word is eternal
"*... when ye see these things come to pass, know ye that the kingdom of God is nigh at hand. Verily I say unto you, This generation shall not pass away, till all be fulfilled. Heaven and earth shall pass away: but...*" Lk. 21:31-33

The Promise:
"*... My Words shall not pass away.*" Lk. 21:33

"*Watch ye therefore, and pray always, that ye may be accounted worthy to escape* (#1628 "to flee out" of) *all these things that shall come to pass, and to stand before the Son of man.*" Lk. 21:36

The promise to the 12 disciples

The Promise:
"*And I appoint unto you a kingdom, as My Father hath appointed unto Me; that ye may eat and drink at My table in My kingdom, and sit on thrones Judging the twelve tribes of Israel.*" Lk. 22:29,30

Promise to Peter
"*And the Lord said, Simon, Simon, behold, Satan hath desired to have you, that he may sift you as wheat: but I have prayed for thee, that thy faith fail not: and when thou art converted, strengthen thy brethren.*" Lk. 22:31,32
Prayer:
Father in heaven, I pray for _____ that they would be converted and that their faith would not fail them just like You did for Peter; so that they can help to strengthen their brothers and sisters in Christ. Thank You in Jesus' name, Amen!

Jesus promised His disciples that they would lack nothing
"*And He* (Jesus) *said unto them, when I sent you without purse, and scrip, and shoes, lacked ye anything? And they said, Nothing.*" Lk. 22:35

Miracle
"And one of them ("Peter" Matt.26:42;Jn.18:11) smote the servant ("Malchus" Jn.18:10) of the high priest, and cut off his right ear..."

The Promise:
"... and He (Jesus) touched his ear, and healed him." Lk. 22:50,51

Jesus told Peter "put your sword back in its place" Matt. 26:52;Jn.18:11.

Promise of the Holy Spirit
"Then (Jesus) opened... their understanding, that they might understand the Scriptures... that repentance and remission of sins should be preached in His name among all nations, beginning at Jerusalem. And ye are witnesses of these things. And, behold, I send the promise of My Father upon you: but tarry ye in the city of Jerusalem, until ye be endued with power from on high. And He led them out as far as to Bethany, and He lifted up His hands, and blessed them." Lk. 24:45,47-51

John

John "... came (as) a witness... that all men through Him (Jesus) might believe." Jn. 1:7
The Condition:
"But as many as received Him..." Jn. 1:12

The Promise:
"... to them gave He power to become the sons of God..." Jn. 1:12

The Condition:
"... even to them that believe on His name..." Jn. 1:12

"... His (Jesus) fullness have all we received, and grace for grace..." Jn. 1:16

Jesus said to Nathaniel "... believest thou? Thou shalt see greater things than these." Jn. 1:50

Miracles
"... many believed in His name, when they saw the miracles which He did." Jn. 2:23

Believe
"If I do not the works of My Father, believe Me not. But if I do, though ye believe not Me, believe the works: that ye may know, and believe, that the Father is in Me, and I in Him." Jn. 10:37,38

"For God so loved the world, that He gave His only begotten Son ..." Jn. 3:16

The Condition:
"... that whosoever believeth in Him ..." Jn. 3:16

> **The Promise:**
> *"... should not perish, but have everlasting life. For God sent not His Son... to condemn the world; but that the world through Him might be saved. He that believeth on Him is not condemned... in the name of the only begotten Son of God."* Jn. 3:16-28

"... light is come into the world." Jn. 3:19
If we believe in Jesus, we won't be condemned!

A *"... man can receive nothing, except it be given him from heaven."* Jn. 3:27
Nothing good or bad can happen to us unless it's God's will.

Promise to Jesus
"... for God giveth not the Spirit by measure unto Him (Jesus). *The Father loveth the Son, and hath given all things into His hand ..."* Jn. 3:34

The Condition:
"... he that believeth on the Son ..." Jn. 3:36

> **The Promise:**
> *"... hath everlasting life ..."* Jn. 3:36

The Condition:
"Jesus answered and said unto her, Whosoever drinketh of this water shall thirst again: but whosoever drinketh of the water that I shall give him ..." Jn. 4:13,14

> **The Promise:**
> *"... shall never thirst; but the water that I shall give him shall be in him a well of water springing up into everlasting life."* Jn. 4:14

"Come... let him take the Water of Life freely." Rev. 22:17

"The woman saith unto Him, I know that Messias cometh, which is called Christ; when He is come..." Jn. 4:25

The Promise:
"... He will tell us all things." Jn. 4:25

Reward for preaching the Gospel
"And he that reapeth..." Jn. 4:36

The Promise:
"... receiveth wages and gathereth fruit unto life eternal: that both he that soweth and he that reapeth may rejoice together." Jn. 4:36

Miracle
A nobleman who's son was sick and dying went to Jesus and asked Him to "... heal his son: for he was at the point of death. Then said Jesus unto him, Except ye see signs and wonders, ye will not believe. The nobleman saith unto him, Sir, come down ere my child die. Jesus saith unto him, Go thy way; thy son liveth. And the man believed the Word that Jesus had spoken unto him, and he went his way... his servants met him, and told him, saying, Thy son liveth. Then inquired he of them the hour when he began to mend. And they said unto him, Yesterday at the seventh hour the fever left him. So the father knew it was the same hour in the which Jesus said unto him Thy son liveth: and himself believed and his whole house." Jn. 4:47-53

Miracle
"The impotent man answered Him, Sir, I have no man (to help me)... Jesus saith unto him, Rise, take up thy bed, and walk... and immediately the man was made whole, and took up his bed, and walked ... afterward Jesus findeth him in the Temple, and said unto him, Behold, thou art made whole ..." Jn. 5:7-9,14

The Condition:
"... sin no more, lest a worse thing come unto thee." Jn. 5:14
Jesus said the same thing to the woman caught in adultery in Jn. 8:11.

The Condition:
"Verily, verily, I say unto you, He that heareth My Word, and believeth on Him that sent Me..." Jn. 5:24

The Promise:
"... hath everlasting life, and shall not come into condemnation; but is passed from death unto life. Verily, verily, I say unto you, The hour is coming, and now is, when the dead shall hear the voice of the Son

of God: and they that hear shall live. For as the Father hath life in Himself; so hath He given to the Son to have life in Himself; and hath given Him authority to execute Judgment also, because He is the Son of man. Marvel not at this: for the hour is coming, in the which all that are in the graves shall hear His voice, and shall come forth; they that have done good, unto the Resurrection of life ..." Jn. 5:24-29

When we believe and strive to obey Jesus, we won't have to be afraid of the Judgment! We pass from Judgment to life because Jesus took our punishment but our works will go through the fire to determine what our eternal rewards will be, I Cor. 3:15.

We must be careful because if we are sons and daughters of God, He will punish us if we do wrong, Heb. 12:6.

The Scriptures show us how to have eternal life in Christ Jesus
"Search the Scriptures; for in them ye think ye have eternal life (and you do)*: and they* (the Scriptures) *are they which testify of Me."* Jn. 5:39
Jesus was saying to them, If you know that the Old Testament Scriptures lead to eternal life, then believe them when they point to Me as the Messiah.

Miracle
"When Jesus then lifted up his eyes, and saw a great company come unto Him, He saith unto Philip, Whence shall we buy bread, that these may eat? And this He said to prove ("test" ESV) *him: for He Himself knew what He would do."* Jn. 6:5,6

Miracle
Jesus feeds the 5,000, Jn. 6:11-14.

Miracle
Jesus walks on water, Jn. 6:19
Jesus said to them, *"... it is I; be not afraid..."* Jn. 6:20
How do we do the works of Jesus? Believe!
"Labour not for the meat which perisheth, but for that meat which endureth
unto everlasting life, which the Son of man shall give unto you; for Him hath God the Father sealed. Then said they unto Him, What shall we do, that we might work the works of God? Jesus answered and said unto them, this is the work of God, that ye believe on Him (Jesus) *whom He hath sent."* Jn. 6: 27-29 (See notes on Mk. 16:17,18,20)

Jesus, the Bread of Life
"Moses gave you not that bread from heaven; but My Father giveth you the true Bread from heaven. For the Bread of God is He (Jesus) which cometh down from heaven, and..." Jn. 6:32,33

The Promise:
"... giveth life unto the world." Jn. 6:33

"Then said they unto Him, Lord, evermore give us this bread. And Jesus said unto them, I Am the Bread of Life..." Jn. 6:34,35

The Condition:
"... he that cometh to Me..." Jn. 6:35

The Promise:
"... shall never hunger..." Jn. 6:35

The Condition:
"...and he that believeth on Me..." Jn. 6:35

The Promise:
"... shall never thirst." Jn. 6:35

The Condition:
"All that the Father giveth me shall come to Me; and him that cometh to Me..." Jn. 6:37

The Promise:
"... I will in no wise cast out." Jn. 6:37

"... I should lose nothing, but should raise it up again at the last day. And this is the will of Him that sent Me, that every one which seeth the Son, and believeth on Him, may have everlasting life: and I will raise him up at the last day..." Jn. 6:39,40,44
We see here that the Resurrection of the righteous is on the last day!

The Condition:
"He that believeth on Me..." Jn. 6:47

The Promise:
"... hath everlasting life." Jn. 6:47

"I am the Bread of Life... the Living Bread which came down from heaven..." Jn. 6:48,51
The Condition:
"... if any man eat of this Bread (through Communion)..." Jn. 6:51

The Promise:
"... he shall live forever..." Jn. 6:51

"... and the bread that I will give is My flesh, which I will give for the life of the world." Jn. 6:51

The Condition:
"... except ye eat the flesh of the Son of man, and drink His blood (through the symbol of Communion) ye have no life in you... whoso eateth My flesh, and drinketh My blood (symbolically through Communion)..." Jn. 6:53,54

The Promise:
"... hath eternal life; and I will raise him up at the last day." Jn. 6:54

The Condition:
"He that eateth My flesh, and drinketh My blood (through Communion)..." Jn. 6:56

The Promise:
"... dwelleth in Me, and I in him..." Jn. 6:56

Communion is one way that we abide or dwell in God and He in us.
Jn. 15:7 tells us that if we abie in Him, we can ask anything.
Jn. 15:10 says that if we keep the Commandments we abide in Him.
Jesus said that the wheat must die (He died on the cross and we die with Him in baptism) or it abides alone.
Jn. 12:24 and He said that if we abide in Him, He wil abide in us, Jn. 15:15.

The Condition:
"... he that eateth of this Bread (through Communion)..." Jn. 6:57

The Promise:
"... even he shall live by Me..." Jn. 6:57

The Condition:
"... he that eateth of this Bread (through Communion)..." Jn. 6:58

The Condition:
"... the Words that I speak unto you..." Jn. 6:63

The Promise:
"... shall live forever... the Spirit that quickeneth..." Jn. 6:63

The Promise:
"... they are Spirit, and they are life." Jn. 6:63

And Jesus is the Word, Jn. 1:4.
"... no man can come unto Me, except it were given unto him of My Father." Jn. 6:65

Prayer:
Father in heaven, please give life to me and my family because of Jesus. Thank You in Jesus' name, Amen!
"Then Jesus said unto the twelve, Will you also go away? Then Simon Peter answered Him, Lord, to whom shall we go? Thou hast the Words of eternal life." Jn. 6:67

We believe and are sure
"And we believe and are sure that Thou art that Christ, the Son of the living God." Jn. 6:69

If you are willing to obey, God will let you know what is truth and what is right!
The Condition:
"If any man will do His will..." Jn. 7:17

> **The Promise:**
> *"... he shall know of the doctrine ("teaching"), whether it be of God, or whether I speak of Myself."* Jn. 7:17

"And many of the people believed on Him, and said, When Christ cometh, will He do more miracles than these which this man hath done?" Jn. 7:31

"... if any man thirst, let him come unto Me, and drink..." Jn. 7:37

The Condition:
"He that believeth on Me, as the Scripture hath said..." Jn. 7:38

> **The Promise:**
> *"... out of his belly shall flow rivers of living water."* Jn. 7:38

"But this spake He of the Spirit, which they that believe on Him should receive ..." Jn. 7:39

I don't condemn you!
"When Jesus had lifted up Himself... He said unto her, Woman, where are ... thine accusers? hath no man condemned thee? She said, No man, Lord. And Jesus said unto her..." Jn. 8:10,11

> **The Promise:**
> *"... neither do I condemn thee..."* Jn. 8:10,11

Jesus said the same thing to the impotent man in Jn. 5:7-9,14.

The Condition:
"... go, and sin no more." Jn. 8:10,11

"Then spake Jesus... saying, I am the light of the world..." Jn. 8:12
The Condition:
"... he that followeth Me..." Jn. 8:12

> **The Promise:**
> *"... shall not walk in darkness, but shall have the light of life."* Jn. 8:12

The Condition:
"If ye had known Me (Jesus)..." Jn. 8:19

> **The Promise:**
> *"... ye should have known My Father also."* Jn. 8:19

The Condition:
"... if ye continue in My Word..." Jn. 8:31

> **The Promise:**
> *"... then are ye My disciples indeed..."* Jn. 8:31

The Condition:
"And ye shall know the truth..." Jn. 8:32

> **The Promise;**
> *"... and the truth shall make you free."* Jn. 8:32

The Condition:
"... the Son abideth forever. If the Son therefore shall make you free..." Jn. 8: 35,36

> **The Promise:**
> *"... ye shall be free indeed..."* Jn. 8:36

The Condition:
"... if a man keep My saying..." Jn. 8:51

> **The Promise:**
> *"... he shall never see death."* Jn. 8:51

Jesus healed the blind man
"Master, who did sin... that he was born blind? Jesus answered, Neither hath this man sinned, nor his parents: but that the works of God should be made

manifest in him. I must work the works of Him that sent Me, while it is day: the night cometh, when no man can work." Jn. 9:2-4

Miracle
"When He (Jesus) had thus spoken, He spat on the ground, and made clay of the spittle, and He anointed the eyes of the blind man with the clay, And said unto him Go, wash in the pool of Siloam, (which is by interpretation, Sent). He went his way therefore, and washed, and came seeing... therefore said they unto him (the blind man who was healed), How were thine eyes opened? He answered and said, A man that is called Jesus made clay, and anointed mine eyes, and said unto me, Go to the pool of Siloam, and wash: and I went and washed, and I received sight." Jn. 9:6-11

God does not hear sinners!
The Condition:
"Now we know that God heareth not sinners: but if any man be a worshipper of God and doeth His will..." Jn. 9:31

> **The Promise:**
> "... him He heareth." Jn. 9:31

So what do we do if God doesn't hear sinners and we are all sinners?
1. We repent
2. We believe and receive Jesus
3. We get baptized
4. God sees us righteous in Christ Jesus

The Condition:
"I am the door: by Me (Jesus) if any man enter in..." Jn. 10:9

> **The Promise:**
> "... he shall be saved, and shall go in and out, and find pasture... I am come that they might have life, and that they might have it more abundantly." Jn. 10:9,10

"abundantly" Gr. – "Perissos" which means, super abundant exceeding, abundantly, above superior, beyond measure".

"My sheep hear My voice, and I know them, and they follow Me..." Jn. 10:27

> **The Promise:**
> "... and I give unto them eternal life; and they shall never perish, neither shall any man pluck them out of My hand. My Father, which gave them Me, is greater than all; and no man is able to pluck them out of My Father's hand." Jn. 10:27-29

Jesus said that we could believe that He is God because He did miracles in the power of His Father and He is still doing miracles today.
"If I do not the works of My Father, believe Me not. But if I do, though ye believe not Me, believe the works: that ye may know, and believe, that the Father is in Me, and I in him." Jn. 10:37,38

Martha said to Jesus
"... I know, that even now, whatsoever Thou wilt ask of God, God will give it Thee..." Jn. 11:22

Miracle
"Jesus saith unto her, Thy brother shall rise again. Martha saith unto Him, I know that he shall rise again in the Resurrection at the last day. Jesus said unto her, I Am the Resurrection and the life..." Jn. 11:23-25
Again we see here that the Resurrection is on the last day.

The Condition:
"... he that believeth in Me, though he were dead..." Jn. 11:25

> **The Promise:**
> *"... yet shall he live..."* Jn. 11:25

The Condition:
"... and whosoever liveth and believeth in Me..." Jn. 11:26

> **The Promise:**
> *"... shall never die."* Jn. 11:26

"Believest thou this? She saith unto Him, yea, Lord: I believe that Thou art the Christ, the Son of God, which should come into the world." Jn. 11:26,27
"Jesus saith unto her (Martha), *Said I not unto thee, that..."* Jn. 11:40
The Condition:
"... if thou wouldest believe..." Jn. 11:40

> **The Promise:**
> *"... thou shouldest see the glory of God..."* Jn. 11:40-42

Jesus prayed, *"Father, I thank Thee that Thou hast heard Me. And I knew that Thou hearest Me always..."* Jn. 11:42
Jesus raised Lazarus from the dead, Jn. 11:43,44.

You must die to self to abide with Christ

"Verily, verily, I say unto you, Except a corn of wheat fall into the ground and die, it abideth alone: but if it die (it doesn't abide alone), *it bringeth forth much fruit."* Jn. 12:24

We must be baptized as a symbol that we are dying to self and being Resurrected with Jesus. The wheat falling into the ground symbolizes baptism by immersion. At baptism we die with Christ and are raised with Resurrection power.

*"Therefore we are **buried with Him by baptism into death**: that like as Christ was raised up from the dead by the glory of the Father, even so we also should walk in newness of life. For if we have been planted together in the likeness of His death, we shall be also in the likeness of His Resurrection..."* Rom. 6:4,5

*"... in whom also ye are circumcised with the circumcision made without hands, in putting off the body of the sins of the flesh, by the circumcision of Christ: **buried with Him in baptism**, wherein also you are risen with Him through the faith of the operation of God, who hath raised Him from the dead."* Col. 2:11,12

The Condition:
"... he that hateth his life in this world..." Jn. 12:25

    The Promise:
    "... shall keep it unto life eternal." Jn. 12:25

The Condition:
"... if any man serve Me..." Jn. 12:26

    The Promise:
    "... him will My Father honour." Jn. 12:26

    The Promise:
    "Now is the Judgment of this world: now shall the prince of this world be cast out." Jn. 12:31

The Condition:
"And I, if I be lifted up from the earth..." Jn. 12:32

    The Promise:
    "... will draw all men unto Me (Jesus).*"* Jn. 12:32

The Condition:
"While ye have light, believe in the light..." Jn. 12:36

    The Promise:
    "... that ye may be the children of light..." Jn. 12:36

The Condition:
"... be converted..." Jn. 12:40

> **The Promise:**
> "... and I should heal them." Jn. 12:40

"... I have not spoken of Myself; but the Father which sent Me, He gave Me a Commandment, what I should say, and what I should speak... I know that His Commandment is life everlasting..." Jn. 12:49,50

"Let not your heart be troubled: ye believe in God, believe... in Me." Jn. 14:1

> **The Promise:**
> "... in My Father's house are many mansions... I go to prepare a place for you. And... I will come again, and receive you unto Myself; that where I am, there ye may be also." Jn. 14:2-3

The Condition:
"... he that believeth on Me..." Jn. 14:12

> **The Promise:**
> "... the works that I do shall he do also; and greater works than these shall he do; because I go unto My Father. And whatsoever ye shall ask in My name, that will I do, that the Father may be glorified in the Son. If ye shall ask anything in My name, I will do it." Jn. 14:12-14

The Condition:
"If ye love Me, keep My Commandments..." Jn. 14:15

> **The Promise:**
> "And I will pray the Father, and He shall give you another Comforter, that He may abide with you forever; even the Spirit of truth; whom the world cannot receive, because it seeth Him not, neither knoweth Him: but ye know Him; for He dwelleth with you, and shall be in you. I will not leave you comfortless: I will come to you." Jn. 14:16-18

The Condition:
"He that hath My Commandments, and keepeth them, he it is that loveth Me: he that loveth Me..." Jn. 14:21

> **The Promise:**
> "... shall be loved of My Father, and I will love him, and will manifest Myself to him..." Jn. 14:21

The Condition:
"... *if a man love Me, he will keep My Words...*" Jn. 14:23

> **The Promise:**
> "... *and My Father will love him, and we will come unto him, and make our abode with him.*" Jn. 14:23

The Holy Spirit teaches us

> **The Promise:**
> "*But the Comforter which is the Holy Ghost, whom the Father will to your remembrance, whatsoever I have said unto You.*" Jn. 14:26

Jesus promises to give us peace
"*Peace I leave with you, My peace I give unto you: not as the world giveth, give I unto you. Let not your heart be troubled, neither let it be afraid.*" Jn. 14: 27

"*Abide in Me...*" Jn. 15:4

> **The Promise:**
> "... *and I* (will abide) *in you.*" Jn. 15:5

The Condition:
"... *as the branch cannot bear fruit of itself, except it abide in the vine; no more can ye, except ye abide in me. I am the vine, ye are the branches: He that abideth in me, and I in him...*" Jn. 15:4,5

> **The Promise:**
> "... *the same bringeth forth much fruit...*" Jn. 15:5

"... *without Me ye can do nothing.*" Jn. 15:5
We are commanded to abide in Christ Jesus. The promise is that God will abide in us if we abide in Him.
The Condition:
"*If ye abide in Me, and My words abide in you...*" Jn. 15:7

> **The Promise:**
> "... *ye shall ask what ye will, and it shall be done unto you.*" Jn. 15:7

The Condition:
"*As the Father hath loved Me, so have I loved you: continue ye in My love. If ye keep My Commandments...*" Jn. 15:9,10

> **The Promise:**
> "... *ye shall abide in My love...*" Jn. 15:10

"... even as I have kept My Father's Commandments, and abide in His love." Jn. 15:10

"These things have I spoken unto you, that My joy might remain in you, and that your joy might be full." Jn. 15:11

> **The Promise:**
> "Ye are My friends..." Jn. 15:14

The Condition:
"... if ye do whatsoever I command you." Jn. 15:14

Jesus calls us friends
"Henceforth I call you not servants; for the servant knoweth not what his lord doeth: but I have called you friends; for all things that I have heard of My Father I have made known unto you. Ye have not chosen Me, but I have chosen you, and ordained you, that ye should go and bring forth fruit, and that your fruit should remain: that..." Jn. 15:15,16

> **The Promise:**
> "... whatsoever ye shall ask of the Father in My name, He may give it you... I have chosen you out of the world..." Jn. 15:16,19

Spirit of Truth
"... when the Comforter is come..." Jn. 15:26

> **The Promise:**
> "... whom I will send unto you from the Father, even the Spirit of truth, which proceedeth from the Father..." Jn. 15:26

"... He shall testify of Me..." Jn. 15:26
The Condition:
"...I tell you the truth; it is expedient for you that I go away: for if I go not away, the Comforter will not come unto you; but if I depart..." Jn. 16:7

> **The Promise:**
> "... I will send Him unto you. And when He is come, He will reprove the world of sin, and of righteousness, and of Judgment; of sin, because they believe not on Me (Jesus); of righteousness, because I go to My Father, and ye see Me no more; of Judgment, because the prince of this world is Judged." Jn. 16:7-11

"I have yet many things to say unto you, but ye cannot bear them now. Howbeit when He, the Spirit of truth, is come..." Jn. 16:12,13

The Promise:
"... He will guide you into all truth: for He shall not speak of Himself; but whatsoever He shall hear, that shall He speak: and He will shew you things to come. He shall glorify Me (Jesus): *for He shall receive of Mine, and shew it unto you."* Jn. 16:13-14

"... you... have sorrow now..." Jn. 16:22 HCSB

The Promise:
"... but I will see you again, and your heart shall rejoice, and your joy no man taketh from you. And in that day ye shall ask Me nothing.

My name, He will give it you." Jn. 16:22,23

"Hitherto have ye asked nothing in My name..." Jn. 16:24

The Condition:
"... ask..." Jn. 16:24

The Promise:
"... and ye shall receive, that your joy may be full." Jn. 16:24

"... I shall no more speak unto you in proverbs..." Jn. 16:25

The Promise:
"... I shall shew you plainly of the Father. At that day ye shall ask in My name... for the Father Himself loveth you..." Jn. 16:25,26

The Condition:
"... and because ye have loved Me, and have believed that I came out from God. I came forth from the Father, and am come into the world: again, I leave the world, and go to the Father." Jn. 16:27

"These things I have spoken unto you..." Jn. 16:33

The Promise:
"... that in Me ye might have peace." Jn. 16:33

"In the world ye shall have tribulation: but be of good cheer; I have overcome the world." Jn. 16:33

Jesus gave us the Words from the Father
"For I have given unto them the Words which Thou gavest Me; and they have received them, and have known surely that I came out from Thee, and they have believed that Thou didst send Me." Jn. 17:8

Jesus prays for His disciples through all time

"... Holy Father, keep through Thine own name those whom Thou hast given Me, that they may be one, as we are. While I was with them in the world, I kept them in Thy name: those that Thou gavest Me I have kept, and none of them is lost, but the son of perdition (Judas)*; that the Scripture might be fulfilled. And now come I to Thee; and these things I speak in the world, that they might have My joy fulfilled in themselves. I have given them Thy Word; and the world hath hated them, because they are not of the world, even as I am not of the world... keep them from the evil... Sanctify them through Thy truth: Thy Word is truth."* Jn. 17:11-15,17

The promise is that Jesus prayed these things and we know the Father answered His prayer. The Father keeps us from evil in Jesus' name – we can have the joy of Jesus – we are Sanctified through the Word of truth!

Prayer:

Father in heaven, please keep me in the Father's name and those You've given to me in my life that none of them will be lost. Help us to be one as You are One in Spirit and in truth and let Your joy be in us. Thank You in Jesus' name, Amen!

We are one in Christ Jesus

"That they all may be one; as Thou, Father, art in Me, and I in Thee, that they also may be one in Us: that the world may believe that Thou hast sent Me. And the glory which Thou gavest Me I have given them; that they may be one, even as We are One: I in them, and Thou in Me, that they may be made perfect in One; and that the world may know that Thou hast sent Me, and hast loved them, as Thou hast loved Me." Jn. 17:21-23

"And I have declared unto them Thy name, and will declare it..." Jn. 17:26

> **The Promise:**
> *"... that the love wherewith Thou hast loved Me may be in them, and I in them."* Jn. 17:26

Blessing of peace
"... peace be unto you.." Jn. 20:21

Jesus gave them the Holy Spirit
"And when He had said this, He breathed on them and saith unto them, Receive ye the Holy Ghost..." Jn. 20:22

> **The Promise:**
> *"... whosoever sins ye remit, they are remitted unto them: and whosoever sins ye retain, they are retained."* Jn. 20:22-23

"If you forgive the sins of any, they are forgiven them; if you retain the sins of any, they are retained." Jn. 20:22,23 HCSB
Dict. *"remit"* means *"payment, cancel, free someone from punishment, lay aside; desist from activity, release from guilt or penalty of, restore."*
Dict. *"retain"* means *"keep, hold, reserve"*.

Blessed
"... be not faithless, but believing... blessed are they that have not seen, and yet have believed." Jn. 20:27,29

The Condition:
"But these are written, that ye might believe that Jesus is the Christ, the Son of God; and that believing..." Jn. 20:31

> **The Promise:**
> *"... ye might have life through His name."* Jn. 20:31

Acts

"And, being assembled together with them, commanded them that they should not depart from Jerusalem, but wait for the promise of the Father, which, saith He, ye have heard of Me. For John truly baptized with water..." Acts 1:4,5

> **The Promise:**
> *"... but ye shall be baptized with the Holy Ghost not many days hence."* Acts 1:4,5

The promise given to the disciples before Pentecost
"But ye shall receive power, after that the Holy Ghost is come upon you: and ye shall be witnesses unto Me both in Jerusalem, and in all Judaea, and in Samaria, and unto the uttermost part of the earth." Acts 1:8
"... ye men of Galilee, why stand ye gazing up into heaven? This same Jesus, which is taken up from you into heaven..." Acts 1:11

> **The Promise:**
> *"... shall so come in like manner as ye have seen Him go into heaven."* Acts 1:11

We see this in Zechariah, *"And His feet shall stand in that day upon the Mount of Olives, which is before Jerusalem on the East, and the Mount of*

Olives shall cleave in the midst thereof toward the East and toward the West, and there shall be **_a very great valley_**... and the Lord my God shall come, **_and all the saints_** with Thee." Zech. 14:4,5

This is a promise that the 1st time Jesus' feet touch the earth it will be on the Mt. of Olives. Jesus promised this as He was ascending from the Mt. of Olives after His Resurrection.

Day of Pentecost
"And they were all filled with the Holy Ghost..." Acts 2:4

Promise of the Holy Spirit
"And it shall come to pass in the last days, saith God, I will pour out of My Spirit upon all flesh: and your sons and your daughters shall prophesy, and your young men shall see visions, and your old men shall dream dreams: and on My servants and on My handmaidens I will pour out in those days of My Spirit; and they shall prophesy. And I will shew wonders in the heaven above, and signs in the earth beneath; blood, and fire and vapour of smoke: the sun shall be turned into darkness, and the moon into blood, before that great and notable day of the Lord come: and it shall come to pass, that whosoever shall call on the name of the Lord shall be saved..." Acts 2:17-21
This promise is also found in Joel 2:28

Miracles
"Jesus of Nazareth, a man approved of God among you by miracles and wonders and signs, which God did by Him in the midst of you, as ye yourselves also know..." Acts 2:22

Jesus is at the right hand of the Father
"For David speaketh concerning Him (Jesus)*, I foresaw the Lord always before My face, for He* (Jesus) *is on My* (God the Father's) *right hand..."* Acts 2:25

The Promise:
"... that I should not be moved ("shaken" NKJV)..." Acts 2:25

The promise to Jesus
"... My flesh shall rest in hope: because Thou wilt not leave My soul in hell, neither wilt Thou suffer Thine Holy One to see corruption. Thou hast made known to me the ways of life; Thou shalt make me full of joy with Thy countenance." Acts 2:25-28

"Then Peter said unto them..." Acts 2:38

The Condition:
"... repent, and be baptized every one of you in the name of Jesus Christ ..." Acts 2:38

> **The Promise:**
> *"... for the remission of sins, and ye shall receive the gift of the Holy Ghost."* Acts 2:38

(Gr. #907 baptizo means, *"dip, submerge, immerse"*)
"Therefore we are buried with Him by baptism into death: that like a s Christ was raised up from the dead by the glory of the Father, even so we also should walk in newness of life (through the Holy Spirit)." Rom. 6:4

"For the promise (of the Holy Spirit) *is unto you, and to your children, and to all that are afar off, even as many as the Lord our God shall call."* Acts 2:39
As many as shall *"... be saved."* Acts 2:40 NKJV

Miracles
"And fear came upon every soul: and many wonders and signs were done by the Apostles." Acts 2:43

God builds up the church
They were *"praising God, and having favour with all the people. And the Lord added to the church daily such as should be saved ... and many wonders and signs were done by the Apostles."* Acts 2:47,48

Prayer
Father in heaven, please continue adding to the church as You did at Pentecost and let us see Your miracles like we see in Your Word. In the name of Jesus, Amen!

Miracle
"Then Peter said, Silver and gold have I none: but such as I have give I thee: in the name of Jesus Christ of Nazareth rise up and walk. And he took him by the right hand, and lifted him up: and immediately his feet and... (ankle) *bones re-ceived strength. And he leaping up stood, and walked, and entered with them into the Temple, walking, and leaping, and praising God... why look ye so earnestly on us, as though by our own power or Holiness we had made this man to walk? The God of Abraham, and of Isaac, and of Jacob, the God of our fathers, hath glorified His Son Jesus... and His name through faith in His name hath made this man strong, whom ye see and know: yea, the faith which is by Him hath given him this perfect soundness in the presence of you all."* Acts 3:6,11-13,16

The Condition:
"Repent ye therefore, and be converted..." Acts 3:19

> **The Promise:**
> *"... that your sins may be blotted out, when the times of refreshing shall come from the presence of the Lord; and He shall send Jesus Christ* (at the 2nd coming)*..."* Acts 3:19

Blessed
"Ye are the children of the prophets, and of the Covenant which God made with our fathers, saying unto Abraham, And in thy Seed shall all the kindreds of the earth be blessed. Unto you first God, having raised up His Son Jesus, sent Him to bless you, in turning away every one of you from His iniquities (sins)*."* Acts 3:26

Prayer
Lord, bless me and my family by turning us away from our sins. Thank You in Jesus' name, Amen!

No other name but Jesus can save us!
"And when they had set them in the midst, they asked, By what power, or by what name, have ye done this? Then Peter, filled with the Holy Ghost, said unto them... if we this day be examined of the good deed done to the impotent man, by what means he is made whole... by the name of Jesus Christ of Nazareth, whom ye crucified, whom God raised from the dead, even by Him doth this man stand here before you whole... neither is there Salvation in any other: for there is none other name under heaven given among men, whereby we must be saved... the which was healed standing with them..." Acts 4:7-12,14

Miracle
"... for that indeed a notable miracle hath been done by them is manifest to all them that dwell in Jerusalem; and cannot deny it." Acts 4:16

Give
"And now, Lord... grant unto Thy servants, that with all boldness they may speak Thy Word, by stretching forth Thine hand to heal; and that signs and wonders may be done by the name of Thy Holy Child Jesus... and they were all filled with the Holy Ghost, and they spake the Word of God with boldness." Acts 4:29-31

Prayer:
Father in heaven, please fill us with Your Holy Spirit and give us boldness to

speak Your Word and please stretch forth Your mighty hand of power to heal us today as You did back then. Thank You in Jesus' name, Amen!

Great grace
"And with great power gave the Apostles witness of the Resurrection of the Lord Jesus: and great grace was upon them all. Neither was there any among them that lacked..." Acts 4:33,34

Miracles
"... by the hands of the Apostles were many signs and wonders wrought among the people; (and they were all with one accord)... believers were the more added to the Lord, multitudes both of men and women." Acts 5:12-14

Miracles
"There came also a multitude out of the cities round about unto Jerusalem, bringing sick folks, and them which were vexed with unclean spirits: and they were healed every one." Acts 5:16

Holy Spirit given
"He (Jesus) *hath God* (the Father) *exalted with His right hand to be a Prince and a Saviour..."* Acts 5:31

> **The Promise:**
> *"... for to give repentance to Israel, and forgiveness of sins."* Acts 5:31

"And we are His witnesses of these things..." Acts 5:32

> **The Promise:**
> *"... and so is also the Holy Ghost whom God hath given ..."* Acts 5:32

The Condition:
"... to them that obey Him." Acts 5:32

Miracles
"And Stephen, full of faith and power, did great wonders and miracles among the people... they were not able to resist the wisdom and the Spirit by which he spake." Acts 6:8,10

"... He promised that He would give it (the land) *to him* (Abraham) *for a possession, and to his seed after him, when as yet he had no child.* Acts 7:5,17

"... and God was with him (Joseph). And delivered him out of all his afflictions, and gave him favor and wisdom in the sight of Pharaoh king of Egypt; and he made him governor over Egypt and all his house." Acts 7:9,10

"But when the time of the promise drew nigh, which God had sworn to Abraham, the people grew and multiplied in Egypt..." Acts 7:17

Moses mighty in words and deeds
"And Moses... was mighty in words and in deeds... for he supposed his brethren would have understood how that God by His hand would deliver them: but they understood not." Acts 7:22,25
Prayer:
Father in heaven, please make us mighty in word and deed like You did for Moses. In Jesus' name, Amen!

Philip performs miracles in Jesus' name
"And the people with one accord gave heed unto those things which Philip spake, hearing and seeing the miracles which he did. For unclean spirits, crying with loud voice, came out of many that were possessed with them: and many taken with palsies, and that were lame, were healed. And there was great joy in that city." Acts 8:6-8

Holy Spirit
"Who, when they were come down, prayed for them, that they might receive the Holy Ghost... (and) they received the Holy Ghost." Acts 8:15,17

Miracle
"... the Spirit of the Lord caught away Philip... And (he) was found at Azotus..." Acts 8:39,40

God gives Paul strength and wisdom
"But Saul increased the more in strength, and confounded the Jews which dwelt at Damascus, proving that this is very Christ." Acts 9:22

The church is comforted
"Then had the churches rest... and in the comfort of the Holy Ghost, were mul-tiplied." Acts 9:31
"... had peace and were edified and walking in the fear of the Lord..." Acts 9:31 NKJV

Miracle
"... Jesus Christ maketh thee whole: arise, and make thy bed. And he arose im-mediately. And all that dwelt at Lydda and Saron saw him, and turned to the Lord." Acts 9:34,35

Miracle
"But Peter put them all forth, and kneeled down, and prayed... turning him to the body said, Tabitha, arise. And she opened her eyes; and when she saw Peter, she sat up." Acts 9:40
"... and he presented her (Dorcas) alive." Acts 9:41 NKJV

Cornelius and his household are saved and receive the Holy Spirit
"There was a certain man in Caesarea called Cornelius, a centurion of the band
called the Italian band, a devout man, and one that feared God with all his house, which gave much alms to the people, and prayed to God always. He saw in a vision evidently about the ninth hour (3 p.m.) of the day an angel of God coming in to him, and saying unto him, Cornelius. And when he looked on him, he was afraid, and said, What is it, Lord? And he said unto him, Thy prayers and thine alms are come up for a memorial before God. And now send men to Joppa, and call for one Simon, whose surname is Peter... "Acts 10:1-5

> **The Promise:**
> "... God is no respecter of persons..." Acts 10: 34

"... God shows no partiality." Acts 10:34 NKJV
The Condition:
"... but in every nation he that feareth Him, and worketh righteousness ..." Acts 10:35
"... acts uprightly" Acts 10:35 NABRE
"... and does what is right" Acts 10:35 NIV
"... do good deeds" Acts 10:35 TLB

> **The Promise:**
> "... is accepted with Him." Acts 10:35

Miracles
"How God anointed Jesus of Nazareth with the Holy Ghost and with power: who went about doing good, and healing all that were oppressed of the devil; for God was with him." Acts 10:38
Jesus healed while on this earth and sometimes we can still see Him healing today.

Holy Spirit poured out
"While Peter yet spake these words, the Holy Ghost fell on all them which heard the Word... on the Gentiles also was poured out the gift of the Holy Ghost..." Acts 10:44,45

The Promise:
"... you will be saved, you and all your household." Acts 11: 14

Prayer
Lord, save me and all my family. Thank You for hearing and answering in Jesus' name, Amen.

"... the Holy Ghost fell on them, as on us at the beginning." Acts 11:15
"And the hand of the Lord was with them: and a great number believed, and turned unto the Lord." Acts 11:21

Full of the Holy Spirit
"Who, when he (Barnabas) came, and had seen the grace of God, was glad, and exhorted them all, that with purpose of heart they would cleave unto the Lord. For he was a good man, and full of the Holy Ghost and of faith: and much people was added unto the Lord." Acts 11:23,24

An angel appears
"... behold, an angel of the Lord suddenly appeared and a light shone in the cell; and he struck Peter's side and woke him up, saying, 'Get up quickly'. And his chains fell off his hands (and the angel takes him out of prison).*"* Acts 12:7,10 NASB

Peter delivered from prison
"... now I know of a surety, that the Lord hath sent His angel, and hath delivered me out of the hand of Herod, and from all the expectation of the people of the Jews." Acts 12:11

"... how that the promise which was made unto the fathers (of Israel), *God hath fulfilled... in that He hath raised up Jesus..."* Acts 13:32,33

Promise to Jesus
"... I will give You the sure mercies of David. Wherefore He saith also in ano-ther Psalm, Thou shalt not suffer Thine Holy One to see corruption." Acts 13: 34,35

"... He (Jesus), whom God raised again, saw no corruption. Be it known unto you therefore, men and brethren, that through this man is preached unto you the forgiveness of sins: and by Him all that believe..." Acts 13:37-39

The Promise:
"... are Justified..." Acts 13:39

I work a work
"... for I work a work in your days, a work which ye shall in no wise believe, though a man declare it unto you." Acts 13:41

Paul and Barnabas go to give Salvation to the Gentiles
"Then Paul and Barnabas waxed bold, and said, It was necessary that the Word of God should first have been spoken to you: but seeing ye put it from you, and Judge yourselves unworthy of everlasting life, lo, we turn to the Gentiles. For so hath the Lord commanded us, saying, I have set thee to be a light of the Gentiles, that Thou shouldest be for Salvation unto the ends of the earth... and as many as were ordained to eternal life believed." Acts 13:47,48

Disciples filled with the Holy Spirit
"And the disciples were filled with joy, and with the Holy Ghost." Acts 13:52

Signs and wonders
"... speaking boldly in the Lord, which gave testimony unto the Word of His grace, and granted signs and wonders to be done by their hands." Acts 14:3

Prayer:
Father in heaven, please grant that we too can do signs and wonders in Jesus' name, Amen!

Miracle
A crippled man *"... heard Paul speak: who stedfastly beholding him, and perceiveing that he had faith to be healed, said with a loud voice, Stand upright on thy feet. And he leaped and walked."* Acts 14:8-10

Prayer
Father in heaven, please give us the faith to heal and be healed. In Jesus' name, Amen!

"Nevertheless He left not Himself without witness, in that He did good, and gave us rain from heaven, and fruitful seasons, filling our hearts with food and gladness." Acts 14:17

God gave the Holy Spirit
"And God, which knoweth the hearts, bare them witness, giving them the Holy Ghost, even as He did unto us and put no difference between us and them..." Acts 15:8,9

The Promise:
"... purifying their hearts by faith." Acts 15:9

Prayer:
Father in heaven, please purify our hearts by faith in Jesus' name and through His blood, Amen!

Saved by grace
"But we believe that through the grace of the Lord Jesus Christ we shall be saved, even as they." Acts 15:11

Miracles
"Then all the multitude kept silence, and gave audience to Barnabas and Paul, declaring what miracles and wonders God had wrought among the Gentiles by them." Acts 15:12

Gospel taken to the Gentiles
"Simeon hath declared how God at the first did visit the Gentiles, to take out of them a people for His name." Acts 15:14-17

"... Lydia... whose heart the Lord opened." Acts 16:14
We can ask God to open the hearts of our loved ones.
Prayer:
Father in heaven, if You could open Lydia's heart to receive Jesus, then please open _____'s heart to receive Jesus as well! Thank You in Jesus' name, Amen!

Miracle
"And suddenly there was a great earthquake, so that the foundations of the prison were shaken: and immediately all the doors were opened, and everyone's bands were loosed." Acts 16:26
Prayer:
Father in heaven, please loose us from every sin and deliver us from every bondage in Jesus' name, Amen!

Believe and be saved
"And they said..." Acts 16:31

The Condition:
"... believe on the Lord Jesus Christ..." Acts 16:31

> **The Promise:**
> *"... and thou shalt be saved, and thy house."* Acts 16:31

Prayer:
Father in heaven, please save my household like You did for them. Thank You in Jesus' name, Amen!

Seek God and find Him
"From one man (Adam) He made all the nations, that they should inhabit the whole earth; and He marked out their appointed times in history and the boundaries of their lands. God did this so that they would seek Him and perhaps reach out for Him and find him..." Acts 17:26,27
God determined ahead of time where we should live and our appointed times.

> **The Promise:**
> *"... though He is not far from any one of us."* Acts 17:27

Those who seek Him find Him, Mt. 7:7
Prayer:
Father in heaven, I thank You that You're not far from any of us. Help us to reach out and find You. In Jesus' name, Amen!

If we look for God, we will find Him
"That they should seek the Lord, if haply they might feel after Him, and find Him, though He be not far from every one of us: for in Him we live, and move, and have our being..." Acts 17:27,28

Promise to Paul
"Then spake the Lord to Paul in the night by a vision, Be not afraid, but speak, and hold not thy peace." Acts 18:9

> **The Promise:**
> *"For I am with thee, and no man shall set on thee to hurt thee: for I have much people in this city."* Acts 18:10

Prayer:
Father in heaven, I thank You that no man can hurt me unless it's Your will. Please be with me as you were with Paul and keep me from harm and danger. Thank You in the name of Jesus, Amen!

Grace
"... which had believed through grace..." Acts 18:27

The Holy Spirit
They that *"... believe... on Christ Jesus. When they heard this, they were baptized in the name of the Lord Jesus. And when Paul had laid his hands upon them, the Holy Ghost came on them..."* Acts 19:4-6

Miracles
"And God wrought special miracles by the hands of Paul: so that from his body were brought unto the sick handkerchiefs or aprons, and the diseases departed from them, and the evil spirits went out of them." Acts 19:11,12

You'll get an inheritance in heaven someday.
"And now, brethren, I commend you to God, and to the Word of His grace, which is able to build you up, and to give you an inheritance among all them which are Sanctified." Acts 20:32

Blessed
"... it is more blessed to give then to receive." Acts 20:35

What are you waiting for?
"And now why tarriest thou?" Acts 22:16

The Condition:
"... arise, and be baptized ("Baptizo" #907 means, "submerge, immerse, dip under")..." Acts 22:16

> **The Promise:**
> *"... wash away thy sins, calling on the name of the Lord."* Acts 22:16

First we repent, then we wash away our sins through the blood of Jesus and baptism.
"... and the blood of Jesus Christ His Son cleanseth us from all sin." I Jn. 1:7
"... except a corn of wheat fall into the ground and die (through baptism)*, it abideth alone: but if it die, it bringeth forth much fruit."* Jn. 12:24
*"Therefore we are **buried with Him by baptism** into death: that like as Christ was raised up from the dead by the glory of the Father, even so we also should walk in newness of life."* Rom. 6:4

"Delivering thee from the people, and from the Gentiles, unto whom now I send thee, to open their eyes, and to turn them from darkness to light, and from the power of Satan unto God..." Acts 26:17,18

Yes, Satan is powerful but God is more powerful!!! You cannot serve God and
Satan; you must choose!

Prayer:
Father in heaven, please open the eyes of my family and loved ones and turn them from darkness to light and from the power of Satan to God. Thank You,
in Jesus' name, Amen!

"... choose you this day whom you will serve ..." Josh. 24:15

> **The Promise:**
> *"... that they may receive forgiveness of sins, and inheritance among them which are Sanctified by faith that is in Me."* Acts 26:18

God promised to deliver all that sailed with Paul
"... be of good cheer: for there shall be no loss of any man's life among you... fear not Paul... God hath given thee all them that sail with thee ... except these abide in the ship, ye cannot be saved." Acts 27:22,24,31
God also gave Rahab all that came into her home where the scarlet cord was, Josh. 6:25.

Prayer:
Father in heaven, please give me all that are with me, my family, and friends. Thank You in the name of Jesus, Amen!
Promise to Paul
"Wherefore I pray you to take some meat: for this is for your health ..." Acts 27:34

> **The Promise:**
> *"... for there shall not an hair fall from the head of any of you."* Acts 27:34

And *"... they escaped all safe to land."* Acts 27:44
Prayer:
Father in heaven, help us to escape when we are in danger. Thank You in Jesus' name, Amen!

Miracle
"And he shook off the beast (snake) *into the fire, and felt no harm."* Acts 28:5
Miracles

"So when this was done, others also, which had diseases in the island, came, and were healed..." Acts 28:9

Romans

The Gospel promised in the Old Testament
"... the Gospel of God, which He had promised afore by His prophets in the Holy Scriptures..." Rom. 1:1,2

Spiritual Gifts
"For I long to see you, that I may impart unto you some Spiritual gift, to the end ye may be established..." Rom. 1:11
Prayer:
Father in heaven, please give me Spiritual gifts through the power of Your Holy Spirit. Thank You, in the name of Jesus, Amen!

The just shall live by faith
"For I am not ashamed of the Gospel of Christ..." Rom. 1:16

The Promise:
"... for it is the power of God unto Salvation to everyone that believeth; to the Jew first, and also to the Greek. For therein is the righteousness of God revealed from faith to faith: as it is written, The just shall live by faith." Rom. 1:16,17

If we aren't ashamed of Jesus, He won't be ashamed of us, Matt. 10:33; II Tim. 2:12.

"... despisest thou the riches of His goodness and forbearance and longsuffering; not knowing that the goodness of God leadeth thee to repentance..." Rom. 2:4

Rewarded according to our works

The Promise:
"Who will render to every man according to his deeds..." Rom. 2: 6

The Condition:
"... who by patient continuance in well doing seek for glory and honour and immortality, eternal life." Rom. 2:7

We are to continue doing what God requires not to be saved but because we love Him and want to please Him and He will reward us someday in heaven for our good works.

God is still faithful
"For what if some did not believe? Shall their unbelief make the faith ("faithfulness" ESV) of God without effect? God forbid: yea, let God be true, but every man a liar; as it is written, That thou might be Justified in thy sayings, and mightest overcome when thou art Judged." Rom. 3:3,4

"... if some did not believe, will their unbelief cancel ("nullify" NASB) God's faithfulness?" Rom. 3:3 HCSB

"By no means! Let God be true though everyone were a liar, as it is written, 'That you may be Justified ("proved true" NIV) in Your words, and prevail when you are Judged." Rom. 3:4 ESV

Righteousness by faith
"Even the righteousness of God which is by faith of Jesus Christ unto all and upon all them that believe: for there is no difference: for all have sinned, and come short of the glory of God..." Rom. 3:22

> **The Promise:**
> *"... being Justified freely by His grace through the Redemption that is in Christ Jesus: whom God hath set forth to be a propitiation through faith in His blood, to declare His righteousness for the remission of sins that are past, through the forbearance of God..."* Rom. 3:22-25

Dict. *"Propitiation"* means *"atoning sacrifice"*. Jesus is our atoning sacrifice for sin.
In the Old Testament the animal sacrifices were a promise that the true Lamb of God, Jesus, would come and die for our sins.
"(from Latin propitiāre, to appease; from propitius, gracious), also called expiation, is the act of appeasing or making well disposed a deity, thus incurring divine favor to avoid divine retribution.
The word propitiation carries the basic idea of appeasement, or satisfaction, specifically towards God. Propitiation is a two-part act that involves appeasing the wrath of an offended person and being reconciled to him." www.wikipedia.com
"The necessity of appeasing God is something many religions have in common. In ancient pagan religions, as well as in many religions today, the idea is taught that man appeases God by offering various gifts or sacrifices. However, the Bible teaches that God Himself has provided the only means

through which His wrath can be appeased and sinful man can be reconciled to Him. In the New Testament, the act of propitiation always refers to the work of God and not the sacrifices or gifts offered by man. The reason for this is that man is totally incapable of satisfying God's justice except by spending eternity in hell. There is no service, sacrifice or gift that man can offer that will appease the Holy wrath of God or satisfy His perfect justice. The only satisfaction, or propitiation, that could be acceptable to God and that could reconcile man to Him, had to be made by God. For this reason God the Son, Jesus Christ, came into the world in human flesh to be the perfect sacrifice for sin and make atonement or 'propitiation for the sins of the people'" Heb. 2:17. www.gotquestions.org

Justified by faith
"But to Him that worketh not, but believeth on Him that Justifieth the ungodly, his faith is counted for righteousness." Rom. 4:5
We are saved by grace alone not by works so that no one can boast, Eph. 28:8. But Col. 1:10 tells us we are to live a life worthy of Jesus and to please Him in everything we do.
"So that you will walk in a manner worthy of the Lord, to please Him in all re-spects, bearing fruit in every good work and increasing in the knowledge of God..." Col. 1:10 NASB
"... created in Christ Jesus unto good works, which God hath before ordained that we should walk in them.." Eph. 2:10
"... so that you would walk in a manner worthy of... God..." I Thess. 2:12 NASB
Let your light shine so they can see your good works, Matt. 5:16.
"Faith without works is dead" Jms. 2:17
Rom. 2:6 tells us that our works are rewarded. So we are saved by grace alone but rewarded for our works.
We strive to please God not to be saved but because we love Him and He rewards us for that. Salvation is a free gift but rewards are earned. It's easy to be saved but hard to earn the rewards otherwise everyone would have the same reward. In the parable of the prodigal son, the father was eagerly looking for the return of his wayward son. He loved his son even though he wasted all his inheritance and squandered it on wild living and debauchery. When he came home, the father reassured him that he was still a son and not a slave. He threw him a party, gave him a place to live, and his signet ring, which was like a credit card today, so that every need was met. His son would want for no good thing and be loved completely; but he lost his inheritance, the land, because he squandered it (Just like us – sometimes we want our rewards now!).

But the son who stayed with his father and worked hard and did those things that were pleasing to his father; well, the land was still his but he needed to learn to love and forgive his brother and see him with the same loving eyes as his father. We can learn a lot from this parable.

"... *thy Father which seeth in secret... shall **reward** thee openly*." Matt. 6:4
Paul says, "*But I discipline my body and keep it under control, lest after preaching to others I myself should be **disqualified for the prize**.*" I Cor. 9:27
"*Look to yourselves* ("*watch out*" NIV), *that we **lose not** those things* ("*lose what we've worked for*" NIV) *which we have wrought, but that we receive a **full reward**.*" II Jn. 1:8
"*Take heed that ye do not your alms before men... otherwise ye **have no reward** of your Father which is in heaven.*" Matt. 6:1

We see here that it is not being disqualified for Salvation but being disqualified for the rewards or the prize that is in heaven.

We don't know what our reward is until we get there; we just keep striving, knowing that we are saved in Jesus and someday in heaven we will get our re-wards.

Blessed
"*Blessed are they whose iniquities are forgiven, and whose sins are covered. Blessed is the man to whom the Lord will not impute sin... faith was reckoned to Abraham for righteousness.*" Rom. 4:7-9

Abraham is the father of those that believe
"*... that righteousness might be imputed unto them also ...*" Rom. 4:11
Promise to inherit the world
"*For the promise, that he should be the heir of the world* ("*inherit the world*" HCSB), *was not to Abraham, or to his seed... but through the righteousness of faith.*" Rom. 4:13
The promises are sure to Abraham's seed
"*Therefore it is of faith, that it might be by grace; to the end the promise might be sure to all thy seed...*" Rom. 4:16
We are adopted sons and daughters of God through faith in Jesus.
"*For ye are all the children of God by faith in Christ Jesus.*" Gal. 3:26
And we are also adopted by Abraham through faith in Jesus and baptism.
"*Know ye therefore that they which are of faith, the same are the children of Abraham... so then they which be of faith are blessed with faithful Abraham...*" Gal. 3:7,9
"*For as many of you as have been **baptized** into Christ have put on Christ... and if ye be Christ's, **then are ye Abraham's seed, and heirs** according to the promise.*" Gal. 3:27,29

Hold on to the promises by faith
"He staggered not at the promise of God through unbelief; but was strong in faith, giving glory to God..." Rom. 4:20
God is able to perform what He has promised
"And being fully persuaded that, what He had promised, He was able also to perform. And therefore it was imputed to him for righteousness." Rom. 4:21,22

We have peace with God through Jesus Christ
"Therefore being Justified by faith, we have peace with God through our Lord Jesus Christ: by whom also we have access by faith into this grace wherein we stand, and rejoice in hope of the glory of God." Rom. 5:1,2

Sometimes Christians have tribulations
"... but we glory in tribulations also: knowing that tribulation worketh patience; and patience, experience; and experience, hope: and hope maketh not ashamed; because the love of God is shed abroad in our hearts by the Holy Ghost which is given unto us. For when we were yet without strength, in due time Christ died for the ungodly... while we were yet sinners, Christ died for us. Much more then, being now Justified by His blood, we shall be saved from wrath through Him. For if, when we were enemies, we were reconciled to God by the death of His Son, much more..." Rom. 5:3-10

The Promise:
"... being reconciled we shall be saved by His life." Rom. 5:10

Atonement in Jesus
"... we also joy in God through our Lord Jesus Christ, by whom we have now received the Atonement." Rom. 5:11

They *"... which receive abundance of grace and of the gift of righteousness..."* Rom. 5:17

The Promise:
"... shall reign in life by One, Jesus Christ..." Rom. 5:17

Free gift of life
"... even so by the righteousness of One the free gift came upon all men unto Justification of life... so by the obedience of one shall many be made righteous... where sin abounded, grace did much more abound... even so might grace reign through righteousness unto eternal life by Jesus Christ our Lord." Rom. 5:18-21

The Condition:
"For if we have been planted together (through baptism) *in the likeness of His death..."* Rom. 6:5

> **The Promise:**
> *"... we shall be also in the likeness of His Resurrection..."* Rom. 6:5

> **The Promise:**
> *"For sin shall not have dominion over you...* (for we are) *made free from sin... ye have fruit unto Holiness, and the end everlasting life... the gift of God is eternal life through Jesus Christ our Lord."* Rom. 6:14,18,22,23

Delivered from death
"... who shall deliver me from the body of this death... Jesus Christ our Lord..." Rom. 7:24,25

> **The Promise:**
> *"There is therefore now no condemnation to them which are in Christ Jesus..."* Rom. 8:1

The Condition:
"... who walk not after the flesh, but after the Spirit." Rom. 8:1
We are not condemned if we are not satisfying the lusts and desires of our flesh. If we sin, we should repent and ask for forgiveness and cleansing by the blood of Jesus and strive to obey God from the heart through the power of the Holy Spirit.

"For the law of the Spirit of life in Christ Jesus hath made me free from... sin and death... God sending His own Son... condemned sin in the flesh... the righteousness of the law might be fulfilled in us, who walk not after the flesh, but after the Spirit." Rom. 8:2-4

Prayer:
Thank You, Lord, that all the righteousness of the law is fulfilled in me because of Jesus. Please help me to always do those things that please You and to walk as Jesus walked so I can bear fruit for Your kingdom according to Your will. Help me to show You how much I love You by obeying You. Give me the victory over the flesh, the world, and the Devil in Jesus' name! Thank You that when I fail, I can repent and receive forgiveness through the blood of Jesus. Help me not to sin presumptuously, taking grace for granted; I understand that grace is not a license for sin. In Jesus' name I pray, Amen!

Be Spiritually minded
> **The Promise:**
> "… *to be Spiritually minded is life and peace."* Rom. 8:6

"But if the Spirit of Him that raised up Jesus from the dead dwell in you, He that raised up Christ from the dead shall also quicken your mortal bodies by His Spirit (at the Resurrection) *that dwelleth in you."* Rom. 8:11

Adoped by God through Jesus
The Condition:
"For as many as are led by the Spirit of God…" Rom. 8:14

> **The Promise:**
> *"… they are the sons of God… ye have received the Spirit of adoption, whereby we cry, Abba, Father. The Spirit itself beareth witness with our spirit, that we are the children of God: and if children, then heirs; heirs of God, and joint heirs with Christ…"* Rom. 8:14-17

Prayer:
Thank You Father in heaven that we are adopted into Your family because of Jesus and now we can call You Abba, Father, because we are Your children in Jesus' name, Amen!

The Condition:
"… *if so be that we suffer with Him…"* Rom. 8:17

> **The Promise:**
> *"… that we may be also glorified together."* Rom. 8:17

Our sufferings seem so hard now but someday it won't even compare with the glory revealed to us in heaven.
"For I reckon that the sufferings of this present time are not worthy to be compared with the glory which shall be revealed in us." Rom. 8:18
"For our light and momentary troubles are achieving for us an eternal glory that far outweighs them all." II Cor. 4:17 NIV
All our trials and tribulations will be compensated for in heaven.

Children of God revealed
"… *creation waits in eager expectation for the children of God to be revealed."* Rom. 8:19

Creation will be delivered from bondage on the New Earth

"Because the creature (#2937 "creation") itself also shall be delivered from the bondage of corruption into the glorious liberty ("freedom" NIV) of the children of God." Rom. 8:21

We have freedom from sin not freedom to sin (Rom. 6:14).

We are promised a new body at the Resurrection
"... ourselves... which have the firstfruits of the Spirit, even we ourselves groan within ourselves, waiting for the adoption, to wit, the Redemption of our body. For we are saved by hope: but hope that is seen is not hope. But if we hope for that we see not, then do we with patience wait for it." Rom. 8:23-25

Sometimes we receive the fulfillment of the promises now and sometimes we have to wait patiently for them to ultimately be fulfilled on the New Earth.

The Holy Spirit helps us to pray
"... the Spirit also helpeth our infirmities: for we know not what we should pray for as we ought: but the Spirit itself maketh intercession for us with groanings which cannot be uttered... because He maketh intercession for the saints according to the will of God. And we know that..." Rom. 8:26,27

> **The Promise:**
> *"... all things work together, for good..."* Rom. 8:28

The Condition:
"... to them that love God, to them who are the called according to His purpose." Rom. 8:28

Called to be glorified
"For whom He did foreknow, He also did predestinate to be conformed to the image of His Son, that He might be the firstborn among many brethren. Moreover whom He did predestinate, them He also called: and whom He called, them He also Justified: and whom He Justified, them He also glorified." Rom. 8:29,30

The Condition:
"... if God be for us..." Rom. 8:31

> **The Promise:**
> *"... who can be against us?"* Rom. 8:31

"He that spared not His own Son, but delivered Him up for us all, how shall He not with Him also..." Rom. 8:32

The Promise:
"... freely give us all things?" Rom. 8:32

"Who shall lay anything to the charge of God's elect?" Rom. 8:33

The Promise:
"... it is God that Justifieth." Rom. 8:33

"... who is he that condemneth?" Rom. 8:33

Jesus makes intercession for us
"It is Christ that died, yea rather, that is risen again, who is even at the right hand of God, who also maketh intercession for us." Rom. 8:34

Jesus will not let go of us
"Who shall separate us from the love of Christ? Shall tribulation, or distress, or persecution, or famine, or nakedness, or peril, or sword..." Rom. 8:35,36
No, nothing can separate us from Christ but ourselves. We choose to walk with God or walk away from God, it's our choice.

We are more than conquerors through Jesus
"Nay, in all these things we are more than conquerors through Him that loved us. For I am persuaded, that neither death, nor life, nor angels, nor princi-palities, nor powers, nor things present, nor things to come. Nor height, nor depth, nor any other creature, shall be able to separate us from the love of God, which is in Christ Jesus our Lord." Rom. 8:37-39

"... Israelites; to whom pertaineth... the promises..." Rom. 9:4
"Neither, because they are the seed of Abraham, are they all children: but, in Isaac shall thy seed be called." Rom. 9:7-9.

"... I will have mercy on whom I will have mercy, and I will have compassion on whom I will have compassion... God that sheweth mercy..." Rom. 9:15,16

God will make known to us His riches in glory
"And that He might make known the riches of His glory on the vessels of mercy, which He had afore prepared unto glory." Rom. 9:23

"... I will call them My people, which were not My people; and her beloved, which was not beloved... a remnant shall be saved... for He will finish the work, and cut it short in righteousness: because a short work will the Lord make upon the earth." Rom. 9:25,27,28 (Hosea 2:23)

"As it is written, behold, I lay in Sion a stumbling Stone and Rock of offence..." Rom. 9:33

The Condition:
"... and whosoever believeth on Him (Jesus)..." Rom. 9:33

> **The Promise:**
> "... shall not be ashamed." Rom. 9:33

Believe and confess with your mouth.
"... righteousness which is of faith... the Word is nigh thee, even in thy mouth, and in thy heart... the Word of faith, which we preach; that if thou shalt confess with thy mouth the Lord Jesus, and shalt believe in thine heart that God hath raised Him from the dead, thou shalt be saved. For with the heart man believeth unto righteousness; and with the mouth confession is made unto Salvation." Rom. 10:6-8

The Condition:
"That if thou shalt confess with thy mouth the Lord Jesus, and shalt believe in thine heart that God hath raised Him from the dead..." Rom. 10:9,10

> **The Promise:**
> "... thou shalt be saved." Rom. 10:9

"For with the heart man believeth unto righteousness; and with the mouth confession is made unto Salvation." Rom. 10:10

You believe it with your heart and you speak it with your mouth.
"... for the same Lord over all is rich unto all that call upon Him... for whosoever shall call upon the name of the Lord..." Rom. 10:12,13

> **The Promise:**
> "... shall be saved." Rom. 10:13

"... how beautiful are the feet of them that preach the Gospel of peace, and bring glad tidings of good things!" Rom. 10:15

We get faith by hearing the Word of God
"... faith cometh by hearing, and hearing by the Word of God." Rom. 10:17
"... I (Jesus) was found of them that sought Me not; I was made manifest unto them that asked not after Me." Rom. 10:20
"Even so then at this present time also there is a remnant according to the election of grace." Rom. 11:5
"... the fall of them (Israel) be the riches of the world... how much more their fullness?" Rom. 11:12

"... the casting away of them... (is) the reconciling of the world... the receiving of them (will) be... life from the dead?" Rom. 11:15

"Behold therefore the goodness and severity of God: on them which fell, severity but toward thee, goodness..." Rom. 11:22

The Condition:
"... if thou continue in His goodness..." Rom. 11:22
"And so all Israel shall be saved: as it is written, There shall come out of Sion the Deliverer (Jesus), *and shall turn away ungodliness from Jacob: for this is My Covenant unto them, when I shall take away their sins... as touching the election, they are beloved for the father's* (Abraham, Isaac, and Jacob) *sakes."* Rom. 11:26-28

> **The Promise:**
> *"... the gifts and calling of God are without repentance."* Rom. 11:29

"For God hath concluded them all in unbelief, that He might have mercy upon all." Rom. 11:32
"O the depth of the riches both of the wisdom and knowledge of God! How unsearchable are His Judgments, and His ways past finding out!" Rom. 11:33

Be transformed
"Do not conform any longer to the pattern of this world, but be transformed by the renewing of your mind. Then you will be able to test and approve what God's will is – His good, pleasing and perfect will." Rom. 12:2 NIV
"Don't copy the behavior and customs of this world..." Rom. 12:2 LB
The promise is that if we renew our minds (through reading the Word), we will be transformed to be like Jesus.

The Condition:
"... every man... (should not) think of himself more highly than he ought to think... but to think soberly, according as..." Rom. 12:3

God gives us faith
> **The Promise:**
> *"... God hath dealt to every man the measure of faith."* Rom. 12:3

"So we, being many, are one body in Christ, and every one members one of another. Having then gifts differing according to the grace that is given to us..." Rom. 12:6

The Condition:
"Dearly beloved, avenge not yourselves, but rather give place unto (God's) *wrath: for it is written..."* Rom. 12:19

> **Promise:**
> *"... vengenace is Mine; I will repay, saith the Lord."* Rom. 12:19

The Condition:
"... do that which is good..." Rom. 13:3

> **The Promise:**
> *"... and thou shalt have praise of the same* (rulers)*..."* Rom. 13:3

The Condition:
"And that, knowing the time, that now it is high time to awake out of sleep ..." Rom. 13:11

> **The Promise:**
> *"... for now is our Salvation nearer than when we believed."* Rom. 13:11

> **The Promise:**
> *"... God is able to make* (us) *stand."* Rom. 14:4

"For to this end Christ both died, and rose, and revived, that He might be Lord both of the dead and living." Rom. 14:9

"For it is written, As I live, saith the Lord..." Rom. 14:11

> **The Promise:**
> *"... every knee shall bow to Me, and every tongue shall confess to God."* Rom. 14:11

*"For the kingdom... *(is) *righteousness, and peace, and joy in the Holy Ghost. For he that in these things serveth Christ..."* Rom. 14:17,18

> **The Promise:**
> *"... is acceptable to God, and approved of men."* Rom. 14:18

"... let us therefore follow after the things which make for peace, and things wherewith one may edify another." Rom. 14:19
God wants us to have peace with each other. We should do everything possible to live in peace; but not at the expense of our conscience. The Bible also says that we should speak the truth in love, Eph. 4:15.
"For even Christ pleased not Himself; but, as it is written, The reproaches ("insults" NIV) *of them that reproached* ("insulted" NIV) *thee fell on Me."* Rom. 15:3

Every time someone reproaches or insults you, it falls on Jesus!
Prayer:
Thank You Jesus for taking the insults and reproaches for me!!!

The Condition:
"... that we through patience and comfort of the Scriptures..." Rom. 15:4

The Promise:
"... might have hope. Now the God of patience and consolation grant you to be likeminded one toward another according to Christ Jesus ..." Rom. 15:4,5

As we become more like Jesus and learn to do things His way, we will be closer to each other.
Prayer
Father in heaven, please help me to have the same mind as Christ Jesus so that I can be likeminded with other Christians who have the mind of Christ. Thank You in Jesus' name, Amen!

Jesus receives us
"*Wherefore receive ye one another, as Christ also received us to the glory of God.*" Rom. 15:7

"*Now the God of hope fill you with all joy and peace in believing, that ye may abound in hope, through the power of the Holy Ghost.*" Rom. 15:13
Prayer
Father in heaven, please fill me with Your joy and peace and let me abound in hope through the power of the Holy Spirit! In the name of Jesus, Amen!

Jesus fills us with His goodness
"*... I myself also am persuaded of you, my brethren, that ye also are full of goodness, filled with all knowledge... nevertheless, brethren, I have written the more boldly unto you in some sort, as putting you in mind, because of the grace that is given to me of God...*" Rom. 15:14,15

Signs and wonders
"*Through mighty signs and wonders, by the power of the Spirit of God...*" Rom. 15:19

Blessing
"*And I am sure that, when I (Paul) come unto you, I shall come in the fullness of the blessing of the Gospel of Christ.*" Rom. 15:29

The Promise:
"And the God of peace shall bruise (#4937 "break by crushing, break in pieces, shatter, broke, broken to pieces, mauling") Satan under your feet shortly…" Rom. 16:20

"… the grace of our Lord Jesus Christ be with you. Amen." Rom. 16:20
"I give unto you power to tread on serpents and scorpions… over all the power of the enemy: and nothing shall by any means hurt you." Lk. 10:19

"Now to Him that is of power to stablish you…" Rom. 16:25

I Corinthians

We are enriched through Jesus
"I thank my God always on your behalf, for the grace of God which is given you by Jesus Christ; that in everything ye are enriched by Him, in all utterance, and in all knowledge…" I Cor 1:4-6

The Promise:
"… so that ye come behind in no gift; waiting for the coming of our Lord Jesus Christ: who shall also confirm you unto the end, that you may be blameless in the day of our Lord Jesus Christ. God is faithful ("reliable, trustworthy, and therefore ever true to His promise - He can be depended on" Amp Bible)… by whom you were called unto the fellowship of His Son, Jesus Christ our Lord." I Cor. 1:7-9

Preaching is the power of God
"For the preaching of the cross is to them that perish foolishness; but unto us which are saved it is the power of God." I Cor. 1:18

God is wiser and stronger
"Because the foolishness of God is wiser than men; and the weakness of God is stronger than men." I Cor. 1:25

God chooses people that are despised and rejected
"But God hath chosen the foolish things of the world to confound the wise; and God hath chosen the weak things of the world to confound the things which are mighty; and base things of the world, and things which are despised, hath God chosen…" I Cor. 1:27,28

Preaching through the power of God
"And my speech and my preaching was not with enticing words of man's wisdom, but in demonstration of the Spirit and of power: that your faith should not stand in the wisdom of men, but in the power of God." I Cor. 2:4,5

> **The Promise:**
> *"But as it is written, Eye hath not seen, nor ear heard, neither have entered into the heart of man, the things which God hath prepared ..."* I Cor. 2:9

The Condition:
"... for them that love Him. But God hath revealed them unto us by His Spirit: for the Spirit searcheth all things, yea, the deep things of God." I Cor. 2:9,10
The Holy Spirit helps us to know what God has given us.
"Now we have received not the spirit of the world..." I Cor. 2:12

> **The Promise:**
> *"... but the Spirit which is of God; that we might know the things that are freely given to us of God."* I Cor. 2:12

The Holy Spirit and the Word of God reveal to us the things that God has already freely given to us through Jesus Christ. Thank You Jesus!

"I have planted, Apollos watered..." I Cor. 3:6

> **The Promise:**
> *"... but God gave the increase."* I Cor. 3:6

"So then neither is he that planteth anything, neither he that watereth; but God that giveth the increase." I Cor. 3:6,7

Rewarded according to works

> **The Promise:**
> *"... and every man shall receive his own reward according to his own labour."* I Cor. 3:8

The Condition:
"Every man's work shall be made manifest: for the day (of Judgment) *shall declare it, because it shall be revealed by fire; and the fire shall try every man's work of what sort it is. If any man's work abide which he hath built there-upon..."* I Cor. 3:13,14

> **The Promise:**
> *"... he shall receive a reward."* I Cor. 3:14

The Condition:
"... if any man's work shall be burned, he shall suffer loss..." I Cor. 3:15

> **The Promise:**
> *"... but he himself shall be saved..."* I Cor. 3:15

The Condition:
"... yet so as by fire..." I Cor. 3:15

"Therefore let no man glory in men..." I Cor. 3:21

> **The Promise:**
> *"... for all things are yours... things present, or things to come; all are yours; and ye are Christ's; and Christ is God's."* I Cor. 3:21-23

We should be careful not to think too highly of any man – we need to put God first in all things

The Condition:
"Therefore Judge nothing before the time, until the Lord come, who both will bring to light the hidden things of darkness, and will make manifest the counsels of the hearts..." I Cor. 4:5

> **The Promise:**
> *"... and then shall every man have praise of God."* I Cor. 4:5

"... what do you have that you did not receive (of God)..." I Cor. 4:7 NASB

> **The Promise:**
> *"Now ye are full, now ye are rich..."* I Cor. 4:8

"... ye have reigned as kings without us: and I would to God ye did reign, that we also might reign with you." I Cor. 4:8

> **The Promise:**
> *"For the Kingdom of God is not in word, but in power... with the power of our Lord Jesus Christ..."* I Cor. 4:20;5:4

"And God hath both raised up the Lord, and will also raise up us by His own power (at the Resurrection)." I Cor. 6:14

> **The Promise:**
> *"But he that is joined unto the Lord is one Spirit."* I Cor. 6:17

The Condition:
"Flee fornication..." I Cor. 6:18
Your body is the Temple of the Holy Spirit

"What? Know ye not that your body is the temple of the Holy Ghost which is in you, which ye have of God, and ye are not your own? For ye are bought with a price: therefore glorify God in your body, and in your spirit, which are God's." I Cor. 6:19,20

Unbeliever Sanctified by spouse

The Promise:
"For the unbelieving husband is Sanctified by the wife, and the unbelieving wife is Sanctified by the husband: else were your children unclean; but now are they Holy... for what knowest thou, O wife, whether thou shalt save thy husband? Or how knowest thou, O man, whether thou shalt save thy wife?" I Cor. 7:14,16

Prayer:
Thank You Lord, that my spouse is Sancitifed and my children are Holy in Jesus!

God knows those who love Him
The Condition:
"But if any man love God..." I Cor. 8:3

The Promise:
"... the same is known of Him." I Cor. 8:3

God knows who really loves Him from the heart and who wants praise from man!

Reward for preaching
The Condition:
If "... I preach the Gospel... willingly..." I Cor. 9:17

The Promise:
"... I have a reward..." I Cor. 9:17

Strive to master
The Condition:
"... run that you may obtain (the prize). And every man that **striveth** (#75 striving as in an athletic contest; contend as with an adversary") **for the mastery** (#3956 "in all things") is temperate in all things. Now they do it to obtain a corruptible crown..." I Cor. 9:24,25
"... refraineth himself from all things..." I Cor. 9:25 Douay Rheims Bible
"Athletes are disciplined ("exercises self-control" ESV)..." I Cor. 9:25 NLT
"... restrains his mind..." I Cor. 9:25 Aramaic Bible in Plain English

The Promise:
"... but we an incorruptible (crown)." I Cor. 9:25

"There hath no temptation taken you but such as is common to man..." I Cor. 10:13

The Promise:
"... but God is faithful, who will not suffer you to be tempted above that ye are able; but will with the temptation also make a way to escape, that ye may be able to bear it." I Cor. 10:13

Prayer
Father in heaven, You promised that You wouldn't let me have more than I could take. When I am tempted, please make a way of escape that I can bear it like You promised. Thank You in Jesus' Name, Amen!

The Condition:
"... no man can say that Jesus is the Lord, but by the Holy Ghost." I Cor. 12:3
The promise is that the Holy Spirit helps us to see that Jesus is Lord and confess Him!

Gifts of the Spirit

The Promise:
"But the manifestation of the Spirit is given to every man to profit to withal. For to one is given by the Spirit the word of wisdom; to another the word of knowledge by the same Spirit; to another faith by the same Spirit; to another faith by the same Spirit; to another the gifts of healing by the same Spirit..." I Cor. 12:7-8

The Promise:
"... to another the performing of miracles, to another, prophecy, to another, distinguishing between spirits, to another, different kinds of languages, to another, interpretation (Gr. #2058 "from the same as #2059 'translation'") of languages." I Cor. 12:9 HCSB

The Promise:
"... love never fails..." I Cor. 13:8 NIV

"... love goes on forever..." I Cor. 13:8 LB
"... love never ends..." I Cor. 13:8 RSV

Someday we will see God face to face
"For now we see through a glass, darkly; but then face to face: now I know in part; but then shall I know even as also I am known." I Cor. 13:12
"For now we see in a mirror dimly... then I shall understand fully, even as I have been fully understood." I Cor. 13:12 RSV

In heaven we will know each other.
"... the Gospel... by which also..." I Cor. 15:1

> **The Promise:**
> *"... ye are saved..."* I Cor. 15:1,2

The Condition:
"... if ye keep in memory ("holdfast" KJV fn) what I preached to you.." I Cor. 15:2

"Behold, I show you a mystery..." I Cor. 15:51

> **The Promise:**
> *"... we shall not all sleep, but we shall all be changed, in a moment, in the twinkling of an eye, at the last Trump: for the trumpet shall sound, and the dead shall be raised incorruptible, and we shall be changed. For this corruptible must put on incorruption, and this mortal must put on immortality. So when this corruptible shall have put on incorruption, and this mortal shall have put on immortality, then shall be brought to pass the saying that is written, Death is swallowed up in victory... but thanks be to God, which giveth us the victory through our Lord Jesus Christ... your labor is not in vain in the Lord."* I Cor 15:51-58

> **The Promise:**
> *"... as God hath prospered him..."* I Cor. 16:2

> **A Promise:**
> *"... a great door for effective work has opened to me."* I Cor. 16:9 NIV

Prayer:
Father in heaven, please open doors for me to be effective as You did for Paul. Thank You! In Jesus' name, Amen!

II Corinthians

God blessed
"Blessed be God, even the Father of our Lord Jesus Christ, the Father of mercies, and the God of all comfort; who comforteth us in all our tribulation, that we may be able to comfort them which are in any trouble, by the comfort wherewith we ourselves are comforted of God." II Cor. 1:4

The Condition:
"For as the sufferings of Christ abound in us..." I I Cor. 1:5

> **The Promise:**
> *"... so our consolation also aboundeth by Christ... whether we be comforted, it is for your consolation and Salvation."* II Cor. 1:5,6

"But we had the sentence of death in ourselves, that we should not trust in ourselves, but in God which raiseth the dead: who delivered us from so great a death, and doth deliver: in whom we trust that..." II Cor. 1:9,10

> **The Promise:**
> *"... He will yet deliver us..."* II Cor. 1:10

All the promises are Yes in Christ Jesus!
"... God is true ("faithful" ESV)... for the Son of God, Jesus Christ, who was preached among you by us... was not yea and nay..." II Cor. 1:18-22

> **The Promise:**
> *"... but in Him was yea. For all the promises of God in Him are yea, and in Him Amen, unto the glory of God by us. Now He which stablishedth us with you in Christ, and hath anointed us, is God; who hath also sealed us, and given the earnest of the Spirit in our hearts... by faith ye stand."* II Cor. 1:19-22,24

"For no matter how many promises God has made, they are 'Yes' in Christ. And so through Him the 'Amen' is spoken by us to the glory of God. Now it is God who makes both us and you stand firm in Christ. He anointed us, set His seal of ownership on us, and put His Spirit in our hearts as a deposit, guaranteeing what is to come." II Cor. 1:20-22 NIV

Prayer:
Father in heaven, I thank You that You give us Your precious promises and that they are all *"Yes"* in Christ Jesus. I say *"Amen"* to Your promises; let it be according to Your Word and Your will. In Jesus' name, Amen!

The Condition:
"For to this end also did I write, that I might know the proof of you, whether ye be obedient in all things." II Cor. 3:9

The Promise:
"To whom ye forgive anything, I forgive also..." II Cor. 2:10

"... lest Satan should get an advantage of us: for we are not ignorant of his devices.' II Cor. 2:10,11
"Now thanks be unto God, which always causeth us to triumph in Christ, and maketh manifest the savour of His knowledge by us in every place. For we are unto God a sweet savour of Christ..." II Cor. 2 14
"... our sufficiency is of God..." II Cor 3:5
"... our competence comes from God." II Cor. 3:5 NIV
"Who also hath made us able ministers of the New Testament..." II Cor. 3:6

The Promise:
"... the Spirit giveth life..." II Cor. 3:6

"Seeing then that we have such hope..." II Cor. 3:12

Moses face shone with the glory of God, II Cor. 3:13 (Ex. 34:29).
"Now the Lord is that Spirit: and where the Spirit of the Lord is there is liberty (from sin not to sin), but we all, with open face beholding as in a glass the glory of the Lord, are changed into the same image from glory to glory, even as by the Spirit of the Lord." II Cor. 3:17,18

We are not destroyed
"But we have this treasure in earthen vessels, that the excellency of the power may be of God, and not of us. We are troubled on every side, yet not distressed; we are perplexed, but not in despair; persecuted, but not forsaken; cast down, but not destroyed..." II Cor. 4:7-9

We believe the promises and we speak the promises out loud
*"We having the same Spirit of faith, according as it is written, I believed, and therefore **have I spoken**; we also believe, and therefore **speak**; knowing that He which raised up the Lord Jesus shall raise up us also by Jesus and shall present us with you. For all things are for your sakes, that the abundant grace might through the thanksgiving of many redound to the glory of God. For which cause we faint not; but though our outward man perish, yet the inward man is renewed day by day. For our light affliction, which is but for a moment..."* II Cor. 4:13-17

The Promise:
"... worketh for us a far more exceeding and eternal weight of glory..." II Cor. 4:17

"... while we look not at the things which are seen, but at the things which are not seen: for the things which are seen are temporal; but the things which are not seen are eternal." II Cor. 4:18

"For we know that if our earthly house of this Tabernacle were dissolved ..." II Cor. 5:1

The Promise:
"... we have a building of God (a new body), an house not made with hands, eternal in the heavens. For in this we groan, earnestly desiring to be clothed upon with our house which is from heaven: if so be that being clothed we shall not be found naked." II Cor. 5:1-3

The Promise:
"... but clothed upon, that mortality might be swallowed up of life. Now he that hath wrought us for the selfsame thing is God, who also hath given unto us the earnest of the Spirit... to be present with the Lord" II Cor. 5:4,5,8

The Condition:
Is "... to be absent from the body..." II Cor. 5:8

The Condition:
"Wherefore we labour, that, whether present or absent..." II Cor. 5:9

The Promise:
"... we may be accepted of Him." II Cor. 5:9

The Condition:
"Therefore if any man be in Christ..." II Cor. 5:17

The Promise:
"... he is a new creature: old things are passed away; behold, all things are become new. And all things are of God, who hath reconciled us to Himself by Jesus Christ, and hath given to us the ministry of reconciliation; to wit, that God was in Christ, reconciling the world unto Himself, not imputing their trespasses unto them; and hath committed unto us the Word of reconciliation." II Cor. 5:17-19

Ambassadors for Christ
"Now then we are ambassadors for Christ, as though God did beseech you

by us: we pray you in Christ's stead, be ye reconciled to God. For He hath made Him to be sin for us, who knew no sin; that we might be made the righteous-ness of God in Him." II Cor. 5:20,21

Now is the time!
The Promise:
"... He saith, I have heard thee in a time accepted, and in the day of Salvation have I succoured ("helped" NIV) thee behold, now is the accepted time; behold, now is the day of Salvation..." II Cor. 6:2

"... by the power of God... as sorrowful, yet always rejoicing; as poor ..." II Cor. 6:7,10
The Promise:
"... yet making many rich..." II Cor. 6:10

"... as having nothing..." II Cor. 6:10
The Promise:
"... and yet possessing all things." II Cor. 6:10

The Condition:
"And what agreement hath the temple of God with idols? For ye are the temple of the living God; as God hath said..." II Cor. 6:16
The Promise:
"... I will dwell in them, and walk in them; and I will be their God, and they shall be My people." II Cor. 6:16

The Condition:
"Wherefore come out from among them, and be ye separate, saith the Lord, and touch not the unclean thing..." II Cor. 6:17
The Promise:
"... and I will receive you, and will be a Father unto you, and ye shall be My sons and daughters, saith the Lord Almighty." II Cor. 6:17,18

Promises cleanse us
"Having... these promises... let us cleanse ourselves from all filthiness of the flesh and spirit, perfecting Holiness in the fear of God." II Cor. 7:1
Here's a promise of cleansing, Rev. 1:5

"... I am filled with comfort... exceeding joyful in all our tribulation." II Cor. 7:4
(See Rev. 16:4.

"But God, who comforts the downcast..." II Cor. 7:6 NIV & RSV
"Then God who cheers those who are discouraged..." II Cor. 7:6 LB

The Promise:
"Nevertheless, God, that comforteth those that are cast down, comforted us..." II Cor. 7:6

"For godly sorrow worketh repentance to Salvation not to be repented of..." II Cor. 7:10

The Promise:
"Therefore, as ye abound in everything, in faith, and utterance, and knowledge, and in all diligence, and in your love to us..." II Cor. 8:7

The Condition:
"... see that ye abound in this grace also." II Cor. 8:7

"For ye know the grace of our Lord Jesus Christ, that, though He was rich, yet for your sakes He became poor..." II Cor. 8:9

The Promise:
"... that ye through His poverty might be rich." II Cor. 8:9

"As it is written, He that had gathered much had nothing over; and he that had gathered little had no lack." II Cor. 8:15
Quoting from Ex. 16:18.

The Condition:
"But this I say, He which soweth sparingly shall reap also sparingly; and he which soweth bountifully..." II Cor. 9:6

The Promise:
"... shall reap also bountifully." II Cor. 9:6

"... for God loveth a cheerful giver." II Cor. 9:7

The Promise:
"And God is able to make all grace abound toward you; that ye, always having all sufficiency in all things, may abound to every good work: (as it is written, He hath dispersed abroad; He hath given to the poor: His righteousness remaineth forever. Now He that ministereth seed to the sower both minister bread for your food, and multiply your seed sown, and increase the fruits of your righteousness): being enriched in everything to all bountifulness, which causeth through us thanksgiving to God." II Cor. 9:8-11

*"Now He who supplies seed to the sower and bread for... food will also supply and increase your store of seed and will enlarge the harvest of your righteousness. You will be made rich in every way so that you can be generous on every occasion, and through us your generosity will result in thanksgiving to God... men will praise God for the **obedience that accompanies your confession** of the Gospel of Christ, and for your generosity in sharing with them..."* II Cor. 9:10-14 NIV
Obedience should accompany our confession of faith!

Prayer:
Father in heaven, please increase my store of seed and enlarge the harvest so that we can see many saved for the glory of God. Give me enough so that I can be generous as it says in Your Word. Help me to be obedient as I confess the Gospel so that glory will be given to God in all things. Thank You in Jesus' name, Amen!

"Thanks be unto God for His unspeakable gift (of Jesus)." II Cor. 9:15

"For the weapons of our warfare are not carnal..." II Cor. 10:4

> **The Promise:**
> *"... but mighty through God to the pulling down of strong holds..."* II Cor. 10:4

Prayer:
Father in heaven, please, through Your mighty power, pull down every stronghold that would put me and my family in bondage. Cast down every imagination and every high thing that exalts itself against the knowledge of God and help us to bring every thought into obedience to You in Jesus' name and by His blood. Thank You, Amen!

The Condition:
"... casting down imaginations, and every high thing that exalteth itself against the knowledge of God, and bringing into captivity every thought to the obedience of Christ... II Cor. 10:5
Even our thoughts should be in obedience to God!

> **The Promise:**
> *"... My grace is sufficient for thee: for My strength is made perfect in weakness that the power of Christ, may rest upon me... for when I am weak, then am I strong."* II Cor. 12:9,10

Miracles
"Truly the signs of an Apostle were wrought among you in all patience in signs, and wonders, and mighty deeds." II Cor. 12:12

"For though He (Jesus) was crucified through weakness, yet He liveth by the power of God. For we also are weak in Him..." II Cor. 13:4

> **The Promise:**
> "... but we shall live with Him by the power of God toward you." II Cor. 13:4

The Condition:
"Examine yourselves, whether ye be in the faith: prove your own selves. Know ye not your own selves..." II Cor. 13:5

> **The Promise:**
> "... how that Jesus Christ is in you..." II Cor. 13:5

The Condition:
"... be perfect, be of good comfort, be of one mind, live in peace..." II Cor. 13:11

> **The Promise:**
> "... and the God of love and peace shall be with you." II Cor. 13:11

"The grace of the Lord Jesus Christ, and the love of God, and the communion of the Holy Ghost, be with you all. Amen." II Cor. 13:14
We can only be perfect in Jesus and He gives us the ability to obey Him in everything.

Galatians

Miracles
"He therefore that ministereth to you the Spirit, and worketh miracles among you..." Gal. 3:5

Those of faith blessed with Abraham
"And the Scripture, foreseeing that God would justify the heathen through faith preached before the Gospel unto Abraham, saying, In thee shall all nations be blessed. So then they which be of faith are blessed with faithful Abraham." Gal. 3:8,9

> **The Promise:**
> "... the just shall live by faith." Gal. 3:11

If we have faith in Jesus, we have the blessings of Abraham."

Redeemed from the curse

The Promise:
"Christ hath Redeemed us from the curse…" Gal. 3:13

The Promise:
"… that the blessing of Abraham might come on the Gentiles through Jesus Christ; that we might receive the promise of the Spirit through faith." Gal. 3:14

"Now to Abraham and his Seed were the promises made. He saith not, and to seeds, as of many; but as of One, and to thy Seed, which is Christ… God gave
it (the inheritance) *to Abraham by promise."* Gal. 3:16-18
We inherit the promises of Abraham them through Jesus, Gal. 3:29.

"Is the law then against ("opposed to" NIV) *the promises of God? God forbid…"* Gal. 3:21

The Promise:
"… that the promise by faith of Jesus Christ might be given to them that believe." Gal. 3:22

God's law is not against the promises but it cannot save us – only Jesus can save us and then He gives us His Holy Spirit to help us to overcome and keep His law. We need to be forgiven and washed clean by Jesus' blood for breaking God's law (Rev. 1:5).

The Promise:
"For ye are all the children of God by faith in Christ Jesus. For as many of you as have been baptized into Christ have put on Christ… ye are all one in Christ Jesus." Gal. 3:26-28

We inherit the promises through Jesus.
"And if ye be Christ's then are ye Abraham's seed, and heirs according to the promise." Gal. 3:29

The Promise:
"To Redeem them… that we might receive the adoption of sons. And because ye are sons, God hath sent forth the Spirit of His Son into your hearts, crying, Abba, Father. Wherefore thou art no more a servant, but a son; and if a son, then an heir of God through Christ." Gal. 4:5-7

The Promise:
"Now we, brethren, as Isaac was are the children of promise..." Gal. 4:28

We wait for the hope
"... we through the Spirit wait for the hope of righteousness by faith." Gal. 5:5

The Condition:
"... walk in the Spirit..." Gal. 5:16

The Promise:
"...and ye shall not fulfil ("gratify" NIV) the lust of the flesh ("sinful nature")." Gal. 5:16

"For the flesh lusteth against the Spirit, and the Spirit against the flesh: and these are contrary the one to the other: so that ye cannot do the things that ye would." Gal. 5:17
"... you do not do what you want." Gal. 5:17 NIV
"Be not deceived; God is not mocked: for whatsoever a man soweth, that shall he also reap." Gal. 6:7
The promise is that if you sow good things, you will reap good things! But it is also true that if you sow sin, you will reap the consequences.
"For he that soweth to the flesh shall of the flesh reap corruption; but he that soweth to the Spirit shall of the Spirit reap life everlasting." Gal. 6:8
"The one who sows to please his sinful nature, from that nature will reap destruction; the one who sows to please the Spirit, from the Spirit will reap eternal life." Gal. 6:8 NIV
We strive to live a Holy life because we love God and want to please Him.

The Condition:
"And let us not be weary in well doing: for in due season..." Gal. 6:9

The Promise:
"... we shall reap..." Gal. 6:9

The Condition:
"... if we faint not." Gal. 6:9
"Let us not become weary in doing good, for at the proper time we will reap a harvest if we do not give up." Gal. 6:8,9 NIV

Ephesians

Blessed
"*Blessed be the God and Father of our Lord Jesus Christ, who hath blessed us with all Spiritual blessings in heavenly places in Christ: according as He hath chosen us in Him before the foundation of the world...*" Eph. 1:3,4

Blessed
"*Blessed be the God and Father of our Lord Jesus Christ, who hath blessed us with all Spiritual blessings; in heavenly places in Christ... having predestinated us unto the **adoption** of children by Jesus Christ to Himself, according to the good pleasure of His will... made us accepted in the beloved. In whom we have Redemption through His blood, the forgiveness of sins, according to the riches of His grace...*" Eph. 1:5-8
"*... that He lavished on us. With all wisdom and understanding...*" Eph. 1:8 NIV

We are adopted by God and Abraham!
"*And if you belong to Christ, then you are Abraham's descendants, ("offspring" ESV) heirs...*" Gal. 3:29
"*Wherefore thou art no more a servant, but a son; and if a son, then an heir of God through Christ.*" Gal. 4:7

He will gather us
"*... when the time is ripe He will gather us all together from wherever we are – in heaven or on earth – to be with Him in Christ, forever.*" Eph. 1:10 LB

We have obtained an inheritance
"*In whom also we have obtained an inheritance, being predestinated accord-ing to the purpose of Him who worketh all things after the counsel of His own will...*" Eph. 1:11
"*In Him we have obtained an inheritance.*" Eph. 1:11 ESV

Sealed with the Holy Spirit
"*In whom ye also trusted, after that ye heard the Word of truth, the Gospel of your Salvation: in whom also after that ye believed, ye were sealed with that Holy Spirit of promise, which is the earnest of our inheritance until the Redemption of the purchased possession...*" Eph. 1:13

That we may know the riches of His inheritance
"That the God of our Lord Jesus Christ, the Father of glory, may give unto you the Spirit of wisdom and revelation in the knowledge of Him: the eyes of your understanding being enlightened; that ye may know what is the hope of His calling, and what the riches of the glory of His inheritance in the saints, and what is the exceeding greatness of His power to usward who believe, according to the working of His mighty power." Eph. 1:17-19
"I pray that your hearts will be flooded with light so that you can see something of the future He has called you to share..." Eph. 1:18 LB

Christ is *"above all principality, and power, and might, and dominion, and every name that is named, not only in this world, but also in that which is to come: and hath put all things under His feet, and gave Him* (Jesus) *to be the head over all things to the church, which is His body, the fullness of Him that filleth all in all."* Eph. 1:21-23
Jesus is the head of the church and we can call on the name of Jesus because He is above everything and we are His body.

> **The Promise:**
> *"And you hath He quickened, who were dead in trespasses and sins..."* Eph. 2:1

"But God, who is rich in mercy, for His great love wherewith He loved us, even when we were dead in sins, hath quickened us together with Christ, (by grace ye are saved); and hath raised us up together, and made us sit together in heavenly places in Christ Jesus... for by grace are ye saved through faith; and that not of yourselves: it is the gift of God..." Eph. 2:4-6,8
The Covenant is a promise
"But now hath He obtained a more excellent ministry, by how much also He is the Mediator of a better Covenant, which was established upon better promises." Heb. 8:6
In the Old Covenant the people promised to obey God and they failed. The better promise is that Jesus promises to save us by His blood and He always keeps His promise.
"... at that time ye were without Christ, being aliens... and strangers from the Covenants of promise..." Eph. 2:12

> **The Promise:**
> *"... but now in Christ Jesus ye who sometimes were far off are made nigh by the blood of Christ."* Eph. 2:13

"... (Jesus) is our peace, who hath made both one, and hath broken down the middle wall of partition between us... and that He might reconcile both unto

God in one body by the cross, having slain the enmity thereby: for through Him we both have access by one Spirit unto the Father." Eph. 2:14,16,18
God wants to reconcile Jew and Gentile into one body through Jesus.

Foundation of Apostles and Jesus, the Cornerstone
"Now therefore ye are no more strangers and foreigners, but fellow citizens with the saints, and of the household of God; and are built upon the foundation of the Apostles and prophets, Jesus Christ Himself being the chief Cornerstone..." Eph. 2:19,20

Fellow heirs
"That the Gentiles should be fellow heirs, and of the same body, and partakers of His promise in Christ by the Gospel: whereof I was made a minister, according to the gift of the grace of God given unto me by the effectual working of His power... that I should preach among the Gentiles the unsearchable riches of Christ..." Eph. 3:6-8
Gentiles are now heirs with Abraham's seed if we receive Jesus and we can now partake of the promises.

The manifold wisdom of God *"... might be known by the church..."* Eph. 3:10

We have boldness in Jesus
"... Christ Jesus our Lord; in whom we have boldness and access with confidence by the faith of Him." Eph. 3:12

Strengthened by the Holy Spirit
"That He would grant you, according to the riches of His glory, to be strengthened with might by His Spirit in the inner man; that Christ may dwell in your hearts by faith; that ye, being rooted and grounded in love, may be able to comprehend with all saints what is the breadth, and length, and depth, and height; and to know the love of Christ, which passeth knowledge ..." Gal. 3:16-19

The Promise:
"... that ye might be filled with all the fullness of God. Now unto Him that is able to do exceeding abundantly above all that we ask or think, according to the power that worketh in us..." Eph. 3:19,20

Jesus was filled with the fullness of the Father and the Holy Spirit
"For it pleased the Father that in Him (Jesus) *should all fullness dwell..."* Col. 1:19
And if we have Jesus, we have the fullness of the Godhead through Him.

"... when He ascended up on high, He led captivity captive..." Eph. 4:8

> **The Promise:**
> "... and gave gifts unto men." Eph. 4:8

The Condition:
"And grieve not the Holy Spirit of God..." Eph. 4:30

> **The Promise:**
> "... whereby ye are sealed unto the day of Redemption... God for Christ's sake hath forgiven you." Eph. 4:30,32

Jesus loves us and gave Himself for us
"And walk in love, as Christ also hath loved us, and hath given Himself for us an offering and a sacrifice to God for a sweet smelling savour." Eph. 5:2

> **The Promise:**
> "Now are ye light in the Lord." Eph. 5:8

We are told to let our light shine so that others can see our good works
"Ye are the light of the world. A city that is set on an hill cannot be hid. Neither do men light a candle, and put it under a bushel, but on a candlestick; and it giveth light unto all that are in the house. Let your **light so shine** before men, that they may **see your good works**, and glorify your Father which is in heav-en." Matt. 5:16
According to this verse, the light that we let shine is Jesus manifested in our good works!

Christ promises to Sanctify and cleanse us
"... even as Christ also loved the church, and gave Himself for it; that He might Sanctify and cleanse it with the washing of water by the Word, that He might present it to Himself a glorious church, not having spot, or wrinkle, or any such thing; but that it should be Holy and without blemish... but nourisheth and cherisheth it, even as the Lord the church..." Eph. 5:25-27

The Condition:
"Honour thy father and mother; which is the first Commandment with promise." Eph. 6:2

> **The Promise:**
> "That it may be well with thee, and thou mayest live long on the earth." Eph. 6:3

Rewarded for good works

> **The Promise:**
> "... because you know that the Lord will reward each one for whatever good they do..." Eph. 6:8 NIV

> **The Promise:**
> "... neither is there respect of persons with Him... be strong in the Lord, and in the power of His might..." Eph. 6:9,10

The Condition:
"Put on the whole armour of God..." Eph. 6:11

> **The Promise:**
> "... that ye may be able to stand against the wiles of the devil ... that ye may be able to withstand in the evil day, and having done all, to stand." Eph. 6:13

Belt of Truth
The Condition:
"Stand therefore, having your loins girt about with truth.. having on the breastplate of righteousness; and your feet shod with the preparation of the Gospel of peace... taking the shield of faith, wherewith..." Eph. 6:14-16

> **The Promise:**
> "... ye shall be able to quench all the fiery darts of the wicked." Eph. 6:16

The Condition:
"And take the helmet of Salvation, and the sword of the Spirit, which is the Word of God... that I may open my mouth boldly, to make known the mystery of the Gospel... that therein I may speak boldly, as I ought to speak..." Eph. 6:17-20

> **The Promise:**
> "... that He might comfort your hearts." Eph. 6:22

Philippians

"Being confident of this very thing, that He which hath begun a good work in you..." Phil. 1:6

> **The Promise:**
> "... will perform it until the day of Jesus Christ..." Phil. 1:6

"... being filled with the fruits of righteousness, which are by Jesus Christ unto the glory and praise of God." Phil. 1:11

The Promise:
"For to me to live is Christ, and to die is gain." Phil. 1:21

The Condition:
"Wherefore, my beloved, as ye have always obeyed... work out your own Salvation with fear and trembling..." Phil. 2:13

The Promise:
"For it is God which worketh in you both to will and to do of His good pleasure." Phil. 2:13

We are to reach for the heavenly prize
"... reach forth unto those things which are before, I press toward the mark for the prize of the high calling of God in Christ Jesus... God shall reveal even this unto you." Phil. 3:13-15
"I press on toward the goal to win the prize..." Phil. 3:14 NIV
"I press on to reach the end of the race and receive the heavenly prize..." Phil. 3:14 NLT
"I pursue as my goal the prize promised..." Phil. 3:14 HCSB
"With my eyes fixed on the goal I push on to secure the prize..." Phil. 3:14 WNT
"... lest by any means, when I have preached to others, I myself should be a castaway." I Cor. 9:27
"Therefore I do not run like a man running aimlessly; I do not fight like a man beating the air... so that after I have preached to others, I myself will not be disqualified for the prize..." I Cor. 9:27 NIV
The promise is that God has a reward/prize for those who do God's will and endure to the end.

The Condition:
"Be careful for nothing; but in everything by prayer and supplication with thanksgiving let your requests be made known unto God. And the peace of God, which passeth all understanding..." Phil. 4:6,7

The Promise:
"... shall keep your hearts and minds..." Phil. 4:7

The Condition:
"... through Christ Jesus." Phil. 4:7

The Condition:
"Those things, which ye have both learned, and received, and heard, and seen in me, do..." Phil. 4:9

> **The Promise:**
> *"... and the God of peace shall be with you."* Phil. 4:9

"I can do all things through Christ which strengtheneth me." Phil. 4:13

> **The Promise:**
> *"But my God shall supply all your need according to His riches in glory by Christ Jesus."* Phil. 4:19

Walk worthy of God and be fruitful
"... to desire that ye might be filled with the knowledge of His will in all wisdom and Spiritual understanding; **that ye might walk worthy of the Lord unto all pleasing, being fruitful in every good work***, and increasing in the knowledge of God; strengthened with all might, according to His glorious power, unto all patience and longsuffering with joyfulness; giving thanks unto the Father..."* Col. 1:9-12

> **The Promise:**
> *"... which hath made us meet to be partakers of the inheritance of the saints in light... delivered us from the power of darkness, and hath translated us into the kingdom of His dear Son: in whom we have Redemption through His blood, even the forgiveness of sins..."* Col. 1:12-14

We see here that it is His blood shed on the cross that Redeems us and forgives us. Thank You Jesus!

> **The Promise:**
> *"Who hath delivered us from the power of darkness, and hath translated us into the kingdom of His dear Son..."* Col. 1:13

"And, having made peace through the blood of His cross, by Him to reconcile all things unto Himself; by Him, I say, whether they be things in earth, or things in heaven. And you, that were sometime alienated and enemies in your mind by wicked works, yet now hath He reconciled... in the body of His flesh through death..." Col. 1:20-22

The Promise:
"... to present you Holy and unblameable and unreproveable in His sight..." Col. 1:22

The Condition:
"If ye continue in the faith grounded and settled, and be not moved away from the hope of the Gospel, which ye have heard, and which was preached..." Col. 1:23

"... to whom God would make known what is the riches of the glory of this mystery among the Gentiles; which is Christ in you, the hope of glory: whom we preach... that we may present every man perfect in Christ Jesus. Whereunto I also labour, striving according to His working..." Col. 1:27-29

The Promise:
"... which worketh in me mightily." Col. 1:29

"That their hearts might be comforted, being knit together in love, and unto all riches of the full assurance of understanding, to the acknowledgement of the mystery of God, and of the Father, and of Christ; in whom are hid all the treasures of wisdom and knowledge." Col. 2:2,3

The Promise:
"And ye are complete in Him..." Col. 2:10

"And you, being dead in your sins and the uncircumcision of your flesh, hath He quickened together with Him, having forgiven you all trespasses..." Col. 2:13

The Promise:
"... as Christ forgave you..." Col. 2:13

The Condition:
"... so also do ye." Col. 2:13
Jesus triumphed over principalities
"... having spoiled principalities and powers, He made a shew of them openly, triumphing over them in it." Col. 2:15

"... the whole body (the church)... grows as God causes it to grow." Col. 2:19 NIV

Reward of inheritance

The Promise:
"... of the Lord ye shall receive the reward of the inheritance..." Col. 3:24

The Condition:
"... for ye serve the Lord Christ." Col. 3:24

"Epaphras, who is... a servant of Christ... always laboring fervently for you in prayers, that ye may stand perfect and complete in all the will of God." Col. 4:12

I Thessalonians

The Gospel came with power
"For our Gospel came not unto you in Word only, but also in power, and in the Holy Ghost, and in much assurance..." I Thess. 1:5

> **The Promise:**
> *"... Jesus, which delivered us from the wrath to come."* I Thess. 1:10

> **The Promise:**
> *"... the Word of God, which effectually worketh also in you..."* I Thess. 2:13

The Condition:
"... that believe." I Thess. 2:13

"For now we live..." I Thess. 3:8
The Condition:
"... if ye stand fast in the Lord." I Thess. 3:8
"And the Lord make you to increase and abound in love one toward another, and toward all men, even as we do toward you..." I Thess. 3:12

> **The Promise:**
> *"... to the end He may stablish your hearts unblameable in Holiness before God, even our Father, at the coming of our Lord Jesus Christ with all His saints."* I Thess. 3:12,13

Abstain from fornication

> **The Promise:**
> *"For this is the will of God, even your Sanctification..."* I Thess. 4:3

The Condition:
"... ye should abstain from fornication: that every one of you should know how to possess his vessel (body) *in Sanctification and honour; not in the lust*

of concupiscence, even as the Gentiles which know not God; that no man go beyond and defraud his brother in ("the" KJV fn)... matter: because that the Lord is the avenger of all such, as we also have forewarned you and testified." I Thess. 4:3-6

> **The Promise:**
> "... God, who hath also given unto us His Holy Spirit..." I Thess. 4:8

You "... are taught of God to love one another." I Thess. 4:9

> **The Promise:**
> "... that ye may have lack of nothing." I Thess. 4:12

Promise of 2nd coming of Jesus

> **The Promise:**
> "For the Lord Himself shall descend from heaven with a shout, with the voice of the archangel, and with the Trump of God: and the dead in Christ shall rise first: then we which are alive and remain shall be caught up together with them in the clouds, to meet the Lord in the air: and so shall we ever be with the Lord." I Thess. 4:16,17

Sanctified
"... God of peace Sanctify you wholly; and I pray God your whole spirit and soul and body be preserved blameless unto the coming of our Lord Jesus Christ. Faithful is He that calleth you..." I Thess. 5:23,24

> **The Promise:**
> "... who also will do it." I Thess. 5:24

II Thessalonians

We can trust that God will pay back those who cause us trouble

> **The Promise:**
> "Seeing it is a righteous thing with God to recompense tribulation to them that trouble you..." II Thess. 1:6

"Wherefore also we pray always for you, that our God would count you worthy of this calling, and fulfil all the good pleasure of His goodness, and the work of faith with power..." II Thess. 1:11

God chose you

> **The Promise:**
> "... God hath from the beginning chosen you to Salvation through Sanctification of the Spirit and belief of the truth... hath given us everlasting consolation and good hope through grace, comfort your hearts ..." II Thess. 2:13,16,17

God wants to establish you in good works
"... and stablish you in every good word and work." II Thess. 2:17

> **The Promise:**
> "But the Lord is faithful who shall stablish you, and keep you from evil." II Thess. 3:3

I Timothy

> **The Promise:**
> "... I obtained mercy..." I Tim. 1:13

"This is a faithful saying, and worthy of all acceptation..." I Tim. 1:16

> **The Promise:**
> "... that Christ Jesus came into the world to save sinners; of whom I am chief. Howbeit for this cause I obtained mercy, that in me first Jesus Christ might shew forth all longsuffering, for a pattern to them which should hereafter believe on Him to life everlasting." I Tim. 1:16

"... that Christ Jesus could use me (Paul) as a prime example of His great pa-tience with even the worst sinners. Then others will realize that they, too, can believe in Him and receive eternal life." I Tim. 1:16 NLT
"... Christ Jesus might display His unlimited patience..." I Tim. 1:16 NIV

"... God our Saviour; who will have all men to be saved, and to come unto the knowledge of the truth." I Tim. 2:4

"For bodily exercise profiteth little..." I Tim. 4:8

> **The Promise:**
> "... but godliness is profitable unto all things, having promise of the life that now is, and of that which is to come." I Tim. 4:8

"Neglect not the gift that is in thee, which was given thee by prophecy, with the laying on of the hands of the presbytery." I Tim. 4:14

The Condition:
"... godliness with contentment..." I Tim. 6:6

> **The Promise:**
> "... is great gain." I Tim. 6:6

Rich in good works

> **The Promise:**
> "... God, who giveth us richly all things to enjoy... be rich in good works... laying up in store for themselves a good foundation against the time to come, that they may lay hold on eternal life." I Tim. 6:17

"... laying up in store for themselves a good foundation against the time to come, that they may lay hold on eternal life." I Tim. 6:19

II Timothy

"... according to the promise of life which is in Christ Jesus..." II Tim. 1:1

"For God hath not given us the spirit of fear..." II Tim. 1:7

> **The Promise:**
> "... but of power, and of love, and of a sound mind... who hath saved us, and called us with an Holy calling... according to His own purpose and grace which was given us in Christ Jesus before the world began..." II Tim. 1:7,9

"... for I know whom I have believed, and am persuaded that..." II Tim. 1:12

> **The Promise:**
> "He is able to keep that which I have committed unto Him against that day." II Tim. 1:12

Abundant grace
"And the grace of our Lord was exceeding abundant with faith and love which is in Christ Jesus. This is a faithful saying, and worthy of all acceptation, that Christ Jesus came into the world..." II Tim. 1:14,15

> **The Promise:**
> "... to save sinners..." II Tim. 1:14,15

Jesus, *"Who gave Himself a ransom..."* II Tim. 2:6

The Condition:
"... if we be dead with Him (we died with Him through baptism, Rom. 6:3,4, 8;Col.2:12)..." II Tim. 2:11

> **The Promise:**
> *"... we shall also live with Him..."* II Tim. 2:11

The Condition:
"If we suffer..." II Tim. 2:12

> **The Promise:**
> *"... we shall also reign with Him..."* II Tim. 2:12

He is faithful
"Even when we are too weak to have any faith left, He remains faithful to us and will help us... and He will always carry out His promises to us. Remind your people of these great facts..." II Tim. 2:13,14 LB

"... the Lord knoweth them that are His..." II Tim. 2:19
The Condition:
"Persecutions, afflictions... I endured..." II Tim. 3:11

> **The Promise:**
> *"... but out of them all the Lord delivered me."* II Tim. 3:11

"... thou hast known the Holy Scriptures, which are able to make thee wise un-to Salvation through faith which is in Christ Jesus." II Tim. 3:15

"All Scripture is given by inspiration of God..." II Tim. 3:16

> **The Promise:**
> *"That the man of God may be perfect, thoroughly furnished unto all good works."* II Tim. 3:17

> **The Promise:**
> *"Henceforth there is laid up for me a crown of righteousness, which the Lord, the righteous Judge, shall give me at that day and not to me only..."* II Tim. 4:8

The Condition:
"... but unto all them also that love His appearing." II Tim. 4:8

God will stand with me and preserve me
> **The Promise:**
> "... the Lord stood with me, and strengthened me ... and the Lord shall deliver me from every evil work, and will preserve me unto His heavenly kingdom..." II Tim.4:18

God promised us eternal life before He even created this earth
> **The Promise:**
> "In hope of eternal life, which God, that cannot lie, promised before the world began..." Titus 1:2

> **The Promise:**
> "For the grace of God that bringeth Salvation hath appeared to all men... looking for that blessed hope, and the glorious appearing of the great God and our Saviour Jesus Christ; who gave Himself for us, that He might Redeem us from all iniquity, and purify unto Himself a peculiar people, **zealous of good works**." Titus 2:11-14

"... *eager to do what is good.*" Titus 2:14 NIV
"... *enthusiasm*..." Titus 2:14 LB
"... *zealous for good deeds.*" Titus 2:17 RSV
Dict. "*zealous*" means, "*full of... ardently active, devote, or diligent*"
Synonyms, "*enthusiastic, eager, fervid, fervent, intense, passionate, warm.*"
Zealous and enthusiastic to do good works!
The grace of God brings the Salvation that Jesus purchased for us on the cross to Redeem us from sin and purify us; to make us a peculiar people that are ready and willing to be obedient.

> **The Promise:**
> "... *according to His mercy He saved us...*" Titus 3:5-7

The Condition:
"... *by the washing of regeneration, and renewing of the Holy Ghost; which He shed on us abundantly through Jesus Christ our Saviour; that being Justi-fied by His grace...*" Titus 3:5-7

> **The Promise:**
> "... *we should be made heirs according to the hope of eternal life.*" Titus 3:7

He saved us because He is merciful and He washed us with the Word and through baptism (Acts 22:16;Eph. 5:26) and renewed us through the Holy Spirit. Now we are justified by faith and have hope of eternal life through His grace.

Hebrews

Jesus loves righteousness and hates sin!
The Condition:
"Thou hast loved righteousness, and hated iniquity..." Heb. 1:9
  The Promise:
  "... God, hath anointed Thee (Jesus) *with the oil of gladness above Thy fellows."* Heb. 1:9

Angels sent to minister to us

  The Promise:
  "Are they (angels) *not all ministering spirits, sent forth to minister for them, who shall be heirs of Salvation?"* Heb. 1:14

God gives signs, wonders, miracles, and gifts as a witness

  The Promise:
  "God also bearing them witness, both with signs and wonders, and with divers miracles, and gifts of the Holy Ghost, according to His own will?" Heb. 2:4

"But we see Jesus, who was made a little lower than the angels (while on earth), *for the suffering of death, crowned with glory and honour in heaven..."* Heb. 2:9

Jesus tasted the second death for all men

  The Promise:
  "... that He by the grace of God should taste death for every man." Heb. 2:9

Jesus promises here to destroy the Devil someday
"... that through death He (Jesus) *might **destroy** him that had the power of death, that is, **the devil**."* Heb. 2:14,15

God delivers us from the fear of death
The Promise:
"And deliver them who through fear of death were all their lifetime subject to bondage." Heb. 2:15

"Wherefore in all things it behooved Him to be made like unto His brethren, that He might be a merciful and faithful high priest in things pertaining to God..." Heb. 2:17

The Promise:
"... to make reconciliation for the sins of the people. For in that He Himself hath suffered being tempted, He is able to succor them that are tempted." Heb. 2:17,18

The Promise:
"For we are made partakers of Christ..." Heb. 3:14

The Condition:
"... if we hold the beginning of our confidence stedfast unto the end..." Heb. 3:14

Let's not fall short of His promise
"Let us therefore fear, lest, a promise being left us of entering into His rest, any of you should seem to come short of it. For unto us was the Gospel preached, as well as unto them: but the Word preached did not profit them, not being mixed with faith in them that heard it. For we which have believed do enter into rest..." Heb. 4:1-11

"For as long, then, as that promise of resting in Him pulls us on to God's goal for us, we need to be careful that we're not disqualified. We received the same promises as those people in the wilderness, but the promises didn't do them a bit of good because they didn't receive the promises with faith. If we believe, though, we'll experience that state of resting. But not if we don't have faith... so this promise has not yet been fulfilled. Those earlier ones never did get to the place of rest because they were disobedient. God keeps renewing the promise... and so this is still a live promise. It wasn't canceled at the time of Joshua... the promise... is still there for God's people. God Himself is at rest. And at the end of the journey we'll surely rest with God. So let's keep at it and... not drop out through some sort of disobedience... so let's walk right up to Him and get what He is so ready to give. Take the mercy, accept the help." Heb. 4:1-11 TM

"For the Word of God is quick, and powerful, and sharper than any two-edged sword, piercing even to the dividing asunder of soul and spirit, and of the joints and marrow, and is a discerner of the thoughts and intents of the heart." Heb. 4:12

The Condition:
"Let us therefore come boldly unto the throne of grace..." Heb. 4:16

> **The Promise:**
> *"... that we may obtain mercy, and find grace to help in time of need."* Heb. 4:16

"For the earth which drinketh in the rain that cometh oft upon it, and bringeth forth herbs meet for them by whom it is dressed..." Heb. 5:7

> **The Promise:**
> *"... the earth... receiveth blessing from God."* Heb. 5:7;6:7

"And being made perfect, He (Jesus) became the author of eternal Salvation..." Heb. 5:9

The Condition:
"... unto all them that obey Him..." Heb. 5:9

Blessing
"For the earth which drinketh in the rain that cometh oft upon it, and bringeth forth herbs meet for them by whom it is dressed..." Heb. 6:7

> **The Promise:**
> *"... receiveth blessing from God."* Heb. 6:7

The Condition:
"... that ye be not slothful, but followers of them who through faith and patience..." Heb. 6:12

We inherit the promises through faith and patience

> **The Promise:**
> *"... inherit the promises."* Heb. 6:12

Blessing
"Saying, Surely blessing I will bless thee..." Heb. 6:14

The Condition:
"... after he had patiently endured..." Heb. 6:15

> **The Promise:**
> *"... he obtained the promise."* Heb. 6:15

Sometimes we have to wait for the promises to be fulfilled and sometimes God answers right away.
We are heirs to the promises

> **The Promise:**
> "Wherein God, willing more abundantly to shew unto the heirs of promise the immutability of His counsel, confirmed it by an oath: that by two immutable things, in which it was impossible for God to lie, we might have a strong consolation, who have fled for refuge to lay hold upon the hope set before us: which hope we have as an anchor of the soul, both sure and stedfast, and which entereth into that within the veil..." Heb. 6:17-19

We can be sure of His promises
"God also bound Himself with an oath, so that those He promised to help would be perfectly sure and never need to wonder whether He might change His plans. He has given us both His promise and His oath, two things we can completely count on, for it is impossible for God to tell a lie... now they can know without doubt that He will give them the Salvation He has promised them. This certain hope of being saved is a strong and trustworthy anchor for our souls..." Heb. 6:17-19 LB

Blessed
Melchisedec "... *blessed him* (Abraham) *that had the promises.*" Heb. 7:6
The promises were given to Abraham and we inherit the promises by being adopted sons and daughters of Abraham through faith and baptism, Gal. 3:14,29.
"... *Jesus made a surety of a better Testament.*" Heb. 7:22
"... *Jesus has become the guarantee of a better Covenant.*" Heb. 7:22 NIV
It is a better Covenant because Jesus' blood is better than animal sacrifices; and because His promise to save is better than man's promise to keep His Covenant..."

> **The Promise:**
> "Wherefore He is able also to save them to the uttermost that come unto God by Him, seeing He ever liveth to make intercession for them." Heb. 7:25

The Condition:
"For this is the Covenant that I will make with the house of Israel after those days, saith the Lord..." Heb. 8:10
"Behold, the days come, saith the Lord, that I will make a New Covenant with the house of Israel..." Jer. 31:31

The Promise:
"I will put My laws into their mind, and write them in their hearts: and I will be to them a God, and they shall be to Me a people: and they shall not teach every man his neighbour, and every man his brother, saying, Know the Lord: for all shall know Me (on the New Earth), *from the least to the greatest. For I will be merciful to their unrighteousness, and their sins and their iniquities will I remember no more."* Heb. 8:10-12

"... I will forgive their wickedness..." Heb. 8:12 NIV
God wants to put His 10 Commandment law in our hearts so that we obey Him willingly not out of duty but out of joy. God will forgive our sins and help us to obey from the heart. Obeying from the heart is not new to the New Covenant. God wanted that in the Old Covenant as well. Here are some Scriptures on obeying from the heart, Jer.31:31;Ps.37:30,31;40:8; 114:34;Prov.7:3;Is.51:7;Jer.32:39;Ez.11:19;18: 31;36:26;Rom2:14,15;7:22;II Cor.3:3;Heb.8:8,10 (see *"heart"* in Topical section).

The Promise:
"How much more shall the blood of Christ, who through the eternal Spirit offered Himself without spot to God, purge your conscience from dead works to serve the living God... for the Redemption of the transgressions that were under the first Testament..." Heb. 9:14,15

The blood of Jesus cleanses us from our sins. The blood of animals in the Old Testament was only a promise of the true sacrifice to come, which was Jesus. He wants to get rid of our dead works and put it in our hearts to do good works willingly from the heart out of love to God. We don't do our good works to be saved but because we love Him and want to please Him from the heart. Love and obey always go hand in hand.

The Promise:
"So Christ was once offered to bear the sins of many; and unto them that look for Him shall He appear the second time without sin unto Salvation." Heb. 9:28

The Promise:
"From henceforth expecting till His enemies be made His footstool. For by one offering He hath perfected forever them that are Sanctified." Heb. 10:13,14

Jesus has perfected and Sanctified us by His offering on the cross.

Our riches are in heaven
"... *knowing... that ye have in heaven a better and an enduring substance.*" Heb. 10:34

"... *I will put My laws into their hearts, and in their minds will I write them; and their sins and iniquities will I remember no more. Now where remission (re-moval) of these is, there is no more offering for sin. Having therefore, brethren, boldness to enter into the Holiest by the blood of Jesus. By a new and living way, which He hath consecrated for us, through the veil, that is to say, His flesh... let us draw near with a true heart in full assurance of faith, having our hearts sprinkled from an evil conscience, and our bodies washed with pure water* (through baptism)... *for He is faithful that promised...*" Heb. 10:16-23
"*Cast not away therefore your confidence...*" Heb. 10:35

The Promise:
"... *which hath great recompence of reward.*" Heb. 10:35

Have patience
The Condition:
"*For ye have need of patience, that, after ye have done the will of God...*" Heb. 10:36

The Promise:
"... *ye might receive the promise.*" Heb. 10:36

The Promise:
"*For yet a little while, and He that shall come will come, and will not tarry.*" Heb. 10:37

Jesus will come again!
"*Now faith is the substance of things hoped for, the evidence of things not seen.*" Heb. 11:1

You must believe that God rewards!
The Condition:
"*But without faith it is impossible to please Him: for he that cometh to God **must believe that He is**...*" Heb. 11:6

The Promise:
"... *and that He is **a rewarder** of them that diligently seek Him...* (Noah) *became heir of the righteousness which is by faith...* (Abraham) *receive*(d) *an inheritance, obeyed; and he went out... sojourned in the land of promise... dwelling in tabernacles with Isaac and Jacob, the heirs with him of the same promise...*" Heb. 11:6-9

God wants us to believe that He will reward us someday. The Bible says *"...we must believe... that He is a rewarder"* Heb. 11:6.

God has a city prepared for us
"Through faith also Sara herself received strength to conceive seed, and was delivered of a child when she was past age, because she judged Him faithful who had promised... these all died in faith, not having received the promises, but having seen them afar off, and were persuaded of them, and embraced them, and confessed... and now they desire a better country... an heavenly: wherefore God is not ashamed to be called their God: for He hath pre-pared for them a city. Abraham... received the promises..." Heb. 11:11,13, 16, 17

Blessed
"By faith Isaac blessed Jacob and Esau concerning things to come." Heb. 11:20

Blessed
"By faith Jacob, when he was... dying, blessed both the sons of Joseph..." Heb. 11:21
Moses respected the reward in heaven

The Promise:
"By faith Moses... esteemed the reproach of Christ greater riches than the treasures in Egypt: for he had respect unto the recompence of the reward." Heb. 11:26

"Who through faith subdued kingdoms, wrought righteousness, obtained promises, stopped the mouths of lions, quenched the violence of fire, escaped the edge of the sword, out of weakness were made strong, waxed valiant in fight, turned to flight the armies of the aliens (foreigners). *Women received their dead raised to life again: and others were tortured, not accepting deliverance; that they might obtain a better Resurrection..."* Heb. 11:33-35

Made perfect with us
"And these all, having obtained a good report through faith, received not the promise: God having provided some better thing for us, that they without us should not be made perfect." Heb. 11:39,40

"... but He (Jesus) *for our profit, that we might be partakers of His Holiness."* Heb. 12:10

"Endure hardship as discipline; God is treating you as sons... God disciplines us for our good, that we may share in His Holiness... it produces a harvest of righteousness and peace for those who have been trained by it." Heb. 12:7-11 NIV

Healed
"... and make straight paths for your feet, lest that which is lame be turned out of the way; but let it rather be healed." Heb. 12:13

The Promise:
"Wherefore we receiving a kingdom which cannot be moved..." Heb. 12:28

"... let us have grace, whereby we may serve God acceptably with reverence and godly fear: for our God is a consuming fire." Heb. 12:28,29
We have received a kingdom, through Jesus the king, that will never be taken away from us!

Condition:
"Let your conversation be without covetousness; and be content with such things as ye have..." Heb. 13:5

The Promise:
"... for He hath said, I will never leave thee, nor forsake thee. So that we may boldly say, The Lord is my helper, and I will not fear what man shall do unto me." Heb. 13:5,6

Jesus will never change

The Promise:
"Jesus Christ the same yesterday... today, and forever." Heb. 13:8

"... we seek (the New Jerusalem)... *to come."* Heb. 13:14

The Promise:
"... our Lord Jesus, that great Shepherd of the sheep, through the blood of the everlasting Covenant, make you perfect in every good work to do His will, working in you that which is well pleasing in His sight, through Jesus Christ; to whom be glory forever and ever, Amen." Heb. 13: 21

We are saved and made perfect through the blood and righteousness of Jesus, but He saves us to do good works through the power of the Holy Spirit. It is the Holy Spirit that helps us to do the things that please God.

James

The trying of our faith works patience
"My brethren, count it all joy when ye fall into divers temptations; knowing this, that the trying of your faith worketh patience. But let patience have her perfect work, that ye may be perfect and entire, wanting nothing." Jms. 1:2-4

Ask for wisdom
The Condition:
"If any of you lack wisdom, let him ask of God..." James 1:5

> **The Promise:**
> *"... that giveth* (wisdom) *to all men liberally, and upbraideth not; and it shall be given him."* Jms. 1:5

The Condition:
"... but let him ask in faith, nothing wavering. For he that wavereth is like a wave of the sea driven with the wind and tossed. For let not that man think that he shall receive anything of the Lord. A double minded man is unstable in all his ways." Jms. 1:6-8

"Let the brother of low degree..." Jms. 1:9

> **The Promise**
> *"... rejoice in that he is exalted..."* Jms. 1:9

"A Christian who doesn't amount to much in this world should be glad, for he is great in the Lord's sight." Jms. 1:9 LB
"Let the lowly brother boast in his exaltation (in heaven), *and the rich in his humiliation...*" Jms. 1:9 RSV
"But the brother of humble circumstances is to glory in his high position (in heaven)." Jms. 1:9 NASB
"Let the brother of low degree rejoice in that he is exalted (in heaven)." Jms. 1:9 AKJV
"Believers in humble circumstances ought to take pride in their high position (in heaven)." Jms. 1:9 NIV
"Let the lowly brother boast in his exaltation (in heaven)." Jms. 1:9 ESV
"Now the believer of humble means should take pride in his high position (in heaven)." Jms. 1:9 Net Bible

We know that the poor are not exalted here on earth most of the time, so it must be talking about in heaven.

Those who are not considered as esteemed as others here on earth will be exalted in heaven; the least shall be the greatest and the greatest shall be the least, Matt.9: 13;23:11.

"... for he that is least among you all,the same shall be great." Lk. 9:48

... he that is greatest among you let him be as the younger and he that is chief as he that doth serve." Lk. 22:26

"... he that is greatest among you shall be your servant." Matt. 23:11

Blessed
The Condition:
"Blessed is the man that endureth temptation: for..." Jms. 1:12

> **The Promise:**
> *"... when he is tried he shall receive the crown of life, which the Lord hath promised to them that love Him."* Jms. 1:12

"Every good gift and every perfect gift is from above, and cometh down from the Father of lights with whom is no variableness (#3883 *"variation, change, mutation"*) *neither shadow of turning..."* Jms. 1:17

The Condition:
"Wherefore lay apart all filthiness and superfluity of naughtiness, and receive with meekness the engrafted Word..." Jms. 1:21

> **The Promise:**
> *"... which is able to save your souls."* Jms. 1:21

The Condition:
"But be ye doers of the Word, and not hearers only, deceiving your own selves. For if any be a hearer of the Word, and not a doer, he is like unto a man beholding his natural face in a glass: for he beholdeth himself, and goeth his way, and straightway forgetteth what manner of man he was. But whoso looketh into the perfect law of liberty (the 10 Commandments), *and continueth therein, he being not a forgetful hearer, but a doer of the work... hearken, my beloved brethren..."* Jms. 1:22-25

Blessed

> **The Promise:**
> *"... this man shall be blessed in his deed."* Jms. 1:25

"This one will be blessed in what he does." Jms. 1:25 NKJV

"Hearken, my beloved brethren..." Jms. 2:5

The Promise:
"... hath not God chosen the poor of this world rich in faith, and heirs of the Kingdom which He hath promised to them that love Him?" Jms. 2:5

God has promised us a Kingdom that is not of this world.

"... yet ye have not, because ye ask not. Ye ask, and receive not, because ye ask amiss, that ye may consume it upon your lusts." Jms. 4:2,3
God wants us to ask Him for what we need but not just for our own selfish desires

The Promise:
"But He giveth more grace ..." Jms. 4:6

The Condition:
"... unto the humble." Jms. 4:6

The Condition:
"Submit yourselves therefore to God. Resist the devil..." Jms. 4:7

The Promise:
"... and he will flee from you." Jms. 4:7

The Condition:
"... draw nigh to God..." Jms. 4:7

The Promise:
"... and He will draw nigh to you." Jms. 4:8

The Condition:
"Cleanse your hands, ye sinners; and purify your hearts, ye double minded. Be afflicted, and mourn, and weep: let your laughter be turned to mourning, and your joy to heaviness. Humble yourselves in the sight of the Lord..." Jms. 4:8-10

The Promise:
"... and He shall lift you up." Jms. 4:10

How do we cleanse our hands and purify our hearts? Through repentance, forgiveness, and cleansing through the blood of Jesus (I Jn. 1:7,9;Rev.1:5).
A prayer you can pray when you sin.
Prayer:
Father in heaven, I confess that I have sinned (name the sin)! I am truly

sorry and ask that You would forgive me and cleanse me by the blood of Jesus. Help me to overcome my sins and do those things that are pleasing in Your sight. I put all my sins under the blood of Jesus. Thank You! In Jesus' name, Amen!

When I confess my sins and put my sins under the blood of Jesus, turn away from my sin and strive to overcome my sins through the power of the Holy Spirit, then no one can Judge me or condemn me because I am righteous in God's eyes because of Jesus.
"Who will bring any charge against those whom God has chosen? It is God who Justifies." Rom. 8:33
Now that isn't to say that you can do anything you want, knowing that God will forgive you. Remember that if we are sons, then He will punish us when need be. So be careful that your sins don't come back on your own head.
"For the Lord disciplines those He loves, and He punishes each one He accepts as His child." Heb. 12:6,7
"... you have sinned against the Lord, and be sure your sin will find you out." Num. 32:23
Jacob deceived his father and then later in his life, his uncle deceived him. His mother said she would take the curse and she never saw her favorite son again on this earth.
David had Uriah killed and took his wife. Later in his life, three of his sons were killed and several of his wives were violated by Absalom. There are many stories in the Bible that illustrate this point. Let us be careful not to presume upon God's grace that leads us to deliberately sin; for there is no sacrifice for deliberate sin.
"For if we sin willfully ("deliberately keep on sinning" NIV) after that we have received the knowledge of the truth, there remaineth no more sacrifice for sins..." Heb. 12:10

The Condition:
"Be patient therefore, brethren, unto the coming of the Lord" Jms. 5:7

   The Promise:
   "... for the coming of the Lord draweth nigh..." Jms. 5:8

Blessed
"Behold, we count them happy (Gr. "blessed") which endure." Jms. 5:11

   The Promise:
   "... the Lord is very pitiful ("full of compassion" NASB), and of tender mercy." Jms. 5:11

The Condition:
"Is any sick among you? let him call for the elders of the church; and let them pray over him, anointing him with oil in the name of the Lord ..." Jms. 5:14

> **The Promise:**
> "And the prayer of faith shall save the sick, and the Lord shall raise him up; and if he have committed sins, they shall be forgiven him." Jms. 5:15

"And the prayer offered in faith will make the sick person well..." Jms. 5:15 NIV

My grandmother did this for my mother when she was sick as a child and my mother was healed (See personal answers to prayer).

The Condition:
"Confess your faults one to another, and pray one for another..." Jms. 5:16

> **The Promise:**
> "... that ye may be healed. The effectual fervent prayer of a righteous man availeth much." Jms. 5:15,16

"... he which converteth the sinner from the error of his way..." Jms. 5:20

> **The Promise:**
> "... shall save a soul from death, and shall hide a multitude of sins." Jms. 5:20

I Peter

"Blessed be the God and Father of our Lord Jesus Christ, which according to His abundant mercy hath begotten us again unto a lively hope by the Resurrection of Jesus Christ from the dead..." I Pet. 1:3

> **The Promise:**
> "... to an inheritance incorruptible, and undefiled, and that fadeth not away, reserved in heaven for you, who are kept by the power of God..." I Pet. 1:3,4

The Condition:
"... through faith unto Salvation ready to be revealed in the last time." I Pet. 1:5

Our inheritance and rewards are kept safe for us in heaven.

The Condition:
"That the trial of your faith, being much more precious than of gold that perisheth, though it be tried with fire..." I Pet. 1:7

> **The Promise:**
> *"... might be found unto praise and honour and glory at the appearing of Jesus Christ (at the 2nd coming)..." I Pet. 1:7*

> **The Promise:**
> *"Receiving the end of your faith, even the Salvation of your souls." I Pet. 1:9*

The Holy Spirit helps the preachers who are preaching the Gospel
"... the glory that should follow... by them that have preached the Gospel unto you with the Holy Ghost sent down from heaven..." I Pet. 1:12

The Condition:
"Wherefore gird up the loins of your mind, be sober, and hope to the end..." I Pet. 1:13

> **The Promise:**
> *"... for the grace that is to be brought unto you at the revelation of Jesus Christ (at the 2nd coming)." I Pet. 1:13*

*"Forasmuch as ye know that ye were not Redeemed with corruptible things, as silver and gold, from your vain conversation received by tradition from your fathers; but with the precious blood of Christ, as of a lamb without blemish and without spot; who verily was foreordained before the foundation of the world, but was manifest in these last times for you, who by Him do believe in God, that raised Him up from the dead, and gave Him glory; that your faith and hope might be in God. Seeing ye have **purified your souls in obeying** the truth through the Spirit... see that ye love one another with a pure heart fervently..." I Pet. 1:18-22*

We are Redeemed by the blood of Jesus and this verse says that we purify our soul by our obedience through the Holy Spirit so that we can love with a pure heart.

Jesus is the Word (Jn.1:1) that endures forever!

> **The Promise:**
> *"... the Word of the Lord endureth forever..." I Pet. 1:25*

That menas we will have the Bible throughout all eternity!

The Condition:
The Word will make you grow spiritually
"As new born babes, desire the sincere milk of the Word..." I Pet. 2:2

> **The Promise:**
> *"... that ye may grow thereby..."* I Pet. 2:2

You are living stones and a Holy priesthood
"If so be ye have tasted that the Lord is gracious. To whom coming, as unto a living stone, disallowed indeed of men, but chosen of God, and precious, ye also, as lively stones, are built up a Spiritual house, an Holy priesthood, to offer up Spiritual sacrifices, acceptable to God by Jesus Christ..." I Pet. 2:3-5

> **The Promise:**
> *"... he that believeth on Him shall not be confounded."* I Pet. 2:6

Even though we weren't His people we have become His people through Jesus

> **The Promise:**
> *"... ye are a chosen generation, a royal priesthood, an Holy nation, a peculiar people; that ye should shew forth the praises of Him who hath called you out of darkness into His marvelous light: which in time past were not a people, but are now the people of God: which had not obtained mercy, but now have obtained mercy."* I Pet. 2:9,10

Endure grief for suffering unjustly
The Condition:
"For this is thankworthy, if a man for conscience toward God endure grief, suffering wrongfully. For what glory is it, if, when ye be buffeted for your faults, ye shall take it patiently but if, when ye do well, and suffer for it, ye take it patiently..." I Pet. 2:19,20

> **The Promise:**
> *"... this is acceptable with God..."* I Pet. 2:20

"... because Christ also suffered for us, leaving us an example, that ye should follow His steps..." I Pet. 2:21
"For one is approved ("commended" NIV) *if, mindful of God, he endures pain while suffering unjustly."* I Pet. 2:19 RSV
"Who His own self bare our sins in His own body on the tree, that we, being dead to sins, should live unto righteousness..." I Pet. 2:24

> **The Promise:**
> *"... by whose stripes ye were healed."* I Pet. 2:24

"For ye were as sheep going astray; but are now returned unto the Shepherd and Bishop of your souls." I Pet. 2:24,25
We are now dead to sin and we want to live in a way that pleases God and not live just to please ourselves.

"... *if any* (husband) *obey not the Word...*" I Pet. 3:1

   The Promise:
   "... *they also may without the Word be won...*" I Pet. 3:1

The Condition:
"... *by the conversation* (Gr. # 391 "conduct") *of the wives; while they behold your chaste conversation coupled with fear* (of God)." I Pet. 3:1,2

The Condition:
"Likewise, ye husbands, dwell with them (wives) *according to knowledge, giving honour unto the wife, as unto the weaker vessel...*" I Pet. 3:7

   The Promise:
   "... *being heirs together of the grace of life...*" I Pet. 3:7

"... *that your prayers be not hindered.*" I Pet. 3:7
Husbands, the Bible promises that if you do not treat your wife right, then your prayers will not heard.

Blessed
The Condition:
"*Not rendering evil for evil, or railing for railing: but contrariwise blessing ...*" I Pet. 3:9

   The Promise:
   "... *knowing that ye are thereunto called, that ye should inherit a blessing.*" I Pet. 3:9

   The Promise:
   "*For the eyes of the Lord are over the righteous, and His ears are open unto their prayers...*" I Pet. 3:12

The Condition:
"... *but the face of the Lord is against them that do evil.*" I Pet. 3:12
Prayer:
Thank You, Jesus, that You watch over us and hear our prayers!

"And who is he that will harm you, if ye be followers of that which is good? But and if ye suffer for righteousness' sake, happy are ye: and be not afraid of their terror, neither be troubled..." I Pet. 3:13,14

"For Christ also hath once suffered for sins, the just for the unjust..." I Pet. 3:18

> **The Promise:**
> *"... that he might bring us to God,"* I Pet. 3:18

"... being put to death in the flesh, but quickened by the Spirit." I Pet. 3:18

The Condition:
"... for he that hath suffered in the flesh..." I Pet. 4:1

> **The Promise:**
> *"... hath ceased from sin..."* I Pet 4:1

Rejoice when you partake of Christ's suffering
"Beloved, think it not strange concerning the fiery trial which is to try you, as though some strange thing happened unto you: but rejoice, inasmuch as ye are partakers of Christ's sufferings..." I Pet. 4:12,13

> **The Promise:**
> *"... that when His glory shall be revealed, ye may be glad also with exceeding joy."* I Pet. 4:13

The Condition:
"If ye be reproached for the name of Christ..." I Pet. 4:14

> **The Promise:**
> *"... happy are ye; for the Spirit of glory and of God resteth upon you ..."* I Pet. 4:14

Blessed
"If you are reproached for the name of Christ, you are blessed..." I Pet. 4:14 RSV

The Condition:
"And when the Chief Shepherd shall appear..." I Pet. 5:4

> **The Promise:**
> *"... ye shall receive a crown of glory that fadeth not away."* I Pet. 5:4

> **The Promise:**
> *"... for God... giveth grace to the humble."* I Pet. 5:5

The Condition:
"Humble yourselves therefore under the mighty hand of God..." I Pet. 5:6

>**The Promise:**
>"... that He may exalt you in due time: Casting all your care upon Him; for He careth for you." I Pet. 5:6,7

The Condition:
"But the God of all grace, who hath called us unto His eternal glory by Christ Jesus, after that ye have suffered a while..." I Pet. 5:10

>**The Promise:**
>"... make you perfect, stablish, strengthen, settle you." I Pet. 5:10

"... to them that have obtained like precious faith with us through the righteousness of God and our Saviour Jesus Christ: grace and peace be multiplied unto you through the knowledge of God, and of Jesus our Lord..." II Pet. 1:1,2

He gives us great and precious promises

>**The Promise:**
>"According as His divine power hath given unto us all things that pertain unto life and godliness, through the knowledge of Him that hath called us to glory and virtue: whereby are given unto us exceeding great and precious promises: that by these ye might be partakers of the divine nature, having escaped the corruption that is in the world through lust." II Pet. 1:3,4

"His divine power has given us everything we need for life and godliness through our knowledge of Him who called us by His own glory and goodness. Through these He has given us His very great and precious promises, so that through them you may participate in the divine nature and escape the corruption in the world caused by evil desires." II Pet. 1:3,4 NIV

The Condition:
"... giving all diligence, add to your faith virtue... to virtue knowledge... to knowledge temperance... to temperance patience... to patience godliness.. to godliness brotherly kindness... to brotherly kindness charity..." II Pet. 1:5-8

The Promise:
"... for if these things be in you, and abound they make you that ye shall neither be barren nor unfruitful in the knowledge of our Lord Jesus Christ." II Pet. 1:8

The Condition:
"... if ye do these things..." II Pet. 1:10

The Promise:
"... ye shall never fall." II Pet. 1:10

The Promise:
"The Lord knoweth how to deliver the godly out of temptations..." II Pet. 2:9

The Lord will deliver us from falling into temptation

The Promise:
"... they have escaped the pollutions of the world through the knowledge of the Lord and Saviour Jesus Christ..." II Pet. 2:20

The Promise:
"The Lord is not slack concerning His promise..." II Pet. 3:9

"... as some men count slackness..." II Pet. 3:9

The Promise:
"... but is longsuffering to usward, not willing that any should perish, but that all should come to repentance." II Pet. 3:9

The Promise:
"Nevertheless we, according to His promise, look for new heavens and a New Earth, wherein dwelleth righteousness." II Pet. 3:13

I John

"... our fellowship is with the Father, and with His Son Jesus Christ. And these things write we unto you, that your joy may be full." I Jn. 1:4
The promise is that we can have fellowship with the Father and Jesus; and He wants our joy to be full.

The Condition:
"But if we walk in the light, as He is in the light..." I Jn. 1:7

The Promise:
"... we have fellowship one with another, and the blood of Jesus Christ His Son cleanseth us from all sin..." I Jn. 1:7

The Condition:
"If we confess our sins..." I Jn. 1:9

The Promise:
"... He is faithful and just to forgive us our sins, and to cleanse us from all unrighteousness." I Jn. 1:9

"My little children, these things write I unto you, that ye sin not. And if any man sin..." I Jn. 2:1

The Promise:
"... we have an advocate with the Father, Jesus Christ the righteous: and He is the propitiation for our sins: and not for ours only, but also for the sins of the whole world." I Jn. 2:1,2

Propitiation means to regain favor.
Gr. #2434 "*atoning sacrifice*" - "*hilasmós – properly, propitiation*; *an offering to appease (satisfy) an angry, offended party... (hilasmós) is only used twice (1 Jn 2:2, 4:10) – both times of Christ's atoning blood that appeases God's wrath, on all confessed sin. By the sacrifice of Himself, Jesus Christ provided the ultimate/ hilasmós ("propitiation")." www.biblehub.com

The Condition:
"... if we keep His Commandments... (and) keepeth His Word ..." I Jn. 2:3,5

The Promise:
"... in him verily is the love of God perfected..." I Jn. 2:5

"I write unto you, little children..." I Jn. 2:12

The Promise:
"... because your sins are forgiven for His name's sake." I Jn. 2:12
"I write unto you, fathers..." I Jn. 2:13

The Promise:
"... because ye have known Him that is from the beginning," I Jn. 2:13

"I write unto you, young men..." I Jn. 2:13

The Promise:
"... because ye have overcome the wicked one." I Jn. 2:13

"... I write unto you, little children..." I Jn. 2:13

> **The Promise:**
> "... because ye have known the Father." I Jn. 2:13

"I have written unto you, young men..." I Jn. 2:14

> **The Promise:**
> "... because ye are strong, and the Word of God abideth in you, and ye have overcome the wicked one." I Jn. 2:14

The Condition:
"... he that doeth the will of God..." I Jn. 2:17

> **The Promise:**
> "... abideth forever." I Jn. 2:17

"... and all of you know the truth." I Jn. 2:20 NIV
"...and all of you have knowledge." I Jn. 2:20 HCSB

> **The Promise:**
> "But ye have an unction from the Holy One, and ye know all things." I Jn. 2:20

The Condition:
"Let that therefore abide in you, which ye have heard from the beginning. If that which ye have heard from the beginning shall remain in you..." I Jn. 2:24

> **The Promise:**
> "... ye also shall continue in the Son." I Jn. 2:24

The Holy Spirit teaches us

> **The Promise:**
> "And this is the promise that He hath promised us, even eternal life... but the anointing which ye have received of Him abideth in you, and ye need not that any man teach you: but as the same anointing teacheth you of all things, and is truth, and is no lie, and even as it hath taught you..." I Jn. 2:25-27

The Condition:
"... ye shall abide in Him. And now, little children, abide in Him; that, when He
shall appear, we may have confidence, and not be ashamed before Him at His coming. If ye know that He is righteous, ye know that every one that doeth righteousness is born of Him." I Jn. 2:27-29

The Promise:
"Behold, what manner of love the Father hath bestowed upon us, that we should be called the sons of God... beloved, now are we the sons of God, and it doth not yet appear what we shall be: but we know that, when He shall appear, we shall be like Him; for we shall see Him as He is." I Jn. 3:1,2

The Condition:
"And every man that hath this hope in him purifieth himself, even as He is pure." I Jn. 3:3
We purify ourselves from sin and strive to overcome through prayer, confession, the blood of Jesus, and the help of the Holy Spirit.

"... for this purpose the Son of God was manifested..." I Jn. 3:8

The Promise:
"... that He might destroy the works of the devil." I Jn. 3:8

The Condition:
"Whosoever is born of God..." I Jn. 3:9

The Promise:
"... doth not commit sin; for His Seed remaineth in him: and he cannot sin..." I Jn. 3:9

"cannot sin" (Gr. #1410 means does not have *"permission"* to sin)

The Condition:
"... because he is born of God. In this the children of God are manifest, and the children of the devil: whosoever doeth not righteousness is not of God, neither he that loveth not his brother." I Jn. 3:9,10
God knows that we will sin but He never gives us permission to sin. He told the woman caught in sin, *"Go and sin no more"* Jn. 8:11. He's made a way for us to stay clean through repentance, confession, asking for forgiveness, through His blood, baptism, and Communion. He wants us to strive to overcome by the power of His Holy Spirit. We should not be Judgmental knowing that we have fallen short ourselves and knowing we are only saved by His death on the cross. (I Jn. 1:9,10;2:1). Because God forgives us, we should also forgive others. In fact, God won't forgive us if we don't forgive others (see the parable in Matt. 18:21-35 of the unforgiving servant).

The Condition:
"Beloved, if our heart condemn us not, then have we confidence toward God. And whatsoever we ask..." I Jn. 3:21, 22

The Promise:
"... *we receive of Him...*" I Jn. 3:22

The Condition:
"... *because we keep His Commandments, and do those things that are pleasing in His sight.*" I Jn. 3:22
Paul said, My conscience is clear but that does not make me innocent, I Cor. 4:4.
(See also Acts 23:1;Rom. 2:15;13:5;I Tim. 1:5,19;4:2;Titus 1:15;Heb. 9:14; 10: 22;13:18;I Pet. 3:16

The Condition:
"... *he that keepeth His Commandments...*" I Jn. 3:23,24

The Promise:
"... *dwelleth in Him, and He in him... we know that He abideth in us, by the Spirit which He hath given us.*" I Jn. 3:24

The Promise:
"*Ye are of God, little children, and have overcome them: because greater is He that is in you, than He that is in the world...*" I Jn. 4:4,5

"... *he that knoweth God heareth us... love is of God and everyone that loveth is born of God, and knoweth God.*" I Jn. 4:6,7

The Promise:
"... *God dwelleth in us, and His love is perfected in us.*" I Jn. 4:12

"... *God abides in us and His love has been perfected in us.*" I Jn. 4:12 NKJV
The Condition:
"... *if we love one another...*" I Jn. 4:12

God dwells in us
"*Whosoever shall confess that Jesus is the Son of God, God dwelleth in him, and he in God. And we have known and believed the love that God hath to us. God is love; and he that dwelleth in love dwelleth in God, and God in him. Herein is our love made perfect, that we may have boldness in the Day of Judgment: because as He is, so are we in this world.*" I Jn. 4:15-17
Love drives out fear
"*There is no fear in love; but perfect love casteth out fear: because fear hath torment. He that feareth is not made perfect in love. We love Him, because He first loved us.*" I Jn. 4:18,19

The Condition:
"For whatsoever is born of God…" I Jn. 5:4

> **The Promise:**
> *"… overcometh the world: and this is the victory that overcometh the world, even our faith."* I Jn. 5:4

> **The Promise:**
> *"… God hath given to us eternal life…"* I Jn. 5:11

The Condition:
"… and this life is in His Son." I Jn. 5:11
As long as you remain in Jesus you can know that you have eternal life

> **The Promise:**
> *"He that hath the Son hath life…"* I Jn. 5:12

The Condition:
"These things have I written unto you that believe on the name of the Son of God…" I Jn. 5:13

> **The Promise:**
> *"… that ye may know that ye have eternal life…"* I Jn. 5:13

"And this is the confidence that we have in Him, that…" I Jn. 5:14

The Condition:
"… if we ask anything according to His will…" I Jn. 5:14

> **The Promise:**
> *"… He heareth us…"* I Jn. 5:14

"… and if we know that He hear us, whatsoever we ask, we know that…" I Jn. 5:15

> **The Promise:**
> *"… we have the petitions that we desired of Him…* I Jn. 5:15

Ask life for another
"… If any man see his brother sin a sin which is not unto death, he shall ask…" I Jn. 5:16

> **The Promise:**
> *"… and He shall give him life for them…"* I Jn. 5:16

The Condition:
"... that sin not unto death. There is a sin unto death: I do not say that he shall pray for it." I Jn. 5:16

The Condition:
"We know that whosoever is born of God sinneth not; but he that is begotten of God keepeth himself..." I Jn. 5:18

> **The Promise:**
> "... and that wicked one toucheth him not." I Jn. 5:18

I Jn. 3:8 tells us that sin is of the Devil, which means that we participate with devils when we sin. In vs. 9 it says that when we are born of God we do not commit sin. The word *"cannot sin"* is Gr. #1410, *"able"* which means, does not have *"permission"* to sin. God knows we will sin and He has made a way for us to be forgiven our sins, but He never gives us permission to sin.

"And we know that the Son of God is come..." I Jn. 5:20

> **The Promise:**
> *"... and hath given us an understanding, that we may know Him that is true, and we are in Him that is true, even in His Son Jesus Christ. This is the true God, and eternal life."* I Jn. 5:20

II John

"Look to yourselves, that we lose not those things which we have wrought, but that we receive a full reward." II Jn. 1:8
We want to receive the full reward in heaven and not lose anything God has prepared for us.

The Condition:
"Whosoever transgresseth, and abideth not in the doctrine of Christ, hath not God. He that abideth in the doctrine of Christ..." II Jn. 1:9

> **The Promise:**
> "... he hath both the Father and the Son." II Jn. 1:9

III John

> **The Promise:**
> "Beloved, I wish above all things that thou mayest prosper and be in health, even as thy soul prospereth." III Jn. 1:2

We should never be afraid to pray for God's will; it's His desire that we be healthy and prosperous, it's His will that we and our family be saved, Lk.12: 32;Jn.6:40. We pray in the Lord's Prayer, "*let Your will be done on earth as it is in heaven*" Matt. 6:9-1.

Jude

A blessing
"*Mercy unto you, and peace, and love, be multiplied.*" Jude 1:2

The Promise:
"*Now unto Him that is able to keep you from falling, and to present you faultless before the presence of His glory with exceeding joy.*" Jude 1:24

Revelation

Blessing
"*Blessed is he that **readeth**, and they that **hear** the words of this prophecy, and **keep** those things which are written therein: for the time is at hand.*" Rev. 1:3
We are promised a three-fold blessing if we read Revelation.
Blessed are those who:
1. Hear
2. Do
3. Keep

No other book in the Bible has this promise, so don't be afraid to read this book. It is the revealing of Jesus Christ and His ultimate victory over the Devil as well as His Kingdom being set up on this earth after the 1000 years (Rev. 20:3;21:1).

"*... and from Jesus Christ, who...*" Rev. 1:5

The Promise:
"*... loved us, and washed us from our sins in His own blood... and ... made us kings and priests unto God and His Father...*" Rev. 1:5,6

The Condition:
"*... to him that overcometh...*" Rev. 2:7

The Promise:
"... will I give to eat of the Tree of Life, which is in the midst of the paradise of God (the New Jerusalem)." Rev. 2:7

"I know thy works, and tribulation, and poverty..." Rev. 2:9

The Promise:
"... but thou art rich (in heaven)... Rev. 2:9

The Condition:
"... be thou faithful unto death..." Rev. 2:10

The Promise:
"... and I will give thee a crown of life." Rev. 2:10

Some say that there are five crowns in the Bible. Is it really five different crowns or five ways of describing one crown? I don't know but we'll find out when we get there.
1. Incorruptible (imperishable) crown – I Cor. 9:24,25
2. Crown of rejoicing – I Thess. 2:19,20
3. Crown of life – Jms. 1:12;Rev. 2:10
4. Crown of righteousness – II Tim. 4:8
5. Crown of glory – I Pet. 5:1-4

The Condition:
"... he that overcometh..." Rev. 1:11

The Promise:
"... shall not be hurt of the second death." Rev. 1:11

The Condition:
"... to him that overcometh..." Rev. 2:17

The Promise:
"... will I give to eat of the hidden manna, and will give him a white stone, and in the stone a new name written which no man knoweth saving he that receiveth it." Rev. 2:17

The Promise:
"... and I will give unto every one of you..." Rev. 2:23

The Condition:
"... according to your works." Rev. 2:23

Again we see that we are rewarded for our works – even though we are saved by grace. We have seen a lot of verses saying this – it must be important!

The Condition:
"And he that overcometh, and keepeth My works unto the end ..." Rev. 2:26
> **The Promise:**
> *"... to him will I give power over the nations... and I will give him the Morning Star (Jesus)."* Rev. 2:26-28

The Condition:
"Thou hast a few names even in Sardis, which have not defiled their garments
..." Rev. 3:4

> **The Promise:**
> *"... and they shall walk with Me in white..."* Rev. 3:4

The Condition:
"... for they are worthy." Rev. 3:4

The Condition
"He that overcometh..." Rev. 3:5

> **The Promise:**
> *"... the same shall be clothed in white raiment; and I will not blot out his name out of the book of life, but I will confess his name before My Father, and before His angels."* Rev. 3:5

"Behold, I will make them of the synagogue of Satan, which say they are Jews, and are not, but do lie..." Rev. 3:9

> **The Promise:**
> *"... behold, I will make them to come and worship before thy feet, and to know that I have loved thee..."* Rev. 3:9

The Condition:
"Because thou hast kept the Word of My patience..." Rev. 3:9

> **The Promise:**
> *"I also will keep (#5083 "to watch carefully, to guard; to keep an eye on") thee from the hour of temptation, which shall come upon all the world, to try them that dwell upon the earth."* Rev. 3:9-10

"For in the Time of Trouble He shall hide me.." Ps. 27:5
"Come My people, enter thou into thy chambers and shut the doors about thee; hide thyself... until the indignation be past." Is. 26:20
"I kept (#5083 "Keep, guard, observe, watch over, maintain, preserve") them in Thy name..." Jn. 17:12
"... to try them that dwell upon the earth." Rev. 3:10

The Promise:
"Behold, I come quickly..." Rev. 3:11

"... hold that fast which thou hast, that no man take thy crown..." Rev. 3:11
This verse tells us that if we aren't careful, we could lose our crown.
The Condition:
"... him that overcometh..." Rev. 3:12

The Promise:
"... will I make a pillar in the Temple of My God, and he shall go no more out: and I will write upon him the name of My God, and the name of the City of My God, which is New Jerusalem, which cometh down out of heaven from My God: and I will write upon him My new name." Rev. 3:12

The Condition:
"Behold, I stand at the door, and knock: if any man hear My voice, and open the door..." Rev. 3:20

The Promise:
"... I will come in to him, and will sup with him, and he with Me." Rev. 3:20

The Condition:
"... to him that overcometh..." Rev. 3:21

The Promise:
"... will I grant to sit with Me in My throne, even as I also overcame, and am set down with My Father in His throne." Rev. 3:20,21

Redeemed by the blood of Jesus
"... Thou hast Redeemed us to God by Thy blood out of every kindred, and tongue, and people, and nation and hast made us unto our God kings and priests: and we shall reign on the earth." Rev. 5:9,10

The Promise:
"They shall hunger no more, neither thirst anymore; neither shall the sun light on them, nor any heat. For the Lamb which is in the midst of the throne shall feed them, and shall lead them unto living fountains of waters: and God shall wipe away all tears from their eyes (Rev. 21:4)." Rev. 7:16,17

The kingdoms of earth will someday belong to Jesus forever!
"... there were great voices in heaven, saying..." Rev. 11:15

The Promise:
"... the kingdoms of this world are become the Kingdoms of our Lord, and of His Christ; and He shall reign forever and ever." Rev. 11:15

God's servants will be rewarded
"... the time of the dead, that they should be Judged..." Rev. 11:18

The Promise:
"... and that Thou shouldest give reward unto Thy servants the prophets, and to the saints..." Rev. 11:18

The Promise:
"... now is come Salvation, and strength, and the kingdom of our God, and the power of His Christ: for the accuser of our brethren is cast down, which accused them before our God day and night." Rev. 12:10

The Promise:
"And they overcame Him by the blood of the Lamb, and by the word of their testimony..." Rev. 12:11

We overcome by calling on the blood of Jesus and speaking the promises!
"Having therefore these promises... let us cleanse ourselves... perfecting Holiness..." II Cor. 7:1

Promise to the woman (who is the church)
"And the earth helped the woman, and the earth opened her mouth, and swallowed up the flood which the dragon cast out of his mouth." Rev. 12:16

Promise to the 144,000
"And I looked, and lo, a Lamb stood on the Mount Sion, and with Him an hundred forty and four thousand... these are they which follow the Lamb whithersoever He goeth. These were Redeemed from among men, being the firstfruits unto God and to the Lamb." Rev. 14:1,4

Blessed
*"Behold, **I come as a thief**, blessed is he that watcheth, and keepeth his garments, lest he walk naked, and they see his shame."* Rev. 16:15

Here is how Jesus comes as a thief
*"But the day of the Lord will come **as a thief in the night** in the which the **heavens shall pass away** with a **great noise** and the **elements shall melt**

with fervent heat, the **earth** also and the works that are therein shall be **burned up**." II Pet. 3:10

At the 2nd Coming of Jesus:
1. The heavens pass away
2. With a great noise
3. The elements melt with a great heat
4. The earth is burned up

The part that is like a thief is that it happens when we don't expect it.
The Bride is now ready

"Let us be glad and rejoice, and give honour to Him: for the marriage of the Lamb is come, and His wife hath made herself ready." Rev. 19:7

The Promise:
"... to her was granted that she should be arrayed in fine linen, clean and white: for the fine linen is the righteousness ("righteous acts" NIV) of saints. And He saith unto me, Write, Blessed are they which are called unto the Marriage Supper of the Lamb..." Rev. 19:7-9

"... and He saith unto me, These are the true sayings of God." Rev. 19:9

"And I saw thrones, and they sat upon them, and Judgment was given unto them: and I saw the souls of them that were beheaded for the witness of Jesus, and for the Word of God, and which had not worshipped the beast, neither his image, neither had received his mark upon their foreheads, or in their hands..." Rev. 20:4

The Promise:
"... and they lived and reigned with Christ a thousand years." Rev. 20:4

The Condition:
"Blessed and Holy is he that hath part in the first Resurrection..." Rev. 20:6

The Promise:
"... on such the second death hath no power, but they shall be priests of God and of Christ, and shall reign with Him a thousand years." Rev. 20:6

After the 1000 years (Rev. 20:7), the New Jerusalem (and the Bride) comes down out of heaven (Rev. 21:2) and then God the Father and the Son come to earth to reign (Rev. 22:3); there is no Temple there (Rev. 21:22) because They are the Temple on the New Earth.

The Promise:
"*And **when the thousand years are expired**... I saw a new heaven and a New Earth: for the first heaven and the first earth were passed away; and there was no more sea. And I John saw the Holy City, New Jerusalem, coming down from God out of heaven, prepared as a bride adorned for her husband. And I heard a great voice out of heaven saying, Behold, the Tabernacle of God is with men, and He will dwell with them, and they shall be His people, and God Himself shall be with them, and be their God. And God shall wipe away all tears from their eyes; and there shall be no more death, neither sorrow, nor crying, neither shall there be any more pain: for the former things are passed away... He that sat upon the throne said, Behold I make all things new... and He said unto me, It is done. I am Alpha and Omega, the beginning and the end. I will give unto him that is athirst of the fountain of the water of life freely*." Rev. 20:7;21:1-6

The Condition:
"*He that overcometh...*" Rev. 21:7

> **The Promise:**
> "*... shall inherit all things; and I will be his God, and he shall be My son.*" Rev. 21:7

The Condition
"*And the nations of them which are saved...*" Rev. 21:24

> **The Promise:**
> "*... shall walk in the light of it: and the kings of the earth do bring their glory and honour into it. And the gates of it shall not be shut at all by day: for there shall be no night there* (in the city)." Rev. 21:24,25

See footnote for Rev. 22:1-5

The Tree of Life produces twelve types of fruit, a new one for each month.

> **The Promise:**
> "*And he* (the angel) *shewed me a pure river of Water of Life, clear as crystal, proceeding out of the throne of God and of the river, was there the Tree of Life, which bare twelve manner of fruits, and yielded her fruit every month: and the leaves of the tree were for the healing of the nations. And there shall be no more curse: but the throne of God and of the Lamb shall be in it; and His servants shall serve Him; and they shall see His face; and His name shall be in their fore-*

heads. And there shall be no night there (New Jerusalem)*; and they need no... light of the sun; for the Lord God giveth them light: and they shall reign forever and ever."* Rev. 22:1-5

The New Jerusalem is so bright from the presence of God that you cannot even see the sun. We know that there is a sun and moon on the New Earth because it says in Isaiah that the moon will be as bright as the sun and the sun will be seven times brighter than now.

"Moreover the light of the moon shall be as the light of the sun, and the light of the sun shall be sevenfold, as the light of seven days, in the day that the Lord bindeth up the breach of His people..." Is. 30:26

There are trees on both sides of the River and leaves for healing, Ez. 47:12.

Rewards

The Promise:
"And, behold, I come quickly; and My reward is with Me, to give every man according as his work shall be." Rev. 22:12

Here again at the very end of the Bible we see that God wants to reward our works. Saved by grace alone and rewarded for our good works, character, and obedience.

The Condition:
"Blessed are they that do His Commandments..." Rev. 22:14

The Promise:
"... that they may have right to the Tree of Life, and may enter in through the gates into the city." Rev. 22:14

"And the Spirit and the bride say, Come, and let him that heareth say, Come. And let him that is athirst come, and whosoever will, let him take the Water of Life freely." Rev. 22:17

The promise is that Jesus is offering the Water of Life to everyone who will receive it.

The promise is that Jesus is coming back very soon, so our prayer is, *"Even so, Come Lord Jesus!"* Rev. 22:20

The Promises of the Bible in Topical Order

Topical Promises

Abba/Father

Matt. 6:26 *"Behold the fowls of the air: for they sow not, neither do they reap, nor gather into barns; yet your heavenly Father feedeth them. Are ye not much better than they?"*
Matt. 7:9-11 *"... how much more shall your Father which is heaven give good things to them that ask Him?"*
Lk. 6:35,36 *"... ye shall be the children of the Highest: for He is kind unto the unthankful and to the evil... your Father also is merciful."*
Lk. 12:32 *"It is your Father's good pleasure to give you the kingdom."*
Lk. 15:20,22-24,31 The prodigal son *"... his father saw him... had compassion... ran... fell on his neck, and kissed him... the father said to his servants, Bring forth the best robe... put it on him... put a ring on his hand, and shoes on his feet... bring hither the fatted calf... kill it; and let us eat... be merry: for this my son was dead, and is alive again; he was lost, and is found... he said unto (his other son)... all that I have is (yours).."*
Jn. 14:2,3 *"In My Father's house are many mansions... I go to prepare a place for you... if I go and prepare a place for you, I will come again, and receive you unto Myself; that where I am, there ye may be also."*
Jn. 16:27 *"... for the Father Himself loveth you, because ye have loved Me (Jesus), and have believed that I came out from God."*
Rom. 8:15 *"... ye have received the Spirit of adoption... we cry, Abba, Father."*
Gal. 4:6 *"And because ye are a son, God hath sent forth the Spirit of His Son into your hearts, crying, Abba, Father."*
I Jn. 3:1 *"Behold, what manner of love the Father hath bestowed upon us, that we should be called the sons of God..."*
When we believe and receive Jesus, we go from being *"children of wrath"* (Eph. 2:11) to adopted children of God and Abraham and inherit the promises of Abraham (See *"Adopt"* in Topical).

Abide/Dwell

Jn. 6:51,56 *"I am the living bread which came down from heaven: if any* man eat of this bread, he shall live forever: and the bread that I will give is My flesh, which I will give for the life of the world... he that eateth of my flesh, and drinketh my blood* (through the symbol of Communion), *dwelleth* (or abideth) *in Me, and I in him."

Jn. 8:31 "... *if ye continue* (abide) *in My word, then are ye My disciples indeed; and ye shall know the truth, and the truth shall make you free."*

Jn. 12:46 "... *whosoever believeth on Me should not abide in darkness."*

Jn. 14:16-18 "*I will pray the Father and He shall give you another Comforter that He may abide with you forever... the Spirit of truth... He dwelleth with you, and... in you. I will not leave you comfortless: I will come to you."*

Jn. 14:23 "*If a man love Me* (Jesus), *he will keep My Words: and My Father will love him, and... come unto him, and make our abode* (abide) *with him."*

Jn. 15:4-6 "*Abide in Me* (Jesus), *and I in you. As the branch cannot bear fruit of itself, except it abide in the vine; no more can ye, except ye abide in Me. I am the vine, ye are the branches: he that abideth in Me, and I in him, the same bringeth forth much fruit: for without Me ye can do nothing..."*

Jn. 15:7 "*If ye abide in Me* (Jesus), *and My Words abide in you, ye shall ask what ye will, and it shall be done unto you."*

Jn. 15:10 "*If ye keep My Commandments, ye shall abide in My love; even as I have kept My Father's Commandments, and abide in His love."*

(Love and obey go together, Deut.5:10;6:2,5;7:9;10:12,13;11:1,13,22;19:9; 30:6,8,16,20;Josh.22:5;I Kings 3:3;Neh.1:5;Ps.119:127,159,165,167;I Jn.1: 6

I Cor. 3:14 "*If any man's work abide... he shall receive a reward."*

I Jn. 2:3-6 "... *hereby we do know that we know Him, if we keep His Commandments... hereby know we that we are* (to abide) *in Him. He that saith he abideth in Him ought himself also so to walk even as He walked."*

I Jn. 3:24 "... *he that keepeth His Commandments dwelleth in Him, and He in him... hereby we know that He abideth in us, by the* (Holy) *Spirit..."*

I Jn. 4:15 "*Whosoever shall confess that Jesus is the Son of God, God dwelleth in him, and he in God."*

Adopt / Adoption / Children

Lk. 6:35 "... *ye shall be children of the Highest..."*
Acts 17:29 "... *we are the offspring of God..."*
Rom. 8:15 "... *ye have received the Spirit of adoption..."*
Rom. 9:8 "... *the children of the promise are counted for the seed* (of Abraham). *For this is the Word of promise..."*

Rom. 11:17,24 *"... thou, being a wild olive tree, wert grafted in among them, and with them partakers of the root and fatness of the olive tree ... and wert grafted contrary to nature into a good olive tree..."*
There is only one olive tree and we are grafted into it.
Rom. 12:5 *"... so we, being many, are one body in Christ, and every one members one of another."*
II Cor. 6:18 *"(I) will be a Father unto you, and ye shall be My sons and daughters, saith the Lord Almighy."*
Gal. 3:9,14,16 *"... they which be of faith are blessed with faithful Abraham ... that the blessing of Abraham might come on the Gentiles through Jesus Christ; that we mght receive the promise of the Spirit through faith ... now to Abraham and his seed were the promises made..."*
Gal. 3:26 *"For ye are all the children of God by faith in Christ Jesus."*
Gal. 3:29 *"And if ye be Christ's, then are ye Abraham's seed, and heirs according to the promise."*
Gal. 4:5-7 *"... that we might receive the adoption of sons. And because ye are sons, God hath sent forth the Spirit of His Son into your hearts, crying, Abba, Father. Wherefore thou art no more a servant, but a son; and if a son, then an heir of God through Christ."*
Gal. 4:31 *"... we are children of the free* (woman)... (New Jerusalem)*"*
Eph. 1:5 *"Having predestinated us unto the adoption of children by Jesus Christ to Himself, according to the good pleasure of His will... He hath made us accepted in the beloved."*
Eph. 3:6 *"... He hath made us accepted in the Beloved."*
I Jn. 3:1 *"Behold, what manner of love the Father hath bestowed on us, that we should be called the sons of God."*
Rev. 21:7 *"He that overcometh shall inherit all things; and I will be his God, and he shall be my son."*

Afraid/Fear

Ex. 23:27 *"I will send My fear before thee..."*
Lev. 26 None shall make you afraid
Judges 6:23 *"And the Lord said unto him* (Gideon), *Peace be unto thee; fear not: thou shalt not die."*
Deut. 7:18,21,24 *"... thou shalt not be afraid of them: but shalt well remember what the Lord thy God did... so shall the Lord thy God do unto all the people of whom thou art afraid... thou shalt not be affrighted at them: for the Lord thy God is among you, a mighty God and terrible... there shall no man be able to stand before thee..."*

Deut. 31:6 *"Be strong and of a good courage, fear not, nor be afraid of them: for the Lord thy God, He it is that doth go with thee; He will not fail thee, nor forsake thee."*
Josh. 10:8 *"... fear them not: for I have delivered them into thine hand; there shall not a man of them stand before thee."*
Josh. 10:25 *"... fear not, nor be dismayed, be strong and of good courage: for thus shall the Lord do to all your enemies against whom ye fight."*
I Sam. 11:7 *"... the fear of the Lord fell on the people..."*
II Chron. 17:10 *"And the fear of the Lord fell upon all the kingdoms of the lands that were round about Judah, so that they made no war..."*
Job 5:22 *"... neither shalt thou be afraid of the beasts of the earth... and the beasts of the field shall be at peace with thee."*
Ps. 3:6-8 *"I will not be afraid of ten thousands of people, that have set themselves against me round about. Arise, O Lord; save me, O my God: for Thou hast smitten all mine enemies upon the cheek bone; Thou hast broken the teeth of the ungodly. Salvation belongeth unto the Lord: Thy blessing is upon Thy people. Selah."*
Ps. 23:4 *"I will fear no evil for Thou art with me."*
Ps. 27:1,3 *"A Psalm of David. The Lord is my light and my Salvation; whom shall I fear? The Lord is the strength of my life; of whom shall I be afraid... though an host should encamp against me, my heart shall not fear: though war should rise against me in this will I be confident."*
Ps. 31:19 *"... how great is Thy goodness... laid up for them that fear thee..."*
Ps. 33:18 *"Behold, the eye of the Lord is upon them that fear Him..."*
Ps. 46:1-3 *"... God is our refuge and strength, a very present help in trouble. Therefore will not we fear, though the earth be removed, and... the mountains be carried into the midst of the sea though the waters thereof roar and be troubled, though the mountains shake with the swelling..."*
Ps. 49:5 PB *"... I will not fear in the days of evil..."*
Ps. 56:3 *"What time I am afraid, I will trust in Thee."*
Ps. 103:13 *"... the Lord pitieth them that fear Him."*
Ps. 112:7,8 *"He shall not be afraid of evil tidings: his heart is fixed, trusting in the Lord. His heart is established, he shall not be afraid..."*
Ps. 118:4,6 *"Let them... that fear the Lord say, that His mercy endureth forever... the Lord is on my side; I will not fear: what can man do unto me?"*
Is. 17:2 *"... and none shall make them afraid."*
Is. 35:4-6 *"Say to them that are of a fearful heart, be strong, fear not: behold, your God will come with vengeance. Even God with a recompence: He will come and save you..."*
Is. 41:10 *"Fear thou not; for I am with thee..."*

Is. 43:3,5 *"For I am the Lord thy God, the Holy One of Israel, thy Saviour... fear not: for I am with thee..."*
Ez. 34:28 *"... they shall dwell safely, and none shall make them afraid."*
Matt. 8:26 *"Why are you fearful, O ye of little faith."*
The promise is that if you have faith, you don't need to be afraid.
Matt. 14:27 *"... be of good cheer; it is I; be not afraid."*
Jn. 14:27 *"Peace I leave with you, My peace I give unto you: not as the world giveth, give I unto you. Let not your heart be troubled, neither let it be afraid."*

Affliction

Affliction Gr. #6869 means, *"Adversary, adversity, anguish, distress, tribulation, trouble"*
Affliction in the Dict. means, *"Anything that causes great suffering, a state of pain, distress, or grief"*
Synonyms, *"adversity, ailment, complaint, disorder, disease, handicap, illness, indisposition, malady, misery, sorrow, tribulation, trouble, woe"*
Gen. 16:11 *"... the Lord hath heard my affliction."*
Gen. 29:32 *"... surely the Lord hath looked upon my affliction."*
Gen. 31:42 *"... God hath seen my affliction..."*
Gen. 41:52 *"... God hath caused me to be fruitful in the land of my affliction."*
Ex. 4:31 *"And the people believed: and when they heard that the Lord had visited the children of Israel, and that He had looked upon their affliction, then they bowed their heads and worshipped."*
Deut. 26:7 *"... when we cried unto the Lord God of our fathers, the Lord heard our voice, and looked on our affliction, and our labour, and our oppression..."*
II Kings 14:26 *"... the Lord saw the affliction of Israel... it was very bitter: for (there was not) any helper for Israel... He saved them..."*
II Kings 14:26 NLT *"For the Lord saw the bitter suffering of everyone in Israel, and how they had absolutely no one to help them."*
Neh. 9:7 *"Thou art the Lord... who didst choose Abram... and found his heart faithful before Thee... and didst see the affliction of our fathers in Egypt, and heardest their cry... and shewedst signs and wonders... for Thou knewest that they dealt proudly against them."*
Job 36:15 *"He delivereth the poor in his affliction, and openeth their ears in oppression.*
Job 36:15 NLT *"But by means of their suffering, He rescues those who suffer. For He gets their attention through adversity."*

Ps. 106:44 "... *He regarded their affliction, when He heard their cry...*"
Ps. 113:4 "*The Lord is high above all nations... His glory above the heavens.*"
Ps. 117:1 "*O praise the Lord, all ye nations: praise Him, all ye people.*"
Ps. 129:2,4 "*Many a time have they afflicted me from my youth: yet they have not prevailed against me...*"
Is. 48:10 "*... I have chosen thee in the furnace of affliction.*"
Is. 48:10 NLT "*I have refined you in the furnace of suffering. I will rescue you...*"
Is. 63:9 "*In all their affliction He was afflicted, and the angel of His presence saved them: in His love and in His pity He Redeemed them...*"
Is. 63:9 NLT " *In all their suffering He also suffered, and He personally rescued them... He carried them through all the years.*"
Jer. 16:19 "*Lord, my strength... my fortress... my refuge in the day of affliction...*"
Nah. 1:9 "*... He (God) will make an utter end: affliction (because of sin) shall not rise up the second time.*"
Acts 7:10 About Joseph "*... God was with him, and delivered him out of all his afflictions, and gave him favour and wisdom...*"
Acts 7:34 "*... I have seen the affliction of My people... I have heard their groaning, and Am come down to deliver them...*"
II Cor. 4:17 "*For our light affliction, which is but for a moment, worketh for us a far more exceeding and eternal weight of glory...*"
II Cor. 4:17 NIV "*For our light and momentary troubles are achieving for us an eternal glory that far outweighs them all ("beyond all comparison" NASB).*"

All / Every / Whole

Gen. 12:1-3 "*Now the Lord had said unto Abram... in thee shall all families of the earth be blessed.*"
Gen. 22:18;26:4 "*In thy seed shall all the naions of the earth be blessed...*"
Num. 14:21 "*... all the earth shall be filled with the glory of the Lord.*"
Num. 21:34 "*... fear him not: for I have delivered him into thy hand, and all his people, and his land...*"
Deut. 14:2 "*... the Lord has chosen thee... above all nations.*"
I Chron. 29:12 "*Both riches and honour come of Thee, and Thou reignest over all; and in Thine hand is power and might; and in Thine hand it is to make great, and to give strength unto all.*"
Ps. 34:19 "*Many are the afflictions of the righteous: but the Lord delivereth him out of them all.*"

Ps. 65:2 *"O Thou that hearest prayer, unto Thee shall all flesh come."*
Ps. 66:4 *"All the earth shall worship Thee, and shall sing unto Thee ..."*
Ps. 67:2 *"That Thy way may be known upon the earth Thy saving health among all nations."*
Ps. 67:7 *"God shall bless us; and all the ends of the earth shall fear Him."*
Ps. 82:8 NIV *"... all the nations are Your inheritance."*
Ps. 86:9 *"All nations whom Thou hast made shall come and worship before Thee, O Lord; and shall glorify Thy name."*
Ps. 103:2,3 *"Bless the Lord... who forgiveth all thine iniquities; who healeth all thy diseases..."*
Ps. 103:18 *"To such as keep His Covenant, and to those that remember His Commandments to do them. The Lord hath prepared His throne in the heavens; and His kingdom ruleth over all."*
Ps. 113:4 *"The Lord is high above all nations, and His glory above the heavens."*
Ps. 145:21 *"... let all flesh bless His Holy name forever and ever."*
Ps. 145:9 *"The Lord is good to all: and His tender mercies are over all His works ("all He has made" ESV)."*
Is. 25:6-8 *"And in this mountain shall the Lord of hosts make unto all people a feast... and He will destroy in this mountain the face of the covering cast over all people, and the vail that is spread over all nations ("He will remove the coud of gloom, the shadow of death that hangs over the earth." NLT "the veil of grief covering all people and the mask covering all nations." Heb. #4541 for veil is, " the web that is woven over all the nations" www.biblehub.com). He will swallow up death in victory; and the Lord God will wipe away tears from off all faces (Rev. 21:4); and the rebuke of His people shall He take away from off all the earth: for the Lord hath spoken it."*
Is. 45:25 *"In the Lord shall all the seed of Israel be Justified..."*
Is. 64:8 *"... we all are the work of Thy hand."*
Is. 66:18 *"... I will gather all nations and tongues..."*
Jer. 31:1 I will be the God *"... of all the families of Israel, and they shall be My People."*
Jer. 3:17 *"... they shall call (the New) Jerusalem the throne of the Lord... all... nations shall be gathered unto it, to the name of the Lord, to Jerusalem: neither shall they walk anymore after the imagination of their evil heart."*
Ez. 18:4 *"... all souls are Mine..."*
Ez. 18:4 NIV *"... everyone belongs to Me..."*
Joel 2:28 *"... I will pour out My Spirit upon all flesh..."*
Joel 3:2 *"I will... gather all nations, and will bring them down into the valley of Jehoshaphat, and will plead with them there for My people..."*

Hag. 2:7 "... I will shake all nations, and the desire of all nations (Jesus) shall come.."

Matt. 6:33 BSB "... seek first the kingdom of God and His righteousness, and all these things will be added to you."

Matt. 10:1 "And when He (Jesus) had called unto Him His twelve disciples, He gave them power against unclean spirits, to cast them out, and to heal all manner of sickness and all manner of disease."

Matt. 12:15 "... He healed them all."

Lk. 10:19 "... I give unto you power to tread on serpents and scorpions, and over all the power of the enemy: and nothing shall by any menas hurt you."

Lk. 15:31 NKJV In the parable of the prodical son the father told the good son, "all that I have is yours."

Jn. 1:7 "The same came... to bear witness of the Light, that all men through Him might believe."

Jn. 1:16 "And His fullness have all we received, and grace for grace."

Jn. 6:45 "It is written in the prophets, 'And they shall all be taught of God...'"

Jn. 12:32 "And I, if I be lifted up from the earth, will draw all men unto Me."

Jn. 17:21 "That they all may be one; as Thou, Father, art in Me, and I in Thee, that they also may be one in Us..."

Acts 2:4 HCSB "Then they were all filled with the Holy Spirit and began to speak in different languages, as the Spirit gave them ability for speech."

Acts 2:17 "And it shall come to pass in the last days, saith God, I will pour out of My Spirit upon all flesh..."

Acts 11:14 To Cornelius, "... whereby thou and all thy house shall be saved."

Acts 14:16 "... He did good, and gave us rain from heaven, and fruitful seasons, filling our hearts with food and gladness."

Acts 17:26,27 "And hath made of one blood all nations of men for to dwell on all the face of the earth..."

Acts 17:30,31 "And the times of this ignorance God winked at: but now commandeth all men everywhere to repent... whereof He hath given assurance unto all men in that He hath raised Him from the dead..."

Rom. 4:11 "... that he might be the father of all that believe..."

Rom. 4:16 "Therefore it is of faith, that it might be by grace; to the end the promise might be sure to all the seed... which is of the faith of Abraham; who is the father of us all (who believe)..."

Rom. 5:18 "Therefore as by the offence of one (Adam) Judgment came upon all men to condemnation; even so by the righteousness of one (Jesus) the free gift came upon all men unto Justification of life."

Rom. 8:28 "And we know that all things work together for good to them that love God, to them who are the called according to His purpose."

Rom. 8:32 *"He (the Father in heaven) that spared not His own Son (Jesus), but delivered Him up for us all, how shall He not with Him also freely give us all things?"*
Rom. 9:5 *"... Christ... who is over all. God blessed forever..."*
Rom. 11:26 *"And so all Israel shall be saved: as it is written, There shall come out of Sion the Deliverer, and shall turn away ungodliness from Jacob..."*
Rom. 11:32 *"For God hath concluded them all in unbelief, that He might have mercy upon all."*
Rom. 11:36 *"For of Him, and through Him, and to Him, are all things..."*
Rom. 14:11,12 *"... it is written... every knee shall bow to Me... every tongue shall confess to God... everyone... shall give account of Himself to God."*
Rom. 15:13,14 *"... the God of hope fill you with all joy and peace... that ye may abound in hope, through the power of the Holy Ghost... ye also are full of goodness, filled with all knowledge, able also to admonish one another."*
I Cor. 1:4-7 *"I thank my God always on your behalf, for the grace of God which is given you by Jesus Christ... so that ye come behind in no gift..."*
I Cor. 3:21,22 *"... for all things are yours; whether... things present, or things to come; all are yours; and ye are Christ's; and Christ is God's. Whether... the world, or life... or present, or things to come; all are yours..."*
I Cor. 4:5 *"... then shall every man have praise of God."*
I Cor. 8:1 *"... we know that we all have knowledge..."*
I Cor. 15:22-28 *"... as in Adam all die, even so in Christ shall all be made alive. But every man in his own order... when He shall have put down all rule and all authority and power. For He must reign, till He hath put all enemies under His feet... when all things shall be subdued unto Him, then shall the Son also Himself be subject unto Him* (the Father) *that put all things under Him* (Jesus), *that God may be all in all."*
I Cor. 15:51 *"We shall not all sleep, but we shall all be changed..."*
II Cor. 1:4 *"Who comforteth us in all our tribulations, that we may be able to comfort them which are in any trouble, by the comfort wherewith we ourselves are comforted of God."*
II Cor. 1:20 *"For all the promises of God in Him are yea, and in Him Amen, unto the glory of God by us."*
II Cor. 5:17 *"Therefore if any man be in Christ, he is a new creature: old things are passed away; behold, all things are become new."*
II Cor. 6:10 *"... always(s) rejoicing... making many rich... yet possessing all things."*
II Cor. 7:1 *"Having therefore these promises, dearly beloved, let us cleanse ourselves from all filthiness of the flesh and spirit, perfecting Holiness in the fear of God."*

II Cor. 9:8 *"And God is able to make all grace abound toward you; that ye, always having all sufficiency in all things, may abound to every good work..."*
II Cor. 13:14 *"The grace of the Lord Jesus Christ, and the love of God, and the communion of the Holy Ghost, be with you all. Amen."*
Gal. 3:8 *"God would Justify the heathen through faith... in Thee shall all nations be blessed."*
Gal. 3:26 *"For ye are all the children of God by faith in Christ Jesus."*
Eph. 1:3 *"Blessed be the God and Father of our Lord Jesus Christ, who hath blessed us with all Spiritual blessings in heavenly places in Christ..."*
Eph. 1:10 *"... that He might gather together in one all things in Christ, both which are in heaven, and which are on earth; even in Him..."*
Eph. 1:22 *"And hath put all things under His feet, and gave Him to be the head over all things to the church, which is His body, the fullness of Him that filleth all in all."*
Eph. 3:10 *"To the intent that now unto the principalities and powers in heavenly places might be now by the church the manifold wisdom of God."*
Eph. 3:19 *"And to know the love of Christ, which passeth knowledge, that ye might be filled with all the fullness of God."*
Eph. 3:21 *"Unto Him be glory in the church by Christ Jesus throughout all ages, world without end. Amen."*
Eph. 4:13 *"Till we all come in the unity of the faith, and of the knowledge of the Son of God, unto a perfect man, unto the measure of the stature of the fullness of Christ."*
Eph. 6:16 *"Above all, taking the shield of faith, wherewith ye shall be able to quench all the fiery darts of the wicked."*
Phil. 4:13 *"I can do all things through Christ which strengtheneth me."*
Phil. 4:19 *"But my God shall supply all your need according to His riches in glory by Christ Jesus."*
Col. 1:9-14 *"... we... do not cease to pray for you, and to desire that ye might be filled with the knowledge of His will in all wisdom and Spiritual understanding; that ye might walk worthy of the Lord unto all pleasing, being fruitful to every good work, and increasing in the knowledge of God; strengthened with all might, according to His glorious power, unto all patience and longsuffering with joyfulness; giving thanks unto the Father, which hath made us meet to be partakers of the inheritance of the saints in light: who hath delivered us from the power of darkness, and hath translated us into the kingdom of His dear Son: in whom we have Redemption through His blood, even the forgiveness of sins..."*
Col. 1:18 *"And He is the head of the body, the church: who is the beginning, the firstborn from the dead; that in all things He might have preeminence."*

Col. 1:20 "... *having made peace through the blood of His cross, by Him to reconcile all things unto Himself...*"
Col. 1:28 "... *teaching every man in all wisdom; that we may present every man perfect in Christ Jesus...*"
Col. 2:2,3 "*That their hearts might be comforted... unto all riches of the full assurance of understanding... and of Christ; in whom are hid all the treasures of wisdom and knowledge.*"
Col. 2:13 "... *having forgiven all your trespasses.*"
Col. 3:11 "... *Christ is all, and in all.*"
Col. 3:16 "*Let the word of Christ dwell in you richly in all wisdom...*"
Col. 4:12 "... *Epaphras... that ye may stand perfect and complete in all the will of God.*"
I Thess. 3:12,13 "*And the Lord make you to increase and abound in love one toward another, and toward all men, even as we do toward you: to the end He may stablish your hearts unblameable in Holiness before God, even our Father, at the coming of our Lord Jesus Christ wth all His saints.*"
I Thess. 4:6 "... *the Lord is the avenger of all such...*"
I Thess. 5:4,5 "*But you brethren, are not in darkness... ye are all the children of light* (who are in Christ Jesus)*...*"
II Thess. 3:16 "*Now the Lord of peace Himself give you peace always by all means. The Lord be with you all.*"
I Tim. 1:16 Paul said, "... *I obtained mercy, that in me first Jesus Christ might shew forth all longsuffering, for a pattern to them which should hereafter believe on Him to life everlasting.*"
I Tim. 2:4 "*Who will have all men to be saved, and to come unto the knowledge of the truth.*"
I Tim. 2:6 "*Who gave Himself a ransom for all...*"
I Tim. 3:15 "*But if I tarry long, that thou mayest know how thou oughtest to behave thyself in the house of God, which is the church of the living God, the pillar and ground of the truth.*"
I Tim. 4:8 "... *godliness is profitable unto all things, having promise of the life that now is, and of that which is to come.*"
I Tim. 4:10 "*For therefore we both labour and suffer reproach, because we trust in the living God, who is the Saviour of all men, specially of those that believe.*"
I Tim. 6:17 "... *the living God, who giveth us richly all things to enjoy.*"
II Tim. 3:11 "*Persecutions, afflictions, which came to me at Antioch... what persecutions I endured: but out of them all the Lord delivered me* (Paul)*.*"
II Tim. 3:16,17 "*All Scripture is given by inspiration of God, and is profitable for doctrine, for reproof, for correction, for instruction in righteousness: that the man of God may be perfect, thoroughly furnished unto all good works.*"

II Tim. 4:8 *"Henceforth there is laid up for me a crown of righteousness, which the Lord, the righteous Judge, shall give me at that day: and not to me only, but unto all them also that love His appearing."*
Titus 2:11 *"... grace of God that bringeth Salvation hath appeared to all men..."*
Titus 2:14 *"Who gave Himself for us, that He might Redeem us from all iniquity, and purify unto Himself a peculiar people, zealous of good works."*
Heb. 1:14 *"Are they not all ministering spirits, sent forth to minister for them who shall be heirs of Salvation?"*
Heb. 5:9 *"And being made perfect, He became the author of eternal Salvation unto all them that obey Him..."*
Heb. 8:11 *"... all shall know Me from the least to the greatest."* (On the New Earth).
Heb. 10:10 *"... we are Sanctified through the offering of the body of Jesus Christ once for all."*
Heb. 11:13 *"These all died in faith, not having received the promises, but having see them afar off, and were persuaded of them, and embraced them ..."*
Jms. 1:5 *"If any of you lack wisdom, let him ask of God, that giveth to all men liberally, and upbraideth not; and it shall be given him."*
I Pet. 5:7 *"Casting all your care upon Him; for He careth for you."*
II Pet. 3:9 *"The Lord is not slack concerning His promise... is longsuffering... not willing that any should perish, but that all should come to repentance."*
I Jn. 1:5 *"... God is light, and in Him is no darkness at all."*
I Jn. 1:7 *"if we walk in the light, as He is in the light, we have fellowship one with another, and the blood of Jesus Christ His Son cleanseth us from all sin."*
I Jn. 1:9 *"If we confess our sins, He is faithful and just to forgive us our sins, and to cleanse us from all unrighteousness."*
I Jn. 2:1,2 *"... these things write I unto you, that ye sin not... if any man sin, we have an advocate with the Father, Jesus Christ the righteous... He is the propitiation for our sins... (and) also for the sins of the whole world."*
I Jn. 2:20 *"But ye have an unction from the Holy One, and ye know all things."*
I Jn. 2:27 *"But the anointing which ye have received of Him abideth in you, and ye need not that any man teach you: but as the same anointing teacheth you of all things, and is truth, and is no lie, and even as it hath taught you, ye shall abide in Him."*
III Jn. 2 *"Beloved, I wish above all things that thou mayest prosper and be in health, even as thy soul prospereth."*
Rev. 7:17 *"For the Lamb which is in the midst of the throne shall feed them, and shall lead them unto living fountains of waters: and God shall wipe away all tears from their eyes."* (On the New Earth)

Rev. 15:4 "*Who shall not fear Thee, O Lord, and glorify Thy name? for Thou only art Holy: for all nations shall come and worship before Thee; for Thy Judgments are made manifest.*"
Rev. 21:4 "*And God shall wipe away all tears from their eyes; and there shall be no more death, neither sorrow, nor crying, neither shall there by anymore pain: for the former things are passed away.*" (On the New Earth)
Rev. 21:5 "*And He that sat upon the throne said, Behold, I make all things new...*" (On the New Earth)
Rev. 21:7 "*He that overcometh shall inherit all things; and I will be his God, and he shall be My son.*"

Angel (s) / Cherubs

Ex. 23:23 "*My angel will go before you...*"
Num. 20:16 "*And when we cried unto the Lord, He heard our voice, and sent an angel, and hath brough us forth...*"
Ps. 8:6 "*What is man, that Thou art mindful of him: and the son of man, that Thou visitest him? For Thou hast made him a little lower than the angels, and hast crowned him with glory and honour ...*"
(At the Resurrection we will be equal to angels, Lk.20:36; we will Judge fallen angels, I Cor.6:3; Jesus is greater than angels, Heb.1:4;2:9)
Ps. 18:6,10 "*... the Lord... and He rode upon a cherub and did fly: yea, He did fly upon the wings of the wind.*"
Ps. 55:18 "*He hath delivered my soul in peace from the battle that was against me; for there were many* (angels) *with me.*"
Ps. 91:11,12 "*For He shall give His angels charge over thee, to keep thee in all thy ways. They shall bear thee up in their hands, lest thou dash thy foot against a stone.*"
Ps. 103:20 "*Bless the Lord, ye His angels, that excel in strength, that do His Commandments, hearkening unto the voice of His Word.*"
Ps. 104:4 (Heb. 1:7) "*Who maketh His angels spirits; His minsters a flaming fire...*"
Is. 37:36 "*Then the angel of the Lord went forth, and smote* (killed) *in the camp of the Assyrians (185,000).*"
If one angel can kill 185,000, then we know that God can take care of us.
Matt. 4:6 "*... He shall give His angels charge concerning thee... in their hands they shall bear thee up, lest at any time thou dash thy foot against a stone.*"
Matt. 18:10 "*Take heed that ye despise not one of these little ones; for I say unto you, that in heaven their angels do always behold the face of My Father which is in heaven.*"

Lk. 4:10,11 "*For it is written, He shall give His angels charge over thee, to keep thee: and in their hands they shall bear thee up, lest at any time thou dash thy foot against a stone.*" (Quoting from Ps. 91:11,12)

Lk. 15:10 "*... there is joy in the presence of the angels of God over one sinner that repenteth.*"

Acts 5:19 "*But the angel of the Lord by night opened the prison doors, and brought them* (Peter and Apostles) *forth...*"

Acts 12:7-11 "*... the angel of the Lord came upon him, and a light shined in the prison: and he smote Peter on the side, and raised him up, saying, Arise up quickly. And his chains fell off from his hands. And the angel said unto him... follow me...* (he) *thought he saw a vision... when Peter was come to himself, he said, Now I know of a surety, that the Lord hath sent His angel, and hath delivered me...*"

Rom. 8:38,39 "*For I am persuaded, that neither death, nor life, nor angels, nor principalities, nor powers, nor things present, nor things to come, nor height, nor depth, nor any other creature, shall be able to separate us from the love of God, which is in Christ Jesus our Lord.*"

Heb. 1:13,14 "*... angels... are they not all ministering spirits sent* (by God) *to minister for them who shall be heirs of Salvation.*"

Anger / Hate / Wrath

Lev. 19:17,18 "*Thou shalt not hate thy brother in thine heart... thou shalt not avenge, nor bear any grudge... but thou shalt love thy neighbor as thyself: I am the Lord.*"

Neh. 9:17 "*... but Thou art a God ready to pardon, gracious and merciful, slow to anger, and of great kindness, and forsookest them not.*

Ps. 4:4 NIV "*In your anger do not sin; when you are on your beds, search your hearts and be silent.*"

(Ps. 4:4 NLT "*Don't sin by letting anger gain control over you. Think about it overnight and remain silent.*"

Ps. 37:8,9 "*Cease from anger, and forsake wrath: fret not thyself in any wise to do evil. For evildoers shall be cut off: but those that wait upon the Lord, they shall inherit the earth... the meek shall inherit the earth; and shall delight themselves in the abundance of peace.*"

Ps. 78:38 "*But He, being full of compassion, forgave their iniquity, and destroyed them not: yea, many a time turned He His anger away, and did not stir up all His wrath.*"

When we think of how many times God has forgiven us and turned His wrath away from us, then we should do the same for others. Remember the

parable of the man who was forgiven much but did not forgive others in Matt. 18:21-35.
Ps. 85:3 *"Thou hast taken away all Thy wrath: Thou hast turned Thyself from the fierceness of Thine anger."*
Ps. 103:8 *"The Lord is merciful and gracious, slow to anger, and plenteous in mercy."*
Ps. 145:8 *"The Lord is gracious, and full of compassion; slow to anger, and of great mercy."*
Prov. 14:17 *"He that is soon angry dealeth foolishly: and a man of wicked devices is hated."*
(Prov. 14:17 NLT *"Those who are short-tempered do foolish things, and schemers are hated."*
Prov. 14:29 *"He that is slow to wrath is of great understanding: but he that is hasty of spirit exalteth folly."*
(Prov. 14:29 NIV *"A patient man has great understanding, but a quick-tempered man displays folly."*
(Prov. 14:29 NASB *"He who is slow to anger has great understanding..."*
Prov. 15:1 *"A soft ("gentle") answer turneth away wrath..."*
Prov. 16:32 *"He that is slow to anger is better than the mighty; and he that ruleth his spirit than he that taketh a city."*
Prov. 19:11 *"The discretion of a man deferreth his anger; and it is his glory to pass over a transgression."*
(Prov. 19:11 NIV *"A man's wisdom gives him patience; it is to his glory to overlook an offense."*
(Prov. 19:11 NLT *"People with good sense restrain their anger; they earn esteem by overlooking wrongs."*
Eccl. 7:9 *"Be not hasty in thy spirit to be angry: for anger resteth in the bosom of fools."*
(Eccl. 7:9 NLT *"Don't be quick-tempered, for anger is the friend of fools."*
Is. 12:1 *"... in that day thou shalt say... Lord, I will praise Thee: though Thou wast angry with me, Thine anger is turned away, and Thou comfortedst me."*
Is. 54:9 *"... I (have) sworn that I would not be wroth with... (or) rebuke thee."*
Hosea 14:4 *"I will heal their backsliding ("waywardness" NIV), I will love them freely: for Mine anger is turned away from him."*
Joel 2:13 *"... rend your heart, and not your garments... turn unto the Lord your God: for He is gracious... merciful, slow to anger... of great kindness, and repenteth Him of the evil."*
(Joel 2:13 NLT *"eager to relent and not punish"*
Jonah 3:9 *"Who can tell if God will turn and repent, ("relent" NIV; "change His mind" NLT) and turn away from His fierce anger, that we perish not?"*

Jonah 4:2 Jonah said, "... *for I knew that Thou art a gracious God, and merciful, slow to anger, and of great kindness, and repentest Thee of the evil.*"
(Jonah 4:2 ISV A God who is "... *reluctant to send trouble...*"
Mic. 7:18 "*Who is a God like unto Thee, that pardoneth iniquity, and passeth by the transgression of the remnant of His heritage? He retaineth not His anger forever, because He delighteth in mercy.*"
Nah. 1:3 "*The Lord is slow to anger, and great in power...*"
Zeph. 2:3 "*Seek ye the Lord, all ye meek of the earth, which have wrought His Judgment; seek righteousness, seek meekness: it may be ye shall be hid in the day of the Lord's anger.*"
(Zeph. 2:3 NIV "... *all you humble of the land, you who do what He commands... seek humility; perhaps you will be sheltered...*"
Matt. 5:22 "... *but I say unto you, That whosoever is angry with his brother without a cause shall be in danger of the Judgment...*"
(Matt. 5:22 NLT "... *if you call someone an idiot, you are in danger of... the high council... if you curse someone, you are in danger of the fires of hell.*"
Lk. 6:24-38 "*But I say unto you which hear, Love your enemies, do good to them which hate you, bless them that curse you, and pray for them which despitefully use you. And unto him that smiteth thee on the one cheek offer also the other; and him that taketh away thy cloke forbid not to take thy coat also... and as ye would that men should do to you, do ye also to them likewise. For if ye love them which love you, what thank have ye? For sinners also love those that love them. And if ye do good to them which do good to you, what thank have ye? For sinners also do even the same.... but love ye your enemies, and do good... hoping for nothing again; and your reward shall be great, and ye shall be the children of the Highest: for He is kind unto the unthankful and to the evil. Be ye therefore merciful, as your Father also is merciful... for with the same measure that ye meteth withal it shall be measured to you again.*"
Rom. 5:9 "*Much more then, being now Justified by His* (Jesus') *blood, we shall be saved from wrath through Him.*"
Rom. 12:17-19 "*Recompense to no man evil for evil. Provide things honest in the sight of all men. If it be possible, as much as lieth in you, live peaceably with all men... avenge not yourselves, but rather give place unto wrath* ("... *leave room for God's wrath...*" NIV): *for it is written, Vengeance is Mine; I will repay, saith the Lord.*"
(Rom. 12:7-19 NLT "*Never pay back evil for evil to anyone. Do things in such a way that everyone can see you are honorable. Do your part to live in peace with everyone, as much as possible... never avenge yourselves. Leave that to God... I will repay those who deserve it, says the Lord.*"

(Rom. 12:19-20 NIV *"Do not take revenge... but leave room for God's wrath, for it is written: "It is mine to avenge; I will repay," says the Lord. On the contrary: If your enemy is hungry, feed him; if he is thirsty, give him something to drink. In doing this, you will heap burning coals on his head."*
Rom. 12:21 *"Do not be overcome by evil, but overcome evil with good."*
Eph. 4:26 *"Be ye angry, and sin not: let not the sun go down upon your wrath: neither give place to the devil."*
(Eph. 4:26 NLT *"And don't sin by letting anger gain control over you. Don't let the sun go down while you are still angry, for anger gives a mighty foothold to the Devil."*
Eph. 4:31,32 *"Let all bitterness, and wrath, and anger, and clamour, and evil speaking, be put away from you, with all malice: and be ye kind ("compasssionate" NIV) one to another, tenderhearted, forgiving one another, even as God for Christ's sake hath forgiven you."*
(Eph. 4:31 NIV *"Get rid of all bitterness, rage and anger, brawling and slander, along with every form of malice."*
Col. 3:8 *"But now you also put off all these; anger, wrath, malice, blasphemy, filthy communication ("abusive speech" NASB) out of your mouth... seeing that ye have put off the old man with his deeds; and have put on the new man, which is renewed in knowledge after the image of Him that created him..."*
I Thess. 1:10 *"... Jesus, which delivered us from the wrath to come."*
I Thess. 5:9 *"God hath not appointed us to wrath, but to obtain Salvation..."*
II Tim. 2:23,24 *"foolish and unlearned questions avoid... they do gender strifes... the servant of the Lord must not strive; but be gentle... apt to teach, patient, in meekness instructing those that oppose themselves..."*
(II Tim. 2:23 NIV *"Don't have anything to do with foolish and stupid arguments, because you know they produce quarrels. And the Lord's servant must not quarrel; instead, he must be kind to everyone... not resentful..."*
(II Tim. 2:23 NLT *"... they must... be patient with difficult people."*
(II Tim. 2:23 NASB *"... patient when wronged..."*
Heb. 10:30 *"For we know Him that hath said, Vengeance belongeth unto Me, I will recompense, saith the Lord. And... shall Judge (My) people."*
Jms. 1:19,20 *"... let every man be swift to hear, slow to speak, slow to wrath: for the wrath of man worketh not the righteousness of God."*
(Jms. 1:19 NIV *"... slow to become angry..."*
(Jms. 1:20 NLT *"Your anger can never make things right in God's sight."*
I Pet. 3:8-14 NASB *"... be harmonious, sympathetic, brotherly, kindhearted... humble in spirit; not returning evil for evil or insult for insult... giving a blessing instead; for you were called for the... purpose that you might inherit a blessing. For, 'the one who desires life, to love and see good days, must*

keep his tongue from evil and his lips from speaking deceit. He must turn away from evil and do good; he must seek peace and pursue it. For the eyes of the Lord are toward the righteous, and His ears attend to their prayer... even if you should suffer for the sake of righteousness, you are blessed... do not fear their intimidation... do not be troubled..."

Answer / Hear / Receive

I Sam. 7:9 "... Samuel cried unto the Lord for Israel; and the Lord heard him."
Job 14:15 NKJV "You shall call and I will answer you..."
Job 22:27 "Thou shalt make thy prayer unto Him, and He shall hear thee..."
Ps. 4:3 "... the Lord will hear when I call unto Him."
Ps. 6:8 UKJV "The Lord heard the voice of my weeping"
Ps. 10:17 "Lord, Thou hast heard the desire of the humble... Thou wilt cause Thine ear to hear..."
Ps. 15:29 "... He heareth the prayer of the righteous."
Ps. 34:15,17,18 "The eyes of the Lord are upon the righteous, and His ears are open unto their cry. The righteous cry, and the Lord heareth, and delivereth them out of all their troubles. The Lord is nigh unto them that are of a broken heart; and saveth such as be of a contrite spirit."
Ps. 37:4,5 "... He shall give thee the desires of thine heart... commit thy way unto the Lord: trust also in Him and He shall bring it to pass."
Ps. 38:15 "... Thou wilt hear, O Lord my God. For I said, Hear me, lest otherwise they should rejoice over me..."
Ps. 40:1 "I waited patiently for the Lord... He... heard my cry."
Ps. 55:19 "God shall hear (when you pray)..."
Ps. 65:5 NIV "You answer us with awesome deeds of righteousness, O God..."
Ps. 66:18-20 "If I regard iniquity in my heart, the Lord will not hear me: but verily God hath heard me; He hath attended to the voice of my prayer. Blessed be God, which hath not turned away my prayer. Nor His mercy...."
Ps. 69:33 "For the Lord heareth the poor..."
Ps. 86:7 "In the day of my trouble I will call upon thee... Thou wilt answer..."
Ps. 91:15,16 "He shall call upon Me... I will answer him; and be with him in trouble..."
Ps. 94:9 "He that planted (created) the ear, shall He not hear..."
Ps. 116:1,2 "I love the Lord, because He hath heard my voice and my supplications. Because He hath inclined His ear unto me, therefore will I call upon Him as long as I live."
Ps. 118:5 "I called upon the Lord in distress: the Lord answered me, and set me in a large place."

Ps. 145:18,19 *"The Lord is nigh unto all them that call upon Him, to all that call upon Him in truth. He will fulfil the desire of them that fear Him: He also will hear their cry and save them."*
Prov. 15:29 *"The Lord is far from the wicked: but He heareth the prayer of the righteous."*
Is. 30:19 *"... He will be very gracious unto thee at the voice of thy cry; when He shall hear it, He will answer thee."*
Is. 49:8 *"Thus saith the Lord, In an acceptable time have I heard thee..."*
Is. 50:2-5 *"... when I called, was there none to answer? Is My hand shortened at all, that it cannot Redeem? or have I no power to deliver? Behold, at My rebuke I dry up the sea, I make the rivers a wilderness..."*
Is. 58:9 *"Then shalt thou call, and the Lord shall answer... and... shall say, Here I am..."*
Is. 65:24 *"... before they call, I will answer; and while they are yet speaking, I will hear."*
Jer. 29:11,12 *"Then shall ye call upon Me, and ye shall go and pray unto Me, and I will hearken unto you. And ye shall seek Me, and find Me, when ye shall search for me with all your heart... I will be found of you, saith the Lord: and I will turn away your captivity..."*
Jer. 33:3 *"... call unto Me, and I will answer thee, and shew thee great and mighty things, which thou knowest not."*
Hosea 2:21 *"And it shall come to pass in that day, I will hear, saith the Lord..."*
Zech. 10:6 *"... for I am the Lord their God, and will hear them."*
Zech. 13:9 *"... they shall call on My name, and I will hear them: I will say, It is My people: and they shall say, The Lord is my God."*
Mal. 3:16 *"Then they that feared the Lord spake often one to another: and the Lord hearkened, and heard it, and a Book of Remembrance was written before Him for them that feared the Lord, and that thought upon His name."*
Mal. 13:9 *"... they shall call on My name, and I will hear them..."*
Lk. 1:13 *"the angel said unto him, Fear not, Zacharias: for thy prayer is heard*
I Pet. 3:12 *"... the eyes of the Lord are over the righteous... His ears are open unto their prayers..."*

Anxiety

Ps. 94:19 NAS *"When I worried (Heb. #8312 "thoughts, disquieting thoughts, anxious thoughts (and) doubts, secrets") about many things, Your assuring Words soothed my soul."*
(Ps. 94:19 NLT, ESV *"... know my anxious thoughts."*

(Ps. 94:19 NIV *"When anxiety was great within me, Your consolation brought me joy ("multiply within me" NASB)."*
(Ps. 94:19 *"... Thy comforts delight my soul..."*
(Ps. 94:19 ISV *"When my anxious inner thoughts become overwhelming, Your comfort encourages me."*
(Ps. 94:19 Net Bible *"When worries threaten to overwhelm me, Your soothing touch makes me happy."*
Ps. 139:23 NKJV *"Search me, O God, and know my heart. Try me and know my anxieties."*
Matt. 6:25 *"Therefore I say unto you, Take no thought for your life, what ye shall eat, or what ye shall drink; nor yet for your body, what ye shall put on. Is not the life more than meat, and the body than raiment? Behold the fowls of the air: for they sow not, neither do they reap, nor gather in to barns; yet your heavenly Father feedeth them. Are ye not much better than they? Which of you by taking thought can add one cubit unto his stature? And why take ye thought for raiment? Consider the lilies of the field, how they grow; they toil not, neither do they spin: and... even Solomon in all His glory was not arrayed like one of these... if God so clothe the grass of the field, which today is, and tomorrow is cast into the oven, shall He not much more clothe you, O ye of little faith? Therefore take no thought, saying, What shall we eat? or, What shall we drink? or, Wherewithal shall we be clothed? (For after all these things do the Gentiles seek): for your heavenly Father knoweth that ye have need of all these things. But seek ye first the kingdom of God, and His righteousness; and all these things shall be added unto you."*

Ashamed

Is. 49:23 *"... for they shall not be ashamed that wait for Me."*
Joel 2:26 *"... God, that hath dealt wonderously with you... shall never be ashamed."*

Ask / Cry / Pray

I Sam. 1:17 *"... go in peace: and the God of Israel grant thee thy petition that thou hast asked of Him."*
II Chron. 1:7 God said to Solomon *"... ask what I shall give thee... let Thy promise unto David my father be established ..."*
Job 6:8 *"Oh that I might have my request; and that God would grant me the thing that I long for!"*

Ps. 21:2 *"Thou hast given him his heart's desire, and hast not withholden the request of his lips..."*
Ps. 56:9 *"When I cry unto Thee, then shall mine enemies turn back: this I know; for God is for me."*
Matt. 7:7,11 *"Ask, and it shall be given you... or what man is there of you, whom if his son ask bread, will he give him a stone? Or if he ask a fish, will he give him a serpent? If ye then, being evil, know how to give good gifts unto your children, how much more shall your Father which is in heaven give good things to them that ask Him?"*
Matt. 21:22 *"... all things, whatsoever ye shall ask in prayer, believing, ye shall receive."*
Lk. 11:9-13 *"And I say unto you, Ask, and it shall be given you... for everyone that asketh receiveth... if a son shall ask bread of any of you that is a father, will he give him a stone? Or if he ask a fish, will he... give him a serpent? Or if he shall ask an egg, will he offer him a scorpion? If ye then, being evil, know how to give good gifts unto your children: how much more shall your heavenly Father give the Holy Spirit to them that ask Him?"*
Jn. 11:22 Martha to Jesus *"But I know, that even now, whatsoever thou wilt ask of God, God will give it thee."*
Jn. 14:13,14 *"... whatsoever ye shall ask in My name, that will I do, that the Father may be glorified... If ye shall ask anything in My name, I will do it."*
Jn. 15:7 *"If ye abide in Me and My Words abide in you, ye shall ask what ye will, and it shall be done unto you."*
Jn. 15:16 *"... that whatsoever ye shall ask of the Father in My name, He may give it* (to) *you."*
Jn. 16:24-27 *"... ask, and ye shall receive, that your joy may be full... at that day ye shall ask in My name... and I say not unto you, that I will pray the Father for you: for the Father Himself loveth you..."*
Eph. 3:20 *"Now unto Him that is able to do exceeding abundantly above all that we ask or think, according to the power that worketh in us..."*
Phil. 4:9 *"Be careful for nothing: but in everything by prayer and supplication with thanksgiving let your requests be made known unto God. And the God of peace shall be with you."*
Jms. 4:2,3 *"... ye have not, because ye ask not. Ye ask, and receive not, because ye ask amiss, that ye may consume it upon your lusts."*
I Jn. 3:22 *"And whatsoever we ask, we receive of Him, because we keep His Commandments, and do those things that are pleasing in His sight."*
I Jn. 5:14,15 *"... this is the confidence that we have in Him, that, if we ask anything according to His will, He heareth us... if we know that He hear us... we know that we have the petitions that we desired of Him."*

Baptize / Baptism

The promise is that when we are baptized, our sins are removed; and that God will baptize us with the Holy Spirit if we ask. The word *"baptize"* comes from the Greek word, #907 *"baptizo"* which means, *"immerse; submerse; literally dip under"* (taken from www.biblehub.com).

Matt. 28:18,20 *"And Jesus came and spake unto them, saying, All power is given unto Me in heaven and in earth. Go ye therefore, and teach all nations, baptizing them in the name of the Father... Son, and... Holy Ghost: teaching them to observe all things whatsoever I have commanded you: and lo, I am with you always, even unto the end of the world..."*

Mk. 1:4 John *"... the baptism of repentance for the remission of sins."*

Mk. 1:8 John said, *"I indeed have baptized you with water: but He shall baptize you with the Holy Ghost... and straightway coming up out of the water, he saw the heavens opened, and the Spirit like a dove descending upon Him (Jesus)..."*

Lk. 3:3 *"... the baptism of repentance for the remission of sins..."*

Lk. 3:16 *"John answered, saying... I indeed baptize you with water; but one mightier than I cometh (Jesus), the latchet of whose shoes I am not worthy to unloose: He shall baptize you with the Holy Ghost and with fire."*

Lk. 3:21,22 *"... when all the people were baptized... Jesus also being baptized, and praying, the heaven was opened. And the Holy Ghost descended in a bodily shape like a dove upon Him, and a voice came from heaven, which said, Thou art My beloved Son; in Thee I am well pleased."*

Jn. 1:33 *"... He that sent me to baptize with water, the same said unto me, Upon Whom thou shalt see the Spirit descending, and remaining on Him, the same is He which baptizeth with the Holy Ghost."*

Jn. 3:3,5-7 *"Jesus... said unto him (Nicodemus), Verily, verily, I say unto thee, Except a man be born again, he cannot see the kingdom of God... except a man be born of water and of the Spirit he cannot enter the kingdom of God... that which is born of the flesh is flesh; and that which is born of the Spirit is Spirit. Marvel not that I said unto thee, Ye must be born again."*

Jn. 3:23 *"... John also was baptizing in Aenon near to Salem, because there was much water there: and they came, and were baptized."*

Acts 1:5 *"... John truly baptized with water; but ye shall be bapized with the Holy Ghost..."*

Acts 2:38,39,41 *"T Peter said unto them, Repent, and be baptized everyone of you in the name of Jesus Christ for the remission of sins, and ye shall receive the gift of the Holy Ghost. For the promise is unto you, and to your* children, and to all that are afar off, even as many as the Lord our God shall call. Then they that gladly received His Word were baptized..."

Acts 8:36-39 "And as they went on their way, they came unto a certain water: and the eunuch said, See, here is water; what doth hinder me to be baptized? And Philip said, If thou believest with all thine heart, thou mayest. And he answerd and said, I believe that Jesus Christ is the Son of God. And he commanded the chariot to stand still: and they went down both into the water, both Philip and the eunuch; and he baptized him. And when they were come up out of the water, the Spirit of the Lord caught away Philip.."

Acts 10:47 "Can any man forbid water, that these should not be baptized, which have received the Holy Ghost as well as we?"

Acts 11:16 "Then rememberd I the Word of the Lord, how that He said, John indeed baptized with water; but ye shall be baptized wth the Holy Ghost."

Because John's baptism was before Jesus' death on the cross and before the outpouring of the Holy Spirit on Pentecost so that they didn't receive the Holy Spirit with John's baptism.

Rom. 6:4 "... we are buried with Him by baptism... like as Christ was raised up from the dead... even so we also should walk in newness of life."

I Cor. 12:13 "For by one Spirit are we all baptized into one body... and have been all made to drink into one Spirit."

Gal. 3:27 "... you (who) have been baptized into Christ have put on Christ."

Eph. 5:25,26 "... Christ also loved the church, and gave Himself for it. That He might Sanctify and cleanse it with the washing of water by the Word..."

Col. 2:12 "Buried with Him in baptism, wherein also ye are risen with Him..."

When you go under the water, it is a symbol of you dying with Christ and when you come up out of the water, it is a symbol of being Resurrected with Him and you receive the Holy Spirit who gives you new life in Christ Jesus. This is part of being born again. Jesus told Nicodemus, You must be born of water and Spirit, Jn. 3:5.

Col. 3:1-3 You are risen with Christ (through baptism).

Titus 3:5 "Not by works of righteousness which we have done, but according to His mercy He saved us, by the washing of regeneration, and renewing of the Holy Ghost..."

Beauty

I Sam. 16:7 "... for the Lord seeth not as man seeth; for man looketh on the outward appearance, but the Lord looketh on the heart."

I Chron. 16:29 ".... worship the Lord in the beauty of Holiness."

Ps. 27:4 "One thing have I desired... to behold the beauty of the Lord..."

Ps. 29:2 *"... worship the Lord in the beauty of Holiness."*
Ps. 50:2 *"Out of Zion, the perfection of beauty..."*
Ps. 90:17 *"... let the beauty of the Lord our God be upon us..."*
Ps. 96:9 *"O worship the Lord in the beauty of Holiness.."*
Ps. 149:4 *"For the Lord taketh pleasure in His people: He will beautify the meek ("humble" NKJV) with Salvation."*
Song of Solomon 7:1 *"How beautiful are thy feet with shoes, O prince's daughter..."*
Prov. 20:29 *"The glory of young men is their strength: and the beauty of old men is the gray head."*
Prov. 31:30 *"Favour is deceitful, and beauty is vain: but a woman that feareth the Lord, she shall be praised."*
Eccl. 3:11 *"He hath made everything beautiful in His time..."*
Is. 4:2 *"In that day shall the branch of the Lord (Jesus) be beautiful and glorious, and the fruit of the earth shall be excellent and comely..."*
Is. 28:5 *"In that day shall the Lord of hosts be for a crown of glory, and for a diadem of beauty..."*
Is. 33:17 *"Thine eyes shall see the king in His beauty: they shall behold the land that is very far off."*
Is. 52:7 *"How beautiful upon the mountains are the feet of him that bringeth good tidings, that publisheth peace; that bringeth good tidings of good, that publisheth Salvation; that saith unto Zion, thy God reigneth!"*
Is. 61:3 *"... to give them beauty for ashes..."*
Ez. 16:8-15 *"... I ...entered into a Covenant with thee, saith the Lord God... thou wast exceeding beautiful, and thou didst prosper into a kingdom. And thy renown went forth among the heathen for thy beauty: for it was perfect through My comeliness, which I had put upon thee, saith the Lord God..."*
Ez. 16:7 HCSB *"... you... became very beautiful..."*
Hosea 14:6 *"... and his beauty shall be as the Olive Tree..."*
Rom. 10:15 *"... how beautiful are the feet of them that preach the Gospel of peace, and bring glad tidings of good things!"*

Believe / Faith / Faithful

Gen. 15:6 *"And he (Abraham) believed in the Lord; and He counted it to him for righteousness."*
Is. 49:7 *"... the Lord that is faithful..."*
Matt. 8:13 *"... as thou hast believed, so be it done unto thee."*
Matt. 9:29 *"... according to your faith be it unto you."*

Mk. 11:22-24 *"... have faith in God... whosoever shall say unto this mountain, Be thou removed, and be thou cast into the sea; and shall not doubt in his heart, but shall believe that those things which he saith shall come to pass; he shall have whatsoever he saith... what things soever ye desire, when ye pray, believe that ye receive them, and ye shall have them."*
Mk. 9:23,24 *"Jesus said unto him, If thou canst believe, all things are possible to him that believeth... I believe; help thou mine unbelief."*
Mk. 11:22-24 *"And Jesus answering saith unto them, Have faith in God. For verily I say unto you, That whosoever shall say unto this mountain, Be thou removed, and be thou cast into the sea; and shall not doubt in his heart, but shall believe that those things which he saith shall come to pass; he shall have whatsoever he saith. Therefore I say unto you, What things soever ye desire, when ye pray, believe that ye receive them, and ye shall have them."*
Lk. 7:50 *"And He said to the woman, Thy faith hath saved thee; go in peace."*
Lk. 8:25 *"... where is your faith..."*
Lk. 8:50 *"... Fear not: believe only... she shall be made whole."*
Lk. 17:5,6 *"... the Apostles said... Lord, Increase our faith... the Lord said, If ye had faith as a grain of mustard seed, ye might say unto this Sycamine tree, Be thou plucked up by the root, and be thou planted in the sea; and it should obey you."*
Lk. 17:19 *"... thy faith hath made thee whole."*
Jn. 1:7 *"The same came for a witness, to bear witness of the Light, that all men through Him might believe."*
Jn. 1:12 *"But as many as received Him, to them gave He power to become the sons of God, even to them that believe on His name..."*
Jn. 1:50 Jesus to Nathanael *"... because I said unto thee, I saw thee under the fig tree, believest thou? Thou shalt see greater things than these..."*
Jn. 2:23 *"... many believed in... when they saw the miracles which He did."*
Jn. 3:16,17 *"For God so loved the world that He gave His only begotten Son, that whosoever believeth in Him should not perish but have everlasting life. For God sent not His Son into the world to condemn the world; but that the world through Him might be saved."*
Jn. 3:36 *"He that believeth on the Son hath everlasting life..."*
Jn. 5:24 *"... he that heareth My Word, and believeth on Him that sent Me, hath everlasting life, and shall not come into condemnation; but is passed from death unto life."*
Jn. 6:29 *"... this is the work of God... believe on Him whom He hath sent."*
Jn. 6:39,40 *"And this is the Father's will which hath sent Me, that of all which He hath given Me I should lose nothing, but should raise it up again at the **last day**. And this is the will of Him that sent Me, that everyone which seeth*

the Son.. believeth on Him, may have everlasting life... I will raise him up at the **last day**."
(The Resurrection is on the last day!
Jn. 6:47 "... He that believeth on Me hath everlasting life."
Jn. 6:69 "... we believe and are sure that (your are) Christ, the Son of the living God."
Jn. 7:31 "And many of the people believed on Him, and said, When Christ cometh, will He do more miracles than these which this man hath done?"
Jn. 7:37-39 "... he that believeth on Me, as the Scripture hath said, out of his belly shall flow rivers of living water. (But this spake He of the Spirit, which they that believe on Him should receive) ..."
Jn. 10:37 "If I do not the works of My Father, believe Me not."
Jn. 11:26 "And whosoever liveth and believeth in Me shall never die..."
Jn. 11:40 "Jesus saith unto her, Said I not unto thee, that, if thou wouldest believe, thou shouldest see the glory of God?"
Jn. 12:36 "While ye have light, believe in the light, that ye may be the children of light..."
Jn. 14:1 "Let not your heart be troubled: ye believe in God believe also in Me."
Jn. 14:29 "And now I have told you before it come to pass, that, when it is come to pass, ye might believe."
Acts 13:39 "And by Him all that believe are Justified from all things ..."
Acts 16:31 "... believe on the Lord Jesus Christ, and thou shalt be saved, and thy house."
Rom. 1:16 "For I am not ashamed of the Gospel of Christ: for it is the power of God unto Salvation to everyone that believeth ..."
Rom. 10:6-8 "... the Word of faith... that if thou shalt confess with thy mouth the Lord Jesus, and shalt believe in thine heart that God hath raised Him from the dead, thou shalt be saved."
II Cor. 4:13 "... I believed, and therefore have I spoken; we also believe, and therefore speak...
Gal. 3:21 "... that the promise by faith of Jesus Christ might be given to them that believe."
Eph. 1:13 "In whom ye also trusted, after that ye heard the Word of truth, the Gospel of your Salvation: in whom also after that ye believed, ye were sealed with that Holy Spirit of promise..."
I Tim. 1:16 "... them which should hereafter believe on Him to life ever-lasting."

Bind/Bound/Binding

Is. 61:1 "The Spirit of the Lord God is upon Me; because the Lord hath anointed Me to preach good tidings unto the meek; He hath sent me to bind up the brokenhearted, to proclaim liberty to the captives, and the opening of the prison to them that are bound...'

Ez. 34:16 "I will seek that which was lost, and bring again that which was driven away, and will bind up that which was broken, and will strengthen that which was sick..."

Hosea 6:1 "Come, and let us return unto the Lord: for He hath torn, and He will heal us; He hath smitten, and He will bind us up."

Matt. 12:29 "Or else how can one enter into a strong man's house, and spoil his goods, except he first bind the strong man? And then he will spoil his house."

Matt. 16:18,19;18:18 "... I will build My church; and the gates of hell shall not prevail against it. And I will give unto thee the keys of the kingdom of heaven: and whatsoever thou shalt bind on earth shall be bound in heaven: and whatsoever thou shalt loose on earth shall be loosed in heaven."

Mk. 3:27 "No man can enter into a strong man's house, and spoil his goods except he will first bind the strong man; and then he will spoil his house."

Bitterness

Heb. 12:15 "... looking diligently lest any man fail of the grace of God; lest any root of bitterness springing up trouble you, and thereby many be defiled..."

Eph. 4:31,32 "Let all bitterness, and wrath, and anger, and clamour, and evil speaking, be put away from you, with all malice: and be ye kind ("compassionate" NIV) one to another, tenderhearted, forgiving one another, even as God for Christ's sake hath forgiven you."

(Eph. 4:31 NIV "Get rid of all bitterness, rage and anger, brawling and slander, along with every form of malice."

Blameless

I Cor. 1:8 "Who shall also confirm you unto the end, that ye may be blameless in the day of our Lord Jesus Christ."

Phil. 2:15 *"That ye may be blameless and harmless, the sons of God, without rebuke, in the midst of a crooked and perverse nation, among whom ye shine as lights in the world..."*
I Thess. 5:23 *"And the very God of peace Sanctify you wholly; and I pray God your whole spirit and soul and body be preserved blameless unto the coming of our Lord Jesus Christ."*

Blessed / Cannot be cursed

Num. 22:12 *"... thou shalt not curse the people: for they are blessed."*
Num. 23:19-23 *"Behold, I have received commandment to bless: and He hath blessed; and I cannot reverse it... surely there is no enchantment against Jacob, neither is there any divination against Israel"*
What God has blessed cannot be cursed unless you step outside of God's umbrella of protection. Balaam cursed Israel, by causing them to sin! Num. 25:1-6.
Num. 24:5-10 *"Blessed is he that blesseth thee, and cursed is he that curseth thee... (Balaam) blessed them these three times."*
Prov. 26:2 *"... so the curse causeless shall not come."*
(Prov. 26:2 NIV *"Like a fluttering sparrow or a darting swallow, an undeserved curse does not come to rest."*
(Prov. 26:2 LB *"An undeserved curse has no effect."*
(Prov. 26:2 RSV *"... a curse that is causeless does not alight."*
(Prov. 26:2 PB *"... so the curse that is causeless shall be driven away."*

Blessed / Blessing / Favor / Give

Gen. 1:28 *"And God blessed them (Adam and Eve), and God said unto them, Be fruitful, and multiply, and replenish the earth, and subdue it: and have dominio..."*
Gen. 2:2,3 *"... and God blessed the seventh day, and Sanctified it: because that in it He had rested from all His work which God created and made."*
Gen. 5:1,2 *"... in the day that God created man, in the likeness of God made He him; male and female created He them; and blessed them..."*
Gen. 9:1 *"And God blessed Noah and his sons, and said unto them, Be fruitful, and multiply, and replenish the earth."*
Gen. 27:29 *"... cursed be every one that curseth thee, and blessed be he that blesseth thee."*
Gen. 48:9 Jacob blessed Ephraim and Manasseh *"... I will bless them."*

Ex. 20:6,11 *"... shewing mercy unto... them that love Me, and keep My Commandments... the Lord blessed the Sabbath day, and hallowed it."*
Ex. 23:25-27 *"And ye shall serve the Lord your God, and He shall bless thy bread, and thy water; and I will take sickness away from the midst of thee. There shall nothing cast their young, nor be barren, in thy land: the number of days I will fulfil. I will send My fear before thee... and I will make all thine enemies turn their backs unto thee."*
Num. 6:24-27 The Blessing *"... ye shall bless the children of Israel, saying.. The Lord bless thee, and keep thee: the Lord make His face shine upon thee, and be gracious unto thee: the Lord lift up His countenance upon thee, and give thee peace. And they shall put My name upon the children of Israel; and I will bless them."*
Num. 22:6 *"... he whom Thou blesses is blessed..."*
Num. 23:11 *"... thou hast blessed them altogether."*
Num. 24:1 NKJV *"... it pleased the Lord to bless Israel."*
Num. 29:18 *"... he that keepeth the law, happy* (blessed) *is he."*
Lev. 25:21 *"... I will command My blessing upon you in the sixth year, and it shall bring forth fruit for three years."*
Deut. 1:11 AMP *"May the Lord, the God of your fathers... bless you as He has promised you!"*
Deut. 2:7 AMP *"... for the Lord your God has blessed you in all the work of your hand... you have lacked nothing."*
Deut. 7:12-15 *"Wherefore it shall come to pass, if ye hearken to these Judgments, and keep, and do them, that the Lord thy God shall keep unto thee the Covenant and the mercy which He sware unto thy fathers: and He will love thee, and bless thee, and multiply thee: He will also bless the fruit of thy womb, and the fruit of thy land... Thou shalt be blessed above all people: there shall not be male or female barren among you, or among your cattle. And the Lord will take away from thee all sickness, and will put none of the evil diseases of Egypt, which thou knowest, upon thee..."*
Deut. 11:26 *"Behold, I set before you this day a blessing and a curse; a blessing, if ye obey the Commandments of the Lord your God... and a curse, if ye will not obey the Commandments of the Lord your God, but* (don't) *turn aside out of the way which I command you this day..."*
(Lk. 16:13 You cannot have two masters
Deut. 14:29 *"... the Lord thy God may bless thee in all the work of thine hand which thou doest."*
Deut. 15:4 *"... for the Lord shall greatly bless thee in the land which the Lord thy God giveth thee for an inheritance to possess it..."*
Deut. 15:6 *"For the Lord thy God blessed thee, as He promised thee..."*
Deut. 15:10 *"... the Lord thy God shall bless thee in all thy works..."*

Deut. 15:18 "... and the Lord thy God shall bless thee in all that thou doest."
Deut. 28:1-14 "... if thou shalt hearken diligently unto the voice of the Lord thy God, to observe and to do all His Commandments... all these blessings shall come on thee, and overtake thee, if thou shalt hearken unto the voice of the Lord thy God. Blessed shalt thou be in the city, and blessed shalt thou be in the field. Blessed shall be the fruit of thy body, and the fruit of thy ground, and the fruit of thy cattle, the increase of thy kind, and the flocks of thy sheep. Blessed shall be thy basket and thy store ("dough, kneading trough" KJV fn). Blessed shalt thou be when thou comest in, and blessed shalt thou be when thou goest out. The Lord shall cause thine enemies that rise up against thee to be smitten before thy face: they shall come out against thee one way, and flee before thee seven ways. The Lord shall command the blessing upon thee in thy storehouses ("barns" KJV fn), and in all that thou settest thine hand unto; and He shall bless thee in the land which the Lord thy God giveth thee. The Lord shall establish thee an Holy people unto Himself... if thou shalt keep the Commandments of the Lord thy God, and walk in His ways. And all people of the earth shall see that thou art called by the name of the Lord; and they shall be afraid of thee. And the Lord shall make thee plenteous in goods, in the fruit of thy body, and in the fruit of thy cattle, and in the fruit of thy ground, in the land which the Lord sware unto thy fathers to give thee. The Lord shall open unto thee His good treasure, the heaven to give the rain unto thy land in his season, and to bless all the work of thine hand: and thou shalt lend unto many nations, and thou shalt not borrow. And the Lord shall make thee the head, and not the tail; and thou shalt be above only, and thou shalt not be beneath; if that thou hearken unto the Commandments of the Lord thy God... to observe and to do them: and thou shalt not go aside from any of the Words which I command thee this day, to the right hand, or to the left..."
Deut. 30:14-16 "... and the Lord thy God shall bless thee in the land whither thou goest to possess it."
Deut. 33:1 "... this is the blessing, (that) Moses the man of God blessed...."
Deut. 33:27-29 NIV "Blessed are you, Israel! Who is like you, a people saved by the Lord? He is your shield and helper and your glorious sword. Your enemies will cower before you, and you will tread on their heights."
Josh. 17:14 "... forasmuch as the Lord hath blessed me hitherto..."
Josh. 22:7,8 "... then he blessed them... saying, Return with much riches..."
Josh. 24:10 "... but I (God) would not hearken unto Balaam; therefore he blessed you still; so I delivered you out of his hand."
Ruth 4:14 To "... Naomi, Blessed be the Lord, which hath not left thee this day without a kinsman that his name may be famous in Israel. And he shall be unto thee a restorer of thy life, and a nourisher of thine old age..."

Jesus is our Kinsman-Redeemer.

I Sam. 2:20,21 *"And Eli blessed Elkannah and his wife, and said, The Lord give thee seed of this woman..."*

II Sam. 6:12 *"And it was told king David, saying, The Lord hath blessed the house of Obed-edom, and all that pertaineth unto him, because of the Ark of God. So David went and brought up the Ark of God from the house of Obed-edom into the city of David with gladness."*

II Sam. 7:28,29;I Chron. 17:26,27 *"... Thou hast promised this goodness unto Thy servant: therefore now let it please Thee to bless the house of Thy servant... with Thy blessing let the house of Thy servant be blessed forever."*

I Kings 8:56 Solomon said, *"Blessed be the Lord, that hath given rest unto His people Israel, according to all that He promised: there hath not failed one Word of all his good promise, which He promised by the hand of Moses His servant."*

I Chron. 4:11 *"And Jabez called on the God of Israel, saying, Oh that Thou wouldest bless me indeed, and enlarge my coast, and that Thine hand might be with me, and that Thou wouldest keep me from evil, that it may not grieve me! And God granted him that which he requested."*

I Chron. 16:2 *"... David... blessed the people in the name of the Lord."*

I Chron. 26:5 Sons of Asaph *"... for God blessed him."*

II Chron. 31:10 *"... since the people began to bring the offerings into the house of the Lord, we have had enough to eat, and have left plenty: for the Lord hath blessed His people; and that which is left is this great store."*

Neh. 13:2 *"... God turned the curse into a blessing."*

Job 1:10 God blessed Job at the beginning and end of his life, *"Hast not Thou made an hedge about him (Job), and about his house, and about all that he hath on every side? Thou hast blessed the work of his hands, and his substance is increased in the land."*

Job 42:12 *"So the Lord blessed the latter end of Job more than his beginning..."*

Ps. 1:1 *"Blessed is the man that walketh not in the counsel of the ungodly, nor standeth in the way of sinners, nor sitteth in the seat of the scornful. But his delight is in the law of the Lord; and in His law doth he meditate day and night. He shall be like a tree planted by the rivers of water..."*

Ps. 3:8 *"... Thy blessing is upon Thy people. Selah."*

Ps. 5:11,12 *"But let all those that put their trust in Thee rejoice: let them ever shout for joy, because Thou defendest them: let them also that love Thy name be joyful in thee. For Thou, Lord, wilt bless the righteous; with favour wilt Thou compass him as with a shield."*

Ps. 21:1-6 *"The king shall joy ("rejoice" NIV) in Thy strength, O Lord; and in Thy Salvation how greatly shall he rejoice! Thou hast given him his heart's* desire, and hast not withholden the request of his lips. Selah. For Thou preventest him with the blessings of goodness: Thou settest a crown of pure gold on his head. He asked life of Thee, and Thou gavest it him, even length of days forever and ever. His glory is great in thy Salvation: honour and majesty hast Thou laid upon him. For Thou hast made him most blessed forever: Thou hast made him exceeding glad with Thy countenance."

Ps. 21:3 NIV "You welcomed him with rich blessings... and made him glad with the joy of Your presence."

Ps. 29:11 "... the Lord will bless His people with peace."

Ps. 31:21 "Blessed be the Lord: for He hath shewed me His marvelous kindness in a strong city."

Ps. 32:1,2 "Blessed is he whose transgression is forgiven, whose sin is covered. Blessed is the man unto whom the Lord imputeth not iniquity, and in whose spirit there is no guile."

Ps. 37:22 "For such as be blessed of Him shall inherit the earth..."

Ps. 37:25,26 "... yet have I not seen the righteous forsaken, nor his seed begging bread. He is ever merciful, and lendeth; and his seed is blessed."

Ps. 41:1-3 "Blessed is he that considereth the poor: the Lord will deliver him in time of trouble. The Lord will preserve him, and keep him alive; and he shall be blessed upon the earth: and thou wilt not deliver him unto the will of his enemies. The Lord will strengthen him upon the bed of languishing: Thou wilt make all his bed in his sickness."

Ps. 41:3 NIV "The Lord will sustain him on his sickbed and restore him from his bed of illness."

Ps. 41:3 LB "He nurses them when they are sick, and soothes their pains and worries."

Ps. 45:2 "... God hath blessed thee forever."

Ps. 65:10 "... Thou makest it soft with showers: Thou blessest the springing thereof."

(Ps. 65:10 NIV "... you soften it with showers and bless its crops."

Ps. 67:6,7 "Then shall the earth yield her increase; and God, even our own God, shall bless us. God shall bless us; and all the ends of the earth shall fear Him."

Ps. 84:4-12 "Blessed are they that dwell in thy house... blessed is the man whose strength is in thee; in whose heart are the ways of them... they go from strength to strength... no good thing will He withhold from them that walk uprightly... blessed is the man that trusteth in thee."

Ps. 89:15 "Blessed is the people that knoweth joyful sound: they shall walk, O Lord, in the light of Thy countenance."

Ps. 94:12 "Blessed is the man whom Thou chastenest, O Lord, and teachest him out of Thy law..."

Ps. 103 1,2 *"Bless the Lord, O my soul: and all that is within me, bless His Holy name. Bless the Lord, O my soul, and forget not all His benefits ..."*
Ps. 103:21 *"Bless ye the Lord, all ye His hosts; ye ministers of His, that do His pleasure."*
Ps. 107:38 *"He blesseth them also..."*
Ps. 112:1-3 *"Praise ye the Lord. Blessed is the man that feareth the Lord, that delighteth greatly in His Commandments. He seed shall be mighty upon earth: the generation of the upright shall be blessed. Wealth and riches sh all be in his house: and his righteousness endureth forever."*
Ps. 115:12,13 *"The Lord hath been mindful of us; He will bless us; He will bless the house of Israel... He will bless them that fear the Lord, both small and great... ye are blessed of the Lord which made heaven and earth."*
Ps. 115:14 LB *"May the Lord richly bless both you and your children."*
Ps. 115:15 *"Ye are blessed of the Lord which made heaven and earth."*
Ps. 118:26 *"Blessed be He that cometh in the name of the Lord: we have blessed you out of the house of the Lord."*
Ps. 119:57 LB *"... and I promise to obey! With all my heart I want Your blessings. Be merciful just as You promised."*
Ps. 119:65 LB *"Lord, I am overflowing with Your blessings, just as You promised."*
Ps. 127:3-5 *"Lo, children are an heritage of the Lord: and the fruit of the womb is his reward. As arrows are in the hand of a mighty man; so are children of the youth. Happy ("Blessed" NIV) is the man that hath his quiver full of them: they shall not be ashamed, but they shall speak with the enemies in the gate."*
Ps. 128:1-6 *"Blessed is every one that feareth the Lord; that walketh in His ways. For thou shalt eat the labour of thine hands: Happy (Gr. "Blessed") shalt thou be, and it shall be well with thee. Thy wife shall be as a fru itful vine by the sides of thine house: thy children like olive plants round about thy table. Behold, that thus shall the man be blessed that feareth the Lord. The Lord shall bless thee out of Zion: and thou shalt see the good of Jerusalem all the days of thy life. Yea, thou shalt see thy children's children, and peace upon Israel."*
(Ps. 128:2 NIV *"... blessings and prosperity will be yours."*
Ps. 132:15-18 *"I will abundantly bless her provision; I will satisfy her poor with bread."*
Ps. 147:13 *"... He hath blessed thy children within thee."*
Prov. 3:33 *"... He (God) blesseth the habitation of the just."*
Prov. 8:32-35 *"... blessed are they that keep My ways... blessed is the man that heareth me, watching daily at my gates, waiting at the posts of my doors. For whoso findeth* (wisdom) *findeth life, and shall obtain favour..."*

Prov. 10:6 "*Blessings are upon the head of the just...*"
Prov. 10:22 "*The blessing of the Lord, it maketh rich, and He addeth no sorrow with it.*"
Prov. 11:8 "*By the blessing of the upright the city is exalted...*"
Prov. 20:7 "*The just man walketh in his integrity: his children are blessed...*"
Prov. 22:9 "*He that hath a bountiful eye shall be blessed; for he giveth of his bread to the poor.*"
Prov. 22:9 NLT "*Blessed are the generous...*"
Prov. 24:25 "*... but to them that rebuke him* (the wicked) *shall be delight, and a good blessing shall come upon them.*"
Prov. 28:20 "*A faithful man shall abound with blessings...*"
Prov. 29:18 "*... he that keepeth the law, happy* ("*blessed*" NIV) *is he.*"
Prov. 31:28 A virtuous woman "*Her children arise up, and call her blessed; her husband also, and he praiseth her.*"
Is. 20:24,25 "*In that day shall Israel be the third with Egypt and with Assyria, even a blessing in the midst of the land; whom the Lord of hosts shall bless, saying, Blessed be Egypt My people, and Assyria the work of My hands, and Israel Mine inheritance.*"
Is. 32:20 "*Blessed are ye that sow beside all waters, that send forth thither the feet of the ox and the* (donkey)."
Is. 32:20 NIV "*... how blessed you will be, sowing your seed by every stream, and letting your cattle and donkeys range free.*"
Is. 44:3 "*For I will pour... My blessing upon thine offspring...*"
Is. 51:2,3 "*... for I called him* (Abraham) *and blessed him, and increased him.*"
Is. 56:2 "*Blessed is the man... that keepeth the Sabbath from polluting it.*
Is. 61:9 "*... all that see them shall acknowledge them, that they are the seed which the Lord hath blessed.*"
Is. 65:23 "*They shall not labour in vain, nor bring forth for trouble; for they are the seed of the blessed of the Lord, and their offspring with them.*"
Jer. 17:7 "*Blessed is the man that trusteth in the Lord... whose hope the Lord is.*"
Jer. 31:23 "*... the Lord bless thee, O habitation of justice, and Mountain of Holiness.*"
Ez. 34:26 "*And I will make them and the places round about My hill a blessing; and I will cause the shower to come down in his season; there shall be showers of blessing.*"
Hag. 2:19 "*... from this day will I bless you.*"
Mal. 3:10 "*Bring ye all the tithes into the storehouse, that there may be meat in Mine house, and prove Me now herewith, saith the Lord of hosts, if I will not open you the windows of heaven, and pour you out a blessing, that there shall not be room enough to receive it.*"

Matt. 11:6 "... *blessed is he, whosoever shall not be offended in Me* (Jesus)."
Matt. 13:16 "... *blessed are your eyes... they see: and your ears... they hear.*"
Matt. 14:19,20 - Jesus blessed the bread
Matt. 16:17 "... *Jesus... said... Blessed art thou, Simon Barjona: for flesh and blood hath not revealed it unto thee, but My Father which is in heaven.*"
Matt. 25:34 "... *the King (will) say unto them on His right... come, ye blessed of My Father, inherit the kingdom prepared for you...*"
Mk. 11:10 "*Blessed be the kingdom of our father David, that cometh in the name of the Lord...*"
Lk. 1:28 An angel said to Mary "... *blessed art thou among women.*"
Lk. 1:42 Elizabeth to Mary "*Blessed art thou among women, and blessed is the fruit of thy womb.*"
(Jesus said that whoever does His will is His mother and brothers, Matt.12: 50;Lk.8:21
Lk. 1:45 "... *blessed is she that believed: for there shall be a performance* (Gr. #5050 *"fulfillment, completion, perfection"*) *of those things which were told her from the Lord.*"
Lk. 1:68 "*Blessed be the Lord God of Israel; for He hath visited and Redeemed His people and hath raised up a Horn of Salvation* (Jesus) *for us in the house of His servant David...*"
Lk. 6:20-22,28 Jesus said, "... *blessed be ye poor: for yours is the Kingdom of God. Blessed are ye that hunger now: for ye shall be filled. Blessed are ye that weep now: for ye shall laugh. Blessed are ye, when men shall hate you, and when they shall separate you from their company, and shall reproach you, and cast out your name as evil, for the Son of man's sake ... bless them that curse you, and pray for them which despitefully use you.*"
Lk. 7:23 "... *blessed is he, whosoever shall not be offended in Me* (Jesus)."
Lk. 12:37,44 "*Blessed are those servants, whom the Lord when He cometh shall find watching: verily I say unto you, that He shall gird Himself, and make them to sit down to meat, and will come forth and serve them... He will make him ruler over all that He hath...*"
Lk. 13:35 ".... *ye shall not see Me* (Jesus), *until the time come when ye shall say, Blessed is He that cometh in the name of the Lord* (at the 2nd coming)."
Lk. 14:13-15 "*But when thou makest a feast, call the poor, the maimed, the lame, the blind: and thou shalt be blessed; for they cannot recompense thee: for thou shalt be recompensed at the Resurrection of the just... blessed is he that shall eat bread in the kingdom of God.*"
Lk. 23:29 "*For behold, the days are coming, in the which they shall say, Blessed are the barren...*"

Lk. 24:48,50,51 *"And behold, I send the promise of My Father upon you... and it came to pass, while He blessed them, He was parted from them, and carried up into heaven..."*
Jn. 13:15,17 *"For I have given you an example, that you should do as I have done... if ye know these things, happy are ye if ye do them."*
Jn. 13:17 NIV *"Now that you know these things, you will be blessed if you do them."*
(I Jn. 2:6 We are to walk as Jesus walked.
Jn. 20:29 *"... blessed are they that have not seen, and yet have believed."*
Acts 3:26 *"... having raised up His Son Jesus, sent Him to bless you, in turning away every one of you from his iniquities."*
Acts 20:35 *"... it is more blessed to give than to receive."*
Rom. 4:7-9 *"... blessed are they whose iniquities are forgiven, and whose sins are covered. Blessed is the man to whom the Lord will not impute sin. Cometh this blessedness then upon the circumcision only, or upon the uncircumcision also? For we say that faith was reckoned to Abraham for righteousness."*
Rom. 12:14 *"Bless them which persecute you: bless, and curse not."*
Rom. 15:29 *"... I am sure that, when I (Paul) come unto you, I shall come in the fullness of the blessing of the Gospel of Christ."*
The Communion cup is called the Cup of Blessing
I Cor. 10:16 *"The Cup of Blessing which we bless, is it not the Communion of the blood of Christ? The bread which we break, is it not the Communion of the body of Christ?"*
Gal. 3:8,9 *"... unto Abraham... in thee shall all nations be blessed. So then they which be of the faith are blessed with faithful Abraham."*
Gal. 3:14 *"That the blessing of Abraham might come on the Gentiles through Jesus Christ; that we might receive the promise of the Spirit through faith."*
Eph. 1:3 *"Blessed be the God and Father of our Lord Jesus Christ, who hath blessed us with all Spiritual blessings in heavenly places in Christ..."*
Heb. 6:14 *"Saying, Surely blessing I will bless thee, and multiplying I will multiply thee."*
Heb. 7:6,7 *"... but he whose descent is not counted from them received tithes of Abraham, and blessed him that had the promises. And without all contradiction the less is blessed of the better..."*
Heb. 11:20,21 *"By faith Isaac blessed Jacob and Esau... by faith Jacob, when he was a dying, blessed both the sons of Joseph..."*
Jms. 1:25 *"But be ye doers of the Word, and not hearers only, deceiving your own selves. For if any be a hearer of the Word, and not a doer, he is like unto a man beholding his natural face in a glass: for he beholdeth himself, and goeth his way, and straightway forgetteth what manner of man he was.*

But whoso looketh into the perfect law of liberty ("perfect law that gives freedom" NIV), and continueth therein, he being not a forgetful hearer, but a doer of the work, this man shall be blessed in his deed."
Jms. 1:12 *"Blessed is the man that endureth temptation: for when he is tried, he shall receive the crown of life, which the Lord hath promised to them that love Him."*
Jms. 5:11 *"Behold, we count them happy (Gr. "blessed") which endure. Ye have heard of the patience of Job, and have seen the end of the Lord; that the Lord is very pitiful, and of tender mercy."*
I Pet. 3:9 *"Not rendering evil for evil, or railing for railing: but contrariwise blessing... ye are thereunto called, that ye should inherit a bless-ing."*
I Pet. 4:14 RSV *"If you are reproached for the name of Christ, you are blessed, because the Spirit of glory and of God rests upon you."*
Rev. 14:13 *"... blessed are the dead which die in the Lord from henceforth."*
Rev. 16:15 *"... blessed is he that watcheth, and keepeth his garments, lest he walk naked, and they see his shame."*
Rev. 20:6 *"Blessed and Holy is he that hath part in the first Resurrection: on such the second death hath no power, but they shall be priests of God and of Christ, and shall reign with Him a thousand years."*
The last blessing in the Bible
Rev. 22:14 *"Blessed are they that do His Commandments, that they may have right to the Tree of Life, and may enter in through the gates into the city (New Jerusalem)."*

Blessing Isaac gives to Jacob

Gen. 27:27-29 *"See, the smell of my son is as the smell of a field which the Lord hath blessed: therefore God give thee of the dew of heaven, and the fatness of the earth, and plenty of corn and... let people serve thee, and nations bow down to thee: be lord over thy brethren, and let thy mother's sons bow down to thee: cursed be every one that curseth thee, and blessed be he that blesseth thee."*

Blessing to 12 Sons / Tribes

Jacob blesses his 12 sons in Gen. 49 and Moses blesses the 12 tribes in Deut. 33.
Deut. 33:8-12 *"Bless, Lord, his substance, and accept the work of his hands; smite through the loins of them that rise against him, and of them that hate him, that they rise not again. "*

"And of Gad he said, Blessed be he that enlargeth Gad: he dwelleth as a lion, and teareth the arm with the crown of the head. And he provided the first part for himself, because there, in a portion of the lawgiver, was he seated; and he came with the heads of the people, he executed the justice of the Lord, and his Judgments with Israel." Deut. 33:20,21

Asher means "happy, joy, blessed"
Gen. 49:22 "... by the Almighty, who shall bless thee with blessings of heaven above, blessings of the deep that lieth under, blessings of the breasts, and of the womb: the blessings of thy father have prevailed above the blessings of my progenitors unto the utmost bound of the everlasting hills: they shall be on the head of Joseph, and on the crown of the head of him that was separate from his brethren."
From Moses
Deut. 33: 13-17 "... Blessed of the Lord be his land... let the blessing come upon the head of Joseph..."
"Let Asher be blessed with children; let him be acceptable to his brethren, and let him dip his foot in oil. Thy shoes shall be iron and brass; and as thy days, so shall thy strength be. There is none like unto the God of Jeshurun (Israel), who rideth upon the heaven in thy help, and in his excellency on the sky. The eternal God is thy refuge, and underneath are the everlasting arms: and he shall thrust out the enemy from before thee; and shall say, Destroy them." Deut. 33:24-27
Gen. 49:28 "All these are the twelve tribes of Israel: and this is it that their father spake unto them, and blessed them; every one according to his blessing he blessed them."

Bless Ephraim & Manasseh

From Jacob
Gen. 48:14-16 "And he blessed Joseph, and said, God, before whom my father's Abraham and Isaac did walk, the God which fed me all my life long unto this day, the Angel which Redeemed me from all evil, bless the lads; and let my name be named on them, and the name of my father's Abraham and Isaac, and let them grow into a multitude in the midst of the earth.... and his (Ephraim's) seed shall become a multitude of nations. And he blessed them that day, saying, In thee shall Israel bless, saying, God make thee as Ephraim and as Manasseh... moreover I have given to thee one portion above thy brethren..."

Blessings / Beatitudes

Matt. 5:3-12 *"Blessed (Happy) are the poor in spirit: for theirs is the kingdom of heaven.*
Blessed (Happy) are they that mourn: for they shall be comforted.
Blessed (Happy) are the meek: for they shall inherit the earth.
Blessed (Happy) are they which do hunger and thirst after righteousness: for they shall be filled.
Blessed (Happy) are the merciful: for they shall obtain mercy.
Blessed (Happy) are the pure in heart: for they shall see God.
Blessed (Happy) are the peacemakers... they shall be called the children of God.
Blessed (Happy) are they which are persecuted for righteousness' sake: for theirs is the Kingdom of heaven.
Blessed (Happy) are ye, when men shall revile you, and persecute you, and shall say all manner of evil against you falsely, for My sake. Rejoice, and be exceeding glad: for great is your reward in heaven: for so persecuted they the prophets which were before you."

(7) Blessings of Revelation

We should not be afraid to read Revelation because there is a blessing promised to those who read it.

1. *"Blessed is he that readeth, and they that hear the words of this pro-phecy, and keep those things which are written therein: for the time is at hand."* Rev. 1:3
2. *"... blessed are the dead which die in the Lord from henceforth: Yea, saith the Spirit, that they may rest from their labours; and their works do follow them."* Rev. 14:13
3. *"Behold, I come as a thief. Blessed is He that watcheth (for the 2nd coming of Jesus), and keepeth his garments, lest he walk naked, and they see his shame."* Rev. 16:15
4. *"Blessed are they which are called unto the Marriage Supper of the Lamb."* Rev. 19:9
5. *"Blessed and Holy is he that hath part in the first Resurrection: on such the second death hath no power, but they shall be priests of God (the Father) and of (Jesus) Christ..."* Rev. 20:6
6. *"Behold, I come quickly: blessed is he that keepeth the sayings of the prophecy of this book."* Rev. 22:7

7. *"Blessed are they that do His Commandments, that they may have right to the tree of life, and may enter in through the gates into the city."* Rev. 22:14

Bold / Boldness

Eph. 3:12 *"In whom we have boldness... confidence by the faith of Him."*
Eph. 6:20-22 *"... therein I may speak boldly, as I ought to speak..."*

Book (s)

Ps. 56:8 NLT *"You keep track of all my sorrows. You have collected all my tears in Your bottle. You have recorded each one in Your book."*
Ps. 69:28 *"Let them be blotted out of the Book of the Living, and not be written with the righteous."* (righteous written in Book of the Living)
Ps. 139:16 NLT *"You saw me before I was born. Every day of my life was recorded in Your Book. Every moment was laid out before a single day had passed."*
Is. 34:16 *"Seek ye out of the Book of the Lord, and read: no one of these (promises) shall fail, none shall want her mate..."*
Mal. 3:16 *"... they that feared the Lord spake often one to another... the Lord hearkened... heard it, and a Book of Remembrance was written before Him for them that feared the Lord, and that thought upon His name. They shall be Mine, saith the Lord of hosts, in that day when I make up My jewels..."*
Lk. 10:20 *"... rejoice, because your names are written in heaven."*
Phil. 4:3 *"... whose names are in the Book of Life."*
Rev. 3:5 *"He that overcometh, the same shall be clothed in white raiment; and I will not blot out his name out of the Book of Life, but I will confess his name before My Father, and before His angels.*
Rev. 17:8 *"... and they that dwell on the earth shall wonder, whose names were not written in the Book of Life from the foundation of the world, when they behold the beast..."*

Born Again / New Birth

Is. 66:9 *"Shall I bring to the birth, and not cause to bring forth..."*
Gal. 4:19,29 *"... I travail in birth again until Christ be formed in you..."*
I Jn. 4:7 *"... everyone that loveth is born of God, and knoweth God."*

I Jn. 5:4 *"For whatsoever is born of God overcometh the world: and this is the victory that overcometh the world, even our faith."*

Bride / Spiritual Virgin

Eve, Isha means, *"woman, wife, softness"*
Ps. 45:9 *"... upon Thy right hand did stand the queen in gold of Ophir."*
(This verse is about Solomon but Heb. 1:8 quotes Ps. 45:6,7 and uses it about Jesus. *"But unto the Son he saith, Thy throne, O God, is forever and ever..."*
Is. 60:10 *"I will greatly rejoice in the Lord, my soul shall be joyful in my God; for He hath clothed me with the garments of Salvation, He hath covered me with the robe of righteousness... as a bride adorneth herself with her jewels."*
Is. 62:5 *"As a young man marrieth a virgin, so shall thy sons marry thee... as the bridegroom rejoiceth over the bride, so shall thy God rejoice over thee."*
Jer. 2:2 *"... thus saith the Lord; I remember thee... the love of thine espousals"*
Jer. 2:2 NIV *"I remember the devotion of your youth, how as a bride you loved Me and followed Me through the dessert..."*
Jer. 2:2 NLT *"... I remember how eager you were to please Me as a young bride long ago, how you loved Me and followed Me..."*
Jn. 3:29 *"He that hath the bride is the Bridegroom..."*
II Cor. 11:2 *"For I am jealous over you with godly jealousy... that I may present* (you as) *a chaste virgin to Christ."*
Eph. 5:25-27 *"... Christ also loved the church, and gave Himself for it..."*
Rev. 19:7-9 *"Let us be glad and rejoice... for the marriage of the Lamb is come, and His wife ("Bride" NIV) hath made herself ready."*
Rev. 21:2 *"And I John saw the Holy City, New Jerusalem, coming down from God out of heaven, prepared as a Bride adorned for her husband."*
Rev. 21:9 *"... Come hither, I will shew thee the Bride, the Lamb's wife."*
Rev. 22:17 *"... the Spirit and the Bride say, Come... and let him that is athirst come... whosoever will, let him take the Water of Life freely."*

Bridegroom / Husband / Jesus

Adam, *"Ish"* means *"husband, protector, master, lord, strength"*
Ps. 19:5 *"Which is as a Bridegroom coming out of His chamber, and rejoiceth as a strong man to run a race."*
Talking about the sun but could also be an allegory about Jesus when He comes to get His Bride,
Is. 54:5 *"For thy Maker is thine husband..."*

Hosea 2:19,20 *"... I will betroth thee unto Me forever... unto Me in righteousness, and in Judgment, and in lovingkindness, and in mercies. I will even betroth thee unto Me in faithfulness: and thou shalt know the Lord."*
Jer. 31:31-33 *"... the days come... that I will make a New Covenant with the house of Israel, and with the house of Judah: not according to the Covenant that I made with their fathers... although I was an husband unto them, saith the Lord... after those days... I will put My law in their inward parts, and write it in their hearts; and will be their God, and they shall be My people."*
Matt. 9:15;Mk. 2:19,20;Lk.5:34,35 *"... can the children of the Bridechamber fast, while the Bridegroom is with them... the days will come, when the Bridegroom shall be taken away from them, and then shall they fast..."*
Matt. 25:1,5,6,10,13 *"Then shall the kingdom of heaven be likened unto ten virgins, which took their lamps, and went forth to meet the Bridegroom... while the bridegroom tarried, they all slumbered and slept. And at midnight there was a cry made, Behold... go ye out to meet Him... the Bridegroom came; and they that were ready went in with Him to the marriage..."*
II Cor. 11:2,3 *"For I am jealous over you with godly jealousy: for I have espoused you to one husband..."*
Eph. 5:25-27 *"Husbands, love your wives even as Christ also loved the church, and gave Himself for it; that He might Sanctify and cleanse it with the washing of water by the Word, that He might present it to Himself a glorious church, nor having spot, or wrinkle, or any such thing (Rev. 29:8); but that it should be Holy and without blemish."*
Eph. 5:29 *"For no man ever yet hated his own flesh; but nourisheth and cherisheth it, even as the Lord the church: for we are members of His body, of His flesh, and of His bones."*
Eph. 5:32 *"This is a great mystery... I speak (of) Christ and the church."*

Brokenhearted

Is. 61:1 *"The Spirit of the Lord God is upon me; because the Lord hath anointed Me to preach good tidings unto the meek; He hath sent Me to bind up the brokenhearted, to proclaim liberty to the captives, and the opening of the prison to them that are bound..."*

Care/Cast

Ps. 55:22 *"Cast thy burden upon the Lord, and He shall sustain thee: He shall never suffer the righteous to be moved."*

Jn. 6:37 *"All that the Father giveth Me shall come to Me; and him that cometh to Me I will in no wise cast out."*
II Cor. 7:6 *"... God that comforteth those who are cast down..."*
I Pet. 5:7 *"Casting all your cares on Him, for He careth for you."*
I Pet. 5:7 BSB *"Cast all your anxiety ("worries" NLT) on Him because He cares for you."*

Children

Promises to have children (It is God who opens and closes the womb)
Gen. 1:27,28 *"... male and female created He them. And God blessed them, and God said unto them, Be fruitful, and multiply, and replenish the earth..."*
Gen. 9:1 *"And God blessed Noah and his sons, and said unto them, Be fruitful, and multiply, and replenish the earth."*
Gen. 16:10 *"And the angel of the Lord said unto her, I will multiply thy seed exceedingly, that it shall not be numbered for multitude."*
Gen. 17:6 About Hagar *"And I will make thee exceeding fruitful, and I will make nations of thee, and kings shall come out of thee..."*
Gen. 17:16 *"And I will bless her, and give thee a son also of her: yea, I will bless her, and she shall be a mother of nations..."*
Gen. 18:14 *"Is anything too hard for the Lord? At the time appointed I will return unto thee... and Sarah shall have a son."*
Gen. 26:24 *"And the Lord appeared unto him the same night, and said, I am the God of Abraham thy father: fear not, for I am with thee, and will bless thee, and multiply thy seed for My servant Abraham's sake."*
Gen. 29:31;30:31 *"And when the Lord saw that Leah was hated, He opened her womb: but Rachel was barren."*
It is God who opens and closes the womb.
Gen. 30:22 *"And God remembered Rachel, and God hearkened to her, and opened her womb. And she conceived, and bare a son; and said, God hath taken away my reproach; and she called his name Joseph; and said, The Lord shall add to me another son."*
Gen. 48:4 Jacob to Joseph, *"... behold, I will make thee fruitful, and multiply thee, and I will make of thee a multitude of people..."*
Gen. 48:9 Joseph said to Jacob *"... they are my sons, whom God hath given me in this place..."*
Joseph acknowledged that it was God who had given him his sons!
Ex. 1:20 *"... God dealt well with* (them): *and the people multiplied, and waxed very mighty."*
God blessed the midwives because they would not kill the baby boys.

Ex. 1:21 ESV *"And because the midwives feared God, He gave them families."*
Ex. 23:26 Blessing - If you serve the Lord none shall be barren
Ex. 32:13 *"... I will multiply your seed as the stars..."*
Lev. 26:9 *"For I will... make you fruitful, and multiply you..."*
Deut. 1:11 AMP *"May the Lord, the God of your fathers, make you a thousand times as many as you are... as He has promised you!"*
Deut. 7:13-15 *"And He will... multiply thee: He will also bless the fruit of thy womb... there shall not be male or female barren among you..."*
(Deut. 7:14,15 AMP *"You shall be blessed above all peoples; there shall not be male or female barren among you..."*
Deut. 28:4,11 *"Blessed shall be the fruit of thy body... and the Lord shall make thee plenteous in... the fruit of thy body..."*
Deut. 30:5 *"And the Lord thy God will... multiply thee..."*
Ruth 4:13 *"So Boaz took Ruth, and she was his wife: and when he went in unto her, the Lord gave her conception, and she bare a son."*
I Sam. 1:27 Hannah said, *"For this child* (Samuel) *I prayed; and the Lord hath given me my petition which I asked of Him..."*
I Sam. 2:20,21 *"And Eli blessed Elkannah and his wife, and said, The Lord give thee seed of this woman... and the Lord visited Hannah, so that she conceived, and bare three sons and two daughters* (after Samuel)*..."*
Job 5:25 *"Thou shalt know also that thy seed shall be great, and thine offspring as the grass of the earth."*
Ps. 108:38 *"... they are multiplied greatly..."*
Ps. 113:9 *"He maketh the barren woman to keep house, and to be a joyful mother of children. Praise ye the Lord."*
Ps. 113:9 NLT *"He gives the barren woman a home, so that she becomes a happy mother."*
Ps. 115:14 *"The Lord shall increase you more and more.. and your children."*
Ps. 127:3 *"Lo, children are an heritage of the Lord: and the fruit of the womb is His reward."*
Ps. 127:4,5 *"As arrows are in the hand of a mighty man; so are children of the youth. Happy is the man that hath his quiver full of them..."*
Ps. 128:3 *"Thy wife shall be as a fruitful vine by the sides of thine house: thy children like olive plants round about thy table."*
Prov. 22:6 *"Train up a child in the way he should go: and when he is old, he will not depart from it."*
Is. 8:18 NIV *"Here am I, and the children the Lord has given me..."*
Is. 48:18,19 *"O that thou hadst hearkened to My Commandments... thy seed also had been as the sand, and the offspring of thy bowels like the gravel thereof; his name should not have been cut off... from before Me."*

Is. 54:1 *"Sing, O barren, thou that didst not bear; break forth into singing, and cry aloud, thou that didst not travail with child: for more are the children of the desolate than the children of the married wife, saith the Lord."*
Is. 65:23 *"...they are the seed of the blessed of the Lord, and their offspring..."*
Is. 66:9 *"Shall I bring to the birth, and not cause to bring forth? Saith the Lord: shall I cause to bring forth, and shut the womb? Saith thy God."*
Jer. 29:6 *"Take ye wives, and beget sons and daughters; and take wives for your sons, and give your daughters to husbands, that they may bear sons and daughters; that ye may be increased there, and not diminished."*
Gal. 4:27 *"For it is written, Rejoice, thou barren that bearest not; break forth and cry, thou that travailest not: for the desolate hath many more children.."*

Children / Offspring / Seed

Promises for your children
Deut. 3:2 *"And the Lord said unto me, Fear him not: for I will deliver him..."* (You can claim this promise for your children)
Prayer: Lord, please deliver my child/children from the evil one!
Deut. 4:40 *"Thou shalt keep... His Commandments... that it may go well with thee, and with thy children..."*
Deut. 5:29,33 *"O that there were such an heart in them, that they would fear Me, and keep all My Commandments always, that it might be well with them, and with their children forever!"*
Deut. 6:4-7;11:19 *"And these words, which I command thee... thou shalt teach them diligently unto thy children, and shalt talk of them when thou sittest... and when thou walkest... when thou liest down, and... risest up."*
Deut. 30:6 *"And the Lord thy God will circumcise thine heart, and the heart of thy seed, to love the Lord thy God with all thine heart, and with all thy soul, that thou mayest live."*
Deut. 30:9 *"... the Lord thy God will make thee plenteous in every work of thine hand, in the fruit of thy body... the fruit of thy cattle... the fruit of thy land, for good: for the Lord will again rejoice over thee for good..."*
Deut. 30:19 *"... choose life, that both thou and thy seed may live..."*
Deut. 32:46,47 *"... command your children to observe to do, all the words of this law. For it is not a vain thing for you; because it is your life: and through this thing ye shall prolong your days in the land..."*
I Chron. 29:19 *"... give unto Solomon, my son, a perfect heart to keep Thy Commandments."*
Prayer: Lord, give my children and family a perfect heart to obey You.

Ps. 25:12 "*What man is he that feareth the Lord... his seed shall inherit the earth.*"
Ps. 37:25,26 "*I have been young, and now am old; yet have I not seen the righteous forsaken, nor his seed begging bread... his seed is blessed.*"
Ps. 72:4 "*... He shall save the children of the needy...*"
Ps. 103:17 "*But the mercy of the Lord is from everlasting to everlasting upon them that fear him, and his righteousness unto children's children... to those that remember His Commandments to do them.*"
Ps. 112:1,2 "*... blessed is the man that feareth the Lord, that delighteth greatly in His Commandments. His seed shall be mighty upon earth: the generation of the upright shall be blessed.*"
(Ps. 112:2 NLT "*Their children will be successful...*"
(Ps. 112:2 NIV "*Their children will be mighty...*"
Ps. 113:9 "*He maketh the barren woman to keep house, to be a joyful mother of children.*"
Ps. 113:9 NIV "*He settles the barren woman in her home as a happy mother.*"
Ps. 115:14 LB "*May the Lord richly bless both you and your children.*"
Ps. 127:3-5 "*... children are an heritage of the Lord... the fruit of the womb is his reward. As arrows... in the hand of a mighty man; so are children of the youth. Happy ("Blessed" NIV) is the man that hath his quiver full of them: they shall not be ashamed, but they shall speak with the enemies...*"
Ps. 128:5,6 "*... thou shalt see thy children's children...*"
Ps. 144:12-15 "*That our sons may be as plants grown up in their youth; that our daughters may be as cornerstones, polished...*"
Ps. 147:13 "*... He hath blessed thy children within thee.*"
Prov. 11:21 "*... the seed of the righteous shall be delivered.*"
Prov. 14:26 "*In the fear of the Lord is strong confidence: and his children shall have a place of refuge.*"
Prov. 17:6 HCSB "*Grandchildren are the crown of the elderly, and the pride of sons is their fathers.*"
Prov. 20:7 "*The just man walketh in his integrity: his children are blessed after him.*"
Prov. 22:6,15 "*Train up a child in the way he should go: and when he is old, he will not depart from it.*"
Prov. 29:17 "*Correct thy son, and he shall give thee rest; yea, he shall give delight unto thy soul.*"
Prov. 31:28 "*... her children arise up, and call her blessed...*"
Is. 8:18 "*Behold, I and the children whom the Lord hath given me...*"
Is. 44:3 "*... I will pour My Spirit upon thy seed, and My blessing upon thine offspring: and they shall spring up as among the grass...*"
Is. 49:18 NLT "*... all your children will come back to you...*"

Is. 49:25 "... *for I will contend with him that contendeth with thee, and I will save thy children.*"
(Is. 49:25 LB "*I will fight those who fight you...*"
Is. 54:1 "*Sing, O barren, thou that didst not bear; break forth into singing, and cry aloud, thou didst not travail with child: for more are the children of the desolate than the children of the married wife...*"
Is. 54:13 "*And all thy children shall be taught of the Lord; and great shall be the peace of thy children.*"
Is. 59:21 "*... this is My Covenant with them... My Spirit that is upon thee, and My words which I have put in thy mouth shall not depart out of thy mouth, nor out of the mouth of thy seed, nor out of the mouth of thy seed's seed, saith the Lord, from henceforth and forever.*"
Is. 61:9 "*And their seed shall be known among the Gentiles, and their offspring among the people: all that see them shall acknowledge them, that they are the seed which the Lord hath blessed.*"
Is. 65:23 "*... for they are the seed of the blessed of the Lord, and their offspring with them.*"
Jer. 3:17-19 "*... neither shall they walk anymore after the imagination of their evil heart. In those days* (on the New Earth)*... the house of Judah shall walk with the house of Israel, and they shall come together out of the land... that I have given for an inheritance unto your fathers.*"
 Jer. 3:20 NIV "*I Myself said, 'How gladly would I treat you like My children and give you a pleasant land, the most beautiful inheritance of any nation.' I thought you would call Me 'Father' and not turn away from following Me.*"
Jer. 24:7 "*And I will give them a heart to know Me, that I am the Lord: and they shall be My people, and I will be their God: for they shall return unto Me with their whole heart.*"
Prayer: Lord, please give my child/children a heart to know You and let them return to You with all their hearts. In Jesus' name, Amen!
Jer. 31:17 "*... thy children shall come again to their own border.*"
Jer. 32:39,40 "*... I will give them one heart, and one way, that they may fear Me forever, for the good of them* ("*for their own good*" ESV)*, and of their children after them. And I will make an everlasting Covenant with them, that I will not turn away from them, to do them good; but I will put My fear in their hearts, that they shall not depart from Me.*"
Prayer: Lord, please put Your fear in the hearts of my child/children so that they will not depart from You. In Jesus' name, Amen!
Ez. 11:19 "*And I will give them one heart, and I will put a new Spirit within you; and I will take the stony heart out of their flesh, and will give them an Heart of flesh...*"

Ez. 36:25-27,29 *"Then will I sprinkle clean water upon you, and ye shall be clean: from all your filthiness, and from all your idols, will I cleanse you. A new heart also will I give you, and a new Spirit will I put within you: and I will take away the stony heart out of your flesh, and I will give you a heart of flesh. And I will put My Spirit within you, and cause you to walk in My Statutes, and ye shall keep My Judgments, and do them... I will also save you from all your uncleannesses..."*

Ez. 36:31 *"Then shall ye remember your own evil ways, and your doings that were not good, and shall loathe yourselves in your own sight for your iniquities and for your abominations."*

You can pray this promise over your children.

Ez. 37:25 *"... they shall dwell therein, even they, and their children, and their children's children forever..."*

Hosea 11:1,4 *"When Israel was a child, then I loved him... I drew them with cords of a man, with bands of love..."*

Prayer: Lord, I know that You love my child/children also. Please draw them with Your cords of love. In Jesus' name, Amen!

Hosea 14:4 *"I will heal their backsliding, I will love them freely: for Mine anger is turned away from him."*

You can pray: Lord, Please heal my child/children's backslidings and show them Your love and don't be angry with them. Thank You in Jesus' name.

Matt. 18:14 *"... it is not the will of your Father which is in heaven, that one of these little ones should perish."*

Jn. 17:11-13 Jesus prayed, *"Father, keep through Thine own name those whom Thou hast given Me, that they may be one, as we are... I have kept them in Thy name... I have kept, and none of them is lost... that they might have My joy fulfilled in themselves."*

Prayer: Lord, please keep my child/children so that none are lost so that they will have Your joy in their hearts. Thank You in Jesus' name, Amen!

Acts 3:26 *"Unto you first God, having raised up His Son Jesus, sent Him to bless you, in turning away every one of you from His iniquities."*

Prayer: Lord, please turn the ones I love away from their sins!

Acts 16:31;11:14 *"... believe on the Lord Jesus Christ, and thou shalt be saved, and thy house..."*

Prayer: Lord, please save all of my family. Thank You in Jesus' name, Amen!

I Cor. 7:13-16 *"And the woman which hath an husband that believeth not, and if he be pleased to dwell with her, let her not leave... or the unbelieving husband is Sanctified by the wife, and the unbelieving wife is Sanctified by the husband: else were your children unclean; but now are they Holy..."*

Our children are Holy if we believe in Jesus.

Chose / Chosen / Choose

I Chron. 16:13 "... *seed of Israel... children of Jacob, His chosen ones.*"
And now, according to I Pet. 2:4, we are also chosen by God.
Ps. 65:4,5 "*Blessed is the man whom thou choosest, and causest to approach unto Thee, that he may dwell in Thy courts: we shall be satisfied with the goodness of Thy house, even of Thy Holy Temple.*"
Ps. 106:23 "*... Moses His chosen...*"
Ps. 132:13;135:4 "*For the Lord hath chosen Zion... (and) Jacob...*"
Is. 41:8 "*But thou, Israel, art My servant, Jacob whom I have chosen, the seed of Abraham My friend.*"
Is. 41:9 "*... thou art My servant; I have chosen thee, and not cast thee away.*"
Is. 43:10 "*Ye are My witnesses... My servant whom I have chosen...*"
Is. 48:10 "*... I have chosen thee in the furnace of affliction.*"
Is. 49:7 "*... the Holy One of Israel... He shall choose thee.*"
Zech. 3:2 "*... the Lord hath chosen Jerusalem...*"
Matt. 22:14 "*... many are called, but few are chosen.*" (Because few respond)
Jn. 6:70 "*... I have chosen you twelve (disciples)...*"
Jn. 13:18 "*... I know whom I have chosen...*"
Jn. 15:16 "*Ye have not chosen Me, but I have chosen you...*"
Jn. 15:19 "*... I have chosen you out of the world...*"
Acts 1:2 "*... Apostles whom He has chosen...*"
Acts 9:15 "*... he (Paul) is a chosen vessel unto Me...*"
Acts 10:41 "*... unto witnesses chosen before of God, even to us...*"
Acts 22:14 "*... the God of our fathers hath chosen thee, that thou shouldest know His will, and see that Just One, and shouldest hear the voice of His mouth. For thou shalt be His witness unto all men...*"
I Cor. 1:27,28 "*... and things which are despised, hath God chosen...*"
Eph. 1:4 "*According as He hath chosen us in Him before the foundation of the world, that we should be Holy and without blame before Him in love...*"
II Thess. 2:13 "*... God hath from the beginning chosen you to Salvation through Sanctification of the Spirit and belief of the truth..*"
II Tim. 2:4 "*No man that warreth entangleth himself with the affairs of this life; that he may please him who hath chosen him to be a soldier.*"
Jms. 2:5 "*... hath not God chosen the poor of this world rich in faith, and heirs of the kingdom which He hath promised to them that love Him?*"
I Pet. 2:4 "*... chosen of God, and precious...*"
I Pet. 2:9 "*...ye are a chosen generation, a royal priesthood, an Holy nation...*"

Church

Matt. 16:18 Jesus said to Peter (petros #4074 means "*small stone or detached stone*"), "*... upon this rock* (Jesus - Rock #4073 means "*a ledge, cliff, huge massive rock rising up from the ground; boulder*") *I will build My church; and the gates of hell shall not prevail against it.*"

Acts 2:47 "*... the Lord added to the church daily such as should be saved.*"

I Cor. 4:4,5 "*For I know nothing by myself; yet am I not hereby Justified: but He that Judgeth me is the Lord. Therefore Judge nothing before the time, until the Lord come, who both will bring to light the hidden things of darkness, and will make manifest the counsels of the hearts: and then shall every man have praise of God.*"

I Cor. 12:28 HCSB "*And God has placed these in the church, first Apostles, second prophets, third teachers, next miracles, then gifts of healing, helping, managing, various kinds of languages.*"

Eph. 1:22 "*And hath put all things under His* (Jesus) *feet, and gave Him to be the head over all things to the church, which is His body, the fullness of Him that filleth all in all.*"

Eph. 3:10 "*To the intent that now unto the principalities and powers in heavenly places might be now by the church the manifold wisdom of God.*"

Eph. 3:21 "*Unto Him be glory in the church by Christ Jesus throughout all ages, world without end. Amen.*"

Eph. 5:23,25 "*... Christ is the head of the church: and He is the Saviour of the body... Christ loved the church, and gave Himself for it.*"

Eph. 5:26,27 "*That He might Sanctify and cleanse it with the washing of water by* (through baptism and) *the Word, that He might present it to Himself a glorious church, not having spot, or wrinkle, or say such thing; but that it should be Holy and without blemish.*"

Col. 1:18 "*And He is the head of the body, the church: who is the beginning, the firstborn from the dead; that in all things He might have preeminence.*"

I Tim. 3:15 "*But if I tarry long, that thou mayest know how thou oughtest to behave thyself in the house of God, which is the church of the living God...*"

Heb. 12:23 "*To the general assembly and church of the firstborn, which are written in heaven, and to God the Judge of all, and to the spirits of just men made perfect.*"

Clean / Cleanse (ed)

Ps. 19:12 "*... Cleanse Thou me from secret faults.*"

Ps. 51:2,3 *"Wash me thoroughly from mine iniquity, and cleanse me from my sin. For I acknowledge my transgressions: and my sin is ever before me."*
Ps. 119:9 *"Wherewithal shall a young man cleanse his way? By taking heed thereto according to Thy Word."*
Jer. 33:8 *"And I will cleanse them from all their iniquity, whereby they have sinned against Me; and I will pardon all their iniquities, whereby they have sinned, and whereby they have transgressed against Me."*
Ez. 36:25-27,29 *"Then will I sprinkle clean water upon you, and ye shall be clean: from all your filthiness, and from all your idols, will I cleanse you. A new heart also will I give you, and a new Spirit will I put within you: and I will take away the stony heart out of your flesh, and I will give you a heart of flesh. And I will put My Spirit within you, and cause you to walk in My Statutes, and ye shall keep My Judgments, and do them... I will also save you from all your uncleannesses..."*
Ez. 36:33 *"... in the day that I shall have cleansed you from all your iniquities"*
Ez. 37:23 *"... neither shall they defile themselves anymore with their idols, nor with their detestable things, nor with any of their transgressions: but I will save them out of all their dwelling places, wherein they have sinned, and will cleanse them: so shall they be My people, and I will be their God."*
Matt. 8:3 *"And Jesus put forth His hand, and touched him, saying, I will; be thou clean. And immediately his leprosy was cleansed."*
Matt. 10:8 *"Heal the sick, cleanse the lepers, raise the dead, cast out devils: freely ye have received, freely give."*
Matt. 11:5 *"... the blind receive their sight, and the lame walk, the lepers are cleansed, and the deaf hear, the dead are raised up, and the poor have the Gospel preached to them."*
Matt. 23:26 *"Thou blind Pharisee, cleanse first that which is within the cup and platter, that the outside of them may be clean also."*
Mk. 1:42 *"And as soon as He had spoken, immediately the leprosy departed from him, and he was cleansed."*
Lk. 5:12,13 A man with leprosy said to Jesus, *"... Lord, if Thou wilt, Thou canst make me clean. And He put forth His hand and touched him, saying, I will: be thou clean. And immediately the leprosy departed from him."*
Lk. 17:14 The lepers healed by Jesus *"... as they went, they were cleansed."*
II Cor. 7:1 *"Having therefore these promises, dearly beloved, let us cleanse ourselves from all filthiness of the flesh and spirit, perfecting Holiness..."*
Jms. 4:8 *"Draw nigh to God, and He will draw nigh to you. Cleanse your hands, ye sinners; and purify your hearts, ye double minded... humble yourselves in the sight of the Lord, and He shall lift you up."*
I Jn. 1:9 *"If we confess our sins, He is faithful and just to forgive us our sins, and to cleanse us from all unrighteousness."*

Clothing / Raiment

Deut. 8:4 "... raiment waxed not old"
Deut. 8:4 NIV "Your clothes did not wear out and your feet did not swell during these forty years."
Deut. 11:18 "He doth execute the Judgment of the fatherless and widow, and loveth the stranger, in giving him... raiment."
Neh. 9:21 "... they lacked nothing; their clothes waxed not old and their feet swelled not."
Matt. 6:28-34;Lk.12:28 "And why take ye thought for raiment? Consider the lilies of the field, how they grow... even Solomon in all his glory was not arrayed like one of these. Wherefore, if God so clothe the grass of the field... shall He not much more clothe you, O ye of little faith... for your heavenly Father knoweth that ye have need of all these things... seek ye first the kingdom of God, and His righteousness; and all these things shall be added unto you. Take therefore no thought for the morrow: for the morrow shall take thought for the things of itself. Sufficient unto the day is the evil thereof."
I Tim. 6:8 "And having food and raiment let us be therewith content."
Here is a promise that you will have food and raiment and God wants us to be content with that.
Prayer: Lord, please clothe us as You have promised in Your Word.

Conquer (ors)

Rom. 8:37 "... in all these things we are more than conquerors through Him that loved us."

Comfort

Ps. 71:21 "Thou shalt increase my greatness, and comfort me on every side."
Ps. 94:19 "... Thy comforts delight my soul."
Ps. 119:52 LB "... Your Word has been my comfort."
Ps. 119:77 LB "... let Your lovingkindness comfort me, just as you promised."
Is. 12:1 "... Thine anger is turned away, and Thou comfortedst me."
Is. 49:13 "... the Lord hath comforted His people..."
Is. 51:2,3 "The Lord shall comfort Zion (and) all her waste places..."
Is. 51:11,12 "... they shall obtain gladness and joy; and sorrow and mourning shall flee away. I, even I, am He that comforteth you..."

Is. 52:9 "... *for the Lord hath comforted His people, He hath Redeemed...*"
Is. 57:18 "... *I will... restore comforts unto him...*"
Is. 61:1,2 "*The Spirit of the Lord God is upon Me... to comfort all that mourn.*"
Is. 66:13 "... *so will I comfort you, and ye shall be comforted in Jerusalem.*"
Jn. 14:16,17,18 "*And I will pray the Father, and He shall give you another Comforter, that He may abide with you forever; even the Spirit of truth... I will not leave you comfortless: I will come to you*"
Jn. 16:7 "*Nevertheless I tell you the truth; it is expedient for you that I go away: for if I go not away, the Comforter will not come unto you; but if I depart, I will send Him unto you.*"
Jn. 14:26 "... *the Comforter... the Holy Ghost, whom the Father will send...*"
Jn. 15:26,27 "*But when the Comforter is come, whom I will send unto you from the Father, even the Spirit of truth, which proceedeth from the Father, He shall testify of Me: and ye also shall bear witness...*"
II Cor. 7:6 "... *God, that comforteth those that are cast down, comforted us...*"
Col. 2:2 "... *that their hearts might be comforted, being knit together in love, and unto all riches in the full assurance of understanding...*"
Eph. 6:22 "... *that He might comfort your hearts.*"
II Thess. 2:17 "*Now the Lord Jesus Christ Himself, and God, even our Father, which hath loved us, and hath given us everlasting consolation and good hope through grace, comfort your hearts, and stablish you in every good word and work.*"

Compassion

Ps. 86:15 "*But Thou, O Lord, art a God full of compassion, and gracious, longsuffering, and plenteous in mercy and truth.*"
Ps. 112:4 "... *He is gracious, and full of compassion, and righteous.*"
Ps. 145:8 "*The Lord is gracious, and full of compassion; slow to anger, and of great mercy. The Lord is good to all: and His tender mercies are over all His works.*"
Is. 30:18 NASB "*Therefore the Lord longs to be gracious to you, and therefore He waits on high to have compassion on you...*"
Jer. 12:15 HCSB "... *I will once again have compassion on them and return each one to his inheritance...*"
Lam. 3:22,23 "*It is the Lord's mercies that we are not consumed, because His compassions fail not. They are new every morning: great is thy faithfulness.*"
Mic. 7:19 "*He will turn again, He will have compassion upon us; He will subdue our iniquities; and... wilt cast all their sins into the depths of the sea.*"

Mk. 8:2 *"I have compassion on the multitude..."*

 Confess

Prov. 28:13 *"... whoso confesseth and forsaketh* (his sins) *shall have mercy."*
Matt. 10:32 *"Whosoever therefore shall confess Me before men, him will I confess also before My Father which is in heaven."*
Lk. 12:8 *"... whosoever shall confess Me before men, him shall the Son of man also confess before the angels of God..."*
Acts 19:18 *"And many that believed came, and confessed, and shewed their deeds ("told their faults" PB)."*
Rom. 10:9 *"... that if thou shalt confess with thy mouth the Lord Jesus, and shalt believe in thine heart that God hath raised Him from the dead, thou shalt be saved. For with the heart man believeth unto righteousness; and with the mouth confession is made unto Salvation."*
Rom. 14:11 *"For it is written, As I live, saith the Lord, every knee shall bow to Me, and every tongue shall confess to God."*
Phil. 2:11 *"... every tongue should confess that Jesus Christ is Lord, to the glory of God the Father..."*
Jms. 5:16 *"Confess your faults... and pray one for another, that ye may be healed. The effectual fervent prayer of a righteous man availeth much."*
I Jn. 1:9 *"If we confess our sins, He is faithful and just to forgive us our sins, and to cleanse us from all unrighteousness."*
I Jn. 4:2 *"Hereby know ye the Spirit of God: every Spirit that confesseth that Jesus Christ is come in the flesh is of God..."*
I Jn. 4:15 *"Whosoever shall confess that Jesus is the Son of God, God dwelleth in him, and he in God."*
Rev. 3:5 *"He that overcometh, the same shall be clothed in white raiment; and I will not blot out his name out of the Book of Life, but I will confess his name before My Father, and before His angels."*

 Confident

Phil. 1:6 *"Being confident of this very thing, that He which began a good work in you will perform it until the day of Jesus Christ..."*

Covenants

The Ten Commandments is the Covenant.
"*There was nothing in the Ark save the two Tables which Moses put therein at Horeb (at this time)... and in it have I put the Ark, wherein is the Covenant of the Lord...*" II Chron. 5:10;6:11
("And He gave unto Moses, when He had made an end of communing with him upon Mount Sionai, two tables of Testimony, tables of stone, written with the finger of God." (stone represents permanence). The Ten Commandments is a Mitzvah (Mitzvah means "*a precept or commandment*".
"*Now therefore come thou, let us make a covenant... Jacob took... stones... this heap is a witness between me and thee this day. Therefore was the name of it called... Mizpah; for he said, The Lord watch between me and thee, when we are absent one from another.*" Gen. 31:44-49
Sometimes in those days they would take a stone and break it in two, one for each party, as a contract or covenant. They would each take a piece of the rock or stone and when they came together, they could see that the two rocks fit together; this was called a Mitzvah. The Ten Commandments are similar to this. Two Tablets, one for each party; a Covenant, will, Testament, or con-tract between God and man that if you obey then God will save and give blessings; Jesus, as a man fulfilled every part of the law and if we receive Him, we have the blessings.
We have the Old and New Testament. Testament means, "*Covenant*".
"*Testament occurs twelve times in the New Testament (Heb. 9:14, etc.) as the rendering of the Gr. 'diatheke', which is twenty times rendered 'covenant' in the Authorized Version, and always so in the Revised Version. The Vulgate translates incorrectly by testamentum, whence the name 'Old' and 'New Testament', by which we now designate the two sections into which the Bible is divided.*" www.biblestudytools.com
"*In most cases a Covenant is conditional. If one party breaks the Covenant, the other party is released from it. But with God, it's different. God's promise is that even when we are faithless, He is faithful. And for every promise with condition. Jesus has met that condition. And the Bible promises that all the promises are yes in Christ Jesus* (I Cor. 1:20).
A "*Covenant is a treaty. A contract, a carefully formulated legal arrangement respecting the union... between God and man.*"
"*Each of the... Covenants is about Jesus Christ (who) is the One who fulfills God's promise to Abraham to bless all people of the earth through Him. Jesus is the One who fulfills God's promise to David of a king who will rule forever... the One whose death and Resurrection marked the beginning of*

the New Covenant... whose coming again will see us transformed and blessed forever. The Covenant commitments that God has made throughout history are all about Jesus... as we study them, we learn about Him. And our trust in God's love grows and grows." Every Promise of the Bible p. 8,9

"The Hebrew word 'Covenant', be'rit, occurs 272 times in the Od Testament. The Greek word, diatheke, is used 33 times in the New Testament... it meant a 'binding agrement' or 'contract'". Every Covenant and Promise in the Bible p. 2

A Covenant is a promise. When you enter into the Covenant of marriage, you are making a commitment. It is a promse you make to each other and to God that you promise to love each other and stay together no matter what!

A *"Covenant"* is a treaty, a contract. A carefully formulated legal arrangement respecting the union.. between God and man.

Judges 2:1 God said, *"I will never break My Covenant with you."*

Neh. 1:5 God keeps His Covenants, "... *the great and terrible God, that keepeth Covenant and mercy for them that love Him and observe His Commandments..."*

Eph. 2:12-14 *"That at that time ye were without Christ, being aliens (#3581 "stranger, foreigners") from the commonwealth of Israel, and strangers from the Covenants of promise, having no hope, and without God in the world: but now in Christ Jesus ye who sometimes were far off are made nigh by the blood of Christ. For He is our peace, who hath made both one, and hath broken down the middle wall of partition between us..."*

Neh. 1:5 *"O Lord God of heaven, the great and terrible God, that keepeth Covenant and mercy for them that love Him and observe His Commandments..."*

Neh. 9:32 *"... the great, the mighty, and the terrible God, who keepest Covenant and mercy..."*

I Kings 8:23-26 *"... there is no God like Thee, in heaven above, or on earth beneath, who keepest Covenant and mercy with Thy servants that walk before thee with all their heart..."*

Ps. 25:14 *"The secret of the Lord is with them that fear Him; and He will shew them His Covenant."*

Ps. 89:34 *"My Covenant will I not break, nor alter the thing that is gone out of My lips."*

Ps. 103:18 *"To such as keep His Covenant, and to those that remember His Commandments to do them. The Lord hath prepared His throne in the heavens; and His kingdom ruleth over all."*

Ps. 106:44:45 *"And He remembered for them His Covenant, and repented according to the multitude of His mercies."*

Ps. 107:45 *"And He remembered for them His Covenant, and repented* (Heb. # 5162 *"had compassion, comforted, changed mind, moved to pity, relent, time of mourning ended, give rest, regret"*) *according to the multitude of His mercies."*

Is. 42:6-8 *"I the Lord have called Thee* (Jesus) *in righteousness, and will hold Thine hand, and will keep Thee, and give Thee for a Covenant of the people, for a light of the Gentiles; to open the blind eyes, to bring out the prisoners from the prison, and them that sit in darkness out of the prison house. I am the Lord; that is My name: and My glory will I not give to another, neither My praise to graven images."*

Jesus was given as a sacrifice for sin which ratified the Covenant with His own blood and that is what made it new. No longer were they to offer animal sacrifices because these pointed to His sacrifice on the cross, the fulfillment of all animal sacrifices.

Is. 49:8 *"... I will ... give Thee* (Jesus) *for a Covenant of the people, to establish the earth, to cause to inherit the desolate heritages..."*

Is. 54:10 *"For the mountains shall depart, and the hills be removed; but My kindness shall not depart from thee, neither shall the Covenant of My peace be removed, saith the Lord that hath mercy on thee."*

Is. 55:3 *"... and I will make an everlasting Covenant with you, even the sure mercies of David."*

Is. 56:4 *"For thus saith the Lord unto the eunuchs that keep My Sabbaths, and choose the things that please Me, and take hold of My Covenant; even unto them will I give in Mine house and within My walls a place and a name better than of sons and of daughters: I will give them an everlasting name, that shall not be cut off. Also the sons of the stranger, that join themselves to the Lord, to serve Him, and to love the name of the Lord, to be His servants, every one that keepeth the Sabbath from polluting it, and taketh hold of My Covenant; even them will I bring to My Holy Mountain* (Rev. 22:14), *and make them joyful in My house of prayer..."*

Is. 59:21 *"... this is My Covenant with them, saith the Lord; My Spirit that is upon Thee, and My words which I have put in Thy mouth, shall not depart out of Thy mouth, nor out of the mouth of Thy seed, nor out of the mouth of Thy seed's seed, saith the Lord, from henceforth and forever."*

Is. 61:8 *"... I will make an everlasting Covenant with them."*

The ultimate fulfillment of every Covenant and promise will be future, on the New Earth.

Covenant (Edenic)

Blessed
God gives Adam dominion on condition of obedience.
Gen. 1:26-30 *"And God said, Let us make man in our image, after our likeness; and let them have dominion over the fish of the sea, and over the fowl of the air, and over the cattle, and over all the earth, and over every creeping thing that creepeth upon the earth. And God created man in His own image, in the image of God created He him; male and female created He them. And God blessed them, and God said unto them, Be fruitful, and multiply, and replenish the earth, and subdue it: and have dominion over the fish of the sea, and over the fowl of the air, and over every living thing that moveth upon the earth. And God said, Behold, I have given you every herb bearing seed, which is upon the face of all the earth, and every tree, in the which is the fruit of a tree yielding seed; to you it shall be for meat. And to every beast of the earth, and to every fowl of the air, and to everything that creepeth upon the earth, wherein there is life, I have given every green herb for meat: and it was so."*

Covenant (Adamic)

Gen. 3:16-19 *"And I will put enmity between thee and the woman, and between thy seed and her seed; it shall bruise thy head, a nd thou shalt bruise his heel..."*

Covenant (Noahic/Rainbow)

The first time we see the word *"Covenant"* in the Bible is with Noah. The flood was a Judgment upon the world... because of sin but Noah found grace.
Gen. 6:8 *"But Noah found grace in the eyes of the Lord... a just man and perfect in his generation."*
After the flood they were afraid that it would flood again. That is why they built the Tower of Babel. We don't have to be afraid every time it rains.
Gen. 6:18;7:1 *"But with thee (Noah) I will establish My Covenant... for thee have I seen righteous before Me in this generation."*
Gen. 8:13-17 *"I do set My bow in the cloud, and it shall be for a token of a Covenant between Me and the earth. And it shall come to pass, when I bring a cloud over the earth, that the bow shall be seen in the cloud: and I will re-*

member My Covenant, which is between Me and you and every living creature of all flesh; and the waters shall no more become a flood to destroy all flesh. And the bow shall be in the cloud; and I will look upon it, that I may remember the everlasting Covenant between God and every living creature of all flesh that is upon the earth. And God said unto Noah, This is the token of the Cov-enant, which I have established between God and every living creature of all flesh that is upon the earth."

Gen. 8:21,22;9:1,2 "... and the Lord said in His heart, I will not again curse the ground anymore for man's sake... neither will I again smite anymore everything living, as I have done. While the earth remaineth, seedtime and harvest, and cold and heat, and summer and winter, and day and night shall not cease. And God blessed Noah and his sons, and said unto them, Be fruitful, and multiply, and replenish the earth. And the fear of you and the dread of you shall be upon every beast... every fowl of the air, upon all that moveth... and... all the fishes... into your hand are they delivered."

Gen. 9:9-17 "... behold, I establish My Covenant with you, and with your seed after you; and with every living creature that is with you, of the fowl, of the cattle, and of every beast of the earth with you; from all that go out of the Ark, to every beast of the earth. And I will establish My Covenant with you; neither shall all flesh be cut off anymore by the waters of a flood; neither shall there anymore be a flood to destroy the earth. And God said, This is the token of the Covenant which I make between Me and you and every living creature that is with you, for perpetual generations: I do set My bow in the cloud, and it shall be for a token of a Covenant between Me and the earth. And it shall come to pass, when I bring a cloud over the earth, that the bow shall be seen in the cloud: and I will remember My Covenant, which is between Me and you and every living creature of all flesh; and the waters shall no more become a flood to destroy all flesh. And the bow shall be in the cloud; and I will look upon it, that I may remember the everlasting Covenant between God and every living creature of all flesh that is upon the earth. And God said unto Noah, This is the token of the Covenant, which I have established between Me and all flesh that is upon the earth."

II Pet.2:5 "And spared not the old world, but saved Noah the eighth person (eight people on the Ark), a preacher of righteousness, bringing in the flood upon the world of the ungodly..."

Covenant (Abrahamic)

Also called the "*Covenant in flesh*" (Gen. 17:13) or "*Covenant of circumcision*" (Acts 7:8).

We inherit the blessings of Abraham through Jesus, Gal. 3:14,29.

God made special promises to Abraham. He promised that his children would be as the stars in heaven, He promised to give the land as a permanent possession (which is ultimately fulfilled on the New Earth). He promised that all the earth would be blessed through Abraham, Gen. 12:3. The Savior of the world came through Abraham and we become adopted sons and daughters of Abraham. God preserved the Ten Commandments through the descendants of Abraham and most of the Bible was written by his descendants. Jesus was called *"the king of the Jews"*, Gen. 27:37. Over and over He is called, *"the God of Israel"*, II Kings 22:15 etc.

Gen. 15:6 *"And he* (Abraham) *believed in the Lord; and He* (God) *counted it to him for righteousness."*

Deut. 4:31 *"... for the Lord thy God... will not... forget the Covenant of thy fathers, which He sware unto them."*

Ther are seven promises made to Abraham
1. Make a great nation (1:2)
2. God will bless you (1:2)
3. Make you a great name (12:2)
4. You will be a blessing (12:2)
5. Bless those who bless you (12:3)
6. In you all families of earth blessed (12:3)
7. Give the land to you (12:7)

1. I will make you a Great Nation - Numerous descendants
   Gen.12:2,3,7 *"And I will make of thee a great nation..."*
   Gen.13:16 *"And I will make thy seed as the dust of the earth..."*
   Gen. 17:2 *"And I will make My Covenant between Me and thee, and will multiply thee exceedingly."*
   Gen. 17:6,7 *"And I will make thee exceeding fruitful, and I will make nations of thee..."*
   I will make you a father of many nations
   Abraham means *"father of a multitude"*
   Gen. 17:4,5 *"... My Covenant is with thee, and thou shalt be a father of many nations..."*
   Gen. 22:15-18 *"... as the sand which is upon the sea shore; and thy seed shall possess the gate of his enemies..."*
   Rom. 4:17 *"... as it is written, I have made thee a father of many nations..."*

2. I will bless you
   Gen. 12:2,3 *"... and I will bless thee, and make thy name great; and thou shalt be a blessing: and I will bless them that bless thee, and curse him that curseth thee: and in thee shall all families of the earth be blessed."*
   Gen. 14:19,20 *"And He (God) blessed him (Abraham), and said, Blessed be Abram of the Most High God..."*
   Gen. 22:15-18 *"... in blessing I will bless thee... in thy seed shall all the nations of the earth be blessed; because thou hast obeyed..."*

3. I will make your name great
   Gen.12:2 *"And I will make... thy name great..."*

4. You will be a blessing
   "... and thou shalt be a blessing..." Gen. 12:2

5. I will those who bless you
   "And I will bless them that bless thee..." Gen. 12:3

6. I will bless all families of earth through you (because of Jesus)
   "... in thee shall all families of the earth be blessed." Gen. 12:3
   Gen. 17:1-21*"... the Lord appeared to Abram, and said.. I am the Almighty God; walk before Me, and be thou perfect (#8549 "complete, sound, blameless, integrity, whole")... this is My Covenant, which ye shall keep.. every man child among you shall be circumcised ... it shall be a token of the Covenant betwixt Me and you..."*
   (In the Old Testament they were circumcised in the flesh to enter into the Covenant with God but in the New Testament we believe and are baptized under water to enter into the Covenant with God; this is the circumcision of the heart.
   (Col. 2:11,12 *"... in whom also ye are circumcised with the circumcision made without hands, in putting off the body of the sins of the flesh, by the circumcision of Christ: buried with Him in baptism, wherein also you are risen with Him through the faith of the operation of God, who hath raised Him from the dead."*
   Gen. 22:17,18;26:4,5;28:13-15 Because Abraham did not withhold his son, *"... that in blessing I will bless thee... in thy seed shall all the nations of the earth be blessed; because thou hast obeyed My voice."*
   Gal. 3:14 *"That the blessing of Abraham might come on the Gentiles through Jesus Christ; that we might receive the promise of the*

Spirit through faith."
*We are adopted sons/daughters of God and Abraham and heirs of the promises
Gal. 3:29 *"And if ye be Christ's then are ye Abraham's seed, and heirs according to the promise."*
Gal. 4:5,7 *"... that we might receive the adoption of sons... and if a son, then an heir of God through Christ."*
Rom. 8:17 *"... if children, then heirs..."*
Rom. 9:8,9 *"... they which are the children of the flesh, these are not the children of God: but the children of the promise are counted for the seed. For this is the Word of promise..."*

7. I give you the land
   Gen. 12:6,7 *"And Abram passed through the land... and the Lord appeared unto Abram, and said, Unto thy seed will I give this land..."*
   Gen. 13:14-17 *"And the Lord said unto Abram... lift up now thine eyes, and look from the place where thou art Northward, and Southward, and Eastward, and Westward: for all the land which thou seest, to thee will I give it, and to thy seed forever* (this will ultimately be fulfilled on the New Earth)*... arise, walk through the land in the length of it and in the breadth of it; for I will give it unto thee."*
   Gen. 15:18 *"In the same day the Lord made a Covenant with Abram, saying, Unto thy seed have I given this land, from the river of Egypt unto the great river, the river Euphrates..."*
   Gen. 17:8-13 *"And I will give unto thee, and to thy seed after thee, the land wherein thou art a stranger, all the land of Canaan, for an everlasting possession; and I will be their God..."*
   I Chron. 16:17,21 *"And hath confirmed the same to Jacob for a law, and to Israel for an everlasting Covenant, saying, Unto thee will I give the land of Canaan, the lot of your inheritance... He suffered no man to do them wrong."*

Covenant (Mosaic)

Deut.11:26-28 *"Behold, I set before you this day a blessing and a curse; a blessing, if ye obey the Commandments of the Lord your God, which I command you this day: and a curse, if ye will not obey the Commandments of the Lord your God, but turn aside out of the way which I command you this*

day, to go after other gods, which ye have not known... it shall come to pass, when the Lord thy God hath brought thee in unto the land whither thou goest to possess it, that thou shalt put the blessing upon mount Gerizim... for ye shall pass over Jordan to go in to possess the land which the Lord your God giveth you... ye shall observe to do all the Statutes and Judgments..."
Deut. 28 – Blessings for obedience and curses for disobedience
Jesus redeemed us from the curse by becoming a curse for us when He hung on the cross. He took our curse and so we can now receive His blessing.
"Christ hath redeemed us from the curse of the law, being made a curse for us: fr it is written, Cursed is everyone that hangeth on a tree." Gal. 3:13

Covenant to Return to the Land

God promised Israel that they would come back to the land after the 70 year Babylonian captivity.
Deut.30:1-10 *"And it shall come to pass, when all these things are come upon thee, the blessing and the curse, which I have set before thee, and thou shalt call them to mind among all the nations whither the Lord thy God hath driven thee, and shalt return unto the Lord thy God, and shalt obey His voice according to all that I command thee this day, thou and thy children, with all thine heart, and with all thy soul; that then the Lord thy God will turn thy captivity, and have compassion upon thee, and will return and gather thee from all the nations, whither the Lord thy God hath scattered thee. If any of thine be driven out unto the outmost parts of heaven, from thence will the Lord thy God gather thee, and from thence will He fetch thee: and the Lord thy God will bring thee into the land which thy fathers possessed, and thou shalt possess it; and He will do thee good, and multiply thee above thy fathers... and with all thy soul, that thou mayest live... and thou shalt return and obey the voice of the Lord, and do all His Commandments which I command thee this day. And the Lord thy God will make thee plenteous in every work of thine hand... for good: for the Lord will again rejoice over thee for good, as He rejoiced over thy fathers: if thou shalt hearken unto the voice of the Lord thy God, to keep His Commandments and His Statutes which are written in this book of the law, and if thou turn unto the Lord thy God with all thine heart, and with all thy soul... but the Word is very nigh unto thee, in thy mouth, and in thy heart, that thou mayest do it. See, I have set before thee this day life and good, and death and evil; in that I command thee this day to love the Lord thy God, to walk in His ways, and to keep His Commandments... that thou mayest live and multiply: and the Lord thy God shall bless thee in the land whither thou goest to possess it... therefore choose life, that*

both thou and thy seed may live: that thou mayest **love** the Lord thy God, and that thou mayest **obey** His voice, and that thou mayest cleave unto Him: for He is thy life, and the length of thy days: that thou mayest dwell in the land which the Lord sware unto thy fathers..."

Again we see that love and obey go together.

Covenant (Davidic)

Some say that this is the 7th Covenant

II Sam. 7:5,9-16 *"Go and tell My servant David, Thus saith the Lord... I was with thee whithersoever thou wentest, and have cut off all thine enemies out of thy sight, and have made thee a great name... I will appoint a place for My people Israel, and will plant them, that they may dwell in a place of their own, and move no more; neither shall the children of wickedness afflict them anymore... the Lord telleth thee that He will make thee an house... and I will establish his kingdom... I will stablish the throne of his kingdom forever. I will be his father, and he shall be My son. If he commit iniquity I will chasten him... but My mercy shall not depart away from him... and thine house and thy kingdom...* (and) *thy throne shall be established forever.*

Prayer: Lord, please go with me wherever I go and cut off my enemies. Don't let Your mercy depart from me or my children.

II Sam. 23:5 *"... yet He hath made with me an everlasting Covenant..."*

Ps. 89:3,4 *"I have made a Covenant with My chosen, I have sworn unto David My servant, thy seed will I establish forever, and build up thy throne to all generations. Selah."*

I Kings 8:23-26; I Chron. 17:8-14

Covenant (New)

(Jer. 31:31 tells us that the New Covenant is obeying God's law from the heart!

Deut. 30:3-13 TM *"... God will restore everything you lost; He'll have compasson on you; He'll come back and pick up the pieces... He will give you a good life... God... will cut away the thick calluses on your heart and your children's hearts, freeing you to love God... with your whole heart and soul and live, really live. And you will make a **new start**, listening obediently to God, keeping all His Commandments... God... will outdo Himself in making things go well for you.. you must return to God... totally, heart and soul, holding nothing back..."*

Jer. 31:31-33 *"Behold, the days come, saith the Lord, that I will make a New Covenant with the house of Israel, and with the house of Judah: not according to the Covenant that I made with their fathers in the day that I took them by the hand to bring them out of the land of Egypt; which My Covenant they brake, although I was an husband unto them... this shall be the Covenant that I will make with the house of Israel; after those days.. I will put My law in their inward parts, and write it in their hearts; and will be their God, and they shall be My people."*

The Old Covenant was based on animal sacrifices and the promises of the people to obey but they couldn't do it. The New Covenant is based on the blood of Jesus and God's promises to us which He will keep.

Jer. 32:40 *"... and I will make an everlasting Covenant with them, that I will not turn away from them, to do them good..."*

Ez. 16:60-63 *"... I will remember My Covenant with thee in the days of thy youth, and... establish unto thee an everlasting Covenant. Then thou shalt remember thy ways, and be ashamed... and I will establish My Covenant with thee; and thou shalt know that I am the Lord: that thou mayest remember, and be confounded... because of thy shame, when I am pacified toward thee for all that thou hast done..."*

Ez. 20:37 *"... and I will bring you into the bond of the Covenant..."*

Hosea 2:18 *"And in that day will I make a Covenant for them..."*

Matt. 26:27,28 *"And He took the cup... saying, Drink ye all of it; for this is My blood of the New Testament ("Covenant" ESV), which is shed for many for the remission of sins."*

Lk. 1:72 *"To perform the mercy promised to our fathers, and to remember His Holy Covenant..."*

Lk. 22:20 *"... the cup after supper, saying, This cup is the New Testament ("Covenant" NIV) in My blood, which is shed for you."*

I Cor. 11:25 *"... this cup is the New Testament ("Covenant" NIV) in My blood..."*

II Cor. 3:6 *"Who also hath made us able ministers of the New Testament ("Covenant" NIV)... of the Spirit... the Spirit giveth life."*

Eph. 2:12 *"... at that time ye were without Christ, being aliens from the commonwealth of Israel, and strangers from the Covenants of promise, having no hope, and without God in the world... made nigh by the blood of Christ."*

Heb. 8:6-8,10 *"... (Jesus has). also He is the Mediator of a better Covenant... established upon better promises... the days come... when I will make a New Covenant with the house of Israel... not according to the Covenant that I made with their fathers in the day when I took them by the hand to lead them out of the land of Egypt; because they continued not in My Covenant...*

this is the Covenant that I will make with the house of Israel after those days... I will put My laws into their mind, and write them in their hearts: and I will be to them a God and they shall be to Me a people... for if that first Covenant had been faultless, then should no place have been sought for the second. For finding fault with them... the days come... this is the Covenant that I will make with the house of Israel after those days... I will put My laws into their mind, and write them in their hearts: and I will be to them a God, and they shall be to Me a people..."

Heb. 9:15-17 *"And for this cause He is the Mediator of the New Testament (Covenant), that by means of death, for the Redemption of the transgressions that were under the first Testament (Covenant), they which are called might receive the promises of eternal inheritance. For where a Testament is, there must also of necessity be the death of the Testator. For a Testament is of force after men are dead: otherwise it is of no strength at all while the Testator liveth."*

Heb. 12:24 *"... to Jesus the mediator of the New Covenant, and to the blood of sprinkling, that speaketh better things than that of Abel* (lamb sacrifice).*"*

Heb. 13:20 *"Now the God of peace, that brought again from the dead our Lord Jesus, that great Shepherd of the sheep, through the blood of the everlasting Covenant, make you perfect in every good work to do His will..."*

Covenant of Peace

"In the KJV translation of Scripture the word 'Covenant' appears 272 times, and the word, 'Peace' appears 400 times. However, the phrase 'Covenant of Peace' occurs only 4 times."

1. An everlasting priesthood (a type of Jesus)
   *"... behold, I give unto him **My Covenant of Peace**... the Covenant of an everlasting priesthood* (in the order of Melchizedek, Heb. 7:17, 24)*..."* Num. 25:12,13
2. After mountains's depart and hills removed (at second coming of Jesus Rev. 6:14)
   *"For the mountains shall depart, and the hills be removed; but My kindness shall not depart from thee, neither shall the **Covenant of My Peace** be removed, saith the Lord that hath mercy on thee."* Is. 54:10
3. When there are no more evil beasts on the earth and everyone dwells safely then *"...I will make with them a **Covenant of Peace**..."* Ez. 34:25
4. When God is the Temple on earth.

*"Moreover I will make a **Covenant of Peace** with them: it shall be an everlasting Covenant with them: and I will place them, and multiply them, and will set My Sanctuary in the midst of them forevermore... I will be their God and they will be My people."* Ez. 37:26

God the Father and Jesus are the Temple on the New Earth and come to dwell with man, Rev. 21:3;22.

 Covenant of Salt

A Covenant of salt is a Covenant of peace

Num. 18:19 *"All the heave offerings of the Holy things, which the children of Israel offer unto the Lord, have I given thee, and thy sons and thy daughters with thee, by a Statute forever: it is a **Covenant of salt** forever before the Lord unto thee and to thy seed with thee."*

Lev. 2:13 *"And every oblation of thy meat offering shalt thou season with salt; neither shalt thou suffer the **salt of the Covenant** of thy God to be lacking from thy meat offering: with all thine offerings thou shalt offer salt."*

II Chron. 13:5 *"Ought ye not to know that the Lord God of Israel gave the kingdom over Israel to David forever, even to him and to his sons by a **Covenant of salt**?"*

Mk. 9:50 *"... have **salt** in yourselves, and have **peace** one with another."*

Salt represent preserving, endurance, stablility, everlasting, forever, cleansing, purifying, and peace. Salt was used to seal the deal, sometimes with a meal. In Ezekiel 47:11 the dead sea will some day be made fresh and alive. Lot's wife obeyed by leaving Sodom but her heart was still there and she was turned into a pillar of salt. Here salt could represent Judgment. I think that the Covenant of Salt represents the Covenant of peace because we see that salt and peace are synomynous in Mk. 9:50. The Covenant of peace will be fulfilled with Jesus reigning on the New Earth after the thousand years. Then there will be peace forever. There will never again be anymore war, Is. 2:4.

Elisha healed the poisonous water with salt in II Kings 2:21,22.

Job says, *"Can that which is unsavoury be eaten without salt?"* Job 6:6.

Here the salt makes bland food worth eating.

Matt. 5:13 *"Ye are the salt of the earth: but if the salt have lost his savour, wherewith shall it be salted? It is thenceforth good for nothing, but to be cast out, and to be trodden under foot of men."*

Everlasting peace will only be on the New Earth.

Convert

Ps. 19:7 *"The law of the Lord is perfect, converting the soul..."*
Is. 6:10 *"... lest they see with their eyes, and hear with their ears, and understand with their heart, and convert, and be healed."*
Matt. 13:15;Jn.12:40 *"... lest at any time they should see with their eyes, and hear with their ears, and should understand with their heart, and should be converted, and I should heal them."* (quoting from Is. 6:10)
Matt. 18:3 *"... be converted, and become as little children... enter into the kingdom of heaven."*
Mk. 4:12 *"... be converted, and their sins should be forgiven them."*
Lk. 22:32 *"But I have prayed for thee, that thy faith fail not... and... thou art converted..."*
Acts 3:19 *"Repent... and be converted, that your sins may be blotted out, when the times of refreshing shall come from the presence of the Lord..."*
Acts. 28:27 *"For the heart of this people is waxed gross, and their ears are dull of hearing, and their eyes have they closed; lest they should see with their eyes, and hear with their ears, and understand with their heart, and should be converted, and I should heal them."*
Jms. 5:19 *"... if any of you do err from the truth, and one convert him; let him know, that he which converteth the sinner from the error of his way shall save a soul from death, and shall hide a multitude of sins."*

Crown

Num. 6:7.8 *"... because the consecration of his God is upon his head. All the days of his separation he is Holy unto the Lord."*
"Crown of Separation – the word is actually translated separation and is the Hebrew word 'nezer' (Heb. #5145) which means consecration, crown, and separation. All the days of his separation he is Holy to the Lord. It could also be termed our Crown of Holiness. We are of God." The Seven Crowns
Ps. 5:12 Crown of Protection – *"For Thou, Lord, wilt bless the righteous with favor wilt Thou compass him as with a shield* (lit. *"... with a shield, with favor will you edge."*)
#5849 "Atar", *"compass - a primitive root; to encircle (for attack or protecttion); especially to crown (lit. or fig.) compass, crown."*
"... God is all powerful and it is He who is our protection which is a blessing reserved for the righteous person." The Seven Crowns

Ps. 8:5 *"What is man, that Thou art mindful of him? And the son of man, that thou visitest him? For Thou hast made him a little lower than the angels, and hast crowned him with glory and honour."*
(Man will be equal to the angels at the Resurrection, Lk.20:35 ,26.)
Ps. 21:3 *"... Thou settest a crown of pure gold on his head."*
Ps. 103:4 *"... who crowneth thee with lovingkindness* (lit. *"... who crowns you with Covenant loyalty"*) *and tender* (#2617 *"favor"*) *mercies* (#7356 *"compas-sion"*)..."
Prov. 4:9 *"She* (wisdom) *shall give to thine head an ornament of grace; a crown of glory shall she deliver to thee."*
Prov. 12:4 *"A virtuous woman is a crown to her husband..."*
Prov. 14:18 *"... the prudent are crowned with knowledge."*
Prudent means *"acting with or showing care and thought for the future."*
Prov. 14:24 *"The crown of the wise is their riches..."*
Prov. 16:31 *"The hoary head* (white hair) *is a crown of glory..."*
Prov. 17:6 *"... children's children are the crown of old men..."*
Is. 28:5 *"In that day shall the Lord of hosts be for a crown of glory, and for a diadem of beauty* (*"beautiful, beauty, boast, glorious, glory, adornment, honor, jewels"*), *unto the residue of His people..."*
Is. 62:3 *"Thou shalt also be a crown of glory in the hand of the Lord, and a royal diadem in the hand of thy God."*
Ez. 16:12 *"And I put a jewel on thy forehead, and earrings in thine ears, and a beautiful* (*"pomp, pride, splendor"*) *crown upon thine head."*
Ez. 21:26 *"... take off the crown* (*"diadem"*)... *exalt him that is low, and abase him that is high."*
Matt. 20:16 *"So the last shall be first, and the first last..."*
Zech. 9:16 *"And the Lord their God shall save them in that day... for they shall be as the stones* (#68 *"jeweler, lapis-lazuli, carbuncle*) *of a crown* (#5145 *"consecration crown, dedication, hair, Nazarite, separation"*), *lifted up as an ensign* (*"#5264 "displayed"*)..."
Jn. 19:2 *"And the soldiers platted a crown of thornes, and put it on His* (Jesus) *head..."* (someday Jesus will wear many crowns and be King of kings)
Jesus wore a crown of thorns so we could wear a crown of glory in eternity!
I Cor. 9:25 *"And every man that striveth for the mastery is temperate in all things. Now they do it to obtain a corruptible crown; but we an incorruptible* (crown)."
I Thess. 2:19 *"For what is our hope, or joy, or crown of rejoicing* (#2746 *"boasting, glory"*)..."
II Tim. 2:5 *"And if a man also strive for masteries, yet is he not crowned, except he strive lawfully."*

II Tim. 4:8 "Henceforth there is laid up for me a crown of righteousness, which the Lord, the righteous Judge, shall give me at that day: and not to me only, but unto all them also that love His appearing."
Heb. 2:6,7 "... what is man that... thou crownedst him with glory and honour, and didst set him over the works of thy hands..."
Heb. 2:9 "But we see Jesus, who was made a little lower than the angels for the suffering of death, crowned with glory and honour; that He by the grace of God should taste death for every man."
Jms. 1:12 "Blessed is the man that endureth temptation: for when he is tried, he shall receive the crown of life, which the Lord hath promised to them that love Him."
I Pet. 5:4 "And when the chief Shepherd shall appear, ye shall receive a crown of glory that fadeth not away."
Rev. 2:10 "... be thou faithful unto death, and I will give thee a crown of life."
Rev. 3:11 "... hold that fast which thou hast, that no man take thy crown."
In other words, it can be taken away from you and you must hold fast to Jesus.
Rev. 14:14 ... upon the cloud One sat like unto the Son of man, having on His head a golden crown..."
Rev. 19:11,12 "And I saw heaven opened, and behold a white horse... on His head were many crowns..."

Cry

See Weep

Curses

Prov. 26:2 "... so the curse causeless shall not come."
Prov. 26:2 PB "... shall be driven away."
Prov. 26:2 NIV "Like a fluttering sparrow or a darting swallow, an undeserved curse does not come to rest."
Prov. 26:2 NLT "... an undeserved curse will not land on its intended victim."
Prov. 26:2 NASB "... does not alight."
Prov. 26:2 HCSB "... goes nowhere."
Prov. 26:2 ABPE "... so an empty curse wanders."
Prov. 26:2 JB 2000 "... shall never come."
Prov. 26:2 DBT "... shall not come."

Dancing

Ps. 30:11 NIV *"You turned my wailing ("mourning" KJV) into ("joyful" NLT) dancing."*

Death / Grave / Resurrection

The promise is that God will raise us from the dead some day.
Ps. 49:15 *"But God will Redeem ("ransom" ESV) my soul from the power of the grave ("Sheol" ESV): for he shall receive me..."*
Ps. 116:8 *"For thou hast delivered my soul from death, mine eyes from tears, and my feet from falling."*
Ps. 118:18 *"The Lord... hath not given me over unto death."*
Prov. 10:2;11:4 *"... righteousness delivereth from death."*
Prov. 12:28 *"In the way of righteousness is life; and in the pathway thereof there is no death."*
Prov. 14:27 *"The fear of the Lord is a fountain of life, to depart from the snares of death."*
Prov. 14:32 *"... the righteous hath hope in his death."*
Is. 25:8 *"He will swallow up death in victory..."*
Is. 27:19 *"Thy dead men shall live, together with my dead body shall they arise. Awake and sing, ye that dwell in dust: for thy dew is as the dew of herbs, and the earth shall cast out the dead* (at the Resurrection)*..."*
Matt. 10:28 *"... do not fear those who kill the body but cannot kill the soul..."*
Lk14:14 *"... for thou shalt be recompensed at the* **Resurrection of the just**.*"*
Jn. 5:28,29 *"Marvel not at this: for the hour is coming, in the which all that are in the graves shall hear His voice, and shall come forth; they that have done good, unto the* **Resurrection of life**...*"*
Jn. 6:39,40,44 *"... of all which He hath given Me I should lose nothing, but should raise it up again at the last day... and I will raise him up..."*
Jn. 8:51 Jesus said, *"If a man keep My saying ("obeys My Word" NIV), he shall never see death."*
Jn. 11:24 *"Martha saith unto Him* (Jesus), *I know that he* (Lazarus) *shall rise again in the Resurrection at the last day. If you believe in Me, you will never die."*
Jn. 11:25,26 *"Jesus said unto her, I am the Resurrection, and the life: he that believeth in Me, though he were dead, yet shall he live: and whosoever liveth and believeth in Me shall never die. Believest thou this?"*
Acts 17:18 *"... (Paul) preached unto them Jesus, and the Resurrection."*

Acts 17:31,32 "... *whereof He hath given assurance unto all men, in that He hath raised Him* (Jesus) *from the dead... the Resurrection of the dead...*"

Acts 24:15 "*And have hope toward God... that there shall be a* **Resurrection** *of the dead, both* **of the just and unjust**."

Again we see only two Resurrections; the Resurrection of the just and the Resurrection of the unjust.

I Cor. 15:21-23 "... *by man* (Jesus) *came also the Resurrection of the dead. For as in Adam all die, even so in Christ shall all be made alive, but every man in his own order: Christ the firstfruits; afterward they that are Christ's at His coming.*"

We see here that the Resurrection (of the righteous) is at the second coming of Jesus, I Thess. 4:13-17

I Cor. 15:26 "*The last enemy that shall be destroyed is death. For He hath put all things under His feet...*"

I Cor. 15:35 "... *how are the dead raised up... with what body do they come?*"

I Cor. 15:42-44 "*So also is the Resurrection of the dead. It is sown in corruption; it is raised in incorruption: it is sown in dishonour; it is raised in glory; it is sown in weakness; it is raised in power: it is sown a natural body; it is raised a Spiritual body...*"

I Cor. 15:51-55 "... *I shew you a mystery; we shall not all sleep, but we shall all be changed, in a moment, in the twinkling of an eye, at the last Trump: for the trumpet shall sound, and the dead shall be raised incorruptible, and we shall be changed. For this corruptible must put on incorruption, and this mortal must put on immortality. So when this corruptible shall have put on incorruption, and this mortal shall have put on immortality, then shall be brought to pass the saying that is written, Death is swallowed up in victory. O death, where is thy sting? O grave, where is thy victory?*"

II Cor. 1:9,10 "... *we had the sentence of death in ourselves, that we should not trust in ourselves, but in God which raiseth the dead: who delivered us from so great a death... in whom we trust that He will yet deliver us...*"

II Cor. 4:14 "... *the Lord Jesus shall raise up us also by Jesus, and present us with you.*"

II Cor. 5:6-8 "*Therefore we are always confident, knowing that, whilst we are at home in the body, we are absent from the Lord... and willing rather to be absent from the body, and to be present with the Lord.*"

Phil. 1:20-24 "... *so now also Christ shall be magnified in my body, whether it be by life, or by death. For to me to live is Christ and to die is gain... for... having a desire to depart, and to be with Christ; which is far better: nevertheless to abide in the flesh is more needful for you.*"

Phil. 3:21 "... *who shall change our vile body, that it may be fashioned like unto His glorious body...*"

Col. 3:3 *"For ye are dead, and your life is hid with Christ in God."*
I Thess. 1:10 *"And to wait for His Son from heaven... which delivered us from the wrath to come."*
I Thess. 4:13-18 *"... I would not have you to be ignorant, brethren, concerning them which are asleep, that ye sorrow not, even as others which have no hope. For if we believe that Jesus died and rose again, even so them also which sleep in Jesus will God bring with Him. For this we say unto you by the Word of the Lord, that we which are alive and remain unto the coming of the Lord shall not prevent them which are asleep. For the Lord Himself shall descend from heaven with a shout, with the voice of the archangel, and with the Trump of God: and the dead in Christ shall rise first; then we which are alive and remain shall be caught up together with them in the clouds, to meet the Lord in the air: and so shall we ever be with the Lord. Wherefore comfort one another with these words."*
Heb. 2:9 *"... that He (Jesus)... should taste death for every man."*
Heb. 11:34 *"... that they might obtain a better Resurrection..."*
Jude 14,15 *"... the Lord cometh with ten thousands of His saints..."*
Rev. 1:18 *"I am He that liveth, and was dead; and, behold, I am alive forevermore, Amen; and have the keys of hell and of death."*
Rev. 2:11 *"... he that overcometh shall not be hurt of the second death."*
Rev. 20:5,6 *"... this is the first Resurrection. Blessed and Holy is he that hath part in the first Resurrection: on such the second death hath no power..."*
Rev. 20:14 *"And death and hell were cast into the lake of fire ..."*
Rev. 21:4 *"... and there shall be no more death..."*

Decree

We must be careful not to decree bad things that are undeserved or they could come back on our own head.
(*"His mischief shall return upon his own head"* Ps. 7:16; *"... as you have done, it will be done to you; your deeds will return upon your own head."* Ob. 1:15)
Job 22:28 *"... thou shalt also decree a thing, and it shall be established unto thee..."*
Job. 22:28 NIV *"... what you decide on will be done."*
Ps. 2:7 *"I will declare the decree..."*
Is. 10:1 *"Woe unto them that decree unrighteous decrees..."*

Defense

Job 22:24-30 "... *The Lord shall be thy defence...*"

Deliver

Ex. 12:27 *"...He... delivered our houses..."*
Ex. 18:18 *"... Moses told his father-in-law all that the Lord had done... and how the Lord delivered them... blessed be the Lord who hath delivered you (and)... who hath delivered His people... the Lord is greater than all gods..."*
Ex. 23:22,23 *"... I will be an enemy unto thine enemies, and an adversary unto thine adversaries... I will cut them off."*
Ex. 23:27 *"I will send My fear before thee, and will destroy all the people to whom thou shalt come, and I will make all thine enemies turn their backs unto thee."*
Ez. 23:31 *"... for I will deliver the inhabitants of the land into your hand..."*
Num. 21:34 *"... the Lord our God delivered all unto us..."*
Deut. 3:2 *"And the Lord said unto me, Fear him not: for I will deliver him, and all his people, and his land, into thy hand..."*
Judges 10:11 *"... did not I deliver you..."*
I Sam. 7:3 *"And prepare your hearts unto the Lord... He will deliver you (from your enemies)..."*
I Sam. 12:11 *"... and delivered you out of the hand of your enemies on every side, and ye dwelled safe."*
I Sam. 14:12 *"... for the Lord hath delivered them into the hand of Israel."*
II Sam. 22:1,2 *"... the Lord had delivered him out of the hand of all his enemies... the Lord is my Rock, and my Fortress, and my Deliverer..."*
II Sam. 22:18 *"He delivered me from my strong enemy, and from them that hated me: for they were too strong for me."*
II Sam. 22:20 *"He brought me forth also into a large place: He delivered me, because He delighted in me."*
II Chron. 16:8,9 *"... because thou didst rely on the Lord, He delivered them into thine hand. For the eyes of the Lord run to and fro throughout the whole earth, to shew Himself strong in the behalf of them whose heart is perfect toward Him..."*
Job 5:19 *"He shall deliver thee in six troubles: yea, in seven there shall no evil touch thee."*
Job 22:29,30 *"When men are cast down, then thou shalt say, There is lifting up; and He shall save the humble person. He shall deliver the island of the innocent: and it is delivered by the pureness of thine hands."*

(Job 22:29 NIV *"When people are brought low and you say, 'Lift them up!' then He will save the downcast."*

(Job 22:29 NASB *"When you are cast down, you will speak with confidence, and the humble person He will save. He will deliver one who is not innocent and he will be delivered through the cleanness of yur hands."*

Ps. 18:16-18 The Lord, *"... He drew me out of many waters. He delivered me from my strong enemy, and from them which hated me: for they were too strong for me... the Lord was my stay."*

Ps. 18:47,48 *"It is God that avengeth me, and subdueth the people under me. He delivereth me from mine enemies: yea, thou liftest me up above those that rise up against me: thou hast delivered me from the violent man."*

Ps. 32:7 *"... Thou shalt compass me about with songs of deliverance..."*

Ps. 33:19 *"To deliver their soul from death..."*

Ps.34:4,6,7,19 *"I sought the Lord, and He heard me, and delivered me from all my fears... the Lord heard him, and saved him out of all his troubles. The angel of the Lord encampeth round about them that fear him, and delivereth them... many are the afflictions of the righteous: but the Lord delivereth him out of them all."*

Ps. 35:10 The *"... Lord... deliverest the poor from him that is too strong for him, yea, the poor and the needy from him that spoileth ("rob" NIV) him?"*

Ps. 37:39,40 *"But the Salvation of the righteous is of the Lord: He is their strength in the time of trouble. And the Lord shall help them, and deliver them: He shall deliver them from the wicked, and save them, because they trust in Him."*

Ps. 41:1-3 *"Blessed is he that considereth the poor: the Lord will deliver him in time of trouble... Thou wilt not deliver him unto the will of his enemies."*

Ps. 50:15 *"And call upon Me in the day of trouble: I will deliver thee, and thou shalt glorify Me."*

Ps. 55:18 *"He hath delivered my soul in peace from the battle that was against me; for there were many* (angels) *with me."*

Ps. 56:13 *"For Thou hast delivered my soul from death: wilt not Thou deliver my feet from falling..."*

Ps. 91:3 *"Surely He shall deliver thee from the snare of the fowler ("hunter's net" HCSB), and from the noisome pestilence ("deadly desease" NLT)."*

Ps. 91:15,16 *"... therefore will I deliver him; I will set him on high, because he hath known My name. He shall call upon Me, and I will answer him: I will be with him in trouble; I will deliver him, and honour him..."*

Ps. 97:10 *"... He delivereth them out of the hand of the wicked."*

Ps. 107:6,7 *"And they cried unto the Lord in their trouble, and He delivered them out of their distresses."*

Ps. 107:19,20 "... and saved them out of their distresses... and delivered them from their destructions."
Ps. 119:170 "... deliver me according to Thy Word."
Ps. 144:2 "... my Deliverer; my shield... He in whom I trust..."
Prov. 2:12 "To deliver thee from the way of the evil man, from the man that speaketh forward things..."
Prov. 11:8,9 "The righteous is delivered out of trouble... through knowledge shall the just be delivered."
Prov. 11:21 "... the seed of the righteous shall be delivered."
Is. 38:17 "... Thou hast... delivered it from the pit of corruption..."
Is. 43:13 "... and there is none that can deliver out of My hand..."
Is. 26:4 "... I... will deliver you."
Jer. 1:19 "And they shall fight against thee; but they shall not prevail against thee; for I am with thee, saith the Lord, to deliver thee."
Jer. 15:20,21 "... they shall not prevail against thee: for I am with thee, saith the Lord. And I will deliver thee out of the hand of the wicked, and I will Redeem thee out of the hand of the terrible."
Jer. 20:13 "... He hath delivered the soul of the poor from the hand of evildoers."
Jer. 39:17,18 "But I will deliver thee in that day, saith the Lord: and thou shalt not be given into the hand of the men of whom thou art afraid. For I will surely deliver thee, and thou shalt not fall by the sword, but thy life shall be for a prey unto thee: because thou hast put thy trust in Me."
Joel 2:32 "And it shall come to pass, that whosoever shall call on the name of the Lord shall be delivered..."
Lk. 1:71,74 "That we should be saved from our enemies, and from the hand of all that hate us... that He (God) would grant unto us, that we being delivered out of the hand of our enemies might serve Him without fear, in Holiness and righteousness before Him, all the days of our life."
Acts 7:9,10 "... Joseph... God was with him and delivered him out of all his afflictions, and gave him favour, and wisdom..."
Acts 26:17,18 "Delivering thee from the people, and from the Gentiles... to open their eyes, and to turn them from darkness to light, and from the power of Satan unto God, that they may receive forgiveness of sins, and inheritance among them which are Sanctified by faith that is in Me (Jesus)."
Rom. 7:24,25 "O wretched man that I am! Who shall deliver me from the body of this death? I thank God through Jesus Christ our Lord..."
Rom. 8:21 "Because the creature (Gr. #2937 "creation") itself also shall be delivered from the bondage of corruption into the glorious liberty..."
The liberty we have is freedom from sin not freedom to sin, Rom. 6:14,

II Cor. 1:10 *"Who delivered us from so great a death, and doth deliver: in whom we trust that He will yet deliver us…"*
Col. 1:13 *"Who hath delivered us from the power of darkness…"*
I Thess. 1:10 *"… Jesus, which delivered us from the wrath to come."*
II Tim. 3:11 *"… what persecutions I endured: but out of them all the Lord delivered me."*
II Tim. 4:17,18 Paul said, *"… I was delivered out of the mouth of the lion. And the Lord shall deliver me from every evil work, and will preserve me unto His heavenly kingdom…"*

Depression / Anxious / Anxiety

Prov. 12:25 *"Heaviness in the heart of man maketh it stoop: but a good word maketh it glad."*
(Prov. 12:25 NIV *"An anxious heart weighs a man down, but a kind word cheers him up."*
II Sam. 22:29 *"… Thou art my lamp… the Lord will lighten my darkness."*
(II Sam. 22:29 NIV *"… the Lord turns my darkness to light."*
Ps. 34:15-19 *"The eyes of the Lord are upon the righteous, and His ears are open ("attentive" NIV) unto their cry… the righteous cry, and the Lord heareth, and delivereth them out of all their troubles. The Lord is nigh ("close" NIV) unto them that are of a broken heart; and saveth such as be of a contrite spirit. Many are the afflictions of the righteous: but the Lord delivereth him out of them all."*
(Ps. 34:15-19 NLT *"The eyes of the Lord watch over those who do right; His ears are open to their cries for help… the Lord hears His people when they call to Him for help. He rescues them from all their troubles. The Lord is close to the brokenhearted; He rescues those who are crushed in spirit."*
Ps. 43:5 *"… unto God my exceeding joy (" … God, my joy and my delight." NIV) … why art thou cast down, O my soul? And why art thou disquieted within me? Hope is God: for I shall yet praise Him, who is the health of my countenance, and my God."*
(Ps. 43:5 NLT *"… God, the source of all my joy… why am I discouraged… Why so sad? I will put my hope in God…"*
Ps. 43:5 NASB *"… God, my exceeding joy… why are you in despair, O my soul? And why are you disturbed within me? Hope in God, for I shall again praise Him, the help of my countenance and my God."*
Ps. 55:22 *"Cast thy burden upon the Lord, and He shall sustain thee: He shall never suffer the righteous to be moved ("shaken" NASB)."*
(Ps. 55:22 NIV *"Cast your cares on the Lord and He will sustain you; He will*

never let the righteous fall."
(Ps. 55:22 NLT *"Give your burdens to the Lord, and He will take care of you. He will not permit the godly to slip and fall."*
Ps. 68:35 NIV *"You are awesome, O God, in Your Sanctuary; the God of Israel gives power and strength to His people..."*
Ps. 71:1-5 *".. I am poor and needy: make haste unto me, O God: Thou art my help and my deliverer; O Lord, make no tarrying. In Thee, O Lord, do I put my trust: let me never be put to confusion. Deliver me in Thy righteousness, and cause me to escape* (from depression)*: incline Thine ear unto me, and save me... Thou hast given commandment to save me* (from depression)*... deliver me... for Thou art my hope, O Lord God: Thou art my trust..."*
Ps. 119:117 *"Hold Thou me up, and I shall be safe* (from depression)*..."*
God delivers us from our enemies and depression is an enemy.
Ps. 136:24 *"And hath Redeemed us from our enemies: for His mercy endureth forever."*
Ps. 143:7-9 *"Hear me speedily, O Lord: my spirit faileth: hide not Thy face from me... cause me to hear Thy lovingkindness in the morning; for in Thee do I trust... deliver me, O Lord... I flee unto Thee to hide me."*
(Ps. 143:7 NLT *"Come quickly, Lord, and answer me, for my depression deepens. Don't turn away from me, or I will die..."*
(Ps. 143:8 NIV *"... let the morning bring me word of Your unfailing love, for I have put my trust in You."*
Ps. 147:3 NAS *"He healeth the broken in heart... bindeth up their wounds."*
Is. 26:3,4 *"Thou wilt keep him in perfect peace, whose mind is stayed on Thee; because he trusteth in Thee. Trust ye in the Lord forever: for in the Lord Jehovah is everlasting strength* (*"Rock eternal"* NIV) *..."*
Is. 35:10 *"And the ransomed of the Lord shall return. And come to Zion with songs and everlasting joy upon their heads: they shall obtain joy and gladness, and sorrow and sighing shall flee away."*
Is. 40:29-31 *"He giveth power to the faint; and to them that have no might He increaseth strength... they that wait upon the Lord shall renew their (*"find new"* NLT; *"gain new"* NASB) strength; they shall mount up with wings as eagles; they shall run, and not be weary; and they shall walk, and not faint."*
(Is. 40:27-31 NLT *"O Israel, how can you say the Lord does not see your troubles? How can you say God refuses to hear your case... He gives power to those who are tired and worn out; He offers strength to the weak... those who wait on the Lord will find new strength..."*
Is. 53:4 *"Surely He hath borne our griefs (*"infirmities"* NIV), and carried our sorrows..."*
(Is. 53:4 NLT *"Yet it was our weaknesses He carried; it was our sorrows that weighed Him down..."*

Jer. 32:27 *"Behold, I am the Lord, the God of all flesh: is there anything too hard for Me?"*
Mic. 4:10 *"... there the Lord shall Redeem thee from the hand of thine enemies* (depression)*."*
Rom. 15:33 *"Now the God of peace be with you all. Amen."*
Phil. 4:6,7 *"Be careful for nothing; but in everything by prayer and supplication with thanksgiving let your requests be made known unto God. And the peace of God, which passeth all understanding ("comprehension" NASB), shall keep your hearts and minds through Christ Jesus."*
Phil. 4:6,7 NIV *"Do not be anxious about anything, but in everything, by prayer and petition, with thanksgiving, present your requests to God. And the peace of God, which transcends all understanding, will guard your hearts and your minds in Christ Jesus."*
(Phil. 4:6-9 NLT *"Don't worry about anything; instead, pray about everything. Tell God what you need, and thank Him for all He has done. If you do this, you will experience God's peace, which is far more wonderful than the human mind can understand. His peace will guard your hearts and minds as you live in Christ Jesus. And now, dear brothers and sisters... fix your thoughts on what is true and honorable and right. Think about things that are pure and lovely and admirable. Think about things that are excellent and worthy of praise. Keep putting into practice all you learned from me and heard from me and saw me doing, and the God of peace will be with you."*
II Cor. 6:2 NLT *"... God is ready to help you right now..."*
II Cor. 7:5 NLT *"But God, who encourages those who are discouraged, encouraged us..."*
II Cor. 7:6 *"But God, that comforteth those that are cast down..."*
(II Cor. 7:6 NIV *"But God, who comforts the downcast, comforted us..."*
(II Cor. 7:6 NASB *"But God, who comforts the depressed, comforted us..."*
Jms. 4:10 *"Humble yourselves in the sight of the Lord... He shall lift you up."*
I Pet. 5:7,10 *"... casting all your care ("anxiety" NASB) upon Him; for He careth for you ("He cares about what happens to you" NLT)... but the God of all grace, who hath called us into His eternal glory by Christ Jesus, after that ye have suffered a while, make you perfect, stablish, strengthen, settle you."*
I Pet. 5:10 NIV *"... ("In His kindness God called you..." NLT)... restore you and make you strong, firm, and steadfast."*
See also the sections on *"Healing"* – *"Help"* – *"Deliver"*

Desire (s) / Desired

Ex. 32:24 *"... neither shall any man desire thy land, when thou shalt go up to appear before the Lord..."*

Prayer: Lord, keep people from desiring my things when I am away. Thank You in Jesus' name, Amen!

II Sam. 23:5 *"... surely He would ... grant me my every desire."*

Ps. 27:4 *"One thing have I desired of the Lord, that will I seek after; that I may dwell in the house of the Lord all the days of my life, to behold the beauty of the Lord, and to inquire in His Temple."*

Ps. 37:4 *"Delight thyself also in the Lord; and He shall give thee the desires of thine heart."*

Ps. 107:30 *"Then are they glad because they be quiet; so He bringeth them unto their desired haven."*

(Ps. 107:30 NIV *"They were glad when it grew calm, and He guided them to their desired haven."*

Ps. 145:19 *"He will fulfil the desire of them that fear Him: He also will hear their cry, and will save them."*

Ps. 21:2 *"Thou hast given him his heart's desire..."*

Ps. 37:39,40 *"But the Salvation of the righteous is of the Lord: He is their strength in the time of trouble. And the Lord shall help them, and deliver them: He shall deliver them from the wicked, and save them, because they trust in Him."*

Prov. 10:24 *"... the desire of the righteous shall be granted."*

Prov. 21:20 *"There is treasure to be desired... oil in the dwelling of the wise..."*

(Prov. 21:20 NLT *"The wise have wealth and luxury..."*

Mk. 11:24 *"Therefore I say unto you, What things soever ye desire, when ye pray, believe that ye receive them, and ye shall have them."*

II Cor. 5:2 *"For in this we groan, earnestly desiring to be clothed upon with our house* (new body) *which is from heaven..."*

II Thess. 1:11 PB *"... and satisfy all your desires."*

I Jn. 5:15 *"And if we know that He hear us, whatsoever we ask, we know that we have the petitions that we desired of Him."*

Dwell / Abide

Ps. 37:27 *"Depart from evil, and do good; and dwell forevermore."*

Ps. 68:18 *"Thou hast ascended on high... that the Lord God might dwell among them."*

Ps. 69:35,36 *"For God will save Zion, and will build the cities of Judah: that they may dwell there, and have it in possession. The seed also of His servants shall inherit it: and they that love His name shall dwell therein."*

Ps. 91:1 *"He that dwelleth in the secret place of the Most High shall abide under the shadow of the Almighty."*

Ps. 140:13 *"... the upright shall dwell in Thy presence."*

Prov. 2:21 *"For the upright shall dwell in the land, and the perfect..."*

Is. 58:12 *"And they that shall be of thee shall build the old waste places: thou shalt raise up the foundations of many generations; and thou shalt be called, The repairer of the breach, The restorer of paths to dwell in."*

Ez. 34:28 *"... but they shall dwell safely, and none shall make them afraid."*

Ez. 38:8 *"... they shall dwell safely all of them."*

Hosea 14:7 *"They that dwell under His shadow shall return; they shall revive as the corn, and grow as the vine..."*

Zech. 2:11 *"And many (#7227 "abundance, much, great, myriads, exceedingly") nations shall be joined to the Lord in that day, and shall be My people: and I will dwell in the midst of thee, and thou shalt know that the Lord of hosts hath sent Me unto thee."*

Rom. 8:11 *"But if the Spirit of Him that raised up Jesus from the dead dwell in you, He that raised up Christ from the dead shall also quicken your mortal bodies by His Spirit that dwelleth in you."*

II Cor. 6:16 *"... I will dwell in them, and walk in them; and I will be their God and they shall be My people."*

Eph. 3:17-19 *"That Christ may dwell in your hearts by faith..."*

Col. 3:16 *"Let the Word of Christ dwell in you richly in all wisdom..."*

I Jn. 4:13 *"Hereby know we that we dwell in Him, and He in us, because He hath given us of His Spirit."*

Rev. 21:3,22 *"... I heard a great voice out of heaven saying, Behold, the Tabernacle of God is with men, and He will dwell with them, and they shall be His people, and God Himself shall be with them, and be their God ... and I saw no Temple therein: for the Lord God Almighty and the Lamb are the Temple of it* (on the New Earth).*"*

Early

See Wakes

Enemy / Enemies

Ex. 23:22 "... I will be an enemy unto thine enemies, and an adversary unto thine adversaries."

Deut. 33:29 "... thine enemies shall be found... liars..."

II Sam. 22:18 "He delivered me from my strong enemy, and from them that hated me: for they were too strong for me."

I Chron. 17:8-14 "... I will subdue all thine enemies..."

Ezra 8:31 "... the hand of our God was upon us, and He delivered us from the hand of the enemy, and of such as lay in wait by the way."

Ps. 18:17 "He delivered me from my strong enemy, and from them which hated me: for they were too strong for me."

Ps. 37:13-17 "The Lord shall laugh at him: for He seeth that his day is coming... their sword shall enter into their own heart... their bows... (and) the arms of the wicked shall be broken.. the Lord, upholdeth the righteous."

Ps. 58:6 "Break their teeth O God, in their mouth: break out the great teeth of the young lions, O Lord."

This is talking about breaking their demonic power through the power of the Holy Spirit.

Ps. 61:3 "For Thou hast been a shelter for me... a strong tower from the enemy."

Ps. 81:13,14 "Oh that My people had hearkened unto Me, and Israel had walked in My ways? I should soon have subdued their enemies and turned My hand against their adversaries."

Ps. 107:2 "Let the Redeemed of the Lord say so, whom He hath Redeemed from the hand of the enemy."

Ps. 108:13 "Through God we shall do valiantly; for He it is that shall tread down our enemies."

Ps. 138:7 "Though I walk in the midst of trouble, Thou wilt revive me: Thou shalt stretch forth Thine hand against the wrath of mine enemies, and Thy right hand shall save me."

Prov. 16:7 "When a man's ways please the Lord, He maketh even his enemies to be at peace with him."

Jer. 15:11 "... Verily it shall be well with thy remnant... I will cause the enemy to entreat thee well in the time of evil and in the time of affliction."

Zeph. 3:15 "The Lord hath taken away thy Judgments, He hath cast out the enemy..."

Lk. 1:71,74 "... we should be saved from our enemies, and from the hand of all that hate us... delivered out of the hand of our enemies..."

Lk. 10:19 *"... I give unto you power to tread on serpents and scorpions, and over all the power of the enemy: and nothing shall by any means hurt you."*
I Cor. 15:25 *"For He must reign, till He hath put all enemies under his feet."*

Eternal Life

Jn. 5:39 *"Search the Scriptures; for in them ye think* (#1380 *"esteem, recognize, regard"*) *ye have eternal life* (and you do)*: and they are they which testify of Me* (Jesus)*."*
I Tim. 6:19 *"Laying up in store for themselves a good foundation against the time to come, that they may lay hold on eternal life."*

Exalted

Lk. 1:52 *"He hath put down the mighty... and exalted them of low degree."*

Eye (s)

Eyes represent the Holy Spirit and the all-knowing power of God.
II Chron. 16:9 *"For the eyes of the Lord run to and fro throughout the whole earth to shew himself strong in the behalf of them whose heart is perfect toward Him..."*
Job 34:21 *"... His eyes are upon the ways of man, and He seeth all his goings."*
Ps. 33:18 *"Behold, the eye of the Lord is upon them that fear Him, upon them that hope in His mercy..."*
Ps. 34:15 *"The eyes of the Lord are upon the righteous... His ears are open unto their cry."*
Prov. 5:21 NIV *"For your ways are in full view of the Lord, and He examines all your paths."*
Prov. 5:21 NKJV *"For the ways of man are before the eyes of the Lord, and He ponders all his paths."*
Prov. 15:3 *"The eyes of the Lord are in every place, beholding the evil and the good."*
Is. 32:3 *"And the eyes of them that see shall not be dim..."*
Zech. 3:9 *"For behold the stone that I have laid before Jesus; upon one Stone shall be seven eyes..."*
Zech. 4:10 *"... with those seven; they are the eyes of the Lord which run to and fro through the whole earth."*

(Rev. 4:5,8 The seven eyes are the "... *seven lamps of fire burning before the throne, which are the seven Spirits of God*.")
I Pet. 3:12 "... *the eyes of the Lord are over the righteous... His ears are open unto their prayers: but the face of the Lord is against them that do evil.*"
Rev. 1:4 "... *the seven Spirits which are before His throne...*"
(Rev. 3:1 The seven eyes are the same as the "... *seven Spirits of God...*"
Rev. 1:7 "... *He cometh with clouds; and every eye shall see Him...*"
Rev. 4:5,6 "*And out of the throne proceeded lightnings and thunderings and voices: and there were seven lamps of fire, burning before the throne, which are the seven Spirits of God. And before the throne there was a sea of glass like unto crystal: and in the midst of the throne, and round about the throne, were four beasts full of eyes before and behind.*"
Rev. 5:6 "... *a Lamb as it had been slain, having seven horns and seven eyes, which are the seven Spirits of God sent forth into all the earth.*"

Faith / Faithful / Faithfulness

Deut. 7:9 "*Know therefore that the Lord thy God, He is God, the faithful God, which keepeth Covenant and mercy with them that love Him and keep His Commandments to a thousand generations...*"
Ps. 31:23 "... *love the Lord, all ye His saints... the Lord preserveth the faithful...*"
Ps. 36:5 "*Thy mercy, O Lord, is in the heavens; and Thy faithfulness reacheth unto the clouds.*"
Ps. 89:33 "*Nevertheless My lovingkindness will I not utterly take from him, nor suffer My faithfulness to fail.*"
Ps. 119:90 "*Thy faithfulness is unto all generations: Thou hast established the earth, and it abideth.*"
Is. 49:7 "... *because the Lord is faithful...*"
Lam. 3:22,23 "*It is of the Lord's mercies that we are not consumed.. His compasssions fail not. They are new every morning: great is Thy faithfulness.*"
Hosea 2:20 "*I will even betroth thee unto Me in faithfulness: and thou shalt know the Lord.*"
Hab. 2:4 "... *the just shall live by his faith.*"
Matt. 9:22 "... *Jesus... said, Daughter, be of good comfort; thy faith hath made thee whole. And the woman was made whole from that hour.*"
Matt. 9:29 "*Then touched He their eyes, saying, According to your faith be it unto you.*"
Matt. 17:20,21 "... *for verily I say unto you, If ye have faith as a grain of mustard seed, ye shall say unto this mountain, Remove hence to yonder*

place; and it shall remove; and nothing shall be impossible unto you. Howbeit this kind goeth not out but by prayer and fasting"

Matt. 21:21 "Jesus answered and said unto them, Verily I say unto you, If ye have faith, and doubt not, ye shall not only do this which is done to the fig tree, but also if ye shall say unto this mountain, Be thou removed, and be thou cast into the sea; it shall be done."

Matt. 25:21,23 "... well done, thou good and faithful servant: thou hast been faithful over a few things, I will make thee ruler over many things: enter thou into the joy of thy Lord."

Mk. 5:34 "And He said unto her, Daughter, thy faith hath made thee whole; go in peace, and be whole of thy plague."

Mk. 10:52 "... Jesus said unto him, Go thy way; thy faith hath made thee whole... immediately he received his sight, and followed Jesus in the way."

Lk. 7:50;8:48 NIV "Jesus said to the woman, 'Your faith has saved you...'"

Lk. 16:10 "He that is faithful in that which is least is faithful also in much..."

Lk. 16:11 NIV "So if you have not been trustworthy ("faithful" KJV) in handling worldy wealth, who will trust you with true riches?"

Lk. 16:12 "And if ye have not been faithful in that which is another man's, who shall give you that which is your own?"

Lk. 17:6 "... if ye had faith as a grain of mustard seed, ye might say unto this Sycamine tree, Be thou plucked up by the root, and be thou planted in the sea; and it should obey you."

Lk. 17:19 "... He said unto him, Arise, go thy way: thy faith hath made thee whole."

Lk. 18:42 "... Jesus said... Receive thy sight: thy faith hath saved thee."

Lk. 19:17 "And He said unto him, Well, thou good servant: because thou hast been faithful in a very little, have thou authority over ten cities."

Acts 14:9 "... perceiving that he had faith to be healed..."

Acts 15:9 "... purifying their hearts by faith."

Acts 26:18 "To open their eyes, and to turn them from darkness to light, and from the power of Satan unto God, that they may receive forgiveness of sins, and inheritance among them which are Sanctified by faith that is in me."

Rom. 1:17 "... the just shall live by faith."

Rom. 3:28 "... man is Justified by faith..."

Rom. 5:1 "Therefore being Justified by faith, we have peace with God through our Lord Jesus Christ..."

Rom. 10:17 "... faith cometh by hearing, and hearing by the Word of God."

Rom. 12:3 "... God hath dealt to every man the measure of faith."

I Cor. 1:9 "... God is faithful..."

I Cor. 10:13 "There hath no temptation taken you but such as is common to man: but God is faithful, who will not suffer you to be tempted above that

ye are able; but will with the temptation also make a way to escape, that ye may be able to bear it."
II Cor. 5:7 "... for we walk by faith, not by sight..."
Gal. 3:8,9 "... the Scripture, foreseeing that God would Justify the heathen through faith, preached before the Gospel unto Abraham, saying, In thee shall all nations be blessed so then they which be of faith are blessed with faithful Abraham."
Gal. 3:11 "... the just shall live by faith."
Gal. 3:14 "That the blessing of Abraham might come on the Gentiles through Jesus Christ; that we might receive the promise of the Spirit through faith."
Gal. 3:24 "... that we might be Justified by faith."
Eph. 2:8 "For by grace are ye saved through faith; and that not of yourselves: it is the gift of God..."
Eph. 3:17 "That Christ may dwell in your hearts by faith..."
Phil. 1:6 "Being confident of this very thing, that He which hath begun a good work in you will perform it until the day of Jesus Christ..."
Phil. 3:9 "... be found in Him, not having mine own righteousness... but that which is through the faith of Christ, the righteousness... of God by faith..."
I Thess. 5:24 "Faithful is He that calleth you, who also will do it ("bring it to pass" NASB; "perform it" American Bible in plain English)."
II Thess. 1:3 "... your faith groweth exceedingly..."
II Thess. 1:11 "Wherefore also we pray always for you, that our God would count you worthy of this calling, and fulfil all the good pleasure of His goodness, and the work of faith with power..."
II Thess. 3:3 "But the Lord is faithful, who shall stablish you, and keep you from evil."
I Tim. 6:12 "Fight the good fight of faith, lay hold on eternal life, whereunto thou art also called, and hast professed a good profession before many witnesses."
Heb. 10:23 "Let us hold fast the profession of our faith without wavering; (for He is faithful that promised)..."
Heb. 10:38 "... the just shall live by faith..."
Heb. 11:1 "Now faith is the substance of things hoped for, the evidence of things not seen."
Heb. 11:7 "By faith Noah... became heir of the righteousness which is by faith."
Heb. 11:11 "Through faith... Sara... Judged Him faithful who had promised."
Hebs. 11:33 "Who through faith subdued kingdoms, wrought righteousness, obtained promises, stopped the mouths of lions..."
Heb. 12:2 "Looking unto Jesus the author and finisher of our faith..."
Jms. 1:3 "... the trying of our faith worketh patience."

Jms. 1:6 *"... let him ask in faith, nothing wavering."*
Jms. 2:5 *"... God* (Hath) *chosen the poor of this world rich in faith, and heirs of the kingdom which He hath promised to them that love Him."*
Jms. 2:22 *"... faith wrought with his works... faith made perfect..."*
Jms. 5:15 *"And the prayer of faith shall save the sick, and the Lord shall raise him up; and if he have committed sins, they shall be forgiven him."*
I Pet. 1:7 *"That the trial of your faith, being much more precious than of gold that perisheth, though it be tried with fire, might be found unto praise and honour and glory at the appearing of Jesus Christ..."*
I Pet. 1:9 *"Receiving the end of your faith, even the Salvation of your souls."*
I Jn. 1:9 *"If we confess our sins, He is faithful and just to forgive us our sins, and to cleanse us from all unrighteousness."*
I Jn. 5:4 *"For whatsoever is born of God overcometh the world: and this is the victory that overcometh the world, even our faith."*

Family / Friends

Promises you can claim for your family and friends
Deut. 3:2 *"And the Lord said unto me... I will deliver him..."*
Deut. 39:27-29 NIV *"He... is your... helper..."*
God is the One who helps us with our family and friends!
Josh. 6:17 Rahab and all that were with her were saved
Job 22:30 *"He shall deliver the island* (means, *"not innocent"*) *of the innocent: and it is delivered by the pureness of thine hands."*
Job 22:30 NIV *"He will deliver even one who is not innocent, who will be delivered through the cleaness of your hands."*
Jer. 24:7 *"And I will give them an heart to know Me... for they shall return unto Me with their whole heart."*
Jer. 32:40 *"... I will put My fear in their hearts, that they shall not depart from Me. Yea, I will rejoice over them to do them good..."*
Ez. 14:11 *"... that* (they) *may go no more astray from Me, neither be polluted anymore with all their transgressions; but that they may be My people, and I may be their God, saith the Lord God."*
Ez. 36:25-33 *"... I* (will) *sprinkle clean water upon you... ye shall be clean: from all your filthiness, and from all your idols, will I cleanse you. A new heart also will I give you... a new Spirit will I put within you... I will take away the stony heart out of your flesh... I will give you a heart of flesh... I will put My Spirit within you, and cause you to walk in My Statutes ... and ye shall be My people, and I will be your God. I will also save you from all your unclean-ness... then shall ye remember your own evil ways, and your doings that*

were not good, and shall loathe yourselves in your own sight for your iniquities and for your abominations. Not for your sakes do I this... be ashamed and confounded for your own ways... in the day that I shall have cleansed you from all your iniquities..."

Jer. 3:17-19 *"... neither shall they walk anymore after the imagination of their evil heart... thou shalt call Me, My Father; and shalt not turn away..."*

Jer. 24:6,7 *"For I will set Mine eyes upon them for good, and I will bring them again to this land: and I will build them, and not pull them down; and I will plant them, and not pluck them up. And I will give them an heart to know Me, that I am the Lord: and they shall be My people, and I will be their God: for they shall return unto Me with their whole heart."*

Jer. 32:37-42 *"... I will cause them to dwell safely: and they shall be My people, and I will be their God: and I will give them one heart, and one way, that they may fear Me forever, for the good of them, and of their children after them: and I will make an everlasting Covenant with them, that I will not turn away from them, to do them good; but I will put My fear in their hearts, that they shall not depart from Me. Yea, I will rejoice over them to do them good, and I will plant them in this land assuredly with My whole heart and with My whole soul. For thus saith the Lord... so will I bring upon them all the good that I have promised them."*

Ez. 11:19,20 *"I will give them one heart... I will put a new Spirit within you; and I will take the stony heart out of their flesh, and will give them an heart of flesh: that they may walk in My Statutes, and keep Mine Ordinances, and do them: and they shall be My people, and I will be their God."*

Hosea 14:4 *"I will heal their backsliding ("waywardness" NIV; "faithlessness" NLT; "apostasy" ESV), I will love them freely: for Mine anger is turned away."*

Joel 2:17 *"... spare Thy people, O Lord..."*

Matt. 18:14 *"... it is not the will of your Father which is in heaven, that one of these little ones should perish."*

Lk. 1:74-77 About John the Baptist *"That He would grant unto us, that we being delivered out of the hand of our enemies might serve Him without fear, in Holiness and righteousness before Him, all the days of our life. And thou, child, shalt be called the prophet of the Highest: for thou shalt go before the face of the Lord to prepare His ways; to give knowledge of Salvation unto His people by the remission* (removal) *of their sins, through the tender mercy of our God; whereby the dayspring from on high hath visited us, to give light to them that sit in darkness and in the shadow of death, to guide our feet into the way of peace. And the child grew, and waxed strong in Spirit."*

Lk. 22:31,32 *"... Satan hath desired to have you... but I have prayed for thee that thy faith fail not..."*

Jn. 17:11-13 *"Father, keep through Thine own name those whom Thou hast given Me, that they may be one, as we are... I have kept them in Thy name... I have kept, and none of them is lost... that they might have My joy fulfilled in themselves."*
Prayer: Lord, I pray that You will keep the ones that You have given to me and that none will be lost that we may have Your joy in ourselves, Amen!
Acts 3:26 *"... sent Him (Jesus) to bless you in turning away every one of you from his iniquities."*
Prayer: Lord, bless my family in turning them away from their sins. Thank You in Jesus' name, Amen!
Acts 11:8 *"... God also... granted repentance unto life."*
Acts 11:14 *"... whereby thou and all thy house shall be saved."*
Acts 16:14 *"... Lydia... whose heart God opened..."*
Prayer: Lord, open the hearts of my loved ones to receive the Gospel also as it says in Your Word.
Acts 16:31 *"... believe on the Lord Jesus Christ, and thou shalt be saved, and thy house..."*
Acts 26:18 *"... to open their eyes... to turn them from darkness to light, and from the power of Satan unto God, that they may receive forgiveness of sins, and inheritance among them which are Sanctified by faith that is in Me."*
Prayer: Lord, please open our eyes and turn us from the darkness to the light – from the power of Satan to God. Forgive our sins and give us an inheritance among the Sanctified. In Jesus' name, Amen!
Acts 27:24 *"... and lo, God hath given thee all them that sail with thee."*
Rom. 6:18 *"Being then made free from sin..."*
I Tim. 2:1 *"I exhort therefore, that, first of all, supllications, prayers, intercessions, and giving of thanks, be made for all men..."*
II Tim. 2:25,26 *"... God... will give them repentance to the acknowledging of the truth; and that they may recover themselves out of the snare of the Devil, who are taken captive by him at his will."*
Prayer: Lord, give my family repentance and deliver them from the snare of the Devil who has taken them captive to do his will. Thank You Jesus!
Heb. 8:10 *"... this is the (New) Covenant that I will make with the house of Israel after those days... I will put My laws into their mind, and write them in their hearts: and I will be to them a God, and they shall be to Me a people..."*
We can ask God to change the hearts of our loved ones so that they will want to obey God from the heart!
Jms. 5:13-16 *"Is any among you afflicted? Let him pray... and the prayer of faith shall save (them)..."*
I Jn. 5:16 *"If any man see his brother sin a sin which is not unto death, he shall ask, and he shall give him life for them that sin not unto death..."*

Fatherless

Ps. 10:14 "... *Thou art the helper of the fatherless...*"

Favor/Favour

Gen. 18:1,3 "... *the Lord appeared to him...* (Abraham) *said... if now I have found favour in Thy sight, pass not away, I pray Thee, from Thy servant...*"
Gen. 39:21 "*But the Lord was with Joseph, and shewed him mercy, and gave him favour in the sight of the keeper of the prison.*"
Ex. 11:3 "*And the Lord gave the people favour in the sight of the Egyptians...*"
Ex. 12:35,36 "... *they borrowed of the Egyptians jewels of silver, and jewels of gold, and raiment: and the Lord gave the people favour in the sight of the Egyptians, so that they lent unto them such things as they required. And they spoiled the Egyptians.*"
I Sam. 2:26 "*And the child Samuel grew on, and was in favour both with the Lord, and also with men.*"
Job 10:2,12 "*I will say unto God... Thou hast granted me life and favour, and Thy visitation hath preserved my spirit.*"
Ps. 5:12 "*For Thou, Lord, wilt bless the righteous; with favour wilt Thou compass him as with a shield.*"
Ps. 30:4,5 "*Sing unto the Lord... in His favour is life...*"
Ps. 102:13 "*Thou shalt arise, and have mercy upon Zion: for the time to favour her* (Jerusalem), *yea, the set time, is come.*"
Ps. 119:57,58 "... *Lord, I have said I would keep Thy Word. I intreated Thy favour with my whole heart: be merciful unto me according to Thy Word.*"
Prov. 3:1-4 "... *forget not My law; but let thine heart keep My Commandments: for length of days, and long life, and peace, shall they add to thee. Let not mercy and truth forsake thee: bind them about thy neck; write them upon the table of thine heart: so shalt thou find favour and good understanding in the sight of God and man.*"
Prov. 8:32-35 "... *blessed are they that keep My ways... blessed is the man that heareth me, watching daily at my gates, waiting at the posts of my doors. For whoso findeth me* (wisdom) *findeth life, and shall obtain favour..*"
Prov. 12:2 "*A good man obtaineth favour of the Lord...*"
Prov. 13:15 "*Good understanding giveth favour...*"
Prov. 14:9 "... *among the righteous there is favour.*"
Prov. 16:15 "... *his favour is as a cloud of the latter rain.*"
Prov. 18:22 "*Whoso findeth a wife findeth a good thing, and obtaineth favour of the Lord.*"

Song of Solomon 8:10 "... *then was I in his eyes as one that found favour.*"
Is. 60:10 "... *in My favour have I had mercy on thee.*"
Dan. 1:9 "*Now God had brought Daniel into favour and tender love with the prince of the eunuchs.*"
Lk. 1:30,31 "... *Mary; for thou hast found favour of God. Thou shalt conceive in thy womb, and bring forth a son, and shalt call His name Jesus.*"
Lk. 2:52 "... *Jesus increased in wisdom and stature... in favour with God and man.*"
Acts 2:46.47 "*And* (the church) *continuing daily with one accord in the Temple, and breaking bread from house to house, did eat their meat with gladness and singleness of heart...*"
Acts 7:10 "... *Joseph... God was with him, and delivered him out of all his afflictions, and gave him favour and wisdom...*"
Acts 7:45,46 "... *David, who found favour before God...*"
Prayer: Lord, You gave them favor in the Bible. Please give me Your favor as You did for them. Thank You in Jesus' name, Amen!

Fear

See Afraid

Fight/Battle

Ez. 14:14 "*The Lord will fight for you...*"
Ez. 14:27 "... *and the Lord overthrew the Egyptians in the midst of the sea.*"
Deut. 1:30 "*The Lord your God which goeth before you, He shall fight for you, according to all that He did for you in Egypt before your eyes.*"
Deut. 3:22 "*Ye shall not fear them... the Lord your God He shall fight for you.*"
Deut. 11:18 "*He doth execute the Judgment of the fatherless and widow, and loveth the stranger....*"
Josh. 23:3,10 "... *for the Lord your God is He that hath fought for you... one man of you shall chase a thousand: for the Lord your God, He it is that fighteth for you, as He hath promised you.*"
I Sam. 17:47 "... *all this assembly shall know that the Lord saveth not with sword and spear... the battle is the Lord's... He will give you into our hands.*"
I Chron. 14:15 "... *God is gone forth before thee to smite... the Philistines.*"
II Chron. 14:11 "... *for we rest on thee, and in Thy name we go against this multitude* ("great army" PB)..."
II Chron. 20:15 "... *thus saith the Lord unto you, Be not afraid nor dismayed by reason of this great multitude; for the battle is not yours, but God's.*"

Ps. 24:8 *"Who is this King of glory? The Lord strong and mighty, the Lord mighty in battle."*
Eccl. 9:11 *"... the race is not to the swift, nor the battle to the strong ..."*
Jer. 1:19 *"And they shall fight against thee; but they shall not prevail against thee; for I am with thee, saith the Lord, to deliver thee."*

Fire

Ps. 66:12 *"... we went through fire and through water: but Thou broughtest us out into a wealthy place."*
Is. 43:2 *"When thou passest through the waters, I will be with thee; and through the rivers, they shall not overflow thee: When thou walkest through the fire, thou shalt not be burnt; neither shall the flame kindle upon thee."*
Lk. 3:16 *"... He shall baptize you with the Holy Ghost and with fire."*
Actsd 2:3,4 *"And there appeared unto them cloven tongues like as of fire, and it sat upon each of them. And they were all filled with the Holy Ghost..."*
Acts 2:19 *"And I will shew wonders in the heaven above, and signs in the earth beneath; blood, and fire, and vapour of smoke ..."*
Acts 7:30 *"... there appeared to him (Moses) in the wilderness of Mt Sinai an angel of the Lord in a flame of fire in a bush."*
Heb. 11:33 *"Who through faith... quenched the violence of fire ..."*
Heb. 12:29 *"For our God is a consuming fire."*
I Pet. 1:7 *"That the trial of your faith, being much more pecious than gold that perisheth, though it be tried with fire, might be found unto praise and honour and glory at the appearing of Jesus Christ."*

Flood / Waters

Gen. 9:15,16 *"And I (God) will remember My Covenant, which is between Me and you and every living creature of all flesh; and the waters shall no more become a flood to destroy all flesh. And the bow shall be in the cloud; and I will look upon it, that I may remember the everlasting Covenant between God and every living creature of all flesh that is upon the earth."*
Job 38:11 *"And said (to the sea), Hitherto shalt thou come, but no further: and here shall thy proud waves be stayed?"*
Is. 59:19-21 *"... when the enemy shall come in like a flood, the Spirit of the Lord shall lift up a standard against him."*
Rev. 13:16,17 *"And the serpent cast out of his mouth water as a flood after the woman... and the earth helped the woman, and the earth opened her mouth, and swallowed up the flood which the dragon cast out of his mouth."*

Food/Water

Gen. 27:28 *"Therefore God give thee of the dew of heaven, and the fatness of the earth, and plenty of corn..."*

Gen. 28:20-22 *"And Jacob vowed a vow, saying, If God will be with me, and will keep me in this way that I go, and will give me bread to eat, and raiment to put on, so that I come again to my father's house in peace; then shall the Lord be my God... and I will surely give the tenth unto Thee."*

Gen. 48:15 *"... the God which fed me all my life..."*

Ex. 16:4 God gives them Manna, *"Then said the Lord unto Moses, Behold, I will rain bread from heaven for you..."*

Ex. 16:13-15 *"And it came to pass, that at even the quails came up, and covered the camp: and in the morning the dew lay round about the host... there lay a small round thing, as small as the hoar frost on the ground... it is manna... this is the bread which the Lord hath given you to eat."*

Ex. 16:18 *"... and he that gathered little had no lack; they gathered every man according to his eating."*

Ex. 23:25,26 *"And ye shall serve the Lord your God, and He shall bless thy bread, and thy water...."*

Lev. 25:18,19 The land will yield her fruit and you shall eat your fill.

Lev. 26:3-5,10 *"If ye walk in My Statutes, and keep My Commandments, and do them then I will give you rain in due season, and the land shall yield her increase, and the trees of the field shall yield their fruit. And your threshing shall reach unto the vintage, and the vintage shall reach unto the sowing time: and ye shall eat your bread to the full, and dwell in your land safely... and ye shall eat old store, and bring forth the old because of the new."*

Lev. 26:3-5,10 NIV *"... the ground will yield its crops and the trees of the field their fruit. Your threshing will continue until grape harvest and the grape harvest will continue until planting, and you will eat all the food you want... You will still be eating last year's harvest when you will have to move it out to make room for the new."*

Deut. 6:10-12 *"... it shall be, when the Lord thy God shall have brought thee into the land which He sware unto thy fathers.. to give thee great and goodly cities, which thou buildedst not, and houses full of all good things, which thou filledst not, and wells digged, which thou diggedst not, vineyards and olive trees, which thou plantedst not; when thou shalt have eaten and be full; then beware lest thou forget the Lord, which brought thee forth out of the land of Egypt, from the house of bondage."*

Deut. 8:3 NIV *"He humbled you, causing you to hunger and feeding you with manna... to teach you that man does not live on bread alone but on every Word that comes from the mouth of the Lord."*

Deut. 8:15 *"... who brought thee forth water out of the rock of flint; who fed thee in the wilderness with manna..."*

Deut. 10:18 *"For the Lord your God is God of gods, and Lord of lords, a great God, a mighty, and a terrible... and loveth the stranger, in giving him food and raiment."*

Deut. 11:14,15 *"That I will give you the rain of your land in his due season, the first rain and the latter rain, that thou mayest gather in thy corn... and thine oil. And I will send ("give" KJV fn) grass in thy fields for thy cattle, that thou mayest eat and be full."*

Deut. 11:18 *"He... loveth the stranger, in giving him food and raiment."*

Deut. 28:1-9 *"Blessed shall be... the fruit of thy ground... thy basket and thy store... the Lord shall command the blessing upon thee in thy storehouses... and the Lord shall make thee plenteous in... the fruit of thy ground..."*

Deut. 32:12-15 *"So the Lord alone did lead him... He made him ride on the high places of the earth, that he might eat the increase of the fields; and He made him to... (get) honey out of the rock, and oil out of the flinty rock; butter of kine ("herd and flock" NIV), and milk of sheep, with fat of lambs, and rams of the breed of Bashan, and goats, with the... ("kernels" NIV) of wheat; and thou didst drink the pure... (juice) of the grape. But Jeshurun (Israel) waxed fat... then he forsook God which made him..."*

Neh. 9:20,21 *"... and withheldest not Thy manna from their mouth, and gavest them water for their thirst... so that they lacked nothing..."*

II Kings 2:20-22 *"And he (Elisha) said, Bring me a new cruse, and put salt therein. And they brought it to him. And he went forth unto the spring of the waters, and cast the salt in there, and said, Thus saith the Lord, I have healed these waters; there shall not be from thence any more death or barren land. So the waters were healed unto this day according to the saying of Elisha which he spake."*

II Chron. 31:10 *"... since the people began to bring the offerings into the house of the Lord, we have had enough to eat, and have left plenty: for the Lord hath blessed His people; and that which is left is this great store."*

II Chron. 31:10 PB *"what is left give to the poor."*

Neh. 9:15 *"Thou camest down also upon Mount Sinai... and gavest them... true laws ("laws of truth" KJV fn) ... and Commandments... and gavest them bread from heaven for their hunger, and broughtest forth water for them out of the rock for their thirst, and promisedst them that they should go in to possess the land which Thou hadst sworn to give them."*

Neh. 9:25 "... they took strong cities, and a fat ("fertile" HCSB) land and possessed houses full of all goods, wells digged, vinyards... oliveyards... fruit trees in abundance: so they did eat, and were filled... ("were well-nourished" NIV; "satiated" ISV) and delighted themselves in Thy great goodness."
Neh. 9:25 NIV "They ate to the full and were well nourished..."
Job 5:20,22 "In famine He shall Redeem thee from death... at destruction and famine thou shalt laugh..."
Job 36:16 "... and that which should be set on thy table should be full of fatness ("best food" NLT)"
Job 36:16 NIV "He wooing you from the jaws of distress to a spacious place free from restriction, to the comfort of your table laden with choice food."
Ps. 23:5 "Thou preparest a table before me in the presence of mine enemies..."
Ps. 33:19 "... to keep them alive in famine."
Ps. 36:8,9 "They shall be abundantly satisfied with the fatness of thy house; and thou shalt make them drink of the river of thy pleasures. For with Thee is the fountain of life..."
Ps. 37:3 "Trust in the Lord, and do good; so shalt thou dwell in the land, and verily thou shalt be fed."
Ps. 37:19 "They shall not be ashamed in the evil time: and in the days of famine they shall be satisfied."
Ps. 65:9,11,13 "Thou visitest the earth, and waterest it: Thou greatly enrichest it with the river of God, which is full of water; Thou preparest them corn, when Thou hast so provided for it... Thou crownest the year with Thy goodness; and Thy paths drop fatness... the valleys also are covered over with corn..."
Ps. 78:15 "He clave ("split" NIV) the rocks in the wilderness, and gave them drink as out of the great depths. He brought streams also out of the rock, and caused waters to run down like rivers."
Ps. 78:24-29 "And had rained down manna upon them to eat, and had given them of the corn of heaven. Man did eat angels' food: He sent them meat to the full. He caused an East wind to blow in the heaven: and by His power He brought in the South wind. He rained flesh also upon them as dust, and feathered fowls like as the sand of the sea: and He let it fall in the midst of their camp, round about their habitations. So they did eat, and were well filled: for He gave them their own desire..."
Ps. 81:10 "... open thy mouth wide, and I will fill it."
Ps. 81:16 "He should have fed them also with the finest of the wheat: and with honey out of the rock should I have satisfied thee."
Ps. 85:12 "Yea, the Lord shall give that which is good; and our land shall yield her increase."

Ps. 103:5 *"Who satisfieth thy mouth with good things..."*
Ps. 105:41 *"He opened the rock, and the waters gushed out; they ran in the dry places like a river."*
Ps. 107:9 *"For He satisfieth the longing soul, and filleth the hungry soul with goodness."*
Ps. 111:5 *"He hath given meat ("provides food" NIV) unto them that fear Him: He will ever be mindful of His Covenant."*
(Ps. 11:5 NLT *"... He always remembers His Covenant."*
Ps. 132:15 HCSB *"I will... bless its food; I will satisfy its needy with bread."*
Ps. 132:15 PB *"I will satisfy her poor with bread."*
Ps. 136:25 *"Who giveth food to all flesh: for His mercy endureth forever."*
Ps. 145:15,16 *"The eyes of all wait upon Thee; and Thou givest them their meat in due season. Thou openest Thine hand, and satisfiest the desire of every living thing."*
Ps. 145:15,16 HCSB *"You give them their food at the proper time ("as they need it" NLT) ..."*
Ps. 146:7 *"... which giveth food to the hungry..."*
Ps. 147:9 *"He giveth to the beast his food... to the young ravens which cry."*
Prayer: Lord, if You can feed the beasts of the field and the ravens, then I know that You can feed me." (Mt. 6:26). Thank You in Jesus' name!
Ps. 147:14 *"He ...filleth thee with the finest of the wheat."*
Prov. 3:9 *"Honour the Lord with thy substance, and with the firstfruits of all thine increase: so shall thy barns be filled with plenty, and thy presses shall burst out with new wine."* (see Mal. 3:10)
Prov. 10:3 *"The Lord will not suffer the soul of the righteous to famish..."*
(Prov. 10:3 NIV *"The Lord does not let the righteous go hungry..."*
Prayer: Thank You Lord, that You won't let me go hungry according to Your Word because my righteousness is in Jesus.
Prov. 12:11,12 *"He that tilleth his land shall be satisfied with bread... the root of the righteous yieldeth fruit."*
Prov. 13:25 *"The righteous eateth to the satisfying of his soul..."*
Prov. 18:20 *"... He filleth thee with the finest wheat..."*
Prov. 28:19 *"He that tilleth his land shall have plenty of bread...*
Is. 1:19 *"If ye be willing and obedient, ye shall eat the good of the land..."*
Is. 12:3 *"... with joy shall ye draw water out of the wells of Salvation..."*
Is. 30:23,25 *"... He (shall) give the rain of thy seed, that thou shalt sow the ground withal; and bread of the increase of the earth... it shall be fat and plenteous: in that day shall thy cattle feed in large pastures... there shall be upon every high mountain... rivers and streams of waters..."*
Is. 33:15-17 *"He that walketh righteously, and speaketh uprightly; he that despiseth the gain of oppressions, that shaketh his hands from holding of*

bribes, that stoppeth his ears from hearing of blood, and shutteth his eyes from seeing evil; he shall dwell on high; his place of defence shall be the munitions of rocks: bread shall be given him; his waters shall be sure."
Is. 41:17,18 "When the poor and needy seek water, and there is none, and their tongue faileth for thirst, I the Lord will hear them, I the God of Israel will not forsake them. I will open rivers in high places, and fountains in the midst of the valleys: I will make the wilderness a pool of water, and the dry land springs of water."
Is. 44:3 "For I will pour water upon him that is thirsty, and floods upon the dry ground..."
Is. 49:10 "They shall not hunger nor thirst; neither shall the heat nor sun smite them: for He that hath mercy on them shall lead them, even by the springs of water shall He guide them."
Is. 55:1 "Ho, every one that thirsteth, come ye to the waters, and he that hath no money; come ye, buy, and eat; yea, come, buy wine and milk without money and without price."
Is. 58:11 "And the Lord shall... satisfy thy soul in drought, and make fat thy bones: and thou shalt be like a watered garden, and like a spring of water, whose waters fail not."
Is. 58:13,14 "If thou turn away (#7725 "return, turn back, bring them back, repent, restore, turn you back, turn you around") thy foot (#7272 " follow, footsteps") from the Sabbath, from doing thy pleasure on My Holy Day; and call the Sabbath a delight, the Holy of the Lord, honourable; and shalt honour Him, not doing thine own ways, nor finding thine own pleasure, nor speaking thine own words: then shalt thou delight thyself in the Lord; and I will cause thee to ride upon the high places of the earth, and feed thee with the heritage of Jacob thy father: for the mouth of the Lord hath spoken it."
Is. 65:13 God said, "Behold, My servants shall eat... behold, My servants shall drink... behold, My servants shall rejoice ..."
Jer. 22:15 NIV "... did not your father have food and drink."
Ez. 34:14 "I will feed them with good pasture, and upon the high mountains of Israel shall their fold be; there shall they lie down in a good fold, and in a fat pasture shall they feed upon the mountains of Israel. I will feed My sheep and I will cause them to lie down, says the Lord God."
Hosea 11:4 "I drew them with cords of a man, with bands of love... I was to them as they that take off the yoke on their jaws, and I laid meat unto them."
Hosea 11:4 PB "I bent over them and fed them."
Hosea 11:4 NIV "I led them with cords of human kindness, with ties of love. To them I was like One who lifts a little child to the cheek, and I bent down to feed them."

Joel 2:19 *"Yea, the Lord will answer and say unto His people, Behold, I will send you corn... and oil, and ye shall be satisfied therewith..."*
Joel 2:24 *"... the floors shall be full of wheat... the fats... with ... oil..."*
Joel 2:26 *"... and ye shall eat in plenty, and be satisfied, and praise the name of the Lord your God, that hath dealt wondrously with you..."*
Zeph. 3:13 *"... they shall feed and lie down... none shall make them afraid."*
Matt. 6:26 *"... the fowls of the air... they sow not, neither do they reap, nor gather into barns; yet your heavenly Father feedeth them. Are ye not much better than they... O ye of little faith? Therefore take no thought, saying, What shall we eat? Or, What shall we drink? Or, Wherewithal shall we be clothed? (For after all these things do the Gentiles seek): for your heavenly Father knoweth that ye have need of all these things. But seek ye first the kingdom of God and His righteousness... all these things shall be added unto you. Take therefore no thought for the morrow: for the morrow shall take thought for the things of itself. Sufficient unto the day is the evil thereof."*
Matt. 14:19,20 Jesus feeds 5,000 *"And He ... looking up to heaven, He blessed, and brake, and gave the loaves to His disciples, and the disciples to the multitude. And they did all eat, and were filled... and they that had eaten were about five thousand men, beside women and children."*
Mk. 6:37,42 *"He answered and said unto them, Give ye them to eat... and they did all eat, and were filled... and they that did eat of the loaves were about five thousand men* (not counting the women and children)."
In those days they counted the men who were of the age for war, Num. 1:3.
Mk. 8:2-8 Jesus feeds 4,000 *"... Jesus ... saith ... I have compassion on the multitude, because they have now been with Me three days, and have nothing to eat... so they did eat, and were filled..."*
Lk. 1:53 *"He hath filled the hungry with good things..."*
Lk. 12:29-31 *"... seek not ye what ye shall eat, or what ye shall drink, neither be ye of doubtful mind. For all these things do the nations of the world seek after: and your Father knoweth that ye have need of these things. But rather seek ye the kingdom of God; and all these things shall be added unto you."*
Jn. 6:27 *"Labour not for the meat which perisheth, but for that meat which endureth unto everlasting life, which the Son of man shall give unto you: for him hath God the Father sealed."*
Jn. 6:32 *"... My Father giveth you the true bread from heaven* (Jesus)."
Jn. 6:35 *"And Jesus said unto them, I am the bread of life: he that cometh to Me shall never hunger; and he that believeth on Me shall never thirst."*
Jn. 6:40,41 *"And this is the will of Him that sent Me, that every one which seeth the Son, and believeth on Him, may have everlasting life... I am the bread which came down from heaven."*

Jn. 6:43,48-51 *"Jesus therefore answered and said unto them... I Am that bread of life... this is the bread which cometh down from heaven, that a man may eat thereof, and not die... if any man eat of this bread, he shall live forever: and the bread that I will give is My flesh* (through the symbol of Communion), *which I will give for the life of the world."*
Jn. 7:38 *"He that believeth on Me, as the Scripture hath said, out of his belly shall flow rivers of living water."*
Acts 14:17 *"... He left not Himself without witness, in that He did good, and gave us rain from heaven, and fruitful season, filling our hearts with food and gladness."*
Rom. 14:17,19 *"For the Kingdom of God is not meat and drink; but righteousness, and peace, and joy in the Holy Ghost... let us therefore follow after the things which make for peace..."*
II Tim. 6:8 *"And having food and raiment, let us be therewith content."*
Rev. 2:7 *"... to him that overcometh will I give to eat of the Tree of Life, which is in the midst of the Paradise of God."*
Rev. 21:6 *"... I will give unto him that is athirst of the fountain of the Water of Life freely."*

Forget

Is. 49:15,16 *"Can a woman forget her...* (nursing) *child, that she should not have compassion on the son of her womb? Yea, they may forget, yet will I not forget thee. Behold, I have graven thee upon the palms of My hands; thy walls are continually before Me."*
Is. 49:15,16 NLT *"See, I have written your name on the palms of My hands always on My mind is a picture of Jerusalem's walls in ruins."*

Forgive / Unforgiveness / Repent

Zech. 3:4 *"... Behold, I have caused thine iniquity to pass from thee..."*
Zech. 3:9 *"... I will remove the iniquity of that land in one day."*
Ps. 32:5 *"... I will confess my transgressions unto the Lord; and Thou forgavest the iniquity of my sin..."*
Ps. 85:2,3 *"Thou hast forgiven the iniquities of Thy people, Thou hast covered all their sin* (by the blood of Jesus). *Selah! Thou hast taken away all Thy wrath: Thou hast turned Thyself from the fierceness of Thine anger."*
Ps. 86:5 *"For Thou, Lord, art good, and ready to forgive; and plenteous in mercy unto all them that call upon Thee."*
Ps. 103:3 *"Who forgiveth all thine iniquities..."*

Ps. 103:10-13 *"He hath not dealt with us after our sins; nor rewarded us according to our iniquities. For as the heaven is high above the earth, so great is His mercy toward them that fear Him. As far as the East is from the West, so far hath He removed our transgressions from us... the Lord pitieth them that fear Him."*
Is. 33:24 *"... the people that dwell therein shall be forgiven..."*
Is. 38:17 *"... for Thou hast cast all my sins behind Thy back."*
Is. 40:2 *"... her iniquity is pardoned..."*
Is. 43:25 *"I, even I, am He that blotteth out thy transgressions for Mine own sake, and will not remember thy sins."*
Is. 44:21 *"... thou art My servant: I have formed thee; thou art My servant: O Israel, thou shalt not be forgotten of Me. I have blotted out, as a thick cloud, thy transgressions, and, as a cloud, thy sins: return unto Me; for I have Redeemed thee."*
Is. 53:6 *"All we like sheep have gone astray; we have turned everyone to his own way; and the Lord hath laid on Him the iniquity of us all."*
Is. 55:7 *"Let the wicked forsake his way, and the unrighteous man his thoughts: and let him return unto the Lord, and He will have mercy upon him; and to our God, for He will abundantly pardon."*
Jer. 33:6 NIV *"... I will cleanse them from all the sin they have committed against me and will forgive all their sins of rebellion..."*
Jer. 33:8 *"And I will cleanse them from all their iniquity, whereby they have sinned against Me; and I will pardon all their iniquities, whereby they have sinned, and whereby they have transgressed against Me."*
(Jer. 33:8 NLT *"I will cleanse them of their sins against Me and forgive all their sins or rebellion."*
Jer. 50:20 *"In those days, and in that time, saith the Lord, the iniquity of Israel shall be sought for, and there shall be none; and the sins of Judah, and they shall not be found: for I will pardon them whom I reserve."*
Matt. 6:12 *"... forgive us our debts, as we forgive our debtors... if ye forgive not men their trespasses, neither will your Father forgive your trespasses."*
We must forgive if we want God to forgive us! Sometimes we must put our will into motion and say, *"I will forgive! Or I choose to forgive!"* Then the bad feelings will leave and we are then able to forgive from the heart. Satan may try to bring the offense back to us but we must again say, *"I will forgive!"*
Matt. 6:14 *"For if ye forgive men their trespasses, your heavenly Father will also forgive you..."*
Matt. 12:31 *"... all manner of sin and blasphemy shall be forgiven unto men; but the blasphemy against the Holy Ghost shall not be forgiven unto men."*

Matt. 12:32 *"And whosoever speaketh a word against the Son of man, it shall be* forgiven *him..."*
Mk. 2:5 *"... thy sins be forgiven thee."*
Mk. 2:10 *"... the Son of man hath power on earth to forgive sins..."*
Mk. 3:28 *"... all sins shall be forgiven unto the sons of men, and blasphemies... they shall blaspheme: but he that shall blaspheme against the Holy Ghost hath never forgiveness, but is in danger of eternal damnation..."*
Mk. 6:37,42 Jesus said, *"... give ye them to eat... and they did all eat and were filled."*
Lk. 1:77 *"To give knowledge of Salvation unto His people by the remission of their sins..."*
Lk. 5:20,21,24,32 *"And when He saw their faith, He said unto him, Man, thy sins are forgiven thee... who can forgive sins, but God alone ... but that ye may know that the Son of man hath power upon earth to forgive sins (because He is God)... (He said unto the sick of the palsy), I say unto thee, Arise and take up thy couch, and go into thine house. And immediately he rose up... I came not to call the righteous, but sinners to repentance."*
Lk. 6:37,38 *"... forgive, and ye shall be forgiven... for with the same measure that ye mete withal it shall be measured to you again."*
Lk. 7:47,48 *"... her sins, which are many, are forgiven; for she loved much: but to whom little is forgiven, the same loveth little. And He said unto her, Thy sins are forgiven."*
Lk. 12:10 *"And whosoever shall speak a word against the Son of man, it shall be forgiven him: but unto him that blasphemeth against the Holy Ghost it shall not be forgiven."*
Jn. 20:23 *"... whosoever sins ye remit, they are remitted unto them; and whosesoever sins ye retain, they are retained."*
Acts 2:38 *"... repent, and be baptized every one of you in the name of Jesus Christ for the remission* (removal) *of sins..."*
Acts 5:31 *"Him hath God exalted with His right hand to be a Prince and a Saviour, for to give repentance to Israel, and forgiveness of sins."*
Acts 10:43 *"... that through His name whosoever believeth in Him shall receive remission of sins."*
Acts 11: 18 *"... hath God also to the Gentiles granted repentance unto life."*
Acts 22:16 *"And now why tarriest thou? Arise, and be baptized, and wash away thy sins, calling on the name of the Lord."*
Acts 26:18 *"To open their eyes, and to turn them from darkness to light, and from the power of Satan unto God, that they may receive forgiveness of sins, and inheritance among them which are Sanctified by faith that is in Me."*
II Cor. 2:10 *"To whom ye forgive anything, I forgive also: for if I forgave anything, to whom I forgave it, for your sakes forgave I it in the person of*

Christ; lest Satan should get an advantage of us: for we are not ignorant of his devices."

Eph. 1:7 "In whom we have Redemption through His blood, the forgiveness of sins, according to the riches of His grace..."

Eph. 4:31,32 "Let all bitterness... wrath... anger... clamour... and evil speaking, be put away from you, with all malice: and be ye kind ("compass-ionate" NIV) one to another, tenderhearted, forgiving one another, even as God for Christ's sake hath forgiven you."

(Eph. 4:31 NIV "Get rid of all bitterness, rage and anger, brawling and sland-er, along with every form of malice.")

Col. 1:14 "In whom we have Redemption through His blood, even the forgiveness of sins..."

Col. 2:13 "... having forgiven you all trespasses..."

Col. 3:12,13 "Put on therefore, as the elect of God, Holy and beloved, bowels of mercies, kindness, humbleness of mind, meekness, longsuffering, for-bear-ing one another, and forgiving one another... if any man have a quarrel against any: even as Christ forgave you, so also do ye.."

Heb. 8:12 "For I will be merciful to their unrighteousness, and their sins and their iniquities will I remember no more."

(Heb. 8:12 NIV "For I will forgive their wickedness and will remember their sins no more.")

I Jn. 1:7 "... if we walk in the light as He is in the light, we have fellowship one with another, and the blood of Jesus Christ His Son cleanseth us from all sin."

I Jn. 1:9 "If we confess our sins, He is faithful and just to forgive us our sins, and to cleanse us from all unrighteousness."

I Jn. 2:12 "... your sins are forgiven you for His name's sake."

Rev. 1:5 "Jesus Christ... loved us... washed us from our sins in His... blood..."

Fortress

Ps. 144:2,3 "... blessed be the Lord my strength... my goodness, and my fortress; my high tower and my deliverer; my shield, and He in whom I trust; who subdueth my people under me. ("... what are human beings that You care for them, mere mortals that you think of them?" NIV)"

Free/Freedom/Freely

Is. 58:6 "Is not this the fast that I have chosen? To loose the bands of wickedness, to undo the heavy burdens, and to let the oppressed go free, and that ye break every yoke?"

Hosea 14:4 *"I will heal their backsliding ("waywardness" NIV; "faithlessness" NLT; "apostasy" ESV), I will love them freely: for Mine anger is turned away from him."*
Matt. 10:8 *"Heal the sick, cleanse the lepers, raise the dead, cast out devils: freely ye have received, freely give."*
Jn. 8:32 NIV *"... you will know the truth, and the truth will set you free."*
Jn. 8:36 *"If the Son therefore shall make ("set") you free, ye shall be free..."*
Rom. 3:24 *"Being Justified freely by His grace through the Redemption that is in Christ Jesus..."*
Rom. 5:18 *"... by the righteousness of one the free gift came upon all men unto Justification of life."*
Rom. 6:18 *"Being then made free from sin, ye became the servants of righteousness."*
Rom. 6:22 *"But now being made free from sin, and become servants to God, ye have your fruit unto Holiness, and the end everlasting life."*
Rom. 6:22 NLT *"But now you are free from the power of sin... you do those things that lead to Holiness and result in eternal life."*
Rom. 8:2 *"... made me free from... sin..."*
Rom. 8:32 *"He that spared not His own Son, but delivered Him up for us all, how shall He not with Him also freely give us all things?"*
I Cor. 2:12 *"Now we have received, not the spirit of the world, but the Spirit which is of God; that we might know the things that are freely given to us..."*
Gal. 5:1 *"Stand fast therefore in the liberty wherewith Christ hath made us free..."* (Freedom from sin, not free to sin (Rom. 6:18).
I Pet. 2:16 *"As free, and not using your liberty for a cloke of maliciousness, but as the servants of God."*
(I Pet. 2:16 NLT *"For you are free... so don't use your freedom as an excuse to do evil."*
Rev. 21:6 *"... I will give to him that is athirst of the fountain of the water of life freely."*
Rev. 22:17 *"And the Spirit and the Bride say, Come. And let him that heareth say, Come. And let him that is athirst come. And whosoever will, let him take the Water of Life freely."*

Friend(s)

Prov. 18:24 *"... there is a friend who sticketh closer than a brother."*
Jn. 15:15 *"... I have called you friends..."*

Forsake Not

Deut. 4:31 *"... for the Lord thy God is a merciful God... He will not forsake thee, neither destroy thee..."*

Deut. 31:6 *"Be strong and of a good courage, fear not, nor be afraid of them: for the Lord thy God, he it is that doth go with thee; he will not fail thee, nor forsake thee."*

Josh. 1:5 *"There shall not any man be able to stand before thee all the days of thy life: as I was with Moses, so I will be with thee* (Joshua): *I will not fail thee, nor forsake thee."*

I Sam. 12:22 *"For the Lord will not forsake His people for His great name's sake: because it hath pleased the Lord to make you His people."*

I Kings 6:13 *"And I will dwell among the children of Israel, and will not forsake My people Israel."*

Neh. 9:31 *"Nevertheless for Thy great mercies' sake Thou didst not utterly consume them, nor forsake them; for Thou art a gracious and merciful God."*

Ps. 9:10 *"... for Thou, Lord, hast not forsaken them..."*

Ps. 37:25 I have not *"... seen the righteous forsaken ("abandoned" HCSB), nor his seed begging for bread."*

Ps. 37:28 *"For the Lord loveth Judgment, and forsaketh not His saints; they are preserved forever..."*

Is. 41:17 *"... I the Lord will hear them, I the God of Israel will not forsake them."*

Zeph. 3:15 *"... the Lord, is in the midst of thee: thou shalt not see evil anymore."*

Prayer: Lord, be in the midst of me and not forsake me so that I will not see evil. Thank You in Jesus' name, Amen!

Heb. 13:5 *"... He hath said, I will never leave thee, nor forsake thee."*

Gifts / Give / Given

Ps. 68:18 YLT *"Thou hast ascended on high. Thou hast taken captive captivity, Thou hast taken gifts for men."*

Ps. 84:11 *"... the Lord will give grace and glory: no good thing will He withhold from them that walk uprightly."*

Matt. 7:11; Lk. 11:13 *"If ye then, being evil, know how to give good gifts unto your children, how much more shall your Father which is in heaven give good things to them that ask Him?"*

Matt. 10:8 *"... freely ye have received, freely give."*

Matt. 13:11,12 The Disciples asked Jesus why He spoke in parables and Jesus said, "... *because it is given unto you to know the mysteries of the kingdom of heaven, but to them it is not given. For whosoever hath, to him shall be given, and he shall have more abundance: but whosoever hath not, from him shall be taken away even that he hath.*"
Lk. 6:38 "*Give, and it shall be given unto you; good measure, pressed down... shaken together, and running over, shall men give into your bosom. For with the same measure that ye mete withal it shall be measured to you again.*"
Lk. 8:10 "*... it is given (you) to know the mysteries of the Kingdom of God...*"
Rom. 5:18 "*... even so by the righteousness of One* (Jesus) *the free gift came upon all men unto Justification of life.*"
Rom. 8:32 "*He that spared not His own Son, but delivered Him up for us all, how shall He not with Him also freely give us all things?*"
I Cor. 1:7 "*So that ye come behind in no gift; waiting for the coming of our Lord Jesus Christ...*"
I Cor. 2:12 We have received "*... the Spirit which is of God; that we might know the things that are freely given to us of God.*"
I Cor. 12:4 "*... there are diversities of gifts...*"
I Cor. 14:1- "*Pursue love and desire Spiritual gifts and above all... prophesy.*"
Eph. 2:8 "*For by grace are ye saved through faith; and that not of yourselves: it is the gift of God...*"
Eph. 4:8 "*... when He ascended up on high, He led captivity captive, and gave gifts unto men.*"
Heb. 2:4 "*God also bearing them witness, both with signs and wonders, and with divers miracles, and gifts of the Holy Ghost, according to His own will?*"

Gold

Gen. 13:2 "*And Abram was very rich in cattle, in silver, and in gold.*"
Gen. 24:53 "*And the servant* (of Abraham) *brought forth jewels of silver, and jewels of gold, and raiment, and gave them to Rebekah: he gave also to her brother and to her mother precious things.*"
Gen. 41:42 "*... Pharaoh took off his ring from his hand, and put it upon Joseph.. arrayed him in vestures of fine linen... put a gold chain* (on him)*...*"
Job 23:10 "*When He hath tried me I shall come forth as gold.*"
Ps. 119:72 "*The law of thy mouth is better unto me than thousands of gold and silver.*"
(Ps. 119:72 HCSB "*Instruction from your lips...*"
Ps. 119:127 "*I love Thy Commandments above gold; yea, above fine gold.*"

Prov. 3:13 *"Happy is the man that findeth wisdom, and the man that getteth understanding. For the merchandise of it is better than the merchandise of silver, and the gain thereof than fine gold. She is more precious than rubies: and all the things thou canst desire are not to be compared unto her. Length of days is in her right hand; and in her left hand riches and honour."*

Prov. 8:12,17-19,21 *"I wisdom... love them that love me; and those that seek me early shall find me. Riches and honour are with me: yea, durable riches and righteousness. My fruit is better than gold, yea, than fine gold; and my revenue than choice silver.... I may cause those that love me to inherit substance; and I will fill their treasures."*

Prov. 16:16 *"How much better is it to get wisdom than gold..."*

Prov. 25:11 *"A word fitly spoken is like apples of gold in pictures of silver."*

Is. 13:12 *"I will make a man more precious than fine gold; even a man than the golden wedge of Ophir."*

Is. 60:6 *"... all they from Sheba shall come: they shall bring gold and incense; and they shall shew forth the praises of the Lord."*

Is. 60:9 *"Surely the isles shall wait for me, and the ships of Tarshish first, to bring thy sons from far, their silver and their gold with them..."*

Is. 60:16,17 *"... thou shalt know that I... am thy Saviour... thy Redeemer, the mighty One of Jacob. For brass I will bring gold, and for iron, silver..."*

Hag. 2:8 *"The silver is Mine and the gold is Mine, saith the Lord..."*

Zech. 13:9 *"And I will bring the third part through the fire, and will refine them as silver is refined, and will try them as gold is tried: they shall call on My name, and I will hear them: I will say, It is My people: and they shall say, The Lord is my God."*

Mal. 3:3 *"And He shall sit as a refiner and purifier of silver: and he shall purify the sons of Levi, and purge them as gold and silver, that they may offer unto the Lord an offering in righteousness."*

Acts 17:29 *"Forasmuch then as we are the offspring of God, we ought not to think that the Godhead is like unto gold, or silver, or stone, graven by art and man's device."*

I Pet. 1:7 *"That the trial of your faith, being much more precious than of gold that perisheth, though it be tried with fire, might be found unto praise and honour and glory at the appearing of Jesus Christ."*

I Pet. 1:18 *"Forasmuch as ye know that ye were not Redeemed with corruptible things, as silver and gold..."*

Rev. 3:18 *"I counsel thee to buy of me gold tried in the fire, that thou mayest be rich; and white raiment, that thou mayest be clothed, and that the shame of thy nakedness do not appear; and anoint thine eyes with eyesalve, that thou mayest see."*

Rev. 21:18 *"... the city* (New Jerusalem) *was pure gold, like unto clear glass."*

Rev. 21:21 "... the street of the city was pure gold, as.. transparent glass."

Grace/Gracious

Grace means free and unmerited favor. It is getting freely something you don't deserve.
Gen. 6:8 "... Noah found grace ("favor" NIV) in the eyes of the Lord."
II Chron. 30:9 "... for the Lord your God is gracious and merciful, and will not turn away His face from you, if ye return unto Him."
II Kings 13;23 "... the Lord was gracious unto them..."
Neh. 9:17 "... Thou art a God ready to pardon, gracious and merciful, slow to anger, and of great kindness, and forsookest them not."
Ps. 39:9 "Be gracious to me, O Lord, for I am in distress; my eye is wasted away from grief, my soul and my body also."
Ps. 86:15 "But Thou, O Lord, art a God full of compassion, and gracious, longsuffering, and plenteous in mercy and truth."
Ps. 84:11 "For the Lord God is a sun and shield: the Lord will give grace and glory: no good thing will He withhold from them that walk uprightly."
Ps. 103:8 "The Lord is merciful and gracious, slow to anger... plenteous in mercy."
Ps. 111:4 "He hath made His wonderful works to be remembered: the Lord is gracious and full of compassion..."
Prov. 3:34 "He... giveth grace unto the lowly."
Prov. 3:34 NIV "He... shows faver to the humble..."
Is. 30:19 "For the people shall dwell in Zion at Jerusalem: thou shalt weep no more: He will be very gracious unto thee at the voice of thy cry; when He shall hear it, He will answer thee."
Zech. 4:7 "Who art thou, O great mountain? Before Zerubbabel thou shalt become a plain: and He shall bring forth the Headstone thereof with shoutings, crying, Grace, grace unto it."
Jn. 1:16 "And of His fullness have all we received, and grace for grace."
Acts 4:33 "... and great grace was upon them all."
Rom. 1:5 "By whom we have received grace and Apostleship, for obedience to the faith among all nations, for His name..."
Rom. 3:24 "Being Justified freely by His grace through the Redemption that is through Christ Jesus."
Rom. 4:16 "Therefore it is of faith, that it might be by grace; to the end the promise might be sure to all the seed... also which is of the faith of Abraham; who is the father of us all..."

Rom. 5:1,2 *"Therefore being Justified by faith, we have peace with God through our Lord Jesus Christ: by whom also we have access by faith into this grace wherein we stand, and rejoice in hope of the glory of God."*
Rom. 5:15 *"... so also is the free gift... much more the grace of God, and the gift by grace, which is by one man, Jesus Christ, hath abounded to many."*
Rom. 5:17 *"... much more they which receive abundance of grace and of the gift of righteousness shall reign in life by One, Jesus Christ..."*
Rom. 5:20 *"... where sin abounded, grace did much more abound..."*
Rom. 12:6 *"Having... gifts... according to the grace that is given to us..."*
II Cor. 9:8 *"And God is able to make all grace abound toward you; that ye, always having all sufficiency in all things, may abound to every good work..."*
II Cor. 12:9 *"My grace is sufficient for thee: for my strength is made perfect in weakness..."*
Eph. 1:7 *"In whom we have Redemption through His blood, the forgiveness of sins, according to the riches of His grace..."*
Eph. 4:7 *"But unto every one of us is given grace according to the measure of the gift of Christ."*
Eph. 6:24 *"Grace be with all them that love our Lord... in sincerity..."*
Titus 3:7 *"That being Justified by His grace, we should be made heirs according to the hope of eternal life."*
Heb. 4:16 *"Let us therefore come boldly unto the throne of grace, that we may obtain mercy, and find grace to help in time of need."*
Jms. 4:6 *"But He giveth more grace. Wherefore He saith, God resisteth the proud, but giveth grace unto the humble."*
I Pet. 3:7 *"... being heirs together of the grace of life..."*
I Pet. 5:5 *"... God resisteth the proud, and giveth grace to the humble."*
II Pet. 1:2 *"Grace and peace be multiplied unto you through the knowledge of God, and of Jesus our Lord..."*
Rev. 1:4 *"... grace be unto you..."*

Guide

Ex. 15:13 *"Thou in Thy mercy hast led forth the people which Thou hast Redeemed: Thou hast guided them in Thy strength unto Thy Holy Habitation."*
Ps. 25:9 *"The meek will He guide in Judgment.. the meek will He teach His way."*
Ps. 32:8 *"... I will guide thee with Mine eye."*
Ps. 48:14 *"For this God is our God forever and ever: He will be our guide even unto death."*

Ps. 73:20,24 *"... O Lord... Thou shalt guide me with Thy counsel, and afterward receive me to glory..."*
Prov. 11:3 *"The integrity of the upright will guide them..."*
Is. 49:10 *"They shall not hunger nor thirst; neither shall the heat nor sun smite them: for He that hath mercy on them shall lead them even by the springs of water shall He guide them."*
Is. 58:11 *"And the Lord shall guide thee continually..."*
Lk. 1:79 *"To give light to them that sit in darkness and in the shadow of death, to guide our feet into the way of peace."*
Jn. 16:13 *"... when He, the Spirit of truth, is come, He will guide you into all truth..."*

Hair

Lk. 12:7 *"But even the very hairs of your head are all numbered. Fear not therefore: ye are of more value than many sparrows."*
Lk. 21:18,19 *"But there shall not an hair of your head perish. In your patience possess ye your souls."*

Hand

Ps. 16:11 *"... at Thy right hand are pleasures forevermore."*
Ps. 18:35 *"Thou hast also given me the shield of Thy Salvation: and Thy right hand hath holden me up, and Thy gentleness hath made me great."*
Ps. 31:15 *"... my times are in Thy hand..."*
Ps. 37:24 *"... the Lord upholdeth him with His hand."*
Ps. 48:10 *"... Thy right hand is full of righteousness."*
Ps. 63:8 *"... Thy right hand upholdeth me."*
Is. 66:14 *"... the hand of the Lord shall be known toward his servants..."*
Lk. 1:66 About John the Baptist, *"And all they that heard them laid them up in their hearts, saying, What manner of child shall this be! And the hand of the Lord was with him."*
Acts 11:21 *"And the hand of the Lord was with them: and a great number believed, and turned unto the Lord."*

Happen

Prov. 12:21 *"There shall no evil happen to the just..."*

Happy

Deut. 33:29 "... happy art thou... O people saved by the Lord..."
Ps. 144:15 "... happy is that people whose God is the Lord."
Prov. 3:13 "Happy is the man that findeth wisdom, and the man that getteth understanding."
Prov. 16:20 "... whoso trusteth in the Lord, happy is he."
Prov. 29:18 "... he that keepeth the law, happy is he."
Matt. 5:3-11 The Beatitudes (The word blessed is Gr. #3107 which means, "happy, blessed, to be envied")
Jn. 13:17 "... if ye know these things, happy are you if you do them."
Jms. 5:11 "... we count them happy which endure..."

Harm

See Hurt

Haven

Ps. 107:30 "... He bringeth them unto their desired haven."

Heal / Healing

(See Miracles)
Ex. 15:26 "... I will put none of these diseases upon thee... for I am the Lord that healeth thee."
Ex. 23:25 "... I will take sickness away from the midst of thee."
Ps. 30:2 "... Thou hast healed me."
Ps. 41:2,3 "... Thou wilt make all his bed in his sickness... heal my soul..."
Ps. 107:20 "He sent His Word, and healed them..."
Ps. 103:3 "Who forgiveth all thine iniquities; who healeth all thy diseases..."
Ps. 146:8 "The Lord openeth the eyes of the blind..."
Ps. 147:3 "He healeth the broken in heart, and bindeth up their wounds."
Prov. 4:20-22 "... attend to My words; incline thine ear unto My sayings... they are life unto those that find them, and health to all their flesh."
Prov. 13:17 NLT "... a reliable messenger bring healing."
Is. 53:5 "... He was wounded for our transgressions, He was bruised for our iniquities: the chastisement of our peace was upon Him; and with His stripes we are healed."

Jer. 17:14 *"Heal me, O Lord, and I shall be healed... for Thou art my praise."*
Jer. 30:17 *"I will heal thee of thy wounds."*
Hosea 6:1 *"Come, and let us return unto the Lord: for He hath torn, and He will heal us; He hath smitten, and He will bind us up."*
Hosea 11:3 *"... they knew not that I healed them."*
Hosea 14:4 *"I will heal their backsliding, I will love them freely: for Mine anger is turned away from him."*
Matt. 8:13 *"... Jesus said unto the centurion, Go thy way... as thou hast believed, so be it done unto thee... his servant was healed* (that) *same hour."*
Matt. 9:35 *"And Jesus went about... healing every sickness and every disease among the people."*
Matt. 10:1 *"And when He* (Jesus) *had called unto Him His twelve Disciples, He gave them power against unclean spirits, to cast them out, and to heal all manner of sickness and all manner of disease."*
Matt. 10:7,8 *"And as ye go, preach, saying, The kingdom of heaven is at hand. Heal the sick, cleanse the lepers, raise the dead, cast out devils: freely ye have received, freely give."*
Matt. 13:15 *"For this people's heart is waxed gross, and their ears are dull of hearing, and their eyes they have closed; lest at any time they should see with their eyes, and hear with their ears, and should understand with their heart, and should be converted, and I should heal them."*
Matt. 14:14 *"And Jesus went forth, and saw a great multitude, and was moved with compassion toward them, and He healed their sick."*
Matt. 19:2 *"... great multitudes followed Him* (Jesus)*... He healed them..."*
Matt. 21:14 *"And the blind and the lame came to Him* (Jesus) *in the Temple; and He healed them."*
Mk. 1:32-34 *"And at even, when the sun did set, they brought unto Him* (Jesus) *all that were diseased, and them that were possessed with devils. And all the city was gathered together at the door. And He healed many that were sick of divers diseases, and cast out many devils; and suffered not the devils to speak, because they knew Him."*
Mk. 3:10,11 *"For He* (Jesus) *had healed many; insomuch that they pressed upon Him for to touch Him, as many as had plagues and unclean spirits, when they saw Him, fell down before Him, and cried, saying, Thou art the Son of God."*
Mk. 3:15 *"... have power to heal sicknesses, and to cast out devils..."*
Mk. 5:34 *"And He said unto her, Daughter, thy faith hath made thee whole: go in peace, and be whole of thy plague."*
Mk. 6:5,6 *"And whithersoever He* (Jesus) *entered... they laid the sick in the streets, and besought Him that they might touch if it were but the border of His garment: and as many as touched Him were made whole."*

Lk. 4:18-21 Jesus quoting from Isaiah, "*The Spirit of the Lord is upon Me, because He hath anointed Me to preach the Gospel to the poor; He hath sent Me to heal the brokenhearted, to preach deliverance to the captives, and recovering of sight to the blind, to set at liberty them that are bruised...*"
Lk. 8:47,48 "*... she was healed immediately. And He* (Jesus) *said unto her, Daughter, be of good comfort: thy faith hath made thee whole; go in peace.*"
Lk. 4:39-41 "*And He* (Jesus) *stood over her, and rebuked the fever; and it left her: and immediately she arose and ministered unto them.*"
Lk. 5:15 "*But so much the more went there a fame abroad of Him* (Jesus): *and great multitudes came together to hear, and to be healed by Him of their infirmities.*"
Lk. 6:17-19 Many "*... came to hear Him* (Jesus), *and to be healed of their diseases... and they that were vexed with unclean spirits: and they were healed. And the whole multitude sought to touch Him: for there went virtue out of Him, and healed them all.*"
Lk. 8:2 While Jesus was preaching the kingdom, His twelve disciples were with Him and some women and one that had been "*... healed of evil spirits and infirmities, Mary called Magdalene, out of whom went seven devils...*"
Lk. 9:1,2,6 "*Then He* (Jesus) *called His twelve disciples together, and gave them power and authority over all devils, and to cure diseases... He set them to preach the Kingdom of God, and to heal the sick... and they departed, and went through the towns, preaching the Gospel, and healing everywhere.*"
Lk. 9:11 "*And the people, when they knew it, followed Him* (Jesus): *and He received them, and spake unto them of the kingdom of God, and healed them that had need of healing.*"
Lk. 9:42,43 "*... Jesus rebuked the unclean spirit... healed the child... delivered him again to his father. And they were all amazed at the mighty power of God...* (and) *they wondered every one at all things which Jesus did...*"
Lk. 10:9 "*... heal the sick that are therein, and say unto them, The Kingdom of God is come nigh unto you.*"
Lk. 22:51 "*... Jesus... touched his ear and healed him.*"
Acts 8:6-8 "*... hearing and seeing the miracles which He* (Jesus) *did. For unclean spirits, crying with loud voice, came out of many that were possessed with them: and many taken with palsies, and that were lame, were healed. And there was great joy in that city.*"
Acts 10:38 "*How God anointed Jesus of Nazareth with the Holy Ghost and with power: who went about doing good, and healing all that were oppressed of the devil; for God was with Him.*"
Jn. 12:40 "*... be converted and I should heal them.*"
Jms. 5:14-16 "*And the prayer of faith shall save the sick, and the Lord shall raise him up; and if he have committed sins, they shall be forgiven him.*"

I Pet. 2:24 *"Heal me, O Lord, and I shall be healed."*

Health

Prov. 3:8 *"... I shall yet praise Him, who is the health of my countenance."*
Prov. 3:5,8 *"Trust in the Lord with all thine heart... it shall be health to thy navel and marrow to thy bones."*

Hear / Heard

II Sam. 22:7 *"In my distress I called upon the Lord, and cried to my God: and He did hear my voice out of His Temple, and my cry did enter unto is ears."*
Neh. 9:27,28 *"... in the time of their trouble, when they cried unto Thee, Thou heardest them from heaven... and many times didst Thou deliver them according to Thy mercies..."*
Ps. 3:4 *"I cried unto the Lord... He heard me out of His Holy Hill."*
Ps. 18:3,6 *"I will call upon the Lord, who is worthy to be praised: so shall I be saved from mine enemies. In my distress I called upon the Lord, and cried unto my God: He heard my voice out of His Temple, and my cry came before Him, even into His ears."*
Ps. 34:4 *"I sought the Lord... He heard me... delivered me from all my fears."*
Ps. 42:11 *"Why art thou cast down, O my soul? And why art thou disquieted within me? Hope thou in God: for I shall yet praise Him, who is the health of my countenance and my God."*
Ps. 55:17 *"Evening, and morning, and at noon, will I pray, and cry aloud: and He shall hear my voice."*
Ps. 55:19 *"God shall hear..."*
Prov. 15:29 *"... He heareth the prayer of the righteous."*
Is. 30:19 *"For the people shall dwell in Zion at Jerusalem: thou shalt weep no more: He will be very gracious unto thee at the voice of thy cry; when He shall hear it, He will answer thee."*
Is. 49:8 God says, *"... in an acceptable time have I heard thee..."*
Is. 49:10 *"I the Lord will hear them..."*
Jer. 30:17 *"... I will restore health unto thee. I will heal thee of thy wounds..."*
Jer. 33:5,6 *"... this city... I will bring it health and cure, and I will cure them."*
Jn. 9:31 *"Now we know that God heareth not sinners: but if any man be a worshiper of God, and doeth His will, him He heareth."*
I Jn. 5:14,15 *".. this is the confidence that we have in Him, that, if we ask anything according to His will, He heareth us... if we know that He hear us... we know that we have the petitions that we desired of Him."*

Heart (Circumcised Heart)

Deut. 5:29 *"O that there were such an heart in them, that they would fear Me, and keep all My Commandments always, that it might be well with them, and with their children forever!"*

Deut. 10:16 NIV *"Circumcise your hearts... do not be stiffnecked..."*

Deut. 30:1-3 *"And it shall come to pass, when all these things are come upon thee, the blessing and the curse, which I have set before thee, and thou shalt call them to mind among all the nations whither the Lord thy God hath driven thee, and shalt return unto the Lord thy God, and shalt obey His voice according to all that I command thee this day, thou and thy children, with all thine heart, and with all thy soul; that then the Lord thy God will turn thy captivity, and have compassion upon thee..."*

Deut. 30:6 *"And the Lord thy God will circumcise thine heart, and the heart of thy seed, to love the Lord thy God with all thine heart, and with all thy soul, that thou mayest live."*

Prayer: Lord, circumcise my heart and the hearts of my child/children (and family) as it says in Your Word. Thank You in Jesus' name, Amen!

I Sam. 10:9 Speaking of king Saul *"... God gave him another heart... and the Spirit of God came upon him, and he prophesied..."*

Prayer: Lord, give me and my family another heart so that we will serve you with all our hearts. Thank You in Jesus' name, Amen!

I Sam. 12:24 *"Only fear the Lord, and serve Him in truth with all your heart: for consider how great things He hath done for you."*

I Kings 3:12 God said to Solomon, *"Behold, I have done according to Thy words... I have given thee a wise and... understanding heart; so that there was none like thee before thee, neither after thee shall any arise..."*

I Kings 8:23 *"... who keepeth Covenant and mercy with Thy servants that walk before Thee with all their heart..."*

II Kings 20:3 *"Remember now, O Lord, I beseech You, how I have walked before You in truth... with a whole heart and have done what is good..."*

I Chron. 28:9 *"... serve Him with a perfect heart and with a willing mind: for the Lord searcheth all hearts, and understandeth all the imaginations of the thoughts: if thou seek Him, He will be found of thee..."*

II Chron. 6:14 *"And he (Solomon) said, O Lord God of Israel there is no God like Thee in the heaven, nor in the earth; which keepest Covenant, and shewest mercy unto (those) that walk before Thee with all their hearts..."*

II Chron. 6:30,31 *"... for Thou only knowest the hearts of the children of men... that they may fear Thee, to walk in Thy ways..."*

II Chron. 6:38 *"If they return to Thee with all their heart and with all their soul... then hear Thou from the heavens, even from Thy dwelling place, their prayer and their supplications, and maintain their cause, and forgive Thy people which have sinned against Thee."*
II Chron. 15:12 *"... they entered into the Covenant to seek the Lord God of their fathers with all their heart and soul..."*
II Chron. 16:9 *"For the eyes of the Lord run to and fro throughout the whole earth, to shew Himself strong in the behalf of them whose heart is perfect toward Him..."*
I Chron. 29:19 *"And give unto Solomon my son a perfect heart, to keep Thy Commandments... and to do all these things..."*
II Chron. 30:12 *"... the hand of God was to give them one heart to do the Commandment of the king... by the Word of the Lord."*
II Chron. 31:21 *"And in every work that he began in the service of the house of God, and in the law, and in the Commandments, to seek his God, he did it with all his heart, and prospered."*
II Chron. 34:31 *"And the king stood in his place, and made a Covenant before the Lord, to walk after the Lord, and to keep His Commandments... with all his heart, and with all his soul, to perform the Words of the Covenant..."*
Job 29:13 *"The blessing of him that was ready to perish came upon me: and I caused the widow's heart to sing for joy."*
Ps. 19:14 *"Let the words of my mouth, and the meditation of my heart, be acceptable in Thy sight, O Lord, my strength, and my Redeemer."*
Ps. 21:1-6 *"... Thou hast given him his heart's desire, and hast not withholden the request of his lips..."*
Ps. 28:7,8 *"The Lord is my strength and my shield; my heart trusted in Him, and I am helped: therefore my heart greatly rejoiceth; and with my song will I praise Him."*
Ps. 31:24 *"Be of good courage, and He shall strengthen your heart, all ye that hope in the Lord."*
Ps. 37:31 *"The law of God is in his heart..."*
Ps. 40:8 *"I delight to do Thy will, O my God: Yea, Thy law is within my heart."*
Ps. 84:4-12 *"... blessed is the man whose strength is in thee; in whose heart are the ways of them... they go from strength to strength... no good thing will He withhold from them that walk uprightly..."*
Ps. 101:2 *"I will walk within my house with a perfect heart..."*
Ps. 112:7 *"He shall not be afraid of evil tidings: his heart is fixed ("steadfast" NASB; "firm" EXV; "Confident" HCSB), trusting the Lord."*
Ps. 119:2 *"Blessed are they that keep His Testimonies, and that seek Him with the whole heart."*

Ps. 119:11 *"Thy Word have I hid in mine heart, that I might not sin against Thee."*
(Ps. 119:11 LB *"I have thought much about your Words, and stored them in my heart so that they would hold me back from sin."*
According to this verse we are to keep the Commandments unto the end.
Ps. 119:57 LB *"... and I promise to obey! With all my heart I want Your bless-ings. Be merciful just as You promised."*
Ps. 119:111,112 *"Thy Testimonies have I taken as an heritage forever: for they are the rejoicing of my heart. I have inclined mine heart to perform Thy Sta-tutes always, **even unto the end**."*
Ps. 141:3,4 *"Set a watch, O Lord, before my mouth; keep the door of my lips. Incline not my heart to any evil thing, to practice wicked works with men that work iniquity..."*
Prov. 3:1,2 *"... forget not My law; but let thine heart keep My Command-ments: for length of days, and long life, and peace, shall they add to thee."*
Prov. 3:3 *"Let not mercy and truth forsake thee: bind them about thy neck; write them upon the table of thine heart: so shalt thou find favour and good understanding in the sight of God and man."*
Prov. 3:5,6 *"Trust in the Lord with all thine heart; and lean not unto thine own understanding. In all thy ways acknowledge Him, and He shall direct thy paths."*
Prov. 4:20-22 *"My son attend to My words... let them not depart from thine eyes; keep them in the midst of thine heart."*
Prov. 4:23 *"Keep thy heart with all diligence; for out of it are the issues of life."*
Prov. 6:20,21 *"My son, keep thy father's commandment, and forsake not the law of thy mother: bind them continually upon thine heart, and tie them about thy neck. When thou goest, it shall lead thee; when thou sleepest, it shall keep thee; and when thou awakest, it shall talk with thee."*
Prov. 7:2,3 *"Keep My Commandments, and live; and My law as the apple of thine eye. Bind them upon thy fingers; write them upon the table of thine heart."*
Prov. 12:25 *"... a good word maketh it (the heart) glad."*
Prov. 14:30 *"A sound heart is the life of the flesh..."*
Prov. 14:33 *"Wisdom resteth in the heart of him that hath understanding..."*
Prov. 15:15 *"... he that is of a merry heart hath a continual feast."*
Prov. 15:30 *"The light of the eyes rejoiceth the heart..."*
Prov. 17:22 *"A merry heart doeth good like a medicine..."*
Prov. 18:15 *"The heart of the prudent getteth knowledge..."*
II Chron. 31:20,21 *"And thus did Hezekiah... in the law, and in the Commandments, to seek his God, he did it with all his heart, and prospered."*

Is. 57:15 *"For thus saith the high and lofty One that inhabiteth eternity, whose name is Holy; I dwell in the high and Holy place, with him also that is of a contrite and humble spirit, to revive the spirit of the humble, and to revive the heart of the contrite ones."*

Jer. 3:17-19 *"At that time they shall call Jerusalem the throne of the Lord; and all the nations shall be gathered unto it, to the name of the Lord, to Jerusalem: neither shall they walk anymore after the imagination of their evil heart..."*

Jer. 24:6,7 *"For I will set Mine eyes upon them for good, and I will bring them again to this land: and I will build them, and not pull them down; and I will plant them, and not pluck them up. And I will give them an heart to know Me, that I am the Lord: and they shall be My people, and I will be their God: for they shall return unto Me with their whole heart."*

Jer. 29:11-14 *"For I know the thoughts that I think toward you, saith the Lord, thoughts of peace, and not of evil, to give you an expected end. Then shall ye call upon Me, and ye shall go and pray unto Me, and I will hearken unto you. And ye shall seek Me, and find Me, when ye shall search for Me with all your heart. And I will be found of you, saith the Lord: and I will turn away your captivity..."*

Jer. 31:33 *"... I will put My law in their inward parts, and write it in their hearts; and will be their God, and they shall be My people."*

Jer. 32:37-42 *"... I will cause them to dwell safely: and they shall be My people, and I will be their God: and I will give them one heart, and one way, that they may fear Me forever, for the good of them, and of their children after them: and I will make an everlasting Covenant with them, that I will not turn away from them, to do them good; but I will put my fear in their hearts, that they shall not depart from Me. Yea, I will rejoice over them to do them good, and I will plant them in this land assuredly with My whole heart and with My whole soul... so will I bring upon them all the good that I have promised them."*

Jer. 32:39,40 *"And I will give them one heart, and one way, that they may fear Me forever, for the good of them, and of their children after them: and I will make an everlasting Covenant with them, that I will not turn away from them, to do them good; but I will put My fear in their hearts, that they shall not depart from Me."*

Prayer: Lord, please put Your fear in my heart and the hearts of my family so that we will not depart from You. Thank You in Jesus' name, Amen!

Ez. 11:19 *"... I will give them one heart, and I will put a new Spirit within you; and I will take the stony heart out of their flesh, and will give them a heart of flesh: that they may walk in My Statutes, and keep Mine Ordinances, and do them: and they shall be My people, and I will be their God."*

Ez. 18:31 *"Cast away from you all your transgressions, whereby ye have transgressed; and make you a new heart and a new Spirit: for why will ye die, O house of Israel... turn... and live..."*

Ez. 36:26-28 *"A new heart also will I give you, and a new Spirit will I put within you: and I will take away the stony heart out of your flesh, and I will give you an heart of flesh. And I will put My Spirit within you, and cause you to walk in My Statutes, and ye shall keep My Judgments, and do them... ye shall be My people, and I will be your God."*

Matt. 12:34;Lk. 6:45 *"A good man out of the good treasure of his heart bringeth forth that which is good... for of the abundance of the heart his mouth speaketh."*

Lk. 6:45 *"A good man out of the good treasure of his heart bringeth forth that which is good... for of the abundance of the heart his mouth speaketh."*

Acts 11:23 *"... when he came, and had seen the grace of God, was glad, and exhorted them all, that with purpose of heart they would cleave unto the Lord."*

Acts 13:22 *"... David... a man after Mine own heart... shall fulfil all My will."*

Acts 16:14 *"... whose heart the Lord opened..."*

Rom. 2:15 *"... which shew the work of the law written in their hearts."*

Rom. 2:29 *"... he is a Jew, which is one inwardly.. circumcision is that of the heart, in the Spirit... whose praise is not of men, but of God."*

Rom. 5:5 *"... the love of God is shed abroad in our hearts by the Holy Ghost which is given unto us."*

Rom. 6:17 *"... but ye have obeyed from the heart..."*

Rom. 7:22 *"For I delight in the law of God after the inward man (the heart)..."*

Rom. 8:27 *"And He that searcheth the hearts knoweth what is the mind of the Spirit, because He maketh intercession for the saints according to the will of God."*

Rom. 10:8-10 *"But what saith it? The Word is nigh thee, even in thy mouth, and in thy heart: that is, the Word of faith, which we preach; that if thou shalt confess with thy mouth the Lord Jesus, and shalt believe in thine heart that God hath raised him from the dead, thou shalt be saved. For with the heart man believeth unto righteousness; and with the mouth confession is made unto Salvation."*

I Cor. 2:9 *"... eye hath not seen, nor ear heard, neither have entered into the heart of man, the things which God hath prepared for them that love Him. But God hath revealed them unto us by His Spirit..."*

II Cor. 3:3 *"... ye are manifestly declared to be the epistle of Christ ministered by us, written not with ink, but with the Spirit of the living God; not in tables of stone, but in fleshy tables of the heart."*

Gal. 4:5-7 "... and because ye are sons, God hath sent forth the Spirit of His Son into your hearts, crying, Abba, Father..."
Eph. 6:5,6 "... in singleness of your heart, as unto Christ... as the servants of Christ, doing the will of God from the heart..."
Eph. 6:22 "... that He might comfort your hearts."
Col. 2:2,3 "That their hearts might be comforted, being knit together in love, and unto all riches of the full assurance of understanding... Christ; in whom are hid all the treasures of wisdom and knowledge."
Col. 3:16 "... singing with grace in your hearts to the Lord."
II Thess. 2:17 "Comfort your hearts, and stablish you in every good word and work."
Heb. 8:8-10 "... behold, the days come, saith the Lord, when I will make a New Covenant with the house of Israel and with the house of Judah: not according to the Covenant that I made with their fathers in the day when I took them by the hand to lead them out of the land of Egypt; because they continued not in My Covenant, and I regarded them not, saith the Lord. For this is the Covenant that I will make with the house of Israel after those days, saith the Lord; I will put My laws into their mind, and write them in their hearts: and I will be to them a God, and they shall be to Me a people..." (Quoting Jer. 31:31)
Heb. 10:16 "This is the Covenant that I will make with them after those days, saith the Lord, I will put My laws into their hearts, and in their minds will I write them; and their sins and iniquities will I remember no more."

Heaven / New Earth - Jerusalem

Deut. 8:7-16 "For the Lord thy God bringeth thee into a good land, a land of brooks of water, of fountains and depths that spring out of valleys and hills; a land of wheat, and barley, and vines, and fig trees, and pomegranates; a land of... olive (oil), and honey; a land wherein thou shalt eat bread without scarceness, thou shalt not lack anything in it; a land whose stones are iron, and out of whose hills thou mayest dig brass. When thou hast eaten and art full, then thou shalt bless the Lord thy God for the good land which He hath given thee. Beware that thou forget not the Lord thy God, in not keeping His Commandments, and His Judgments, and His Statutes, wich I command thee this day: lest when thou hast eaten and art full, and hast built goodly houses, and dwelt therein... then thine heart be lifted up, and thou forget the Lord thy God which brought thee forth water out of the rock of flint; who fed thee in the wilderness with manna, which thy fathers knew not, that He might humble thee... that He might prove thee, to do thee good at thy latter end ..."

These verses are about Canaan which is symbolically the New Earth.

Lev. 26:4-6,11-13 "... *Then I will give you rain in due season, and the land shall yield her increase, and the trees of the field shall yield their fruit. And your threshing shall reach unto the vintage, and the vintage shall reach unto the sowing time: and ye shall eat your bread to the full, and dwell in your land safely. And I will give peace in the land, and ye shall lie down, and none shall make you afraid: and I will rid evil beasts out of the land, neither shall the sword go through your land... and I wil set My Tabernacle among you: and My soul shall not abhor you. And I will walk among you, and will be your God, and ye shall be My people. I am the Lord your God... I have broken the bands of your yoke, and made you go upright.*"

Job 19:25 "*For I know that my Redeemer liveth, and that He shall stand at the latter day* (Heb. #314 "*at the end, last, coming after, last time, later, afterwards*") *upon the earth.*"

Ps. 16:11 "*Thou wilt shew me the path of life: in Thy presence is fullness of joy; at Thy right hand there are pleasures for evermore.*"

Ps. 46:4,5 "*There is a river, the streams whereof shall make glad the city of God, the Holy place of the Tabernacles of the Most High. God is in the midst of her* (New Jerusalem); *she shall not be moved: God shall help her, and that right early.*

Ps. 46:5 ESV "*... God will help her when morning dawns.*"

Ps. 46:5 God's Word Translation "*... at break of dawn.*"

Ps. 46:9 "*He maketh wars to cease unto the end of the earth...*" (fulfilled on the New Earth)

Ps. 50:2 "*Out of Zion, the perfection of beauty, God hath shined... gather My saints together unto Me; those that have made a Covenant with Me by sacrifice.*"

Ps. 72:8 "*He shall have dominion also from sea to sea, and from the river unto the ends of the earth.*"

Ps. 102:13-16 "*Thou shalt arise, and have mercy upon Zion: for the time to favour her, yea, the set time, is come. For Thy servants take pleasure in her stones...* (Rev. 21:19)"

Ps. 104:30 "*Thou sendest forth Thy Spirit, they are created: and Thou renewest the face of the earth. The glory of the Lord shall endure forever: the Lord shall rejoice in His works.*"

Ps. 107:36 "*He turneth the wilderness into a standing water, and dry ground into watersprings. And there He maketh the hungry to dwell., that they may prepare a city for habitation; and sow the fields, and plant vineyards, which may yield fruits of increase. He blesseth them also ...*"

Eccl. 3:11 "*He hath made everything beautiful in His time; also He hath set the world* (Gr. #5769 "*eternal, eternity, ages, long duration, antiquity &*

futurity, perpetual, forevermore, forever and ever, everlasting") in their heart, so that no man can find out ("fathom" NIV; "fully comprehend" ISV) the work that God maketh from the beginning to the end."

Is. 2:2-5 "And it shall come to pass in the last days, that the mountain of the Lord's house shall be established in the top fo the mountains, and shall be exalted above the hills; and all nations shall flow unto it. And many people shall go and say, Come ye, and let us go up to the mountain of the Lord, to the house of the God of Jacob; and He will teach us of His ways, and we will walk in His paths: for out of Zion shall go forth the law, and the Word of the Lord from Jerusalem... He shall Judge among the nations, and shall rebuke many people: and they shall beat their sword into plowshares, and their spears into pruninghooks: nation shall not.. learn war anymore... come ye, and let us walk in the light of the Lord."

Is. 2:11,17 " The lofty looks of man shall be humbled.. the haughtiness of men shall be bowed down, and the Lord alone shall be exalted in that day."

Is. 4:2-6 "In that day shall the branch of the Lord be beautiful and glorious, and the fruit of the earth shall be excellent and comely for them that are escaped of Israel. And it shall come to pass, that he that is left in Zion... shall be called Holy, even everyone that is written among the living in Jerusalem: when the Lord shall have washed away the filth of the daughters of Zion, and shall have purged the blood of Jerusalem from the mdist thereof by the Spirit of Judgment, and by the Spirit of burning: and the Lord will create upon every dweling place of Mt Zion, and upon her assemblies, a cloud and smoke by day, and the shining of a flaming fire by night: for upon all the glory shall be a defence. And there shall be a Tabernacle for a shadow in the daytime from the heat... for a place of refuge... for a covert from storm... from rain."

(The Father, Jesus, the New Jerusalem) are the Temple on the New Earth.

(Rev. 20;7;21:1-3,22 "And when the thousand years are expired... I saw a new heaven and a new earth... and I... saw the Holy City, New Jerusalem, coming down from God out of heaven... behold, the Tabernacle of God is with men, and He will dwell with them... and I saw no Temple therein: for the Lord God Almighty and the Lamb are the Temple of it."

Is. 5:27 "None shall be weary nor stumble among them; none shall slumber nor sleep; neither shall the girdle of their loins be loosed, nor the latchet of their shoes be broken..."

Is. 9:7 "Of the increase of His Government and peace there shall be no end, upon the throne of David, and upon His kingdom, to order it, and to establish it with Judgment and with justice from henceforth even forever. The zeal of the Lord of hosts will perform this."

Is. 11:6-10,16 "The wolf also shall dwell with the lamb, and the leopard shall lie down with the kid; and the calf and the young lion and the fatling together; and a little child shall lead them. And the cow and the bear shall feed; their young ones shall lie down together: and the lion shall eat straw like the ox. And the... (nursing) child shall play on the hole of the asp, and the weaned child shall put his hand on the cockatrice' den. They shall not hurt nor destroy in all My Holy Mountain: for the earth shall be full of the knowledge of the Lord, as the waters cover the sea. And in that day there shall be a root of Jesse (Jesus), which shall stand for an ensign ("... as a banner for the people [to gather around]" God's Word Translation; Gr. #5251 "a standard, ensign, signal, sign") of the people... and there shall be a highway for the remnant of His people"

Is. 12:6 "Cry out and shout, thou inhabitant of Zion: for great is the Holy One of Israel (Jesus) in the midst of thee."

Is. 14:7,8 "The whole earth is at rest, and is quiet: they break forth into singing. Yea, the fir trees rejoice.. and the cedars of Lebanon...."

Is. 16:5 "And in mercy shall the throne be stablished: and He shall sit upon it in truth in the Tabernacle of David, Juding, and seeking Judgment, and hasting righteousness."

(Rev. 20;7;21:1-3,22 "And when the thousand years are expired... I saw a new heaven and a new earth... and I... saw the Holy City, New Jerusalem, coming down from God out of heaven... behold, the Tabernacle of God is with men, and He will dwell with them... and I saw no Temple therein: for the Lord God Almighty and the Lamb are the Temple of it."

Is. 17:7 "At that day shall a man look to his Maker, and his eyes shall have respect to the Holy One of Israel (on New Earth)."

Is. 18:7 "... the present be brought unto the Lord of hosts of a people scattered and peeled, and from a people terrible from their beginning hitherto; a nation meted out and trodden under foot, whose land the rivers have spoiled, to the place of the name of the Lord of hosts, the Mt. Zion."

Is. 18:7 NIV "At that time gifts will be brought to the Lord Almighty... the gifts will be brought to Mt. Zion, the place of the Name of the Lord..."

Is. 19:20-25 "... Egypt: for they shall cry unto the Lord because of the oppressors, and he shall send them a Saviour... a great One... He shall deliver them. And the Lord shall be known to Egypt, and the Egyptians shall know the Lord in that day, and shall do sacrifice and oblation; yea, they shall vow a vow unto the Lord, and perform it. And the Lord shall smite Egypt: he smite and heal it: and they shall return even to the Lord and He shall be intreated of them, and shall heal them. In that day shall there be a highway out of Egypt to Assyria, and the Assyrian shall come into Egypt, and the Egyptian into Assyria, and the Egyptians shall serve with the Assyrians. In that day shall Israel be the third with Egypt and with Assyria, even a blessing in the midst *of the land: whom the Lord of hosts shall bless, saying, Blessed be Egypt My people, and Assyria the work of My hands and Israel Mine inheritance."*

Is. 24:23 *"Then the moon shall be confounded... the sun ashamed, when the Lord of hosts shall reign in Mt. Zion... in Jerusalem, and before His ancients..."* (They're ashamed because, even though the sun is seven times brighter and the moon is as bright as the day (Is. 30:26), the light from the New Jerusalem is so bright (because of God's presence) that you cannot even see the sun and there will be no night (Rev. 21:23,25).

Is. 25:6,7 *"And in this mountain* (on the New Earth) *shall the Lord of hosts make unto all people a feast* ("lavish feast" PB)*... and He will destroy in this mountain the face of the covering cast over all people, and the vail* (Heb. #4541 "web woven over all nations") *that is spread over all nations... He will swallow up death in victory: and the Lord God will wipe away tears from off all faces* (Rev.21:4)*; and the rebuke of His people shall He take away from off all the earth: for the Lord hath spoken it. And it shall be said in that day, Lo, this is our God; we have waited for Him, and He will save us: this is the Lord; we have waited for Him, we will be glad and rejoice in His Salvation. For in this mountain shall the hand of the Lord rest..."*

Is. 27:6 *"He shall cause them that come of Jacob to take root: Israel shall blos-som and bud and fill the face of the world with fruit."*

Is. 27:13 *"And it shall come to pass in that day, that the great trumpet shall be blown, and they shall come which were ready to perish in the land of Assyria, and the outcasts in the land of Egypt, and shall worship the Lord in the Holy Mount at Jersalem."*

Is. 29:17-19 *"Is it not yet a very little while, and Lebanon shall be turned into a fruitful field, and the fruitful field shall be esteemed as a forest... in that day shall the deaf hear the Words of the Book... the eyes of the blind shall see out of obscurity, and out of darkness. The meek also shall increase their joy in the Lord... the poor among men shall rejoice in the Holy One of Israel."*

Is. 30:23-26 *"... the food that comes from the land will be rich and plentiful... in that day your cattle will graze in broad meadows... streams of water will flow on every high mountain and every lofty hill. The moon will shine like the sun, and the sunlight will be seven times brighter, like the light of seven full days, when the Lord binds up the bruises of His people and heals the wounds He inflicted."*

Is. 32:1 *"Behold, a King* (Jesus) *shall reign in righteousness, and princes shall rule in Judgment."*

Is. 32:15-18 *"Until the Spirit be poured upon us from on high, and the wilderness be a fruitful field, and the fruitful field be counted for a forest... Judgment shall dwell in the wilderness... righteousness remain in the fruitful field... the work of righteousness shall be peace; and the effect of righteous-*

ness quietness and assurance forever. And My people shall dwell in a peaceable habitation, and in sure dwellings, and in quiet resting places ..."
Is. 33:17 "Thine eyes shall see the King in His beauty: they shall behold the land that is very far off (on New Earth)."
Is. 33:20-22,24 "... thine eyes shall see Jerusalem a quiet habitation, a Tabernacle that shall not be taken down; not one of the stakes thereof shall ever be removed, neither shall any of the cords thereof be broken. But there the glorious Lord will be unto us a place of broad rivers and streams... the Lord is our King; He will save us... and the inhabitant shall not say, I am sick: the people that dwell therein shall be forgiven their iniquity."
Is. 34:16 "... none shall want her mate."
Is. 35:1,2 "The wilderness and the solitary place shall be glad for them; and the desert shall rejoice, and blossom as the rose. It shall blossom abundantly and rejoice even with joy and singing: the glory of Lebanon shall be given unto it. The excellency of Carmel and Sharon. They shall see the glory of the Lord, and the excellency of our God."
Is. 35:5-8 "Then the eyes of the blind shall be opened, and the ears of the deaf shall be unstopped. Then shall the lame man leap as a hart, and the tongue of the dumb sings: for in the wilderness shall waters break out, and streams in the desert. And the parched ground shall become a pool, and the thirsty land spring of water... and an highway shall be there, and a way, and it shall be called The Way of Holiness; the unclean shall not pass over it: but it shall be for those: the wayfaring men..."
Is. 35:6-10 "... in the wilderness shall waters break out... streams in the desert... the parched ground shall become a pool.. the thirsty land springs of water... (and) grass with reeds and rushes. And an highway shall be there, and a way, and it shall be called the Way of Holiness (the streets of gold, Rev. 21:21); the unclean shall not pass over it; but it shall be for those: the wayfaring men, though fools, shall not err therein. No lion shall be there, nor any ravenous beast shall go up thereon, it shall not be found there; but the Redeemed shall walk there: and the ransomed of the Lord shall return, and come to Zion with songs and everlasting joy upon their heads: they shall obtain joy and gladness, and sorrow and sighing shall flee away."
(Is. 35:6 NLT "The lame will leap like a deer, and those who cannot speak will sing for joy..."
Is. 40:5 "And the glory of the Lord shall be revealed, and all flesh shall see it together: for the mouth of the Lord hath spoken it."
Is. 41:18 "... I will open rivers in high places... fountains in the midst of the valleys: I will make the wilderness a pool of water... the dry land springs of water."

Is. 41:19,20 *"I will plant in the wilderness the cedar, the shittah tree, and the myrtle, and the oil tree; I will set in the desert the fir tree, and the pine, and the box tree together: that they may see, and know and consider, and understand together, that the hand of the Lord hath done this, and the Holy One of Israel hath created it."*

Is. 42:16 *"... I will bring the blind by a way that they knew not; I will lead them in paths that they have not known: I will make darkness light before them, and crooked things straight. These things will I do unto them, and not forsake them."*

Is. 51:3,4 *"For the Lord shall comfort Zion: He will comfort all her waste places; and He will make her wilderness like Eden, and her desert like the garden of the Lord; joy and gladness shall be found therein, thanksgiving, and the voice of melody... ("the Law will go out from Me" NIV)..."*

Is. 54:11 *"So shall My Word be that goeth forth out of My mouth: it shall not return unto Me void, but it shall accomplish that which I please, and it shall prosper in the thing whereto I sent it."*

Is. 55:12,13 *"For ye shall go out with joy and be led forth with peace: the mountains and the hills shall break forth before you into singing, and all the trees of the field shall clap their hands. Instead of the thorn shall come up the fir tree, and instead of the brier shall come up the myrtle tree: and it shall be to the Lord for a name, for an everlasting sign that shall not be cut off."*

Is. 56:5-7 *"For thus says the Lord: To the eunuchs who keep My Sabbaths and choose what pleases Me, and hold fast My Covenant. Even to them I will give in My house and within My walls a place and a name better than that of sons and daughters; I will give them an everlasting name that shall not be cut off. Also the sons of the foreigner who join themselves to the Lord, to serve Him, and to love the name of the Lord, to be His servants – everyone who keeps from defiling the Sabbath, and holds fast My Covenant – even them I will bring to My Holy Mountain, and make them joyful in My house of prayer... for My house shall be called a house of prayer for all nations."*

Is. 57:15 *"... the high and lofty One that inhabiteth eternity, whose name is Holy: I dwell in the high and Holy place..."*

Is. 60:11,13-15 *"Therefore Thy gates shall be open continually; they shall not be shut day nor night; that men may bring unto Thee the forces ("wealth" KJV fn) of the Gentiles, and that their kings may be brought ("kings led in triumphal entry" NIV)... the glory of Lebanon shall come unto Thee, the fir tree, the pine tree, and the box together, to beautify the palce of My Sanctuary: and I will make the place of My feet glorious. The sons also of them that afflicted thee shall come bending unto thee; and all they that despised thee shall bow themselves down at the soles of thy feet: and they* shall call thee, The city of the Lord, The Zion of the Holy One of Israel (Jesus)... I will make thee an eternal excellency, a joy of many generations."

Is. 60:15-21 "... I will make thee (the New Jerusalem) an eternal excellency, a joy of many generations... ("powerful kings and mighty nations will satisfy your every need, as though you were a child nursing at the breast of a queen." vs. 16 NLT) and thou shalt know that I the Lord am thy Saviour... for brass I will bring gold, and for iron I will bring silver, and for wood brass, and for stones iron: I will also make thy officers peace, and thine exactors right-eousness. Violence shall no more be heard in thy land, wasting nor destructtion within thy borders... thou shalt call thy walls Salvation... thy gates Praise. The sun shall be no more thy light by day; neither for brightness shall the moon give light unto thee: but the Lord shall be unto thee an everlasting light, and thy God thy glory (Rev. 21:23). Thy sun shall no more go down; neither shall thy moon withdraw itself: for the Lord shall be thine everlasting light, and the days of thy mourning shall be ended. Thy people also shall be all righteous: they shall inherit the land forever, the branch of My planting, the work of My hands, that I may be glorified. A little one shall become a thousand, and a small one a strong nation: I the Lord will hasten it..."

It is in the New Jerusalem that there will be no need for the sun or moon because the glory of God will be so bright you won't need the sun or moon. The Bible promises in Is. 30:26 that the moon will be as bright as the sun and the sun will be seven times brighter.

Is. 61:4 "And they shall build the old wastes, they shall raise up the former desolations, and they shall repair the waste cities, the desolations of many generations. And strangers shall stand and feed your flocks, and the sons of the alien shall be your plowmen and your vinedressers... men shall call you the Ministers of our God: ye shall eat the riches of the Gentiles, and in their glory shall ye boast yourselves."

Is. 65:17-19,21-25 "For, behold, I create new heavens and a New Earth: and the former shall not be remembered, nor come into mind. But be you glad and rejoice forever in that which I create: for behold, I create Jerusalem a rejoicing, and her people a joy. And I will rejoice in Jerusalem, and joy in My people: and the voice of weeping shall be no more heard in her, nor the voice of crying... and they shall build houses, and inhabit them; and they shall plant vineyards, and eat the fruit of them. They shall not build, and another inhabit; they shall not plant, and another eat: for as the days of a tree are the days of My people, and mine elect shall long enjoy the work of their hands. They shall not labour in vain, nor bring forth for trouble; for they are the seed of the blessed of the Lord, and their offspring with them. And it shall come to pass, that before they call, I will answer; and whiles they are yet speaking, I will hear. The wolf and the lamb shall feed together, and the lion shall eat straw like the bullock: and dust shall be the serpent's meat. They shall not hurt nor destroy in all My Holy Mountain, saith the Lord."

Is. 66:3 "He that killeth an ox is as if he slew a man; he that sacrificeth a lamb, as if he cut off a dog's neck..."

Is. 66:12 "... I will extend peace to her (the New Jerusalem) like a river, and the glory of the Gentiles like a flowing stream..."

Is. 66:22,23 "... as the new heavens and the New Earth which I will make, shall remain before Me.. so shall your seed and your name remain... it shall come to pass, that from one New Moon to another, and from one Sabbath to another, shall all flesh come to worship before Me, saith the Lord."

Jer. 3:17-19 "At that time they shall call Jerusalem the throne of the Lord; and all the nations shall be gathered unto it, to the name of the Lord, to Jerusalem: neither shall they walk anymore after the imagination of their evil heart. In those days the house of Judah shall walk with the house of Israel, and they shall come together out of the land of the North to the land that I have given for an inheritance unto your fathers. But I said, How shall I put thee among the children ("I will consider you as children" PB), and give thee a pleasant land, a goodly heritage of the hosts of nations? And I said, Thou shalt call Me, My Father; and shalt not turn away from Me."

Jer. 4:2 "... the Lord liveth, in truth, in Judgment, and in righteousness; and the nations shall bless themselves in Him, and in Him shall they glory."

Jer. 17:12,13 "A glorious high throne from the beginning is the place of our Sanctuary... Lord, the hope of Israel... the fountain of living waters (Rev.22:1)..."

Jer. 30:9,10 "But they shall serve the Lord their God, and David their king, whom I will raise up unto them... lo, I will save thee from afar, and thy seed from the land of their captivity; and Jacob shall return, and shall be in rest, and be quiet, and none shall make him afraid."

Jer. 31:6,7 "For there shall be a day, that the watchmen upon the mount Ephraim shall cry, Arise ye, and let us go up to Zion unto the Lord our God... sing with gladness for Jacob, and shout among the chief of the nations: publish ye, praise ye..."

Jer. 31:34 "And they shall teach no more every man his neighbor, and every man his brother, saying, Know the Lord: for they shall all know Me, from the least of them unto the greatest of them, saith the Lord: for I will forgive their iniquity, and I will remember their sin no more."

Jer. 32:38-42 "... I will cause them to dwell safely: and they shall be My people, and I will be their God: and I will give them one heart, and one way, that they may fear Me forever, for the good of them, and of their children after them: and I will make an everlasting Covenant with them, that I will not turn away from them, to do them good; but I will put My fear in their hearts, that they shall not depart from Me. Yea, I will rejoice over them to do them good, and I will plant them in this land assuredly with My whole heart and with My whole soul... I will bring upon them all the good that I have promised them.

Jer. 33:14-17 "Behold, the days come, saith the Lord, that I will perform that good thing which I have promised unto them..."

Jer. 33:16 "In those days shall Judah be saved... Jerusalem shall dwell safely... this is the name wherewith she shall be called, The Lord our Righteousness."

Ez. 28:26 "And they shall dwell safely therein, and shall build houses, and plant vineyards; yea, they shall dwell with confidence, when I have executed Judgments upon all those that despise them round about them; and they shall know that I Am the Lord ther God."

Ez. 34:22-31 "... therefore will I save My flock, and they shall no more be a prey; and I will Judge... and I will set up one Shepherd over them, and He shall feed them, even My servant David; He shall feed them, and He shall be their Shepherd. And the Lord will be their God, and My servant David a prince among them; I the Lord have spoken it. And I will make with them a Covenant of peace, and will cause the evil beasts to cease out of the land: and they shall dwell safely in the wilderness, and sleep in the woods. And I will make them and the places round about My hill a blessing; and I will cause the shower to come down in his season; there shall be showers of blessing. And the tree of the field shall yield her fruit, and the earth shall yield her increase, and they shall be safe in their land, and shall know that I am the Lord, when I have broken the bands of their yoke, and delivered them out of the hand of those that serve themselves of them. And they shall no more be a prey to the heathen, neither shall the beast of the land devour them; but they shall dwell safely, and none shall make them afraid. And I will raise up for them a plant of renown, and they shall be no more consumed with hunger in the land, neither bear the shame of the heathen anymore. Thus shall they know that I the Lord their God am with them, and that they, even the house of Israel, are My people, saith the Lord God. And ye My flock, the flock of My pasture, are men, and I am your God, saith the Lord God."

Ez. 43:7 "... the place of My throne, and the place of the soles of My feet, where I will dwell in the midst of the children of Israel forever..."

Ez. 47:1,7,9,12 "... waters issued out from under the threshold of the house eastward... now when I had returned behold, at the bank of the river were very many trees on the one side and on the other... and it shall come to pass, that everything that liveth, which moveth, whithersoever the rivers shall come, shall live... and by the river upon the bank thereof, on this side and on that side, shall grow all trees for meat, whose leaf shall not fade, neither shall the fruit thereof be consumed: it shall bring forth new fruit according

to his months, because their waters they issued out of the Sanctuary: and the fruit thereof shall be for meat, and the leaf thereof for medicine."
(This is the same as the water of life and the tree of life in Rev. 22. (Rev. 20;7;21:1-3,22 "And when the thousand years are expired... I saw a new heaven and a new earth... and I... saw the Holy City, New Jerusalem, coming down from God out of heaven... behold, the Tabernacle of God is with men, and He will dwell with them... and I saw no Temple therein: for the Lord God Almighty and the Lamb are the Temple of it."
Ez. 48:31,35 "And the gates of the city shall be after the names of the tribes of Israel (Rev. 21:17)... the name of the city from that day shall be, The Lord is there."
Joel 3:17,18 "So shall ye know that I Am the Lord your God dwelling in Zion, My Holy Mountain: then shall Jerusalem be Holy, and there shall no strangers pass through her anymore. And it shall come to pass in that day, that the mountains shall drop down new wine, and the hills shall flow with milk, and all the rivers of Judah shall flow with waters, and a fountain shall come forth of the house of the Lord, and shall water the valley of Shittim."
Amos 9:13-15 "... the mountains shall drop sweet wine and all the hills shall melt. And I will bring again the captivity of My people of Israel, and they shall build the waste cities, and inhabit them; and they shall plant vineyards, and drink the wine thereof; they shall also make gardens, and eat the fruit of them. And I will plant them upon their land, and they shall no more be pulled up out of their land which I have given them, saith the Lord thy God."
Mic. 4:2 "... He will teach us of His ways, and we will walk in His paths: for the law shall go forth of Zion, and the Word of the Lord from Jerusalem (on the New Earth)."
Mic. 4:1-9 "But in the last days it shall come to pass, that the Mountain of the house of the Lord shall be established in the top of the mountains, and it shall be exalted above the hills; and people shall flow unto it. And many nations shall come, and say, Come, and let us go up to the mountain of the Lord, and to the house of the God of Jacob; and He will teach us of His ways, and we will walk in His paths: for the law shall go forth of Zion, and the Word of the Lord from Jerusalem. And He shall Judge among many people, and rebuke strong nations afar off; and they shall beat their swords into plowshares, and their spears into pruning hooks: nation shall not lift up a sword against nation, neither shall they learn war anymore. But they shall sit every man under his vine and under his fig tree; and none shall make them afraid for the mouth of the Lord of hosts hath spoken it. For all people will walk everyone in the name of his God, and we will walk in the name of the Lord our God forever and ever. In that day, saith the Lord will I assemble her that halteth, and I wil gather her that is driven out, and her that I have

afflicted; and I will make her that halted a remnant, and her that was cast far off a strong nation: and the Lord (Jesus Christ) *shall reign over them in Mount Zion from henceforth... forever... O tower of the flock, the stronghold of the daughter of Zion, unto thee shall it come, even the first dominion; the kingdom shall come to the daughter of Jerusalem. Now why dost thou cry out aloud? Is there no king in thee? Is thy counseller perished..."*
Nahum 1:9 ESV *"... trouble ("Affliction"* KJV;*"oppression"* HCSB;Heb. #6869 *"adversary, tribulation, anguish, distress, trouble, rival") will not rise up a second time."*
(This will happen after God creates everything new.
Nahum 1:15 *"... the wicked shall no more pass through thee* (New Jerusalem)*; he is utterly cut off."*
Hab. 2:14 *"For the* (New) *earth shall be filled with the knowledge of the glory of the Lord, as the waters cover the sea."*
Zeph. 3:11-17 *"In that day shalt thou not be ashamed for all thy doings, wherein thou hast transgressed against Me; for then I will take away out of the midst of thee them that rejoice in thy pride, and thou shalt no more be haughty because of My Holy Mountain... they shall trust in the name of the Lord... they shall feed and lie down, and none shall make them afraid... be glad and rejoice with all the heart... the Lord hath taken away thy Judgments, He hath cast out thine enemy; the king of Israel... is in the midst of thee; thou shalt not see evil anymore... the Lord thy God in the midst of thee is mighty; He wll save, He will rejoice over thee with joy: He will rest in Hiis love, He will joy over thee with singing."*
Zech. 2:5 *"For I, saith the Lord, will be unto her* (New *"Jerusalem"* vs. 2) *a wall of fire round about, and will be the glory in the midst of her."*
Zech. 2:10-12 *"Sing and rejoice, O daughter of Zion: for, lo, I come, and I will dwell in the midst of thee, saith the Lord. And many nations shall be joined to the Lord in that day, and shall be My people: and I will dwell in the midst of thee, and thou shalt know that the Lord of hosts hath sent Me unto thee. And the Lord shall inherit Judah his portion in the Holy land, and shall choose ("be pleased with"* PB) *Jerusalem again."*
Zech. 3:7 *"... I will give thee places to walk among these..."*
Zech. 3:10 *"In that day, saith the Lord of hosts, shall ye call every man his neighbor under the vine and under the fig tree."*
Zech. 3:9,10 *"... I will remove the iniquity of that land in one day. In that day, saith the Lord of hosts, shall ye call every man his neighbor under the vine and under the fig tree."*
Zech. 9:8 *"... and no oppressor shall pass through them anymore..."*
Zech. 9:10,16,17 *"... He shall speak peace unto the heathen: and His dominion shall be from sea even to sea, and from the river even to the ends of the*

earth... and the Lord their God shall save them in that day as the flock of His people: for they shall be as the stones of a crown, lifted up as an ensign upon His land. For how great is His goodness, and how great is is beauty! Corn shall make the young men cheerful, and new wine the maids."

Zech. 12:8 "In that day shall the Lord defend the inhabitants of Jerusalem; and he that is feeble among them at that day shall be as David; and the house of David shall be as God, as the angel of the Lord before them."

Zech. 13:1 "In that day there shall be a fountain opened to the house of David and to the inhabitants of Jerusalem for sin and for uncleanness."

Zech. 13:1,2 "In that day there shall be a fountain opened to the house of David and to the inhabitants of Jerusalem for sin and for uncleanness. And it shall come to pass that day, saith the Lord of hosts, that I will cut off the names of idols out of the land, and they shall no more be remembered: and also I will cause the prophets and the unclean spirit to pass out of the land.

Zech. 14:1 "Behold, the day of the Lord cometh, and thy spoil shall be divided in the midst of thee."

Zech. 14:3-11 "... His feet shall stand in that day upon the Mt. of Olives, which is before Jerusalem on the East, and the Mt. of Olives shall cleave in the midst thereof toward the East and toward the West, and there shall be a very great valley; and half of the mountain shall remove toward the North, and half of it toward the South... my God shall come, and all the saints with Thee... living waters shall go out from Jerusalem; half of them toward the former sea, and half of them toward the hinder sea... and the Lord shall be King over all the earth: in that day shall there be One Lord, and His name One... and there shall be no more utter destruction; but Jerusalem shall be safely inhabited."

Zech. 14:4-11 "And His feet shall stand in that day upon the Mount of Olives, which is before Jerusalem on the East. And the Mount of Olives shall cleave in the midst... there shall be a very great valley; and half of the mountain shall remove toward the North, and half of it toward the South. And ye shall flee to the valley of the mountains... shall flee... and the Lord my God shall come, and all the saints with Thee... it shall be in that day, that living waters shall go out from Jerusalem: half of them toward the former sea, and half of them toward the hinder sea: in summer and in winter shall it be. And the Lord shall be King over all the earth: in that day shall there be one Lord, and His name One. All the land shall be turned as a plain... and it shall be lifted up, and inhabited in her place... and men shall dwell in it, and there shall be no more utter destruction; but Jerusalem shall be safely inhabited..."

Zech. 14:14,16 "... and the wealth of all the heathen round about shall be gathered together, gold, and silver, and apparel, in great abundance... and it shall come to pass, that everyone that is left of all the nations which came

against Jerusalem shall even go up from year to year to worship the King, the Lord of hosts, and to keep the Feast of Tabernacles."
Zech. 14:20 *"In that day shall there be upon the bells of the horses, Holiness unto the Lord..."*
Mal. 3:17 *"And they shall be Mine, saith the Lord of hosts, in that day when I make up My jewels; and I will spare them, as a man spareth his own son..."*
Mal. 4:2,3 *"... unto you that fear My name shall the Sun of righteousness arise with healing in His wings; and ye shall go forth, and grow up as calves of the stall. And ye shall tread down the wicked; for they shall be ashes under the soles of your feet in the day that I shall do this, saith the Lord of hosts."*
Matt. 5:3 *"Blessed are the poor in spirit: for theirs is the kingdom of heaven."*
Matt. 5:5 *"Blessed are the meek: for they shall inherit the earth."*
Matt. 5:10 *"Blessed are they which are persecuted for righteousness sake: for theirs is the kingdom of heaven."*
Matt. 5:19 *"... whosoever shall do and teach them* (the Law/Commandments) *the same shall be called great in the kingdom of heaven."*
Lk. 19:17,19 *"... well* (done), *thou good servant: because thou hast been faithful in a very little, have thou authority over ten cities... and he said likewise to* (the second man)*... be thou also over five cities."*
Lk. 23:43 *"... you will be with Me in Paradise* (Gr. #3857 *"... an ancient Persian word meaning enclosure, garden, park..."*)
Acts 1:11 *"... this same Jesus, which is taken up from you into heaven, shall so come in like manner as ye have seen Him go into heaven."*
Acts 3:21 *"And He shall send Jesus Christ... whom the heaven must receive until the times of restitution of all things* (on the New Earth)*..."*
(Acts 3:21 HCSB *"Heaven must welcome Him* (Jesus) *until the times of the restoration of all things* (on the New Earth)*..."*
Rom. 8:21 NLT *"... the creation looks forward to the day when it will join God's children in glorious freedom from death and decay."*
Eph. 3:21 *"... world without end. Amen."*
Phil. 3:20 *"... our conversation is in heaven..."*
Col. 3:1-4 *"If ye then be risen with Christ, seek those things which are above, where Christ sitteth on the right hand of God. Set your affection on things above, not on things on the earth. For ye are dead, and your life is hid with Christ in God. When Christ, who is our life, shall appear, then shall ye also appear with Him in glory."*
(The promise is that we have an inheritance in heaven so that is where our affections should be.
I Pet. 1:3,4 *"... according to His abundant mercy hath begotten us again unto a lively hope by the Resurrection of Jesus Christ... to an inheritance incorruptible, and undefiled, and that fadeth not away, reserved in heaven for you..."*

II Pet. 3:13 "... *we, according to His promise, look for new heavens and a New Earth, wherein dwelleth righteousness.*"
Rev. 2:7 "... *to him that overcometh will I give to eat of the tree of life, which is in the midst of the paradise of God.*"
Rev. 3:11,12 "... *I come quickly: hold that fast which thou hast, that no man take thy crown. Him that overcometh will I make a pillar in the Temple of my God... he shall go no more out... I will write upon him the name of my God... the name of the city of my God, which is New Jerusalem, which cometh down out of heaven from my God: and I will write upon him My new name.*"
Rev. 7:16,17 "*They shall hunger no more, neither thirst anymore; neither shall the sun light on them, nor any heat. For the Lamb which is in the midst of the throne shall feed them, and shall lead them unto living fountains of waters: and God shall wipe away all tears from their eyes.*"
Rev. 20:7;21:1-7 "... *when the thousand years are expired... I saw a new heaven and a New Earth: for the first heaven and the first earth were passed away; and there was no more sea. And I John saw the Holy City, New Jerusalem, coming down from God out of heaven, prepared as a bride* (Gr. #3565 "*bridal chamber*) *adorned for her husband. And I heard a great voice out of heaven saying, Behold, the Tabernacle of God is with men, and He will dwell with them, and they shall be His people, and God Himself shall be with them, and be their God. And God shall wipe away all tears from their eyes; and there shall be no more death, neither sorrow, nor crying, neither shall there be anymore pain: for the former things are passed away. And He that sat upon the throne said, Behold, I make all things new. And He said unto me, Write: for these words are true and faithful. And he said unto me, It is done. I am Alpha and Omega, the beginning and the end. I will give unto him that is athirst of the fountain of the Water of Life freely. He that overcometh shall inherit all things: and I will be his God, and He shall be my son.*"
Rev. 21:9-12,14 "... *come hither, I will shew thee the Bride, the Lamb's wife. And he carried me away in the Spirit to a great and high mountain, and shewed me that Great City, the Holy Jerusalem, descending out of heaven from God, having the glory of God: and her light was like unto a stone most precious, even like a jasper stone, clear as crystal; and had a wall great and high, and had twelve gates, and at the gates twelve angels, and names written thereon, which are the names of the twelve tribes of the children of Israel... and the wall of the city had twelve foundations, and in them the names of the twelve Apostles of the Lamb...*"
Rev. 21:16-27 "*And the city lieth foursquare, and the length is as large as the breadth: and he measured the city with the reed, twelve thousand furlongs. The length and the breadth and the height of it are equal. And he measured the wall thereof, an hundred and forty and four cubits... the building of the*

wall of it was of jasper: and the city was pure gold... and the foundations of the wall of the city were garnished with all manner of precious stones... and the twelve gates were twelve pearls... and the street of the city was pure gold, as it were transparent glass... I saw no Temple therein: for the Lord God Almighty and the Lamb are the Temple of it... the city had no need of the sun (or) moon... for the glory of God did lighten it.. the Lamb is the light thereof* (This is just in the city because Is. 30:26 tells us that the sun is seven times brighter and the moon is as bright as the sun)... *the nations of them which are saved shall walk in the light of it... the kings of the earth do bring their glory and honour into it... the gates of it shall not be shut at all by day: for there shall be no night there... they shall bring the glory and honour of the nations into it... there shall in no wise enter into it anything that defileth... but they which are written in the Lamb's Book of Life."*

Rev. 22:1-5 *"... he shewed me a pure river of water of life... proceeding out of the throne of God and of the Lamb. In the midst of the street of it, and on either side of the river, was there the Tree of Life, which bare twelve manner of fruits, and yielded her fruit every month... the leaves of the tree were for the healing of the nations... there shall be no more curse; but the throne of God and of the Lamb shall be in it; and His servants shall serve Him; and they shall see His face... His name shall be in their foreheads... there shall be no night there.. they need no candle, neither light of the sun; for the Lord God giveth them light: and they shall reign forever..."* See Ez. 47:12.

Rev. 22:17 *"... let him that is athirst come, and whosoever will, let him take the Water of Life freely."*

Heir

See Inherit

Hell / Pit / Grave

Job 23:27 *"He will deliver his soul from going into the pit."*
Ps. 16:9-11 *"... my heart is glad... my glory rejoiceth: my flesh also shall rest in hope.. Thou wilt not leave my soul in hell; neither wilt Thou suffer Thine Holy One* (Jesus) *to see corruption. Thou wilt shew me the path of life: in Thy presence is fullness of joy; at Thy right hand there are pleasures forever."*
Ps. 30:3 *"O Lord, Thou hast brought up my soul from the grave* (Heb. #7585 "sheol"): *Thou hast kept me alive, that I should not go down to the pit."*
Ps. 40:2 *"He brought me up also out of an horrible pit, out of the miry clay, and set my feet upon a Rock, and established my goings."*

Ps. 49:15 *"But God will Redeem my soul from the power of the grave (Heb. #785 "sheol"): for He shall receive me. Selah."*
Ps. 86:13 *"For great is Thy mercy toward me: and thou hast delivered my soul from the lowest hell."*
Is. 38:15-17 *"... Thou hast in love to my soul delivered it from the pit of corruption: for Thou hast cast all my sins behind Thy back."*
Zech. 9:11 *"As for thee also, by the blood of Thy Covenant I have sent forth thy prisoners out of the pit wherein is no water."*
Acts 2:26,27 *"... my flesh shall rest in hope because Thou wilt not leave My soul in hell (Heb. #86 "Hades"), neither wilt Thou suffer Thine Holy One to see corruption."* (Quoting from Ps. 16:2-11)

Help

I Chron. 22:16 PB *"The Lord will help you..."*
I Chron. 22:18 PB *"He will help you and relieve you on every side."*
II Chron. 20:9 *"... then Thou wilt hear and help."*
Ps. 3:6,7 *"I will not be afraid of ten thousands of people, that have set themselves against me round about. Arise, O Lord; save m... for Thou hast smitten all mine enemies upon the cheek bone; Thou hast broken the teeth of the ungodly."*
Ps. 33:20 *"... He is our help and our shield."*
Ps. 37:40 *"And the Lord shall help them, and deliver them: He shall deliver them from the wicked, and save them, because they trust in Him."*
Ps. 42:5 NIV *"Hope in God, for I shall yet praise Him for the help of His countenance."*
Ps. 58:6 *"Break their teeth, O God, in their mouth: break out the great teeth of the young lions O Lord."*
God breaks their teeth by breaking Satan's power, I Pet. 5:8.
Ps. 71:6 *"By Thee have I been holden up from the womb: Thou art He that took me out of my mother's bowels..."*
Ps. 86:17 *"... Thou, Lord, hast... ("helped" PB) me, and comforted me."*
Ps. 94:17 *"Unless the Lord had been my help, my soul had almost dwelt in silence."*
Ps. 107:28 *"Then they cry unto the Lord in their trouble, and He bringeth them out of their distresses. He maketh the storm a calm, so that the waves thereof are still. Then are they glad because they be quiet; so He bringeth them unto their desired haven."*
Ps. 108:12 *"... O God... give us help from trouble: for vain is the help of man."*
Ps. 116:6 *"(God) preserveth the simple: I was brought low... He helped me."*

Ps. 118:13 "... *the Lord helped me.*"

Ps. 119:81 LB "*I expect Your help...*"

Ps. 121:1,2 "*I will lift up mine eyes unto the hills, from whence cometh my help. My help cometh from the Lord, which made heaven and earth. He will not suffer thy foot to be moved... the Lord shall preserve thee from all evil: He shall preserve thy soul. The Lord shall preserve thy going out and thy coming in from this time forth, and even forevermore.*"

Ps. 124:6-8 "*Blessed be the Lord, who hath not given us as a prey to their teeth. Our soul is escaped as a bird out of the snare of the fowlers: the snare is broken, and we are escaped. Our help is in the name of the Lord, who made heaven and earth.*"

Prov. 12:18 "*... but the tongue of the wise is health.* ("brings healing" NIV). *The lip of truth shall be established forever...*"

Prov. 12:19 NLT "*Truthful words stand the test of time...*"

Is. 8:13 PB "*... He is your God and He is your helper.*"

Is. 37:40 "*And the Lord shall help them, and deliver them: He shall deliver them from the wicked, and save them, because they trust in Him.*"

Is. 41:10 "*Fear thou not; for I am with thee: be not dismayed; for I am thy God: I will strengthen thee: yea, I will help thee; yea, I will uphold thee with the right hand of My righteousness.*"

Is. 41:13,14 "*For I the Lord thy God will hold thy right hand, saying unto thee, Fear not: I will help thee. Fear not... saith the Lord, and thy Redeemer, the Holy One of Israel.*"

Is. 49:8 "*Thus saith the Lord, In an acceptable time have I heard thee, and in a day of Salvation have I helped thee...*"

Is. 50:7 "*... the Lord God will help me... I* (shall) *not be confounded: therefore have I set my face like a flint, and I know that I shall not be ashamed.*"

Is. 50:9 "*... Lord God will help me; who is he that shall condemn me...*"

Jer. 49:11 NLT "*... I will protect the orphans who remain among you. Your wi-dows, too, can depend on Me for help.*"

Lk. 1:54 "*He hath...* (helped) *His servant... in remembrance of His mercy...*"

Heb. 2:18 "*For in that He Himself hath suffered being tempted, He is able to succor* (#997 "send aid, help, support") *them that are tempted.*"

Heb. 13:6 "*... the Lord is my helper... I will not fear what man shall do to me.*"

Holy Spirit / Power / Strength

Seven represents the Holy Spirit, "*Seven Spirits before His throne*" Rev. 1:4; "*Seven Spirits of God*" Rev. 4:5.

Ex. 15:2 *"The Lord is my strength and song and He is become my Salvation: He is my God, and I will prepare him an habitation..."*
Deut. 7:19 *"... and the signs, and the wonders, and the mighty hand, and the stretched out arm, whereby the Lord thy God brought thee out: so shall the Lord thy God do unto all the people of whom thou art afraid."*
Deut. 7:21 *"... for the Lord thy God is among you, a mighty God and terrible."*
Deut. 33:25 To the Tribe of Asher, *"... as thy days, so shall thy strength be."*
Josh. 1:5,7 To Joshua, *"There shall not any man be able to stand before thee all the days of thy life: as I was with Moses, so I will be with thee: I will not fail thee, nor forsake thee. Be strong and of a good courage: for unto this people shalt thou divide for an inheritance the land..."*
Judges 14:6,9;15:14 *"... the Spirit of the Lord came mightily (on Samson)..."*
I Sam. 10:6,7,9,10 To king Saul, *"And the Spirit of the Lord will come upon thee, and thou shalt prophesy with them, and shalt be turned into another man... that thou do as occasion serve thee; for God is with thee ... God gave him another heart... and the Spirit of God came upon him, and he prophesied among them."*
II Sam. 22:33,36 *"God is my strength and power: and He maketh my way perfect... Thy gentleness hath made me great."*
I Chron. 29:12,14 *"... Thou reignest over all; and in Thine hand is power and might; and in Thine hand it is to make great, and to give strength unto all... for all things come of Thee, and of Thine own have we given Thee."*
II Chron. 16:9 *"... the eyes of the Lord run to and fro throughout the whole earth, to shew Himself strong in the behalf of them whose heart is perfect toward Him..."*
Prayer: Lord, please show Yourself strong on my behalf as You promised in Your Word. Thank You in Jesus' name, Amen!
Prayer: II Chron. 20:6 *"... O Lord God of our fathers, art not Thou God in heaven? And rulest not Thou over all the kingdoms... and in Thine hand is there not power and might, so that none is able to withstand Thee? Art not Thou our God, who didst drive out the inhabitants of this land before Thy people Israel, and gavest it to the seed of Abraham Thy friend forever?"*
Neh. 8:10 *"... for the joy of the Lord is your strength."*
Neh. 9:20 *"Thou gavest also Thy good Spirit to instruct them..."*
Ps. 27:1 *"The Lord is my light and my Salvation; whom shall I fear? The Lord is the strength of my life; of whom shall I be afraid?"*
Ps. 28:7,8 *"The Lord is my strength and my shield; my heart trusted in Him, and I am helped... my heart greatly rejoiceth... with my song will I praise Him. The Lord is their strength, and He is the saving strength of His anointed."*
Ps. 29:11 *"The Lord will give strength unto His people; the Lord will bless His people with peace."*

Ps. 31:24 *"Be of good courage, and He shall strengthen your heart, all ye that hope in the Lord."*
Ps. 37:39 *"... He is their strength in the time of trouble."*
Ps. 41:3 *"The Lord will strengthen him upon the bed of languishing ("The Lord sustains them on their sickbed..." NIV)..."*
Ps. 66:3 *"... through the greatness of Thy power shall Thine enemies submit themselves unto Thee."*
Ps. 68:18 *"... Thou hast received gifts* (of the Holy Spirit) *for men..."*
Ps. 68:35 *"... God... that giveth strength and power unto His people..."*
Ps. 84:4-12 *"... Blessed is the man whose strength is in thee; in whose heart are the ways of them... they go from strength to strength... no good thing will He withhold from them that walk uprightly..."*
Ps. 89:8-10 *"O Lord God of hosts, who is a strong Lord like unto Thee? or to Thy faithfulness round about Thee? Thou rulest the raging of the sea: when the waves thereof arise, Thou stillest them... Thou hast scattered Thine enemies with Thy strong arm."*
Ps. 105:24 About Israel, *"And He increased His people greatly; and made them stronger than their enemies."*
Ps. 119:49,50 LB *"... Your promises... give me strength..."*
Ps. 138:3 *"In the day when I cried Thou answeredst me, and strengthenedst me with strength in my soul."*
Ps. 144:1,2 *"Blessed be the Lord my strength, which teacheth my hands to war, and my fingers to fight: my goodness, and my fortress; my high tower, and my deliverer; my shield, and He in whom I trust; who subdueth my people under me."*
Prov. 24:5 *"A wise man is strong; yea, a man of knowledge increaseth strength."*
Prov. 28:4 PB *"... those who keep the law receive strength."*
Is. 12:2 *"... the Lord Jehovah is my strength and my song..."*
Is. 25:4 *"For Thou hast been a strength ("refuge" NIV; "stronghold" ESV; "defense" NASB) to the poor, a strength to the needy in his distress, a refuge from the storm, a shadow from the heat, when the blast of the terrible ones is as a storm against the wall ("the breath of the ruthless is like a storm against a wall." ESV)."*
Is. 26:4 *"... trust ye in the Lord forever: for in the Lord Jehovah is everlasting strength..."*
Is. 27:5 *"... let him take hold of My strength, that he may make peace with Me; and he shall make peace with Me."*
Is. 30:15 *"... thus saith the Lord God... in returning and rest shall ye be saved; in quietness and in confidence shall be your strength..."*

Is. 29:5 "And now, saith the Lord that formed me from the womb to be his servant... my God shall be my strength."

Is. 40:29-31 "He giveth power to the faint; and to them that have no might He increaseth strength... but they that wait upon the Lord shall renew their strength; they shall mount up with wings as eagles; they shall run, and not be weary; and they shall walk, and not faint."

Is. 42:5 "Thus saith God the Lord, He that created the heavens, and stretched them out; He that spread forth the earth, and that which cometh out of it; He that giveth breath unto the people upon it, and Spirit to them that walk there-in..."

Is. 44:3 "For I will pour water upon him that is thirsty... and floods upon dry ground: I will pour My Spirit upon thy seed..."

Is. 45:24 "Surely, shall one say, in the Lord have I righteousness and strength..."

Is. 55:1 "Ho, everyone that thirsteth, come ye to the waters, and he that hath no money; come ye, buy, and eat; yea, come, buy wine and milk without money and without price."

Is. 61:1 "The Spirit of the Lord God is upon Me... the Lord hath anointed Me to preach good tidings unto the meek; He hath sent Me to bind up the brokenhearted, to proclaim liberty to the captives... the opening of the prison to them that are bound; to proclaim the acceptable year of the Lord... to comfort all that mourn; to appoint unto them that mourn in Zion to give unto them beauty for ashes, the oil of joy for mourning, the garment of praise for the spirit of heaviness; that they might be called trees of righteousness, the planting of the Lord, that He might be glorified."

Jer. 16:21 "... I will cause them to know Mine hand and My might; and they shall know that My name is The Lord."

Ez. 36:26 "A new heart also will I give you, and a new Spirit will I put within you: and I will take away the stony heart out of your flesh, and I will give you an heart of flesh. And I will put My Spirit within you, and cause you to walk in My Statutes, and ye shall keep My Judgments, and do them."

Joel 2:23 "... for He hath given you the former rain moderately, and He will cause to come down for you the rain, the former rain, and the latter rain in the first month."

Joel 2:25-29 "And it shall come to pass afterward, that I will pour out My Spirit upon all flesh... in those days will I pour out My Spirit."

Joel 3:10 "... let the weak say, I am strong."

Mic. 3:8 "But truly I am full of the power by the Spirit of the Lord... and of might... to declare unto Jacob his transgression, and to Israel his sin."

Zeph. 3:17 "*The Lord thy God in the midst of thee is mighty; He will save, He will rejoice over thee with joy; He will rest in His love, He will joy over thee with singing.*"

Zech. 4:6,7 "*... not by might, nor by power, but by My Spirit, saith the Lord of hosts. Who art thou, O great mountain? Before Zerubbabel thou shalt be-come a plain...*"

I can say to the mountains in my life, "*Who are you O great mountain?!!! You will become a plain!*"

Zech. 12:5 "*... the inhabitants of Jerusalem shall be My strength in the Lord of hosts their God*"

Zech. 12:5 PB "*The inhabitants of Jerusalem are stronger than we through the Lord...*"

Zech. 12:5 NIV "*The people of Jerusalem are strong, because the Lord Almighty is their God.*"

Matt. 10:19 "*... when they deliver you up, take no thought how or what ye shall speak: for it shall be given you in that same hour what ye shall speak... it is not ye that speak but the Spirit of your Father which speaketh in you.*"

Mk. 1:8 "*I indeed have baptized you with water: but He shall baptize you with the Holy Ghost.*"

Mk. 13:11 "*... take no thought beforehand what ye shall speak, neither do ye premeditate: but whatsoever shall be given you in that hour, that speak ye: for it is not ye that speak, but the Holy Ghost.*"

Lk. 1:31 "*... the Holy Ghost shall come upon thee, and the power of the Highest shall overshadow thee...*"

Lk. 1:51 "*He hath shewed strength with His arm; He hath scattered the proud in the imagination of their hearts. He hath put down the mighty from their seats, and exalted them of low degree.*"

Lk. 2:25,26 "*... Simeon; and the same man was just and devout, waiting for the consolation of Israel: and the Holy Ghost was upon Him. And it was revealed unto him by the Holy Ghost, that he should not see death, before he had seen the Lord's Christ.*"

Lk. 3:16 "*... He (Jesus) shall baptize you with the Holy Ghost and with fire...*"

Lk. 4:36 "*... with authority and power He commandeth the unclean spirits, and they come out.*"

Lk. 5:17 "*... and the power of the Lord was present to heal them.*"

Lk. 9:1,2 "*Then He called His twelve disciples... and gave them power and au-thority over all devils, and cure diseases. And He sent them to preach the King-dom of God, and to heal the sick.*"

Lk. 9:42,43 "*... and Jesus rebuked the unclean spirit, and healed the child, and delivered him again to his father. And they were all amazed at the mighty power of God...*"

Lk. 10:19 *"Behold, I give unto you power (Gr. 1849 "authority, weight, influence, power") to tread on serpents and scorpions, and over all the power of the enemy: and nothing shall by any means hurt you."*
Lk. 11:13 *"If ye then, being evil, know how to give good gifts unto your children: how much more shall your heavenly Father give the Holy Spirit to them that ask Him?"*
Prayer: Lord, please baptize me new every morning with Your Holy Spirit! For Your Word says that Your mercy is new every morning, Lam. 3:23!
Lk. 12:12 *"... the Holy Ghost shall teach you.. what ye ought to say."*
Lk. 24:49 *"And, behold, I send the promise of My Father upon you: but tarry ye in the city of Jerusalem, until ye be endued with power from on high."*
Jn. 1:12 *"But as many as received Him, to them gave He power to become the sons of God even to them that believe on His name ..."*
Jn. 7:37-39 *"... if any man thirst, let him come unto Me, and drink. He that believeth on Me, as the Scripture hath said, out of his belly shall flow rivers of living water. (But this spake He of the Spirit, which they that believe on Him should receive: for the Holy Ghost was not yet given; because that Jesus was not yet glorified)."*
Jn. 14:16,18 *"And I will pray the Father, and He shall give you another Comforter, that He may abide with you forever; even the Spirit of truth; whom the world cannot receive, because it seeth Him not, neither knoweth Him; but ye know Him; for He dwelleth with you, and shall be in you. I will not leave you comfortless: I will come to you."*
Jn. 14:26 *"But the Comforter, which is the Holy Ghost, whom the Father will send in My name, He shall teach you all things, and bring all things to your remembrance, whatsoever I have said unto you."*
Jn. 15:26 *"But when the Comforter is come, whom I will send unto you from the Father, even the Spirit of truth, which proceedeth from the Father, He (the Holy Spirit) shall testify of Me (Jesus)..."*
Jn. 16:7-14 *"... it is expedient for you that I go away: for if I go not away, the Comforter will not come unto you; but if I depart, I will send Him unto you. And when He is come, He will reprove the world of sin... because they believe not on Me... when He, the Spirit of truth, is come, He will guide you into all truth... He will shew you things to come. He shall glorify Me ..."*
Jn. 20:21-23 *"... He breathed on them... Receive... the Holy Ghost..."*
Lk. 1:51 *"He hath shewed strength with His arm; He hath scattered the proud in the imagination of their hearts. He hath put down the mighty from their seats, and exalted them of low degree."*
Lk. 11:11-13 *"... how much more shall your heavenly Father give the Holy Spirit to them that ask Him?"*

Lk. 24:49 "... behold, I send the promise of My Father upon you... tarry... in the city of Jerusalem, until ye be endued with power from on high."
Acts 1:4,5 "... but wait for the promise of the Father... but ye shall be baptized with the Holy Ghost not many days hence."
Acts 1:8 "But ye shall receive power, after that the Holy Ghost is come upon you: and ye shall be witnesses unto Me both in Jerusalem, and in all Judea, and in Samaria, and unto the uttermost part of the earth."
Acts 2:4 "And they were all filled with the Holy Ghost..."
Acts 2:17-19 "And it shall come to pass in the last days, saith God, I will pour out of My Spirit upon all flesh: and your sons and your daughters shall prophesy, and your young men shall see visions, and your old men shall dream dreams: and on My servants and on My handmaidens I will pour out in those days of My Spirit; and they shall prophesy..."
Acts 2:33 "... having received of the Father the promise of the Holy Ghost, He hath shed forth this, which ye now see and hear."
Acts 2:38,39 "... repent, and be baptized every one of you in the name of Jesus Christ for the remission of sins, and ye shall receive the gift of the Holy Ghost. For the promise is unto you, and to your children, and to all that are afar off, even as many as the Lord our God shall call."
Acts 3:19 "... when the times of refreshing shall come from the presence of the Lord..."
Acts 4:31 "... they were all filled with the Holy Ghost, and they spake the Word of God with boldness"
Acts 4:33 "And with great power gave the Apostles witness of the Resurrection of the Lord Jesus: and great grace was upon them all."
Acts 5:32 "And we are His witnesses of these things; and so is also the Holy Ghost, whom God hath given to them that obey Him."
Acts 6:3,5 "... seven men of honest report, full of the Holy Ghost and wisdom... Stephen, a man full of faith and of the Holy Ghost..."
Acts 7:55 "But he (Stephen), being full of the Holy Ghost, looked up stedfastly into heaven, and saw the glory of God, and Jesus standing on the right hand of God..."
Acts 8:15-18 "Who, when they were come down, prayed for them, that they might receive the Holy Ghost... through laying on of the Apostles' hands the Holy Ghost was given..."
Acts 9:31 "Then had the churches rest... and were edified; and walking in the fear of the Lord, and in the comfort of the Holy Ghost, were multiplied."
Acts 10:45 "... on the Gentiles... was poured out the gift of the Holy Ghost."
Acts 11:15-18 "... and as I began to speak, the Holy Ghost fell on them, as on us at the beginning... but ye shall be baptized with the Holy Ghost... as God

gave them the like gift as He did unto us, who believed on the Lord Jesus Christ..."

Acts 19:6 "... when Paul had laid his hands upon them, the Holy Ghost came on them..."

Rom. 1:11 "For I long to see you, that I may impart unto you some Spiritual gift, to the end ye may be established..."

Rom. 1:16 "... the Gospel of Christ: for it is the power of God unto Salvation to everyone that believeth; to the Jew first, and also to the Greek."

Rom. 8:26,27 "Likewise the Spirit also helpeth our infirmities: for we know not what we should pray for as we ought: but the Spirit itself maketh intercession for us with groanings which cannot be uttered."

Rom. 9:17 "... even for this same purpose have I raised thee up, that I might shew My power in thee..."

Rom. 14:17,19 "For the kingdom of God is not meat and drink; but righteousness, and peace, and joy in the Holy Ghost... let us therefore follow after the things which make for peace..."

Rom. 15:13 "Now the God of hope fill you with all joy and peace in believing, that ye may abound in hope, through the power of the Holy Ghost."

Rom. 15:19 "Through mighty signs and wonders, by the power of the Spirit of God..."

I Cor. 1:18 "For the preaching of the cross is to them that perish foolishness; but unto us which are saved it is the power of God."

I Cor. 2:4,5 "And my speech and my preaching was not with enticing words of man's wisdom, but in demonstration of the Spirit and of power: that your faith should not stand in the wisdom of men, but in the power of God."

I Cor. 2:10-14 ".. God hath revealed them unto us by His Spirit: for the Spirit searcheth all things... the deep things of God... we have received... the Spirit which is of God; that we might know the things that are freely given to us of God... but which the Holy Ghost teacheth... but the natural man receiveth not the things of the Spirit of God: for they are foolishness unto him: neither can he know them, because they are Spiritually discerned."

Prayer: Lord, please send Your Holy Spirit to help me to know the things that You have freely given to me. Thank You in Jesus' name, Amen!

I Cor. 4:20,21 "For the kingdom of God is not in word, but in power... in the Spirit of meekness..."

I Cor. 6:14 "And God hath both raised up the Lord (Jesus), and will also raise up us by His own power."

I Cor. 6:19 "... know ye not that your body is the Temple of the Holy Ghost which is in you, which ye have of God, and ye are not your own?"

I Cor. 12:1,3-13 "... concerning Spiritual gifts ... no man can say that Jesus is the Lord, but by the Holy Ghost... there are diversities of gifts, but the same

Spirit... the manifestation of the Spirit is given to every man to profit withal... for by one Spirit are we all baptized into one body... to drink into one Spirit."
I Cor. 12:3 Lit. in the Gr. "... no one in the Spirit of God says Jesus is accursed and no one is able to say Jesus is Lord if not in the Holy Spirit..."
I Cor. 12:31 "... covet earnestly the best gifts..."
I Cor. 14:1 NASB "Pursue love, yet desire earnestly Spiritual gifts, but especially that you may prophesy."
II Cor. 1:22 "Who hath also sealed us, and given the earnest of the Spirit in our hearts."
II Cor. 3:6 "Who also hath made us able ministers of the New Testament... the Spirit giveth life."
II Cor. 3:13,14 "We having the same Spirit of faith... I believed, and therefore have I spoken; we also believe, and therefore speak. Knowing that He which raised up the Lord Jesus shall raise up us also by Jesus..."
II Cor. 3:17,18 "Now the Lord is that Spirit: and where the Spirit of the Lord is, there is liberty (from sin, not to sin), but we all, with open face beholding as in a glass the glory of the Lord, are changed into the same image from glory to glory, even as by the Spirit of the Lord."
II Cor. 5:5 "... who also hath given unto us the earnest of the Spirit."
II Cor. 10:4 "... (for the weapons of our warfare are not carnal, but mighty through God to the pulling down of strongholds); casting down imaginations, and every high thing that exalteth itself against the knowledge of God, and bringing into captivity every thought to the obedience of Christ..."
II Cor. 12:10 "... for when I am weak, then am I strong."
II Cor. 13:4 "... He (Jesus) liveth by the power of God. For we also are weak in Him, but we shall live with Him by the power of God toward you... Jesus Christ is in you."
II Cor. 13:14 "The grace of the Lord Jesus Christ, and the love of God, and the communion of the Holy Ghost, be with you all. Amen."
Gal. 3:14 "That the blessing of Abraham might come on the Gentiles through Jesus Christ; that we might receive the promise of the Spirit through faith."
Gal. 4:5-7 "To Redeem them... that we might receive the adoption of sons. And because ye are sons, God hath sent forth the Spirit of His Son into your hearts, crying, Abba, Father. Wherefore thou art no more a servant, but a son; and if a son, then an heir of God through Christ."
Eph. 1:13 "... you were sealed with that Holy Spirit of promise."
Eph. 1:17-19 "... the God of our Lord Jesus... Father of glory... give unto you the Spirit of wisdom and revelation in the knowledge of Him: the eyes of your understanding being enlightened; that ye may know... the riches of... His inheritance in the saints, and what is the exceeding greatness of His power to usward who believe, according to the working of His mighty power..."

Eph. 3:6 "*That the Gentiles should be fellowheirs, and of the same body, and partakers of His promise in Christ by the Gospel... according to the gift of the grace of God given unto me by the effectual working of His power.*"
Eph. 3:7 "*Whereof I was made a minister, according to the gift of the grace of God given unto me by the effectual working of His power.*"
Eph. 3:16-21 "*... that He would grant you, according to the riches of His glory, to be strengthened with might by His Spirit in the inner man; that Christ may dwell in your hearts by faith; that ye, being rooted and grounded in love, may be able to comprehend with all saints what is the breadth, and length, and depth, and height; and to know the love of Christ, which passeth knowledge, that ye might be filled with all the fullness of God. Now unto Him that is able to do exceeding abundantly above all that we ask or think, according to the power that worketh in us, unto Him be glory in the church by Christ Jesus throughout all ages, world without end. Amen.*"
Eph. 3:19,20 "*And to know the love of Christ, which passeth knowledge, that ye might be filled with all the fullness of God. Now unto Him that is able to do exceeding abundantly above all that we ask or think, according to the power that worketh in us, unto Him be glory...*"
Eph. 4:8 "*... He... gave gifts unto men.*"
Eph. 4:30 "*And grieve not the Holy Spirit of God, whereby ye are sealed unto the day of Redemption.*"
Eph. 6:10 "*... be strong in the Lord, and in the power of His might.*"
Eph. 6:16,17 "*Above all, taking the shield of faith, wherewith ye shall be able to quench all the fiery darts of the wicked. And take the helmet of Salvation, and the sword of the Spirit, which is the Word of God...*"
Col. 1:29 NLT "*... I depend on Christ's mighty power... in me.*"
I Thess. 1:5 "*For our Gospel came not unto you in word only, but also in power, and in the Holy Ghost, and in much assurance...*"
I Thess. 4:8 "*... God who hath also given unto us His Holy Spirit.*"
II Tim. 1:7 "*For God hath not given us the spirit of fear; but of power, and of love, and of a sound mind.*"
Titus 3:5 "*Not by works of righteousness which we have done, but according to His mercy He saved us, by the washing of regeneration, and renewing of the Holy Ghost; which He shed on us abundantly through Jesus Christ...*"
Heb. 2:4 "*God also bearing them witness, both with signs, and wonders, and with divers miracles, and gifts of the Holy Ghost, according to His own will...*"
Heb. 4:12 "*For the Word of God is quick... powerful... sharper than any twoedged sword, piercing even to the dividing asunder of soul and spirit... joints and marrow... a discerner of the thoughts and intents of the heart.*"
Heb. 11:33-35 "*Who through faith subdued kingdoms, wrought righteousness, obtained promises, stopped the mouths of lions, quenched the*

violence of fire, escaped the edge of the sword, out of weakness were made strong, waxed valiant in fight, turned to flight the ("foreign" NIV) armies... women received their dead raised to life again..."

Home / House / Habitation

Hosea 11:11 *"... I will place them in their houses, saith the Lord."*
(Hosea 11:11 NIV *"... I will settle them in their homes..."*

Honey

Ps. 19:8-10 *"The Commandment of the Lord is pure, enlightening the eyes. The fear of the Lord is clean, enduring forever; the Judgments of the Lord are true and righteous altogether. More to be desired are they than gold, yea, than much fine gold: sweeter also than honey and the honeycomb."*
Ps. 81:16 *"He should have fed them also with the finest of the wheat: and with honey out of the rock should I have satisfied thee."*
Ps. 119:103,104 *"How sweet are Thy Words unto my taste! Yea, sweeter than honey to my mouth! Through Thy precepts I get understanding: therefore I hate every false way."*
Is. 7:14,15 *"... Immanuel. Butter and honey shall He eat, that He may know to refuse the evil, and choose the good."*

Honor

I Sam. 2:30 *"... them that honor Me I will honor..."*

Hunger

See Food

Hurt / Harm

Lk. 10:19 *"Behold, I give unto you power to tread on serpents and scorpions, and over all the power of the enemy: and nothing shall by any means hurt ("harm" NIV "injure" NLT & NASB) you."*

Acts 18:9,10 *"Then spake the Lord to Paul in the night by a vision, Be not afraid, but speak, and hold not thy peace: for I am with thee, and no man shall set on thee to hurt thee: for I have much people in this city."*

Impossible

Lk. 1:37 *"For with God nothing shall be impossible."*

Inherit / Inheritance / Heritage

Ex. 6:8 *"... I will bring you in unto the land... I will give it you for an heritage..."*
Deut. 12:10 *"... the land which the Lord your God giveth you to inherit... when He giveth you rest from all your enemies... so that ye dwell in safety..."*
Deut. 15:4 *"... for the Lord shall greatly bless thee in the land which the Lord thy God giveth thee for an inheritance to possess it..."*
Josh. 14:9 *"And Moses sware on that day, saying, Surely the land whereon thy feet have trodden shall be thine inheritance, and thy children's forever, because thou hast wholly followed the Lord my God."*
Josh. 14:13 *"And Joshua blessed him, and gave unto Caleb... Hebron for an inheritance."*
I Chron. 28:8 *"... keep and seek for all the Commandments of the Lord your God: that ye may possess this good land, and leave it for an inheritance for your children after you forever."*
Ps. 16:5,6 *"The Lord is the portion of mine inheritance and of my cup: thou maintainest my lot... I have a goodly heritage."*
Ps. 25:10-13 *"All the paths of the Lord are mercy and truth unto such as keep His Covenant and His Testimonies... him shall He teach in the way... His soul shall dwell at ease; and his seed shall inherit the earth. The secret of the Lord is with them that fear Him... He will shew them His Covenant."*
Ps. 37:9 *"... those that wait upon the Lord, they shall inherit the earth... the meek shall inherit the earth; and shall delight themselves in the abundance of peace."*
Ps. 37:18 *"The Lord knoweth the days of the upright: and their inheritance shall be forever."*
Ps. 37:22,29 *"For such as be blessed of Him shall inherit the earth... the righteous shall inherit the land..."*
Ps. 37:34 *"Wait on the Lord, and keep His way, and He shall exalt thee to inherit the land..."*
Ps. 47:3,4 *"He shall subdue the people under us, and the nations under our feet. He shall choose our inheritance for us..."*

Ps. 60:5 "... *Thou hast given me the heritage of those that fear Thy name*."
Ps. 69:35 "*For God will save Zion, and will build the cities of Judah: that they may dwell there, and have it in possession. The seed also of His servants shall inherit it: and they that love His name shall dwell therein*."
Ps. 78:55 "... *and divided them an inheritance*..."
Ps. 119:111 "*Thy Testimonies have I taken as an heritage forever: for they are the rejoicing of my heart. I have inclined mine heart to perform Thy Statutes always, even unto the end.*"
Ps. 127:3 "*Lo, children are an heritage of the Lord: and the fruit of the womb is his reward.*"
Prov. 3:35 "*The wise shall inherit glory*..."
Prov. 8:21 "*That I* (wisdom) *may cause those that love me to inherit substance; and I will fill their treasures.*"
Prov. 8:21 NLT "... *to inherit wealth for I fill their treasures*..."
Prov. 28:10 PB "... *inherit good things*"
Is. 49:8 "*Thus saith the Lord, In an acceptable time have I heard thee, and in a day of Salvation have I helped thee: and I will preserve thee, and give thee for a Covenant of the people, to establish the earth, to cause to inherit the desolate heritages*..."
Is. 54:17 "*No weapon that is formed against thee shall prosper; and every tongue that shall rise against thee in Judgment thou shalt condemn. This is the heritage of the servants of the Lord, and their righteousness is of Me*..."
Is. 57:13 "... *he that putteth his trust in Me shall possess* ("*inherit*" PB) *the land, and shall inherit My Holy Mountain.*"
Is. 58:13,14 "... *if thou turn away thy foot from the Sabbath, from doing thy pleasure on My Holy Day; and call the Sabbath a delight*... *then shalt thou delight thyself in the Lord; and I will cause thee to ride upon the high places of the earth, and feed thee with the heritage of Jacob thy father: for the mouth of the Lord hath spoken it.*"
Is. 60:20,21 About the New Jerusalem, "*Thy sun shall no more go down; neither shall thy moon withdraw itself: for the Lord shall be thine everlasting light, and the days of thy mourning shall be ended. Thy people also shall be all righteous: they shall inherit the land forever, the Branch of My planting, the work of My hands, that I may be glorified.*"
Is. 61:7 "*For your shame ye shall have double; and for confusion they shall rejoice in their portion: therefore in their land they shall possess the double: everlasting joy shall be unto them.*"
Is. 61:7 NIV "*Instead of your shame you will receive a double portion, and instead of disgrace you will rejoice in your inheritance. And so you will inherit a double portion in your land, and everlasting joy will be yours.*"
Is. 61:7 NLT "*Instead of shame and dishonor, you will enjoy a double share

of honor. You will possess a double portion of prosperity in your land, and everlasting joy will be yours."
Is. 65:9 *"And I will bring forth a Seed out of Jacob* (Jesus), *and out of Judah an inheritor of My mountains: and Mine elect shall inherit it, and My servants shall dwell there."*
Jer. 12:15 *"And it shall come to pass, after that I have plucked them out I will return, and have compassion on them, and will bring them again, every man to his heritage, and every man to his land."*
Matt. 5:5 *"Blessed are the meek for they shall inherit the earth."*
Matt. 19:29 *"And every one that hath forsaken houses, or brethren, or sisters, or father, or mother, or wife, or children, or lands, for My name's sake, shall receive an hundredfold, and shall inherit everlasting life."*
Matt. 25:34 *"Then shall the King say unto them on His right hand, Come, ye blessed of My Father, inherit the kingdom prepared for you from the foundation of the world..."*
Acts 20:32 *"... Word of His grace, which is able to build you up, and to give you an inheritance among all them which are Sanctified."*
Acts 26:18 *"To open their eyes, and to turn them from darkness to light, and from the power of Satan unto God, that they may receive forgiveness of sins, and inheritance among them which are Sanctified by faith that is in Me."*
Rom. 8:13-17 *"... but if ye through the Spirit do mortify the deeds of the body, ye shall live. For as many as are led by the Spirit of God, they are the sons of God. For ye have not received the spirit of bondage* (sin) *again to fear; but ye have received the Spirit of adoption, whereby we cry, Abba, Father. The Spirit itself beareth witness with our spirit, that we are the children of God: and if children, then heirs; heirs of God, and joint-heirs with Christ; if so be that we suffer with Him, that we may be also glorified together."*
I Cor. 2:9 *"But as it is written, Eye hath not seen, nor ear heard, neither have entered into the heart of man, the things which God hath prepared for them that love Him. But God hath revealed them unto us by His Spirit..."*
Gal. 3:29 *"And if ye be Christ's, then are ye Abraham's seed, and heirs according to the promise."*
Gal. 4:5-7 *"... we might receive the adoption... because ye are sons, God hath sent forth the Spirit of His Son into your hearts, crying, Abba, Father... thou art no more a servant, but a son; and... an heir of God through Christ."*
Gal. 4:30,31 *"... for the son of the bondwoman* (those who won't accept Jesus) *shall not be heir with the son of the freewoman* (anyone who accepts Jesus)*... we are not children of the bondwoman, but of the free."*
Eph. 1:11 ESV *"In Him* (Jesus) *we have obtained an inheritance..."*

Eph. 1:13,14 "... *after you believed, ye were sealed with that Holy Spirit of promise, which is the earnest of our inheritance until the Redemption of the purchased possession...*"

Eph. 1:17-19 "*That the God of our Lord Jesus Christ... may give unto you the Spirit of wisdom... revelation in the knowledge of Him: the eyes of your understanding being enlightened; that ye may know... the riches of... His inheritance... what is the exceeding greatness of His power to usward who believe, according to the working of His mighty power...*"

Col. 1:12 "... *the Father, which hath made us meet to be partakers of the inheritance of the saints in light...*"

Col. 3:24 "*Knowing that of the Lord ye shall receive the reward of the inheritance: for ye serve the Lord Christ.*"

Titus 3:7 "*That being Justified by His grace, we should be made heirs...*"

Heb. 1:14 "*Are they* (angels) *not all ministering spirits, sent forth to minister for them who shall be heirs of Salvation?*"

Heb. 6:12 "... *who through faith and patience inherit the promises.*"

Heb. 6:17 "... *God, willing more abundantly to shew unto the heirs of promise the immutability of His counsel, confirmed it by an oath...*"

Heb. 9:15 "... *they which are called might receive the promise of eternal inheritance.*"

I Pet. 1:3,4 "*Blessed be the God and Father of our Lord Jesus Christ, which ac-cording to His abundant mercy hath begotten us again unto... an inheritance incorruptible, and undefiled, and that fadeth not away, reserved in heaven for you* ("for us" KJV fn)."

I Pet. 3:7 "... *ye husbands, dwell with them according to knowledge, giving honour unto the wife... being heirs together of the grace of life...*"

I Pet. 3:9 "*Not rendering evil for evil, or railing for railing: but contrariwise blessing... that ye should inherit a blessing.*"

Jms. 2:5 "... *hath not God chosen the poor of this world rich in faith, and heirs of the kingdom which he hath promised to them that love him?*"

Rev. 21:7 "*He that overcometh shall inherit all things; and I will be his God, and he shall be my son.*"

Intercession

Rom. 8:34 "*Who is he that condemneth? It is Christ that died... is risen again... at the right hand of God, who also maketh intercession for us.*"

Heb. 7:25 "... *He is able also to save them to the uttermost that come unto God by Him* (Jesus) *seeing He ever liveth to make intercession for them.*"

Jesus as King

Is. 16:5 "*And in mercy shall the throne be established: and He shall sit upon it in truth in the Tabernacle of David...*"
Jn. 12:15 "*Fear not, daughter of Sion: behold thy King cometh, sitting on a (donkey's) colt.*"
Jn. 18:37 "*Pilate therefore said unto Him, Art Thou a King then? Jesus answered, Thou sayest that I am a King. To this end was I born, and for this cause came I into the world...*"
Jn. 18:37 NASB "*... you say correctly that I am a King...*"
Acts 2:30 "*... God had sworn with an oath to him, that...* ("one of his descendants" NIV) *according to the flesh, He would raise up Christ to sit on his (David's) throne...*"
I Tim. 6:15 "*... until the appearing of our Lord Jesus Christ... who is the blessed and only Potentate, the King of kings, and Lord of lords...*"
I Pet. 1:3,4 "*Blessed be the God and Father of our Lord Jesus Christ, which according to his abundant mercy hath begotten us again unto a lively hope by the Resurrection of Jesus Christ... to an inheritance incorruptible, and undefiled, and that fadeth not away, reserved in heaven for you.*"
Rev. 17:14 "*These shall make war with the Lamb, and the Lamb shall overcome them: for He is Lord of lords, and King of kings: and they that are with Him are called, and chosen, and faithful.*"
Rev. 19:16 "*And He hath on His vesture and on His thigh a name written, King of kings, and Lord of lords.*"

Joy / Gladness / Pleasures

Ezra 6:22 "*... for the Lord had made them joyful...*"
Neh. 8:10 "*The joy of the Lord is my strength.*"
Job 8:21 "*Till He fill thy mouth with laughing, and thy lips with rejoicing.*"
Ps. 4:7 "*Thou hast put gladness in my heart...*"
Ps. 5:11,12 "*But let all those that put their rust in Thee rejoice: let them ever shout for joy, because Thou defendest them: let them also that love Thy name be joyful in Thee. For Thou, Lord, wilt bless the righteous; with favour wilt Thou compass him as with a shield.*"
Ps. 14:7 "*... the Lord bringeth back the captivity of His people, Jacob shall rejoice, and Israel shall be glad.*"
Ps. 15:11 "*Thou wilt shew me the path of life: in Thy presence is fullness of joy; at Thy right hand there are pleasures forevermore.*"
Ps. 16:9 "*Therefore my heart is glad, and my glory rejoiceth...*"

Ps. 16:11 *"Thou wilt shew me the path of life: in Thy presence is fullness of joy; at Thy right hand are pleasures forevermore."*
Ps. 21:1-6 *"The king shall joy ("rejoice" NIV) in Thy strength, O Lord; and in Thy Salvation how greatly shall he rejoice… Thou hast made him exceeding glad with Thy countenance."*
Ps. 30:5 *"… weeping may endure for a night but joy cometh in the morning."*
Ps. 30:11 *"Thou hast turned for me my mourning into dancing… and girded me with gladness…"*
(Ps. 30:11 NIV *"You turned my wailing ("mourning" KJV) into ("joyful" NLT) dancing."*
(Ps. 30:11 NLT *"… clothed me with joy."*
Ps. 36:8 *"They shall be abundantly satisfied with the fatness of thy house; and thou shalt make them drink of the river of Thy pleasures."*
(Ps. 36:8 NLT *"You feed them from the abundance of Your own house, letting them drink from Your river of delights."*
Ps. 45:7 *"… God, hath anointed thee with the oil of gladness above thy fellows."*
Ps. 51:12 *"Restore unto me the joy of Thy Salvation; and uphold me with Thy free Spirit."*
(Ps. 51:12 NLT *"Restore to me again the joy of Your Salvation, and **make me willing to obey You**."*
Is. 51:11,12 *"… they shall obtain gladness and joy; and sorrow and mourning shall flee away. I, even I, am He that comforteth you…"*
Is. 61:1 *"The Spirit of the Lord God is upon me; because the Lord hath anointed me to preach good tidings unto the meek; He hath sent Me to bind up the brokenhearted, to proclaim liberty to the captives, and the opening of the prison to them that are bound… to comfort all that mourn; to appoint unto them that mourn in Zion, to give unto them beauty for ashes, the oil of joy for mourning, the garment of praise for the spirit of heaviness; that they might be called trees of righteousness… that He might be glorified."*
Neh. 8:10 *"The joy of the Lord is my strength."*
Ps. 97:11 *"Light is sown for the righteous, and gladness for the upright in heart."*
Ps. 105:43 *"… He brought forth His people with joy, and His chosen with gladness…"*
Ps. 126:5 *"They that sow in tears shall reap in joy. He that goeth forth and weepeth, bearing precious seed, shall doubtless come again with rejoicing, bringing his sheaves with him."*
Ps. 132:16 *"I will also clothe her priests with Salvation: and her saints shall shout aloud for joy."*
Ps. 144:15 *"Happy is that people… whose God is the Lord."*

Prov. 14:21 "... *He that hath mercy on the poor, happy is he.*"
Prov. 15:13 "*A merry heart maketh a cheerful countenance...*"
Prov. 16:20 "*He that handleth a matter wisely shall find good: and whoso trusteth in the Lord, happy is he.*"
Eccl. 2:26 "*For God giveth to a man that is good in His sight wisdom, and knowledge, and joy... to gather and to heap up, that He may give to him that is good before God.*"
Is. 12:3 "*Therefore with joy shall ye draw water out of the wells of Salvation.*"
Is. 29:19 "*The meek also shall increase their joy in the Lord, and the poor among them shall rejoice in the Holy One of Israel.*"
Is. 35:10 "*And the ransomed of the Lord shall return, and come to Zion with songs and everlasting joy upon their heads; they shall obtain joy and gladness, and sorrow and sighing shall flee away.*"
Is. 51:11 "*Therefore the Redeemed of the Lord shall return, and come with singing unto Zion; and everlasting joy shall be upon their head: they shall obtain gladness and joy; and sorrow and mourning shall flee away.*"
Is. 52:9 "*Break forth into joy, sing together, ye waste places of Jerusalem: for the Lord hath comforted His people, He hath Redeemed Jerusalem.*"
Is. 61:3 "*To appoint unto them that mourn in Zion, to give unto them beauty for ashes, the oil of joy for mourning, the garment of praise for the spirit of heaviness; that they might be called trees of righteousness...*"
Is. 61:7 "*For your shame ye shall have double; and for confusion they shall rejoice in their portion: therefore in their land they shall possess the double: everlasting joy shall be unto them.*"
Is. 65:13 "*... thus saith the Lord God... behold, My servants shall rejoice...*"
Jer. 31:4 "*Again I will build thee, and thou shalt be built, O virgin of Israel: thou shalt again be adorned with thy tabrets, and shalt go forth in the dances of them that make merry.*"
Jer. 31:13,14 "*Then shall the virgin rejoice in the dance, both young men and old together: for I will turn their mourning into joy, and will comfort them, and make them rejoice from their sorrow... I will satiate the soul of the priests with fatness, and My people shall be satisfied with My goodness...*"
Zeph. 3:17 "*The Lord thy God in the midst of thee is mighty; He will save, He will rejoice over thee with joy; He will rest in His love, He will joy over thee with singing.*"
Jn. 15:11 "*These things have I spoken unto you, that My joy might remain in you, and that your joy might be full.*"
Jn. 16:23,24 "*And in that day ye shall ask Me nothing. Verily, verily, I say unto you, Whatsoever ye shall ask the Father in My name, He will give it you. Hitherto have ye asked nothing in My name: ask, and ye shall receive, that your joy may be full.*"

Jn. 17:13 *"... that they might have My joy fulfilled in themselves."*
Acts 2:28 *"Thou hast made known to me the ways of life; Thou shalt make me full of joy with Thy countenance."*
Rom. 14:17 *"For the kingdom of God is... righteousness, and peace, and joy in the Holy Ghost."*
Rom. 15:13 *"Now the God of hope fill you with all joy and peace in believing, that ye may abound in hope, through the power of the Holy Ghost."*
II Cor. 1:24 *"Not for that we have dominion over your faith, but are helpers of your joy: for by faith ye stand."*
II Cor. 1:24 NLT *"But that does not mean we want to dominate you by telling you how to put your faith into practice. We want to work together with you so you will be full of joy..."*
II Cor. 7:4 Paul said, *"... I am filled with comfort, I am exceeding joyful in all our tribulation."*
I Pet. 4:13 *"But rejoice, inasmuch as ye are partakers of Christ's sufferings; that, when His glory shall be revealed, ye may be glad also with exceeding joy. If ye be reproached for the name of Christ, happy are ye; for the Spirit of glory and of God resteth upon you..."*
I Jn. 1:4 *"And these things write we unto you, that your joy may be full.*

Judgment

Is. 54:17 *"... every tongue that shall rise against thee in Judgment thou shalt condemn..."*
Jn. 5:24 *"... He that heareth My Word; and believeth on Him* (the Father) *that sent Me* (Jesus), *hath everlasting life, and shall not come into condemnation; but is passed from death unto life."*
Jn. 5:24 NIV *"... will not be Judged..."*
Jn. 5:24 ESV *"... he does not come into Judgment..."*
Jms. 2:13 *"... mercy rejoiceth against Judgment."*
I Jn. 4:17 *"Herein is our love made perfect, that we may have boldness in the Day of Judgment: because as He is, so are we in this world."*

Justified

Is. 50:7-9 *"... He is near who Justifieth me..."*
Matt. 11:19 *"But wisdom is Justified of her children..."*
Acts 13:39 *"And by Him all that believe are Justified from all things..."*
Rom. 2:13 *"For not the hearers of the law are just before God, but the doers of the law shall be Justified."*

Rom. 3:4 "... *as it is written, That thou mightest be Justified in thy sayings, and mightest overcome when thou art Judged.*"
Rom. 3:24 "... *being Justified freely by His grace through the Redemption that is in Christ Jesus...*"
Rom. 3:26 "... *the Justifier of him which believeth in Jesus.*"
Rom. 3:28 "*Therefore we conclude that a man is Justified by faith...*"
Rom. 4:5 ".... *believeth on Him that Justifieth the ungodly, his faith is counted for righteousness.*"
Rom. 5:1 "*Therefore being Justified by faith, we have peace with God through our Lord Jesus Christ...*"
Rom. 5:9 "... *being now Justified by His blood...*"
Rom. 5:18 "*Therefore as by the offence of one Judgment came upon all men to condemnation; even so by the righteousness of one the free gift came upon all men unto Justification of life.*"
Rom. 8:30 "... *and whom He called, them He also Justified...*"
Rom. 8:33 "*Who shall lay anything to the charge of God's elect? It is God that Justifieth.*"
I Cor. 6:11 "... *but ye are washed, but ye are Sanctified, but ye are Justified in the name of the Lord Jesus, and by the Spirit of our God.*"
Gal. 2:16 "*Knowing that a man is... Justified... by the faith of Jesus... even we have believed in Jesus Christ, that we might be Justified by the faith...*"
Gal. 2:17 "... *Justified by Christ.*"
Gal. 3:8 "*And the Scripture, foreseeing that God would Justify the heathen through faith...*"
Gal. 3:24 "... *Justified by faith...*"
Titus 3:7 "*That being Justified by His grace...*"

Keys

Is. 22:22 "*And the key of the house of David will I lay upon His shoulder; so He shall open, and none shall shut; and He shall shut, and none shall open.*"
Matt. 16:18,19 Jesus said about the church, "... *I will build My church; and the gates of hell shall not prevail against it. And I will give unto thee the keys of the Kingdom of heaven: and whatsoever thou shalt bind on earth shall be bound in heaven: and whatsoever thou shalt loose on earth shall be loosed in heaven.*"
Rev. 3:7 "... *these things saith He that is Holy, He that is true, He that hath the key of David, He that openeth, and no man shutteth; and shutteth, and no man openeth.*"

Kindness

II Sam. 2:6 *"And now the Lord shew kindness and truth unto you ..."*
Neh. 9:17 *"... but Thou art a God ready to pardon, gracious and merciful, slow to anger, and of great kindness, and forsookest them not."*
Ps. 117:2 *"For His merciful kindness is great toward us: and the truth of the Lord endureth forever..."*
Ps. 119:76 *"Let, I pray Thee, Thy merciful kindness be for my comfort, according to Thy Word unto Thy servant."*
(Ps. 119:76 NIV *"May Your unfailing love be my comfort, according to Your promise to Your servant."*
Is. 54:8 *"In a little wrath I hid My face from thee for a moment; but with everlasting kindness will I have mercy on thee, saith the Lord thy Redeemer."*
Is. 54:10 *"... the mountains shall depart... the hills be removed; but My kindness shall not depart from thee, neither shall the Covenant of My peace be removed, saith the Lord that hath mercy on thee."*
Joel 2:13 *"... rend your heart, and not your garments, and turn unto the Lord your God..."*
Jonah 4:2 *"... Thou art a gracious God... merciful, slow to anger... of great kindness..."*
Lk. 6:35 *"... love... your enemies... do good.. lend, hoping for nothing again... your reward shall be great... ye shall be the children of the Highest: for He is kind unto the unthankful and to the evil."*
Eph. 2:4-7 *"... God... rich in mercy... His great love wherewith He loved us, even when we were dead in sins, hath quickened us together with Christ, (by grace ye are saved); and hath raised us up together, and made us sit together in heavenly places in Christ Jesus: that in the ages to come He might shew the exceeding riches of His grace in His kindness towards us..."*

Kingdom

Ps. 145:13 *"Thy kingdom is an everlasting kingdom, and Thy dominion endureth throughout all generations."*
Obadiah 1:21 *"... the kingdom shall be the Lord's."*
Matt. 3:2 *"... repent... for the kingdom of heaven is at hand."*
Matt. 5:3;Lk.6:20 *"Blessed are the poor in spirit... theirs is the kingdom of heaven."*
Matt. 5:10 *"Blessed are they which are persecuted for righteousness' sake: for theirs is the kingdom of heaven."*

Matt. 5:19 "... *whosoever shall do and teach them* (the Commandments) *the same shall be called great in the kingdom of heaven."*
Matt. 7:21 "... *he that doeth the will of My Father which is in heaven* (will enter the kingdom of heaven)."
Matt. 11:11;Lk.7:28 "... *John the Baptist... he that is least in the kingdom of heaven is greater than he."*
Matt. 12:28 "... *then the kingdom of God has come unto you..."*
Matt. 13:11;Lk.8:10 "... *because it is given unto you to know the mysteries of the kingdom of heaven..."*
Matt. 16:19 "... *I will give unto thee the keys of the kingdom of heaven: and whatsoever thou shalt bind on earth shall be bound in heaven and whatsoever thou shalt loose on earth shall be loosed in heaven."*
Matt. 24:14 "... *this Gospel of the kingdom shall be preached in all the world for a witness unto all nations; and then shall the end come."*
Matt. 25:34 *"Then shall the King say unto them on His right hand, Come, ye blessed of My Father, inherit the kingdom prepared for you from the foundation of the world."*
Mk. 12:34 Jesus said to the rich young ruler, "... *thou art not far from the kingdom of God."*
Lk. 1:33 *"And He shall reign over the house of Jacob forever; and of His kingdom there shall be no end."*
Lk. 12:31,32 *"But rather seek ye the kingdom of God; and all these things shall be added unto you. Fear not, little flock; for it is your Father's good pleasure to give you the kingdom."*
Lk. 13:29 "... *when ye shall see Abraham... Isaac... Jacob... all the prophets, in the kingdom of God... they shall come from the East, and from the West, and from the North, and from the South, and shall sit* (#347 *"recline... at the table as at feasts"*) *down in the kingdom of God ("of heaven"* Matt. 8:11)."
Lk. 17:21 "... *the kingdom of God is within you..."*
Lk. 18:29,30 "... *there is no man that hath left house... parents... brethren... wife... children, for the kingdom of God's sake, who shall not receive... more in this present time, and in the world to come life everlasting."*
Lk. 21:27,28 *"And then shall they see the Son of man coming in a cloud with power and great glory. And when these things begin to come to pass, then look up and lift up your heads; for your Redemption draweth nigh."*
Lk. 22:29 *"And I appoint unto you a kingdom, as My Father hath appointed unto Me; that ye* (the 12 disciples) *may eat and drink at My table in My kingdom, and sit on thrones Judging the twelve trives of Israel."*
Jn. 18:36 "... *My kingdom is not of this world..."*
(Jesus will never set up His Kingdom on this earth; it is only on the New Earth (Rev. 21:1) that He comes (after the 1000 years, Rev. 20:5) to set up

His kingdom. Then His kingdom will last forever and ever. Acts 3:21 tells us that Jesus must remain in heaven until the heavens and the earth are completely restored. If they say, He's over here or over there, don't belive it.
(Matt. 24:26 *"Wherefore if they shall say unto you, Behold, He is in the desert; go not forth: behold, He is in the secret chambers; believe it not."*
(Lk. 17:23 *"And they shall say to you, See here; or, see there: go not after them, nor follow them."*
(Acts 3:21 "(Jesus) *Whom the heaven must receive until the times of restitution of all things, which God hath spoken by the mouth of all His Holy prophets since the world began."*
(Acts 3:21 HCSB *"Heaven must welcome Him* (Jesus) *until the times of the restoration of all things.."*
(Acts 3:21 ISV *"He* (Jesus) *must remain in heaven until the time of universal restitution..."*
Rom. 14:17 *"For the kingdom of God is not meat and drink; but righteousness, and peace, and joy in the Holy Ghost."*
Jms. 2:5 *"... hath not God chosen the poor of this world rich in faith, and heirs of the kingdom which He hath promised to them that love Him?"*

Kinsmsn-Redeemer

Ruth 4:14 *"Blessed be the Lord, which hath not left the this day without a kinsman, that his name may be famous in Israel* (through Jesus)."
Jesus is our Kinsman-Redeemer

Knock

Lk. 11:9 *"... knock and it shall be opened unto you..."*

Land / Earth / World

Gen. 15:18 *"In the same day the Lord made a Covenant with Abram, saying, Unto thy seed have I given this land, from the river of Egypt unto the great river, the river Euphrates."*
Ps. 24:1 *"The earth is the Lord's and the fullness thereof: the world, and they that dwell therein..."*
Ps. 37:11 *"But the meek shall inherit the earth; and shall delight themselves in the abundance of peace."*
Ps. 37:29 *"The righteous shall inherit the land, and dwell therein forever."*

Ps. 50:10-12 *"For every beast of the forest is Mine, and the cattle upon a thousand hills...the whole world is Mine, and the fullness thereof."*
Matt. 5:5 *"Blessed are the meek, for they shall inherit the earth."*
Rom. 4:13 *"For the promise, that he* (Abraham and his seed) *should be the heir of the world... through the righteousness of faith."*

Language

Zeph. 3:8,9 *"... all the earth shall be devoured with the fire of My jealousy ... then will I turn to the people a pure language, that they may all call upon the name of the Lord, to serve Him with one consent."*
When does this happen? After the earth is devoured by *"the fire of His jealousy"* at the second coming of Jesus and the Lake of Fire, II Pet. 3:10;Rev. 20:14,15.

Latter Rain / Early Rain

Lev. 26:4 *"... I wil give you rain in due season..."*
Deut. 11:14 *"... I will give you the rain of your land in his due season, the first rain and the latter rain, that thou mayest gather in thy corn... and... oil. And I will send grass in thy fields for thy cattle, that thou mayest eat and be full."*
Deut. 32:2 NCV *"My teaching will drop like rain; My Words will fall like dew; they will be like showers on the grass; they will pour down like rain..."*
Job 29:23 *"And they waited for Me as for the rain; and they opened their mouth wide as for the latter rain."*
Ps. 72:6 *"He shall come down like rain upon the mown grass: as showers that water the earth."*
Prov. 16:15 *"In the light of the king's countenance is life; and his favour is as a cloud of the latter rain."*
Is. 20:19 NLT *"The humble will be filled with fresh joy from the Lord..."*
Is. 32:15 *"Until the Spirit be poured upon us from on high..."*
Is.44:3 *"For I will pour water upon him that is thirsty, and floods upon the dry ground: I will pour My Spirit upon thy seed, and My blessing upon thine offspring..."*
Is. 45:8 *"Drop down, ye heavens, from above, and let the skies pour down righteousness* (like rain)*: let the earth open... let them bring forth Salvation, and let righteousness spring up together; I the Lord have created it..."*
Jer.3:3 *"Therefore the showers have been withholden; and there hath been no latter rain..."*

Jer. 5:24 "... let us now fear the Lord... that giveth rain, both the former and the latter, in His season.. your sins have withholden good things from you."

Ez. 34:26 "... I will cause the shower to come down in his season; there shall be showers of blessing."

Hosea 6:3 "... and He shall come unto us as the rain, as the latter and former rain unto the earth."

Hosea 10:12 "Sow to yourselves in righteousness, reap in mercy; break up your fallow ground: for it is time to seek the Lord, till He come and rain righteousness upon you."

Joel 2:23 "Be glad then, ye children of Zion, and rejoice in the Lord your God: for He hath given you the former rain moderately. And He will cause to come down for you the rain, the former rain, and the latter rain in the first month... and I will restore to you the years that the locust hath eaten ..."

Joel 2:28,29 "And it shall come to pass afterward, that I will pour out My Spirit upon all flesh; and your sons and your daughters shall prophesy, your old men shall dream dreams, your young men shall see visions... in those days will I pour out My Spirit."

Zech. 10:1 "Ask ye of the Lord rain in the time of the latter rain; so the Lord shall make bright clouds, and give them showers of rain, to everyone grass in the field."

(Zech.10:1 NASB "Ask rain from the Lord at the time of the spring rain – the Lord who makes the storm clouds; and He will give them showers of rain, vegetation in the field to each man."

Matt. 3:11,12 "... He shall baptize you with the Holy Ghost, and with fire..."

Acts 2:17-19,21 (quoting Joel 2:28,29) "And it shall come to pass in the last days, saith God, I will pour out of My Spirit upon all flesh: and your sons and your daughters shall prophesy, and your young men shall see visions, and your old men shall dream dreams: and on My servants and on My handmaidens I will pour out in those days of My Spirit; and they shall prophesy: and I will shew wonders in the heaven above, and signs in the earth beneath; blood, and fire, and vapour of smoke... and it shall come to pass, that whosoever shall call on the name of the Lord shall be saved."

Rom. 5:5 NKJV "The love of God has been poured out in our hearts by the Holy Spirit who was given to us."

Jms. 5:7,8 "Be patient... unto the coming of the Lord, Behold, the husbandman waiteth for the precious fruit of the earth, and hath long patience for it, until He receive the early and latter rain. Be ye also patient..."

(See Rain

Life / Live / Long life

Gen. 15:15 *"And thou shalt go to thy fathers in peace; thou shalt be buried in a good old age."*
Ex. 20:12 *"... that thy days may be long upon the land which the Lord thy God giveth thee."*
Ex. 23:26 *"... the number of thy days I will fulfil."*
Deut. 4:40,41 *"Thou shalt keep therefore His... Commandments... that thou mayest prolong thy days upon the earth..."*
Deut. 5:29,32,33 *"O that there were such an heart in them, that they would fear Me, and keep all My Commandments always, that it might be well with them, and with their children forever... ye shall observe to do therefore as the Lord your God hath commanded you: ye shall not turn aside to the right hand or to the left. Ye shall walk in all the ways which the Lord your God hath commanded you, that ye may live, and that it may be well with you, and that ye may prolong your days in the land which ye shall possess."*
Deut. 6:2 *"... and that thy days may be prolonged."*
Deut. 30:20 *"... He is thy life, and the length of thy days..."*
Deut. 32:46,47 *"... command your children to observe to do, all the words of this law. For it is not a vain thing for you; because it is your life: and through this thing ye shall prolong your days in the land..."*
I Kings 3:14 God said to Solomon, *"And if thou wilt walk in My ways, to keep My Statutes and My Commandments, as thy father David did walk, then I will lengthen thy days."*
I Chron. 29:28 David *"... died in a good old age..."*
Job 5:26 *"Thou shalt come to thy grave in a full age, like as a shock of corn cometh in his season."*
Ps. 21:1-6 *"... He asked life of Thee, and Thou gavest it him, even length of days forever and ever..."*
Ps. 91:16 *"With long life will I satisfy him, and shew him my Salvation."*
Prov. 3:13,16 *"Happy is the man that findeth wisdom, and the man that getteth understanding... length of days is in her right hand..."*
Prov. 8:35 *"For whoso findeth me (Wisdom) fineth life..."*
Prov. 9:11 *"For by me (wisdom) thy days shall be multiplied, and the years of thy life shall be increased."*
Prov. 10:11 *"The mouth of a righteous man is a well of life..."*
Prov. 10:27 *"The fear of the Lord prolongeth days..."*
Prov. 12:28 *"In the way of righteousness is life..."*
Prov. 13:14;14:27 *"The law of the wise is a fountain of life, to depart from the snares of death."*

Prov. 14:30 *"A sound heart is the life of the flesh…"*

Prov. 19:23 *"The fear of the Lord tendeth to life: and he that hath it shall abide satisfied; he shall not be visited with evil."*

Is. 38:16 *"… so wilt Thou recover me, and make me to live."*

Is. 46:3,4 *"Hearken unto Me… which are carried from the womb: and even to your old age I am He; and even to hoar* (gray) *hairs will I carry you: I have made, and I will bear; even I will carry, and will deliver you."*

Is. 55:3 *"Incline your ear, and come unto Me: hear, and your soul shall live…"*

Lk. 17:33 *"Whosoever shall seek to save his life shall lose it; and whosoever shall lose his life shall preserve it."*

Lk. 18:29,30 *"… there is no man that hath left houses… parents… brethren… wife… children, for the kingdom of God's sake, who shall not receive… more in this present time, and in the world to come life everlasting."*

Jn. 6:63 *"For the Bread of God is He which cometh down from heaven, and giveth life unto the world."*

Jn. 6:51,54 *"I am the living Bread which came down from heaven: if any man eat of this Bread, he shall live forever: and the Bread that I will give is My flesh* (through the symbol of Communion)*, which I will give for the life of the world… whoso eateth My flesh, and drinketh My blood, hath eternal life; and I will raise him up at the last day."*

Jn. 10:9,10 *"I am the door: by Me if any man enter in, he shall be saved, and shall go in and out, and find pasture… I am come that they might have life, and that they might have it more abundantly."*

Jn. 10:27,28 *"My sheep hear My voice, and I know them, and they follow Me: and I give unto them eternal life; and they shall never perish, neither shall any man pluck them out of My hand."*

Jn. 11:25 *"And Jesus said…* (to Martha)*, I am the Resurrection, and the life: he that believeth in Me, though he were dead, yet shall he live: and whosoever liveth and believeth in Me shall never die. Believest thou this… Yea, Lord: I believe that Thou art the Christ, the Son of God…"*

Jn. 12:50 *"And I know that His Commandment is life everlasting…"*

Jn. 20:31 *"But these are written, that ye might believe that Jesus is the Christ, the Son of God; and that believing ye might have life through His name."*

Acts 2:28 *"Thou hast made known to me the ways of life; Thou shalt make me full of joy with Thy countenance (*"presence" PB*)."*

Eph. 6:2,3 *"Honour thy father and mother; (which is the first Commandment with promise;) that it may be well with thee, and thou mayest live long on the earth."*

Jms. 1:12 *"Blessed is the man that endureth temptation… when he is tried, he shall receive the crown of life, which the Lord hath promised to them that love Him."*

Light / Shine / Shone

Ex. 34:29,30 "... when Moses came down from Mount Sinai... his face shone... the skin of his face shone..."
Ex. 34:34 "... Israel saw the face of Moses... shone..."
Judges 5:31 "... let them that love Him be as the sun when he goeth forth in his might..."
Job 11:17 "... thou shalt shine forth, thou shalt be as the morning."
Job 22:28 "... and the light shall shine upon thy ways."
Job 29:3 "... by His light I walked through darkness..."
Ps. 27:1 "The Lord is my light..."
Ps. 31:16 "Make Thy face shine upon Thy servant..."
Ps. 34:5 "They looked unto Him, and were lightened ("radiant" NIV)..."
Ps. 37:5,6 "... He shall bring forth thy righteousness as the light, and thy Judgment as the noonday."
Ps. 50:2 "Out of Zion, the perfection of beauty, God hath shined."
Ps. 84:11 "For the Lord God is a sun and shield..."
Ps. 97:11 "Light is sown for the righteous, and gladness for the upright.."
(Ps. 97:11 NLT "Light shines on the godly..."
Ps. 112:4 "... unto the upright there ariseth light in the darkness..."
(Ps. 112:4 HCSB "... light shines in the darkness for the righteous."
Ps. 121:5 "The Lord is thy keeper: the Lord is thy shade upon thy right hand. The sun shall not smite thee by day, nor the moon by night."
Ps. 139:11,12 "... even the night shall be light around me. Yea, the darkness hideth not from Thee; but the night shineth as the day: the darkness and the light are both alike to Thee."
Prov. 4:18 "But the path of the just is as the shining light, that shineth more and more unto the perfect day."
Prov. 6:23 "For the Commandment is a lamp; and the law is light..."
Prov. 13:19 "The light of the righteous shines brightly..."
Dan. 12:3 "... they that be wise shall shine as the brightness of the firmament; and they that turn many to righteousness as the stars forever..."
Mic. 7:8 "... when I sit in darkness, the Lord shall be a light unto me."
Matt. 5:16 "Let your light so shine before men, that they may see your good works, and glorify your Father which is in heaven."
Matt. 13:43 "Then shall the righteous shine forth as the sun in the kingdom"
Lk. 1:79 "... to give light to them that sit in darkness..."
Lk. 2:32 Jesus is "A light to lighten the Gentiles, and the glory of Thy people."
Jn. 8:12 "I am the light of the world: he that followeth me shall not walk in darkness, but shall have the light of life."

Jn. 12:36 *"While ye have light (Jesus), believe in the light, that ye may be the children of light."*
Rom. 13:12 *"... let us put on the armor of light."*
Phil. 2:15 *"That ye may be blameless and harmless, the sons of God, without rebuke, in the midst of a crooked and perverse nation, among whom ye shine as lights in the world..."*
Col. 1:12 *"Giving thanks unto the Father, which hath made us meet to be partakers of the inheritance of the saints in light..."*
Eph. 5:8 *"... now are ye light in the Lord: walk as children of light..."*
Eph. 5:14 *"... Christ shall give thee light."*
Phil. 2:15 *"... among whom ye shine as lights in the world..."*
I Thess. 5:5 *"Ye are all the children of light... children of the day."*
I Pet. 2:9,10 *"But ye are a chosen generation, a royal priesthood, and Holy nation, a peculiar people; that ye should shew forth the praises of Him who hath called you out of darkness into His marvelous light..."*
I Jn. 1:7 *"But if we walk in the light, as He is in the light, we have fellowship one with another, and the blood of Jesus Christ His Son cleanseth us..."*
Rev. 7:16 *"They shall hunger no more, neither thirst anymore; neither shall the sun light on them, nor any heat."*

Likeminded

Rom. 15:4,5 *"... whatsoever things were written aforetime were written for our learning, that we through patience and comfort of the Scriptures might have hope. Now the God of patience and consolation grant you to be like-minded one toward another according to Christ Jesus: that ye may with one mind and one mouth glorify God even the Father of our Lord Jesus Christ."*

Loose

Matt. 16:18,19 *"... My church... I wll give unto thee the keys of the kingdom of heaven: and whatsoever thou shalt bind on earth shall be bound in heaven and whatsoever thou shalt loose on earth shall be loosed in heaven."*
Matt. 18:18 Jesus speaking to His Disciples said, *"... whatsoever ye shall bind on earth shall be bound in heaven: and whatsoever ye shall loose on earth shall be loosed in heaven."*

Love

The promise is that God loves us; and because He loves us, we are to love each other.

Ps. 85:7NIV *"Show us Your unfailing love, O Lord..."*

Ps. 86:5,13 NIV *"You are forgiving and good O Lord, abounding in love to all who call to You... for great is Your love toward me..."*

Hosea 14:4 *"... I will love them freely... Mine anger is turned away from him."*

Jn. 3:16 *"For God so loved the world that He gave His one and only Son, that whoever believes in Him shall not perish but have eternal life. For God did not send His Son into the world to condemn the world, but to save the world through Him. Whoever believes in Him is not condemned..."*

Jn. 13:1 *"... (Jesus) having loved His own which were in the world, He loved them unto the end."*

Jn. 13:34 *"A new commandment I give unto you, that ye love one another; as I have loved you, that ye also love one another. By this shall all men know that ye are My disciples, if ye have love one to another."*

(I Jn. 2:7 *"Brethren, I write no new commandment unto you, but an old Commandment which ye had from the beginning. The old Commandment is the Word which ye have heard from the beginning. Again, a new commandment I write unto you, which thing is true in Him and in you..."*

(It's the same Commandment but made new because Jesus showed us how to love and gave us His Holy Spirit to help us obey!

Jn. 14:21 *"He that hath My Commandments, and keepeth them, he it is that loveth Me: and he that loveth Me shall be loved of My Father, and I will love him, and will manifest Myself to him."*

Jn. 15:9 *"As the Father hath loved Me, so have I loved you: continue ye in My love. If ye keep My Commandments, ye shall abide in My love; even as I have kept My Father's Commandments, and abide in His love."*

Jn. 15:12 *"This is My Commandment, that ye love one another, as I have loved you... ye are My friends, if ye do whatsoever I command you."*

Jn. 15:17 *"These things I command you, that ye love one another."*

Jn. 17:26 Jesus prayed to the Father in heaven, *"... that the love wherewith Thou hast loved Me may be in them, and I in them."*

Eph. 2:4 *"... God... rich in mercy, for His great love wherewith He loved us..."*

Jn. 17:23,26 *"... You (the Father) ... have loved them even as you have loved Me (Jesus)... that the love You have for Me may be in them and that I myself may be in them."*

Rom. 5:5 *"... because the love of God is shed abroad in our hearts by the Holy Ghost which is given unto us."*

Rom. 5:8 *"God commendeth His love toward us, in that, while we were yet sinners, Christ died for us."*

Rom. 8:35 *"Who shall separate us from the love of Christ? Shall tribulation, or distress, or persecution, or famine, or nakedness, or peril, or sword... nay, in all these things we are more than conquerors through Him that loved us."*

Rom. 8:39 *"For I am persuaded, that neither death, nor life, nor angels, nor principalities, nor powers, nor things present, nor things to come, nor height, nor depth, nor any other creature, shall be able to separate us from the love of God, which is in Christ Jesus our Lord."*

I Cor. 8:3 *"But if any man love God, the same is known of Him."*

Eph. 1:4 *"... according as He hath chosen us in Him before the foundation of the world, that we should be Holy and without blame before Him in love ..."*

Eph. 5:1,2 *"Be ye therefore followers of God... and walk in love, as Christ also hath loved us, and hath given Himself for us an offering and a sacrifice to God for a sweet smelling savour."*

Eph. 5:25 *"... Christ also loved the church, and gave Himself for it..."*

Phil. 1:9 *"And this I pray, that your love may abound yet more and more in knowledge and in all Judgment; that ye may approve things that are excellent; that ye may be sincere and without offence till the day of Christ; being filled with the fruits of righteousness... by Jesus Christ..."*

II Thess. 2:16 *"Now the Lord Jesus Christ Himself, and God, even our Father, which hath loved us..."*

I Tim.1:14 *"And the grace of our Lord was exceeding abundant with faith and love which is in Christ Jesus."*

I Pet. 1:22 *"Seeing ye have purified your souls in obeying the truth through the Spirit unto unfeigned love of the brethren, see that ye love one another with a pure heart fervently..."*

I Jn. 2:5 *"But whoso keepeth His Word, in him verily is the love of God perfected: hereby know we that we are in Him. He that saith he abideth in Him ought himself also so to walk, even as He walked."*

I Jn. 2:10 *"He that loveth his brother abideth in the light, and there is none occasion of stumbling in him."*

I Jn. 3:1 *"Behold, what manner of love the Father hath bestowed upon us, that we should be called the sons of God..."*

I Jn. 3:16 *"Hereby perceive we the love of God, because He laid down His life for us: and we ought to lay down our lives for the brethren... let us not love in word neither in tongue; but in deed and in truth."*

I Jn. 4:7-12 *"... let us love one another: for love is of God; and everyone that loveth is born of God, and knoweth God. He that loveth not, knoweth not God; for God is love. In this was manifested the love of God towards us, because that God sent His only begotten Son into the world, that we might*

live through Him. Herein is love, not that we loved God, but that He loved us, and sent His Son to be the propitiation (Gr. # 2434 "atoning sacrifice") for our sins. Beloved, if God so loved us, we ought also to love one another... if we love one another, God dwelleth in us, and His love is perfected in us. "
I Jn. 4:16-21 "And we have known and believed the love that God hath to us. God is love; and he that dwelleth in love dwelleth in God, and God in him. Herein is our love made perfect, that we may have boldness in the Day of Judgment: because as He is, so are we in this world. There is no fear in love; but perfect love casteth out fear... he that feareth is not made perfect in love. We love Him, because He first loved us. If a man say, I love God and hateth his brother, he is a liar: for he that loveth not his brother whom he hath seen, how can he love God whom he hath not seen? And this commandment have we from Him, that he who loveth God love his brother also."
II Jn 5,6 "... not as though I wrote a new commandment unto thee, but that which we had from the beginning, that we love one another... this is love, that we walk after His Commandments. This is the Commandment... from the beginning, ye should walk in it."
Jude 2 "... mercy unto you, and peace, and love, be multiplied."
Rev. 1:5 "... unto Him that loved us, and washed us from our sins in His own blood."

Lovingkindness/Goodness

Ps. 17:7 "Shew Thy marvelous lovingkindness, O Thou that savest by Thy right hand them which put their trust in Thee from those that rise up against them."
Ps. 25:6 "Remember, O Lord, Thy tender mercies and Thy lovingkindnesses; for they have been ever of old."
Ps. 26:3 "For Thy lovingkindness is before mine eyes: and I have walked in Thy truth."
Ps. 36:10 "O continue Thy lovingkindness unto them that know Thee; and Thy righteousness to the upright in heart."
Ps. 40:10,11 "I have not hid Thy righteousness within my heart; I have declared Thy faithfulness and Thy Salvation: I have not concealed Thy lovingkindness and Thy truth from the great congregation."
Ps. 42:7,8 "Yet the Lord will command His lovingkindness in the daytime..."
Ps. 69:16 "Hear me, O Lord; for Thy lovingkindness is good: turn unto me according to the multitude of Thy tender mercies."
Ps. 89:33,49 "Nevertheless My lovingkindness will I not utterly take from him, nor suffer My faithfulness to fail."

Ps. 92:2 *"To shew forth Thy lovingkindness in the morning, and Thy faithfulness every night."*

Ps. 103:4 *"Who Redeemeth thy life from destruction; who crowneth thee with lovingkindness and tender mercies; who satisfieth thy mouth with good things; so that thy youth is renewed like the eagle's."*

Ps. 107:43 *"Whoso is wise, and will observe these things, even they shall understand the lovingkindness of the Lord."*

Ps. 119:76 *"Let, I pray Thee, Thy merciful kindness be for my comfort, according to Thy Word unto Thy servant. Let Thy tender mercies come unto me, that I may live: for Thy law is my delight."*

Ps. 119:88 *"Quicken me after Thy lovingkindness; so shall I keep the Testimony of Thy mouth. Forever, O Lord, Thy Word is settled in heaven."*

Ps. 119:49 *"Remember the Word unto Thy servant, upon which Thou hast caused me to hope. This is my comfort in my affliction: for Thy Word hath quickened me."*

Ps. 143:8,9,12 *"Cause me to hear Thy lovingkindness in the morning; for in Thee do I trust: cause me to know the way wherein I should walk; for I lift up my soul unto Thee. Deliver me, O Lord from mine enemies: I flee unto Thee to hide me... and of Thy mercy cut off mine enemies, and destroy all them that afflict my soul: for I am Thy servant."*

Ps. 144:2 *"My goodness, and my fortress; my high tower, and my deliverer, my shield, and He in whom I trust; who subdueth my people under me."*

Is. 63:7,8 *"I will mention the lovingkindnesses of the Lord... according to the multitude of His lovingkindnesses."*

Jer. 31:3 *"... I have loved thee with an everlasting love: therefore with lovingkindness have I drawn thee."*

Hosea 2:19 *"And I will betroth thee unto me forever; yea, I will betroth thee unto Me in righteousness, and in Judgment, and in lovingkindness, and in mercies. I will even betroth thee unto Me in faithfulness: and thou shalt know the Lord."*

Marriage / Spouse

Also see section on Family

Gen. 2:18 *"It is not good that the man should be alone; I will make him a help meet..."*

(It is God who did not want man to be alone; marriage began in the Garden of Eden. Woman was not an afterthought but God wanted Adam to want a mate before He gave her to him so that he would appreciate her.

Gen. 2:20-24 *"... but for Adam there was not found a help meet for him. And the Lord God caused a deep sleep to fall upon Adam, and he slept: and He took one of his ribs, and closed up the flesh instead thereof; and the rib, which the Lord God had taken from man, made he a woman, and brought her unto the man. And Adam said, This is now bone of my bones, and flesh of my flesh: she shall be called Woman, because she was taken out of Man. Therefore shall a man leave his father and his mother, and shall cleave unto his wife: and shall be one flesh."*
If God could provide a mate for Adam, He can provide one for us. It is God who makes us one flesh.
Deut. 3:2 *"... fear him not, I will deliver him..."*
(God can deliver your spouse from the things that hold them in bondage.
Deut. 30:6 "And the Lord thy God will circumcise thine heart, and the heart of thy seed, to love the Lord thy God with all thine heart, and with all thy soul, that thou mayest live."
(God is the one who changes the heart. Here is a prayer you could pray over your spouse.
Prayer: Lord, please circumcise the heart of my spouse that they will love You with all their heart. Thank You in Jesus' name, Amen!
I Sam. 10:6,7,9,10 *"... and the Spirit of the Lord will come upon thee... and (you will)... be turned into another man... God gave him another heart..."*
This is a prayer you could pray over your spouse or loved one.
Prayer: Lord, please send the Holy Spirit to turn my spouse into another person and give them a new heart. Thank You in Jesus' name, Amen!
I Chron. 29:19 *"... give unto Solomon my son a perfect heart, to keep Thy Commandments... and to do all these things..."*
Prayer: Lord, give my spouse a perfect heart to obey You in everything. In Jesus' name, Amen!
II Chron. 30:12 *"Also in Judah the hand of God was to give them one heart... by the Word of the Lord."*
Prayer: Lord, give me and my spouse one heart as you did those in the Bible in Jesus' name, Amen!
Ezra 6:22 *"... for the Lord... turned the heart of the king..."* (If God can turn the king's heart then He can turn anyone's heart; see Prov. 21:1)
A prayer you could pray for an unbelieving spouse
Prayer: Lord, if you could turn the heart of the king, then I know you could turn my spouse's heart toward You. In Jesus' name, Amen!
Job 22:30 NIV *"He will deliver even one who is not innocent, who will be delivered through the cleanness of your hands."*

(We keep our hands clean by the righteousness of Jesus (I Cor.6:11), baptism (Eph.5:26;I Pet.3:21), confession, forgiveness, (I Jn. 1:9) and being washed by His blood (Rev. 1:5).

A prayer you could pray for someone who needs help but is undeserving.

Prayer: Lord, please deliver _____ even though he/she is not innocent according to Your Word. Thank You, in Jesus' name, Amen!

Prov. 5:18,19 NLT *"Let your wife be a fountain of blessing for you. Rejoice in the wife of your youth… may you always be captivated by her love."*

Prov. 18:22 *"Whoso findeth a wife findeth a good thing, and obtaineth favour of the Lord."*

Prov. 19:14 *"… a prudent wife is from the Lord."*

Prov. 21:1 *"The king's heart is in the hand of the Lord, as the rivers of water: He turneth it whithersoever He will"*

Is. 34:16 *"… no one of these* (promises) *shall fail, none shall want her mate: for my mouth it hath commanded, and His Spirit it hath gathered them."*

Is. 34:16 NIV *"… for it is His mouth that has given the order, and His Spirit will gather them together."*

Is. 34:16 NLT *"… none will lack a mate, for the Lord has promised this. His Spirit will make it all come true."*

Is. 54:5 *"For thy Maker is thine husband…"*

When your spouse is not the person they should be or you are a widow/widower let Jesus be more than a spouse to you.

Jer. 3:22 *"Return, ye backsliding children, and I will heal your backslidings…"*

A prayer you could pray for your spouse.

Prayer: Lord, heal the backsliding of my spouse in Jesus' name, Amen!

Jer. 32:39-41 *"And I will give them one heart, and one way, that they may fear Me forever, for the good of them, and of their children after them… I will put My fear in their hearts, that they shall not depart from Me… I will rejoice over them to do them good…"*

Ez. 6:9,10 *"They will loathe themselves for the evils which they have committed."*

You could pray: Lord, help my loved one to loathe the evils in their life so they will quit doing what is wrong. In Jesus' name, Amen!

Ez. 11:19,20 *"… I will give them one heart… I will put a new Spirit within you… I will take the stony heart out of their flesh, and will give them an heart of flesh: that they may walk in My Statutes… and do them: and they shall be My people, and I will be their God."*

Ez. 14:11 *"That the house of Israel may go no more astray from Me, neither be polluted any more with all their transgressions; but that they may be My people, and I may be their God, saith the Lord God."*

You could pray: Lord, help my spouse to stop going astray or polluting themselves with sin. Be their God and let them be Your people.

Ez. 16:61 "... *then thou shalt remember thy ways, and be ashamed...*" You could pray this prayer if your spouse is doing something they shouldn't do and need to be ashamed of it.

Prayer: Lord, help my spouse to remember what they've done and be ashamed of their ways and repent in Jesus' name, Amen!

Ez. 36:25-31 "*Then will I sprinkle clean water upon you, and ye shall be clean: from all your filthiness, and from all your idols, will I cleanse you. A new heart also will I give you, and a new Spirit will I put within you: and I will take away the stony heart out of your flesh, and I will give you a heart of flesh. And I will put My Spirit within you, and cause you to walk in My Statutes, and ye shall keep My Judgments, and do them. And ye shall dwell in the land that I gave to your fathers; and ye shall be My people, and I will be your God. I will also save you from all your uncleannesses... then shall ye remember your own evil ways, and your doings that were not good, and shall loathe yourselves in your own sight for your iniquities and for your abominations.*"

Hosea 14:4 "*I will heal their backsliding, I will love them freely: for Mine anger is turned away from him.*"

You could pray: Lord, please heal the backsliding of my spouse and love them freely. Let Your anger be turned away in Jesus' name, Amen!

Matt. 19:4-6;Mk. 10:6-8 "*... have ye not read, that He which made them at the beginning made them male and female, and said, For this cause shall a man leave father and mother, and shall cleave to his wife: and they twain shall be one flesh? Wherefore they are no more twain, but one flesh. What therefore God hath joined together, let not man put asunder.*"

Lk. 22:31,32 "*... Satan hath desired to have you, that he may sift you as wheat; but I have prayed for thee, that thy faith fail not: and when thou art converted, strengthen thy brethren.*"

Prayer: You could pray, Lord, I know that Satan desires to have my spouse. I pray for him/her that his/her faith would not fail like You did for Peter and that You would convert him/her so that they could minister to others. Thank You in Jesus' name, Amen!

Acts 26:18 "*... to open their eyes, and to turn them from darkness to light, and from the power of Satan unto God, that they may receive forgiveness of sins, and inheritance among them which are Sanctified by faith that is in Me.*"

Prayer: Lord, please open the eyes of my spouse and turn him/her from darkness to light, from Satan's power to God's power. Forgive them and let him/ her receive an inheritance among the Redeemed in Jesus' name, Amen!

I Cor. 7:13-16 *"And the woman which hath an husband that believeth not, and if he be pleased to dwell with her, let her not leave him. For the unbelieving husband is Sanctified by the wife, and the unbelieving wife is Sanctified by the husband: else were your children unclean; but now are they Holy... for what knowest thou, O wife, whether thou shalt save thy husband? Or how knowest thou, O man, whether thou shalt save thy wife?"*

I Cor. 7:32 *"... he that is married careth for the things... how he may please his wife."*

God wants us to please our spouse except when it would go against what God commands us to do.

I Tim. 2:1-4 God wants all men saved (including your spouse).

II Tim. 2:25 *"In meekness instructing those that oppose themselves; if God peradventure will give them repentance to the acknowledging of the truth; and that they may recover themselves out of the snare of the devil, who are taken captive by him at his will."*

(II Tim. 2:25 AMPC *"That God may grant that they will repent and come to know the truth."*

You could pray: Lord, please give my spouse repentance and let him/her acknow-ledge truth as found in Your Word. Recover them from the traps and tricks of the devil who wants to take them captive to do his will.

Heb. 8:10,11 *"... I will put My laws into their mind, and write them in their hearts: and I will be to them a God, and they shall be to Me a people... for all shall know Me, from the least to the greatest. For I will be merciful to their unrighteousness, and their sins and their iniquities will I remember no more."*

You could pray,

Prayer: Lord, put Your law in my spouse's mind and heart. Be their God and let them be part of Your people. Let them know You and forgive their sins so they won't be remembered anymore. Thank You in Jesus' name, Amen!

Heb. 13:4 *"Marriage is honourable in all..."*

I Jn. 5:16 *"If any man see his brother sin a sin which is not unto death, he shall ask, and he shall give him life for them that sin not unto death..."*

You could pray: Lord, please give life to my spouse so that they will not die the eternal death. Thank You in Jesus' name, Amen!

I Pet. 3:1 *"... if any obey not the Word, they also may without the Word be won by the conversation (Gr. #391 "conduct") of the wives..."*

Meek

Ps. 37:11 *"But the meek shall inherit the earth; and shall delight themselves in the abundance of peace."*

Ps. 147:6 *"The Lord lifteth up the meek..."*
Is. 61:1 *"The Spirit of the Lord is upon Me; because the Lord hath anointed Me to preach good tidings unto the meek..."*
Matt. 5:5 *"Blessed are the meek: for they shall inherit the earth."*

Mercy / Gracious / Kind

Deut. 4:31 *"... for the Lord thy God is a merciful God..."*
II Sam. 22:26 *"With the merciful Thou wilt shew Thyself merciful, and with the upright man Thou wilt shew Thyself upright. With the pure Thou wilt shew Thyself pure; and with the forward Thou wilt shew Thyself unsavory."*
Neh. 9:31 *"... for Thou art a gracious and merciful God."*
Ps. 59:17 *"Unto thee, O my strength, will I sing: for God is my defense, and the God of my mercy."*
Ps. 85:15 *"But Thou, O Lord, art a God full of compassion, and gracious, long-suffering, and plenteous in mercy and truth."*
Ps. 86:5 *"For Thou, Lord, art good, and ready to forgive; and plenteous in mercy unto all them that call upon Thee."*
Ps. 86:13 *"For great is Thy mercy toward me: and thou hast delivered my soul from the lowest hell."*
Ps. 94:18 *"... Thy mercy, O Lord, held me up."*
Ps. 98:3 *"He hath remembered His mercy and His truth toward the house of Israel: all the ends of the earth have seen the Salvation of our God."*
Ps. 102:13 *"Thou shalt arise, and have mercy upon Zion: for the time to favour her, yea, the set time, is come."*
Ps. 103:8 *"The Lord is merciful and gracious, slow to anger..."*
Ps. 103:17 *"But the mercy of the Lord is from everlasting to everlasting upon them that fear Him..."*
Ps. 109:29 *"O give thanks unto the Lord; for He is good: for His mercy endureth forever."*
Ps. 123:2 *"... our eyes wait upon the Lord our God, until that He have mercy upon us."*
Ps. 136:26 *"O give thanks unto the God of heaven: for His mercy endureth forever."*
Ps. 138:7,8 *"Though I walk in the midst of trouble, Thou wilt revive me: Thou shalt stretch forth Thine hand against the wrath of mine enemies, and Thy right hand shall save me. The Lord will perfect that which concerneth me: Thy mercy, O Lord, endureth forever..."*
Prov. 14:21 *"... he that hath mercy on the poor, happy is he."*

Is. 49:13 "... for the Lord hath comforted His people, and will have mercy upon His afflicted."
Is. 54:7 "... but with great mercies will I gather thee... with everlasting kindness will I have mercy on thee, saith the Lord thy Redeemer."
Is. 55:7 "Let the wicked forsake his way, and the unrighteous man his thoughts: and let him return unto the Lord, and He will have mercy..."
Jer. 33:11 "His mercy endureth forever..."
Zech. 10:6 "And I will strengthen the house of Judah, and I will save the house of Joseph, and I will bring them again to place them; for I have mercy upon them... for I am the Lord their God, and will hear them."
Matt. 5:7 "Blessed are the merciful: for they shall obtain mercy."
Lk. 1:50 "... His mercy is on them that fear him from generation to generation."
Lk. 1:54 "He hath (helped) His servant Israel, in remembrance of His mercy"
Lk. 1:72,78 "To perform the mercy promised to our fathers... through the tender mercy of our God..."
Lk. 6:35,36 "... He is kind unto the unthankful and to the evil. Be ye therefore merciful, as your Father also is merciful."
Acts 2:33 "... having received of the Father the promise of the Holy Ghost, He hath shed forth this, which ye now see and hear."
Eph. 2:4 "... God... rich in mercy, for His great love wherewith He loved us..."
Heb. 4:16 "Let us therefore come boldly unto the throne of grace, that we may obtain mercy, and find grace to help in time of need."
Heb. 8:12 "For I will be merciful to their unrighteousness, and their sins and their iniquities will I remember no more."
I Tim. 1:13 Paul said, "... I obtained mercy..."
I Tim. 1:16 "Howbeit for this cause I obtained mercy..."
I Pet. 1:3,4 "Blessed be the God and Father of our Lord Jesus Christ, which ac-cording to His abundant mercy hath begotten us again unto... an inheritance incorruptible, and undefiled, and that fadeth not away, reserved in heaven for you ("for us" KJV fn)."

Miracles / Healing / Signs

Ex. 23:25 "... and I will take sickness away from the midst of thee."
Deut. 28:15,58-61 Sickness (part of the curse for disobedience)
Gal. 3:13,14 Jesus Redeemed us from the curse
Ex. 15:26 "If thou wilt diligently hearken to the voice of the Lord thy God, and wilt do that which is right in His sight and wilt give ear to His

Commandments, and keep all His Statutes, I will put none of these diseases on thee... I am the Lord that healeth thee"

Ex. 23:25,26 "And ye shall serve the Lord thy God, and He shall bless... and ... will take sickness away from the midst of thee."

Deut. 7:15 "And the Lord will take away from thee all sickness, and will put none of the evil diseases... upon thee..."

II Kings 2:20-22 Elisha heals the poisonous water with salt

II Kings 5:1-19 Naaman healed by Elisha

II Kings 20:5 "... I have heard thy prayer (and) seen thy tears... I will heal thee"

II Chron. 30:20 "And the Lord hearkened to Hezekiah, and healed the people."

Job 5:18 "For He maketh sore, and bindeth up: He woundeth, and His hands make whole."

Job 5:18 NASB "For He inflicts pain, and gives relief; He wounds, and His hands also heal."

Ps. 30:2 "... Thou hast healed me."

Ps. 41:1-3 "... the Lord will strengthen him upon the bed of languishing: Thou wilt make all his bed in his sickness."

Ps. 41:3 NIV "The Lord sustains them on their sickbed and restores them from their bed of illness."

Ps. 41:3 NLT "The Lord nurses them when they are sick and restores them to health."

Ps. 41:3 RSV "The Lord sustains him on his sickbed; in his illness Thou healest all his infirmities."

Ps. 41:4 "... Lord... heal my soul"

Ps. 42:11 "... for I shall yet praise Him, who is the health of my countenance, and my God."

Ps. 67:2 "That Thy way may be known upon earth, Thy saving health among all nations."

Ps. 103:3 "... who healeth all thy diseases..."

Ps. 107:20 "He sent His Word, and healed them..."

Ps. 118:17 "I shall not die, but live, and declare the works of the Lord."

Ps. 146:7-9 "... the Lord openeth the eyes of the blind: the Lord raiseth them that are bowed down: the Lord loveth the righteous..."

Ps. 147:3 "He healeth the broken in heart, and bindeth up their wounds."

Prov. 3:7,8 "... fear the Lord, and depart from evil. It shall be health to thy na-vel, and marrow to thy bones."

Prov. 4:20-23 "... attend unto My words... for they are life unto those that find them, and health to all their flesh."

Prov. 12:18 "... but the tongue of the wise is health."

Prov. 14:30 "A sound heart is the life of the flesh..."

Prov. 16:24 *"Pleasant words are as an honeycomb, sweet to the soul, and health to the bones."*
Prov. 17:22 *"A merry heart doeth good like a medicine..."*
Is. 19:22-25 *"And the Lord shall smite... and heal it... and they shall return even to the Lord, and He shall be intreated of them, and shall heal them."*
Is. 20:22 *"... He shall smite and heal it... and shall heal them."*
Is. 29:18 *"And in that day shall the deaf hear the Words of the book, and the eyes of the blind shall see out of obscurity, and out of darkness."*
Is. 30:26 *"... the Lord bindeth up the breach of His people, and healeth the stroke of their wound."*
Is. 33:24 *"And the inhabitant shall not say, I am sick..."* (on the New Earth)
Is. 35:5,6 *"Then the eyes of the blind shall be opened, and the ears of the deaf shall be unstopped. Then shall the lame man leap as an hart, and the tongue of the dumb sing..."*
Is. 38:16 *"... so wilt Thou recover me, and make me to live."*
Is. 38:21;39:1 Hezekiah asked God to heal him and God answered and told him to put a poultice of figs on his boil and he recovered.
Is. 42:7 *"To open the blind eyes..."*
Is. 42:16 *"And I will bring the blind by a way that they knew not; I will lead them in paths that they have not known: I will make darkness light before them, and crooked things straight. These things will I do unto them, and not forsake them."*
Is. 53:4,5,16 *"... with His stripes we are healed."* (I Pet. 2:24)
Is. 57:18,19 *"I have seen his ways, and will heal him..."*
Is. 58:8 *"Then shall thy light break forth as the morning, and thine health shall spring forth speedily..."*
Jer. 3:22 *"Return, ye backsliding children, and I will heal your backslidings..."*
Jer. 8:22 *"Is there no balm in Gilead; is there no physician there? Why then is not the health of the daughter of My people recovered?"*
Jer. 17:14 *"Heal me, O Lord, and I shall be healed..."*
Jer. 30:17,18 *"For I will restore health unto thee, and I will heal thee of thy wounds, saith the Lord..."*
Jer. 33:6 *"Behold, I will bring it health and cure, and I will cure them..."*
(Jer. 33:6 NIV *"... I will bring health and healing to it; I will heal My people and will let them enjoy abundant peace and security..."*
Ez. 34:16 AMP *"I will seek that which was lost and bring back that which has strayed, and I will bandage the hurt and the crippled and will strengthen the weak and the sick..."*
Hosea 6:1-3 *"Come, and let us return unto the Lord... He will heal us..."*
Hosea 7:1 *"When I would have healed Israel..."*
Hosea 11:3 NKJV *"... they did not know that I healed them."*

Hosea 14:4 "*I will heal their backsliding, I will love them freely: for Mine anger is turned away from him.*"
Joel 2:30 "*And I will shew wonders in the heavens and in the earth, blood, and fire, and pillars of smoke.*"
Mal. 4:2 NKJV "*But to you who fear My name the Sun of Righteousness shall arise with healing in His wings…*"
Matt. 4:23 "*… healing all manner of sickness and all manner of disease among the people.*"
Matt. 4:24 "*… He healed them.*"
Matt. 6:33 "*But seek ye first the kingdom of God, and His righteousness; and all these things shall be added unto you.*"
Matt. 8:2,3 "*… Lord, if Thou wilt, Thou canst make me clean…* (Jesus said) *I will; be thou clean.*"
Matt. 8:7,8 "*… Jesus saith unto him, I will come and heal him… but speak the Word only, and my servant shall be healed.*"
Matt. 8:14 Jesus healed Peter's mother-in-law, "*… and the fever left her…*"
Matt. 8:16,17 "*… He… healed all that were sick… Himself took our infirmities, and bare our sicknesses.*"
Matt. 8:25-27 "*And His Disciples came to Him* (Jesus), *and awoke Him, saying, Lord save us: we perish. And He saith unto them, Why are ye fearful, O ye of little faith? Then He arose, and rebuked the winds and the sea; and there was a great calm… men marveled, saying, What manner of man is this, that even the winds and the sea obey Him!*"
Matt. 9:2-8 "*And, behold, they brought to Him* (Jesus) *a man sick of the palsy, lying on a bed: and Jesus seeing their faith said unto the sick of the palsy; Son, be of good cheer; thy sins be forgiven thee… that ye may know that the Son of man hath power on earth to forgive sins,* (then saith He to the sick of the palsy), *Arise, take up thy bed, and go unto thine house. And he arose, and departed to his house. But when the multitudes saw it, they marveled, and glorified God, which had given such power unto men.*"
Matt. 9:21 "*… if I may but touch His garment, I shall be whole.*"
Matt. 9:22 AMP "*Your faith has made you well. And at once the woman was restored to health.*"
Matt. 9:23-26 Jesus raises the twelve year old from the dead.
Matt. 9:28,29 "*And when Jesus departed thence, two blind men followed Him, crying, and saying, Thou Son of David, have mercy on us. And when He was come into the house, the blind men came to Him: and Jesus saith unto them, Believe ye that I am able to do this? They said unto Him, Yea, Lord. Then touched He their eyes, saying, According to your faith be it unto you.*"
Matt. 9:33 "*And when the devil was cast out, the dumb spake: and the multitudes marveled, saying, It was never so seen in Israel.*"

Matt. 9:35 "... healing every sickness and every disease..."
Matt. 10:1 "... He gave them power against unclean spirits, to cast them out, and to heal all manner of sickness and all manner of disease."
Matt. 10:7,8 "And as ye go, preach, saying, The kingdom of heaven is at hand. Heal the sick, cleanse the lepers, raise the dead, cast out devils; freely ye have received, freely give."
Matt. 11:5 "The blind receive their sight, and the lame walk, the lepers are cleansed, and the deaf hear, the dead are raised up, and the poor have the Gospel preached to them."
Matt. 12:13 "Then saith He (Jesus) to the man, Stretch forth thine hand And he stretched it forth; and it was restored whole, like as the other."
Matt. 12:15 "... He healed them all."
Matt. 12:22 "... He healed him..."
Matt. 12:28 Jesus said, "... if I cast out devils by the Spirit of God, then the king-dom of God is come unto you. Or else how can one enter into a storng man's house, and spoil his goods, except he first bind the strong man and then he will spoil his house."
Matt. 13:15 "... and should be converted, and I should heal them."
Matt. 14:14 "And Jesus... moved with compassion toward them, and He healed their sick."
Matt. 14:19-32 Jesus fed 5,000 with five loaves and two fish.
Matt. 14:35,36 "... that they might only touch the hem of His garment: and as many as touched were made perfectly whole."
Matt. 15:28 "Then Jesus answered and said unto her, O woman, great is thy faith: be it unto thee even as thou wilt. And her daughter was made whole from that very hour."
Matt. 15:30-32 "And great multitudes came unto Him (Jesus), having with them those that were lame, blind, dumb, maimed, and many others, and cast them down at Jesus' feet: and He healed them: insomuch that the multitude wondered, when they saw the dumb to speak, the maimed to be whole, the lame to walk, and the blind to see: and they glorified the God of Israel. Then Jesus called His disciples unto Him, and said, I have compassion on the multitude..."
Matt. 15:32-38 Jesus fed 4,000 with seven loaves and a few fish.
Matt. 19:2 "And great multitudes followed him; and He healed them there."
Matt. 20:30-34 "... two blind men sitting by the wayside, when they heard that Jesus passed by, cried out, saying, Have mercy on us, O Lord, Thou son of David... what will ye that I shall do unto you... that our eyes may be opened. So Jesus had compassion on them, and touched their eyes: and immediately their eyes received sight, and they followed Him."

Matt. 21:14 *"And the blind and the lame came to Him in the Temple; and He healed them."*

Matt. 21:19-22 *"And when He (Jesus) saw a fig tree in the way, He came to it, and found nothing thereon, but leaves only, and said unto it, Let no fruit grow on thee henceforward forever. And presently the fig tree withered away. And when the disciples saw it, they marveled, saying, How soon is the fig tree withered away! Jesus answered and said unto them, Verily I say unto you, If ye have faith, and doubt not, ye shall not only do this which is done to the fig tree, but also if ye shall say unto this mountain, Be thou removed, and be thou cast into the sea; it shall be done. And all things, whatsoever ye shall ask in prayer, believing, ye shall receive."*

Mk. 1:32-34 *"... at even... they brought unto Him all that were diseased, and them that were possessed with devils. And all the city was gathered together at the door. And He healed many that were sick of divers diseases..."*

Mk. 1:40,41 *"... if Thou wilt, Thou canst make me clean. And Jesus, moved with compassion, put forth His hand, and touched him, and saith unto him, I will; be thou clean. And as soon as He had spoken, immediately the leprosy departed from him, and he was cleansed."*

Mk. 2:5,10-12 *"When Jesus saw their faith, He said unto the sick of the palsy, Son, thy sins be forgiven thee... but that ye may know that the Son of man hath power on earth to forgive sins, (He saith to the sick of the palsy), I say unto thee, Arise, and take up thy bed, and go thy way into thine house. And immediately he arose, took up the bed, and went forth before them all; insomuch that they were all amazed, and glorified God, saying, We never saw it on this fashion."*

Mk. 3:5 *"... He saith unto the man, Stretch forth thine hand. And he stretched it out: and his hand was restored whole as the other."*

Mk. 3:10,11 *".. (Jesus) healed many; insomuch that they pressed upon Him for to touch Him, as many as had plagues. And unclean spirits, when they saw Him fell down before Him, and cried, saying, Thou art the Son of God."*

Mk. 3:15 *"... to have power to heal sicknesses, and to cast out devils..."*

Mk. 5:27-31,34 *"... she... touched His garment. For she said, If I may touch but His clothes, I shall be whole. And straightway the fountain of her blood was dried up; and she felt in her body that she was healed of that plague... Jesus, immediately knowing in Himself that virtue had gone out of Him..."*

Mk. 5:36 *"... be not afraid, only believe."*

Mk. 6:5,6,7 *"... He laid His hands upon a few sick folk, and healed them. And He marveled because of their unbelief."*

Mk. 6:7 *"... and gave them power over unclean spirits..."*

Mk. 6:13 *"... anointed with oil many that were sick, and healed them."*

Mk. 6:56 "... they laid the sick in the streets, and besought Him that they might touch if it were but the border of His garment: and as many as touched Him were made whole."

Mk. 7:32-35 "And they bring unto Him one that was deaf, and had an impediment in his speech... and He took him aside from the multitude, and put His fingers into his ears, and He spit, and touched his tongue; and looking up to heaven, He sighed, and saith unto him, Eph-pha-tha, that is, Be opened. And straightway his ears were opened, and the string of his tongue was loosed, and he spake plain."

Mk. 7:37 "... He hath done all things well: He maketh both the deaf to hear, and the dumb to speak."

Mk. 8:2 " I have compassion on the multitude..." (by healing them)

Mk. 8:22-25 "... they bring a blind man unto Him, and besought Him to touch him. And He took the blind man by the hand, and led him out of the town; and when he had spit on his eyes, and put His hands upon him, He asked him if he saw ought... he looked up, and said, I see men as trees, walking. And that He put His hands again upon his eyes, and made him look up: and he was restored, and saw every man clearly."

Mk. 10:27 "... with God all things are possible."

Mk. 10:52 "... thy faith hath made thee whole. And immediately he received his sight, and followed Jesus..."

Mk. 11:13-24 "And seeing a fig tree afar off having (nothing but) leaves.. Jesus... said... No man eat fruit of thee hereafter forever..."

Mk. 16:17 HCSB "And these signs will accompany those who believe: in My name they will drive out demons; they will speak in new languages..."

Mk. 16:18,20 "... they shall lay hands on the sick, and they shall recover... confirming the Word with signs following. Amen."

Lk. 1:64 "And his mouth was opened immediately, and his tongue loosed, and he spake, and praised God."

Lk. 4:18-21 "... He hath sent Me to heal the brokenhearted... and recovering of sight to the blind..."

Lk. 4:39-41 "And He... rebuked the fever; and it left her: and immediately she arose..."

Lk. 5:12,13,16-26 "... a man full of leprosy: who seeing Jesus fell on his face, and besought Him, saying Lord if Thou wilt, Thou canst make me clean. And He put forth His hand, and touched him, saying, I will: be thou clean. And immediately the leprosy departed from him."

Lk. 6:18,19 "... and they were healed... and (Jesus) healed them all."

Lk. 7:7,10 "... say in a word, and my servant shall be healed... and.. returning to the house, found the servant whole that had been sick."

Lk. 7:13-16 *"And when the Lord saw her, He had compassion on her, and said unto her, Weep not. And He came and touched the bier: and they that bare him stood still. And He said, Young man, I say unto thee, Arise. And he that was dead sat up, and began to speak... God hath visited His people."*

Lk. 7:21 *"And in that same hour He cured many of their infirmities and plagues, and of evil spirits; and unto many that were blind He gave sight... the blind see, the lame walk, the lepers are cleansed, the deaf hear, the dead are raised, to the poor the Gospel is preached."*

Lk. 8:2 *"And certain women, which had been healed of evil spirits and infirmities, Mary called Magdalene, out of whom went seven devils..."*

Lk. 8:24 The disciples said to Jesus, *"... Master, we perish. Then He arose, and rebuked the wind and the raging of the water: and they ceased, and there was a calm. And He said unto them, Where is your faith? An... saying one to another, What manner of man is this? For He commandeth even the winds and water, and they obey Him."*

Lk. 8:43 *"... a woman having an issue of blood... touched the border of His garment: and immediately her issue of blood... ("stopped" NIV)... thy faith has made thee whole..."*

Lk. 8:46 Jesus said, *"... I perceive that virtue is gone out of Me... she was healed immediately... thy faith hath made thee whole; go in peace..."*

Lk. 8:49-55 *"... thy daughter is dead... fear not: believe only, and she shall be made whole... and took her by the hand, and called, saying, Maid, arise. And her spirit came again, and she arose straightway..."*

Lk. 9:1,2 Jesus *"... gave* (the disciples) *power and authority over all devils, and to cure diseases. And He sent them to... heal the sick."*

Lk. 9:6 *"And they departed, and went through the towns, preaching the Gospel, and healing everywhere."*

Lk. 9:11 *"... and healed them that had need of healing."*

Lk. 9:42,43 *"... Jesus rebuked the unclean spirit, and healed the child, and delivered him again to his father. And they were all amazed at the mighty power of God..."*

Lk. 10:9 *"... heal the sick that are therein, and say unto them, The kingdom of God is come nigh unto you."*

Lk. 13:12,14 *"... woman, thou art loosed from thine infirmity.. He laid His hands on her: and immediately she was made straight, and glorified God."*

Lk. 13:32 *"And He* (Jesus) *said unto them, Go ye, and tell that fox* (Herod), *Behold, I cast out devils, and I do cures today and tomorrow, and the third day I shall be perfected."*

Lk. 17:12-19 Ten lepers cried, *"... Master, have mercy on us... they were cleansed..."*

Lk. 18:40-43 *"And Jesus stood, and commanded him to be brought unto Him: and when he was come near, He asked him, saying, What wilt thou that I shall do unto thee? And he said, Lord, that I may receive my sight. And Jesus said unto him, Receive thy sight: thy faith hath saved thee. And immediately he received his sight, and followed Him, gloriying God: and all the people, when they saw it, gave praise unto God."*

Lk. 22:51 *"... and He touched his ear, and healed him."*

Jn. 2:23 *"Now when He was in Jerusalem at the Passover, in the Feast day, many believed in His name, when they saw the miracles... He did."*

Jn. 4:47-54 *"... and besought Him* (Jesus) *that He would come down, and heal his son: for he was at the point of death... the nobleman saith unto Him, Sir, come down ere my child die. Jesus saith unto him, Go thy way; thy son liveth. And the man believed the Word that Jesus had spoken unto him, and he went his way. And as he was now going down, his servants met him, and told him, saying, Thy son liveth. Then inquired he of them the hour when he began to amend. And they said unto him, Yesterday at the seventh hour the fever left him. So the father knew that it was at the same hour, in the which Jesus said unto him, Thy son liveth: and himself believed, and his whole house. This is again the second miracle that Jesus did..."*

Jn. 5:14 *"... thou art made whole: sin no more, lest a worse thing come..."*

Jn. 6:5-14 Jesus feeds 5,000 with two loaves of bread and two fish.

Jn. 6:19 *"... they see Jesus walking on the sea...* (and) *He saith unto them, It is I; be not afraid. Then they willingly received Him into the ship: and immediately the ship was at the land whither they went."*

Jn. 6:29 *"Jesus answered and said unto them, This is the work of God, that ye believe on Him* (Jesus) *whom He* (the Father in heaven) *hath sent."*

Jn. 9:3 *"... that the works of God* (the Father) *should be made manifest in Him* (Jesus)*... He spat on the ground, and made clay of the spittle... He anointed the eyes of the blind man with the clay, and said unto him, Go, wash in the pool of Siloam... washed, and came seeing."*

Jn. 10:10 *"... I am come that they might have life, and that they might have it more abundantly."*

Jn. 10:37,38,42 *"If I do not the works of My Father, believe Me not. But if I do... believe the works: that ye may know and believe, that the Father is in Me, and I in Him... and many believed on Him there."*

Jn. 12:40-44 *"Jesus saith unto her, Said I not unto thee, that, if thou wouldest believe, thou shouldest see the glory of God... Jesus lift up His eyes, and said, Father, I thank Thee that Thou hast heard Me. And I knew that thou hearest Me always... He cried with a loud voice, Lazarus, come forth. And he that was dead came forth..."*

Acts 2:22 "... *Jesus of Nazareth, a man approved of God* (the Father) *among you by miracles and wonders and signs, which God did by Him...*"

Acts 2:43 "*And fear came upon every soul: and many wonders and signs were done by the Apostles.*"

Acts 3:6-10 "*Then Peter said, Silver and gold have I none; but such as I have give I thee: In the name of Jesus Christ of Nazareth rise up and walk. And he took him by the right hand, lift him up: and immediately his feet and ankle bones received strength, and he leaping up stood, and walked, and entered with them into the Temple, walking, and leaping, and praising God.*"

Acts 4:14,16 "*... the man which was healed... for that indeed a notable miracle hath been done by them is manifest to all them that dwell in Jerusalem; and we cannot deny it.*"

Acts 4:22 "*... miracle of healing...*"

Acts 4:23 "*And fear came upon every soul: and many wonders and signs were done by the Apostles.*"

Acts 4:30 "*By stretching forth Thine hand to heal; and that signs and wonders may be done by the name of Thy Holy child Jesus.*"

Acts 4:33 "*And with great power gave the Apostles witness of the Resurrection of the Lord Jesus: and great grace was upon them all. Neither was there any among them that lacked...*"

Acts 5:12 "*And by the hands of the Apostles were many signs and wonders wrought among the people...*"

Acts 5:16 "*There came also a multitude out of the cities round about unto Jeru-salem, bringing sick folks, and them which were vexed with unclean spirits: and they were healed everyone.*"

Acts 6:8 "*And Stephen, full of faith and power, did great wonders and miracles among the people.*"

Acts 8:6-8 "*... hearing and seeing the miracles which he did. For unclean spirits, crying with loud voice, came out of many that were possessed with them: and many taken with palsies, and that were lame, were healed. And there was great joy in that city...*"

Acts 8:13 "*... beholding the miracles and signs which were done.*"

Acts 8:39,40 "*And when they were come up out of the water, the Spirit of the Lord caught away Philip, that the eunuch saw him no more: and he went on his way rejoicing. And Philip was found at Azotus...*"

Acts 9:33,34 "*And Peter said unto him, Aeneas, Jesus Christ maketh thee whole: arise, and make thy bed. And he arose immediately.*"

Acts 9:40,41 Peter brought Tabitha/Dorcas to life in Jesus' name!

Acts 10:38 "*... how God* (the Father) *anointed Jesus of Nazareth with the Holy Ghost and with power: who went about doing good, and healing all that were oppressed of the devil; for God* (the Father) *was with Him* (Jesus).*"

Acts 14:3 "... *speaking boldly in the Lord, which gave Testimony unto the Word of His grace, and granted signs and wonders to be done...*"
Acts 14:8-10 "... *a cripple... who never had walked: the same heard Paul speak... perceiving that he had faith to be healed, said with a loud voice, Stand upright on thy feet. And he leaped and walked.*"
Acts 19:12 "*And God wrought special miracles by the hands of Paul: so that from his body were brought unto the sick handkerchiefs... and the diseases de-parted from them, and the evil spirits went out of them.*"
Acts 28:5 "*And he* (Paul) *shook off the beast* (snake) *and felt no harm.*"
Acts 28:8,9 "... *the father of Publius lay sick of a fever and of a bloody flixe* ("dysentery" NIV) ... *Paul... prayed laid his hands on him, and healed him. So when this was done, others also, which had diseases in the island, came, and were healed...*"
Rom. 8:11 '*But if the Spirit of him that raised up Jesus from the dead dwell in you, He that raised up Christ from the dead shall also quicken your mortal bodies by His Spirit that dwelleth in you.*"
Gal. 3:5 "*He therefore that ministereth to you the Spirit, and worketh miracles among you...*"
Heb. 2:4 "*God also bearing them witness, both with signs and wonders, and with divers miracles, and gifts of the Holy Ghost, according to His own will...*"
Heb. 12:13 "... *but let it rather be healed.*"
Jms. 5:13-16 "*Is any among you afflicted? Let him pray... is any sick among you? Let him call for the elders of the church; and let them pray over him, anointing him with oil in the name of the Lord: and the prayer of faith shall save the sick, and the Lord shall raise him up; and if he have committed sins, they shall be forgiven him. Confess your faults one to another, and pray one for another, that ye may be healed. The effectual fervent prayer of a righteous man availeth much* (is "powerful and effective" Jms. 5:16 NIV; "accomplish much" NASB)."
I Pet. 2:24 "... *by whose stripes ye were healed.*" (Is.53:4,5, 16)
III Jn. 2 "*Beloved, I wish above all things that thou mayest... be in health...*"
It is God's will you be in health and if we know it is God's will, we know He will answer our prayers, I Jn. 5:14,15.

Money/Mammon

See also section on Riches
Lk. 16:11 "*If... ye have not been faithful in the unrighteous mammon, who will commit to your trust the true riches? And if ye have not been faithful in that which is another man's, who shall give you that which is your own?*"

The promise is that if you are faithful with money on this earth, God will give you the true riches that can never be taken away from you in heaven!

Mountain / Move Mountains

Ps. 30:6 "And in my prosperity I said, I shall never be moved... by Thy favour Thou hast made my mountain to stand strong..."
Zech. 4:7 "Who art thou, O great mountain? Before Zerubbabel thou shalt become a plain: and he shall bring forth the Headstone (Jesus) thereof with shoutings, crying, Grace, grace unto it."
Mk. 11:23,24 "For verily I say unto you, That whosoever shall say unto this mountain, Be thou removed, and be thou cast into the sea; and shall not doubt in his heart, but shall believe that those things which he saith shall come to pass; he shall have whatsoever he saith. Therefore I say unto you, What things soever ye desire, when ye pray, believe that ye receive them, and ye shall have them."

Mystery

Eph. 1:9 "... having made known unto us the mystery of His will, according to His good pleasure which He had purposed in Himself..."
Eph. 3:3-6 "... how that by revelation He made known unto me the mystery... (that) ye may understand my knowledge in the mystery of Christ... is now revealed unto His Holy Apostles, and prophets by the Spirit; that the Gentiles should be fellow heirs, and of the same body, and partakers of His promise in Christ by the Gospel..."
Eph. 3:9 "... and to make all men see what is the fellowship of the mystery, which from the beginning of the world hath been hid in God, who created all things by Jesus Christ."

Names

Lk. 10:20 "... rejoice because your names are written in heaven."

Never Fails

Deut. 31:6 *"Be strong and of a good courage, fear not, nor be afraid of them: for the Lord thy God, He it is that doth go with thee; He will not fail thee, nor forsake thee."*

New Earth / New Jerusalem

See section on Heaven

New Name

Is. 62:2 *"... thou shalt be called by a new name, which the mouth of the Lord shall name."*
Rev. 2:17 *"... and I will give him a white stone, and in the stone a new name written, which no man knoweth saying he that receiveth it."*

Ocean / Sea / Storms / Waves

I Kings 19:12 God was not in the storm with Elijah but spoke to him in a still small voice.
Job 38:1 God spoke to Job out of the storm
Ps. 55:6,8 *"I said, Oh that I had wings like a dove! For then would I fly away, and be at rest... I would hasten my escape from the windy storm and tempest."*
Ps. 93:4 *"The Lord on high is mightier than the noise of many waters, yea, than the mighty waves of the sea."*
Ps. 89:8,9 *"O Lord God of hosts, who is a strong Lord like unto Thee? Or to Thy faithfulness round about Thee? Thou rulest the raging of the sea: when the waves thereof arise, Thou stillest them."*
Ps. 107:29,30 *"He maketh the storm a calm, so that the waves thereof are still. Then are they glad because they be quiet; so He bringeth them unto their desired haven."*
Is. 4:6 *"And there shall be a Tabernacle for a shadow in the daytime from the heat, and for a place of refuge, and for a covert from storm and... rain."*
Is. 25:4,5 *"For Thou hast been a strength to the poor, a strength to the needy in his distress, a refuge from the storm, a shadow from the heat, when the blast of the terrible ones is as a storm against the wall. Thou shalt bring*

down the noise of strangers, as the heat in a dry place: even the heat with the shadow of a cloud: the branch of the terrible ones shall be brought low."
Matt. 8:26 "... why are ye fearful, O ye of little faith? Then He arose, and rebuked the winds and the sea... even the winds and the sea obey Him!"
Mk. 4:39-41 "And He arose, and rebuked the wind, and said unto the sea, Peace, be still. And the wind ceased, and there was a great calm. And He said unto them, Why are ye so fearful? How is it that ye have no faith?"
Lk. 8:24-25 "(they) awoke Him, saying, Master, Master, we perish. Then He arose, and rebuked the wind and the raging of the water: and they ceased, and there was a calm. And He said unto them, Where is your faith? And they being afraid wondered, saying one to another, What manner of man is this? For He commandeth even the winds and water, and they obey Him."

Old Age

Deut. 33:25 "... as thy days, so shall thy strength be..."
Ruth 4:15 "And he shall be unto thee a restorer of thy life, and a nourisher of thine old age: for thy daughter in law, which loveth thee, which is better to thee than seven sons, hath born him."
Ps. 71:9 "Cast me not off in the time of old age; forsake me not when my strength faileth."
Ps. 71:18 "... when I am old and grayheaded, O God, forsake me not..."
Ps. 92:12-14 "The righteous shall flourish like the palm tree: he shall grow like a cedar in Lebanon. Those that be planted in the house of the Lord shall flourish in the courts of our God. They shall still bring forth fruit in old age; they shall be fat and flourishing..."
Ps. 92:14 NLT "... they will remain vital and green."
Prov. 16:31 "The ("gray head" HCSB) is a crown of glory, if it be found in the way of righteousness."
Is. 46:4 "And even to your old age I am He; and even to... (silver) hairs will I carry you: I have made, and I will bear; even I will carry, and will deliver you."
Is. 46:4 TLB "I will be your God through all your lifetime, yes, even when your hair is white with age. I made you and I will care for you. I will carry you along and be your Savior."
I Cor. 1:8,9 "Who shall also confirm ("strengthen" HCSB) you unto the end, that ye may be blameless in the day of our Lord Jesus Christ. God is faithful, by whom ye were called unto the fellowship of His Son Jesus Christ our Lord."
II Cor. 4:16,17 "For which cause we faint not; but though our outward man perish ("is wasting away" ESV) yet the inward man is renewed day by day."

Oppression / Oppressor(s) / Terrify

Ps. 9:9 *"The Lord also will be a refuge ("shelter" NLT) for the oppressed, a refuge in times of trouble."*

Ps. 10:17,18 *"Lord, Thou hast heard the desire of the humble: Thou wilt prepare their heart, Thou wilt cause Thine ear to hear: to Judge the fatherless and the oppressed, that the man of the earth may no more oppress."*
(Ps. 10:18 NIV *"... man, who is of the earth, may terrify no more."*
(Ps. 10:18 NLT *"... so people can no longer terrify them."*

Ps. 72:4 *"He shall Judge the poor of the people, He shall save the children of the needy, and shall break in pieces the oppressor."*

Ps. 103:6 *"The Lord executeth righteousness and Judgment for all that are oppressed."*

Ps. 107:13,19 *"Then they cried unto the Lord in their trouble, and He saved them out of their distresses..."*

Prov. 20:22 *"... wait on the Lord, and He shall save thee* (from oppression)" (God will plead our case against Oppressors

Prov. 22:22,23 *"... neither oppress the afflicted in the gate: for the Lord will plead their cause, and spoil the soul of those that spoiled them."*

Prov. 22:22,23 NIV *"Do not exploit the poor because they are poor and do not crush the needy in court, for the Lord will take up their case and will plunder those who plunder them."*

Is. 14:3-5 *"And it shall come to pass in the day that the Lord shall give thee rest from thy sorrow, and from thy fear, and from the hard bondage wherein thou wast made to serve, that thou shalt take up this proverb... how hath the oppresssor ceased... the Lord hath broken the staff of the wicked, and the scepter of the rulers..."*

Jer. 30:20 *"... I will punish all that oppress ("hurts" NLT) them."*

Acts 7:34 *"I have seen... the affliction of My people... I have heard their groaning, and am come down to deliver them..."*

Jer. 50:33,34 *"... the children of Israel and the children of Judah were oppressed together: and all that took them captives held them fast: they refused to let them go. Their Redeemer is strong; the Lord of hosts is His name: He shall thoroughly plead their cause, that He may give rest to the land..."*

Path / Steps / Lead / Led

Ps. 37:23 *"The steps of a good man are ordered by the Lord: and He delighteth in his way."*

Prov. 3:5,6 *"Trust in the Lord with all thine heart; and lean not unto thine own understanding. In all thy ways acknowledge Him, and He shall direct thy paths."*
Prov. 4:11 *"I have taught thee in the way of wisdom; I have led thee in right paths."*
Prov. 8:20 *"I lead ("walk"* NASB) *in the way of righteousness, in the midst of the paths of Judgment..."*
Prov. 16:9 *"A man's heart deviseth his way: but the Lord directeth his steps."*
Is. 42:16 *"And I will bring the blind by a way that they knew not; I will lead them in paths that they have not known: I will make darkness light before them, and crooked things straight. These things will I do unto them, and not forsake them."*
Is. 58:10 *"... if thou draw out thy soul to the hungry, and satisfy the afflicted soul; then... the Lord shall guide thee continually ..."*

Peace

Ps. 29:11 *"... the Lord will bless His people with peace."*
Ps. 37:11 *"But the meek shall inherit the earth; and shall delight themselves in the abundance of peace."*
Ps. 37:37 *"Mark the perfect man, and behold the upright: for the end of that man is peace."*
Ps. 72:3,7 *"The mountains shall bring peace to the people... in his days shall the righteous flourish; and abundance of peace so long as the moon endureth."*
Ps. 85:8 *"I will hear what God the Lord will speak: for He will speak peace unto His people, and to His saints: but let them not turn again to folly."*
Ps. 119:165 *"Great peace have they which love Thy law: and nothing shall offend them."*
Prov. 16:7 *"When a man's ways please the Lord, He maketh even his enemies to be at peace with him."*
Is. 26:3,4 *"Thou wilt keep him in perfect peace, whose mind is stayed on Thee: because he trusteth in Thee. Trust ye in the Lord forever: for in the Lord Jehovah is everlasting strength..."*
Is. 26:12 *"Lord, Thou wilt ordain peace for us: for Thou also hast wrought all our works in us."*
Is. 48:18 *"O that thou hadst hearkened to My Commandments! Then had thy peace been as a river, and thy righteousness as the waves of the sea..."*

Is. 54:10 *"For the mountains shall depart, and the hills be removed; but My kindness shall not depart from thee, neither shall the Covenant of My peace be removed, saith the Lord that hath mercy on thee."*
Is. 57:2 *"He shall enter into peace: they shall rest in their beds, each one walking in his uprightness."*
Is. 57:19 *"... peace, peace to him who is far off, and him that is near, saith the Lord..."*
Is. 47:2 LB *"For the godly who die shall rest in peace."*
Is. 66:12 *"For thus saith the Lord, Behold, I will extend peace to her* (New Jerusalem) *like a river, and the glory of the Gentiles like a flowing stream..."*
Jer. 29:11,12 *"For I know the thoughts that I think toward you, saith the Lord, thoughts of peace, and not of evil, to give you an expected end."*
Jn. 14:27 *"Peace I leave with you, My peace I give unto you: not as the world giveth, give I unto you. Let not your heart be troubled, neither let it be afraid*
Jn. 20:21 *"Then said Jesus to them again, Peace be unto you..."*
Rom. 5:1 *"Therefore being Justified by faith, we have peace with God through our Lord Jesus Christ..."*
Rom. 14:17,19 *"For the kingdom of God is not meat and drink; but righteousness, and peace, and joy in the Holy Ghost... let us therefore follow after the things which make for peace..."*
Rom. 15:13 *"Now the God of hope fill you with all joy and peace in believing, that ye may abound in hope, through the power of the Holy Ghost."*
Phil. 4:9 *"Be careful for nothing: but in everything by prayer and supplication with thanksgiving let your requests be made known unto God. And the God of peace shall be with you."*
II Tim. 1:2 *"... grace, mercy, and peace, from... the Father and Christ Jesus..."*

Perfect / Faultless

Matt. 5:48 *"Be ye therefore perfect, even as your Father in heaven is perfect."* The power to be perfect is in the promise; our perfection is in Jesus!
Col. 4:12 *"... that ye may stand perfect and complete in all the will of God."*

Perish

Matt. 18:14 *"It is not the will of your Father which is in heaven that one of these little ones should perish."*
Lk. 21:18 *"... but there shall not an hair of your head perish..."*

Jn. 3:15,16 *"That whosoever believeth in Him should not perish, but have eternal life. For God so loved the world, that He gave His only begotten Son, that whosoever believeth in Him should not perish, but have everlasting life."*
Jn. 10:28 *"And I give unto them eternal life; and they shall never perish, neither shall any man pluck them out of My hand."*
II Cor. 4:16 *"... though our outward man perish, yet the inward man is renewed day by day."*
II Pet. 3:9 *"The Lord is not slack concerning His promise, as some men count slackness; but is longsuffering to usward, not willing that any should perish, but that all should come to repentance."*

Plagues

Solomon's prayer
I Kings 8:35-40 *"When heaven is shut up and there is no rain, because they have sinned against Thee; if they pray toward this plac (now we pray toward heaven) and confess Thy name, and turn from their sin, when Thou afflictest them: then hear Thou in heaven, and forgive the sin of Thy servants, and of Thy people Israel, that Thou teach them the good way wherein they should walk, and give rain upon Thy land, which Thou hast given to Thy people for an inheritance. If there be in the land famine, if there be pestilence, blasting, mildew, locust, or if there be caterpillar; if their enemy besiege them in the land of their cities; whatsoever plague, whatsoever sickness there be; what prayer and suppli-cation soever be made by any man, or by all Thy people Israel, which shall know every man the plague of his own heart, and spread forth his hands toward this house: then hear Thou in heaven Thy dwelling place, and forgive, and do, and give to every man according to his ways whose heart Thou knowest; (for Thou, even Thou only, knowest the hearts of all the children of men); that they may fear Thee all the days that they live in the land which Thou gavest unto our fathers."* Ps. 91:1-10
"He that dwelleth in the secret place place of the Most High shall abide under the shadow of the Almighty. I will say of the Lord, He is my refuge and my fortress: my God; in Him will I trust. Surely He shall deliver thee from the snare of the fowler, and from the noisome pestilence. He shall cover thee with His feathers, and under His wings shalt thou trust: His truth shall be thy shield and buckler. Thou shalt not be afraid for the terror by night; nor for the arrow that flieth by day... for the arrow that flieth by day; nor for the pestilence that walketh in darkness; nor for the destruction that wasteth at noonday. A thousand shall fall at thy side, and ten thousand at thy right hand; but it shall not come nigh thee. Only with thine eyes shalt thou behold

and see the reward of the wicked. Because thou hast made the Lord, which is my refuge, even the Most High, thy habitation. There shall no evil befall thee, neither shall any plague come nigh thy dwelling."

Plans

Jer. 29:10-14 NIV "For I (God) know the plans I have for you... plans to prosper you and not to harm you, plans to give you hope and a future."
Jer. 29:10-14 "... I will visit you, and perform My good Word toward you in causing you to return to this place. For I know the thoughts that I think toward you, saith the Lord, thoughts of peace, and not of evil, to give you an expected end. Then shall ye call upon Me, and ye shall go and pray unto Me, and I will hearken unto you. And ye shall seek Me, and find Me, when ye shall search for Me with all your heart. And I will be found of you, saith the Lord: and I will turn away your captivity, and I will gather you from all the nations.. and I will bring you again into the place whence I caused you to be carried away captive."

Pleasure / Please (ing)

I Chron. 29:17 "... my God, that Thou triest the heart, and hast pleasure in up-rightness..."
Ps. 16:11 "Thou wilt shew me the path of life: in Thy presence is fullness of joy; at Thy right hand there are pleasures forevermore."
Ps. 35:27 "Let the Lord be magnified, which hath pleasure in the prosperity of His servant."
Ps. 69:30,31 "I will praise the name of God with a song, and will magnify Him with thanksgiving. This also shall please the Lord..."
Ps. 147:11 "The Lord taketh pleasure in them that fear Him, in those that hope in His mercy."
Ps. 149:4 "For the Lord taketh pleasure in His people: He will beautify the meek with Salvation."
Prov. 16:7 "When a man's ways please the Lord, He maketh even His enemies to be at peace with Him."
Is. 55:11 "So shall My Word be that goeth forth out of My mouth: it shall not return unto Me void, but it shall accomplish that which I please, and it shall prosper in the thing whereto I sent it."
Is. 56:4 "For thus saith the Lord unto the eunuchs that keep My Sabbaths, and choose the things that please Me, and take hold of My Covenant..."
Lk. 12:32 "... it is your Father's good pleasure to give you the kingdom."

Jn. 8:29 "... the Father hath not left Me (Jesus) alone; for I do always those things that please Him."
(We are to walk as He walked, I Jn.2:6.)
Rom. 8:8 "So then they that are in the flesh cannot please God. But ye are not in the flesh, but in the Spirit, if so be that the Spirit of God dwell in you."
Rom. 15:3 "For even Christ pleased not Himself..."
I Cor. 7:32 "... he that is unmarried careth for the things that belong to the Lord, how he may please the Lord..."
I Cor. 12:18 "But now hath God set the members every one of them in the body, as it hath pleased Him."
Eph. 1:9 HCSB "He made known to us the mystery of His will, according to His good pleasure..."
Phil. 2:13 "... God... worketh in you... to will and to do of His good pleasure."
Col. 1:19 "For it pleased the Father that in Him should all fullness dwell..."
I Thess. 4:1 "... walk and... please God, so ye would abound more..."
II Thess. 1:11 "Wherefore also we pray always for you, that our God would count you worthy of this calling, and fulfill all the good pleasure of His goodness, and the work of faith with power..."
II Tim. 2:4 "No man that warreth entangleth himself with the affairs of this life; that he may please Him who hath chosen him to be a soldier."
Heb. 11:5,6 "... he (Enoch) had this testimony, that he pleased God. But without faith it is impossible to please Him..."
Heb. 13:16 "But to do good and to communicate forget not: for with such sac-rifices God is well pleased."
Rev. 4:11 "Thou art worthy (Lord) to receive glory.. honour... power: for Thou hast created all things, and for Thy pleasure they are and were created."

Poor

Ps. 40:17 "But I am poor and needy; yet the Lord thinketh upon me: Thou art my help and my deliverer; make no tarrying, O my God."
Ps. 72:12 NKJV "For He will deliver the needy when he cries, the poor also, and him who has no helper."
Ps. 113:7 "He raiseth up the poor out of the dust, and lifteth the needy out of the dunghill; that He may set him with princes, even with the princes of His people."
Prov. 14:31 "He that oppresseth the poor reproacheth his Maker: but he that honoureth Him hath mercy on the poor."
Prov. 22:9 "He that hath a bountiful eye shal be blessed; for he giveth of his bread to the poor."

Prov. 28:27 *"Better is the poor that walketh in his uprightness, than he that is perverse in his ways, though he be rich."*
Matt. 19:21 *"... if thou would be perfect, go and sell that thou hast... give to the poor... thou shalt have treasure in heaven... come and follow Me."*
Gal. 2:10 *"... we should remember the poor..."*

Power

See Holy Spirit

Prayer / Pray

II Chron. 30:27 *"... their voice was heard, and their prayer came up to His Holy dwelling place, even unto heaven."*
Ps. 6:9 *"The Lord hath heard my supplication* (and) *will receive my prayer."*
Ps. 102:16,17 *"When the Lord shall build up Zion, He shall appear in His glory. He will regard the prayer of the destitute."*
Prov. 15:29 *"... He heareth the prayer of the righteous..."*
Jer. 29:11-14 *"For I know the thoughts that I think toward you, saith the Lord, thoughts of peace, and not of evil, to give you an expected end. Then shall ye call upon Me, and ye shall go and pray unto Me, and I will hearken unto you. And ye shall seek Me, and find Me, when ye shall search for Me with all your heart."*
Mk. 11:24 *"Therefore I say unto you, What things soever ye desire, when ye pray, believe that ye receive them, and ye shall have them."*
Lk. 1:13 *"... the angel said unto... (Zacharias) Fear not... thy prayer is heard..."*
Lk. 22:32 *"... I have prayed for thee, that thy faith fail not; and when thou art converted, strengthen thy brethren."*
I Pet. 3:12 *"For the eyes of the Lord are over the righteous, and His ears are open unto their prayers..."*

Preserve

Ps. 97:10 *"Ye that love the Lord, hate evil: He preserveth the souls of His saints; He delivereth them out of the hand of the wicked."*

Prisoner

Ps. 146:7,8 "... the Lord looseth the prisoner..."

Prize

I Cor. 9:24 "Know ye not that they which run in a race run all, but one receiveth the prize? So run, that ye may obtain... they do it to obtain a corruptible crown; but we an incorruptible."
Phil. 3:14 "I press toward the mark for the prize of the high calling of God in Christ Jesus."
(See also Crown and Race

Promises (s) / The Word

Deut. 1:11 AMP "May the Lord... bless you as He has promised you."
Josh. 23:10 "One of your men puts to flight a thousand, for the Lord your God is He who fights for you, just as He promised you."
Josh. 23:14,15 "... not one thing hath failed of all the good things which the Lord your God spake concerning you; all are come to pass unto you, and not one thing hath failed therof... as all good things are come upon you, which the Lord your God promised you..."
I Kings 8:23 "... there is no God like Thee, in heaven above, or on earth beneath, who keepest Covenant and mercy with Thy servants that walk before Thee with all their heart: who hast kept with Thy servant David my father that Thou promisedst him: Thou spakest also with Thy mouth, and hast fulfilled it with Thine hand, as it is this day."
I Kings 8:56 "Blessed be the Lord, that hath given rest unto His people Israel, according to all that He promised: there hath not failed one word of all his good promises..."
II Kings 20:9 "... the Lord will do the thing that He hath spoken (promised)..."
I Chron. 17:26,27 "And now, Lord, Thou art God, and hast promised this goodness unto Thy servant: now therefore let it please Thee to bless the house of Thy servant, that it may be before Thee forever: for Thou blessedst, O Lord, and it shall be blessed forever."
Ps. 105:42 "For He remembered His Holy promise..."
Ps. 119:38 LB "Reassure me that Your promises are for me, for I trust and revere You."
Ps. 119:42 LB "... for I trust Your promises."

Ps. 119:49,50 LB *"Never forget Your promises to me Your servant, for they are my only hope. They give me strength in all my troubles; how they refresh and revive me!"*

Ps. 119:57 LB *"... and I promise to obey! With all my heart I want Your blessings. Be merciful just as You promised."*

Ps. 119:65 LB *"... I am overflowing with Your blessings, just as You promised."*

Ps. 119:76 LB *"... let Your lovingkindness comfort me, just as you promised."*

Ps. 119:81,82 TLB *"I faint for Your Salvation; but I expect your help, for you have promised it. My eyes are straining to see Your promises come true. When will You comfort me with your help?"*

Ps. 119:82 NIV *"My eyes fail, looking for Your promise..."*

Ps. 119:95 TLB *"Though the wicked hide along the way to kill me, I will quietly keep my mind upon Your promises."*

Ps. 119:116 *"Uphold me according unto Thy Word ("promise" NIV)..."*

Ps. 119:148 NIV *"My eyes stay open through the watches of the night, that I may meditate on Your promises."*

Ps. 119:162 NIV *"I rejoice in Your promise like one who finds great spoil."*

Ps. 119:170 NIV *"May my supplication come before You; deliver me according to Your promise."*

Ps. 145:13 NIV *"Your kingdom is an everlasting kingdom, and Your dominion endures through all generations. The Lord is trustworthy in all He promises and faithful in all He does."*

Is. 34:16 *... no one of these* (promises) *shall fail, none shall want her mate..."*

Is. 55:11 *"So shall My Word be that goeth forth out of My mouth; it shall not return unto me void, but it shall accomplish that which I please, and it shall prosper in the thing whereto I sent it."*

Jer. 1:12 *"Then said the Lord unto me, Thou hast well seen: for I will hasten My Word to perform it."*

Jer. 29:10 NLT *"... I will... do for you all the good things I have promised..."*

Jer. 32:42 *"... so will I bring upon them all the good that I have promised..."*

Jer. 33:14 *"... the days come... that I* (God) *will perform that good thing which I have promised unto the house of Israel, and to the house of Judah."*

Lk. 1:72 *"To perform the mercy promised to our fathers..."*

Lk. 24:49 At Pentecost, *"... I send the promise of My Father upon you... tarry ye in the city of Jerusalem, until ye be endued with power from on high."*

Acts 1:4,5 At Pentecost, *"... wait for the promise of the Father... ye shall be baptized with the Holy Ghost not many days hence."*

Acts 2:39 *"For the promise is unto you, and to your children, and to all that are afar off, even as many as the lord our God shall call."*

Acts 13:33,34 NLT *"... I am here to bring you this Good News. God's promise to our ancestors has come true in our own time, in that God raised Jesus.*

This is what the second Psalm is talking about when it says concerning Jesus, 'You are My Son. Today I have become Your Father. For God had promised to raise Him from the dead, never again to die. This is stated in the Scripture that says, 'I will give you the sacred blessings I promised to David'."

Rom. 1:1,2 *"Paul... separated unto the Gospel... (Which He had promised afore by His prophets in the Holy Scriptures), concerning His Son Jesus..."*

Rom. 4:16 *"Therefore it is of faith, that it might be by grace; to the end the promise might be sure to all thy seed, not to that only which is of the law, but to that also which is of the faith of Abraham; who is the father of us all..."*

Rom. 4:21 *"And being fully persuaded that, what He had promised, He was able also to perform."*

Rom. 9:4 *"... Israelites... to whom pertaineth the adoption... the glory... the Covenants... the giving of the law... the service of God, and the promises..."*

Rom. 9:8 *"... the children of the promise are counted for the seed. For this is the Word of promise..."*

Rom. 15:8,9 *"... Jesus... to confirm the promises made unto the fathers..."*

II Cor. 1:20 *"For all the promises of God in Him are yea, and in Him Amen..."*

II Cor. 7:1 *"Having therefore these promises, dearly beloved, let us cleanse ourselves from all filthiness of the flesh and spirit, perfecting Holiness in the fear of God."*

Gal. 3:14,16 *"... that we might receive the promise of the Spirit through faith... to Abraham and his Seed were the promises made... which is Christ."*

Gal. 3:21,22 *"Is the law then against the promises of God? God forbid... that the promise by faith of Jesus Christ might be given to them that believe..."*

Gal. 3:29 *"... heirs according to the promise."*

Gal. 4:23 *"... he of the freewoman was by promise."*

Gal. 4:28,29 *"... we... as Isaac... are the children of promise..."*

Eph. 1:13,14 *"... in whom also after that ye believed, ye were sealed with that Holy Spirit of promise, which is the earnest of our inheritance until the Redemption of the purchased possession..."*

Eph. 2:12 *"That at that time ye were without Christ... strangers from the Cove-nants of promise, having no hope... without God in the world.."*

Eph. 3:6 *"That the Gentiles should be fellowheirs, and of the same body, and partakers of His promise in Christ by the Gospel..."*

Eph.6:2,3 *"Honour thy father and mother; (which is the first Commandment with promise); that it may be well with thee, and thou mayest live long on the earth."*

I Tim. 4:8 *"... but godliness is profitable unto all things, having promise of the life that now is, and of that which is to come."*

II Tim. 1:1 *"Paul, an Apostle of Jesus Christ by the will of God, according to the promise of life which is in Christ Jesus..."*

II Tim. 2:13,14 LB "... *If we are unfaithful, He remains faithful... and He will always carry out His promise to us...*"

Titus 1:2 "*In hope of eternal life, which God, that cannot lie, promised before the world began...*"

Heb. 6:12-15,18 "*... who through faith and patience inherit the promises. For when God made promise to Abraham... saying, Surely blessing I will bless thee, and multiplying I will multiply thee... after he had patiently endured, he obtained the promise... God, willing more abundantly to shew unto the heirs of promise the immutability of His counsel, confirmed it by an oath...*"

(Heb. 6:15-18 NIV "*Then Abraham waited patiently, and he received what God had promised. When people take an oath, they call on someone greater than themselves to hold them to it. And without any question that oath is binding. God also bound Himself with an oath, so that those who received the promise could be perfectly sure that He would never change His mind. So God has given us both His promise and His oath. These two things are unchangeable because it is impossible for God to lie. Therefore, we who have fled to Him for refuge can take new courage, for we can hold on to His promise with confidence.*"

(Heb. 6:18 PB "*... by the promise and by the oath... hope that is promised...*"

Heb. 7:6,7 Melchizedek "*... whose descent is not counted from them received tithes of Abraham, and blessed him that had the promises. And without all contradiction the less is blessed of the better...*"

Heb. 8:6 "*... He (Jesus) is the mediator of a better Covenant, which was established upon better promises.*"

Heb. 9:15 "*... they which are called might receive the promise of eternal inheritance.*"

Heb. 10:23 "*Let us hold fast the profession of our faith without wavering; (for He is faithful that promised)...*"

Heb. 10:36 "*For ye have need of patience, that, after ye have done the will of God, ye might receive the promise.*"

Heb. 11:11,13 "*... because she (Sara) Judged Him faithful who had promised ... these all died in faith, not having received the promises, but having seen them afar off...*"

Heb. 11:17 "*By faith Abraham... received the promises...*"

Heb. 11:33-35 "*Who through faith subdued kingdoms, wrought righteousness, obtained promises, stopped the mouths of lions, quenched the violence of fire, escaped the edge of the sword, out of weakness were made strong, waxed valiant in fight, turned to flight the armies of the aliens* ("put foreign armies to flight" ESV). *Women received their dead raised to life again...*"

Jms. 1:12 *"Blessed is the man that endureth temptation: for when he is tried, he shall receive the crown of life, which the Lord hath promised to them that love Him."*

Jms. 2:5 *"... hath not God chosen the poor of this world rich in faith, and heirs of the kingdom which He hath promised to them that love Him?"*

II Pet. 1:3,4 *"According as His divine power hath given unto us all things that pertain unto life and godliness, through the knowledge of Him that hath called us to glory and virtue: whereby are given unto us exceeding great and precious promises: that by these you might be partakers of the divine nature, having escaped the corruption that is in the world through lust ..."*

II Pet. 3:9 *"The Lord is not slack concerning His promise... not willing that any should perish, but that all should come to repentance."*

II Pet. 3:13 *"Nevertheless we, according to His promise, look for new heavens and a new earth, wherein dwelleth righteousness."*

I Jn. 2:25 *"... this is the promise that He hath promised us, even eternal life."*

Propitiation

Some people don't like this word because they don't understand it.

"Propitiation, that by which God is rendered propitious, i.e., by which it becomes consistent with his character and government to pardon and bless the sinner. The propitiation does not procure His love or make Him loving; it only renders it consistent for Him to exercise His love towards sinners. In Rom. 3:25 and Heb. 9:5 (A.V., 'mercy-seat') the Greek word hilasterion is used. It is the word employed by the LXX. Translators in Ex. 25:17 and elsewhere as the equivalent for the Hebrew kapporeth, which means 'covering' and is used of the lid of the Ark of the Covenant (Ex.25:21;30:6). This Greek word (hilasterion) came to denote not only the mercy seat or lid of the Ark, but also propitiation or reconciliation by blood. On the great day of Atonement the high priest carried the blood of the sacrifice he offered for all the people within the veil and sprinkled with it the 'mercy seat', and so made propitiation.

In I Jn.2:2;4:10, Christ is called the "propitiation for our sins". Here a dfferent Greek word is used (hilasmos). Christ is 'the propitiation', because by His becoming our substitute and assuming our obligations he expiated our guilt, covered it, by the vicarios punishment which He endured. (Compare Heb. 2:17, where the expression 'make reconciliation' of the A.V. is more correctly in the RSV 'make propitiation')."

www.biblestudytools.com/dictionary/propitiation

Rom. 3:25 "*Whom God hath set forth to be a propitiation through faith in His blood, to declare His righteousness for the remission of sins that are past, through the forbearance of God...*"
Heb. 2:17 NASB "*Therefore, He had to be made like His brethren in all things, so that He might become a merciful and faithful high priest in things pertaining to God, to make propitiation ("reconciliation" KJV; "atonement" BSB) for the sins of the people.*"
I Jn. 2:1,2 "*... if any man sin, we have an advocate with the Father, Jesus Christ the righteous: and He is the propitiation for our sins: and not for ours only, but also for the sins of the whole world.*"
I Jn. 4:10 "*Herein is love, not that we loved God, but that He loved us, and sent His Son to be the propitiation for our sins.*"

Protect / Protection / Hedge

II Sam. 22:3,4 "*... You save me from violence. I call upon the Lord, who is worthy to be praised, and I am saved from my enemies.*"
Job 1:10 NLT "*Hast not Thou made an hedge about him, and about his house, and about all that he hath on every side? Thou hast blessed the work of his hands, and his substance is increased in the land.*"
(Job 42:10,12 "*And the Lord turned the captivity of Job, when he prayed for his friends: also the Lord gave Job twice as much as he had before... so the Lord blessed the latter end of Job more than his beginning...*"
Ps. 124:2-8 NIV "*If the Lord had not been on our side when people attacked us, they would have swallowed us alive when their anger flared against us; the flood would have engulfed us, the torrent would have swept over us, the raging waters would have swept us away. Praise be to the Lord, who has not let us be torn by their teeth. We have escaped like a bird from the fowler's snare; the snare has been broken, and we have escaped. Our help is in the name of the Lord, the Maker of heaven and earth.*"
Ps. 138:7 "*Though I walk in the midst of trouble, You preserve My life; You stretch out Your hand against the wrath of my enemies, and Your right hand delivers me.*"
II Thess. 3:3 "*... the Lord is faithful, who shall stablish you, and keep you from evil.*"
II Tim. 4:8 "*The Lord will rescue me from every evil deed and bring me safely into His heavenly kingdom. To Him be the glory forever and ever. Amen!*"

Race

Ps. 19:5 *"Which is as a bridegroom coming out of his chamber, and rejoiceth as a strong man to run a race."*
Talking about the sun which is an allegory of Jesus at the second coming.
Eccl. 9:11 *"... the race is not to the swift, nor the battle to the strong..."*
Matt. 24:13 *"He that endures (perseveres) to the end will be saved."*
I Cor. 9:24 *"Know ye not that they which run in a race run all, but one receiveth the prize? So run, that ye may obtain."*
Phil 2:15,16 *"That ye may be blameless and harmless, the sons of God, without rebuke, in the midst of a crooked and perverse nation among whom ye shine as lights in the world; holding forth the Word of life; that I may rejoice in the day of Christ, that I have not run (the race) in vain, neither labored in vain."*
Phil. 3:14 *"I press on toward the goal to win the prize for which God has called me heavenward in Christ Jesus."*
Heb. 12:1 *"Wherefore seeing we also are compassed about with so great a cloud of witnesses, let us lay aside every weight, and the sin which doth so easily beset us, and let us run with patience the race, that is set before us looking unto Jesus the author and finisher of our faith..."*
See Prize

Rain

See also Latter Rain
Lev. 26:4-13 rain in season/land yield her increase
Deut. 11:14,15 *"That I will give you the rain of your land in his due season, the first rain and the latter rain... and I will send ("give" KJV fn) grass in thy fields for thy cattle, that thou mayest eat and be full."*
Deut. 28:12 *"The Lord shall open unto thee His good treasure, the heaven to give the rain unto thy land in his season..."*
Job 28:26 *"When He made a decree for the rain, and a way for the lightning of the thunder..."*
Job 29:23 *"And they waited for Me as for the rain; and they opened their mouth wide as for the latter rain."*
Ps. 65:9 *"Thou visitest the earth, and waterest it: Thou greatly enriches it with the river of God, which is full of water: thou prepares them corn... Thou waterest the ridges thereof abundantly: Thou settlest the furrows thereof: Thou makest it soft with showers: Thou blessest the springing thereof. Thou crownest the year with Thy goodness; and Thy paths drop fatness. They drop*

upon the pastures of the wilderness; and the little hills rejoice on every side. The pastures are clothed with flocks; the valleys also are covered over with corn; they shout for joy, they also sing."

Ps. 68:9 "Thou, O God, didst send a plentiful rain..."

Ps. 72:6 "He shall come down like rain upon the mown grass: as showers that water the earth."

Ps. 147:8,9 "Who covereth the heaven with clouds, who prepareth rain for the earth, who maketh grass to grow upon the mountains. He giveth to the beast his food, and to the young ravens which cry."

Prov. 16:15 "... and His favour is as a cloud of the Latter Rain."

Is. 30:23 "Then shall He give the rain of thy seed, that thou shalt sow the ground withal..."

Is. 30:23 NASB "Then He will give you rain for the seed which you will sow in the ground, and bread from the yield of the ground, and it will be rich and plenteous; on that day your livestock will graze in a roomy pasture."

Is. 44:3 "For I will pour water upon him that is thirsty, and floods upon the dry ground: I will pour My Spirit upon thy seed, and My blessing upon thine off-spring..."

Is. 45:8 "... let the skies pour down righteousness: let the earth open and let them bring forth Salvation, and let righteousness spring up together; I the Lord have created it."

Jer. 5:24 "Neither say they in their heart, Let us now fear the Lord our God, that giveth rain, both the former and the latter, in His season: He reserveth unto us the appointed weeks of the harvest."

Jer. 3:3 "Therefore the showers have been withholden, and there hath been no latter rain..."

Jer. 5:24 "But this people hath a revolting and a rebellious heart... neither say they in their heart, Let us now fear the Lord our God, that giveth rain, both the former and the latter, in His season: He re-serveth unto us the appointed weeks of the harvest. Your iniquities have turned away these things, and your sins have withholden good things from you."

Ez. 34:26 "... I will cause the shower to come down in his season; there shall be showers of blessing."

Joel 2:23 "... for He hath given you the former rain moderately, and He will cause to come down for you the rain, the former rain, and the latter rain in the first month."

Joel 2:28,29 "And it shall come to pass afterward, that I will pour out My Spirit upon all flesh; and your sons and your daughters shall prophesy, your old men shall dream dreams, your young men shall see visions... in those days will I pour out My Spirit."

Hosea 6:3 "... *and He shall come unto us as the rain, as the latter and former rain unto the earth.*"

Hosea 10:12 "*Sow to yourselves in righteousness, reap in mercy; break up your fallow ground: for it is time to seek the Lord, till He come and rain righteousness upon you.*"

Zech. 10:1 "*Ask ye of the Lord rain in the time of the latter rain; so the Lord shall make bright clouds, and give them showers of rain, to everyone grass in the field.*"

Matt. 3:11,12 "*... He shall baptize you with the Holy Ghost, and with fire...*"

Matt. 5:45 "*... for He maketh His sun to rise on the evil and on the good, and sendeth rain on the just and on the unjust.*"

Acts 2:17-19,21 "*And it shall come to pass in the last days, saith God, I will pour out of My Spirit upon all flesh: and your sons and your daughters shall prophesy, and your young men shall see visions, and your old men shall dream dreams: and on My servants and on My handmaidens I will pour out in those days of My Spirit; and they shall prophesy: and I will shew wonders in the heaven above, and signs in the earth beneath; blood, and fire, and vapour of smoke... and it shall come to pass, that whosoever shall call on the name of the Lord shall be saved.*"

Acts 14:17 "*Nevertheless He left not Himself without witness, in that He did good, and gave us rain from heaven...*"

Jms. 5:7,8 "*Be patient therefore, brethren, unto the coming of the Lord. Behold, the husbandman waiteth for the precious fruit of the earth, and hath long patience for it, until he receive the early and latter rain.*"

Jms. 5:17,18 "*Elias was a man subject to like passions as we are, and he prayed earnestly that it might not rain: and it rained not on the earth by the space of three years and six months. And he prayed again, and the heaven gave rain, and the earth brought forth her fruit.*"

Rainbow

Every time we see a rainbow it is a promise!

Gen. 9:13-17 "*I do set My bow in the cloud, and it shall be for a token of a Covenant between Me and the earth. And it shall come to pass, when I bring a cloud over the earth, that the bow shall be seen in the cloud: and I will remember My Covenant, which is between Me and you and every living creature of all flesh; and the waters shall no more become a flood to destroy all flesh. And the bow shall be in the cloud; and I will look upon it, that I may remember the everlasting Covenant between God and every living creature of all flesh that is upon the earth. And God said unto Noah, This is the token* of the Covenant, which I have established between Me and all flesh that is upon the earth."

Ez. 1:28 *"As the appearance of the (rain)bow that is in the cloud in the day of rain, so was the appearance of the brightness round about (Gods throne)... this was the appearance of the likeness of the glory of the Lord..."*

Rev. 4:3 *"And He (God) that sat (on the throne) was to look upon like a jasper and a sardine stone: and there was a rainbow round about the throne, in sight like unto an emerald."*

Rev. 10:1 *"And I saw another mighty angel come down from heaven, clothed with a cloud: and a rainbow was upon his head, and his face was as it were the sun, and his feet as pillars of fire..."*

Rearguard/From Behind

Is. 52:12 *"... for the Lord will go before you; and the God of Israel will be your rereward ("rearguard" HCSB)."*
Is. 52:12 NLT *"The God of Israel will protect you from behind."*
Is. 58:8 *"... the glory of the Lord shall be thy rereward ("rearguard" NASB)."*

Received

Ps. 68:18 *"Thou hast ascended on high, Thou hast led captivity captive: Thou hast received gifts for men; yea, for the rebellious also, that the Lord God might dwell among them."* (a prophecy about Jesus)
Matt. 7:8 *"For every one that asketh receiveth; and he that seeketh findeth; and to him that knocketh it shall be opened."*
Matt. 10:8 *"Heal the sick, cleanse the lepers, raise the dead, cast out devils: freely ye have received, freely give."*
Jn. 1:16 *"And of His fullness have all we received, and grace for grace."*
Jn. 1:16 NIV *"Out of His fullness we have all received grace in place of grace already given."*
Acts 2:33 *"Therefore being by the right hand of God exalted, and having received of the Father the promise of the Holy Ghost, He hath shed forth this, which ye now see and hear."*
Rom. 1:5 NIV *"Through Him we received grace and Apostleship to call all the Gentiles to the obedience that comes from faith for His name's sake."*
I Cor. 2:12 *"Now we have received, not the spirit of the world, but the Spirit which is of God; that we might know the things that are freely given to us of God."*

Heb. 6:7 NASB *"For ground that drinks the rain which often falls on it and brings forth vegetation useful to those for whose sake it is also tilled, receives a blessing from God..."*
Heb. 11:17 *"By faith Abraham.... received the promises..."*
Heb. 12:28 *"Wherefore we receiving a kingdom which cannot be moved, let us have grace, whereby we may serve God acceptably with reverence and godly fear..."*
I Pet. 1:9 *"Receiving the end of your faith, even the Salvation of your souls."*
I Pet. 4:10 *"As every man hath received the gift, even so minister the same one to another, as good stewards of the manifold grace of God."*
I Pet. 4:10 NIV *"Each of You should use whatever gift you have received to serve others..."*

Reconcile / Reconciliation

Rom. 5:10 *"For if, when we were enemies, we were reconciled to God by the death of His Son, much more, being reconciled, we shall be saved by His life."*
II Cor. 5:18,19 *"... God who hath reconciled us to Himself by Jesus Christ, and hath given to us the ministry of reconciliation... God was in Christ reconciling the world unto Himself, not imputing their trespasses unto them; and hath committed unto us the Word of reconciliation.*
Eph. 2:15-17 *"... so making peace; and that He might reconcile both unto God in one body by the cross, having slain the enmity thereby; and came and preached peace to you which were afar off, and to them that were nigh..."*
Col. 1:20,21 *"... and, having made peace through the blood of His cross, by Him to reconcile all things unto Himself; by Him, I say, whether they be things in earth, or things in heaven. And you, that were sometime alienated and enemies in your mind by wicked works, yet now hath he reconciled in the body of His flesh through death, to present you Holy and unblameable and un-reproveable in His sight..."*
Heb. 2:9,17 *"But we see Jesus... to make reconciliation for the sins of the people."*

Redeem / Redeemed / Redemption

Ex. 6:6 God to the Israelites *"I will Redeem you with a stretched out arm, and with great Judgments..."*
Neh. 1:10 *"Now these are Thy servants and Thy people, whom Thou hast Redeemed by Thy great power, and by Thy strong hand..."*
Ps. 31:5 *"... Thou hast Redeemed me, O Lord God of truth."*

Ps. 34:22 *"The Lord Redeemeth the soul of His servants: and none of them that trust in Him shall be desolate."*
Ps. 103:4 *"Who Redeemeth thy life from destruction; who crowneth thee with lovingkindness and tender mericies..."*
Ps. 106:8,10 *"... and He saved them from the hand of him that hated them, and Redeemed them from the hand of the enemy."*
Ps. 130:8 *"And He shall Redeem Israel from all his iniquities."*
Job 5:20 *"In famine He shall Redeem thee from death: and in war from the power of the sword."*
Is. 35:9 *"... an highway shall be there, and a way, and it shall be called The Way of Holiness; the unclean shall not pass over it; but it shall be for those: the wayfaring men... the Redeemed shall walk there..."*
Is. 43:1 *"... now thus saith the Lord that created thee, O Jacob, and He that formed thee, O Israel, Fear not: for I have Redeemed thee, I have called thee by thy name; thou art mine."*
Is. 44:22 *"I have blotted out, as a thick cloud, thy transgressions and, as a cloud, thy sins: return unto me; for I have Redeemed thee."*
Is. 52:3 *"For thus saith the Lord... ye shall be Redeemed without money."*
Is. 62:12 *"And they shall call them, The Holy people, The Redeemed of the Lord..."*
Is. 63:4 *"For the day of vengeance is in Mine heart, and the year of My Redeemed is come."*
Micah 4:10 *"... there shalt thou be delivered; there the Lord shall Redeem thee from the hand of thine enemies."*
Lk. 1:68 *"... He hath Redeemed His people..."*
LK. 21:28 *"And when these things begin to come to pass, then look up, and lift up your heads; for your Redemption draweth nigh."*
Gal. 3:13 *"Christ hath Redeemed us from the curse of the law, being made a curse for us..."*
Eph. 4:30 *"And grieve not the Holy Spirit of God, whereby ye are sealed unto the day of Redemption."*
I Pet. 1:18,19 *"... ye know that ye were not Redeemed with corruptible things, as silver and gold, from your vain conversation received by tradition from your fathers; but with the precious blood of Christ, as of a lamb without blemish and without spot..."*
Rev. 5:9 *"... Thou... hast Redeemed us to God by Thy blood out of every kindred, and tongue, and people, and nation..."*

Refuge

Deut. 33:27 *"The eternal God is thy refuge, and underneath are the everlasting arms: and He shall thrust out the enemy from before thee..."*
II Sam. 7:11 *"... and have caused thee to rest from all thine enemies..."*
II Sam. 22:3 *"The God of my Rock; in him will I trust: He is my shield, and the horn of my Salvation, my high tower, and my refuge, my Saviour; Thou savest me from violence."*
I Kings 5:4 *"But now the Lord my God hath given me rest on every side, so that there is neither adversary nor evil occurrent."*
Ps. 9:9 *"The Lord also will be a refuge for the oppressed, a refuge in times of trouble..."*
Ps. 14:6 *"Ye have shamed the counsel of the poor, because the Lord is his refuge. The Lord also will be a refuge for the oppressed, a refuge in times of trouble."*
Ps. 46:1 *"... God is our refuge and strength, a very present help in trouble."*
Ps. 46:7,11 *"The Lord of hosts is with us; the God of Jacob is our refuge..."*
Ps. 57:1 *"... be merciful unto me, O God, be merciful unto me: for my soul trusteth in Thee: yea, in the shadow of Thy wings will I make my refuge, until these calamities be overpast."*
Ps. 59:16 *"But I will sing of Thy power; yea, I will sing aloud of Thy mercy in the morning: for Thou hast been my defence and refuge in the day of my trouble."*
Ps. 62:7,8 *"In God is my Salvation and my glory: the Rock of my strength, and my refuge, is in God. Trust in Him at all times; ye people, pour out your heart before Him: God is a refuge for us..."*
Ps. 71:7 *"... Thou art my strong refuge."*
Ps. 91:9 *"Because thou hast made the Lord, which is my refuge, even the Most High thy habitation."*
Ps. 94:22 *"... the Lord is my defence... the Rock of my refuge."*
Ps. 142:5 *"I cried unto Thee, O Lord: I said, Thou art my refuge and my portion in the land of the living."*
Prov. 14:26 *"In the fear of the Lord is strong confidence: and his children shall have a place of refuge."*
Is. 4:6 *"And there shall be a Tabernacle for a shadow in the daytime from the heat, and for a place of refuge, and for a covert from storm and from rain."*
Is. 25:4 *"For thou hast been a strength to the poor, a strength to the needy in his distress, a refuge from the storm, a shadow from the heat, when the blast of the terrible ones is as a storm against the wall."*

Jer. 16:19 *"O Lord, my strength, and my fortress, and my refuge in the day of affliction, the Gentiles shall come unto thee from the ends of the earth..."*
Heb. 6:18 *"... therefore, we who have fled to Him for refuge can take new cour-age, for we can hold on to His promise with confidence."*
Heb. 8:18 *"That by two immutable things, in which it was impossible for God to lie, we might have a strong consolation, who have fled for refuge to lay hold upon the hope set before us..."*

Repent / Repentance

Matt. 4:17 *"... Jesus began to preach, and to say, Reptent: for the kingdom of heaven is at hand."*
Mk. 6:12 *"And they went out, and preached that men should repent."*
Lk. 5:32 *"... I came not to call the righteous but sinners to repentance."*
Acts 2:38 ... repent, and be baptized every one of you in the name of Jesus Christ for the remission of sins, and ye shall receive the gift of the Holy Ghost."
II Pet. 3:9 *"The Lord is not slack concerning His promise... but is longsuffering to usward, not wiling that any should perish, but that all should come to repentance."*

Rest

Ex. 33:14 *"... My presence shall go with thee, and I will give thee rest..."*
Josh. 14:15 *"... and the land had rest from war."*
Josh. 22:4 *"And now the Lord your God hath given rest unto your brethren, as He promised them..."*
Job 11:18 *"And thou shalt be secure, because there is hope... and thou shalt take thy rest in safety."*
Ps. 116:7 *"Return unto thy rest, O my soul; for the Lord hath dealt bountifully with thee."*
Is. 57:2 *"He shall enter into peace: they shall rest in their beds, each one walk-ing in his uprightness."*
Jer. 6:16 *"Thus saith the Lord, Stand ye in the ways, and see, and ask for the old paths, where is the good way, and walk therein, and ye shall find rest for your souls..."*
Matt. 11:28,29 *"Come unto Me all ye that labor and are heavey laden and I will give you rest."*

Jer. 6:16 *"Thus saith the Lord, Stand ye in the ways, and see and ask for the old paths, where is the good way, and walk therein, and ye shall find rest for your souls..."*

Matt. 11:28 Jesus said, *"Come unto Me, all ye that labour and are heavy laden, and I will give you rest."*

Restore (er)

This next verse is talking about Boaz the kinsman redeemer but could also be true about Jesus our kinsman Redeemer who came from the line of Ruth and Boaz.

Ruth 4:14 *"And the women said unto Naomi, Blessed be the Lord, which hath not left thee this day without a kinsman, that his name may be famous in Israel... he shall be unto thee a restorer of thy life, and a nourisher of thine old age..."*

Ps. 51:12 *"Restore unto me the joy of Thy Salvation; and uphold me with Thy free Spirit."*

Is. 57:18 *"... I will lead him also, and restore comforts unto him..."*

Is. 58:12 *".. they that shall be of thee shall build the old waste places... thou shalt be called, The repairer of the breach, The restorer of paths to dwell in ."*

Jer. 30:17 *"For I will restore health unto thee, and I will heal thee of thy wounds, saith the Lord..."*

Joel 2:25 *"... I will restore to you the years that the locust have eaten..."*

Matt. 17:11 *"Elijah is coming and will restore all things..."*

Resurrection / Raised / Risen

See section on Death

Job 19:25,26 *"For I know that my Redeemer liveth, and tht He shall stand at the latter day upon the earth: and though after my skin worms destroy this body, yet in my flesh shall I see God: whom I shall see for myself, and mine eys shall behold..."*

Is. 26:19 *"Thy dead men shall live, together with my dead body shall they arise. Awaek and sing, ye that dwell in dust: for thy dew is as the dew of herbs, and the earth shall cast out the dead."*

Dan. 12:2 *"And many of them that sleep in the dust of the earth shall awake, some to everlasting life, and some to shame and everlasting contempt."*

Matt. 22:23-32 *"The same day came to Him the Sadducees, which say that there is no Resurrection, and asked Him, saying, Master, Moses said, If a man die, having no children, his brother shall marry his wife, and raise up* seed unto his brother. Now there were with us seven brethren: and the first, when he had married a wife, deceased, and having no issue, left his wife unto his brother: and likewise the second also, and the third, unto the seventh. And last of all the woman died also. Therefore in the Resurrection whose wife shall she be of the seven? For they all had her. Jesus answered and said unto them, Ye do err, not knowing the Scriptures, nor the power of God. For in the Resurrection they neither marry, nor are given in marriage, but are as the angels of God in heaven. But as touching the Resurrection of the dead, have ye not read that which was spoken unto you by God, sayig, I Am the God of Abraham, and the God of Isaac, and the God of Jacob? God is not the God of the dead but of the living."

Matt. 27:52,53;Mk. 12:18-27;Lk. 20:27-40 After Jesus' Resurrection, "... the earth did quake, and the rocks rent; and the graves were opened; and many bodies of the saints which slept arose, and came out of the graves after His Resurrection, and went into the Holy City, and appeared unto many."

Lk. 14:13,14 "... thou shalt be blessed; for they cannot recompense thee: for thou shalt be recompensed at the Resurrection of the just."

Jn. 6:39 "And this is the Father's will which hath sent Me, that of all which He hath given Me I should lose nothing, but should raise it up again at the last day."

Jn. 5:24-29 "... he that heareth My Word, and believeth on Him that sent Me, hath everlasting life, and shall not come into condemnation; but is passed from death unto life... the hour is coming, and now is, when the dead shall hear the voice of the Son of God: and they that hear shall live. For as the Father hath life in Himself; so hath He given to the Son to have life in Himself; and hath given Him authority to execute Judgment also because He is the Son of man... the hour is coming, in the which all that are in the graves shall hear His voice, and shall come forth; they that have done good, unto the Resurrection of life; and thy that have done evil, unto the Resurrection of damnation."

Jn. 6:39 "... this is the Father's will which hath sent Me, that of all which He hath given Me I should lose nothing, but should raise it up again at the last day."

(The Resurrection is on the last day of this earth's history.

Jn. 11:21-27 "Jesus said unto her, I am the Resurrection, and the life: he that believeth in Me, though he were dead, yet shall he live: and whosoever liveth and believeth in Me shall never die..."

Acts 1:21,22 They picked Matthias to replace Judas because he was "... a witness with us (the twelve dsciples) of His (Jesus') Resurrection."

Acts 2:29-36 "... David... is both dead and buried, and his sepulchre is with us unto this day. Therefore being a prophet, and knowing that God had sworn with an oath to him, that of the fruit of his loins, according to the flesh, he would raise up Christ to sit on his throne; he seeing this before spake of the Resurrection of Christ, that His soul was not left in hell, neither His flesh did see corruption. This Jesus hath God raised up, whereof we all are witnesses... being by the right hand of God exalted, having received of the Father the promise of the Holy Ghost... for David is not ascended into the heavens: but he saith himself, The Lord said unto my Lord, Sit Thou on My right hand, until I make Thy foes Thy foostool. Therefore let all the house of Israel know assuredly, that God hath made that same Jesus whom ye have crucified, both Lord and Christ."

Acts 4:33 "With great power the Apostles continued to testify to the Resurrection of the Lord Jesus. And God's grace was so powerfully at work in them all."

Acts 23:6 "... the hope of the Resurrection..."

Acts 24:15 "And have hope toward God... that there shall be a Resurrection of the dead, both of the just (1st Resurrection) and unjust (2nd Resurection)..."

Rom. 1:3-5 "... His Son Jesus Christ our Lord, which was made of the seed of David according to the flesh; and declared to be the Son of God with power, according to the Spirit of Holiness, by the Resurrection from the dead: by whom we have received grace and Apostleship, for obedience to the faith..."

Rom. 6:3-11 "Therefore we are buried with Him by baptism into death: that like as Chrsit was raised up from the dead by the glory of the Father, even so we also should walk in newness of life. For if we have been planted together in the likeness of His death, we shall be also in the likeness of His Resurrection... now if we be dead with Christ, we believe that we shall also live with Him: knowing that Christ being raised from the dead dieth no more; death hath no more dominion over him."

I Cor. 1:9,10 "... trust... in God which raiseth the dead."

I Cor. 15:51 "We shall not all sleep, but we shall all be changed, in a moment, in the twinkling of an eye, at the last Trump; for the Trumpet shall sound, and the dead shall be raised incorruptible, and we shall be changed. For this corruptible must put on incorruption, and this mortal must put on immortality. So when this corruptible shall have put on incorruption, and this mortal shall have put on immortality, then shall be brought to pass the saying that is written, Death is swallowed up in victory. O death where is thy sting? O grave, where is thy victory?"

Col. 2:12 "Buried with Him in baptism, wherein also ye are risen with Him through the faith of the operation of God, who hath raised Him from the dead"

Phil. 3:10,11 *"That I may know Him, and the power of His Resurrection... if by any means I might attain unto the Resurrection of the dead."*
I Thess. 1:9,10 *"... to serve the living and true God; and to wait for His Son from heaven, whom He raised from the dead, even Jesus, which delivered us from the wrath to come."*
I Thess. 4:13-18 *"But I would not have you to be ignorant, brethren, concerning them which are asleep, that ye sorrow not, even as others which have no hope. For if we believe that Jesus died and rose again, even so them also which sleep in Jesus will God bring with Him. For this we say unto you by the Word of the Lord, that we which are alive, and remain unto the coming of the Lord shall not prevent them which are asleep. For the Lord Himself shall descend from heaven with a shout, with the voice of the archangel, and with the Trump of God: and the dead in Christ shall rise first: then we which are alive and remain shall be caught up together with them in the clouds, to meet the Lord in the air: and so shall we ever be with the Lord. Wherefore comfort one another with these words."*
Heb. 11:35 *"... a better Resurrection..."*
I Pet. 1:3,4 *"... a lively hope by the Resurrection of Jesus Christ from the dead."*
Rev. 20:4-8 *"... this is the first Resurrection."*

Reward(s) / Recompense

Even though we are saved by grace (it is a free gift of God through the blood of Jesus that we cannot earn), we are rewarded for our good works done on earth. Sometimes we get our reward on earth, but most of the time we must wait patiently for it in heaven. Jesus will say to some people, You already received your reward, which means you lost the heavenly reward. Even though our righteousness is as filthy rags, He still rewards us; so even our rewards are by grace. Once we get to heaven, there will be no more chance to earn certain rewards that He has for us. Our greatest reward is to be with Jesus.
Gen. 15:1 *"After these things the Word of the Lord came unto Abram in a vision, saying, Fear not, Abram: I am thy shield, and thy exceeding great reward."*
Ruth 2:12 *"The Lord recompense thy work, and a full reward be given thee of the Lord God of Israel, under whose wings thou art come to trust."*
(Ruth 2:12 NLT Boaz to Ruth, *"May the Lord, the God of Israel, under whose wings you have come to take refuge, reward you fully."*

I Sam. 24:19 *"... the Lord reward thee good for that thou hast done unto me this day."*

II Sam. 22:18-21 *"He delivered me from my strong enemy, and from them that hated me: for they were too strong for me. They prevented me in the day of my calamity: but the Lord was my stay. He brought me forth also into a large place: and delivered me, because He delighted in me. The Lord rewarded me according to my righteousness: according to the cleanness of my hands hath He recompensed me."*

II Sam. 22:25,26 *"Therefore the Lord hath recompensed me according to my righteousness; according to my cleanness in His eyesight. With the merciful Thou wilt shew Thyself merciful, and with the upright man Thou wilt shew Thyself upright. With the pure Thou wilt shew Thyself pure ..."*

II Chron. 15:7 *"Be strong therefore, and let not your hands be weak: for your work shall be rewarded."*

Ps. 18:20,24 *"The Lord rewarded me according to my righteousness; according to the cleanness of my hands hath He recompensed me ... therefore hath the Lord recompensed me according to my righteousness, according to the cleanness of my hands in His eyesight."*

Ps. 19:7,11 *"The law of the Lord is perfect... and in keeping of them there is great reward."*

Ps. 58:11 *"... verily there is a reward for the righteous ..."*

Ps. 62:12 *"... for Thou renderest to every man according to his work."*

Ps. 103:10 *"He hath not dealt with us after our sins; nor rewarded us according to our iniquities."*

Ps. 127:3 *"... the fruit of the womb is his reward."*

Ps. 128:2 NIV *"... blessings and prosperity will be yours."*

Prov. 10:22 *"The blessing of the Lord, it maketh rich... He addeth no sorrow with it."*

Prov. 11:18 *"... to him that soweth righteousness shall be a sure reward."*

Prov. 11:30,31 *"The fruit of the righteous is a Tree of Life; and he that winneth souls is wise. Behold, the righteous shall be recompensed in the earth..."*

Prov. 12:14 *"A man shall be satisfied with good by the fruit of his mouth: and the recompence of a man's hands shall be rendered unto him."*

Prov. 13:13 *"Whoso despiseth the Word shall be destroyed: but he that feareth the Commandment shall be rewarded."*

Prov. 13:21 *"... to the righteous good shall be repayed."*

Prov. 20:17 *"He that hath pity upon the poor lendeth unto the Lord; and that which he hath given will he pay him again."*

Prov. 23:18 *"For surely there is an end ("reward" KJV fn)..."*

Prov. 24:12,14 "... He that keepeth thy soul... shall not He render to every man according to his works... there shall be a reward, and thy expectation shall not be cut off."

Prov. 25:21,22 "If thine enemy be hungry, give him bread to eat; and if he be thirsty, give him water to drink: for thou shalt heap coals of fire upon his head, and the Lord shall reward thee."

Is. 35:4 "... your God will come with vengeance, even God with a recompence..."

Is. 40:10 "... behold, His reward is with Him..."

Is. 62:11,12 "... say ye to the daughter of Zion, Behold, thy Salvation cometh; Behold, His reward is with Him, and His work before Him."

Jer. 25:14 "... and I will recompense them according to their deeds, and according to the works of their own hands."

Jer. 31:16 "... thy work shall be rewarded..."

Jer. 32:19 "... to give everyone according to his ways, and according to the fruit of his doings..."

Hosea 4:9 "... reward them their doings."

Matt. 5:3-10 "Blessed are the poor in spirit: for theirs is the kingdom of heaven. Blessed are they that mourn: for they shall be comforted. Blessed are the meek: for they shall inherit the earth. Blessed are they which do hunger and thirst after righteousness: for they shall be filled. Blessed are the merciful: for they shall obtain mercy. Blessed are the pure in heart: for they shall see God. Blessed are the peacemakers: for they shall be called the children of God. Blessed are they which are persecuted for righteousness' sake: for theirs is the kingdom of heaven."

Matt. 5:11,12 "Blessed are ye, when men shall revile you, and persecute you, and shall say all manner of evil against you falsely, for my sake. Rejoice, and be exceeding glad: for great is your reward in heaven..."

Matt. 5:19 "... whosoever shall do and teach them (the Ten Commandments), the same shall be called great in the kingdom of heaven."

Matt. 5:46 "For if ye love them which love you, what reward have ye..."

It is implied that you will be rewarded for loving someone who doesn't return your love.

Matt. 6:4 "But when thou doest alms, let not thy left hand know what thy right hand doeth: that thine alms may be in secret: and thy Father which seeth in secret Himself shall reward thee openly."

Matt. 6:6,18 "But thou, when thou prayest, enter into thy closet, and when thou hast shut thy door, pray to thy Father which is in secret; and thy Father which seeth in secret shall reward thee openly."

Matt. 6:20,21 *"But lay up for yourselves treasures in heaven, where neither moth nor rust doth corrupt, and where thieves do not break through nor steal: for where your treasure is, there will your heart be also."*

Matt. 10:41,42 *"He that receiveth a prophet in the name of a prophet shall receive a prophet's reward; and he that receiveth a righteous man in the name of a righteous man shall receive a righteous man's reward. And whosoever shall give to drink unto one of these little ones a cup of cold water only in the name of a disciple, verily I say unto you, he shall in no wise lose his reward."*

Matt. 16:17,18 *"But thou, when thou fastest, anoint thine head, and wash thy face; that thou appear not unto men to fast, but unto thy Father which is in secret: and thy Father, which seeth in secret, shall reward thee openly."*

Matt. 16:27 *"For the Son of man shall come in the glory of His Father with His angels: and then He shall reward every man according to his works."*

Matt. 19:21 *"... if thou wilt enter into* (Gr. *"the"*) (path of) *life, keep the Commandments...* (but) *if thou wilt be perfect* (have a greater reward in heaven), *go and sell that thou hast, and give to the poor, and thou shalt have treasure* (rewards) *in heaven: and come and follow Me."*

(Ps. 119:1 *"... the way... the law..."*

(Ps. 119:35 *"... the path of Thy Commandments..."*

Matt. 19:29 *"And every one that hath forsaken houses, or brethren, or sisters, or father, or mother, or wife, or children, or lands, for My name's sake, shall receive an hundredfold, and shall inherit everlasting life. But many that are first shall be last; and the last shall be first."*

Matt. 23:12 (Mk.10:43,44) *"... and he that shall humble himself shall be exalted."*

Matt. 25:21 *"... thou hast been faithful over a few things, I will make thee ruler over many things: enter thou into the joy of thy Lord."*

Mk. 4:24 *"... with what measure ye mete, it shall be measured to you: and unto you that hear shall more be given. For he that hath, to him shall be given..."*

Mk. 9:41 *"For whosoever shall give you a cup of water to drink in My name, because ye belong to Christ, verily I say unto you, he shall not lose his reward."*

Mk. 10:21 *"... go thy way, sell whatsoever thou hast, and give to the poor, and thou shalt have treasure in heaven..."*

Mk. 10:30 *"Verily I say unto you, There is no man that hath left houses, or brethren, or sisters, or father, or mother, or wife, or children, or lands, for My sake, and the Gospel's but he shall receive an hundredfold now in this time, houses, and brethren, and sisters, and mothers, and children, and* lands, with persecutions; and in the world to come eternal life... the last (shall be) *first."*

Lk. 6:22,23 *"Blessed are ye, when men shall hate you, and when they shall separate you from their company, and shall reproach you, and cast out your name as evil, for the Son of man's sake. Rejoice ye in that day, and leap for joy: for behold, your reward is great in heaven: for in the like manner did their fathers unto the prophets."*

Lk. 6:35 *"But love ye your enemies, and do good, and lend, hoping for nothing again; and your reward shall be great, and ye shall be the children of the Highest: for He is kind unto the unthankful and to the evil."*

Lk. 7:35 *"... your reward shall be great..."*

Lk. 12:33 *"But rather seek ye the kingdom of God; and all these things shall be added unto you. Fear not, little flock; for it is your Father's good pleasure to give you the kingdom. Sell that ye have, and give alms; provide yourselves bags which wax not old, a treasure in the heavens that faileth not, where no thief approacheth, neither moth corrupteth. For where your treasure is, there will your heart be also."*

Lk. 12:43 *"Blessed is that servant, whom his Lord when He cometh shall find so doing. Of a truth I say unto you, that He will make him ruler over all that He hath."*

Lk. 14:11 *"... he that humbleth himself shall be exalted."*

Lk. 14:14 *"But when thou makest a feast, call the poor, the maimed, the lame, the blind: and thou shalt be blessed; for they cannot recompense thee: for thou shalt be recompensed at the Resurrection of the just."*

Lk. 18:14 *"... and he that humbleth himself shall be exalted."*

Lk. 18:29,30 *"... there is no man that hath left house, or parents, or brethren, or wife, or children, for the Kingdom of God's sake, who shall not receive manifold more in this present time, and in the world to come life everlasting."*

Lk. 19:17,19 *"... thou hast been faithful in a very little, have thou authority over ten cities. And the second came... be thou also over five cities."*

Rom. 2:6,7 *"Who will render to every man according to his deeds: to them who by patient continuance in well doing seek for glory and honour and immortality, eternal life..."*

I Cor. 3:8 *"... every man shall receive his own reward according to his own labour."*

I Cor. 3:14 *"If any man's work abide which he hath built thereupon, he shall receive a reward."*

I Cor. 9:17 *"For if I do this thing* (preach) *willingly, I have a reward..."*

Gal. 6:7 *"... for whatsoever a man soweth, that shall he also reap.'*

Eph. 3:24 *"Knowing that of the Lord ye shall receive the reward of the inheritance: for ye serve the Lord Christ."*
Eph. 6:8 NIV *"... because you know that the Lord will reward each one for whatever good they do..."*
Phil. 3:13,14 *"... I count not myself to have apprehended* (taken hold of it yet)*: but this one thing I do, forgetting those things which are behind... reaching forth unto those things which are before, I press toward the mark* (goal) *for the prize of the high calling of God in Christ."*
Phil. 4:17 *"... I desire fruit that may abound to your account."*
God is keeping a record of your good works in heaven! It's going on your account for what God wants to reward you for.
Col. 2:18 *"Let no man beguile you of your reward..."*
You see here that you can lose your rewards in heaven (even though you may not lose your Salvation).
Col. 3:23,24 *"... and whatsoever ye do, do it heartily, as to the Lord, and not unto men; knowing that of the Lord ye shall receive the reward of the inheritance: for ye serve the Lord Christ."*
I Tim. 5:18 *"... the labourer is worthy of his reward."*
I Tim. 6:18,19 *"... be rich in good works... laying up in store for themselves a good foundation against the time to come, that they may lay hold on eternal life."*
II Tim. 4:7,8 *"I have fought a good fight, I have finished my course, I have kept the faith: henceforth there is laid up for me a crown of righteousness, which the Lord, the righteous Judge, shall give me at that day: and not to me only, but unto all them also that love His appearing."*
Heb. 10:35,36 *"Cast not away therefore your confidence, which hath great re-compence of reward. For ye have need of patience, that, after ye have done the will of God, ye might receive the promise."*
Heb. 11:6 *"... for he that cometh to God must believe that He is, and that He is a rewarder of them that diligently seek Him."*
God wants us to believe that He will reward those who seek to please Him by their good works.
Heb. 11:26 *"Esteeming the reproach of Christ greater riches than the treasures in Egypt... for he had respect unto the recompence of the reward."*
Moses respected the reward that was his in heaven.
Jms. 1:12 *"Blessed is the man that endureth temptation: for when he is tried, he shall receive the crown of life, which the Lord hath promised to them that love Him."*
Jms. 1:25 *"... whoso looketh into the perfect law of liberty... a doer of the work, this man shall be blessed in his deed."*

Jms. 1:25 LB "... if anyone keeps looking steadily into God's law... he will do what it says, and God will greatly bless him in everything he does."

II Jn. 8 "Look to yourselves, that we lose not those things which we have wrought, but that we receive a full reward."

Rev. 2:23 "... I will give unto every one of you according to your works."

Rev. 3:11,12 "Behold, I come quickly: hold that fast which thou hast, that no man take thy crown. Him that overcometh will I make a pillar in the Temple of my God, and he shall go no more out: and I will write upon him the name of My God, and the name of the city of My God, which is New Jerusalem, which cometh down out of heaven from My God: and I will write upon him My new name."

Rev. 3:21 "To him that overcometh will I grant to sit with Me in My throne, even as I also overcame, and am set down with My Father in His throne."

Rev. 11:18 "And the nations were angry, and Thy wrath is come, and the time of the dead, that they should be Judged, and that Thou shouldest give reward unto Thy servants the prophets, and to the saints, and them that fear Thy name, small and great..."

Rev. 22:12 "And behold, I come quickly; and My reward is with Me, to give every man according as his work shall be."

Riches/Prosperity/Wealth

There are many promises about riches but we must be careful of riches also (see the next section on Be careful of Riches). We should never seek riches just to consume it on our own lusts, Jms. 4:3. Riches do not show us our acceptace with God; we see that in the parable of the rich man and Lazarus, Lk. 16:19-31. Also, the Bible tells us that we should not show partiality to someone who is rich, Jms. 2:1-6. But when we really need something, God promises to give it to us, Phil. 4:19.

(Deut. 28:8,11,12 "This is one of the blessings for obedience.

I Chron. 22:13 "Then shalt thou prosper, if thou takest heed to fulfil the Statutes and Judgments..."

I Chron. 22:13 PB "Then shall you prosper if you take heed to observe these Comandments..."

Job 9:4,5 "He is wise in heart, and mighty in strength: who hath hardened him-self against Him, and hath prospered? Which removeth the mountains, and they know not: which overturneth them in His anger."

Job 9:4,5 NKJV "God is wise in heart and mighty in strength. Who has harden-ed himself against Him and prospered. He removes the mountains, and they do not know when He overturns them in His anger; He shakes the *earth out of its place, and its pillars tremble* (at the second coming of Jesus)..."

If you harden yourself against God, you cannot prosper.

Ps. 112:1-3 *"Praise ye the Lord. Blessed is the man that feareth the Lord, that delighteth greatly in His Commandments. His seed shall be mighty upon earth: the generation of the upright shall be blessed. Wealth and riches shall be in his house: and his righteousness endureth forever."*

Gen. 13:2 *"And Abram was very rich in cattle, in silver, and in gold."*

And we inherit the blessings of Abraham through Jesus, Gal. 3:14!

Gen. 15:14 *"... and afterward shall they come out with great substance."*

Gen. 22:14 *"And Abraham called the name of that place Jehovah-jireh* (meaning *"the Lord provides"*) ... *in the Mount of the Lord it shall be seen."*

Gen. 24:35 *"And the Lord hath blessed my master* (Abraham) *greatly; and he is become great: and he hath given him flocks, and herds, and silver, and gold, and menservants, and maidservants, and camels, and* (donkeys).*"*

Gen. 24:40 *"... the Lord, before whom I* (Abraham) *walk, will send His angel with thee, and prosper thy way..."*

Gen. 24:35,56 Abraham's servant, Eliezer said, *".... the Lord hath prospered my way..."*

Gen. 30:43 *"And the man increased exceedingly, and had much cattle, and maidservants, and menservants, and camels, and* (donkeys).*"*

Gen. 32:9 *"... I will deal well with thee..."*

Gen. 32:9 AMP *"... I will do you good..."*

Gen. 39:2,4 *"And the Lord was with Joseph, and he was a prosperous man ... and his master saw that the Lord was with him, and that the Lord made all that he did to prosper in his hand... and Joseph found grace in his sight..."*

Gen. 39:5 *"... the Lord blessed the Egyptian's house for Joseph's sake; and the blessing of the Lord was upon all that he had in the house, and in the field. And he left all that he had in Joseph's hand... and Joseph was a goodly person, and well favoured."*

Gen. 39:21 *"But the Lord was with Joseph, and shewed him mercy, and gave him favour in the sight of the keeper of the prison... the Lord was with him, and that which he did, the Lord made it to prosper."*

Gen. 39:23 *"The keeper of the prison looked not to anything that was under his hand; because the Lord was with him* (Joseph), *and that which he did, the Lord made it to prosper."*

Deut. 2:7 *"For the Lord your God has blessed you in all the work of your hand... you have lacked nothing."*

Deut. 5:29,32,33 *"O that there were such an heart in them, that they would fear Me, and keep all My Commandments always, that it might be well with them, and with their children forever... ye shall observe to do therefore as* the Lord your God hath commanded you: ye shall not turn aside to the right hand or to the left. Ye shall walk in all the ways which the Lord your God hath commanded you, that ye may live, and that it may be well with you, and that ye may prolong your days in the land which ye shall possess."

Deut. 5:33 NIV "Walk in obedience to all that the Lord your God has commanded you, so that you may live and prosper and prolong your days in the land that you will possess."

Deut. 8:18 "But thou shalt remember the Lord thy God: for it is He that giveth thee power to get wealth, that He may establish His Covenant which He sware unto thy fathers, as it is this day."

Deut. 29:9 "Keep (obey) therefore the words of this Covenant, and do them, that ye may prosper in all that ye do."

Deut. 30:9,10 "And the Lord thy God will make thee plenteous in every work of thine hand, in the fruit of thy body, and in the fruit of thy cattle, and in the fruit of thy land, for good: for the Lord will again rejoice over thee for good, as He rejoiced over thy fathers: if thou shalt hearken unto the voice of the Lord thy God, to keep His Commandments... with all thine heart, and with all thy soul..."

Josh. 1:8 "This book of the law shall not depart out of thy mouth; but thou shalt meditate therein day and night, that thou mayest observe to do according to all that is written therein: for then thou shalt make thy way prosperous, and then thou shalt have good success."

Josh. 22:7,8 "... then he blessed them, and he spake unto them, saying, Return with much riches to your tents..."

Judges 18:5 "... ask counsel, we pray thee, of God, that we may know whether our way which we go shall be prosperous."

I Sam. 2:7-10 "The Lord maketh poor, and maketh rich: He bringeth low, and lifteth up. He raiseth up the poor out of the dust, and lifteth up the beggar from the dunghill, to set them among princes, and make them inherit the throne of glory... He will keep ("guard" NIV) the feet of His saints... for by strength shall no man prevail."

I Chron. 22:11,13 "... the Lord be with thee; and prosper thou... then shalt thou prosper, if, thou takest heed to fulfil the Statutes and Judgments..."

I Chron. 29:12 "... riches and honour come of Thee... and Thou reignest over all... the Lord was with him; and he prospered whithersoever he went."

I Chron. 29:11-14 NIV "Yours, Lord, is the greatness and the power and the glory and the majesty and the splendor, for everything in heaven and earth is yours... wealth and honor come from You... in Your hands are strength and power to exalt and give strength to all... but who am I... that we should be able to give as generously as this? Everything comes from You..."

I Chron. 29:28 David *"... died in a good old age, full of days, riches, and honour..."*

II Chron. 1:8-12 *"Wisdom and knowledge is granted unto thee; and I will give thee riches, and wealth, and honour..."*

II Chron. 14:7 *"... He hath given us rest on every side. So they built and prospered..."*

II Chron. 17:5 *"... and he* (Jehoshaphat) *had riches and honour in abundance."*

II Chron. 20:20,25,26 *"... believe in the Lord... so shall ye prosper... and when Jehoshaphat and his people came to take away the spoil of them, they found among them in abundance both riches... and precious jewels, which they stript off for themselves, more than they could carry away: and they were three days in gathering of the spoil, it was so much. And on the fourth day they assembled themselves in the valley of Berachah ("Blessing" NLT); for there they blessed the Lord; therefore the name of the same place was called, the Valley of Berachah ("Blessing" NLT), unto this day."*

Prayer: Lord, please bring me to Your Valley of Blessing in Jesus' name, Amen!

II Chron. 25:9 *"... the Lord is able to give thee much more than this."*

II Chron. 26:5 *"... as long as he sought the Lord, God made him to prosper."*

II Chron. 26:15 PB *"... until he became very rich."*

II Chron. 31:21 *"And in every work that he* (king Hezekiah) *began in the service of the house of God, and in the law, and in the Commandments, to seek His God, he did it with all his heart, and prospered."*

II Chron. 32:27-31 Hezekiah *"... prospered in all his works..."*

I Kings 2:3 *"... to keep... His Commandments... that thou mayest prosper in all that thou doest, and whithersoever thou turnest thyself..."*

I Kings 3:13 *"... I have also given thee that which thou hast not asked, both riches, and honour..."*

II Kings 18:3,5,7 Hezekiah did what was right in God's eyes

Josh. 22:7,8 *"... then he blessed them, and he spake unto them, saying, Return with much riches to your tents..."*

Ezra 6:14 *"The elders of the Jews builded* (and)*... they prospered..."*

Neh. 1:11 *"Prosper... I pray Thee"*

Neh. 2:20 *"... the God of heaven, He will prosper us..."*

Job 8:6,7 Make thy habitation prosperous

Job 22:21,24,25 *"Acquaint now thyself with Him, and be at peace: thereby good shall come unto thee. Receive... the law... lay up His Words in thine heart... then shalt thou lay up gold as dust... as the stones of the brooks... and thou shalt have plenty of silver."*

Job 22:21 NIV *"Submit to God, and be at peace with Him in this way prosperty will come to you... if you remove wickedness far from your tent... then the Almighty will be your gold, the choicest silver for you..."*

Job 36:11 *"If they obey and serve Him, they shall spend their days in prosperity, and their years in pleasures."*

Ps. 1:3 *"... his delight is in the law of the Lord; and in His law doth he meditate day and night. And he shall be like a tree planted by the rivers of water, that bringeth forth his fruit in his season... and whatsoever he doeth shall prosper."*

Ps. 24:1 *"The earth is the Lord's, and the fullness thereof; the world, and they that dwell therein."*

Ps. 25:12,13 NKJV *"Who is the man that fears the Lord? Him shall He teach in the way He chooses. He Himself shall dwell in properity..."*

Ps. 30:6 *"And in my prosperity I said, I shall never be moved... by Thy favour Thou hast made my mountain to stand strong..."*

Ps. 34:9,10 *"O fear the Lord, ye His saints: for there is no want to them that fear Him... they that seek the Lord shall not want any good thing."*

Ps. 35:27 *"... let the Lord be magnified, which hath pleasure in the prosperity of his servant."*

Ps. 50:10 *"For every beast of the forest is Mine, and the cattle upon a thousand hills."*

Ps. 66:12 *"... Thou broughtest us out into a wealthy place ("place of abundance" NIV)."*

Ps. 67:10 *"... Thou, O God, hast prepared of Thy goodness for the poor."*

Ps. 67:10 NIV *"... You provided for the poor. ("needy" ESV)"*

Ps. 68:6 ESV *"... He leads out the prisoners to prosperity."*

Ps. 104:24 *"... the earth is full of Thy riches."*

Ps. 112:1-3 *"... blessed is the man that feareth the Lord, that delighteth greatly in His Commandments... wealth and riches shall be in his house..."*

Ps. 115:14 *"The Lord shall increase you more and more, you and your children."*

(Ps. 115:14 NIV *"May the Lord make ("give" RSV) you increase both you and your children...."*

Ps. 118:25 Prayer for prosperity, *"... O Lord, I beseech Thee, send now prosperity."*

(Ps. 118:25 NHEB *"... Lord, we beg You, send prosperity now."*

Ps. 119:111 TLB *"Your laws are my joyous treasure forever."*

(Ps. 119:162 NLT *"I rejoice in Your Word like one who finds a great treasure."*

Ps. 122:6 *"Pray for the peace of Jerusalem: they shall prosper that love thee. Peace be within thy walls, and prosperity within thy palaces."*

Ps. 128:1,2 *"Blessed is every one that feareth the Lord; that walketh in His ways. For thou shalt eat the labour of thine hands: happy shalt thou be, and it shall be well with thee."*
Prov. 1:13 *"We shall find all precious substance ("possessions" NKJV), we shall fill our houses with spoil..."*
Prov. 3:10,13-18 *"So shall thy barns be filled... happy is the man that findeth wisdom, and the man that getteth understanding... she is more precious than rubies: and all the things thou canst desire are not to be compared unto her... and in her left hand riches and honour."*
Prov. 8:10-12 *"Receive my instruction, and not silver; and knowledge rather than choice gold. For wisdom is better than rubies; and all the things that may be desired are not to be compared to it."*
(Prov. 8:10-12 Aramaic Bible in Plain English *"We will find all His wealth and His stuff and fill our houses with loot."*
(Prov. 8:10-12 Jubilee Bible *"We will find all kinds of riches."*
(Prov. 8:10-12 NIV *"We will get all sorts of valuable things and fill our houses(with plunder."*
(Prov. 8:10-12 NLT *"... think of the great things we will get. We'll fill our houses with all the stuff we take."*
(Prov. 8:10-12 NASB *"... we will find all kinds of precious wealth..."*
(Prov. 8:12,17-19,21 *"I wisdom... love them that love me (wisdom); and those that seek me early shall find me. Riches and honour are with me: yea, durable riches and righteousness. My fruit is better than gold, yea, than fine gold; and my revenue than choice silver... that I may cause those that love me to inherit substance; and I will fill their treasures."*
Prov. 10:4 *"He becometh poor that dealeth with a slack hand: but the hand of the diligent maketh rich."*
(Prov. 10:4 NIV *"Lazy hands make a man poor, but diligent hands bring wealth."*
(Prov. 10:4 NLT *"Lazy people are soon poor; hard workers get rich."*
Prov. 10:22 *"The blessing of the Lord, it maketh rich, and He addeth no sorrow with it."*
Prayer: Lord, let it be according to Your Word! Amen!
Prov. 11:24,25 *"There is that scattereth, and yet increaseth... the liberal soul shall be made fat: and he that watereth shall be watered also himself."*
(Prov. 11:25 God's Word Translation *"A generous person will be made rich."*
Prov. 11:30,31 *"The fruit of the righteous is a Tree of Life; and he that winneth souls is wise. Behold the righteous shall be recompensed ("repaid" WEB) in the earth..."*
Prov. 13:4 PB *"... the soul of the diligent shall be enriched."*
(Prov. 13:4 NLT *"... those who work hard will prosper."*

Prov. 13:11 "*Wealth gotten by vanity shall be diminished: but he that gathereth by labour shall increase.*"

Prov. 13:21,22 "*... to the righteous good shall be repayed... the wealth of the sinner is laid up for the just.*"

Prov. 14:23 "*In all labour there is profit... the crown of the wise is their riches...*"

Prov. 15:6 "*In the house of the righteous is much treasure...*"

Prov. 16:20 NIV "*Whoever gives heed to instruction prospers, and blessed is he who trusts in the Lord.*"

Prov. 19:17 "*He that hath pity upon the poor lendeth unto the Lord; and that which he hath given will he pay him again.*"

(Prov. 19:17 NIV "*Whoever is kind to the poor lends to the Lord, and He will reward them for what they have done.*"

(Prov. 19:17 WEB "*He who has pity on the poor lends to Yahweh; He will reward him.*"

Prov. 21:5 "*Good planning and hard work lead to prosperity...*"

(Prov. 21:5 NLT "*Steady plodding brings prosperity...*"

Prov. 22:2,4,9 "*The rich and poor meet together: the Lord is the maker of them all... by humility and the fear of the Lord are riches, and honour, and life.*"

Prov. 24:3-5 "*Through wisdom is an house builded; and by understanding it is established: and by knowledge shall the chambers be filled with all precious and pleasant riches.*"

Prov. 24:14 "*So shall the knowledge of wisdom be unto thy soul: when thou hast found it, then there shall be a reward, and thy expectation shall not be cut off.*"

Prov. 28:10 "*... the upright shall have good things in possession.*"

(Prov. 28:10 PB "*... inherit good things*"

Prov. 28:13 "*... whoso confesseth and forsaketh them shall have mercy.*"

Prov. 28:25 "*... he that putteth his trust in the Lord shall be made fat ("will prosper" NIV).*"

Prov. 28:27 "*He that giveth unto the poor shall not lack...*"

Prov. 31:21 NIV "*... the righteous are rewarded with good things.*"

Eccl. 2:26 NIV "*... but to the sinner He gives the task of gathering and storing up wealth to hand it over to the one who pleases God.*"

Eccl. 5:18-20 "*Behold that which I have seen: it is good and comely for one to eat and to drink, and to enjoy the good of all his labour that he taketh under the sun all the days of his life, which God giveth him: for it is his portion. Every man also to whom God hath given riches and wealth, and hath given him power to eat thereof... this is the gift of God... because God answereth him in the joy of his heart.*"

Eccl. 5:18:20 NASB "... this is his reward. Furthermore, as for every man to whom God has given riches and wealth, He has also empowered him to eat from them and to receive his reward and rejoice in his labor; this is the gift of God. For he will not often consider the years of his life, because God keeps him occupied with the gladness of his heart."

The gift of God is to be able to enjoy wealth and possessions and be happy in your labor as long as you are doing God's will and helping others.

Eccl. 7:14 "In the day of prosperity be joyful..."

Is. 30:23-26 NASB "... it will be rich and plenteous..."

Is. 33:6 "... the fear of the Lord is His treasure."

Is. 40:10 "... the Lord God will come with strong hand... His reward is with Him..."

Is. 45:3 "... I will gve thee the treasures of darkness, and hidden riches of secret places, that thou mayest know that I... am the God of Israel."

Is. 48:15 "I have called him; I have brought him, and he shall make his way prosperous."

Is. 48:15 PB "... I have made his way prosperous."

Is. 51:2,3 "... Abraham... for I called him alone, and blessed him, and increased him."

(The blessing of Abraham is ours in Jesus, Gal. 3:14.

Is. 55:11 "So shall My Word be that goeth forth out of my mouth; it shall not return unto Me void, but it shall accomplish that which I please, and it shall prosper in the thing whereto I sent it."

Is. 55:11 "So shall My Word be that goeth forth out of My mouth: it shall not return unto Me void, but it shall accomplish that which I please, and it shall prosper in the thing whereto I sent it."

Is. 61:6 "... ye shall eat the riches of the Gentiles, and in their glory shall ye boast yourselves."

Jer. 23:4 "And I will set up shepherds over them which shall feed them: and they shall fear no more, nor be dismayed neither shall they be lacking, saith the Lord."

Jer. 32:40 "... I will not turn away from them to do them good..."

Jer. 33:9 "... which shall hear all the good that I do unto them: and they shall fear and tremble for all the goodness and for all the prosperity that I procure unto it."

Ez. 16:10-14 "... I entered into a Covenant with thee (Israel), saith the Lord God, and thou becamest Mine... I clothed thee also with broidered work, and shod thee with badgers' skin, and I girded thee about with fine linen, and I covered thee with silk. I decked thee also with ornaments, and I put bracelets upon thy hands, and a chain on thy neck. And I put a jewel on thy forehead, and earrings in thine ears, and a beautiful crown upon thine head.

Thus wast thou decked with gold and silver; and thy raiment was of fine linen, and silk, and broidered work; thou didst eat fine flour, and honey, and oil: and thou wast exceeding beautiful, and thou didst prosper into a kingdom. And thy renown went forth among the heathen for thy beauty: for it was perfect through My comeliness, which I had put upon thee, saith the Lord God."

Dan. 6:28 "So this Daniel prospered..."

Zech. 1:17 "... thus saith the Lord of hosts; My cities through prosperity shall yet be spread abroad; and the Lord shall yet comfort Zion, and shall yet choose Jerusalem."

Matt. 19:29,30 "And every one that hath forsaken houses, or brethren, or sisters, or father, or mother, or wife, or children, or lands, for My name's sake, shall receive an hundredfold, and shall inherit everlasting life..."

Mk. 10:30 "... man that hath left houses, or brethren, or sisters, or father, or mother, or wife, or children, or lands, for My sake, and the Gospel's, but he shall receive an hundredfold now in this time, houses, and brethren, and sisters, and mothers, and children, and lands, with persecutions; and in the world to come eternal life..."

Lk. 6:38 "Give, and it shall be given unto you; good measure, pressed down, and shaken together, and running over, shall men give into your bosom. For with the same measure that ye mete withal it shall be measured to you again."

Acts 4:34 "... neither was there any among them that lacked..."

Rom. 1:10 "... making request, if by any means now at length I might have a prosperous journey by the will of God to come unto you."

Rom. 9:23 "... and that He might make known the riches of His glory on the vessels ("objects" NIV) of ("His" NIV) mercy..."

Rom. 10:12 "For there is no difference between the Jew and the Greek: for the same Lord over all is rich unto all that call upon Him."

(Rom. 10:12 NIV "... the same Lord is Lord of all and richly blesses all who call on Him..."

(Rom. 10:12 LB "...the same Lord who generously gives His riches to all those who ask Him for them."

(Rom. 10:12 RSV "... the same Lord is Lord of all and bestows His riches upon all who call upon Him."

Rom. 11:12 "Now if the fall of them be the riches of the world, and the diminishing of them the riches of the Gentiles; how much more their fullness?"

Rom. 11:33 "O the depth of the riches both of the wisdom and knowledge of God!"

I Cor. 3:21 "... all things are yours... things present, or things to come; all are yours..."
I Cor. 4:8 "Now ye are full, now ye are rich..."
I Cor. 16:2 "... let every one of you lay by him in store as God hath prospered him..."
II Cor. 6:10 "As poor, yet making many rich; as having nothing, and yet possessing all things."
II Cor. 8:9 "... Jesus Christ, that, though He was rich, yet for your sakes He became poor, that ye through His poverty might be rich."
II Cor. 9:6-11"... he which soweth bountifully shall reap also bountifully... God loveth a cheerful giver. And God is able to make all grace abound toward you; that ye, always having all sufficiency in all things, may abound to every good work... He hath given to the poor... being enriched in everything to all bounty-fulness, which causeth through us thanksgiving to God."
II Cor. 9:10-14 NIV "... you will be made rich in every way so that you can be generous on every occasion..."
Eph. 1:7 Riches of grace
Eph. 1:18 "... that ye may know... the riches of the glory of His inheritance in the saints..."
Eph. 2:7 "... that in the ages to come He might shew the exceeding riches of His grace in His kindness towards us through Christ Jesus."
Eph. 3:8 "Unto me, who am less than the least of all saints, is this grace given, that I should preach among the Gentiles the unsearchable riches of Christ..."
Eph. 3:16 "... that He would grant you, according to the riches of His glory, to be strengthened with might by His Spirit in the inner man..."
Phil. 4:19 "But my God shall supply all your need according to His riches in glory by Christ Jesus."
Col. 1:27 "To whom God would make known what is the riches of the glory of this mystery among the Gentiles; which is Christ in you, the hope of glory..."
Col. 1:27 NLT "For it has pleased God to tell His people that the riches and glory of Christ are for you Gentiles, too."
Col. 2:2,3 "... that their hearts might be comforted, being knit together in love, and unto all riches of the full assurance of understanding, to the acknowledge-ment of the mystery of God and of the Father, and of Christ; in whom are hid all the treasures of wisdom and knowledge."
I Thess. 4:12 "... that ye may have lack of nothing."
II Tim. 2:12 "... if we suffer, we shall also reign with Him..."
Jms. 2:5 "... rich in faith..."

II Pet. 1:3 NIV *"His divine power has given us everything we need for life and godliness..."*
III Jn. 2 *"Beloved, I wish above all things that thou mayest prosper..."*
Rev. 3:18 *"I counsel thee to buy of Me gold tried in the fire* (which is Jesus), *that thou mayest be rich..."*
Rev. 2:9 *"I know thy works, and tribulation, and poverty, (but thou art rich)..."*

(Be careful of) Riches

There are so many promises of riches in the Bible, but there are also verses that tell us to be careful of riches and be content with what we have. We should never ask God for riches to use on our own selfish lusts and pleasures. Also we should not use wealth as a measuring rod of God's acceptance of us because the Bible says that the *"greatest shall be the least and the least shall be the greatest"*. It also says that the poor will be exalted. *"Let the brother of low degree rejoice in that he is exalted* (in heaven): *but the rich, in that he is made low* (in heaven)" Jms. 1:9,10. God loves the humble and the poor. We should never trust in our riches but always put our trust in God. The rich and the poor are both saved by grace and not by their riches. But it is also true that God wants to provide for our needs and He blesses us when we obey Him.

II Kings 5:26 *"Is it a time to receive money?"*
Ps. 19:9-11 *"The fear of the Lord is clean, enduring forever: the Judgments of the Lord are true and righteous altogether, more to be desired are they than gold, yea, than much fine gold: sweeter also than honey and the honeycomb... in keeping them is great reward."*
Lk. 12:31 *"But rather seek ye the kingdom of God; and all these things shall be added unto you..."*
Deut. 8:11-18 *"Beware that thou forget not the Lord thy God, in not keeping His Commandments... lest when thou hast eaten and art full, and hast built goodly houses, and dwelt therein; and when thy herds and thy flocks multiply, and thy silver and thy gold is multiplied, and all that thou hast is multiplied; then thine heart be lifted up, and thou forget the Lord thy God, which brought thee forth..."*
II Chron. 1:11 *"And God said to Solomon, Because... thou hast not asked riches, wealth, or honour, nor the life of thine enemies, neither yet hast asked long life; but hast asked wisdom and knowledge for thyself, that thou mayest Judge My people, over whom I have made thee king. Wisdom and*

knowledge is granted unto thee; and I will give thee riches, and wealth, and honour, such as none of the kings have had that have been before thee, neither shall there any after thee have the like."

Ps. 19:9,10 "The fear of the Lord is clean, enduring forever: the Judgments of the Lord are true and righteous altogether. More to be desired are they than gold, yea, than much fine gold: sweeter also than honey and the honey-comb."

Ps. 36:7 "Rest in the Lord, and wait patiently for Him..."

Ps. 37:5 "Commit thy way unto the Lord; trust also in Him; and He shall bring it to pass... rest in the Lord, and wait patiently for Him: fret not thyself because of him who prospereth in his way... those that wait upon the Lord, they shall inherit the earth."

Ps. 37:16 "A little that a righteous man hath is better than the riches of many wicked."

Ps. 39:6 "... he heapeth up riches, and knoweth not who shall gather them."

Ps. 49:5,6 The wicked who "... trust in their wealth, and boast themselves in the multitude of their riches; none of them can by any means Redeem his brother, nor give to God a ransom for him..."

Ps. 49:16 NIV Do not be overawed when a man grows rich

Ps. 49:20 NIV A man who has riches without understanding is like the beasts that perish.

Ps. 52:7 "Lo, this is the man that made not God his strength, but trusted in the abundance of his riches, and strengthened himself in his wickedness."

Ps. 62:10a NLT "Don't try to get rich by extortion or robbery..."

Ps. 62:10b NIV "... though your riches increase, do not set your heart on them."

Ps. 73:3 "For I was envious at the foolish, when I saw the prosperity of the wicked."

Ps. 73:12 "Behold, these are the ungodly, who prosper in the world; they increase in riches."

Ps. 119:14 "I have rejoiced in the way of Thy Testimonies, as much as in all riches."

Ps. 119:13,14 LB "I have recited Your laws, and rejoiced in them more than in riches."

Ps. 119:72 "The law of thy mouth is better unto me than thousands of gold and silver."

(Ps. 119:72 HCSB "Instruction from your lips..."

Ps. 119:36 LB "Help me to prefer obedience to making money!"

Prov. 1:19 NIV "Such are the paths of all who go after ill-gotten gain; it takes away the life of those who get it."

Prov. 3:9 NIV Honor the Lord with your wealth

Prov. 3:14 NIV Wisdom *"... is more profitable than silver and yields better returns than gold."*

Prov. 8:10,11 *"Receive My instruction, and not silver; and knowledge rather than choice gold. For wisdom is better than rubies; and all the things that may be desired are not to be compared to it."*

Prov. 9:5 *"... who hath hardened himself against Him* (God), *and hath prospered?"*

Prov. 11:4 *"Riches profit not in the day of wrath: but righteousness delivereth from death."*

Prov. 11:28 *"He that trusteth in his riches shall fall..."*

(Prov. 11:28 NLT *"Trust in your money and down you go!"*

Prov. 13:7 *"There is that maketh himself* (look) *rich, yet hath nothing: there is that maketh himself* (look) *poor, yet hath great riches."*

Prov. 13:11 *"Wealth gotten by vanity shall be diminished: but he that gathereth by labour shall increase."*

Prov. 15:16 *"Better is little with the fear of the Lord than great treasure* ("wealth" NIV) *and trouble* ("turmoil" NASV) *therewith."*

Prov. 15:17 NIV *"A greedy man brings trouble to his family, but he who hates bribes will live."*

Prov. 15:27 *"He that is greedy of gain troubleth his own house; but he that hateth gifts shall live."*

Prov. 16:16 *"How much better is it to get wisdom than gold..."*

Prov. 18:11 *"The rich think of their wealth as an impregnable defense; they imagine it is a high wall of safety."*

Prov. 18:10 NASB God is our safety, not money, *"The name of the Lord is a strong tower; the righteous runs into it and is safe."*

Prov. 21:6 *"Wealth created by lying is a vanishing mist and a deadly trap."*

Prov. 22:1,4,7 *"A good name is rather to be chosen than great riches, and loving favour rather than silver and gold. The rich and poor meet together: the Lord is the maker of them all... by humility and the fear of the Lord are riches..."*

Prov. 23:4 *"Labour not to be rich..."*

Prov. 27:24 *"For* (earthly) *riches are not forever..."*

Prov. 28:6 *"Better is the poor that walketh in his uprightness, than he that is perverse in his ways, though he be rich."*

Prov. 28:11 *"The rich man is wise in his own conceit; but the poor that hath understanding searcheth him out."*

Prov. 28:13 *"He that covereth his sins shall not prosper..."*

Prov. 28:22 ESV *"A stingy man hastns after wealth and does not know that poverty will come upon him."*

I Jn. 1:9 We must confess our sins and receive forgiveness for them.

Prov. 28:20 "... but he that maketh haste to be rich shall not be innocent. To have respect of persons is not good... he that hasteth to be rich hath an evil eye, and considereth not that poverty shall come..."
Prov. 30:8 "... give me neither poverty nor riches; feed me with food convenient for me: lest I be full, and deny Thee, and say, Who is the Lord? Or lest I be poor, and steal, and take the name of my God in vain."
Eccl. 5:10 "He that loveth silver shall not be satisfied with silver; nor he that loveth abundance with increase: this is also vanity."
Eccl. 5:10-12 NLT "Those who love money will never have enough. How absurd to think that wealth brings true happiness! The more you have, the more people come to help you spend it. So what is the advantage of wealth – except perhaps to watch it run through your fingers! People who work hard sleep well... but the rich are always worrying and seldom get a good night's sleep."
We should not love money but love God and others. Money is not the root of all evil, but the love of money is, I Tim. 6:10.
Is. 14:32 "... and the poor of His people shall trust in it (the walls of Jerusalem)."
Jer. 9:23,24 "... let not the rich man glory in his riches (but rather glory in God)..."
Jer. 17:11 "... he that getteth riches, and not by right, shall leave them in the midst of his days, and at his end shall be a fool."
Jer. 17:11 NLT "Like a partridge that hatches eggs she has not laid, so are those who get their wealth by unjust means. At midlife they will lose their riches; in the end, they will become poor old fools."
Ez. 7:19 "They shall cast their silver in the streets, and their gold shall be removed: their silver and their gold shall not be able to deliver them in the day of the wrath of the Lord..."
Only Jesus can save us - not riches!
Matt. 6:24 "No man can serve two masters: for.. he will hate the one, and love the other... Ye cannot serve God and mammon ("money" NIV; "wealth" NASV; "riches" ISV)."
Matt. 6:20 "But lay ("store" NIV) up for yourselves treasures in heaven, where nether moth nor rust doth corrupt ("destroy" NLT), and where thieves Do not break through nor steal..."
Matt. 6:25-33 "Therefore I say unto you, Take no thought for your life, what ye shall eat, or what ye shall drink; nor yet for your body, what ye shall put on. Is not the life more than meat, and the body than raiment?"
Matt. 13:34 "... the kingdom of heaven is like unto treasure hid in a field; the which when a man hath found, he hideth, and for joy thereof goeth and selleth all that he hath, and buyeth that field. Again, the kingdom of heaven is

like unto a merchant man, seeking goodly pearls: who, when he had found one pearl of great price, went and sold all that he had and bought it."
Matt. 19:21 "Jesus said unto him, If thou wilt be perfect, go and sell that thou hast, and give to the poor, and thou shalt have treasure in heaven: and come and follow me."
Mk. 10:24,25 "... how hard is it for them that trust in riches to enter into the kingdom of God! It is easier for a camel to go through the eye of a needle, than for a rich man to enter into the kingdom of God."
If you have riches, don't trust them but trust in God and give your tithes and offerings to God and help the poor.
Lk. 1:53 "... the rich He hath sent empty away." Because they didn't feel their need for Him!
Lk. 6:24 "But woe unto you that are rich (who are not rich toward God): for ye have ("already" NIV) received your consolation."
Lk. 12:19-21 Parable of rich man, "... I will say to my soul, Soul, thou hast much goods laid up for many years; take thine ease, eat, drink, and be merry. But God said unto him, Thou fool, this night thy soul shall be required of thee: then whose shall those things be, which thou hast provided? So is he that layeth up treasure for himself, and is not rich toward God."
Lk. 12:31,33 "But rather seek ye the kingdom of God; and all these things shall be added unto you... sell that ye have, and give alms; provide yourselves bags which wax not old, a treasure in the heavens that faileth not, where no thief approacheth, neither moth corrupteth."
Lk. 16:11 "If therefore ye have not been faithful in the unrighteous mammon, who will commit to your trust the true riches? And if ye have not been faithful in that which is another man's, who shall give you that which is your own? No servant can serve two masters: for either he will hate the one, and love the other; or else he will hold to the one, and despise the other. Ye cannot serve God and mammon (money)."
Acts 3:6 "Then Peter said, Silver and gold have I none; but such as I have give I thee: in the name of Jesus Christ of Nazareth rise up and walk."
Acts 8:18 "And when Simon saw that through laying on of the Apostles' hands the Holy Ghost was given he offered them money, saying, Give me also this power, that on whomsoever I lay hands, he may receive the Holy Ghost. But Peter said unto him, Thy money perish with thee, because thou hast thought that the gift of God may be purchased with money, Thou hast neither part nor lot in this matter: for thy heart is not right in the sight of God. Repent therefore of this thy wickedness, and pray God, if perhaps the thought of thine heart may be forgiven thee."
II Cor. 6:10 "As sorrowful, yet always rejoicing; as poor, yet making many rich; as having nothing, and yet possessing all things."

Phil. 4:11-13 *"... for I have learned, in whatsoever state I am, therewith to be content. I know both how to be abased, and I know how to abound* ("have plenty" NIV; "live in prosperity" NASB)... *to be full and to be hungry... to a-bound and to suffer need. I can do all things through Christ which strength-eneth me.."*

I Tim. 6:5-12 *"... supposing that gain is godliness* (but being rich is not a sign of God's acceptance)*: from such withdraw thyself. But godliness with contentment is great gain. For we brought nothing into this world, and it is certain we can carry nothing out. And having food and raiment, let us be therewith content. But they that will be rich fall into temptation and a snare, and into many foolish and hurtful lusts, which drown men in destruction and perdition. For the love of money is the root of all evil: which while some coveted after, they have erred from the faith, and pierced themselves through with many sorrows. But thou, O man of God, flee these things: and follow after righteousness, godliness, faith, love, patience, meek-ness. Fight the good fight of faith, lay hold on eternal life, whereunto thou art also called, and hast professed a good profession before many witnesses."*

(I Tim. 6:9 PB *"For those who desire to be rich fall into temptation, and snares, and into many foolish and hurtful lusts which drown men in degeneration and destruction."*

I Tim. 6:17-19 *"Charge them that are rich in this world, that they be not highminded, nor trust in uncertain riches, but in the living God, who giveth us richly all things to enjoy... laying up in store for themselves a good foundation against the time to come, that they may lay hold on eternal life."*

If you are rich, don't trust your riches, but put your trust in God. Don't be proud and think you're better than those with less money than you, you might find that you have a lower position in heaven because you had it easier in this

World, Jms. 1:9;2:5,6.

II Tim. 3:1,2 NIV *"... there will be perilous times in the last days... people will be lovers of money..."*

Heb. 11:26 Moses *"Esteeming the reproach of Christ greater riches than the treasures in Egypt..."*

Heb. 13:5,6 *"Let your conversation be without covetousness; and be content with such things as ye have: for He hath said, I will never leave thee, nor forsake thee... the Lord is my helper..."*

Jms. 1:9-12 *"Let the brother of low degree rejoice in that he is exalted* (in heaven)*: but the rich, in that he is made low: because as the flower of the grass he shall pass away."*

Jms. 2:5,6 *"... hath not God chosen the poor of this world rich in faith, and heirs of the kingdom which He hath promised to them that love Him... do not rich men oppress you..."*

Jms. 5:1-3 *"Go to now, ye rich men, weep and howl for your miseries that shall come upon you. Your riches are corrupted, and your garments are moth eaten. Your gold and silver is cankered; and the rust of them shall be a witness against you, and shall eat your flesh as it were fire. Ye have heaped treasure together for the last days."*

Jms. 5:5 *"Ye have lived in pleasure on the earth, and been wanton; ye have nourished your hearts, as in a day of slaughter."*

I Pet. 1:7 *"The trial of your faith, being much more precious than of gold that perisheth..."*

Rev. 3:17,18 *"Because thou sayest, I am rich, and increased with goods, and have need of nothing; and knowest not that thou art wretched, and miserable, and poor, and blind, and naked. I counsel thee to buy of Me gold tried in the fire, that thou mayest be rich..."*

Jesus is the gold tried in the fire – then you'll have the true riches that won't fade away.

Righteousness (Christ's)

Ps. 37:6 *"And He shall bring forth thy righteousness as the light, and thy Judgment as the noonday."*

Ps. 37:30-33 *"The righteous shall inherit the land and dwell therein forever. The mouth of the righteous speaketh wisdom, and his tongue talketh of Judgment. The law of his God is in his heart; none of his steps shall slide."*

Ps. 37:39 *"But the Salvation of the righteous is of the Lord: He is their strength in the time of trouble."*

Is. 54:17 *"No weapon that is formed against thee shall prosper; and every tongue that shall rise against thee in Judgment thou shalt condemn. This is the heritage of the servants of the Lord, and their righteousness is of Me, saith the Lord."*

Rom.13:14 *"But put ye on the Lord Jesus Christ, and make not provision for the flesh, to fulfil the lusts thereof."*

II Cor. 5:21 *"For He hath made Him to be sin for us, who knew no sin; that we might be made the righteousness of God in Him."*

Gal.3:27 *"For as many of you as have been baptized into Christ have put on Christ."*

Is. 58:8 *"... and thy righteousness shall go before thee; and the glory of the Lord shall be thy rereward ("rearguard")."*

Is. 60:21 *"Thy people also shall be all righteous..."*
I Pet. 3:12 *"For the eyes of the Lord are over the righteous, and His ears are open unto their prayers..."*

Ruler

Matt. 25:21-23 *"His lord said unto him, Well done, thou good and faithful servant: thou hast been faithful over a few things, I will make thee ruler over many things: enter thou into the joy of thy Lord..."*

Safe / Safety

Lev. 25:18 *"... You shall dwell in the land in safety..."*
Deut. 12:10 *"... when He giveth you rest from all your enemies round about, so that ye dwell in safety..."*
Deut. 33:28 *"Israel then shall dwell in safety alone..."*
I Sam. 12:11 *"And the Lord... delivered you out of the hand of your enemies on every side, and ye dwelled safe."*
I Chron. 16:21,22 *"He suffered no man to do them wrong: yea, He reproved (them) for their sakes, saying, Touch not Mine anointed, and do My prophets no harm."*
Job 5:11 NIV *"The lowly He sets on high, and those who mourn are lifted to safety. He thwarts the plans of the crafty, that their hands achieve no success."*
Ps. 4:8 *"I will both lay me down in peace, and sleep: for Thou, Lord, only makest me dwell in safety."*
Ps. 12:5 *"For the oppression of the poor, for the sighing of the needy, Now will I arise, saith the Lord; I will set him in safety from him that puffeth at him."*
Ps. 59:9 NLT *"You are my strength; I wait for You to rescue me, for You, O God, are my place of safety."*
Prov. 1:33 *"But whoso hearkeneth unto Me shall dwell safely, and shall be quiet from fear of evil."*
Prov. 18:10 *"The name of the Lord is a strong tower: the righteous runneth into it, and is safe."*
Prov. 21:31 *"The horse is prepared against the day of battle: but safety is of the Lord.'*
Prov. 24:6 *"... in multitude of counselors there is safety."*
Prov. 29:25 *"... whoso putteth his trust in the Lord shall be safe."*
Is. 14:30 *"... the needy shall lie down in safety..."*

Jer. 32:37 *"... I will cause them to dwell safely..."*
Jer. 33:16 *"In those days shall Judah be saved, and Jerusalem shall dwell safely..."*
Ez. 34:25 *"And I will make with them a Covenant of peace, and will cause the evil beasts to cease out of the land: and they shall dwell safely in the wilderness, and sleep in the woods."*
Ez. 34:27,28 *"... they shall be safe in their land, and shall know that I am the Lord, when I have broken the bands of their yoke, and delivered them out of the hand of those that served themselves of them. And they shall no more be a prey to the heathen... they shall dwell safely, and none shall make them afraid."*
Acts 27:34 *"... there shall not an hair fall from the head of any of you."* (Paul said to those on the ship)

Salvation / Save / Savior

Ex. 14:13 *"... fear ye not, stand still, and see the Salvation of the Lord, which He will shew to you today... the Lord shall fight for you, and ye shall hold your peace..."*
Ex. 15:2 *"The Lord is my strength and song and He is become my Salvation: He is my God, and I will prepare him an habitation..."*
I Sam. 10:19 *"... God, who Himself saved you out of all your adversities and your tribulations..."*
II Sam. 22:28 *"And the afflicted people Thou wilt save..."*
II Sam. 22:51 *"He is the tower of Salvation for his king: and sheweth mercy to His anointed, unto David, and to his seed forevermore."*
II Sam. 23:5 *"... this is all my Salvation, and all my desire..."*
II Sam. 23:5 NIV *"If my house were not right with God... surely He would not bring to fruition my Salvation and grant me my every desire."*
II Kings 13:5 *"... and the Lord gave Israel a savior..."*
Neh. 9:27 *"... who saved them out of the hand of their enemies."*
Ps. 7:10 *"My defence is of God, which saveth the upright in heart."*
Ps. 27:1 *"The Lord is my light and my Salvation; whom shall I fear..."*
Ps. 34:18 *"The Lord is nigh unto them that are of a broken heart: and saveth such as be of a contrite spirit."*
Ps. 37:39,40 *"But the Salvation of the righteous is of the Lord... and the Lord shall help them, and deliver them: He shall deliver them from the wicked, and save them, because they trust in Him."*
Ps. 44:7 *"But thou hast saved us from our enemies, and hast put them to shame that hated us."*

Ps. 50:23 *"Whoso offereth praise glorifieth Me: and to him that ordereth his conversation aright will I shew the Salvation of God."*
Ps. 62:1,2 *"Truly my soul waiteth upon God: from Him cometh my Salvation. He only is my Rock and my Salvation; He is my defence; I shall not be greatly moved."*
Ps. 68:20 *"He that is our God is the God of Salvation..."*
Ps. 71:3 *"... Thou hast given commandment to save me; for Thou art my Rock and my fortress."*
Ps. 80:7 *"Turn us again, O God of hosts, and cause Thy face to shine; and we shall be saved."*
Ps. 85:9 *"Surely His Salvation is nigh them that fear Him..."*
Ps. 91:16 *"With long life will I satisfy him, and shew him my Salvation."*
Ps. 98:2 *"The Lord hath made known His Salvation: His righteousness hath He openly shewed in the sight of the heathen."*
Ps. 103:3 *"Who Redeemeth thy life from destruction..."*
Ps. 106:8,10 *"... He saved them for His name's sake, that He might make His mighty power to be known... and He saved them from the hand of him that hated them, and Redeemed them from the hand of the enemy."*
Ps. 107:6,13,19 *"... He saveth them out of their distresses. He ... delivered them from their destructions."*
Ps. 109:31 *"For He shall stand at the right hand of the poor, to save him from those that condemn his soul."*
Ps. 118:21 *"I will praise Thee: for Thou hast heard me, and art become my Salvation."*
Ps. 132:16 *"I will also clothe her priests with Salvation: and her saints shall shout aloud for joy."*
Ps. 137:7,8 *"... Thou wilt revive me: Thou shalt stretch forth Thine hand against the wrath of mine enemies, and Thy right hand shall save me. The Lord will perfect that which concerneth me: Thy mercy, O Lord, endureth forever..."*
Ps. 138:7,8 *"Though I walk in the midst of trouble, Thou wilt revive me: Thou shalt stretch forth Thine hand against the wrath of mine enemies, and Thy right hand shall save me. The Lord will perfect that which concerneth me: Thy mercy, O Lord, endureth forever..."*
Ps. 145:19,20 *"He will fulfil the desire of them that fear Him: He also will hear their cry, and will save them. The Lord preserveth ("watches over" NIV; "protects" LB; "keeps" NASB) all them that love Him..."*
Is. 1:18 *"... though your sins be as scarlet, they shall be as white as snow; though they be red like crimson, they shall be as wool."*
See my book "The Crimson Worm" at www.thecrimsonworm.com

Is. 12:2 "Behold, God is my Salvation; I will trust, and not be afraid: for the Lord Jehovah is my strength and my song; He also is become my Salvation."
Is. 19:20 "... He shall send them a Saviour..."
Is. 25:9 "And it shall be said in that day, Lo, this is our God; we have waited for Him, and He will save us: this is the Lord; we have waited for Him, we will be glad and rejoice in His Salvation."
Is. 30:15 "For thus saith the Lord God, the Holy One of Israel; in returning and rest shall ye be saved; in quietness and in confidence shall be your strength..."
Is. 33:6 "... wisdom and knowledge shall be the stability of thy times, and strength of Salvation..."
Is. 33:22 "... the Lord is our King; He will save us."
Is. 35:4 "... He will come and save you."
Is. 43:11 "I, even I, am the Lord; and beside Me there is no Saviour."
Is. 44:21 "... thou art My servant: I have formed thee... O Israel, thou shalt not be forgotten of Me. I have blotted out, as a thick cloud, thy transgressions, and, as a cloud, thy sins: return unto Me; for I have Redeemed thee."
Is. 45:21 "... a just God and a Saviour; there is none beside Me. Look unto Me, and be ye saved, all the ends of the earth: for I am God, and there is none else."
Is. 46:13 "... My Salvation shall not tarry: and I will place Salvation in Zion for Israel My glory."
Is. 49:6 "... I will also give Thee for a light to the Gentiles, that Thou mayest be my Salvation unto the end of the earth..."
Is. 49:26 "... and all flesh shall know that I the Lord am thy Saviour and thy Redeemer, the mighty One of Jacob."
Is. 52:7 "How beautiful upon the mountains are the feet of him that bringeth good tidings, that publisheth peace; that bringeth good tidings of good, that publisheth Salvation..."
Is. 56:1 "... for My Salvation is near to come, and My righteousness to be revealed."
Is. 59:16 "... His (Jesus) own arm brought Salvation."
Is. 61:10 "... He hath clothed me with the garments of Salvation, He hath covered me with the robe of (Christ's) righteousness..."
Jer. 17:14 "... save me, and I shall be saved..."
Jer. 33:16 "In those days shall Judah be saved... Jerusalem shall dwell safely..."
Lam. 3:26 "It is good that a man should both hope and quietly wait for the Salvation of the Lord."

Zeph. 3:17 *"The Lord thy God in the midst of thee is mighty; He will save, He will rejoice over thee with joy; He will rest in His love, He will joy over thee with singing."*

Zech. 9:9 *"Rejoice greatly, O daughter of Zion; shout, O daughter of Jerusalem: behold, thy King cometh unto thee: He is just, and having Salvation..."*

Zech. 9:16 *"And the Lord their God shall save them in that day as the flock of His people..."*

Matt. 1:21 *"... Jesus: for He shall save His people from their sins."*

Matt. 8:25 *"... Lord, save us: we perish."*

Matt. 18:11 *"For the Son of man is come to save that which was lost."*

Matt. 24:13;Mk.13:13 *"But he that shall endure unto the end, the same shall be saved."*

Mk. 16:16 *"He that believeth and is baptized shall be saved..."*

Lk. 1:68,69,71 *"... for He hath visited and Redeemed His people. And hath raised up an horn of Salvation for us in the house of His servant David... that we should be saved from our enemies, and from the hand of all that hate us..."*

Lk. 1:77 *"To give knowledge of Salvation unto His people by the remission of their sins..."*

Lk. 2:30 Simeon to baby Jesus, *"... for mine eyes have seen Thy Salvation."*

Lk. 3:6 *"And all flesh shall see the Salvation of God."*

Lk. 7:50 *"... thy faith hath saved thee; go in peace."*

Lk. 9:24 *"... whosoever will lose his life for My sake... shall save it."*

Lk. 9:56 *"For the Son of man is not come to destroy men's lives, but to save them"*

Lk. 19:10 *"For the Son of man is come to seek and to save that which was lost."*

Jn. 3:15-17,36 *"... for God so loved the world, that He gave His only begotten Son, that whosoever believeth in Him should not perish, but have everlasting life... the world through Him might be saved. He that believeth on Him is not condemned..."*

Jn. 10:9 *"I am the door: by Me if any man enter in, he shall be saved, and shall go in and out, and find pasture... I am come that they might have life, and that they might have it more abundantly."*

Acts 2:21 *"And it shall come to pass, that whosoever shall call on the name of the Lord shall be saved."*

Acts 2:4 *"... save yourselves from this untoward generation."*

Acts 2:47 *"... and the Lord added to the church daily such as should be saved."*

Acts 13:48 *"... as many as were ordained to eternal life believed."*

Acts 15:11 *"But we believe that through the grace of the Lord Jesus Christ we shall be saved, even as they."*
Acts 16:31 *"... believe on the Lord Jesus Christ, and thou shalt be saved, and thy house..."*
Rom. 1:16 *"For I am not ashamed of the Gospel of Christ: for it is the power of God unto Salvation to everyone that believeth; to the Jew first, and also to the Greek. For therein is the righteousness of God revealed from faith to faith: as it is written, The just shall live by faith."*
Rom. 5:9 *"Much more then, being now Justfied by His blood, we shall be saved from wrath through Him* (Jesus). *For if, when we were enemies, we were rec-onciled to God by the death of His Son much more, being reconciled, we shall be saved by His life... by whom we have now received the Atonement."*
Rom. 10:9 *"... if thou shalt confess with thy mouth the Lord Jesus, and shalt believe in thine heart that God hath raised Him from the dead, thou shalt be saved. For with the heart man believeth unto righteousness; and with the mouth confession is made unto Salvation."*
Rom. 10:13 *"For whosoever shall call upon the name of the Lord shall be saved."*
Rom. 13:11 *"And that, knowing the time, that now it is high time to awake out of sleep: for now is our Salvation nearer than when we believed."*
I Cor. 1:18 *"For the preaching of the cross... unto us which are saved it is the power of God."*
I Cor. 3:15 *"... and the fire shall try every man's work of what sort it is. If any man's work shall be burned, he shall suffer loss: but he himself shall be saved; yet so as by fire."*
II Cor. 6:2 *"(For He saith, I have heard thee in a time accepted, and in the day of Salvation have I succoured thee: behold, now is the accepted time; behold, now is the day of Salvation)."*
Eph. 1:7 *"... in whom we have Redemption through His blood, the forgiveness of sins, according to the riches of His grace..."*
Eph. 1:13 *"... in whom ye also trusted, after that ye heard the Word of truth, the Gospel of your Salvation..."*
Eph. 2:8,9 *"For by grace are ye saved through faith: and that not of yourselves; it is the gift of God, not of works lest any man should boast."*
Eph. 2:4 *"But God, who is rich in mercy, for His great love wherewith He loved us... by grace ye are saved..."*
II Thess. 2:13 *"... because God hath from the beginning chosen you to Salvation through Sanctification of the Spirit and belief of the truth ..."*

II Tim. 1:9 *"Who hath saved us, and called us with an Holy calling... according to His own purpose and grace, which was given us in Christ Jesus before the world began..."*
II Tim. 3:15 *"... and that from a child thou hast known the Holy Scriptures, which are able to make thee wise unto Salvation through faith which is in Christ Jesus."*
Titus 2:11 *"... the grace of God that bringeth Salvation hath appeared to all men"*
Titus 3:5 *"... according to His mercy He saved us, by the washing of regeneration, and renewing of the Holy Ghost."*
Heb. 5:7 *"(Jesus) who in the days of His flesh, when He had offered up prayers and supplications with strong crying and tears unto Him* (the Father) *that was able to save Him from death, and was heard in that He feared; though He were a Son, yet learned He obedience by the things which He suffered; and being made perfect, He became the author of eternal Salvation unto all them that obey Him..."*
Heb. 7:25 *"Wherefore He is able also to save them to the uttermost that come unto God by Him seeing He ever liveth to make intercession for them."*
I Pet. 1:9 *"... receiving the end of your faith, even the Salvation of your souls. Of which Salvation the prophets have inquired and searched diligently..."*
I Jn. 5:13 *"These things have I written unto you that believe on the name of the Son of God; that ye may know that ye have eternal life..."*
Jms. 1:21 *"Wherefore lay apart all filthiness and superfluity of naughtiness, and receive with meekness the engrafted Word, which is able to save your souls."*
Jude 24 *"Now unto Him that is able to keep you from falling, and to present you faultless before the presence of His glory with exceeding joy..."*
Rev. 21:24 *"... and the nations of them which are saved shall walk in the light of it* (the New Jerusalem)*..."*

(Pray) Salvation for Another

Job 22:30 NIV *"He will deliver even one who is not innocent, who will be delivered through the cleanness of your hands."*
Job 29:27-30 NIV *"You will pray to Him, and He will hear you... what you decide on will be done, and light will shine on your ways. When people are brought low and you say, Lift them up! Then He will save the downcast. He will deliver even one who is not innocent, who will be delivered through the cleanness of your hands."*

I Jn. 5:16 *"If any man see his brother sin a sin which is not unto death, he shall ask, and he shall give him life for them that sin not unto death."*

Sanctify / Sanctification

Sanctify means to set apart as Holy to the Lord

Gen. 2:2 *"And on the seventh day God ended His work which he had made; and He rested on the seventh day from all His work which He had made. And God blessed the seventh day, and Sanctified it: because that in it He had rested from all His work which God created and made."*

Lev. 22:32 NKJV *"... I am the Lord who Sanctifies you."*

Ex. 31:13 *"Speak thou also unto the children of Israel, saying, Verily My Sabbaths ye shall keep: for it is a sign between Me and you throughout Your generations; that ye may know that I am the Lord that doth Sanctify you. Ye shall keep the Sabbath therefore; for it is Holy unto you... for whosoever doeth any work therein, that soul shall be cut off from among His people."*

Ez. 36:23 *"... when I shall be Sanctified in you before their eyes."*

Jn. 17:17,19 *"Sanctify them through Thy truth: Thy Word is truth... I Sanctify myself, that they also might be Sanctified through the truth."*

Acts 20:32 *"And now, brethren, I commend you to God, and to the Word of His grace, which is able to build you up, and to give you an inheritance among all them which are Sanctified."*

Acts 26:18 *"... that they may receive forgiveness of sins, and inheritance among them which are Sanctified by faith that is in Me."*

I Cor. 6:11 *"... ye are washed, but ye are Sanctified, but ye are Justified in the name of the Lord Jesus, and by the Spirit of our God."*

I Cor. 7:13-16 *"For the unbelieving husband is Sanctified by the wife, and the unbelieving wife is Sanctified by the husband: else were your children unclean; but now are they Holy."*

Eph. 5:25 *"... Christ also loved the church, and gave Himself for it; that He might Sanctify and cleanse it with the washing of water by the Word, that He might present it to Himself a glorious church, not having spot, or wrinkle, or any such thing; but that it should be Holy and without blemish."*

I Thess. 4:3-8 *"For this is the will of God, even your Sanctification.. God, who hath also given unto us His Holy Spirit."*

I Thess. 5:23 *"And the very God of peace Sanctify you wholly; and I pray God your whole spirit and soul and body be preserved blameless unto the coming of our Lord Jesus Christ."*

II Thess. 2:13,14 *"But we are bound to give thanks always to God for you, brethren beloved of the Lord, because God hath from the beginning chosen* you to Salvation through Sanctification of the Spirit and belief of the truth: whereunto He called you..."

II Tim. 2:21 "If a man therefore purge himself from these, he shall be a vessel unto honour, Sanctified, and meet for the master's use, and prepared unto every good work."

Heb. 10:10 "By the which will we are Sanctified through the offering of the body of Jesus Christ once for all."

Heb. 10:14 "For by one offering He hath perfected forever them that are Sanctified."

Satan Cannot Touch Us

Lk. 10:17,19 "... the devils are subject unto us through Thy name... I give unto you power to tread on serpents and scorpions, and over all the power of the enemy: and nothing shall by any mean's hurt you."

Col. 1:13 "... who hath delivered us from the power of darkness..."

Col. 2:15 "... having spoiled principalities and powers, He made a shew of them openly, triumphing over them in it."

Eph. 6:10-16 "... be strong in the Lord, and in the power of His might. Put on the whole armour of God, that ye may be able to stand against the wiles of the devil. For we wrestle not against flesh and blood, but against principalities, against powers, against the rulers of the darkness of this world, against spiritual wickedness in high places. Wherefore take unto you the whole armour of God, that ye may be able to withstand in the evil day, and having done all, to stand. Stand therefore, having your loins girt about with truth, and having on the breastplate of righteousness; and your feet shod with the preparation of the Gospel of peace; above all, taking the shield of faith, wherewith ye shall be able to quench all the fiery darts of the wicked."

Heb. 2:14 "... that through death He (Jesus) might destroy him that had the power of death, that is, the devil..."

I Jn. 4:4 "Ye are of God, little children, and have overcome them: because greater is He that is in you, than he that is in the world."

I Jn. 5:18 "... he that is begotten of God keepeth himself, and that wicked one toucheth him not."

Satisfy / Satiate

Neh. 9:25 "And they took strong cities, and a fat land, and possessed houses

full of all goods, wells digged, vineyards, and oliveyards, and fruit trees in abundance: so they did eat, and were filled (satisfied), and became fat, and delighted themselves in Thy great goodness."
Ps. 36:8 "They shall be abundantly satisfied with the fatness of Thy house; and Thou shalt make them drink of the river of Thy pleasures."
Ps. 37:19 "They shall not be ashamed in the evil time: and in the days of fam-ine they shall be satisfied."
Ps. 91:16 "With long life will I satisfy him, and shew him My Salvation."
Ps. 103:5 "Who satisfieth thy mouth ("desires" NIV) with good things; so that thy yourh is renewed like the eagle's."
Ps. 107:9 "For He satisfieth the longing soul, and filleth the hungry soul with goodness."
Ps. 145:15,16 "The eyes of all wait upon Thee; and Thou givest them their meat in due season. Thou openest Thine hand, and satisfiest the desire of every living thing."
Ps. 132:15 PB "I will satisfy the poor with bread."
Prov. 12:14 "A man shall be satisfied with good by the fruit of his mouth: and the recompence of a man's hands shall be rendered unto him."
Prov. 13:25 "The righteous eateth to the satisfying of his soul ("has enough to satisfy his appetite" ESV): but the belly of the wicked shall want."
Prov. 18:20 "A man's belly shall be satisfied with the fruit of his mouth; and with the increase of his lips shall he be filled."
(Prov. 18:20 ISV "The positive words that a man speaks fill his stomach"
Is. 58:11 "And the Lord shall guide thee continually, and satisfy thy soul in drought, and make fat thy bones ("strengthen your frame" NIV; "keep healthy" LB): and thou shalt be like a watered garden, and like a spring of water, whose waters fail not."
Jer. 31:14 "... and I will satiate the soul of the priests with fatness, and My people shall be satisfied with My goodness, saith the Lord..."
Jer. 31:14 NASB "I will fill the soul of the priests with abundance, and My people will be satisfied with My goodness..."
Jer. 31:25 "For I have satiated the weary soul, and I have replenished every sorrowful soul."
Joel 2:19,21,26 "... I will send you corn... and oil, and ye shall be satisfied... re-joice for the Lord will do great things... you shall eat in plenty, and be satisfied."

Seal / Sealed

Eph. 1:13 "... the Gospel of your Salvation: in whom also after that ye

believed, ye were sealed with that Holy Spirit of promise. Which is the earnest of our inheritance until the Redemption of the purchased possession unto the praise of His glory."
Eph. 4:30 "And grieve not the Holy Spirit of God, whereby ye are sealed unto the day of Redemption."

Second Coming

Bible verses about the second coming is a promise that He will Come back!
Is. 21:12 – "... *the morning cometh...*"
Is. 25:8,9 "*He will swallow up death in victory... the Lord God will wipe away tears from off all faces; and the rebuke of His people shall He take away from off all the earth: for the Lord hath spoken it. And it shall be said in* **that day**, *Lo, this is our God; we have waited for Him, and He will save us: this is the Lord; we have waited for Him, we will be glad and rejoice in His Salvation.*"
Is. 27:19 "*Thy dead men shall live, together with my dead body shall they arise. Awake and sing, ye that dwell in dust: for thy dew is as the dew of herbs, and the earth shall cast out the dead* (at the 1st Resurrection)*...*"
Is. 30:27,28 NIV "*See,* **the Lord comes** *from afar... the people of God will sing a song of solemn joy, like songs in the night when Holy feasts are held; His people will have gladness of heart, as when a flutest leads a pilgrim band to Jerusalem to the Mountain of the Lord, the Rock of Israel. And the Lord shall cause His majestic voice to be heard...*"
Is. 35:4 "*Say to them that are of a fearful heart, Be strong, fear not... your God will come with vengeance... with a recompence.. and save you.*"
Is. 40:5 "*... the glory of the Lord shall be revealed and all flesh shall see it...*"
Is. 40:10 "*...* **the Lord God will come** *with strong hand... His arm shall rule for Him: behold, His reward is with Him* (Rev.22:12)*, and His work before Him.*"
Is. 40:10 LB "*...* **the Lord God is coming** *with mighty power; He will rule with awesome strength. See, His reward is with Him, to each as he has done.*"
Is. 66:5 "*... Let the* **Lord** *be glorified: but* **He shall appear** *to your joy...*"
Hosea 6:3 "*... His going forth is prepared as the morning...*"
Hag. 2:6,7 "*... the* **desire of all nations shall come***...*"
Zech. 14:5 "*... and* **the Lord my God shall come***, and all the saints with Thee.*"
Matt. 24:26-31 (Rev.19:17). *Immediately after the tribulation* (time of the anti-Christ)*... shall appear the sign of the Son of man in heaven... they shall see the* **Son of man coming** *in the clouds of heaven with power and great glory* (the 2nd coming of Jesus)*. And He shall send His angels with a great sound of a trumpet, and they shall gather together His elect from the four winds, from one end of heaven to the other.*"

Matt. 24:35-50 *"... Who then is a faithful and wise servant, whom his Lord hath made ruler over His household, to give them meat in due season? Blessed is that servant, whom his Lord when He cometh shall find so doing. Verily I say unto you, That He shall make him ruler over all His goods (Matt. 25:6)..."*

Matt. 25:6,10,13 *"And at midnight there was a cry made, Behold, the bridegroom cometh; go ye out to meet him. And while they* (the five virgins) *went to buy, the Bridegroom came; and they that were ready went in with Him to the marriage: and the door was shut..."*

Matt. 25:31 *"When the **Son of man shall come** in His glory, and all the Holy angels with Him, then shall He sit upon the throne of His glory..."*

Lk. 12:35-40 *"... blessed are those servants, whom the **Lord when He cometh** shall find watching..."*

Lk. 14:14 *"... for thou shalt be recompensed at the Resurrection of the just."*

Lk. 17:34-37 (Matt.24:28;Rev. 19:17,18)."

Lk. 21:27,28 *"... then shall they see the Son of man coming in a cloud with power and great glory... when these things begin to come to pass.. look up... lift up your heads... your Redemption draweth nigh."*

Jn. 5:28 *"Marvel not at this: for the hour is coming, in the which all that are in the graves shall hear His voice, and shall come forth; they that have done good, unto the Resurrection of life* (1st Resurrection)*..."*

Jn. 11:23,24 *"... Jesus said... I am the Resurrection, and the life: he that believeth in Me, though he were dead, yet shall he live: and whosoever liveth and believeth in Me shall never die..."*

Jn. 14:33 *"And if I go and prepare a place for you, **I will come** again, and receive you unto Myself; that where I am, there ye may be also."*

Acts 1:11 *"... this same Jesus, which is taken up from you into heaven, **shall so come** in like manner as ye have seen Him go into heaven."*

Rom. 6:5 *"For if we have been planted together in the likeness of His death, we shall be also in the likeness of His Resurrection..."*

Rom. 8:11 *"But if the Spirit of Him that raised up Jesus from the dead dwell in you, He that raised up Christ from the dead shall also quicken your mortal bodies by His Spirit that dwelleth in you."*

I Cor. 1:8 *"... that ye may be blameless in the **day of our Lord** Jesus Christ."*

I Cor. 15:22,23 *"For as in Adam all die, even so in Christ shall all be made alive, but every man in his own order..."*

I Cor. 15:51-55 *"Behold, I shew you a mystery; we shall not all sleep, but we shall all be changed, in a moment, in the twinkling of an eye, at the **last trump**: for the trumpet shall sound, and the dead shall be raised incorruptible, and we shall be changed. For this corruptible must put on incorruption, and this mortal must put on immortality. So when this* corruptible shall have put on incorruption, and this mortal shall have put on immortality, then shall be brought to pass the saying that is written, Death is swallowed up in victory. O death, where is thy sting? O grave, where is thy victory?"

II Cor. 5:2 "... we have a building (body) of God, an house not made with hands, eternal in the heavens... being clothed we shall not be found naked."

I Thess. 1:10 "... to wait for His Son from heaven... which delivered us from the wrath to come."

I Thess. 2:19 "For what is our hope, or joy, or crown of rejoicing? Are not even ye in the presence of our Lord Jesus Christ **at His coming**?"

I Thess. 3:13 "To the end He may stablish your hearts unblameable in Holiness before God, even our Father, at the **coming of our Lord** Jesus Christ with all His saints."

I Thess. 4:13-18 "But I would not have you to be ignorant, brethren, concerning them which are asleep, that ye sorrow not, even as others which have no hope. For if we believe that Jesus died and rose again, even so them also which sleep in Jesus will God bring with Him. For this we say unto you by the Word of the Lord, that we which are alive and remain unto the coming of the Lord shall not prevent them which are asleep. For the Lord Himself shall descend from heaven with a shout, with the voice of the archangel, and with the Trump of God; and the dead in Christ shall rise first: then we which are alive and remain shall be caught up together with them in the clouds, to meet the Lord in the air: and so shall we ever be with the Lord. Wherefore comfort one another with these words."

I Thess. 5:2-4 "For yourselves know perfectly that the **day of the Lord** so cometh as a thief in the night (II Pet.3:10). For when they shall say, Peace and safety; then sudden destruction cometh upon them, as travail upon a woman with child; and they shall not escape. But ye, brethren, are not in darkness, that that day should overtake you as a thief."

I Thess. 5:23,29 "... and I pray God your whole spirit and soul and body be preserved blameless unto the **coming of our Lord** Jesus Christ..."

II Thess. 1:7-10 "... when the Lord Jesus shall be revealed from heaven with His mighty angels, in flaming fire taking vengeance on them that know not God, and that obey not... He shall come to be glorified... and... admired in all them that believe... in that day."

II Tim. 4:8 "... there is laid up for me a crown of righteousness, which (He) shall give me **at that day**: and not to me only but unto all them also that love **His appearing**."

Titus 2:13 "... looking for that blessed hope... the glorious **appearing** of the great God... Jesus Christ.. that He might Redeem us from all iniquity, and purify unto Himself a peculiar people, zealous of good works."

Heb. 9:28 "...*unto them that look for Him shall He **appear the second time**...*"
Heb. 10:37 "*... yet a little while... **He that shall come** will come... not tarry.*"
Heb. 11:35 "*... that they might obtain a better Resurrection...*"
Jms. 5:7,8 "*Be patient therefore, brethren, unto the **coming of the Lord**. Behold, the husbandman waiteth for the precious fruit of the earth, and hath long patience for it, until He receive the early and latter rain. Be ye also patient; stablish your hearts: for the **coming of the Lord** draweth nigh.*"
I Pet. 1:7 "*... that the trial of your faith, being much more precious than of gold that perisheth, though it be tried with fire, might be found unto praise and honour and glory at the **appearing of Jesus Christ**... receiving the end of your faith, even the Salvation of your souls.*"
I Pet. 1:13 "*... hope to the end for the grace that is to be brought unto you at the **revelation of Jesus** Christ (at His second coming)...*"
I Pet. 5:4 "*And when the **Chief Shepherd shall appear**, ye shall receive a crown of glory that fadeth not away.*"
I Jn. 2:28 "*And now, little children, abide in Him; that, when He **shall appear**, we may have confidence, and not be ashamed before Him **at His coming**.*"
I Jn. 3:2 "*... now are we the sons of God.. it doth not yet appear what we shall be... we know that, **when He shall appear**, we shall be like Him; for we shall see Him as He is.*"
Jude 14,15 "*... behold, the **Lord cometh** with ten thousands of His saints, to execute Judgment upon all...*"
Jude 21 "*... looking for the mercy of our Lord Jesus Christ unto eternal life.*"
Rev. 1:7 "*Behold, **He cometh with clouds**; and every eye shall see Him, and they also which pierced Him: and all kindreds of the earth shall wail because of Him...*"
Rev. 11:18,19 "*... Thou shouldest give reward unto Thy servants the prophets, and to the saints, and them that fear Thy name, small and great..*"
Rev. 16:15 "*... I come as a thief. Blessed is he that watcheth, and keepeth his garments....*"
Rev. 19:7-9 "*... for the marriage of the Lamb is come, and His wife ("Bride" NIV, ESV, NASB) hath made herself ready. And to her was granted that she should be arrayed in fine linen, clean and white: for the fine linen is the righteousness of saints. And he saith unto me, Write, Blessed are they which are called unto the marriage supper of the Lamb...*"
Rev. 19:11-19 "*And I saw heaven opened and behold a white horse; and He that sat upon him was called Faithful and True.. and on His head were many crowns; and He had a name written, that no man knew, but He Himself. And He was clothed with a vesture dipped in blood (Is. 63:1): and His name is called The Word of God. And the armies which were in heaven followed Him*

upon white horses, clothed in fine linen, white and clean... He hath on His vesture and on His thigh a name written, King of kings, and Lord of lords.."
Rev. 20:5,6 "But the **rest of the dead lived not again until the thousand years were finished**. This is the first Resurrection. Blessed and Holy is he that hath part in the first Resurrection: on such the second death hath no power..." (We see here that the 2nd Resurrection is after the 1000 years)
Rev. 22:12 "... I come quickly... My reward is with Me (Jesus), to give every man according as his work shall be."
Rev. 22:20 "... surely I come quickly. Amen, even so, come, Lord Jesus."
(More Scriptures - I Sam.2:10;Job 34:20;Ps.19:4-6;50:3;97:3-6;Is.5:30;11:4; 13:4-11,13;22:5;24:19-22;29:5-7;30:27,28;34:2,10,15;41:15;51:5,6;54:10; 66:15;Jer.4:26-29;25:30,31;Ez.39:18-23;Joel 2:1-11;Mic.1:3,4;Nah.1:5,6;Ez. 30:2-4;Zeph.1:2,3,7,8;Lk.9:26;13:35;17:24;17:26;21:34;Mk.8:38;Jn.6:39,40, 44;Acts17:18;II Thess.2:1-8;II Tim.4:1;Heb.10:27;46:10;II Pet.3:10,12;Rev.3: 3,11;6:14;10:6,7;11:15;14:14-16;14:18-20;6:17-21

Seek

Lk. 11:9 "... seek and ye shall find..."

See / Seen / Look

Gen. 16:13 "She called the name of the Lord that spake unto her, Thou God seest me: for she said, Have I also here looked after Him that seeth me..."
Ex. 3:16 God said, "... I have... seen that which is done to you..."
Job 28:24 "For He looketh to the ends of the earth, and seeth under the whole heaven..."
Ps. 33:13 "The Lord looketh from heaven; He beholdeth all the sons of men."
Matt. 6:4 "... thy Father which seeth in secret... shall reward thee openly."

Seed / Sons

"Rom. 8:13-17 "... if ye through the Spirit do mortify the deeds of the body, ye shall live... as many as are led by the Spirit of God, they are the sons of God... ye have received the Spirit of adoption, whereby we cry, Abba, Father. The Spirit itself beareth witness with our spirit, that we are the children of God: and if children, then heirs; heirs of God, and joint-heirs with Christ; if so be that we suffer with Him, that we may be also glorified together."

Separate

Rom. 3:37-39 "*Nay, in all these things we are more than conquerors through Him that loved us. For I am persuaded, that neither death, nor life, nor angels, nor principalities, nor powers, nor things present, nor things to come, nor height, nor depth, nor any other creature, shall be able to separate us from the love of God, which is in Christ Jesus our Lord.*"

Sick

See Healing or Health
Lk. 5:31 "*... they that are whole need not a physician; but they that are sick...*"

Sin / Sin Not

The promise is that Jesus will forgive us and cleanse us of our sins by His blood. He wants to free us and deliver us from sins. After being set free, we should not go back to our sins because that is like a dog returning his vomit or a pig returning to the slop, Prov. 26:11; II Pet. 2:22.

Num. 32:23 "*... ye have sinned against the Lord: and be sure your sin will find you out.*"

Job 5:24 "*And thou shalt know that thy Tabernacle shall be in peace; and thou shalt visit thy habitation, and shalt not sin ("or err" KJV fn).*"

II Chron. 6:26,27 "*When the heaven is shut up, and there is no rain, because they have sinned against Thee; yet if they pray toward this place, and confess Thy name, and turn from their sin, when Thou dost afflict them; then hear Thou from heaven, and forgive the sin of Thy servants, and of Thy people Israel, when Thou hast taught them the good way, wherein they should walk; and send rain upon Thy land, which Thou hast given unto Thy people for an inheritance.*"

The promise is that if we pray and confess, God will hear.

Ps. 32:1-5 "*Blessed is he whose transgression is forgiven, whose sin is covered. Blessed is the man unto whom the Lord imputeth not iniquity, and in whose spirit there is no guile... for day and night Thy hand was heavy upon me: my moisture is turned into the drought of summer. Selah. I acknowledged my sin unto Thee, and mine iniquity have I not hid. I said, I will confess my transgressions unto the Lord; and Thou forgavest the iniquity of my sin...*"

The promise is that God forgives.
Ps. 78:38,39 *"But He, being full of compassion, forgave their iniquity, and destroyed them not: yea, many a time turned He His anger away, and did not stir up all His wrath. For He remembered that they were but flesh..."*
Ps. 85:2 *"Thou hast forgiven the iniquity of Thy people Thou hast covered all their sin. Selah."*
Ps. 86:5 *"For Thou, Lord art good, and ready to forgive; and plenteous in mercy unto all them that call upon Thee..."*
Ps. 119:11 *"Thy Word have I hid in mine heart, that I might not sin against Thee."*
Is. 1:18 *"Come now, and let us reason together, saith the Lord: though your sins be as scarlet, they shall be as white as snow; though they be red like crimson, they shall be as wool."*
Is. 6:7 *"... thine iniquity is taken away, and thy sin purged."*
Jer. 31:34 *"... for they shall all know Me* (on the New Earth), *from the least of them unto the greatest of them, saith the Lord: for I will forgive their iniquity, and I will remember their sin no more."*
Ez. 33:15,16 *"If the wicked restore the pledge, give again that he had robbed, walk in the Statutes of life, without committing iniquity; he shall surely live, he shall not die. None of his sins that he hath committed shall be mentioned unto him: he hath done that which is lawful and right; he shall surely live."*
Nah. 1:9 *"Affliction* (Heb. #6869 *"adversary, distress, trouble, rival"*) *shall not rise up the second time."*
Matt. 12:31 *"... all manner of sin and blasphemy shall be forgiven unto men..."*
Jn. 1:29 *"... behold the Lamb of God, which taketh away the sin of the world."*
Jn. 10:11 *"... and Jesus said unto her, Neither do I condemn thee: go, and sin no more."*
Rom. 2:4,5 *"... the goodness of God leadeth thee to repentance..."*
Rom. 4:7,8 *"... blessed are they whose iniquities are forgiven, and whose sins are covered* (by the blood of Jesus) *Blessed is the man to whom the Lord will not impute sin."*
Rom. 5:20 *"... where sin abounded, grace did much more abound..."*
Rom. 6:1 *"What shall we say then? Shall we continue in sin, that grace may abound? God forbid..."*
Rom. 6:6,7 *"Knowing this, that our old man is crucified with Him, that the body of sin might be destroyed, that henceforth we should not serve sin. For he that is dead is freed from sin."*
Rom. 6:4,18 *"... we are buried with Him* (Jesus) *by baptism into death... being then made free from sin, ye became the servants of righteousness."*

Rom. 6:22 *"But now being made free from sin, and become servants to God, ye have your fruit unto Holiness, and the end everlasting life."*
Rom. 8:2 *"For the law of the Spirit of life in Christ Jesus hath made me free from the law of sin and death."*
Rom. 8:2,3,8 *"... Jesus... hath made me free from... sin and death..."*
Rom. 14:23 *"... for whatsoever is not of faith is sin."*
II Cor. 5:21 *"For He* (the Father in heaven) *hath made Him* (Jesus) *to be sin for us, who knew no sin; that we might be made the righteousness of God in Him* (Jesus).*"*
Heb. 4:26 *"... but now once in the end of the world hath He appeared to put away sin by the sacrifice of Himself... so Christ was once offered to bear the sins of many..."*
I Jn. 1:7 *"... if we walk in the light, as He is in the light, we have fellowship one with another, and the blood of Jesus Christ His Son cleanseth us from all sin."*
I Jn. 1:9 *"If we confess our sins, He is faithful and just to forgive us our sins, and to cleanse us from all unrighteousness."*
I Jn. 2:1,2 *"My little children, these things write I unto you, that ye sin not. And if any man sin, we have an advocate with the Father, Jesus Christ the righteous: and He is the propitiation for our sins: and not for ours only, but also for the sins of the whole world."*
I Jn. 2:12 *"... your sins are forgiven you for His name's sake."*
I Jn. 3:4 *"Whosoever committeth sin transgresseth also the law: for sin is the transgression of the Law. And ye know that He was manifested to take away our sins; and in Him is no sin. Whosoever abideth in Him sinneth not: whosoever sinneth hath not seen Him, neither known Him."*
I Jn. 3:8,9 *"He that committeth sin is of the devil; for the devil sinneth from the beginning... whosoever is born of God doth not commit sin... he cannot* (#1410 does not have *"permission"* to) *sin, because he is born of God In this the children of God are manifest, and the children of the devil: whosoever doeth not righteousness is not of God..."*
I Jn. 5:17,18 *"All unrighteousness is sin... but he that is begotten of God keepeth himself* (from sin)*, and that wicked one toucheth him not."*

Ps. 29:10 *"The Lord sitteth upon the flood; yea, the Lord sitteth king forever."*
Ps. 29:10 NIV *"The Lord sits enthroned over the flood..."*
Eph. 2:6 *"... and hath raised us up together, and made us sit together in heavenly places in Christ Jesus..."*

Sleep / Weary

Ex. 33:14 "... My presence shall go with thee, and I will give thee rest."
Job 11:18 "... thou shalt take thy rest in safety. Also thou shalt lie down, and none shall make thee afraid..."
Ps. 3:5 "I laid me down and slept; I awaked; for the Lord sustained me."
Ps. 4:8 "I will both lay me down in peace, and sleep: for Thou, Lord, only makest me dwell in safety."
Ps. 42:8 "... in the night His song shall be with me..."
Ps. 127:2 "... for so He giveth His beloved sleep."
Ps. 127:2 NIV "... for He grants sleep to those He loves."
Prov. 3:24 "When thou liest down, thou shalt not be afraid: yea, thou shalt lie down, and thy sleep shall be sweet."
Prov. 19:23 NASB "The fear of the Lord leads to life, so that one may sleep satisfied, untouched by evil."
Is. 14:30 "... and the needy shall lie down in safety..."
Is. 57:2 "He shall enter into peace: they shall rest in their beds, each one walking in his uprightness."
Jer. 31:25 "For I have satiated the weary soul, and I have replenished every sorrowful soul."
Jer. 31:26 "Upon this I awaked... and my sleep was sweet unto me."

Song / Sing

Ps. 32:7 "... Thou shalt compass me about with songs of deliverance...."
Ps. 65:9 "... the valleys also are covered over with corn; they shout for joy, they also sing."
Is. 30:29 "Ye shall have a song, as in the night..."
Zeph. 3:13,14 "The remnant of Israel shall not do iniquity, nor speak lies; neither shall a deceitful tongue be found in their mouth: for they shall feed and lie down, and none shall make them afraid. Sing, O daughter of Zion; shout, O Israel; be glad and rejoice with all the heart, O... Jerusalem."
Zeph. 3:17 "The Lord thy God in the midst of thee is mighty; He will save, He will rejoice over thee with joy; He will rest in His love, He will joy over thee with singing."

Speak / Words / Mouth

Deut. 30:14 "... the Word is very nigh unto thee, **in thy mouth**, and in thy heart,
that thou mayest do it."
Num. 13:30 "... for we are well able to overcome it."
Num. 13:30 NIV "... we can certainly do it..."
Caleb and Joshua spoke faith and the other ten spoke doubt.
I Kings 8:24,26 "... that Thou promisedst him: Thou **spakest also with thy mouth**, and hast fulfilled it with Thine hand, as it is this day... and now, O God of Israel, let Thy Word, I pray Thee, be verified, which **Thou spakest** unto thy servant David my father."
Ps. 2:7 "I will declare the decree..."
Ps. 19:14 "Let the **words of my mouth**, and the meditation of my heart, be acceptable in Thy sight, O Lord, my strength, and my Redeemer."
Ps. 91:2 "**I will say** of the Lord, He is my refuge and my fortress: my God; in Him will I trust."
Prov. 10:11 "The **mouth** of a righteous man is a well of life..."
Prov. 10:19 NASB "When there are many words, transgression is unavoidable, but he who restrains his lips is wise."
Prov. 12:6 "... but the **mouth** of the upright shall deliver them."
Prov. 12:14 "A man shall be satisfied with good by the fruit ("words" NCSB) of his **mouth**: and the recompence of a man's hands shall ("will" NKJV) be rendered unto him."
Prov. 12:18 "... **the tongue** of the wise brings healing."
Prov. 12:25 "Anxiety weighs down the heart, but a kind **word** cheers it up."
Prov. 15:1 "A soft answer turneth away wrath..."
Prov. 15:4 "A wholesome ("gentle" ESV) **tongue** is a tree of life..."
Prov. 15:23 "A man hath joy by the answer of his **mouth**: and a word spoken in due season, how good is it?"
Prov. 15:28 NLT "The heart of the godly thinks carefully before **speaking**; the mouth of the wicked overflows with evil words."
Prov. 16:24 "Pleasant ("gracious" ESV) **words** are as an honeycomb, sweet to the soul and health to the bones."
Prov. 18:4 "The **words of a man's mouth** are as deep waters, and the wellspring of wisdom as a flowing brook."
Prov. 18:20 "A man's belly shall be satisfied with the **fruit of his mouth**; and with the increase of **his lips** shall he be filled."
Prov. 18:21 "Death and life are in the **power of the tongue**: and they that love it shall eat the fruit thereof."

Prov. 21:23 "*Whoso keepeth his **mouth** and his tongue keepeth his soul from troubles.*"
Prov. 25:11 "*A word fitly **spoken** is like apples of gold in pictures of silver.*"
Eccl. 10:12 "*The **words** of a wise man's mouth are gracious; but the lips of a fool will swallow up himself.*"
Prov. 25:15 "*... a soft **tongue** breaketh the bone.*"
Is. 44:26 NIV "*... who carries out the **words** of His servants and fulfills the predictions of His messengers.*"
Is. 46:11 God said, "*yea, I have **spoken** it, I will do it.*"
Is. 46:11 NIV "*What I have **said**, that will I bring to pass...*"
Is. 50:4 "*The Lord God hath given me the tongue of the learned, that I should know how to **speak** a word in season to him that is weary...*"
Is. 55:11 "*... so shall My Word be that goes out from **My mouth**; it shall not return to me void, but it shall accomplish that which I please, and shall prosper in the thing for which I sent it.*"
Jer. 1:7 "*... say not, I am a child: for thou shalt go to all that I shall send thee, and whatsoever I command thee thou shalt speak. Be not afraid of their faces: for I am with thee to deliver thee, saith the Lord. Then the Lord put forth His hand, and touched my mouth. And the Lord said unto me, Behold, I have put my **Words in thy mouth**.*"
Jer. 12:2 "*... Thou art near in their **mouth**...*"
Matt. 8:8 "*... **speak** the Word only, and my servant shall be healed.*"
Matt. 12:37 "*For by thy **words** thou shalt be Justified, and by thy words thou shalt be condemned.*"
Mk. 11:23 "*... have faith in God. For verily I say unto you that whosoever **shall say** unto this mountain, Be thou removed, and be thou cast into the sea; and shall not doubt in his heart, but shall believe that those things which **he saith** shall come to pass; he shall have whatsoever **he saith**. Therefore I say unto you, What things soever ye desire, when ye pray, believe that ye receive them, and ye shall have them.*"
Lk. 6:45 "*... for of the abundance of the heart his **mouth** speaketh.*"
Acts 4:31 "*... they **spake** the Word of God with boldness.*"
Rom. 4:17 "*Before him whom He believed, even God, who quickeneth, even God, who quickeneth the dead, and calleth those things which be not as though they were.*"
Rom. 10:8-10 "*But what saith it? The Word is nigh thee, even **in thy mouth**, and in thy heart: that is, the word of faith, which we preach; that if thou shalt confess with thy **mouth** the Lord Jesus, and shalt believe in thine heart that God hath raised Him from the dead, thou shalt be saved. For with the heart man believeth unto righteousness; and **with the mouth** confession is made unto Salvation.*"

I Cor. 2:13 "... which things also we **speak** ..."
II Cor. 4:13;Ps.116:10 "*We having the same Spirit of faith... I believed, and therefore have I **spoken**; we also believe and therefore **speak**...*"
Eph. 4:29 "*Let no corrupt communication proceed out of your **mouth**, but that which is good to the use of edifying, that it may minister grace unto the hearers... let all bitterness, and wrath, and anger, and clamour, and **evil speaking**, be put away from you, with all malice... as God for Christ's sake hath forgiven you.*"
Jms. 1:26 "*If any man among you seem to be religious, and bridleth not his **tongue**, but deceiveth his own heart, this man's religion is vain... keep himself unspotted from the world.*"
Jms. 3:2 NIV "*... if anyone does not stumble in what he says, he is a perfect man, able also to bridle his whole body...*"
I Pet. 3:10 NLT "*... if you want to enjoy life and see many happy days, keep your tongue from speaking evil and your lips from telling lies.*"
Rev. 12:11 "*And they overcame him by the blood of the Lamb, and by the **word of their testimony**...*"

Spoil principalities

Col. 2:15 "*And having spoiled principalities and powers, He made a shew of them openly, triumphing over them in it.*"

Spouse

See Marriage

Step (s) / Days

Ps. 37:23 "*The steps of a good man are ordered by the Lord: and He delighteth in his way.*"
Ps. 139:16 HSCB "*Your eyes saw me when I was formless; all my days were written in Your book and planned before a single one of them began.*"
(Ps. 139:16 LB "*You saw me before I was born and scheduled each day of my life before I began to breath. Every day was recorded in Your book.*"
Prov. 16:9 "*A man's heart deviseth his way: but the Lord directeth his steps.*"
Prov. 20:24 NLT "*The Lord directs our steps, so why try to understand everything along the way?*"

Stones / Jewels / Gold

Is. 13:12 *"I will make a man more precious than gold..."*
Is. 49:18 NLT *"... all your children will come back to you... they will be like jewels... to display."*
Zech. 9:16 *"... the Lord... shall save them... they shall be as the stones of a crown..."*
Mal. 3:16 *"They shall be Mine... in that day when I make up My jewels."*
I Pet. 2:5 *"ye also as lively ("living") stones, are being built up as a Spiritual house..."*

Sun / Shine

See Light

Strength

See Holy Spirit

Strongman

Matt. 12:29 *"... how can one enter into a strongman's house and spoil his goods, except he first bind the strongman? And then he will spoil his house."*
Mk. 3:27 *"No man can enter into a strongman's house, and spoil his goods, except he will first bind the strongman; and then he will spoil his house."*
Lk. 11:21,22 *"... a strongman armed keepeth hs palace, his goods are in peace... when a stronger than he shall come... and overcome him, he taketh from him all his armour wherein he trusted, and divideth his spoils."*

Stronghold

Nah.1:7 *"The Lord is good, a stronghold in the day of trouble; and He knoweth them that trust in Him."*
II Cor. 10:4 *"For the weapons of our warfare are not carnal, but mighty through God to the pulling down of strongholds..."*

Teach

Ex. 4:12,15 To Moses "... go, and I will be with thy mouth, and teach thee what thou shalt say... and I will be with thy mouth, and with his (Aaron's) mouth, and wilt teach you what ye shall do."
I Sam. 12:23 "... I will teach you the good and the right way..."
I Kings 8:36 "... teach them the good way wherein they should walk..."
Ps. 25:8,9,12 "... therefore will He teach sinners in the way. The meek will He guide in Judgment: and the meek will He teach His way... what man is he that feareth the Lord? Him shall he teach in the way that he shall choose."
Ps. 32:8 "I will instruct thee and teach thee in the way which thou shalt go: I will guide thee with Mine eye."
Ps. 34:11 "... I will teach you the fear of the Lord."
Ps. 90:12 "... teach us to number our days, that we may apply our hearts unto wisdom."
Is. 2:3;Mic.4:2 "... He will teach us of His ways... we will walk in His paths: for out of Zion shall go forth the law, and the Word of the Lord from Jerusalem."
Is. 28:9 "Whom shall He teach knowledge... whom shall He make to understand doctrine? Them that are weaned from the milk... precept... upon precept... line upon line... here a little, and there a little..."
Jer. 32:33 NKJV "I taught them rising up early and teaching them."
Lk. 12:12 "... the Holy Ghost shall teach you... what ye ought to say."

Tell

Is. 42:9 "Behold, the former things are come to pass, and new things do I declare: before they spring forth I tell you of them."

Think / Thoughts

Ps. 189:17,18 LB David's prayer, "Think how precious it is, Lord, to realize that You are thinking about me constantly! I can't even count how many times a day Your thoughts turn towards me and when I waken You are still thinking of me!"
Jer. 29:11 "For I know the thoughts that I think toward you, saith the Lord, thoughts of peace, and not of evil, to give you an expected end.'
Eph. 3:20 "Now unto him that is able to do exceeding abundantly above all that we ask or think, according to the power that worketh in us..."

Tithe / Tithing / Offerings

The promise is that if we pay one tithes and offerings, God, will bless us!

Gen. 13:2 Because Abraham paid tithe he "... *was very rich in cattle, in silver, and in gold."*

Gen. 28:20-22 *"... Jacob vowed a vow.. If God will be with me, and will keep me in this way that I go, and will give me bread to eat, and raiment to put on, so that I come again to my father's house in peace; then shall the Lord be my God: and this stone, which I have set for a pillar, shall be God's house: and of all that Thou shalt give me I will surely give the tenth unto Thee."*

Lev. 27:30,32 *"So shall thy barns be filled with plenty, and thy presses shall burst out with new wine... and concerning the tithe of the herd, or of the flock, even of whatsoever passeth under the rod, the tenth shall be Holy..."*

Deut. 8:17,18 *"... thou shalt remember the Lord thy God: for it is He that giveth thee power to get wealth.."*

Deut. 14:22,24,26 *"... tithe all the increase of thy seed, that the field bringeth forth year by year... when the Lord thy God has blessed thee..."*

Deut. 16:17 *"... give.. according to the blessing... which He hath given thee."*

II Chron. 31:10 *"... since the people began to bring the offerings into the house of the Lord, we have had enough to eat, and have left plenty: for the Lord hath blessed His people; and that which is left is this great store."*

Prov. 3:9,10 *"Honour the Lord with thy substance, and with the firstfruits of all thine increase: so shall thy barns be filled with plenty..."*

Prov. 11:24 ESV *"One gives freely, yet grows all the richer..."*

Is. 1:19 *"... if ye be willing and obedient, ye shall eat the good of the land..."*

Mal. 3:7-11 *"... bring ye all the tithes into the storehouse... prove Me now.. saith the Lord... if I will not open... the windows of heaven, and pour... out a blessing, that there shall not be room enough to receive it... I will rebuke the devourer... he shall not destroy the fruits of your ground; neither... cast her fruit before the time..."*

Mal. 3:11 NIV *"... I will prevent pests from devouring your crops, and the vines in your fields will not drop their fruit before it is ripe..."*

Mal. 3:11 NLT *"Your crops will be abundant, for I will guard them from insects and disease."*

Mal. 3:11 ISV *"And I'll prevent the devourer from harming you, so that he does not destroy the crops of your land."*

Mal. 3:11 NET Bible *"I will stop the plague from ruining your crops..."*

Matt. 6:1-4 *"... thy Father which seeth in secret Himself shall reward thee..."*

Matt. 6:33 *"But seek ye first the kingdom of God, and His righteousness; and all these things shall be added unto you."*

Matt. 9:29;22:21;23:23 (KJV & NIV);Mk. 12:41-44;Lk. 6:38 *"Give, and it shall be given unto you; good measure, pressed down, and shaken together, and running over, shall men give into your bosom. For with the same measure that ye mete withal it shall be measured to you again."*
II Cor. 9:6,7 *"... he which soweth bountifully shall reap also bountifully..."*
Gen.4:4;28:22;14:20;Ex.25:2;Num.18:28NASB;Deut.18:4;Neh.10:38;Neh.12:44;Mal.3:3,4;Matt.5:23,24;6:19-21;Lk.11:42;16:10,13;18:12;Acts 4:34,35; 11:29;20:35,I Cor.4:2 (KJV & NIV);9:13,14;13:3;16:2,II Cor. 8:1-9:15 ESV;Phil. 2:17,I Tim.4:12,18,II Tim.3:16,17,Heb.7:1-28 ESV;7:8

Tongue / Gossip

See Speak
Job 5:21 *"Thou shalt be hid from the scourge of the tongue..."*
(Job 5:21 AKJ *"... whip of the tongue..."*
(Job 5:21 ESV *"... the lash of the tongue..."*
(Job 5:21 NLT *"You will be safe from slander..."*
(Job 5:21 ISV *"You will be protected from the accusing tongue..."*
(Job 5:21 NET *"You will be protected from malicious gossip..."*
Lk. 1:64 *"And his mouth was opened immediately, and his tongue loosed, and he spake, and praised God."*

Touch (ed)

I Jn. 5:18,19 *"We know that whosoever is born of God sinneth not... he that is begotten of God keepeth himself, and that wicked one toucheth him not."*

Trample / Tread / Touch (ed)

Ps. 108:13 *"Through God we shall do valiantly: for He it is that shall tread down our enemies."*
Ruth 2:9 Boaz to Ruth *"... have I not charged the young men that they shall not touch thee..."*
I Chron.16:22;Ps.105:15 *"... touch not Mine anointed, and do My prophets no harm."*
Jer. 1:9 *"Then the Lord put forth His hand, and touched my mouth. And the Lord said unto me, Behold, I have put My Words in thy mouth."*
Zech. 2:8 *"... he that toucheth you toucheth the apple of His eye."*
Matt. 8:15 *"... He touched her hand, and the fever left her..."*

Matt.9:20-22;Lk.8:44 *"... a woman, which was diseased with an issue of blood twelve years, came behind Him, and touched the hem of His garment: (saying) If I may but touch His garment, I shall be whole... He said, Daughter, be of good comfort; thy faith hath made thee whole. And the woman was made whole from that hour."*

Matt. 9:29,30 *"... then touched He their eyes saying, According to your faith be it unto you. And their eyes were opened..."*

Mk. 6:56 *".. whithersoever He entered, into villages... cities...* (or) *country, they laid the sick in the streets... besought Him that they might touch... the border of His garment: and as many as touched Him were made whole..."*

Mk. 16:18 *"They shall take up serpents; and if they drink any deadly thing, it shall not hurt them; they shall lay hands on the sick, and they shall recover... confirming the Word with signs following. Amen."*

This verse is not saying that we should go get deadly poisonous snakes and play with them (which is presumptuous). It is saying that if we are bitten by a snake by accident and we have the faith, it won't hurt us. We see that in the story of Paul who was bitten by a snake jumping out of the fire, and it didn't hurt him (Acts 28:1-6).

Lk. 5:13 *"And He put forth His hand, and touched him, saying, I will: be thou clean. And immediately the leprosy departed from him."*

Lk. 10:19 *".. I give unto you power to tread on serpents and scorpions, and over all the power of the enemy: and nothing shall by any means hurt you."*

Lk. 22:51 *"... He touched his ear and healed him..."*

Heb. 4:14-16 *"Seeing then that we have a great high priest, that is passed into the heavens, Jesus the Son of God, let us hold fast our profession. For we have not an high priest which cannot be touched with the feeling of our infirmities; but was in all points tempted like as we are, yet without sin. Let us therefore come boldly unto the throne of grace, that we may obtain mercy, and find grace to help in time of need."*

Treasure

Mk. 10:21 *"Then Jesus beholding him loved him, and said unto him, One thing thou lackest: go thy way, sell whatsoever thou hast, and give to the poor, and thou shalt have treasure in heaven: and come, take up the cross, and follow Me."*

Lk. 12:33,34 *"Sell that ye have, and give alms; provide yourselves bags which wax not old, a treasure in the heavens that faileth not, where no thief approacheth, neither moth corrupteth. For where your teasure is, there will your heart be also."*

Lk. 18:22 "... He said... lackest thou one thing: sell all that thou hast... distribute unto the poor... thou shalt have treasure in heaven.. follow Me."

Trouble / Tribulation / Trials

Ps. 27:5 "For in the time of trouble He shall hide me in His pavilion: in the secret of His Tabernacle shall He hide me; He shall set me up on a Rock. And now shall mine head be lifted up above mine enemies..."
Ps. 32:7 "Thou art my hiding place; Thou shalt preserve me from trouble..."
Ps. 34:6 "This poor man cried, and the Lord heard him, and saved him out of all his troubles."
Ps. 37:39 "... He is their strength in the time of trouble. And the Lord shall help them, and deliver them: He shall deliver them from the wicked, and save them, because they trust in Him."
Ps. 41:1-3 "Blessed is he that considereth the poor: the Lord will deliver him in time of trouble. The Lord will preserve him, and keep him alive; and he shall be blessed upon the earth: and thou wilt not deliver him unto the will of his enemies. The Lord will strengthen him upon the bed of languishing: thou wilt make all his bed in his sickness."
Ps. 50:15 "Call upon Me in the day of trouble: I will deliver thee, and thou shalt glorify Me..."
Ps. 54:7 "For He hath delivered me out of all trouble: and mine eye hath seen His desire upon mine enemies."
Ps. 59:16,17 "But I will sing of Thy power; yea, I will sing aloud of Thy mercy in the morning: for Thou hast been my defence and refuge in the day of my trouble. Unto Thee, O my strength, will I sing: for God is my defence, and the God of my mercy."
Ps. 86:7 "In the day of my trouble I will call upon Thee.. Thou wilt answer..."
Ps. 91:15,16 "He shall call upon Me, and I will answer him: I will be with him in trouble; I will deliver him, and honour him. With long life will I satisfy him, and shew him my Salvation."
Ps. 107:6 "Then they cried unto the Lord in their trouble, and He delivered them out of their distresses... led them forth by the right way."
Ps. 107:19 "Then they cry unto the Lord in their trouble, He saveth them out of their distresses."
Ps. 107:27-30 "They reel to and fro, and stagger like a drunken man, and are at their wit's end. Then they cry unto the Lord in their trouble, and He bringeth them out of their distresses. He maketh the storm a calm, so that the waves thereof are still. Then are they glad because they be quiet; so He bringeth them unto their desired haven."

Ps. 137:7,8 *"Though I walk in the midst of trouble, Thou wilt revive me: Thou shalt stretch forth Thine hand against the wrath of mine enemies, and thy right hand shall save me. The Lord will perfect that which concerneth me: Thy mercy, O Lord, endureth forever..."*
Ps. 138:7,8 *"Though I walk in the midst of trouble, Thou wilt revive me: Thou shalt stretch forth Thine hand against the wrath of mine enemies, and Thy right hand shall save me."*
Prov. 11:8 *"The righteous is delivered out of trouble..."*
Prov. 12:13 *"... the just shall come out of trouble."*
Is. 65:16 *"... the former troubles are forgotten, and because they are hid from mine eyes."*
Nah. 1:7 *"The Lord is good, a stronghold in the day of trouble; and He knoweth them that trust in Him."*
Nah. 1:9 ESV *"... trouble will not rise up a second time."*
Eph. 6:13 *"Wherefore take unto you the whole armour of God, that ye may be able to withstand in the evil day..."*

Trust

II Sam. 22:3 *"The God of my Rock; in Him will I trust: He is my shield... the horn of my Salvation... my high tower... my refuge, my Saviour; Thou savest me from violence."*
II Sam. 22:31 *"As for God, His way is perfect; the Word of the Lord is tried: He is a buckler to all them that trust in Him."*
Job 13:15 *"Though He slay me, yet will I trust in Him... He also shall be my Sal-vation..."*
Ps. 11:1,2 *"In the Lord put I my trust: how say ye to my soul, Flee as a bird to your mountain? For, lo, the wicked bend their bow, they make ready their ar-row upon the string, that they may privily shoot at the upright in heart."*
Ps. 22:4 *"... they trusted, and Thou didst deliver them... (they) were not con-founded."*
Ps. 28:7 *"The Lord is my strength and my shield; my heart trusted in Him, and I am helped..."*
Ps. 32:10 *"... he that trusteth in the Lord, mercy shall compass him about."*
Ps. 33:21 *"For our heart shall rejoice in Him, because we have trusted in His Holy name."*
Ps. 34:8 *"O taste and see that the Lord is good: blessed is the man that trustest in Him."*
Ps. 34:22 *"The Lord Redeemeth the soul of His servants: and none of them that trust in Him shall be desolate ("guilty" KJV fn; "condemned" PB)*

Ps. 36:7 *"How excellent is Thy lovingkindness, O God! Therefore the children of men put their trust under the shadow of Thy wings."*

Ps. 37:5,6 *"Commit thy way unto the Lord; trust also in Him; and He shall bring it to pass. And He shall bring forth thy righteousness as the light, and thy Judgment as the noonday."*

Ps. 37:40 *"And the Lord shall help them... He shall deliver them from the wicked, and save them, because they trust in Him."*

Ps. 40:4 ABPE *"Blessed is the son of man ("one" NIV) who trusts upon The Name of Lord Jehovah, and has not returned to futility..."*

Ps. 56:3,4 *"What time I am afraid, I will trust in Thee. In God I will praise His Word, in God I have put my trust; I will not fear what flesh can do unto me."*

Ps.84:4-12 *"... O Lord of hosts, blessed is the man that trusteth in thee."*

Ps. 119:41,42 NASB *"May Your lovingkindnesses also come to me, O Lord, Your Salvation according to Your Word; so I will have an answer for him who reproaches me, for I trust in Your Word."*

Ps. 119:66 NIV *"Teach me knowledge and good Judgment, for I trust your com-mands ("Commandments" KJV)."*

Ps. 125:1 *"They that trust in the Lord shall be as Mt. Zion, which cannot be removed, but abideth forever. As the mountains are round about Jerusalem, so the Lord is round about His people from henceforth even forever."*

Prov. 3:5,6 *"Trust in the Lord with all thine heart; and lean not unto thine own understanding. In all thy ways acknowledge Him, and He shall direct thy paths."*

Prov. 16:20 NIV *"Whoever gives heed to instruction prospers, and blessed is he who trusts in the Lord."*

Is. 12:2 *"... God is my Salvation; I will trust, and not be afraid: for the Lord Jehovah is my strength and my song..."*

Is. 26:3 *"Thou wilt keep him in perfect peace, whose mind is stayed on Thee: because he trusteth in Thee."*

Is. 50:10 *"... let him trust in the name of the Lord, and stay upon his God."*
(Is. 50:10 NLT *"... if you are walking in darkness without a ray of light, trust in the Lord and rely on your God."*

Is. 51:5 NKJV *"... on My arm they shall trust..."*

Is. 57:13 *"... he that putteth his trust in Me shall possess the land, and shall inherit My Holy Mountain..."*

Jer. 17:7 *"Blessed is the man that trusteth... whose hope the Lord is."*

Jer. 29:18 *"... I will... deliver them..."*

Nah. 1:7 *"The Lord is good, a stronghold in the day of trouble; and He knoweth them that trust in Him."*

Zeph. 3:12 *"I will also leave in the midst of thee an afflicted and poor people, and they shall trust in the name of the Lord."*

Matt. 12:21 *"And in His name the Gentiles shall trust ("hope" NIV)."*
Rom. 15:12 *"... there shall be a root of Jesse, and He that shall rise to reign over the Gentiles; in Him shall the Gentiles trust ("hope" NIV)."*

Truth

Jn. 8:32 *"And ye shall know the truth, and the truth shall make you free."*
Jn. 14:16-18 *"And I will pray the Father and He shall give you another Comforter that He may abide with you forever: even the Spirit of truth... ye know Him: for He dwelleth with you, and shall be in you."*
Jn. 17:17,19 *"Sanctify them through Thy truth: Thy Word is truth..."*
II Cor. 4:2 *"... by manifestation of the truth commending ourselves to every man's conscience in the sight of God."*
II Cor. 6:4,7 *"... in all things approving ourselves as the ministers of God... by the Word of Truth, by the power of God, by the armour of righteous-ness..."*
Rom. 2:20 *"... which hath the... truth in the law."*
I Jn. 3:19 *"And hereby we know that we are of the truth, and shall assure our hearts before Him... if our heart condemn us not, then have we confidence toward God. And whatsoever we ask, we receive of Him, because we keep His Commandments, and do those things that are pleasing in His sight..."*
I Jn. 2:21 *"I have not written unto you because ye know not the truth, but because ye know it, and that no lie is of the truth."*
I Jn. 4:6 *"We are of God: he that knoweth God heareth us; he that is not of God heareth not us. Hereby know we the Spirit of Truth..."*
I Jn. 5:6 *"... it is the Spirit that beareth witness, because the Spirit is truth."*

Vindication

Is. 54:17 *"No weapon that is formed against thee shall prosper; and every tongue that shall rise against thee in Judgment thou shalt condemn. This is the heritage of the servants of the Lord..."*
(Is. 54:17 NIV *"... this is their vindication from Me, declasres the Lord."*

Violence

See War

Wait

Ps. 37:5 *"Commit thy way unto the Lord; trust also in Him; and He shall bring it to pass... rest in the Lord, and wait patiently for Him: fret not thyself because of him who prospereth in his way... those that wait upon the Lord, they shall inherit the earth."*

Lam. 3:26 *"It is good that a man should both hope, and quietly wait for the Salvation of the Lord."*

Rom. 8:25 *"But if we hope for that we see not, then do we with patience wait for it."*

Wakes / Early

Ps. 57:8 *"... I myself will awake early. I will praise Thee, O Lord..."*
Is. 26:9 *"... with my spirit within me will I seek Thee early..."*
Is. 50:4 *"... He wakeneth morning by morning, He wakeneth mine ear..."*
Jer. 26:5 *"To hearken to the words of My servants the prophets, whom I sent unto you, both rising up early, and sending them..."*
Jer. 32:33 *"... I taught them, rising up early and teaching them..."*
Ps. 3:5 *"I laid me down and slept; I awaked; for the Lord sustained me."*
Prov. 8:17 *"... those who seek Me early shall find Me (wisdom)."*
Lam. 3:22,23 *"Because of the Lord's gracious love we are not consumed, since His compassions never end. They are new every morning..."*

War / Enemies / Violence

Lev. 6:4 *"... he shall restore that which he took violently away, or the thing which he hath deceitfully gotten, or that which was delivered him to keep, or the lost thing which he found."*

II Sam. 22:49 *"And that bringeth me forth from mine enemies: Thou also hast lifted me up on high."*

Job 5:20 *"In famine He shall Redeem thee from death: and in war from the power of the sword."*

Ps. 18:48 *"He delivereth me from mine enemies... Thou liftest me up above those that rise up against me: Thou hast delivered me from the violent man."*

Ps. 140:1,4 *"Deliver me, O Lord, from the evil man: preserve me from the violent man... keep me... from the hands of the wicked; preserve me from the violent man; who have purposed to overthrow my goings."*

Is. 60:18 *"Violence shall no more be heard in thy land..."*

Mic. 4:3 "... *they shall beat their swords into plowshares, and their spears into pruning hooks: nation shall not lift up a sword against nation, neither shall they learn war anymore* (on the New Earth)."
II Cor. 10:3 "*For though we walk in the flesh, we do not war after the flesh... casting down imaginations, and every high thing that exalteth itself against the knowledge of God, and bringing into captivity every thought to the obedience of Christ...*"

Watch

Jer. 31:28 "... *so will I watch over them, to build, and to plant, saith the Lord.*"
Matt.26:41;Mk.14:38 "*Watch and pray lest ye enter into temptation.*"
The promise is that if we watch and pray, we won't succumb to temptation.

Water

Deut. 8:15,25 "... *who brought forth water out of the rock...*"
II Kings 2:20-22 Elisha poured salt into the bad water that was killing people and the Lord said, "... *I have healed these waters...*"
Neh. 9:20 "*Thou gavest also Thy good Spirit... and... water for their thirst.*"
Ps. 18:16 "... *He drew me out of many waters...*"
Ps. 36:8,9 NASB "*They drink their fill of the abundance... and You give them to drink of the river of Your delights. For with You is the fountain of life...*"
Ps. 65:9 "*Thou visitest the earth, and waterest it: Thou greatly enriches it with the river of God, which is full of water...*"
Ps. 78:15 "*He clave the rocks in the wilderness, and gave them drink as out of the great depths.*"
Ps. 105:41 "*He opened the rock, and the waters gushed out; they ran in the dry places like a river.*"
Prov. 8:29 NKJV "*When He assigned to the sea its limit, so that the waters would not transgress His command, when He marked out the foundations of the earth.*"
Is. 12:3 "... *with joy shall ye draw water out of the wells of Salvation.*"
Is. 41:17,18 "*When the poor and needy seek water, and there is none, and their tongue faileth for thirst, I the Lord will hear them, I the God of Israel will not forsake them.*"
Is. 43:2 "*When thou passest through the waters, I will be with thee; and through the rivers they shall not overflow thee...*"

Is. 43:16 "... the Lord which maketh a way in the sea, and a path in the mighty waters... I give waters in the wilderness and rivers in the desert... to give drink to My people, My chosen..."

Is. 43:20 "... I give waters in the wilderness, and rivers in the desert, to give drink to my people, My chosen."

Is. 44:3,4 "For I will pour water upon him that is thirsty, and floods upon the dry ground: I will pour My Spirit upon thy seed, and My blessing upon thy offspring. And they shall spring up as among the grass, as willows by the water courses."

Is. 49:10 "They shall not hunger nor thirst; neither shall the heat nor sun smite them: for He that hath mercy on them shall lead them, even by the springs of water shall He guide them."

Is. 55:1 "Ho, everyone that thirsteth, come ye to the waters, and he that hath no money; come ye, buy, and eat; yea, come, buy wine and milk without money and without price."

How do we buy these things without money? Jesus paid for them with His blood and freely gives them to us.

Is. 58:11 "And the Lord shall guide thee continually, and satisfy (Heb. #7646 "saturate, sated, drink their fill, have plenty") thy soul in drought, and make fat thy bones: and thou shalt be like a watered garden, and like a spring of water, whose waters fail not ("giving you water when you are dry" NLT)."

Is. 65:13 "... thus saith the Lord God, Behold, My servants shall eat... behold, My servants shall drink... behold, My servants shall rejoice..."

Jer. 22:15 NIV "... did not your father (Josiah) have food and drink? He did what was right and just, so all went well with him."

Lk. 8:24 "... they came to (Jesus)... saying.. we perish... He arose... rebuked the wind... the raging of the water... they ceased... and there was a calm."

Jn. 4:13,14 "Jesus answered... whosoever drinketh of the water that I shall give him shall never thirst: but the water that I shall give him shall be in him a well of water springing up into everlasting life."

Jn. 6:35 "And Jesus said... I am the Bread of Life: he that cometh to Me shall never hunger; and he that believeth on Me shall never thirst."

Jn. 7:38 "He that believeth on Me, as the Scripture hath said, out of his belly shall flow rivers of living water."

Rom. 14:17 "For the kingdom of God is not meat and drink; but righteousness, peace, and joy in the Holy Ghost."

Weapon

Is. 54:17 "No weapon that is formed against thee shall prosper; and every

tongue that shall rise against thee in Judgment you shalt condemn. This is the heritage of the servants of the Lord, and their righteousness is of Me, saith the Lord."
II Cor. 10:4 "For the weapons of our warfare are not carnal (Gr. #4559 "fleshly"), but mighty through God to the pulling down of strongholds."
II Cor. 10:4 NIV "The weapons we fight with are not the weapons of the world. On the contrary, they have divine power to demolish ("destroy" ESV) strongholds."

Weary

Is. 32:1,2 "Behold, a king shall reign in righteousness and princes shall rule in Judment. And a man shall be as an hiding place from the wind, and a covert from the tempest; as rivers of water in a dry place, as the shadow of a great rock in a weary land."
Is. 40:31 "He giveth power to the faint; and to them that have no might He increaseth strength. Even the youths shall faint and be weary, and the young men shall utterly fall: but they that wait upon the Lord shall renew their strength; they shall mount up with wings as eagles; they shall run, and not be weary: and they shall walk, and not faint."
Is. 50:4 "The Lord God hath given me the tongue of the learned, that I should know how to speak a word in season to him that is weary..."
Jer. 31:25 "For I have satiated the weary soul, and I have replenished every sorrowful soul..."
Matt 11:28 "Come unto Me, all ye that labour ("are weary" NIV) and are heavy laden ("burdened" NIV), and I will give you rest."

Wedding Feast

The promise is that there will be a Wedding Feast!
Matt. 8:11 "... many shall come from the East and West, and shall sit (#347 "recline at a table or feast") down with Abraham, and Isaac, and Jacob, in the kingdom of heaven."
(Matt. 8:11 INT "... will come and will recline [at table]..."
Matt. 22:2-14 Parable of Wedding Feast "The kingdom of heaven is like unto a certan king, which made a marriage (Gr. #1062 "wedding feast or celebration"; "banquet" NIV; "feast" NLT) for his son... all things are ready: come unto the marriage... the wedding (Feast) is ready... and the wedding was funrnished with guests... (they had to put on a) wedding garment..."

Matt. 25 1-13 Parable of the ten virgins "... *the bridegroom came; and they that were ready went in with Him to the marriage* (Gr. #1062 "banquet" NIV; "feast" NLT): *and the door was shut.*"

Lk. 12:36,37 "*And ye yourselves like unto men that wait for their Lord, when He will return from the wedding: that when He comeh and knocketh, they may open unto Him immediately... verily I say unto you, that He shall gird Himself, and make them to sit down to meat* (Gr. #347 "will make them recline" like those reclining at a feast), *and will come forth and serve them...*"

Lk. 14:15-24 Parable of Wedding Feast "*Blessed is he that shall eat bread in the kingdom of God... come: for all things are now ready... bring in hither the poor, and the maimed, and the halt, and the blind... yet there is room... go out into the highways and hedges, and compel them to come in, that My house may be filled... taste My Supper.*"

Lk. 22:30 Jesus said to His twelve disciples, "*That ye may eat and drink of My table in My kingdom...*"

Rev. 19:7-9 "*Let us be glad and rejoice, and give honour to Him: for the marriage of the Lamb is come, and His wife hath made herself ready. And to her was granted that she should be arrayed in fine linen, clean and white... blessed are they which are called unto the marriage supper* ("feast" NLT) *of the Lamb. And he saith unto Me, These are the true sayings of God.*"

Rev. 22:17 The Wedding invitation, "*The Spirit and the Bride say come...*"

Weep / Weeping / Cry / Tears

Ps. 30:5 "*Weeping may last for a night, but joy comes in the morning.*"
Ps. 31:9 "*Be gracious to me, O Lord, for I am in distress; my eye is wasted away from grief, my soul and my body also.*"
(We ask God to be gracious and He will.
Ps. 56:8 NASB "*You have taken account of my wanderings; put my tears in Your bottle. Are they not in Your book?*"
(Ps. 56:8 NLT "*You keep track of all my sorrows...*"
(Ps. 56:8 NIV "*Record my misery; list my tears on Your scroll...*"
Ps. 116:7-9 "*Return to your rest, O my soul, for the Lord has dealt bountifully with you. For You have rescued my soul from death, my eyes from tears, my feet from stumbling. I shall walk before the Lord in the land of the living.*"
Ps. 126:5 "*They that sow in tears shall reap in joy.*"
Is. 25:8 "*He will swallow up death for all time, and the Lord God will wipe tears away from all faces, and He will remove the reproach of His people from all the earth; for the Lord has spoken.*"

Is. 30:19 *"For the people shall dwell in Zion at Jerusalem: thou shalt weep no more: He will be very gracious unto thee at the voice of thy cry; when He shall hear it, He will answer thee."*
Lk. 6:21 *"Blessed are you who weep now, for you shall laugh."*
Rev. 7:17 *"... God will wipe every tear from their eyes."*
Rev. 21:4 *"And God will wipe away every tear from their eyes; there shall be no more death, nor sorrow, nor crying, There shall be no more pain, for the former things have passed away."*

Widow / Widowhood

Ex. 22:22 *"You shall not mistreat any widow."*
This verse shows you that God cares about widows!
Deut. 14:29 *"... the stranger, and the fatherless, and the widow... shall come, and shall eat and be satisfied; that the Lord thy God may bless thee in all the work of thine hand which thou doest."*
Job 29:13 *"The blessing of him that was ready to perish came upon me: and I caused the widow's heart to sing for joy."*
Ps. 68:5 *"A father of the fatherless, and a Judge of the widows, is God in Holy habitation."*
Ps. 146:9 *"The Lord preserveth the strangers; He relieveth the fatherless and widow..."*
Ps. 147:3 *"He healeth the broken in heart, and bindeth up their wounds."*
Prov. 15:25 ESV *"The Lord... maintains the widows boundaries."*
Is. 54:4 *"... and shalt not remember the reproach of thy widowhood anymore. For thy Maker is thine husband..."*
Jer. 49:11 NLT *"But I will protect the orphans who remain among you. Your widows, too, can depend on Me for help."*
Jer. 29:11 ESV *"Let your widows trust in Me."*
Lk. 18:1-8 *"... there was a widow... I will give her justice."*
I Tim. 5:3 *"Honor widows..."*

Wings / Arms

Ex. 19:4 *"... I bare you on eagle's wings and brought you unto Myself..."*
Deut. 32:11 *"As an eagle stirreth up her nest, fluttereth over her young, spreadeth abroad her wings, taketh them, beareth them on her wings: so the Lord alone did lead him, and there was no strange god with him. He made him ride on the high places of the earth, that he might eat the increase of the fields..."*

Deut. 33:27 *"The eternal God is thy refuge, and underneath are the everlasting arms... He shall thrust out the enemy from before thee ..."*
Ruth 2:12 *"The Lord recompense thy work, and a full reward be given thee of the Lord God of Israel, under whose wings thou art come to trust."*
Ruth 3:9 *"He (Boaz) said, Who are you? And she answered, I am Ruth your maid. So spread your covering over your maid, for you are a...* ("near kinsman" KJV; *"family Redeemer"* NLT)."
Jesus is our near kinsman Redeemer and wants to spread His covering of protection over us.
Ps. 36:7 *"How excellent is Thy lovingkindness, O God! Therefore the children of men put their trust under the shadow of Thy wings."*
Ps. 18:10 *"And He (God) rode upon a cherub, and flew; He flew upon the wings of the wind."*
Ps. 57:1 *"... O God, be merciful unto me: for my soul trusteth in Thee: yea, in the shadow of Thy wings will I make my refuge, until these calamities be overpast."*
Ps. 63:7 *"Because You have been my help, therefore in the shadow of Your wings I will rejoice."*
Ps. 91:4 *"He shall cover thee with his feathers, and under His wings shalt thou trust: His truth shall be thy shield and buckler."*
Ez. 16:8 *"... I spread My wing over you and covered (you)... Yes, I swore an oath to you and entered into a Covenant with you, and you became Mine, says the Lord God."*

Wisdom / Wise / Knowledge

I Kings 5:12 *"And the Lord gave Solomon wisdom, as He promised him: and there was peace..."*
Ps. 19:7 *"The law of the Lord is perfect, converting the soul: the Testimony of the Lord is sure, making wise the simple..."*
Prov. 1:33 *"But whoso hearkeneth unto Me (wisdom) shall dwell safely, and shall be quiet from fear of evil."*
Prov. 2:4,5 *"If thou seekest her (wisdom) as silver, and searchest for her as for hid treasures... then shalt thou... find the knowledge of God."*
Prov. 2:6 *"For the Lord giveth wisdom: out of His mouth cometh knowledge and understanding. He layeth up sound wisdom for the righteous: He is a buckler to them that walk uprightly."*
Prov. 3:10,13-18 *"So shall thy barns be filled... happy is the man that findeth wisdom, and the man that getteth understanding. For the merchandise of it is better than the merchandise of silver, and the gain thereof than fine*

gold. She is more precious than rubies: and all the things thou canst desire are not to be compared unto her. Length of days is in her right hand; and in her left hand riches and honour. Her ways are ways of pleasantness, and all her paths are peace. She is a Tree of Life to them that lay hold upon her: and happy is every one that retaineth her."

Prov. 4:1-12 "... attend to know understanding. For I give you good doctrine, forsake ye not My law... keep My Commandments, and live. Get wisdom, get understanding, forget it not... forsake her not, and she shall preserve thee: love her, and she shall keep thee. Wisdom is the principal thing; therefore get wisdom: and with all thy getting get understanding. Exalt her and she shall promote thee: she shall bring thee to honour, when thou dost embrace her. She shall give to thine head an ornament of grace: a crown of glory shall she deliver to thee... I have taught thee in the way of wisdom, I have led thee in right paths... when thou runnest, thou shalt not stumble."

Prov. 8:11 "For wisdom is better than rubies; and all the things that may be desired are not to be compared to it."

Prov. 8:12,17-19,21 "I wisdom... love them that love me; and those that seek me early shall find me. Riches and honour are with me: yea, durable riches and righteousness. My fruit is better than gold, yea, than fine gold; and my revenue than choice silver... I may cause those that love me to inherit substance; and I will fill their treasures."

Prov. 8:30-32 NKJV "Then I (Wisdom) was beside Him as a master craftsman; and I was daily His delight, rejoicing always before Him, rejoicing in His inhabited world, and my delight was with the sons of men. Now therefore, listen to me, my children, for blessed are those who keep my ways."

Prov. 8:33-35 "... blessed are they that keep my ways... blessed is the man that heareth me... whoso findeth me (wisdom) findeth life, and shall obtain favour of the Lord."

Prov. 9:1 "Wisdom hath builded her house, she hath hewn out her seven pillars."

Prov. 9:10 "The fear of the Lord is the beginning of wisdom, and the knowledge of the Holy One is understanding."

Prov. 9:11 "For by me (wisdom) thy days shall be multiplied, and the years of thy life shall be increased."

Prov. 10:8 "The wise in heart will receive Commandments..."

Prov. 11:2 "... with the lowly ("humble" NASB) is wisdom."

Prov. 11:30,31 "The fruit of the righteous is a Tree of Life; and he that winneth souls is wise. Behold, the righteous shall be recompensed in the earth..."

Prov. 12:18 "... the tongue of the wise is health."

Prov. 13:20 "He that walketh with wise men shall be wise..."

Prov. 24:5 *"A wise man is strong..."*
Is. 50:4 *"The Lord God hath given me the tongue of the learned, that I should know how to speak a word in season to him that is weary..."*
Lk. 2:52 *"And Jesus increased in wisdom and stature, and in favour with God and man."*
Lk. 21:15 *"For I wll give you a mouth and wisdom, which all your adversaries shall not be able to gainsay nor resist."*
Eph. 1:8 *"... wherein He hath abounded toward us in all wisdom and prudence..."*
Eph. 1:17 *"... that the God of our Lord Jesus Christ, the Father of glory, may give unto you the Spirit of wisdom and revelation in the knowledge of Him..."*
Eph. 3:12 *"... in whom we have boldness and access with confidence by the faith of Him..."*

With you

God is with you and will not leave you
Deut. 2:7 *"For the Lord your God* (is) *with you..."*
Deut. 31:6 *"Be strong and of a good courage, fear not, nor be afraid of them: for the Lord thy God, He it is that doth go with thee; He will not fail thee, nor forsake thee."*
Josh. 1:9 *"... be strong and of a good courage; be not afraid, neither be thou dismayed: for the Lord thy God is with thee whithersoever thou goest."*

Womb

Ps. 22:10 *"I was cast upon Thee from the womb: Thou art my God from my mother's belly."*
Ps. 71:6 *"By Thee have I been holden up from the womb: Thou art He that took me out of my mother's bowels: my praise shall be continually of Thee."*
Ps. 139:13-15 *"For Thou hast possessed my reins* ("You created my inmost being" NIV): *Thou hast covered me in my mother's womb. I will praise Thee; for I am fearfully and wonderfully made... my substance was not hid from Thee, when I was made in secret, and curiously wrought in the lowest parts of the earth* ("Reference to the womb... and it shares with the depths of the earth." NIV fn)."
Is. 46:3,4 *"... all the remnant of the house of Israel, which are borne by me from the belly, which are carried from the womb: and even to your old age I am He; and even to hoar* (grey) *hairs will I carry you: I have made, and I will bear; even I will carry, and will deliver you."*

Jer. 1:5 To God said to Jeremiah, "*Before I formed thee in the belly I knew thee; and before you came forth out of the womb I Sanctified thee, and I ordained thee a prophet unto the nations.*"

Word(s)

See also Speak
Is. 44:26 NIV "*Who carries out the words of His servants and fulfills the predictions of His messengers*
Is. 55:11 "*So shall My Word be that goeth forth out of My mouth: it shall not return unto Me void, but it shall accomplish that which I please, and it shall prosper in the thing whereto I sent it.*"

Worry

Do not worry
Matt. 6:25-34;Lk.12:22-31 "*Therefore I say unto you, Take no thought for your life, what ye shall eat, or what ye shall drink; nor yet for your body, what ye shall put on. Is not the life more than meat, and the body than raiment? Behold the fowls of the air: for they sow not, neither do they reap, nor gather into barns; yet your heavenly Father feedeth them. Are ye not much better than they? Which of you by taking thought can add one cubit unto his stature? And why take ye thought for raiment? Consider the lilies of the field, how they grow; they toil not, neither do they spin: and yet I say unto you, That even Solomon in all his glory was not arrayed like one of these. Wherefore, if God so clothe the grass of the field, which today is, and tomorrow is cast into the oven, shall He not much more clothe you, O ye of little faith? Therefore take no thought, saying, What shall we eat? Or, What shall we drink? or, Where-withal shall we be clothed? (for after all these do the Gentiles seek:) for your heavenly Father knoweth that ye have need of all these things. But seek ye first the kingdom of God, and His righteousness; and all these things shall be added unto you. Take therefore no thought for the morrow: for the morrow shall take thought for the things of itself. Sufficient unto the day is the evil thereof.*"

Youth

Ps. 103:5 "*... so that thy youth is renewed like the eagle's.*"
Is. 55:4 "*... for thou shalt forget the shame of thy youth...*"

Every name of God holds a promise

"... this is My name forever, and this is My memorial unto all generations." Ex. 3:15
"... they that know Thy name will put their trust in Thee ..." Ps. 9:9,10
"I remember Your name in the night" Ps. 119:55
We should praise and exalt God's name because it is great!
"Let them praise the name of the Lord: for His name alone is excellent; His glory is above the earth and heaven." Ps. 148:13
"Glorify the Lord with me; let us exalt His name together." Ps. 34:3
"Thy name is from everlasting" Is. 63:16
"... there is none like unto Thee, O Lord; Thou art great, and Thy name is great in might." Jer. 10:6
"I will Sanctify My great name.." Ez. 36:23
God's name has always been and will always be.

His name is Holy and we must not disrespect it or take it in vain
"... Hallowed be Your name..." Matt.6:9; Lk.11:2
"Thou shalt not take the name of the Lord thy God in vain; for the Lord will not hold him guiltless that taketh His name in vain." Ex. 20:7

We are not to forget His name!
"Which think to cause My people to forget My name ..." Jer. 23:27
"... yet have we not forgotten Thee... if we have forgotten the name of our God, or stretched out our hands to a strange god; shall not God search this out? For He knoweth the secrets of the heart..." Ps. 44:17, 20,21

His name protects us and blesses us.
"They shall put My name on (them)... I will bless them." Num. 6:27
"The name of the Lord is a strong tower: the righteous runneth into it, and is safe." Heb. 18:10

Someday His name will be worshipped by all.
"That My name may be throughout all the earth." Ex. 9:16
"For from the rising of the sun even unto the going down of the same My name shall be great among the Gentiles; and in every place incense shall be offered unto My name, and a pure offering: for My name shall be great among the heathen, saith the Lord of hosts." Mal. 1:11

Someday Jesus will write His new name on us, Rev. 3:12.

Names/Titles of God, Jesus

"Those who know Your name put their trust in You, for You, O Lord, have not forsaken those who seek You." Ps. 9:10 ESV
"... what is His name and His Son's name..." Prov.30:4-6
"He that cometh in the name of the Lord" Matt.21:9;Mk.11;9
"I Am come in My Father's name" Jn.5:43
"... and they shall know that My name is the Lord." Jer. 16:21

A Teacher come from God (Jn.3:2)
Abba Father – He's our Father (Rom.8:15)
ABHIR – Mighty One (Gen.49:24;Deut.10:17)
Adonai – Lord and Master (Gen.18:17 - Can be plural and possessive)
Advocate of the Father [An] (I Jn.2:1)
Almighty [The] (Rev.1:8;4:8;16:7)
Almighty God (Gen.17:1)
Alpha and Omega – the beginning and end; first and last (Rev.1:8,11,17;2:8, 22:13;Is.44:6)
Amen (Rev.3:14)
Apostle [The] (Heb.3:1)
A Prophet (Jn.4:19)
Author and Finisher of our Faith (Heb.12:2)
Beginning of the Creation of God [The] (Rev.3:14)
  Beginning, #746 means, *"from the beginning, chief, foremost, has priority, preeminent, ruler"*
Beloved [The] (Eph.1:5)
Beloved Son (Mk.9:7;Lk.3:22;II Pet.1:17)
Beloved Son of God [The] (Matt. 3:1717:5;Mk.9:7;Lk.3:22)
Bishop of souls (I Pet.2:25)
Blessed of God (Ps.45:2)
Branch [The] (Is.4:2;Jer.23:5;Zech.3:8)
Branch of righteousness (Jer.33:15)
Bread of Life [The] (Jn.6:35,41)
Bridegroom [The] (Ps.19:5;Is.61:10;62:5;Jer.7:34;16:9;25:10:33:11; Joel 2: 16;Matt.9:15;25:1,5,6,10;Mk.2:19,20;Lk.5:34,35;Jn.2:9;3:29; Rev.18:23)
Bright and Morning Star (Rev.2:28;22:16)
Carpenter [The] (Mk.6:3)
Carpenter's Son [The] (Mat.13:55)
Chief Cornerstone (Eph.2:2:20;Pet. 2:6)
Chief Shepherd (1 Pet.5:4)
Christ of God [The] (Lk.9:20)
Christ [The] (Mk.14:61)
Christ Jesus (I Tim.2:5)
Christ our Rock (Ps.61:2;I Cor.10:4)

Chosen of God [The] (Lk.23:35)
Chosen One (Ps.89:19;Lk.9:35)
Consolation of Israel [The] (Lk.2:25)
Counsellor (Is.9:6)
Creator (Is.40:28;Jn.1:1-3)
Creator of all life (Rev.4:11)
Dayspring (Lk.1:78)
Deliverer, Delivered [The] (Joel 2:32;Rom.11:26)
Door [The] - Door of the Sheep (Jn.10:7,9)
El (means God)
El-Elyon – the Most High God (Gen.14:18,22)
El-Kanna – Jealous God (Ex.34:14)
  He's not jealous of you, He's jealous if you serve other gods! His jealousy shows how much He loves you because if you don't love much, you aren't jealous much!
Elohim – Creator God (Gen. 1:1) – the plural form of God, the Godhead (Father, Son, and Holy Spirit)
El-Olam – The everlasting, eternal God (Gen.21:33;Is.61:3)
El-Roi – God of seeing (Gen.16:13)
El-Shaddai – the Lord God Almighty (Gen.17:1)
Emmanuel – God with us (Is.7:14:8:8;Matt.1:23)
Everlasting Father (Is.9:6)
Everlasting God (Gen.21:33;Is.40:28)
Everlasting King (Jer.10:10)
Exalted One (Ps.89:19)
Father (Is.63:16) – "And call no man your father upon the earth: for One is your Father, which is in heaven." Matt.23:9
  "For unto us a child is born, unto us a Son is given: and the government shall be upon His shoulder: and His name shall be called Wonderful, Counseller, the Mighty God, The everlasting Father, The Prince of Peace." (Is.9:6)
Faithful and True (Rev.19:11)
Faithful and True Witness [The] (Rev.1:5;3:14)
First and Last (Is.49:12;Rev.1:8,17;2:8;22:13)
First Begotten [The] (Heb.1:61)
First Begotten of the dead [The] (Rev.1:5)
Firstborn (Ps.89:27)
God (Is.9:6)
God Almighty (Gen.28:3;Ex. 6:3)
God's Anointed (Acts 4:27)
God's Holy Child (Acts 4:27,30)
God of Abraham, Isaac, & Jacob (Ex.3:15)
God of Israel (I Kings 8:23)
Good Shepherd (Jn.10:11,14)
Governor – someday He will govern the world on the New Earth (Ps.22:28)

Governor that rules Israel (Matt.2:6)
Great God (Neh.9:32)
Great King (Matt.5:35)
Great Shepherd of the sheep [The] (Heb.13:20;I Pet.5:4)
He that hath the Key of David (Rev.3:7)
He that is Holy (Rev.3:7)
He that is True (Rev.3:7)
High and Lofty One (Is.57:15)
High Priest (Heb.2:17;3:1)
Him that is True (I Jn.5:20)
Holy Child Jesus (Thy) (Acts 4:30)
Holy - Whose name is Holy (Is.57:15)
Holy One (Ps.16:10;89:19;Acts 3:14;I Jn.2:20)
Holy One and Just (Acts 3:14)
Holy One of Israel [The] (Ps.71:22;Is.1:4;30:15,19,24)
Hope of Israel (The) (Acts 28:20)
Horn of Salvation (Lk.1:68)
I Am who I Am (Ex.3:14) – I Am everything you need (Jesus identified Himself as the I Am in Jn.8:58). I Am the Lord that healeth thee (Ex. 15: 26). I Am the first and last (Rev.1:17). I Am He who lives, and was dead (Rev.1:18). I Am alive forevermore (Rev.1:18).
Immanuel – God with us (Is.7:14:Matt.1:23)
Ishi means *"my man" "my husband"* (Hosea 2:14-16) Ishi was the name given to Adam but it also applies to Jesus, The Bridegroom
Jealous (Ex.34:14) (see note on El-Kanna)
Jehovah (YHWH) – The Lord (Ex.6:2,3)
Jehovah-Adon Kal Ha'arets – Lord of all the Earth (Josh.3:13)
Jehovah-Bara – Lord Creator (Is.40:28)
Jehovah-Chereb – Lord the Glorious Sword (Deut.33:29)
Jehovah-Eli – The Lord my God (Ps.18:2)
Jehovah-Elohenu – The Lord our God (Ex.8:10)
Jehovah Ezer – The Lord our helper (I Sam.7:12)
Jehovah-Gibbor Milchamah – The Lord mighty in battle (Ps.24:8)
Jehovah-Go'el – The Lord God Redeemer (Is.49:26,60:16)
Jehovah-'Izuz' Gibbor – The Lord strong and Mighty (Ps.24:8)
Jehovah-Jireh – The Lord will provide (Gen.22:14)
Jehovah-Kabodhi – The Lord my Glory (Ps.3:3)
Jehovah-Hamelech – The Lord King (Ps.96:6)
Jehovah-Hashopet – The Lord Judge (Judg.11:27)
Jehovah-Hoshe'ah – The Lord who saves (Ps.20:9)
Jehovah-Keren-Yish'I – The Lord horn of My Salvation (Ps.18:2)
Jehovah-Machsi – The Lord my refuge (Ps.46:1;91:9)
Jehovah-Magen – The Lord shield (Deut.33:29)
Jehovah-Makeh – The Lord who strikes you (Ez.7:9)
Jehovah-Ma'ozi – My Lord my fortress (Jer.16:19)

Jehovah Mekoddishkem, Mekeddeshem – The Lord who Sanctifies you and makes you Holy (Ex.31:13)
Jehovah-Melech 'Olam – The Lord King forever (Ps.10:16)
Jehovah-Mephalti – The Lord my Deliverer (Ps.18:2)
Jehovah-Moshi'ech – The Lord your Savior (Is.49:26;60:16)
Jehovah-Nissi – The Lord my banner (Ex.17:15)
Jehovah-'Ori – The Lord my light (Ps.27:1)
Jehovah-Raah – The Lord my Shepherd (Ps.23)
Jehovah-Rapha – The Lord that heals (Ex.15:26;Deut.32:39)
Jehovah-Rohi – The Lord my Shepherd (Ps.23:1)
Jehovah-Rophe – The Lord who heals you (Ex.15:26)
Jehovah-Shammah – The Lord is there (Ez.48:35)
Jehovah-Shalom – The Lord is Peace (Judges 6:24)
Jehovah-Sabaoth – The Lord of Hosts (I Sam.1:3)
Jehovah-Sel'I – The Lord my Rock (Ps.18:2)
Jehovah-Tsidkenu – The Lord our Righteousness (Jer.32:5,6)
Jehovah-Uzi – The Lord my Strength (Ps.28:7)
Jesus [Yawshua, Yeshua, Yehoshua] (Matt.1:21)
   Iesous is the Greek #2424 *"God saves"* – Jesus is the Greek transliteration
Jesus of Galilee (Matt.26:69)
Jesus of Nazareth (Matt.26:71;Mk.1:24)
Joseph's Son (Lk.4:22;Jn.1:45;6:42;)
Judge (Ps.7:8;96:3)
Judge of Quick and Dead (Acts 10:42)
Just (Acts 3:14)
Just One [The] - (Acts 7:52;22:14)
Kadosh – Holy One (Ps.71:22;Is.40:25)
King that cometh in the name of the Lord [The] (Lk.19:38;Jn.12:13)
King of Israel [The] (Matt.27:42;Mk.15:32;Jn.1:49;12:13)
King of the ages (Rev. 15:3)
King of the Jews (Matt.2:2;27:11,37:Mk.15:9,12,18,26;Lk.23:3,38;Jn.18:33 39; 19:3,14,15,19,21)
King of kings and Lord of lords (Rev.17:14;19:16)
King of nations (Jer.10:7)
King of Sion (Matt.21:5;Jn.12:15)
Lamb [The] (Rev.5:6,8,12,13;16:16; 7:9,14;12:11;14:1,4,10;15:3;17:14;)
Lamb of God [The] (Jn.1:29,36;Rev.17:14;19:9;21:9,14,22,27;22:1,3)
Life [The] (Jn.1:4)
Light [The] (Jn.1:7)
Light of the World (Jn.1:7,8;8:12)
Lily of the Valley [The] (Son of Songs 2:1 about Solomon, a type of Christ)
Living Bread (Jn.6:51)
Lion of the Tribe of Judah (Rev.5:5)
Lord [The] (Ex.6:3;Matt.28:6;Mk.16:19,20;Lk.2:11)
Lord God (Gen.2:4)

Lord God Almighty (Rev.16:7)
Lord God Omnipotent [all powerful] (Rev.19:6)
Lord Jehovah (Is.26:4)
Lord Jesus [The] (Lk.24:3;Acts 7:59;8:16;9:29;11:7,20;15:11,26;16:31;19:5)
Lord of all (Lk.10:36)
Lord of Glory [The] (I Cor.2:8;Jms.2:1)
Lord of hosts (II Sam.6:18;Is.5:24;Jer.50:34)
Lord of lords (Rev.17:14;19:16)
Lord our Righteousness [The] (Jer.23:6;33:16;Mal.4:2)
Lord of the Sabbath (Mk.2:28)
Lord Sabaoth – Lord of hosts (Jer.50:34;Rom.9:29)
Lord's Christ [The] (Lk.2:26)
Lord, thy God (Ex.3:6)
Lord, the Righteous Judge (II Tim.4:8)
Maker [his] (Prov.14:30)
Man of war *"the Lord is a man of war"* (Ex.15:3) (*"a warrior"* NIV)
Meek & Lowly (Matt.21:5;see also Zech.9:9;Matt.12:19)
Messenger of the Covenant [The] (Mal.3:1)
Messias [The] (Jn.1:41;4:25)
Messiah *"the Prince"* [The] (Dan.9:25)
Mediator between God and man (I Tim.2:5)
Mighty – One that is Mighty (Ps.89:19)
Mighty God (Neh.9:32;Is.9:6)
Mighty God of Jacob (Gen.49:24)
Mighty One of Israel (Is.30:29)
Mighty One of Jacob (Is.60:16)
Mighty Terrible One (Jer.20:11)
M'Kaddesh – to make whole – set apart, Sanctify (Lev.20:8)
Most Upright (Is.26:7)
Morning Star (Rev.2:28;22:16)
My Elect One (Is.42:1)
My Righteous Servant (Is.53:11 NKJV)
My Servant (Is.42:1;Zech.3:8)
Nazarene [A] (Matt.2:23)
One (Zech.4:1)
One with the Father (Jn.10:30)
Only Begotten of the Father (Jn.1:14,18)
Our Passover (I Cor.5:7)
Overseer of your souls (I Pet.2:25)
Patience & Consolation (Rom.15:5)
Prince [A]
  "Exalted Prince & Savior" (Acts 5:31)
  "Him (Jesus) hath God exalted... to be a Prince" (Acts 5:31)
  "Messiah the Prince" (Dan.9:25)
  "The Prince of the kings of the earth" (Rev.1:5)

"*Prince of Life*" (Acts 3:15)
"*Prince of peace*" (Is.9:6)
"*Prince of the Covenant*" (Dan.11:22)
"*Prince of the Host*" (Dan.8:11)
Prophet [A] (Jn.4:19;7:40;9:17;Acts 5:31)
Prophet [The] (Deut.18:18;Matt.7:40;14:5;21:11;Jn.6:14)
Prophet of Nazareth [The] (Matt.21:11)
Qanna [Kanna] – Jealous (Ex.20:5;34:14;Josh.24:19)
   (God is not jealous of anyone, but He is jealous if we love anyone or anything more than Himself because He created us and Redeemed us).
Rabbi – Teacher (Jn.1:38)
Rabboni (Jn.20:16)
Redeemer [Our] (Job 19:25;Ps.78:39;Is.59:20;60:16;63:16)
Redeemer [Your] (Is.60:16)
Repairer of the breach (The) (Es. 58:12)
Restorer of paths to dwell in (The) (Is.58:12)
Resurrection of Life (Jn.11:25)
Righteous Branch (Jer.23:5)
Righteous Judge (II Tim.4:8)
Righteous Man [A] (Lk.23:47)
Rock (I Cor.10:4)
Rock of ages (KJV fn Is. 26:4 - everlasting strength)
Root of Jesse (Is.11:10)
Rock of our Salvation (Ps.18:2;62:6)
Root and Offspring of David (Rev.22:16)
Root of David (Rev.5:5)
Rose of Sharon (Song of Songs 2:1) (about Solomon, a type of Christ)
Same yesterday, today, and forever [The] (Heb.13:8)
Savior [Your] (Is.60:16;Matt.1:21;Lk.2:11;Acts 5:31;13:23;II Pet.1:1,11)
Savior of Israel (Acts 13:23)
Savior of the world [The] (Jn.4:42)
Seed (Lk.1:55)
Seed of Abraham (Acts 3:25;Gal.3:16)
Seed of the Woman (Gen.3:15)
Seed – The Seed of David (Ps.132:11;Jn.7:42;Rom.1:3)
Shaphat – Judge (Ex.20:5,34;Is.40:25)
Shepherd (Gen.49:24;Ps.23;Ps.80:1;I Pet.2:25)
Servant [My] (Is.42:1;52:13;Zech.3:8;Acts 3:26)
Servant of the Lord (Is.42:1-7)
Shepherd of our souls [The] (I Pet. 2:25)
Shiloh (Gen.49:10)
Spiritual Rock (I Cor.10:4)
Son of Abraham [The] (Matt.1:1)
Son of David [The] (Matt.1:1;9:27;Mk.10: 47,48;12:35;Lk.18:38,39;20:41;)
Son of Mary [The] (Mk.6:3)

Son of the blessed (Mk.14:61)
Son of the Highest (Lk.1:32)
Son of the Living God (Matt.3:17;16:16)
Son of the Most High God (Mk.5:7;Lk.8:28)
Son [of God] (Ps.2:7;Matt.3:17;Rom.1:4;Heb.1:5)
Spiritual Rock [The] (I Cor.10:4)
Stem of Jesse (Is.11:1)
Stone of Israel (Gen.49:24)
Stone with seven eyes (Zech.3:9)
Sun of Righteousness – healing in His wings (Ps.19:1-6;Mal.4:2) Jesus is not the sun in our sky to be worshipped but He is greater than any sun; He is clothed in light and at His coming the wicked are killed by His brightness (II Thess. 2:8 *"destroy with the brightness of His coming"*) in Rev.1:14 His eyes are like flames of fire. In Rev. 22:5 the New Jerusalem doesn't need the sun because God is the light that is greater than the sun. He is the sun of all suns, He lights the suns on fire; He is the beginning of suns.
Sure Foundation (A) (Is.28:16)
Teacher-Master - *"But be not ye called Rabbi: for One is your Master, even Christ; and all ye are brethren."* (Matt.23:8)
Teacher come from God (Jn. 3:2)
Terrible God (Neh.9:32)
True Vine (Jn.15:5)
Which is, and Which was, and Which is to come (Rev.1:8;4:8;11:17)
Word of God [The] (Rev.19:13)
Word of Life (I Jn.1:1)
Wonderful (Is.9:6)
Wonderful – Counselor – Mighty God (Is.9:6)
Yeshua – means Yahweh is Salvation (Matt.1:21) or Yehoshuah, which means, *"Adonai saves"*. His name is a promise that He will save you.
Yah the Lord (Is.12:2)
Yahweh – Lord Jehovah (Ex.6:2;9:2;10:2) *"I am Yahweh and I showed to Abraham, to Isaac, and to Jacob, as El-Shaddai, and by My name 'Yahweh', I did not make Myself known to them."*
You-Are-The-God-Who-Sees [This is what Hagar *"called the name of the Lord who spoke to her"*] (Gen.16:13)

Names of the New Jerusalem

There is also a promise in every name of the New Jerusalem
A city not forsaken (Is. 62:12)
Ariel (The hearth of God) (Is.29:1;Rev.21:21)
Beaulah Land (means married) (Is. 62:4)
(No more called Desolate, "Shemamah" but Hephzibah, "*My delight is in her*" and Beulah, "*married*" because God delights in you, your land will be married, Is. 62:4)
Bride – "*prepared as a Bride*" (Is. 62:2 NLT;Rev.21:2)
City of David (II Sam.6:12)
City of God (Ps.46:4;48:1;87:3)
City of God's delight (Is. 62:2 NLT)
City of the Great King (Ps.48:2;Matt.5:35)
City of Jebus (the Jebusite) (Judges 19:11)
City of the Lord [The] (Ps.60:14;Is.60:10)
City of the Lord of Hosts [The] (Ps. 48:8)
City of Righteousness [The] (Is. 1:26)
City of Truth [The] (Zech. 8:3)
Faithful City [The] (Is.1:26)
Great City [That] (Rev. 21:9-14)
Ha-Kodesh – City of Holiness
Hephzibah – means My delight is in her (Is. 62:4)
Holy City [The] (Is.48:2;52:1;Matt.4:5)
Holy Hill (Ps. 3:4)
Holy Jerusalem (Rev .21:9-14)
Holy One of Jacob (Is.29:23)
Holy One of Israel (Is.30:11-13)
Home of Justice (Jer. 31:23)
Joy of the whole earth [The] (Lam. 2:15)
Lord is there [The] (Ez. 48:35)
Lord our Righteousnes [The] (Jer.33:16;23:6)
Mountain of Holiness (Jer. 31:23)
Mountain of the Lord of Hosts (Zech. 8:3)
(The Holy) Mountain (Zech.8:3)
Mt. Moriah (II Chron. 3:1)
My Holy Mountain (Is. 65:25)
Oasis of Justice (Jer. 31:22)
Perfection of Beauty (Lam. 2:15)
Shalom/Salem/Peace (Gen. 14:18)
   (Jerusalem was originally Salem, which means, peace; Jeru-Salem)
Sought Out (Is. 62:12)
Zion (Is.60:14;Heb. 12:22)

Personal answers to prayer

Grandma quits smoking
The Promise:
"I can do all things through Christ who strengthens me" (Phil. 4:13)

When my grandma came to Jesus years before I was even born, she had been a heavy smoker. She wanted to quit to please Jesus, not to be saved. She wanted this real bad but just couldn't get the victory over the habit. One day she was very determined; she was not going to let this habit get the best of her by the grace of God. So every time that she had the urge to smoke she would say, *"I can do all things through Christ who strengthens me"* Phil. 4:13. It took many days of reciting that text but she finally did get the victory and never smoked again.
Thank You Jesus for Your great and precious promises that help us to overcome!

Vicious Coyote
The Promise:
"Call unto Me, and I will answer thee." Jer. 33:3

When I was only 6 yrs. old, we lived in Carson City, Nevada. My mother taught a little Christian school there and I was in the 1st grade. I had to walk home across a large field about half a mile with sage brush everywhere to the trailer park we lived in. Just as I got outside the area where the school was I saw a very skinny, mangy looking Coyote or some kind of wild dog. It seemed larger than a coyote and it was baring its teeth and giving a low growl. It looked very mean and almost as big as I was. I was scared and didn't know what to do so I prayed and asked God to tell me what to do. He spoke very clearly to my heart and said to back up very slowly and not to run. So I did exactly as God told me to do. I had backed up quite a way then God told me to turn around and walk slowly back to the school. When I got there I told my mom that I had seen an angry, mean dog. Well, when I went back outside I couldn't see the coyote or whatever it was anywhere so I ran home as fast as I could, looking over my shoulder to see if he was following me but he was nowhere in sight and I made it home safely. I never did see him again.
Thank You Jesus for keeping me safe and telling me what to do!

This far and no further
The Promise:
"... hitherto shalt thou come, but no further: and here shall thy proud waves be stayed?" Job 38:11

When we moved to Fargo, North Dakota in 1981, we lived right on the Red River. The Red River flooded most years because it thaws out in the South before the

North thaws out and this is one of very few rivers that runs North. Since I knew that the river usually flooded into the basement of our house, I prayed and claimed the verse in the Bible that says God speaks to the waters "This far an d no further" Job 38:, Ps.104;9. We lived there four years and it flooded the year before we moved in and the year after we moved out but it never flooded the four years that we lived there. The waters would come halfway into the yard but never up to the basement. Some would say that it was a coincidence but I say that if was then it was a wonderful conincidence!
Thank You Jesus for fulfilling Your Word for me!

A Still Small Voice
The promise:
"... the Lord passed by (Elijah), and a great and strong wind rent the mountains, and brake in pieces the rocks before the Lord; but the Lord was not in the wind: and after the wind an earthquake; but the Lord was not in the earthquake: and after the earthquake a fire; but the Lord was not in the fire: and after the fire a still small voice." I Kings 9:11,12

One day I was coming home and just as I got to the house the sun was right in my eyes blinding me so that I couldn't see anything. I was right in front of the driveway so was just going to pull in but a still s mall voice said, "Go very slow". I started to argue with that voice and think, "I'm just going to pull into the driveway, what's the big deal?" But I've learned to listen to that still small voice and so I listened and didn't argue. I thought, "O.K. I'll just go slowly". The neighbor lady was sitting on the lawn smiling at me while I went slowly into the driveway and as the sun lifted from my eyes, standing in the driveway right in front of me was the neighbor's two year old son. I could hardly believe my eyes. I wondered why the neighbor hadn't warned me or tried to get her son out of the way. I stopped and let the toddler walk away then looked at the neighbor and said, "You know, the sun was blinding me and I could not see your son standing there." She just laughed! I thought, "She wouldn't be laughing if she knew how close I came to hitting him." I am so glad that God warned me that day and that I listened. That could have been a terrible day for me to have to live with.
Thank You Jesus for that still small voice!!! Help me to always listen to You when You speak to me!

Lost in Seattle
The Promise:
"God is our refuge and strength, a very present help in trouble ." Ps. 46:1
"Then shalt thou call, and the Lord shall answer." Is. 58:9

Not too long ago I went to Seattle for my nephew's wedding. My sister, another nephew, my daughter, and I went to a ball game and it was pretty late when we got out. My oldest nephew had gotten directions from the internet to show me and my sister how to get back to our Motel from the ball game. Well, what we didn't know was that the street we were looking for was in two locations; only they were a few miles apart and not connected. We followed the directions explicitly and ended up on the correct street name but the one that was in the wrong place. I drove and drove up and down these streets but couldn't find the Motel we were in. I called my nephew who had gotten the directions originally but he didn't know how to help us. I called my parents at the Motel but they didn't know how to help us and I was going to run out of gas in the middle of the night with no gas station in sight if I just kept driving around in circles. My sister did not know what to do so we stopped at a store and asked if anyone could give us directions to the correct street where our Motel was but no one there could help us and then we stopped at another store and no one there could help us either. I was getting very worried about our situation because I don't have a very good sense of direction anyway and here I am lost in the middle of the night in a large city with no help in sight. So I was standing there in the store and started praying very seriously. Now I had already prayed many times but this time I really focused on God and said, Lord, I'm in a very serious situation here and I really need You to pay attention to me; I really need help here. I have no one to help me and I can't find my way back to the Motel. This is serious! Please help me right now! Because if You don't help me I'm in deep trouble! Please help me in Jesus' name; Amen!

And immediately, just as soon as I was done praying an older man came in the store. He looked very different from the people in the store or in that area. He looked like he had just stepped off the farm in the Midwest. He seemed like a very meek and gentle man. Anyway, he came in the store and looked right at me and without me saying a word he asked me if I needed help and I said, Yes, do you know how to get to this certain Motel on this same street we're on? He said, Yes; and then proceeded to give me very simple instructions (because I needed simple right then) on how to get back on the highway and then I would see the exit off the highway that would take me to the Motel. From that point on I remembered how to get to the Motel. I don't know if he was sent by God or just a man coming into the store or an angel but I know one thing for sure, God answered my prayer right then and helped me get back to the motel safely! I am so grateful God heard me and helped me at that very moment I needed Him. Thank You Jesus for listening and helping me in my time of need!

Saved cat from Coyote
The Promise:
"Before they call, I will answer" Is. 65:24

We live in an area where there are wild animals, even in town sometimes. We see bears, coyotes, raccoons, and deer on occasion. One day I knew my friend was repainting the inside of her house with her husband and two friends so I thought, wouldn't it be a nice surprise for them if I brought doughnuts because they might not have time to fix anything to eat. So I bought some doughnuts and

drove right over. As I got there I noticed a beautiful coyote standing in the middle of the road in front of their house. I thought, Wow that is the healthiest and prettiest coyote I've ever seen; I wish I had my camera. But then I noticed my friend's cat a few feet away and the coyote was in the process of getting ready to pounce on it. I thought, Oh no!!! What should I do?!!! Then I felt impressed to honk the horn. So very quickly (within seconds of seeing the coyote) I laid on that horn as loud as I could and it scared the coyote mid-air and he ran away. Again, God had me in the right place at the right time because if I had been a few minutes earlier or a few minutes later it would have been too early or too late. From the time I drove up that cat had about 5 seconds before the coyote would have gotten it. My friend had already had one cat eaten by a coyote and she was glad that this cat was O.K.!
Thank you Jesus for helping me to save my friend's cat!

Dogs eat poison
The Promise:
"*Direct my foosteps according to Your Word.*" Ps. 119:133

My mom just moved so she could be closer to her family. And just the other day I felt like I needed to go to her house about two hours away. I was tired and didn't feel like driving 4 hours round trip there and back but I really felt compelled at the time not realizing that it was God who was urging me to go. When I got there, we visited and I was admiring the house and all the work she had done to move in (with help from family) and then as we stepped out onto the porch I saw my youngest nephew coming out of the shed he had just built a few weeks ago for a pantry. I said, Mom let's go into the shed and you can show me the new shelves that my nephew had just finished building. She said, O.K. So we went down into the shed and after I had admired the shelves we came out of the shed and I was going to leave the door open because it was open when we went in. Now that is where the miracle began because as I walked out mom said, Be sure and close the door there's rat poison in there and the dog's can get into it if the door's not kept shut. Well, my nephew had just come from there and we had just walked in. Just then I noticed the dogs were eating something and I said, "What are the dogs eating?" As they investigated, it became apparent that they had eaten the poison. We caught it immediately and were able to induce vomiting and get the two dogs to the vet quickly. Once at the vet's the Doctor induced more vomiting and gave them Vitamin K-1 to keep their blood from getting too thin for a month. If I hadn't asked to see the shed at that very moment, nobody would have noticed that the dogs ate the poison before it was too late. That day everything happened at precisely the right moment so that those dogs were safe. God even cares for our animals.
Thank You Jesus that You had me there at the right moment to save the dogs lives!

Out of Gas
The promise:
"... before they call, I will answer; and while they are yet speaking, I will hear." Is. 65:24

One day I took our daughter and her friend to Eugene. We were coming home and it was starting to get dark when I ran out of gas on a stretch of road too far from any town to walk. We desperately needed someone to take us to a gas station.
I told the girls, We better pray, because sometimes it can be dangerous. So I prayed that God would send someone nice to help us. I no sooner said, Amen, when a young couple who taught school in a town nearby stopped to help us. After we go back with the gas and started to leave, my daughter said, Mom you prayed for someone nice and they were really nice! Yes, I said, God really does answer prayer! That day our daughter learned that we can call on God when we need help. The next time we had car trouble, she was the first one to ask if we could pray.
Thank You Jesus for answering my prayer that day and sending someone nice to help us!

$100 for school clothes
"If ye then, being evil, know how to give good gifts uno your children: how much more shall your heavenly Father give he Holy Spiritto them that ask Him?" Lk. 11:13

This happened when our daughter was in the 3rd grade and we lived in Myrtle Creek, Oregon. My husband gave me a $100 dollar bill to buy some school clothes for our daughter. We weren't making much money at that time so I needed to be careful with that $100. My daughter and I were looking around in stores and we had just left one store and went to another when we saw something we liked and I went to pay for it. That's when I noticed the $100 was gone. Oh no, I thought! I must have dropped it somewhere because I had just seen it not too long ago. So we went back to the last store as I offered up a quick prayer.
Lord, please help me find this money because you know we can't replace this right now.
As I entered the last store I saw the $100 bill laying on the ground. A lady was standing almost on it but didn't notice it. I ran over and picked it up wihout her even seeing me. It had been at least around 15 minutes since I had been in that store and it was a miracle that nobody had seen it and picked it up. Especially since a woman was almost standing on it.
Thank You Jesus for answering my prayer and keeping anyone from taking that money when we needed it for school clothes and couldn't replace it.

Clean house
"He shall call upon Me and I will answer him…" Ps. 91:15
"Call to Me and I will answer you…" Jer. 33:3
"… a very present help in trouble…" Ps. 46:1

I have been working on this book and the last book, Let Them Pray for a couple of years. It has taken up a lot of my time and I have had to put some things on a shelf to do after I'm done. I keep my house clean but have not done a lot of the deep cleaning. So just the other day I prayed and said, Lord I really need help cleaning my house because there is just too much for me to get done and I'm feeling overwhelmed. It was one of the prayers I couldn't imagine how God would answer. Who would want to clean my house anyway? No one I could think of but I prayed it anyway; out of desperation. A few days after I had prayed, a friend who had just started up a business of housecleaning came to me and said that for Pastor's Appreciation she would like to clean our house a few times. Wow, that was amazing!!! I told her that she could not have given us any better gift than that! What a blessing!!
Thank You Jesus that you hear my prayers and answer them!!!

God helps me publish first book
God gives you the desires of you heart, Ps. 37:4

I felt that God wanted me to publish a book called, The Crimson Worm. I was getting ready to publish it and had to step out in faith because I didn't really have the money. As I was preparing to publish, without me even asking for help, my mom and a good friend said they wanted to contribute to the publishing and gave me about half the money I would need; which was a huge help. I was able to publish it and have gone on to publish two more books to date.
Thank You Jesus for watching over me!

How to be reconciled to God

Being reconciled to God is a growing experience; just like a seed grows in the garden, so we grow in Jesus

1st Step to Jesus
Repent - Acts 3:19
"Repent ye therefore, and be converted, that your sins may be blotted out..." Ps. 44:22

Why do we need to repent?
We are all sinners and need a Saviour.
"For all have sinned and come short of the glory of God." Rom. 3:23
"While we were sinners Christ died for us." Rom. 5:8
"... having raised up His Son Jesus, sent Him to bless you, in turning away every one of you from his iniquities (sins)." Acts 3:26

"Repent ye therefore, and be converted (changed) that your sins may be blotted out..." Acts 3:19
"... let the wicked forsake his ways..." Is.55:7

The Good News is that Jesus won't turn anyone away!
"... and him that cometh to Me I will in no way cast out." Jms. 6:37
In the parable of the Wedidng Feast He says, Call the good and the bad, Matt. 22:10. He doesn't want us to stay bad but to be changed and to grow more and more like Jesus every day.

What is sin?
"Sin is the transgression of the law" I Jn. 3:4
It is through the law that we have a knowledge of what sin is, Rom. 3:20.
The Bible says that if we break one, we break them all, Jms. 2:10
We don't know what sin is without the law so even though the law doesn't save us, it still helps us to know what sin is so that we can know what to repent of and know what needs to be overcome in our lives through the power of the Holy Spirit.

Every time we break God's law, we sin!
Sin is not pleasing to God!
The penalty for sin is death!
Someone had to die for sin! Either the sinner or Jesus (if you accept Him) who took our place, our punishment and died instead of us! Jesus gave His life to free us from sin and to cleanse us by His blood, Titus 2:14 NLT
No one can earn Salvation, we are Justified by faith without works, Eph. 2:8,9.
We are saved by His life (I Jn. 5:12) and Justified by His blood (Rom. 5:9,10).

2nd step to Jesus
Believe
We must believe that Jesus is God and came to this earth in the flesh!
"Unless you believe that I Am, you will die in your sins" Jn. 8:4
"And every spirit that confesseth not that Jesus Christ is (God) come in the flesh is not of God: and this is that spirit of antichrist..." I Jn. 4:3

Jesus identified Himself as the I Am.
"Jesus said unto them, Verily, verily, I say unto you, Before Abraham was, I Am."
At the burning bush Moses asked, What is Your name? And He answered *"I Am"*. The people at that time understood that He was saying that He was God because they tried to stone Him for blasphemy. In fact, the very reason they crucified Jesus was because He claimed to be God and they con-sidered that blasphemy. Now it is blasphemy to claim to be God if you are not God but Jesus really was God so it wasn't blasphemy for Him. He proved He was God by the miracles He performed. Thomas cried, My Lord and my God, Jn. 20:28.
Jesus is God come in the flesh. He came to earth and lived a perfect life and died on the cross for our sins. There is no other way to God but through Jesus because He is the only One who never sinned! And He is our Creator and Redeemer.
"No man cometh unto the Father, but by Me." Jn. 14:6
"Neither is there Salvation in any other: for there is none other name under heaven given among men, whereby we must be saved." Acts 4:12
"That if thou shalt confess with thy mouth the Lord Jesus, and shalt **believe in thine heart** *that God hath raised him from the dead, thou shalt be saved."* Rom. 10:9
"But God, who is rich in mercy, for His great love wherewith He loved us, even when we were dead in sins, hath quickened us together with Christ... and hath raised us up together... for by grace are ye saved through faith; and that not of yourselves: it is the gift of God: not of works, lest any man should boast..." Eph. 2:4-9
"Whoever calls on the name of the Lord shall be saved... that if thou shalt confess with thy mouth the Lord Jesus, and shalt believe in thine heart that God hath raised Him from the dead, thou shalt be saved." Rom. 10:13
"Create in me a clean heart, O Lord, and renew a right Spirit within me." Ps. 51:10.

3rd Step to Jesus
Receive
Then we **receive Him** as our Lord and Savior. We make Him our only Lord and Master which means that we will do what He wants us to. We will obey Him above all others; we put Him first in everything. We accept His death on the cross for our sins.
"But as many as received Hm, to them gave He power to become the sons of God, even to them that believe on His name..." Jn. 1:12

"For he hath made him to be sin for us, who knew no sin; that we might be made the righteousness of God in Him." II Cor. 5;21
"Whoever believes in the Son has eternal life, but whoever rejects the Son will not see life, for God's wrath remains on them." Jn. 3:36 NIV

We receive the Holy Spirit
"Acts 2:38 *"... repent, and be baptized every one of you in the name of Jesus Christ for the remission of sins, and ye shall receive the gift of the Holy Ghost."*
"For as many as are led by the Spirit of God, they are the sons of God." Rom. 8:14
"Which is the earnest of our inheritance until the Redemption of the pur-chased possession." Eph. 1:14

Prayer of Salvation
You can pray something like this but it must be from the heart.
"Dear Father in Heaven, I confess that I am a sinner and need a Savior. I repent of my sins and confess them to You; please forgive me and wash me clean by Your blood (Rev. 1:5). I believe that Jesus is God and came to earth to die for my sins. I receive You, Jesus, as my Lord and Savior. I am willing, with Your help, to obey You. Thank you for Your great work on the cross for me. Teach me Your will and help me to do it. In the name of Jesus, my Creator, Redeemer, Amen!"

Now you are saved like the thief on the cross was saved that very mo-ment!
"I write these things to you who believe in the name of the Son of God so that you may know that you have eternal life." I Jn. 5:13 NIV
"These things have I written unto you that believe on the name of the Son of God; that ye may know that ye have eternal life, and that ye may be-lieve on the name of the Son of God." I Jn. 5:13

Now that I'm saved by grace how do I live?
"... through whom we have received grace... to bring about the obedience of faith..." Rom. 1:5

Now that you are saved and Jesus is your Lord and Master, you need to learn what it is that God wants you to do. God saved you by grace alone not of works lest anyone should boast but he saved you to do good works, which He will rewrd someday in heaven (Eph.2:8-10).
 If Jesus is your Lord, then you will do what He asks. We will want to please Him if we truly love him. (If you love Me, keep My Commandments, Jn. 14:15) Sometimes people say being a Christian is too hard when they realize that God has a very high standard and learn how God wants them to live. Well, it's easy to be saved (Jesus did that for you – it's a free gift) but it's true that it is hard to get the rewards. If it was easy, then everyone would have the same reward. Matt. 5:19 tells us that some are least and some are great in the kingdom of heaven

according to their obedience. Only God knows who gets rewards and what they'll be and we'll only know when we get to heaven.
Sometimes people do good works only to be applauded by men and then God says, you've already received your reward, Matt. 6:2. So we shouldn't Judge others; only Judge ourselves.
"For if we would Judge ourselves, (then) *we should not be Judged."* I Cor. 11:31
In other words, if I judge myself now & overcome my sins, then I won't be judged at the Great White Throne Judgment. The righteous are not judged to see if they are saved at the Judgment but our works go through the fire to see what our reward will be, I Cor. 3:15.

The next step in obedience is baptism by immersion
"Go ye therefore, and teach all nations, **baptizing them** *in the name of the Father, and of the Son, and of the Holy Ghost:* **teaching them to observe** *("obey" NIV) all things whatsoever I have commanded you: and lo, I am with you always, even unto the end of the world. Amen."* Matt. 28:19,20
"... repent, and be baptized every one of you in the name of Jesus Christ fo r the remission of sins, and ye shall receive the gift of the Holy Ghost ..." Acts 2:38
Bible baptism is by immersion. Jesus went down into the water and came up out of the water and He is our example.
The Greek word for baptism is, #907 *"baptizo"* which means, "... 'submerge' hence... to immerse (literally, 'dip under')... implies submersion ('immersion'), in contrast to #472 "sprinkle".
John the Baptist found a place where there was much water to baptize.
"And John also was baptizing in Aenon near to Salim, because **there was much water there***: and they came, and were baptized."* Jn. 3:23
"And Jesus, when He was baptized, went **up straightway out of the water***: and lo, the heavens were opened unto Him and He saw the Spirit of God descending like a dove, and lighting upon Him: and lo a voice from heaven, saying This is My beloved Son, in whom I am well pleased."* Matt. 3:16,17
Philip went down into the water with the Ethiopian and they came up out of the water.
"And as they went on their way, they came unto a certain wate r: and the eunuch said, See, here is water; what doth hinder me to be baptized? And Philip said, If thou believest with all thine heart, thou mayest. And he answered and said, I believe that Jesus Christ is the Son of God. And he commanded the chariot to stand still: and they **went down both into the water***, both Philip and the eunuch; and he baptized him. And when they were* **come up out of the water***, the Spirit of the Lord caught away Philip, that the eunuch saw him no more: and he went on his way rejoicing."* Acts 8:36-39

Remember the story of Namaan. Elijah told Naaman to "*Go and wash yourself seven times in the Jordan River*." But he became angry and walked away. He wanted Elijah to wave his hands over him or tell him to wash in some other way.

He wanted to do things his own way but if we want the blessing, we have to do things God's way.

"... his officers tried to reason with him and said, Sir, if the prophet had told you to do some great thing, wouldn't you have done it? So you should certainly obey him when he says simply to go and wash and be cured! So Naaman went down to the Jordan River and dipped himself (under the water) *seven times, as the man of God had instructed him. And his flesh became as healthy as a young child's and he was healed!"* II Kings 5:10-14.

We are to walk as Jesus walked and He went down into the water and came up out of the water. Being baptized by immersion is not that hard to do; God tells you to do it, so just do it! Like the Ethiopian Eunuch said, "What's hindering you?" There are blessings that come with baptism that you don't want to lose out on.

After baptism, take Communion regularly

"...this do in remembrance of Me" Lk. 22:20

"Whoso eateth My flesh, and drinketh My blood (through the symbol of Communion), *hath eternal life; and I will raise him up at the last day."* Jn. 6:53

"For as often as ye eat this bread, and drink this cup, ye do shew the Lord's death till he come." 1 Cor. 11:26

Pray

"Lord, teach us to pray" Lk. 11:1

"Rejoice always, pray continually, give thanks in all circumstances; for this is God's will for you in Christ Jesus." I Thess. 5:16-18

"Is any among you afflicted ("suffering" NASV *"suffering hardships"* NLT *"in trouble"* NIV)*? Let him pray."* Jms. 5:13

See my book, Let Them Pray, with all the prayers in the Bible.

Read the Word and Do (obey) the Word

(Can you try? Just try!)

First of all, we can't know what God requires of us if we don't read the Word. You can't just take the preachers word for it, you must look it up yourself so you won't be deceived. The Bereans were considered more noble because they *"searched the Scriptures daily, whether those things were so ("They searched the Scriptures day after day to see if Paul and Silas were teaching the truth.")"* Acts 17:11. So if it was a noble thing to compare Paul's teachings to the Bible, then it's O.K. to check up on anyone to see if they are preaching the Word correctly.

The Word will tell us what pleases God and what doesn't. Obedience is a work of a lifetime. We are always striving to do those things that please God; knowing that if we fail, we can repent and receive forgiveness and cleansing by the blood of Jesus, Rev. 1:5. Forgiveness is our greatest wea-pon against the Devil. Don't get discouraged, you're already saved; so do it out of a willing heart, not out of compulsion and God will help you and reward you someday.

"... teaching them **to obey** everything I have commanded you." Matt. 28:20 NIV
"For by grace are you saved... created in Christ Jesus unto **good works**, which God hath before ordained that we should walk in them." Eph. 2:8

How do we know what God wants us to do? The Word will tell us what pleases God and what we are commanded to do. We need to read the Word and do the Word like the parable of the wise man in the Bible, Matt. 7:24-27.
But you have to read the Bible to know what it says!
"Study to shew thyself approved unto God, a workman that needeth not to be ashamed, rightly dividing the word of truth." II Tim. 2:15
"As newborn babes, desire the sincere milk of the word, that ye may grow thereby..." 1 Peter 2:2
"That ye might walk worthy of the Lord unto all pleasing, being fruitful in every good work, and increasing in the knowledge of God." Col. 1:10
"I beat my body (figuratively speaking) and make it my slave so that after I have preached to others I myself will not be **disqualified for the prize**." I Cor. 9:27
You notice he wasn't disqualified for eternal life but for the prize.
You see that this verse doesn't say that we are lost, it says our works are lost.
Some people want their reward now; they want their pleasures now and the Bible says that they already have their reward so they won't be getting one in heaven.
"Therefore when thou doest thine alms, do not sound a trumpet before thee, as the hypocrites do in the Synagogues and in the streets, that they may have glory of men. Verily I say unto you, They have their reward (already)." Matt. 6:2

No one can serve two masters.
But be clear about one thing, you can't serve God and the Devil at the same time. You have to choose.
"No man can serve two masters: for either he will hate the one, and love the other; or else he will hold to the one, and despise the other..." Matt. 6:24
"Doth a fountain send forth at the same place sweet water and bitter? Can the fig tree, my brethren, bear olive berries? either a vine, figs? So can no fountain both yield salt water and fresh." Jms.. 3:11
God is light and there is no darkness in Him! Those who choose to serve Satan and want the advantages he can give in this world cannot go to heaven unless they renounce Witchcraft and the things of the Devil.
So you have to ask yourself, Is it worth losing eternity to have the pleasures of sin for a season?
"What does it profit to gain the whole world and lose your soul?" Matt.16:26; Mk.8:36
"For what will it profit a man if he gains the whole world and forteits his soul? Or what shall a man give in return ("exchange" NIV) for his soul?" Matt. 16:26 ESV
Moses chose "... to suffer affliction with the people of God, than to enjoy the pleasures of sin for a season..." Heb. 11:25
What is 70+ years compared to eternity!!!

So if you're:
  Happy – give God the glory and praise Him!
  Sad - pray for help, claim the promises, and trust Him!
  Suffering for God - endure it, knowing you will be rewarded in heaven
  Rich - be generous & put your trust in God not money!
  Poor - trust God & know that you have true riches in heaven someday!
As you grow in Jesus you will be looking for Jesus to come back and take you home to live with Him forever.
"*Looking for and hasting unto the coming of the day of God...*" II Pet. 3:12

The most important thing about your life is where you go when you die. The Bible says, "*Do not deceive yourselves; God is not mocked: for whatever a man sows that shall he also reap*." Gal. 6:7 Jubilee Bible 2000
It also says, "*For many are called, but few are chosen.*" Matt. 22:14
That means many get the call but only a few respond to it. So be one of those who respond to the call and come to Jesus!

Our light and momentary trials and tribulations are working out an eternal weight of glory in heaven for us someday, II Cor. 4:17.

"*The Crimson Worm*" on www.thecrimsonworm.com
"*Let Them Pray*" on www.morningloribooks.com
If you order directly from me, I will send you a signed copy & a Bible reading plan on an easy way to read the whole Bible through!

Index

Chronological Order
Old Testament

	pg.#
Introduction	4
Genesis	28
Exodus	45
Leviticus	58
Numbers	60
Deuteronomy	66
Joshua	84
Judges	91
Ruth	93
I Samuel	94
II Samuel	98
I Kings	103
II Kings	105
I Chronicles	108
II Chronicles	113
Ezra	121
Nehemiah	122
Esther	124
Job	124
Psalms	130
Proverbs	180
Ecclesiastes	203
Song of Solomon	205
Isaiah	205
Jeremiah	237
Lamentations	252
Ezekiel	253
Daniel	259
Hosea	263
Joel	266
Amos	268
Obadiah	269
Jonah	269
Micah	269
Nahum	270
Habakkuk	271

Zephaniah	272
Haggai	273
Zechariah	274
Malachi	278

New Testament

Matthew	281
Mark	305
Luke	313
John	332
Acts	348
Romans	361
I Corinthians	374
II Corinthians	380
Galatians	386
Ephesians	389
Philippians	393
Colossians	395
I Thessalonians	397
II Thessalonians	398
I Timothy	399
II Timothy	400
Titus	402
Hebrews	403
James	411
I Peter	415
II Peter	420
I John	421
II John	427
III John	427
Jude	428
Revelation	428

Topical Order

Abba/Father	436
Abide/Dwell	436
Adopt/Adoption	437
Afraid/Fear	438
Affliction	440
All	441
Angel(s)	448
Anger/Wrath	449
Answer/Hear/Receive	453

Anxiety	454
Ashamed	455
Ask/Cry/Pray	455
Baptize/Baptism	457
Beauty	458
Believe/Faith/Faithfulness	459
Bind/Bound/Binding	462
Bitterness	462
Blameless	462
Blessed (cannot be cursed)	463
Blessed/Blessing/Favor/Give	463
Blessing to Jacob	472
Blessing to 12 sons	472
Bless Ephraim & Manasseh	473
Blessings/Beatitudes	474
(7) Blessings of Revelation	474
Bold/Boldness	475
Book(s)	475
Born Again/New Birth	475
Bride/Spiritual Virgin	476
Bridegroom/Husband/Jesus	476
Brokenhearted	477
Care/Cast	477
Children	478
Children/Offspring/Seed	480
Chose/Chosen/Choose	484
Church	485
Clean/Cleanse(d)	485
Clothing/Raiment	487
Comfort	487
Compassion	488
Confess	489
Confident	489
Covenants	490
Covenant (Edenic)	493
Covenant (Adamic)	493
Covenant (Noahic-Rainbow)	493
Covenant (Abrahamic)	494
Covenant (Mosaic)	497
Covenant to Return to the Land	498
Covenant (Davidic)	499
Covenant (New)	499
Covenant of Peace	501

Covenant of Salt	502
Convert	503
Crown	503
Cry (see Weep)	505
Curses	505
Dancing/Joy	506
Death/Grave/Resurrection	506
Decree	508
Defense	509
Deliver	509
Depression	512
Desire(s)	515
Dwell/Abide	515
Early (see Wakes)	516
Enemy/Enemies	517
Eternal Life	518
Exalted	518
Eye(s)	518
Faith/Faithful(ness)	519
Family/Friends	522
Fatherless	525
Favor	525
Fear (see Afraid)	526
Fight/Battle	526
Fire	527
Flood/Waters	527
Food/Water	528
Forget	534
Forgive/Remove Sins/Repent	534
Fortress	537
Free/Freedom/Freely	537
Friend(s)	538
Forsake Not	539
Gifts/Give/Given	539
Gold	540
Grace/Gracious	542
Guide	543
Hair	544
Hand	544
Happen	544
Happy	545
Harm (see Hurt)	545
Haven	545

Heal/Healing	545
Health	548
Hear/Heard	548
Heart (Circumcised)	549
Heaven/New Earth-Jerusalem	554
Heir (see Inherit)	569
Hell/Pit/Grave	569
Help	570
Holy Spirit/Power/Strength	571
Home/House/Habitation	581
Honey	581
Honor	581
Hunger (see Food)	581
Hurt/Harm	581
Impossible	582
Inherit/Inheritance/Heritage	582
Intercession	585
Jesus as King	586
Joy/Gladness/Pleasures	586
Judgment	589
Justified	589
Keys	590
Kindness	591
Kingdom	591
Kinsman Redeemer	593
Knock	593
Land/Earth/World	593
Language	594
Latter Rain/Early Rain	594
Life/Live/Long Life	596
Light/Shine	598
Likeminded	599
Loose	599
Love	600
Lovingkindness	602
Marriage/Spouse	603
Meek	607
Mercy/Gracious/Kind	608
Miracles/Healing/Signs	609
Money/Mammon	619
Mountain/Move Mountains	620
Mystery	620
Names	620

Never Fails	621
New Earth/New Jerusalem (see Heaven)	621
New Name	621
Ocean/Sea/Storms/waves	621
Old Age	622
Oppression	623
Path/Steps/Lead/Led	623
Peace	624
Perfect/Faultless	625
Perish	625
Plagues	626
Plans	627
Pleasure/Please/Pleasing	627
Poor	628
Power (see Holy Spirit)	629
Prayer/Pray	629
Preserve	629
Prisoner	630
Prize	630
Promises(s)/The Word	630
Propitiation	634
Protection	635
(the) Race	636
Rain	636
Rainbow	638
Rearguard/From Behind	639
Received	639
Reconcile/Reconciliation	640
Redeem(ed)/Redemption	640
Refuge	642
Repent/Repentance	643
Rest	643
Restore(er)	644
Resurrection/Risen	644
Reward/Recompense	647
Riches/Prosperity/Wealth	653
(Be careful of) Riches	663
Righteousness (Christ's)	669
Ruler	670
Safe/Safety	670
Salvation/Savior/Redemption	671
(Pray) Salvation for Another	676

Sanctify/Sanctification	677
Satan (Cannot touch us)	678
Satisfy/Satiate	678
Seal/Sealed	679
Second Coming	680
Seek	684
See/Seen/Eyes/Look	684
Seed/Sons	684
Separate	685
Sick	685
Sin/Sin Not	685
Sit	687
Sleep/Weary	688
Song/Sing	688
Speak/Words/Mouth	689
Spoil Principalities	691
Spouse (see Marriage)	691
Step(s)/Days	691
Stones/Jewels/Gold	692
Sun/Shine (see Light)	692
Strength (see Holy Spirit	692
Strongman	692
Stronghold	692
Teach	693
Tell	693
Think	693
Tithe/Tithing/Offerings	694
Tongue	695
Touch	695
Trample/Tread	695
Treasure	696
Trouble/Tribulation/Trials	697
Trust	698
Truth	700
Vindication	700
Violence (see War)	700
Wait	701
Wakes/Early	701
War/Enemies/Violence	701
Watch	702
Water	702
Weapon	703
Weary	704

Wedding Feast	704
Weep/Weeping/Cry/Tears	705
Widow/Widowhood	706
Wings/Arms	706
Wisdom/Wise/Knowledge	707
With You	709
Womb	709
Word	710
Worry	710
Youth	710
Every name of God is a promise	**711**
Names/Titles of God – Jesus	**712**
Names of New Jerusalem	**719**
Personal Answers to Prayer	**720**
How to be Reconciled to God	**726**
Index	**733**

www.ingramcontent.com/pod-product-compliance
Lightning Source LLC
Chambersburg PA
CBHW031641170426
43195CB00035B/121